G000149805

THE SEMANTICS OF SYNTAX

Denis Bouchard

THE **SEMANTICS**
OF **SYNTAX**

A Minimalist Approach to Grammar

THE **UNIVERSITY OF CHICAGO PRESS** • Chicago & London

DENIS BOUCHARD is professor of linguistics at the University of Quebec at Montreal.

THE UNIVERSITY OF CHICAGO PRESS, CHICAGO 60637
THE UNIVERSITY OF CHICAGO PRESS, LTD., LONDON

©1995 by The University of Chicago
All rights reserved. Published 1995
Printed in the United States of America

04 03 02 01 00 99 98 97 96 95   1 2 3 4 5

ISBN: 0-226-06732-7 (cloth)
0-226-06733-5 (paper)

Library of Congress Cataloging-in-Publication Data

Bouchard, Denis.
    The semantics of syntax : a minimalist approach to grammar / Denis
Bouchard.
        p.   cm.
    Includes bibliographical references and index.
    1. Semantics.   2. Grammar, Comparative and general—Syntax.
3. Generative grammar.   I. Title.
    P325.B628   1995
    415—dc20   95-8405
                                                                    CIP

⊗ The paper used in this publication meets the minimum requirements of the
American National Standard for Information Sciences—Permanence of Paper for
Printed Library Materials, ANSI Z39.48-1984.

To Catherine and Evelyne

If a lion could talk, we could not understand him.
Ludwig Wittgenstein

Contents

Acknowledgments

In the course of the last six years, I presented aspects of this work at various stages of its development to several audiences, and I have greatly benefited from their reactions. But it would have been impossible to obtain these preliminary, but already substantive, results without the help of a small group of enthusiastic students—Jacques Lamarche, Louise Lavoie, Valérie Lanctôt, Yannick Morin, and Christine Poulin—and a remarkable research partner, Jan van Voorst. The task at hand required a slow pace, with every point being reconsidered many times, in order not to come to any hasty conclusion. They checked my methodological rigor and contributed constant feedback. Without their stimulating enthusiasm and intellectual openness, the task would have been much harder—and much less fun. Thanks to them for the joy and their sparkling eyes. I thank John Goldsmith and Jane Grimshaw for their suggestions and criticisms of an earlier version of the manuscript, as well as two anonymous reviewers. Their comments have led to many improvements. I would also like to express my profound gratitude to Geoffrey Huck of the University of Chicago Press for his unfailing support and his insightful comments. This research would not have been possible without grants from the Social Sciences and Research Council of Canada (grants 410-89-1452 and 410-92-0766) and the Fonds du Québec pour la Formation des Chercheurs et l'Avancement de la Recherche (grant 95-ER-1637): these resources allowed the team to concentrate on the task at hand. A grant from L'Université du Québec à Montréal helped to pay part of the copyediting work done by Jennifer Ormston. For the many things that I thought I was saying, and that you made me realize I wasn't, and for helping me turn my "Frenglish" into English, thank you, Jennifer. Finally, I would like to thank my "ghost readers," those two individuals whom I constantly had in the back of my mind while writing, hoping that I could at the same time live up to the very different and very demanding standards of Noam Chomsky and Nicolas Ruwet.

PART I: THE RELATIONSHIP BETWEEN FORM AND MEANING

1 The Semantics of Syntax
Defining the Object of Inquiry

The main thesis of this book is that most linguistic theories are based on the wrong semantics. They are GLOBAL approaches to semantics, in that they, to a large extent, incorporate information that is part of the background knowledge shared by speakers. Such theories are "too concrete"; they involve elements that play no explanatory role in grammar. The assumption that information from background knowledge is involved in the mapping from semantic structures to syntactic structures has led researchers to postulate semantic representations which are very different from the syntactic representations they assume. The correspondence between semantics and syntax is then so distorted that it is practically impossible to state.

I will argue that the appropriate semantics for linguistic description is what I call selective mentalist semantics. Under this approach, semantic representations are purged of the background knowledge shared by speakers. The much more abstract semantic representations of this approach are related to the syntactic representations by principled, straightforward correspondence rules. This mapping is subject to Full Identification, which says that every syntactic element must correspond to something in the semantic representation and that every semantic element must be identified by something in the syntactic representation.

This principle follows from economy—no element can be introduced in either the syntax or the semantic representation unless it is traceable to linguistic evidence. Viewing economy in this way has important repercussions for syntactic structures and operations, as we will see in chapter 2.

In chapter 3, case studies of the effects of the approach on the analysis of lexical properties are presented. It is shown, for a class of French verbs (*aller* 'go', *venir* 'come', *arriver* 'arrive', *partir* 'leave', *sortir* 'go out', *entrer* 'enter'), that the correspondence rules mapping semantic representations to syntax are homomorphic. This requires lexical semantic representations constructed on two assumptions: that nonrelevant material should be excluded and that meaning is encoded in the form of representations themselves. Moreover, the various uses of these verbs in different semantic fields such as Space, Time, and Identification can be accounted for without recourse to metaphoric extensions of "basic uses."

In chapters 4 and 5, the effects on the syntax are presented. Given that vacuous projection is ruled out in principle, syntactic structures with non-branching nodes and "open" positions as landing sites for transformations are strictly impossible. We will see two constructions where this has an effect. First, in chapter 4, we will look at Psych verb constructions, for which NP movement into an open position has been proposed. Second, a case of head movement, that of Verb raising in French and English, will be studied in chapter 5. The potential effects on A-bar movement are examined, through Wh-movement and agreement effects in French, as we go along.

In accordance with the initial program of generative grammar, a mentalist view of semantics is adopted. I assume that Grammar is autonomous from other cognitive capacities, since not all aspects of mentally represented meaning have effects on the Grammar. The autonomy of Grammar is usually assumed in terms of the autonomy of syntax from meaning. This is not a possible definition in my approach because the representations themselves have meaning. The nature of autonomy must therefore be reassessed.

There are three tasks that are usually attributed to semantic representations: (1) semantic representations must describe the meaning of a word, phrase, or sentence; (2) semantic representations must account for semantic properties, such as synonymy, entailment, inconsistency, anomaly, judgments of superordination and subordination, and the like; (3) semantic representations must be mapped onto syntactic structures by correspondence rules. An important question that arises is whether these tasks are accomplished using the *same* semantic representations. This is an empirical question. In a global mentalist approach, it is assumed that the same semantic representations are used for the three tasks. In the selective mentalist approach I am advocating, tasks (1) and (3) are accomplished using the same representations, but these representations will look very different from those assumed in a global approach because background knowledge is excluded. As for task (2), most of it is considered not to be accomplished by the Grammar because it involves knowledge, not meaning. For instance, consider the dictionary definition of a synonym—a word or phrase identical and coextensive in sense and usage with another of the same language (*The Concise Oxford Dictionary of Current English*). Some relations of synonymy are systematic and involve nearly the same sense, such as the relation that holds between actives and passives (although, as Ruwet (1991) points out, the subject of a passive must have a referential autonomy, which is not required of the object of an active). Accounting for these relations is part of the task of Grammar. But most relations of synonymy do not involve the same meaning—the two expressions provide similar information only about a given situation and involve a relation of knowledge rather than meaning. This is the case for pairs such as *I already went to Paris twice this year/I've already been to Paris twice this year* and *John sent Mary a letter/Mary received a letter from John.* Moreover, as we will see below, substitution in these cases is never exactly equivalent. It is not the task of Grammar to account for these relations.

In the next sections, I present a detailed analysis of the properties of global approaches to the representation of meaning so that we can understand why and where they fail (section 1.1). This will allow us to elaborate a selective mentalist approach, which avoids these problems, in section 1.2. The theory will be shown to be an improvement, in that the abstract meanings arrived at allow a highly constrained linking between semantics and syntax, which explains some syntactic phenomena and provides a better descriptive adequacy in lexical semantics. Also crucial is the fact that the approach allows one to do semantics without having to wait for a theory of the knowledge of the world, since it abstracts away from such knowledge—Grammar is autonomous from the theory of the knowledge of the world. The approach also affects how the relationship between Form and Meaning is viewed, which I explore in section 1.3.

1.1 GLOBAL APPROACHES TO MEANING

Most current approaches, including the actantial structures of Tesnière and Greimas, the Cases of Fillmore, the thematic roles of Chomsky and Jackendoff, the cognitive models of Lakoff and Langacker, and the associations with real or possible worlds of most model-theoretic approaches, to some extent make use of features of our knowledge of the world. These approaches are "global," and in many respects they are more a representation of knowledge than a representation of meaning, since the distinction between concept and signification is not clearly made. For example, Ray Jackendoff assumes such a global approach: for him, there is a *single* level of mental representation, Conceptual Structure, at which information conveyed by language is compatible with information from other systems such as vision, nonverbal audition, smell, or kinesthesia. Moreover, "syntactic form is mapped by the correspondence rules directly into Conceptual Structure, without an intermediate level that accounts for purely linguistic inference. . . . If this is the case, the distinction between "semantic" rules of linguistic inference and "pragmatic" rules of linguistic interaction with general knowledge is less marked than is often supposed" (Jackendoff 1983, 105).

Chomsky has always assumed, echoing Bloomfield (1933), that we have only very imperfect knowledge of the world we live in. This leads him to conclude that a scientific theory of such knowledge is not imminent, and he is thus reluctant to appeal to such knowledge in grammatical explanation. But in the minimalist program of Chomsky (1992), the representation of meaning takes on such an important role that it is impossible to further postpone the discussion of the specific content of these representations of meaning, if the theory is to be testable. The problem that we have poor theories of knowledge of the world and need representations of meaning to complete the theory of grammar can be solved if we distinguish between the *reference* of a sentence, the situation to which it can refer in a given use, and its actual *meaning,* its abstract semantic representation. If reference and meaning are kept separate, we can elaborate a theory of meaning without having to understand knowledge itself. In other words, it is crucial to take into account that the representation of meaning is an INTERFACE level; it does not bluntly and globally incorporate the elements of the representation of knowledge with which it is interfacing.[1] In the minimalist program that I propose here, knowledge of the world is not part of the representation of meaning. However, our knowledge of the world does play an essential part in our interpretation of a sentence. It provides information, which combines with the abstract semantic representation of the sentence itself, so that we can determine the actual situation referred to. This is a selective mentalist approach to semantics because only a small, abstract part of meaning is relevant to grammatical processes; situational aspects of meaning are not part of Grammar. The problem that we have poor theories of knowledge of the world but need representations of meaning to complete the theory of grammar, arises only if we build this knowledge into the grammar, not if we build onto it to compute the situation.

The fact that most linguistic theories take a global approach to semantics is in large part due to the influence of logic on the study of language. As Jackendoff puts it, "The avowed purpose of truth-conditional semantics is to explicate Truth, a relation between language and reality, independent of language users. In turn, truth-conditions can be treated as speaker-independent only if both reality *and* the language that describes it are speaker-independent as well. Hence a truth-conditional semantics in the Tar-skian or Davidsonian sense requires a theory of E-language, of language as an abstract artifact extrinsic to speakers" (Jackendoff 1990*a,* 12). But, as Milner (1989, 341–44) observes, if the proposed formalism is intended to be a hypothesis about the synthetic properties of language, rather than a rigorous representation of what is relevant for the logician in language, then not just any representation of the meaning of a sentence will be acceptable. A pro-posal must be evaluated according to its ability to answer questions such as "What are the properties that distinguish a natural language from what is not a natural language?" "What is a possible word?" and "What is a possible sentence?" In short, if a theory is concerned with synthetic properties of lan-guage, then its formalism is subject to a linguistic relevance criterion.

On the other hand, "the purpose of generative grammar has always been to explicate I-language, the principles internalized by speakers that constitute knowledge of language" (Jackendoff 1990a, 12). Thus, there is a fundamental difference between such a mentalist approach and a logic-based approach to meaning. The contrast between the two positions is expressed nicely in Stan-ley Rosen's discussion of Frege's idea that there must be an objective, global approach to meaning:[2]

> Frege offers a metaphor by way of explanation: geographers do not create seas by drawing border lines on a map. Unfortunately this meta-phor overlooks the fact that maps are already images or conceptualiza-tions of the earth, constructed in accordance with human intentions and perceptions. Needless to say, neither a Platonist nor a Kantian would claim that man creates the seas. But the significance or sense of the seas may be man-made: this is the central question of both ontol-ogy and semantics, and Frege leaves it unanswered if not entirely un-asked. (Rosen 1980, 25)

The internalized principles of language, the I-language, relate to internalized principles of conceptualization of reality. The speaker does not create reality in doing so, but the speaker does give it a significance that it would not otherwise have.

Although many more theories of semantics espouse a mentalist approach to language, they nevertheless incorporate a good deal of the global view of meaning which a logic-based approach requires, where knowledge of the world is the relevant concept. This can be seen in some of the primitives adopted in global mentalist approaches, such as thematic roles, which try to represent our knowledge of the situation referred to by a sentence. My contention is that without a corresponding shift from a global to a selective approach to meaning the transition to a mentalist approach is bound to fail because language does not say anything directly about events, it only provides a very abstract outline of events and we use our shared background knowledge to fill in the details. I will examine this issue with respect to some central questions of linguistic theory: the linking problem (section 1.1.1), the problem of accounting for polysemy (section 1.1.2), and problems of descriptive adequacy in lexical semantics (section 1.1.3).

1.1.1 THE LINKING PROBLEM

If inadequate semantic representations are adopted, then the correspondence between semantics and syntax is impossible to state because one of the elements in the relation does not have the appropriate properties. Ray Jackendoff is among the linguists who are critical of applying some of the formalism of logic to the study of language because many notions of logic are understood analogically with natural language. He also has qualms about the use of such formalism because it fails to explain generalizations about syntax. He gives an example from traditional quantificational logic, where a sentence like "Floyd broke the glass" is represented as (1a), or, in the notation of restricted quantification, as (1b) (Jackendoff 1983, 14–15).

(1)   Floyd broke the glass
    a. $\exists x \, (glass(x) \, \& \, break \, (Floyd, x))$
    b. $\exists x_{glass(x)} \, (break \, (Floyd, x))$

There are three linking problems with these representations. First, there are symbols such as & (*and*) which have no syntactic equivalent. Second, the syntactic constituent "the glass" does not correspond to any semantic constituent; the same problem arises for the syntactic constituent "break the glass". Finally, these representations severely distort the dominance relations of the sentence.[3]

This criticism has often been raised against traditional quantificational logic, and it has been answered by the widespread adoption of generalized quantifiers and restricted quantification. The main difficulty that I want to underscore is not with the scattering of syntactic constituents that may result from the formalism adopted for semantic representations. This can be corrected, and it has been in many instances. However, having one's semantic representations based on properties of use rather than of meaning raises problems in addressing the task of representation of meaning of lexical items and in accounting for the correspondence with syntactic structure, regardless of the formalism that is adopted. Thus, an approach that is global and mentalist does not fare better than a global approach based on logic. For example, in a global mentalist approach like the one advocated by Ray Jackendoff, correspondence is established between syntactic structure and the whole Conceptual Structure (CS), which includes much background knowledge. Including this knowledge about use in the semantic representation of a sentence, as if it were part of the meaning, makes the representation of the meaning of the sentence much more complex. For example, consider the use of the verb *hit* illustrated in (2):

(2)   Sue hit Fred with a stick. (see Jackendoff 1987a)

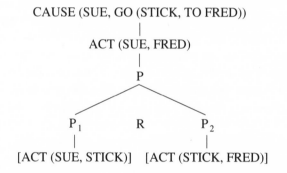

CAUSE (SUE, GO (STICK, TO FRED)) is the thematic tier, and it is directly related to the action tier ACT (SUE, FRED). This action tier is, in turn, related to P, a point on the temporal tier. This temporal point P is decomposed into an initial temporal point P_1, a temporal region R, and a final temporal point P_2. A second action tier, ACT (SUE, STICK), is associated with P_1, and a third action tier, ACT (STICK, FRED), is associated with P_2. The representation expresses that Sue causes a stick to go to Fred and that by doing this, Sue acts on Fred; this action begins with an action of Sue on the stick and ends with an action of the stick on Fred.

Because of the complexity introduced by the inclusion of background knowledge, this kind of representation faces the same three problems that Jackendoff discussed with respect to logic-based representations like (1) above.

First, there are symbols, such as the temporal tier, and elements of the action tiers, such as ACT, that have no syntactic equivalent.

Second, the correspondence between syntactic constituents and semantic constituents is very indirect: the argument *Sue* appears in three different positions in the Conceptual Structure; the VP is as scattered in the representation (2) as the NP *a glass* and the VP *broke the glass* are in (1).

Third, the representation in (2) also distorts some dominance relations of the sentence: thus, if the order of arguments in (2) expresses some relative order of composition, with the first element entering last into composition, STICK precedes FRED on two tiers and so should presumably be higher than FRED in syntax, but it is not.

Because a given argument is typically scattered and enters into many relations, in a Conceptual Structure and similar representations that try to describe the situation that the sentence refers to, argument linking with syntax is forced to be indexical. That is, some additional mechanism is needed to indicate the appropriate linking. Typically in global approaches, a list (sometimes ordered) is extracted from the semantic structure and another list (also sometimes ordered) is extracted from the syntactic structure. Then the two lists are matched up. The organizational aspects of the semantic representation and of the syntactic representation are totally irrelevant, as far as argument linking is concerned. There is nothing in the basic architecture of such an approach that leads us to expect any regularities in linking; these have to be stipulated in statements such as Perlmutter and Postal's UAH (1984) or Baker's UTAH (1988). There is so much to list in these stipulations, if sufficiently detailed (e.g., Jackendoff 1990a, especially chapter 11), that explanatory adequacy is very low and the outcome not very revealing. The process leads us to expect that the relation between semantic and syntactic structure is essentially arbitrary.

One can incorporate redundancy statements like UTAH so as to disallow nonoccurring forms. But as Carter (1988, 3) puts it, "If, however, the redundancies are very great and universal, the question arises whether it might not be preferable to shop around for a theory which would exclude the non-occurring cases on principle." Like Carter, I believe that an approach based on redundancy statements is misguided and is likely to lead to confusion because the linking regularities are more abstract in nature. Specifically, they are based on a homomorphic relationship between the syntactic and semantic representations, as will be discussed in chapter 2.

1.1.2 THE EFFECT OF GLOBALITY ON POLYSEMY:
GENERALIZED HOMONYMY

The complexity of the semantic representations, which is caused by the incorporation of background knowledge, has another detrimental effect. There is an explosition of semantic representations: a lexical item with *n* uses will have *n* different semantic representations. Because situational material from one particular use of the lexical item is entered as part of the representation of its meaning, it is virtually impossible to relate that lexical entry to another use in which different situational material is represented. Technically, therefore, each of the various representations of a lexical item corresponds to only one meaning of that element. A polysemous element, one which can correspond to various situations, is treated as if it were many different lexical items, each with its own meaning; polysemy is dealt with as homonymy. Jackendoff (1990a) acknowledges this problem, but he offers no solution. His attempts at solving the problem (in chapter 4 of Jackendoff 1990a) by using dashed underlines and angled brackets to express optionality fail to express that in *Sue hit Fred* the object in motion is a part of Sue's body (and not necessarily her hand as Jackendoff suggests), as he recognizes in note 9, p. 295. Furthermore, he underestimates the problem of polysemy. (This will be clear in our discussion of HIT in (43)–(51) in section 1.5.2.2.2 below and in Part II on French verbs of movement).

The problem is that if these multiple uses of lexical items are dealt with as separate lexical entries, the Grammar then fails to account for the fact that closely related lexical items across languages are consistently used in similar situations. To give one simple example, why is it that in so many languages the verb that expresses a movement similar to the English 'go' also expresses FUTURE? In Part II, I will argue that this follows from the meaning of these lexical items, once a proper level of abstraction has been reached.

1.1.3 DESCRIPTIVE ADEQUACY IN LEXICAL SEMANTICS

Because global approaches to semantics do not distinguish between background knowledge and linguistic meaning, they include elements from the context of use in semantic representations. This has two important effects: an explosive effect as discussed above, since a word with *n* different uses is assigned *n* different representations, and a reductive effect, in that two elements with the same use and, thus, the same truth conditions tend to be given the same semantic representation.

But as Vandeloise (1986) observes, language is not created in a vacuum, and it makes an intense use of the shared conceptual knowledge of speakers. An example of the distinction between linguistic knowledge and conceptual knowledge is found in his careful study of spatial prepositions in French. He observes that language differs significantly from geometry or logic in that, "contrary to those exact sciences which aspire to offer exhaustive and autonomous information to an interlocutor who is completely ignorant of the context, language ignores all detail not useful for its immediate means and maximally exploits knowledge common to participants in the discourse. That shared knowledge, which both logic and geometry ignore, constitutes the necessary web on which language is woven."[4] Not taking into consideration the distinction between linguistic and conceptual knowledge creates problems of descriptive adequacy.

Consider the descriptive problems created by the reductive effect. It has frequently been observed that logically equivalent expressions are not conceptually equivalent. For example, Pinker (1989) notes that, for verbs that undergo the dative alternation in English, "the meaning change accompanying dativization is logically vacuous: causing Y to go into possession of Z is barely different from causing Z to possess Y. It is not psychologically vacuous, however, as it does have discourse consequences, allowing the speaker to focus either on what is done to the possessor or on what is done to the possession." (83)

A similar point is made by Vandeloise (1986, 20), who notes that some prepositional expressions are said to be converse because equivalence relations like the following hold:

(3) a is in front of $b = b$ is behind a

But the function of these prepositions in their spatial use is to locate a small and mobile object with respect to a larger and more stable object, hence the contrast between (4) and (5).

(4)   The stick is in front of the house.

(5)   #The house is behind the stick.

As for the descriptive problems induced by the explosive effect, they can be illustrated by the French preposition DANS ('in'). The objects related to one another by this preposition can be objects with one, two, or three dimensions.

(6)   les bijoux sont dans la boîte
        the jewels are in the box

(7)   la vache est dans la prairie
        the cow is in the prairie

(8)   le curé est dans la file
        the priest is in the line

In a global approach, three different representations of DANS would be required here. But as Vandeloise points out, the appropriateness of DANS depends on the potential of the object of DANS to function as a container, regardless of the number of dimensions it has. Three-dimensional objects satisfy this requirement more often than one- or two-dimensional objects, but this is a property of these objects as we conceive of them in space, not of the preposition DANS; it should not be encoded in the representation of DANS. As long as an object is a potential container, regardless of how many dimensions it has, it is appropriate as the complement of DANS, as the following contrast shows:

(9)   la ligne est dans le coin de la page
        the line is in the corner of the page

(10)   #la ligne est dans la page
        the line is in the page

As Vandeloise (1986, 15) observes, in a world where entities can be conceived of according to one, two, or three dimensions, there is nothing surprising if the same options are found in the objects that are complements of spatial prepositions. But again, this is not an essential property of these prepositions. Logico-geometric generalizations are likely to mask the real nature of these prepositions because the way we perceive the spatial world has some consequences on their use. But these consequences are never necessary on linguistic grounds. What is linguistically relevant for the preposition DANS is the container/containee relationship. Therefore, only this relationship should be expressed in the abstract representation of DANS. How this relationship applies to a given object—that is, what factors count in determining whether an object is a potential container or not—depends on the nature of the object and will vary accordingly. If we are dealing with objects that are spatial in nature, as is the case in the examples above, then I see three factors at play:

(11) *Factor A:* The container controls the position of the containee and
   not vice versa.
   Factor B: The containee is included, at least partially, in the container.
   Factor C: An object contains its interior, but not its boundaries.

However, factor C does not really need to be specified, if we assume that
boundaries delimit the containing area and that a boundary does not control itself.

So, in a container/containee relationship in the spatial field, the container
controls the containee in an area delimited by boundaries which are determined by the container. Crucially, the boundaries are determined by extralinguistic factors which are field-specific, not by something about the preposition. By removing these factors from the realm of linguistics, it is possible to
give a general and precise definition of the preposition. Because a container
controls the position of a containee in all directions, there is nothing surprising or marked about the use of DANS with one- or two-dimensional objects:
there are simply fewer directions involved in these cases.

We can see the effects of these two factors in the following examples. First,
control is a key factor, regardless of size, as we see in the following contrast:

(12)a. *la bouteille est dans le capuchon
      *the bottle is in the cap
   b.   l'arbre est dans le pot
      the tree is in the pot

The effects of the control factor are also seen in the following two contrasts:

(13)a. *Le fil est dans la pince à linge
      *the line is in the clothespin
   b.   le fil est dans la pince
      the line is in the pliers

(14)a.   l'aiguille est dans le champ de l'aimant
      the needle is in the field of the magnet
   b.   *l'allumette est dans le champ de l'aimant
      the match is in the field of the magnet

The following examples show that, contrary to what a superficial analysis
would lead one to expect, factor B is not sufficient to determine containment:

(15)a.   le camembert est sous (*dans) la cloche à fromage
      *the camembert is under (*in) the cheese bell*

b.   le camembert est dans le plat
      the camembert is in the dish

DANS is not possible in (15a) because of the absence of control: moving the dish will induce a change in the position of the camembert, but lifting the cheese bell will not. On the other hand, there are opposite control relationships between dish and bell and a gas: hence the contrast in (16).

(16)a.   le gaz précieux est dans la cloche à fromage
        the precious gas is in the cheese bell
   b.   *le gaz précieux est dans le plat
        * *the precious gas is in the dish*

Still, the potential of the container to act as a boundary, expressed by factor B is needed to account for the impossibility of the following:[5]

(17)   *l'éléphant est hors de la boîte d'allumettes
      * *the elephant is out of the matchbox*

(18)   *le ruisseau est hors de la maison
      * *the brook is out of the house*

Under the hypothesis that linguistically relevant semantics is highly abstract and contextually determined, in interaction with general knowledge, only semantic representations based on sufficiently abstract notions will be able to account for language use adequately. The foregoing discussion shows that this is, indeed, the case and that a very abstract representation of prepositions is required, even to account only for their spatial uses. In the case of DANS, it is the container/containee relationship that is linguistically relevant. Speakers' general knowledge will identify the factors that determine whether an object is a potential container in a given semantic field (spatial or otherwise). It is because these factors are removed from the linguistic definitions that generalizations are possible in the definitions of such prepositions. A selective approach to semantics, in which the knowledge factors specific to particular semantic domains are not part of Grammar, does not have the problem for descriptive adequacy that is raised by the explosion of semantic representations for every single lexical item.[6]

1.1.4 Summary of Global Approaches to Meaning

Global approaches fail empirically because they do not distinguish between background knowledge and linguistic meaning. This prevents them from making generalizations at the level of abstractness appropriate for linguistic analysis. For example, we saw with DANS that a consequence of including elements from the context of use in the semantic representation of sentences is the failure to account for its actual use in a revealing way. These empirical problems arise from an improper definition of the object of inquiry. Global approaches consider that the object of inquiry is the relationship between linguistic form and situational semantics—the semantics of background knowledge, causing both reductive and explosive effects, which in turn cause problems with linking and polysemy.

1.2 A SELECTIVE APPROACH TO MEANING

The selective mentalist position taken here is closer to Chomsky's original views than are the various positions of recent conceptual semantics because it holds that a large part of meaning is *not* relevant to Grammar. Crucially, all aspects of meaning that are situational must be removed from the study of Grammar, since they overload the Grammar with redundant material and prevent the formulation of important empirical generalizations. Global approaches tend to incorporate the web of the shared conceptual knowledge of speakers into the Grammar. I argue that it is important to understand exactly what those general conceptual properties are in order to remove them from the Grammar. The notion of theta roles, among others, will be seen to be part of situational notions that have no effect on the grammar.

The second important point of the approach presented here is that semantics has more effect on syntax than simply to determine the projection of lexical semantic properties. I assume that the very form of semantic representations has meaning and, crucially, that this meaning affects the syntax adopted. Hence, as is the case in mathematics, a purely formal approach to syntax in a technical sense, à la Hilbert, is abandoned.

These two points correspond to two possible interpretations of the title of this book. On the one hand, "the semantics of syntax" can refer to the semantics which is relevant to syntax, excluding other aspects of meaning; on the other hand, it can refer to the meaning present in the syntactic representations themselves. Both of these views have major effects on the relationship between syntax and semantics, since they radically affect the form of the semantic representations. Given this change in the approach to semantic representations, I will argue in chapter 2 that a form of homomorphic correspondence holds between syntactic representations and lexical semantic representations. This correspondence is highly constrained in a way that follows from the architecture of the theory, in contrast to the usual "indexical" approaches to correspondence which require stipulations of the UAH or UTAH type (Perlmutter and Postal 1984; Baker 1988). Syntax is reduced to the bare essentials of structural concatenation; every node must be licensed by a corresponding homomorphic relation in the semantic representation. Hence, vacuous projections in syntax are not possible in this approach.

Furthermore, I argue that Conceptual Structure must have some internal substructure because not all information in Conceptual Structure is available to the Grammar; for example, although it is in Conceptual Structure, background knowledge plays no role in Grammar, per se. This partitioning effect is caused by the way conceptual properties are organized in our mental representations. They are not all represented in the same way, and only a certain class of representations are accessible to correspondence rules that map onto syntactic form—namely, those representations that take the form of tree structures. This claim will affect the location of the cut-off point for the autonomy of Grammar: it is not between syntax and semantics, but rather between two types of semantics. I will go even further and argue that meaning lies on three planes. As illustrated in figure 1, a first, important part of meaning belongs to general cognitive capacities and has no direct bearing on linguistic analysis. On the contrary, one must abstract from this background knowledge in order to get to the linguistically relevant aspects of meaning, i.e., those that affect the form of the sentence (its structure and what elements appear in each of the positions in this structure). I will call this background knowledge Situational Semantics (S-semantics). Second, of the linguistically relevant aspects of meaning, some affect syntactic form (I call them Grammar Semantics (G-semantics)) while others do not (I call them Linguistic Semantics (L-semantics)).

Conceptual Structure

Situational Semantics	Linguistic Semantics
	Grammar Semantics

We shall see that G-semantics is formally different from L-semantics and that its relationship to actual situations is much coarser than S-semantics (but not vague). The autonomy of Grammar lies in the distinct formal properties of G-semantics, properties which directly determine formal properties of the syntax.

How does such a program fit into the generative enterprise initiated by Chomsky some four decades ago? As we will see, it addresses questions now at the forefront because of a gradual shift that has taken place with respect to the position of semantics in grammar. At its outset, generative grammar was a formal approach to language in the strictest of senses: it set itself the task of explaining the distribution of formal elements of language. Gradually, however, semantics has come to play an increasingly important role in grammatical explanation for linguists of all allegiances. As McCawley (1976, 6) writes, semantics first started to play a role in generative grammar with the advent of *Aspects,* which "brought semantics out of the closet. Here was finally a theory of grammar that not only incorporated semantics (albeit very programmatically) but indeed claimed that semantics was systematically related to syntax and made the construction of syntactic analyses a matter of much more than just accounting for the distribution of morphemes." Generative Semanticists took this position in its extreme form, departing from the distributional orientation to an approach where the mediational orientation dominates and in which the goal of linguistic analysis is seen as an attempt to discover and explain the relationship between sound and meaning: "a grammar is a specification of what the relationship between semantic structures and surface structures is, and the claim that a distinction between syntactic rules and semantic rules must be drawn is a claim requiring justification" (McCawley 1976, 10–11). Huck and Goldsmith (forthcoming) provide an enlightening discussion of these distributional and mediational orientations.

The idea that some aspects of the compositional semantics of a sentence project fairly directly onto its syntactic structure, so that syntax is dependent on semantics in some of its formal aspects, is also found in Montague grammar, an approach that had a lot of influence on generativists. Montague grammar has an explicit projection principle, which essentially states that syntactic and compositional semantic structures are isomorphic; that is, logico-semantic relations are the source of grammatical relations.[7]

In Chomsky's own work, we find the same shift toward a more mediational orientation, although the shift was more gradual. Thus, the notion of projection played an increasingly important role, mostly via the level of Logical Form introduced in Chomsky (1975a). A few years later, in *Lectures on Government and Binding,* we find a highly relativized notion of autonomy of syntax, where it is assumed that essentially all dynamic properties of syntax are projected from lexical structures (LS), with X-bar theory handling the remaining, purely geometric, properties of syntactic structures. There were soon an abundance of studies on LS, since it became of great importance to determine the nature of these LS from which Syntactic Structures (SS) are projected, in order to better understand both. Chomsky's shift from a dominantly distributional orientation to a dominantly mediational orientation culminated in his minimalist approach (Chomsky 1992), where Deep Structure disappears and the only two linguistic levels are the interface levels A-P and C-I, which provide the instructions for the articulatory-perceptual and conceptual-intentional systems, respectively. A computational system mediates between the two levels. Conditions on representations—those of Binding Theory, Case Theory, Theta Theory, etc.—hold only at the interface and are motivated by properties of the interface.

There has been a second shift in generative grammar that will be very important for the proposals that I will make; it is the shift in the form of semantic and syntactic representations. Early on, under the influence of Zellig Harris, it was generally assumed that the structure of meaning differed from the structure of form (for example, see Harris 1951). He recognized that language has a special relation to meaning. But the relation is not simple, and, for him, the forms of language are structured independently from the meanings of language. Harris establishes a correspondence between the structure of language and the structure of objective experience from which we presumably draw our meanings. Like his predecessor Bloomfield and his successor Chomsky, Harris' perception that form and meaning differ greatly comes from an assumption about the nature of these two objects rather than from an examination of the process of correspondence itself: meaning is assumed to incorporate background knowledge.

But semantics was brought much closer to syntax under the influence of McCawley (1968a), who argued that semantic representations had the form of labeled trees. His tree structures expressed certain aspects of standard logic: the predicate-argument organization of the clause, quantificational scope, and anaphor-antecedent relations. Chomsky (1975a) incorporated most of this in his LF level.

This double shift, in the effects of meaning on syntax and in the form of semantic representations, brings some basic questions to the forefront. If the semantic interface has such strong effects on the syntax, it becomes imperative to address the following questions:

(19) (i)   How are semantic properties organized in our mental representa-
           tion of them?
     (ii) How directly do semantic properties map onto syntactic
           structure?
     (iii) Which properties of Conceptual Structure participate in the map-
           ping onto syntactic structures and which do not?

Clearly, the three questions are interrelated. The answers to (i) and (iii) will
greatly determine the answer to (ii). If situational aspects of meaning are
removed from Grammar, as I argue, then syntactic structure is related to a
much less "concrete" semantic representation, a semantic representation that
could have formal properties that are quite different from other aspects of
Conceptual Structure. In fact, I will argue that the formal properties of semantic representations are like those of syntactic representations; it is for this
reason that semantic representations map onto syntactic representations. We
must therefore reconsider our answers to the three questions above.

1.3 A MINIMALIST APPROACH TO GRAMMAR

The selective approach to meaning adopted here assumes semantic representations that are much less cluttered and more abstract: all redundancy with
the content of background knowledge is avoided, and only what is minimally
necessary is retained. Given the assumption that tree structures have meaning, the effect of the selective approach is that syntactic structures are also
pared down. What can appear in syntax is severely constrained; no vacuous
projection is possible, which results in minimal syntactic structures. In the
selective approach, there is a convergence of semantic and syntactic representations, since both are more minimal. Therefore, we must reconsider what
constitutes a semantic representation and a syntactic representation.

This book is therefore an invitation to live a mild case of "Cartesian
doubt," in the sense of the *Discours de la méthode*. Without going so far as to
reject as absolutely false everything that could possibly be doubted, "in order
to see if there would be anything left after that in one's belief which would
be entirely indubitable," it invites the linguist to set aside temporarily the
numerous tools and traditionally accepted ideas of the trade and to go back
to some very basic questions and give them a fresh look.

Suppose we momentarily forget the host of analytical tools at our disposal
and ask ourselves what we need to assume, minimally, about language to
account for the relation between form and meaning. How little can we get
away with?

Consider first *form*. It seems to be difficult to get by without a notion of units that have an independent and verifiable distribution—words. Distributional factors, some morphological, others having to do with order, indicate that we also need a notion of category for these words, such as Noun, Verb, Adjective, and Preposition. Finally, additional distributional factors tell us that words are grouped into higher level units. To express these subgroupings among words, I will assume the minimal branching relation in (20).

(20)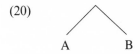

Now consider *meaning*. We can distinguish between elements expressing different meanings, so, minimally, we need some semantic primitives. These primitives combine into larger units, so we need a means of expressing a combination function. The form of this combination function follows from the fact that we perceive distinctiveness, according to Plato, as a dichotomy. Since all distinctions can be reduced to a system of dichotomy, the minimal expression of the combination of primitives into larger units is a binary association, as in (21).

(21) $[_\gamma \, \alpha \, \beta]$

In determining semantic primitives, we can either assume that all factors relevant in computing the situations to which a given sentence can refer must be included in its semantic representation or assume that only the information directly expressed by the linguistic elements in the sentence are included in the semantic representation. One way to determine what constitutes this limited information is to exclude what is built from the context, hence to incorporate only what is common to all uses of a given word or phrase (or, more realistically, to as many uses as we can come up with). Since speakers have in common a vast store of knowledge about the contexts of use of any given sentence, knowledge which is independent of language, the minimal assumption is that the second, much more abstract, representation of meaning is all that is needed. The hearer can compute the situation being referred to by combining the abstract semantic representation of the sentence with the extralinguistic information of the context.

Situational information should be excluded from semantic representations because to include it would make the system massively redundant.[8] Overcrowding the semantic representations in this way would render them quite different from the comparatively simple syntactic forms. Such an approach would incorrectly lead us to expect that there are no regularities in the correspondence between form and meaning; for example, it would predict that the relation between argument type and syntactic position is essentially arbitrary. Furthermore, since under this approach, features of use are incorporated into the semantic representations as if they are part of the meaning, each word would have to be listed with all its possible contexts of use—this would result in generalized homonymy. On the whole, therefore, there are several reasons to assume *prima facie* that situational factors are not part of Grammar and should only be part of a linguistic description as a very last resort. This selective aspect of the level of G-semantics, which excludes features of use, is what distinguishes G-semantics from other widely assumed semantic levels, such as LF, the underlying structures of Generative Semantics, and the semantic levels assumed by GPSG, HPSG, LFG, and Montague Grammar. Generally, these levels are global, in the sense that they incorporate situational features that are based on equivalence of use, not of meaning.

Finally, consider the two relations in (20) and (21). They can both be seen as instances of a basic associative relation, so a minimal hypothesis is that the two are represented similarly. Since there is strong syntactic evidence for (20), we can assume that the minimal binary semantic association is also expressed in the form of a tree structure relation like the one in (20).

The elements of form, meaning, and structure outlined above are the bare minimum that is required, given observed data. If we adopt a strategy of minimalist economy toward Grammar, any additional notions will have to be traceable to linguistic evidence. This idea can be embodied in the following principle:

(22) *Principle of Full Identification:* Every (morpho-)syntactic formative of a sentence must have a corresponding element in the semantic representation. Every formative of a semantic representation must be identified by a (morpho-)syntactic element in the sentence, which is associated with that representation.

As we will see, Full Identification restricts the syntax—there can be no vacuous projections in syntax. So, for example, the syntactic structure of an N^{max} like *John* must be $[_N$ John$]$, not $[_{N''} [_{N'} [_N$ John$]]]$. Full Identification also constrains the semantics—no semantic primitive that is not identified by a morphosyntactic element can be postulated in the semantic representation of a sentence. For example, we will not postulate several entries for the

French verb *aller* in order to account for the fact that it can be used in several contexts, three of which are illustrated in (23):

(23)a. Ce nuage va de Montréal à Longueuil.
        That cloud goes from Montreal to Longueuil
          (i) movement
          (ii) extension
    b. Bruno va voir Marie.
        Bruno is-going-to see Marie
          (iii) future

All that *aller* expresses, I will argue, is that its subject is oriented toward its being in relation with the antideictic center ω, the complement of the deictic center ME-HERE-NOW (I will discuss these concepts fully in chapter 3). There is no primitive in the semantic representation of *aller* that expresses movement: a movement interpretation is possible for a sentence like (23a) because, given the nature of clouds, a likely way for such a spatio-temporal entity to establish a relation with ω is to move to it. But it is not the only way. Extension is a second possible context of use for (23a)—if the cloud is big enough, it could extend across the Saint Lawrence River, between Montreal and Longueuil. This difference is due not to a change in the predicate *aller,* but to our knowledge of clouds. However, these facts about the size of clouds have no effect on the Grammar. As for (23b), the fact that it can have a temporal interpretation is not due to the fact that there is a different, temporal *aller:* the same abstract relation is established as in (23a), but this time one of the arguments, *voir Marie,* is of a temporal rather than a spatial nature, so the situation computed is very different from the one in (23a). As far as meaning is concerned, *aller* remains constant in all of its uses. Situational primitives, such as MOVEMENT and EXTENSION (and thematic roles, which are situational notions derived from such primitives) appear to play no role in the semantics of verbs like *aller.*

How far can we go with this minimum, where syntax is pared down and semantics is purged of background knowledge? Surprisingly far, I will argue. Suppose we assume that a lexical item is a correspondence rule (Jackendoff 1987a, 1990a). Under this assumption, a lexical item is a rule that associates a specific semantic representation with a syntactic representation. Only two things have to be specified: (1) what semantic representation is an input to the rule and (2) what part of that semantic representation the lexical item itself identifies. The rest follows from Full Identification. First, any material identified by the lexical item, such as relations between arguments or the presence of constants, will not appear additionally in the syntax. Second, semantic elements not identified by the lexical item have to be linked to syntactic constituents, or a binder, in order to be identified. Third, what these elements link to is also determined by Full Identification. The syntactic and semantic formatives mentioned in the Principle of Full Identification include formatives of the tree structures, among which are the dominance relations. Therefore, the mapping between semantic representations and syntactic representations will be homomorphic: it will preserve the relative relations of the elements involved.

One consequence of Homomorphic Mapping is that promotion effects follow directly. Normally, the highest argument in a semantic representation will appear as the highest grammatical function in the syntactic structure, i.e., in subject position. But if this argument is neutralized, because of passive morphology, for example, and cannot map onto the syntactic representation, the next-highest argument will become the highest and map onto the subject position. The promotion effect is caused by a general linking convention that is derived from Full Identification. There is no need to postulate any convention about argument linking or possible promotion effects—relativized linking follows from Homomorphic Mapping, which derives from the architecture of the theory. The overall approach to language is, therefore, more autonomous than one that relies on situational notions like Agent, Patient, etc., because it is more abstract.

The minimalist approach I propose requires a shift in what counts as the semantics of syntax, since situational notions are purged from Grammar. This shift to greater abstractness has a wide range of consequences. In the lexicon, the main effect is that the semantic representations better express meaning, so that polysemy is not just listed. In terms of structure, we will see that it becomes possible to give a much more precise content to the following questions and their answers:

—What is a possible word? Answer: It must respect Homomorphic Mapping, hence endocentricity properties from the semantic representation (section 2.2.1).

—What is a possible syntactic node? Answer: It must correspond to a node of the semantic representation (section 2.1.1).

—What is a possible semantic primitive of Grammar? Answer: It is nonsituational (section 1.5.2).

—What is a possible syntactic structure? Answer: It is homomorphic with a semantic structure, so it is binary and contains no vacuous projections (section 2.2).

—What is a possible transformation? Answer: It can involve only Homomorphic Mapping. If a transformation involves two positions, the elements in both of these have to be licensed by nodes in the semantic representation, so there cannot be semantically unlicensed "open" positions, which only appear as landing sites for syntactic operations.[9]

The selective approach to meaning that I am advocating is akin to the insight that a number of people like Jerry Morgan, Lauri Karttunen, Ellen Prince, Jerry Sadock, Deirdre Wilson, and Ruth Kempson sought to build on in the attempt to develop a theory of pragmatics alongside a somewhat stripped-down theory of semantics. Important features that distinguish my approach from these earlier ones are the severe restriction imposed on semantic and syntactic representations by the Principle of Full Identification, and the role attributed to the meaning of the structure itself.

1.4 EFFECTS ON AUTONOMY

Proponents of the specificity of linguistic rules and principles generally see the issue in terms of the autonomy of the purely formal concepts of grammar from semantic notions: "the crucial question is whether these systematic relations involving the full range of semantic concepts enter into the determination (and perhaps the function) of the categories and rules of formal grammar, or whether they simply set conditions on the construction of a theory of linguistic form" (Chomsky 1977, 44). But there is something circular about this position, since the technical notion of "formal" is, by definition, independent of meaning (in the general acceptance of the term, not the restricted sense of "use" found in *Syntactic Structures*).

The question can be put more generally. In order to determine the degree of autonomy of syntax with respect to semantics, it is necessary to have a system of representation of syntax and a system of representation of semantics, as well as correspondence rules that relate the two. Only then can we determine the degree of autonomy of syntax. The more the systems of representation are different in their format, the more complicated the correspondence rules, and the impression that there is more autonomy may result from this complexity.

It is crucial to determine what syntax is autonomous from. The notion of meaning with respect to autonomy discussed by Chomsky has always been close to the notion of use—thus, for him, syntax is autonomous from the web of knowledge on which language is built, a position that I strongly endorse. Aside from "use," the semantic notions that Chomsky considers are rather coarse and general. For him, "the core notions of semantics" are notions like "synonymous," "significant," "denotes," and "refers to concrete objects." Some followers argue that notions like "specific" or "generic" (Hale, La Verne, and Platero 1977) and "affective" (Liberman 1974) should also be excluded from syntax. However, there are many semantic notions that are more abstract than these and more remote from use, and it is much less obvious that syntax is autonomous from some of these notions, as we will see later on. Moreover, the exclusion of semantic properties from syntax that Chomsky proposes is essentially limited to the transformational component: in most cases, it reduces to the following two claims (Newmeyer 1980, 237):

A. *The Semantic Motivation Prohibition:* Semantic evidence may not be used to motivate the existence of a transformational rule.
B. *The Semantic Construct Prohibition:* Semantic constructs may not appear in the formulation of a transformational rule.[10]

I will argue that in searching below the surface, going beyond such coarse notions, and looking at the base component instead of the transformational component, a very different picture emerges: most aspects of the base—and, indirectly, many aspects of the transformational component—derive from semantic properties, once an appropriate level of abstraction has been reached. Essentially, I take the position that although syntax might not be driven by semantic features, it is highly determined by semantic structure.

This proposal is in the same vein as other changes that have taken place since Chomsky's initial proposals. In syntactic theory, many approaches now incorporate some notion of projection of lexical semantic properties: these theories allow some aspects of the compositional semantics of a sentence to project fairly directly into syntax, so syntactic structure is dependent on semantics in some of its formal aspects. On the other hand, some semanticists have proposed a generative approach to Conceptual Structures in which Conceptual Structures have an internal structure formally similar to that of syntactic structures. This is more or less the position in Chomskian circles today. The convergence of syntax and semantics was also central in Generative Semantics, which was based in part on the idea that the underlying categories and structural organization of syntax and of semantics are very similar. These changes are highly significant for the issue of autonomy. It means that if we find any autonomy effects at all, they might not be in the notion of "formal" after all. The technical notion of "formal," in the sense of being absolutely independent from elements of meaning, is rendered inoperative by the idea of projection of lexical semantic properties. The practical notion of "formal," in the sense of precision and exhaustivity, can give an impression of autonomy, if the correspondence rules are highly complex; but if the structural organization of semantics is found to be much closer to that of syntactic structures and the correspondences get significantly simpler, then the impression of autonomy is lessened.

Since the systems of representation of linguistic form and of conceptual form are quite different than when the question of autonomy was raised in the early days of generative grammar, it is likely that the question of the interdependence of syntactic structures and semantic structures will be answered quite differently today. The additional step of reconsidering which aspects of semantics interact directly with grammar, excluding background knowledge, as I have suggested, has dramatic effects on autonomy. I will argue that semantic principles adequately account for many of the syntactic facts of particular languages: the empirical results presented in the rest of this book suggest that most of the configurational aspects of the sentence are determined by abstract semantics, not abstract syntax.

Before closing this section, I would like to comment briefly on some anecdotal arguments that are often proposed in favor of autonomy, sometimes by Chomsky himself, as in the following passage:

> There are, in fact, striking and *obvious* [my emphasis] differences between language learning and the learning (or discovery) of physics. In the first case, a rich and complex system of rules and principles is attained in a uniform way, rapidly, effortlessly, on the basis of limited and rather degenerate evidence. In the second case, we are forced to proceed on the basis of consciously articulated principles subjected to careful verification with the intervention of individual insight and often genius. It is clear enough that the cognitive domains in question are quite different. Humans are designed to learn language, which is nothing other than what their minds construct when placed in appropriate conditions; they are not designed in anything like the same way to learn physics. Gross observations suffice to suggest that very different principles of "learning" are involved. (Noam Chomsky in Piattelli-Palmarini 1980, 320)

Such comparisons are misleading because of the differences in the levels of the objects that are compared. First, the type of unconscious learning involved in language is also involved in some aspects of physics and music. For example, all individuals have the ability to do simple musical tasks like follow a beat. In physics, there is a great deal of unconscious knowledge, too (consider what Plato's slave boy knew or look at a child bouncing a ball against a wall, following numerous ballistic rules "in a uniform way, rapidly, effortlessly, on the basis of limited and rather degenerate evidence") (see also Jackendoff (1983, 128ff) for a technical discussion of the perceptual principles organizing collections of shapes and sounds, in particular the principle of proximity and the principle of similarity, which interact to reinforce or weaken one's judgment). Second, the converse is also true: there are aspects of language that do involve conscious learning. Thus, Jacques Mehler (in Piattelli-Palmarini 1980, 349) correctly points out that to write an alexandrine, compose a symphony, or master advanced physics are activities that all go beyond the shared capacities to speak, follow a beat, and get around in the physical world. Anecdotal arguments add nothing of interest to the discussion.

1.5 EFFECTS ON THE RELATIONSHIP BETWEEN FORM AND MEANING

There are four basic aspects to the selective approach adopted in this book. In section 1.5.1, I argue that classical categorization is used in Semantic Representations relevant for Grammar: categorization based on principles other than necessary and sufficient conditions appears to have no effect on the form and functioning of the Grammar, so, for example, I exclude fuzzy categorization from representations. In section 1.5.2, I look at the consequences of the proposed selective approach on the choice of semantic primitives. In section 1.5.3, I discuss formal differences that exist between the representations of the different kinds of semantics (S-semantics, L-semantics, and G-semantics). These three sections deal with the *relevance* side of the semantics of syntax: they have to do with what aspects of semantics are relevant to the form and functioning of Grammar. A fourth proposal, which is discussed in section 1.5.4, has to do with the *content* side of the semantics of syntax: I consider the general problem of the kind of meaning that structures have.

1.5.1 FUZZINESS AND CATEGORIZATION

If syntactic form maps onto a general Conceptual Structure, we expect aspects of syntax to reflect characteristics of elements in that general CS. Jackendoff (among many others) presents an argument to that effect: in grammatical categorization, he argues, we find fuzziness of the same type as that found in conceptual categorization. Words, contrary to common-sense intuition, do not have definite and precise meanings which can be exhaustively decomposed into necessary and sufficient conditions. Jackendoff (1983) discusses several examples to illustrate his point. Here are a few.

a)   COLOR: what exhaustive decomposition of RED can one give? Once the feature COLOR is stated, what is left to decompose further and how can one make sense of redness minus coloration? (112)[11]

b)   BIRD: This is the old problem of accounting for the fact that a robin is a better example of a BIRD than an ostrich or a penguin.

c)   VASE, CUP, and BOWL: a famous example ever since it was discussed in Labov (1973), who showed that at certain height-width ratios, the choice of label is highly sensitive to context, but it is not at others. "Such a graded response pattern shows that the boundaries of 'vase,' 'cup,' and 'bowl' are not precisely defined, as they should be if the [TYPES] were necessary and sufficient conditions" (Jackendoff 1983, 85–86).

d)   GAME: Wittgenstein's (1953) discussion of this word convinced many of the inadequacy of necessary and sufficient conditions in characterizing a word.

e)   KILL: Although Jackendoff (1990a, 150–51) shows that Fodor's celebrated (1970) argument against decomposing KILL as CAUSE TO BECOME NOT ALIVE is not so strong after all, the problem of the exact decomposition of the verb and of finding the "real" primitives still exists and is revealed in small descriptive inadequacies: "A rock's being not alive does not qualify it as dead. One can die slowly or horribly, but it is odd to talk of becoming dead slowly or horribly" (Jackendoff 1983, 113). This difficulty in pinning down the primitives is supposed to show, once again, the inadequacy of necessary and sufficient conditions.

f)   PERCEPTUAL WORDS: "Since among the possible words must be those for perceptual concepts, the theory of word meanings must be at least expressive enough to encompass the kinds of conditions such concepts require" (Jackendoff 1983, 128). He then argues that human beings make use of a whole system of grouping well-formedness rules and preference rules in deciding whether a particular collection of pitch-events in a musical stream is identified as a #group# and concludes that these rules must therefore be contained in the sense of the word (musical) *group*. "The complexity of this system thus sets a lower bound on the potential complexity of word meanings" (Jackendoff 1983, 135).

g)   MOVEMENT VERBS: walk, run, lope, jog, sprint, scurry. . . . These verbs also form a class of fuzzy and graded words.

Jackendoff concludes from such examples that fuzziness is widespread in language: "The moral is that fuzziness must not be treated as a defect in language; nor is a theory of language defective that countenances it. Rather . . . fuzziness is an inescapable characteristic of *the concepts that language expresses* [my emphasis]. To attempt to define it out of semantics is only evasion" (1983, 11).

But do these examples really show anything about how some aspects of syntax reflect characteristics of elements in general Conceptual Structure? Does fuzziness affect the linguistic behavior of any word? For example, can it be shown that some words are better examples of the categories Noun or Verb and that this has grammatically testable effects on the sentence? The examples do not show any such effects. Rather, as the words I emphasized in the quotation from Jackendoff indicate, it is not some grammatically relevant properties of words that are graded, but rather the concepts that are expressed. This gradience plays no role in the Grammar, as Jackendoff himself recognizes in his discussion of movement verbs:

> The differences among these verbs are not of particular grammatical import. . . . In this respect they resemble the color words, which also are grammatically homogeneous and can be really distinguished only by ostension. This suggests that these verbs share a set of necessary conditions having to do with travelling in physical space. . . . However, each will have its own centrality condition of manner, containing a central visual and/or motor pattern that specifies a characteristic gait and speed" (1983, 149).

Clearly, these differences are not relevant for any grammatical process. Similarly, how we decide whether or not some entity is red, and whether we have difficulty in doing so, is irrelevant to the Grammatical behavior of the NP referring to the entity or of the adjective *red.* Such gradience effects *should* be defined out of Grammar Semantics and put in Situational Semantics, the web on which language is built. Therefore, my position is close to the one taken by Fodor (1975, 62), who showed that, for certain objects, it is difficult to determine whether or not they are a "chair." He proposes to attribute the fuzziness of "chair" to the concept rather than to the actual word. Jackendoff criticizes this position because "it leaves unaddressed how to characterize the fuzziness of the concept, *the issue that should be of concern*" [my emphasis] (1983, 124). I disagree on the last point: fuzziness is of interest, but since it has no effects that are relevant to the behavior of grammatical entities such as words, it is *not* of concern to the linguist, but rather to the psychologist.

Claims have been made about cognitive categorization actually affecting Grammar. For example, Lakoff (1987, chapter 3) reviews several arguments to the effect that there are prototype effects in linguistic categories. Consider the most famous one, that *syntactic categories exhibit prototype effects,* which is based on Ross's argument (1981). He argues that nouns should be classified hierarchically, as in (24).

(24)   toe > breath > way > time (where "x > y" indicates that x is "nounier" than y).

Ross gives three syntactic environments in which only the nounier nouns follow the rule:

(25) *Modification by a passive participle:*
    a.   A *stubbed toe* can be very painful.
    b.   *Held breath is usually fetid when released.
    c.   *A lost way has been the cause of many a missed appointment.
    d.   *Taken time might tend to irritate your boss.

(26) *Gapping:*
    a.   I stubbed my toe, and she hers.
    b.   I held my breath, and she hers.
    c.   *I lost my way, and she hers.
    d.   *I took my time, and she hers.

(27) *Pluralization:*
    a.   Betty and Sue stubbed their toes.
    a'.   *Betty and Sue stubbed their toe.

    b.   Betty and Sue held their breaths.
    b'.   Betty and Sue held their breath.

    c.   *Betty and Sue lost their ways.
    c'.   Betty and Sue lost their way.

    d.   *Betty and Sue took their times.
    d'.   Betty and Sue took their time.

Lakoff adds a fourth test to differentiate *way* and *time.*

(28) *Pronominalization:*
    a.   I stubbed my toe, but didn't hurt *it.*

  b.   Sam held his breath for a few seconds and then released *it*.
  c.   Harry lost his way, but found *it* again.
  d.   *Harry took his time, but wasted *it*.

Notice that all these tests depend on the referentiality of the noun phrase in some way or another. Thus, both (26) and (28) involve pronominalization of the object NP; the contrast between the two seems to have to do with the fact that the subject is the same on both sides of the coordination in (28), but not in (26). Compare (28c) with (29).

(29)   *Harry lost his way, but she found *it* again.

On the other hand, it seems that it is not the pronominalization of *his time* that is problematic in (28d), but rather the oddness of the situation described by the sentence. Compare it to (30).

(30)   Instead of giving his time to a good cause, Harry wasted it.

Pluralization in (27) raises the problem of distributive effects and of factors like the count/mass distinction; again, aspects of referentiality. Even passivization as in (25) involves referentiality: in his study on idioms, Ruwet (1991) notes that a passive subject must have a certain referential autonomy (see Higgins 1979, Keenan 1975). One example of this is discussed by Giry-Schneider (1978), who shows that some syntactic idioms in French with no determiner in the active must have a determiner and a modifying element, such as an adjective, in the passive.[12]

(31)a. Glaucon a pris part/une part importante à cette discussion.
         Glaucon took (an important) part in this discussion
     b. Une part importante/*part a été prise par Glaucon à cette discussion.
         (An important) part was taken by Glaucon in this discussion

Interestingly, if the NPs in (25) are made more referentially autonomous by similar modification, the examples are much better:

(32)a. Improperly held breath is many a swimmer's biggest problem.
     b. Way lost because of negligence has been the cause of many a missed appointment.
     c. Time taken on the job might tend to irritate your boss.

To summarize, the fuzziness effects we have seen do not arise from grammatical categorization, but rather from the conceptual entities to which grammatical elements are linked. For example, the grammatical category N is not fuzzy in any sense: *toe* is not a better example of a N than *time;* it is a better example of a THING. I fully agree with Jackendoff's claim that "fuzziness is an inescapable characteristic of *the concepts that language expresses.*" But contrary to his claim, I think that fuzziness is not present in Grammar in any way, as the discussion of the examples above indicates. Rather, fuzziness is in the web, the background knowledge on which language is woven, and therefore it has no effect on the form and function of language.

Of course, much more could be said on the topic of fuzziness. Let me briefly discuss four more cases. (Thanks to John Goldsmith, personal communication, for bringing these to my attention.) First, modal verbs are a well-known example of words that have a fuzzy status, as far as rules applying to verbs are concerned. But in fact, assuming that these are rules applying to *verbs,* per se, biases the discussion. Such an assumption has no status in most current theories in any event, since movement is typically triggered by morphophonological or semantic properties, such as the need for some element to bear a Tense affix or to be bound by a Tense operator, as in the analyses of Pollock (1989) or Chomsky (1991) (see chapter 5 below). Until we know precisely what forces an element to appear in a given position or with a certain inflection, we cannot decide whether, for example, it is a requirement based on categorial or semantic reasons.

A second example has to do with serial verb constructions in West African languages, which are built by stringing together things that look like VPs with other VPs or PPs. The problem is that the governing element sometimes oscillates between the behavior of a verb, a preposition, or something else. But why call the construction "serial VERB" in the first place? If it is a misnomer, if the proper notion is instead something like "argument-taking element," then the categorial problem is unfounded.

A third case of what looks like fuzziness can be built on extraction facts: bounding nodes often leak, and extraction out of relative clauses or coordinate structures is often fine, under the appropriate semantic and lexical conditions. But this is an argument for fuzziness of categorization only if bounding nodes are the right account of extraction facts. As will be clear from the discussion in section 4.4.11, there is a plausible analysis along the lines of Erteschik-Shir (1973), based on the notion of Dominance, in which the fuzziness of bounding nodes is not an issue because the notion of bounding node is irrelevant.

As a final example, consider the category of the word *faim* 'hunger' in

French. It appears to be a noun, since it has a fixed gender (it is feminine) rather than the two possible genders we would expect if it were an adjective. However, sometimes it appears to behave like an adjective, in that it can be modified by the degree adverb *très,* as in *J'ai très faim* 'I am very hungry' (literally, I have very hunger). Thus, its category appears to be fuzzy. In order to understand what is going on, we must first observe that *très* is only possible with *faim* when the latter does not have a DET. Thus, whereas *J'ai une faim de loup* 'I have a hunger of a wolf = I am as hungry as a wolf' is fine, **J'ai une très faim de loup* 'I have a very hunger of a wolf' is totally impossible. One possibility is that a degree adverb like *très* is possible with an N, but not a DP. A closer look at the phenomenon may reveal that referential autonomy is at work here, too, just like in the Ross (1981) examples discussed above. Thus, it may be that one of the conditions of whether *très* can be an N modifier is the weak referential autonomy of the noun. This predicts that any predicative N could be modified by *très,* all things being equal, and indeed this seems to be the case; for example, *Celui-là, je te dis qu'il est très avocat* 'That one, I tell you, he's really lawyer.'[13] If the distribution of *très* is based on the category of the element being modified, *J'ai très faim* is indeed odd; but if the distribution of *très* is not based on the category, but on semantic aspects of the modified element—such as its referential autonomy—the problem of category fuzziness disappears.

The foregoing discussion suggests that words do have definite and precise meanings that can be exhaustively decomposed into necessary and sufficient conditions, once the effects of the background have been removed. This is why, as we will see in Part II, verbs used to describe movements are often used to describe other situations, such as Extension, Time, Identification, etc., again and again across languages: they are not movement verbs, per se, but their semantic representations are such that they are predisposed for many uses, including movement.

In short, my position is that the speaker "knows" when and where a word or sentence can apply: fuzziness arises when the speaker has some difficulty in determining whether such a situation is present. Therefore, fuzziness is not in the realm of Grammar.

There are two objections to such a view: it is too abstract, and having fuzziness in general conceptualization, but not in language, which is a subpart of general conceptualization, is incongruous. Consider first the abstractness problem: "The classical theory of categories does not do very well on the treatment of polysemy. In order to have a single lexical item, the classi-

cal theory must treat all of the related senses as having some abstract meaning in common—usually so abstract that it cannot distinguish among the
cases and so devoid of real meaning that it is not recognizable as what people
think of as the meaning of a word. And where there are a large number of
related senses that don't all share a property, then the classical theory is
forced to treat such cases as homonomy, the same way it treats the case of
the two words *bank*. Moreover, the classical theory has no adequate means
of characterizing a situation where one or more senses are 'central' or 'most
representative'" Lakoff 1987, 416; see also Jackendoff 1983, 112ff, who has
similar qualms about categorization and necessary and sufficient conditions).
Although some aspects of this objection do indeed hold against a classical
theory of categorization, they do not hold against the position advocated
here. First, although very abstract, the representations that will be proposed
can distinguish among the cases because, contrary to the classical theory, the
present approach crucially assumes that language is not used in a vacuum.
For example, although the meaning of French *venir* that I will give in Part II
is very abstract, it can account for what is common to the three uses in (33)
because the nature of the arguments gives us sufficient information to determine the kind of situation to which the whole utterance can correspond.

(33)a.   Jean vient de Paris. (movement)
          Jean is coming from Paris
    b.   Jean vient de Paris. (origin)
          Jean comes from Paris (He is a Parisian)
    c.   Cette route vient de Québec. (extension)
          This road comes from Québec

The second point raised by Lakoff is an odd one: why should the "real
meaning" of a word correspond to what people think of as the meaning of
that word? Folk theories should no more be a criterion in semantics than
they are in syntax or any other aspect of linguistics. The problem with lexical
meanings is that, in general, there is such an immediacy to the situation in
which the word is used that we tend to attribute these situational properties
to the word itself, as if they were part of its semantic representation, instead
of abstracting away from them.

As for the "large number of related senses that don't all share a property,"
this may apparently be true when all the background factors are taken into
account and blur our view, but once we abstract away from such factors,
shared properties do emerge, as we will see in the case studies in subsequent

chapters. Finally, the fact that one or more senses are "central" or "most representative" can be captured in the present approach, but this is done by cognitive principles that form the background for language. As argued above, they have no effect in the Grammar and so must be removed from it.

The second possible objection takes the following form: "Considering that categorization enters fundamentally into every aspect of language, it would be very strange to assume that the mind *in general* [my emphasis] used one kind of categorization and that language used an entirely different one" (Lakoff 1987, 182). But how general is the use of fuzzy categorization compared to classical categorization? Both Lakoff and Jackendoff provided numerous examples where fuzzy categorization is indeed found in dealing with the "external" or "projected" world. Does this leave classical categorization completely out? Not at all, for either Lakoff or Jackendoff. Millenniums spent studying categorization based on necessary and sufficient conditions are not swept aside by these authors: "I should make it clear that I will not be claiming that classical categories are never relevant to cognition. . . . The point is that not all categories—either of mind or of nature—are classical, and therefore we cannot assume, a priori, as objectivist metaphysics does, that all nature is structured by classical categories" (Lakoff 1987, 160). More crucially for our point, both authors make extensive use of classical categorization in their linguistic analyses. Thus, Jackendoff (1983, 115) subscribes to the following passage from Putnam (1975, 133) ". . . words in natural language are not generally 'yes-no': there are things of which the description 'tree' is clearly true and things of which the description 'tree' is clearly false, to be sure, but there are a host of borderline cases." But this really hinges only on whether one can decide whether a given THING is actually a tree or not; it is of no consequence to the syntactic behavior of *tree*. Thus, this kind of fuzziness never affects how that N should project in a structure, or whether it occupies the position [$_s$ NP . . .] ('subject of S'), or how it will agree with the verb or a pronoun, or whether it is governed. Notions like "subject of," "governed by," "c-commands x," and so forth are all "yes-no." In some case, it might be hard to determine whether such a relation holds because of the complexity of the construction, but either it holds or it does not; there is nothing indeterminate about it.

Thus, both classical and fuzzy categorization are needed. Therefore, what kind of categorization is relevant for the form and functioning of grammar is an empirical question. In looking at studies on Grammar, including those of the two authors cited above, the overwhelming evidence is that fuzzy categorization is involved only in the processes dealing with perception or beliefs about the "external world" and that it is not intrinsically involved in the functioning of Grammar. Externalizing processes such as perception and belief must "reach out," whereas grammatical processes are strictly internal.[14] If fuzziness is a property of externalizing processes only, grammatical processes could very well be strictly classical. It is very important to bear in mind the distinction between the form of the sentence, that is, *how* it expresses something, and *what* it expresses. Only the former is relevant to Grammar.

I therefore conclude that there is nothing strange in the possibility that language uses only classical categorization and that preliminary observations point in this direction. I will argue in Part II that there are good empirical reasons to support this position.

1.5.2 SELECTIVE SEMANTICS AND CHOICE OF PRIMITIVES

The claim that no properties of situational semantics are part of Grammar is related to the general question of how one determines what must be covered by the theory—the question of exhaustivity. This, in turn, raises the question of the choice of which primitives are appropriate to cover what is determined to be relevant data. The choice of primitives is extremely important, since it ultimately determines whether an approach has explanatory adequacy. The primitives must be coherent with the metaphysical and epistemological stance that one takes. I will argue that situational roles are not coherent with a mentalist approach to language because they arise from assuming that sentences and situations are paired globally. They treat the fact that language takes place in human beings who share a vast amount of knowledge as almost irrelevant. Moreover, we cannot use situational roles to describe linguistic experience because they are not really part of the meaning of lexical items, but only describe some prototypical uses. Thus, situational roles can play no role in explanation: "A theory of UG meets the conditions of *explanatory adequacy* to the extent that it provides descriptively adequate grammars under the boundary conditions met by experience" (Chomsky 1985a, 53). Again, no such linguistic experience is available for situational roles.

I will first outline the general guidelines that I adopt (section 1.5.2.1). Then, in order to give the reader a clear idea of what is compatible with these guidelines, I will discuss two familiar types of theories that are not compatible with the selective semantics approach—theta theory (section 1.5.2.2) and theories based on the centrality of space (1.5.2.3). In section 1.5.2.4, I address the fact that polysemy is a central property of language and that this should give us an indication of the kind of semantic primitives that are operative in Grammar.

1.5.2.1 GENERAL GUIDELINES

A theory of Semantic Representations should be evaluated according to the criteria that are used to evaluate and compare theories in general: (a) the clarity and precision with which the theory is formulated, (b) the explanatory and predictive power of the system, (c) the formal simplicity of the theoretical system, and (d) the extent to which the data confirm the theory.

The predictions of the theory and the confirmation of the data should ideally be exhaustive. There are two possible extensions of this exhaustivity for a linguistic theory of meaning: (1) depth of analysis—the decomposition of a text into its constituent elements must be exhaustive, in that it must attain a certain limit; (2) coverage of the analysis—the domain of application of the analytical procedure must exhaustively cover the set of possible texts (see, among others, Piotrowski 1991).

These two aspects of exhaustivity each raise important questions. First, with respect to depth of analysis, how "deeply" does one decompose the primitives? That is, what are the ultimate units? Second, with respect to coverage, how do we determine whether an element is part of the set to be covered? That is, what data are relevant? Both questions fall under a general problem of relevance. Relevance depends on how one defines one's domain of inquiry. But there is no absolute, "objective" way of determining such relevance: "In the sciences, at least, disciplines are regarded as conveniences, not as ways of cutting nature at its joints or as the elaboration of certain fixed concepts; and their boundaries shift or disappear as knowledge and understanding advance" (Chomsky 1985a, 35). I will take it that a theory is a *linguistic* one if the formalism proposed is intended to be a hypothesis about the synthetic properties of language. Therefore, a proposal will be evaluated according to its ability to answer questions like "What are the properties that distinguish a natural language from what is not a natural language?" "What is a possible word?" and "What is a possible sentence?"

A *linguistic primitive* is not absolute in the sense that it can likely be further decomposed, but that decomposition would not be linguistically relevant. Primitives are not an ultimate goal that must be reached. Instead, they are something determined by the system of the theory. In our case, a primitive is understood with respect to certain hypotheses about the acquisition of language.

A *linguistic datum* is a sentence, or one of its components, with which grammaticality judgments are associated. A linguistic theory should therefore explain how humans produce and understand a sentence. One way to do this is to have a grammatical system that generates exclusively grammatical sentences.

If, as a selective mentalist approach claims, the background knowledge encoded in Conceptual Structures has no direct role in the production and understanding of grammatical sentences and only a subpart of the properties that determine our total understanding of a sentence are represented in the semantic representations, then a linguistic theory should provide a system of principles and primitives that are not defined on such background properties. On the other hand, this linguistic system should be structured in such a way that it may interact with general cognition to explain actual use of language, while allowing us to distinguish between natural languages and other possible objects of study. Hence, the strictly grammatical system and the conceptual system must be studied together, in order to correctly determine the role of each in calculating the total situational meaning of the utterance. However, they must be kept separate if a proper understanding of the phenomenon of natural languages is to be attained. At least, this is my claim.

I am not claiming that the study of Conceptual Structures should be removed from the study of language. On the contrary, Conceptual Structures are crucial in understanding language use,[15] but a large part of them, which I refer to as background knowledge, plays no role in Grammar, per se, and no primitive or principle of Grammar should be defined on the basis of such knowledge. Whether one wants to call "linguistics" the study of language use (including background knowledge) or restrict the term to the study of Grammar is a purely terminological problem of little importance. What is important, I claim, is that Conceptual Structures do not interact with Grammar globally and that only a restricted aspect of these structures, the semantic representations, determines the meaning and projection in syntax of lexical items.

The idea that there are two kinds of semantics, one linguistically relevant and the other not, is not new, of course. From the very first studies on language, it has been clear that not all of situational semantics is relevant to language. For example, take an event and the chain of causality that leads to it. As Vendler (1976) observes, along the lines of the tradition in philosophy, "For every event there is a set of facts, each of them being a necessary condition of the occurrence of that event, and all of them jointly amounting to a sufficient condition. This principle I call the *transcendental principle of causality* which sets us the task of completely accounting for the occurrence of every event in terms of the laws of science. The selection, therefore, of the facts causally relevant to a given event will depend upon the totality of the scientific knowledge we possess" (713). But as is well known, lexical causation is very different from this situational view of causation. Thus, if one considers the verb *break* to be a causative verb, it is obvious that only a very small subset of the situational causes involved can be its subject. If John broke the vase by bumping into its pedestal and making it crash to the floor, gravity (or the natural state of the vase, if one prefers) was an important factor in the breaking; yet, while *John broke the vase* is fine, *Gravity broke the vase* is incorrect. Similarly, as Voorst (1993) observes, when one eats sugar, the situation is always such that a limited amount of sugar is eaten, the exact quantity of which could be measured by instruments. Nevertheless, due to the presence of the mass noun, the aspectual interpretation differs from the situational semantics: the event is aspectually not delimited—it is an activity—and it is immeasurable, in terms of linguistics. Another example of this distinction is found in Claude Vandeloise's study of spatial prepositions in French (discussed in 1.1.3 above), in which he shows that one must distinguish between an abstract representation of a preposition and the situational factors that determine its use in spatial relations.

The theoretical importance of the distinction between content and use has been recognized again and again in the tradition of studies on language. Hjelmslev's work can be seen as the epitome of this distinction between semantics of the grammatical system and semantics of a more general nature. He warned against the use of extralinguistic judgments: what is crucial is *how* ideas are expressed by the linguistic system, not our intuitive interpretations of a given situation. In this respect, his approach was very similar to Chomsky's later methodological proposals for formal analyses in generative grammar, which also leave no room in linguistic description for the implicit contributions of the linguist.

We must be consistent on this point. We take an objective position on the problem of what distinguishes humans from other species, with respect to language—whether this is due to a distinct faculty or to generalized cognitive capacities is not a topic for speculation or *a priori* reasoning, but for empirical inquiry; we must determine what system of knowledge has been attained and what initial state of the mind could account for it. In order to be consistent, we must restrict ourselves to the strictly linguistic data and not appeal to intuitive interpretations that belong to general cognitive capacities. Otherwise, we end up in the contradictory position of arguing for the thesis of autonomy of the language faculty on the basis of notions grounded in general, situational semantics. Following in the tradition of Hjelmslev and Chomsky, I will focus not on *what* the situation expressed by a linguistic unit is like, but on *how* language expresses it.

1.5.2.2 THE INADEQUACY OF THETA THEORY

One domain that is not restricted to strictly linguistic data is theta theory. Theta roles play no role in grammar because they are situational; they belong to the wrong semantics to have grammatical relevance. This is not to claim merely that theta roles are not primitives of the theory and are defined in terms of positions in some Lexical Conceptual Structure: the claim is that the very notions on which theta roles are based are external to Grammar. While theta roles may sometimes appear to be relevant, this is only an artifact of the methodological procedure. In most cases, too few situations have been investigated, with the result that situational properties of a subset of the relevant constructions are mistakenly attributed to the lexical item itself. An investigation of more data shows that we must abstract away from the situational factors. This is clearly illustrated by Jean-Paul Boons's remarkable work on locative verbs in French. To give one example, consider the French verb *enfermer* 'to shut up' in (34).

(34)   Jean a enfermé le chat dans le salon.
        Jean shut the cat up in the living room

In terms of theta roles, the sentence can be analyzed as follows:

(35)   Jean is the AGENT
        le chat is the THEME
        le salon is the GOAL

These theta roles describe a situation where one entity caused another to move from a source to a goal. But this is not what the sentence means. As Boons (1985) observes, nothing is said about whether the cat moves in (34). All we know is the cat's final state: it ends up shut up in the living room. How this came about is not part of the linguistic information. Even less is said about Jean. We do not know what he did that caused this state; all we know is that he brought it about that the cat is shut up in the living room. Because of this lack of specificity, the sentence can correspond to several situations. Jean might have put the cat in the room and closed the door; the cat might already have been in the room when Jean closed the door. Furthermore, the latter may or may not have been intentional on Jean's part; he might not even have been aware that the cat was in the room and simply closed the door behind himself, with the result that the cat was shut up. This is not the same as his unintentionally shutting the cat up, which could be conscious: "Oops, I just shut the cat up in the living room." Thus, a wide variety of situational interpretations are possible, but there is only one linguistic interpretation.[16]

The numerous situations could be described by varying the theta roles assigned, as is frequently done, and the different entries of *enfermer* could then be related in some way. If these various entries were *not* related, it would imply that there is generalized homophony in language because most words behave like *enfermer*. However, one look at any nontrivial case indicates that it is not at all obvious how these numerous entries can be related. In any case, the enterprise would be headed in the wrong direction, since meaning is not simply a description of the multiple situations in which an item can be used.

1.5.2.2.1 Sense and Reference

Coming back to sentence (34), one could ask "Is it not the case that this sentence is true, if Jean actually took the cat and shut it up in the living room, as described by (35)?" Granted, but this is asserting the truth of one use of the sentence, but truth and falsity are characteristics of the uses of a sentence, not of the sentence itself, as P. F. Strawson emphasized.[17] Thus, "the king of France is wise" is neither true nor false: it depends on its use—who says it, when it is said, and so on. This is a very old problem—that of distinguishing between sense and reference. A reminder of Strawson's criticism of Russell's treatment of reference and truth-values may be useful at this point:

> The same expression can have different mentioning-uses, as the same sentence can be used to make statements with different truth-values. "Mentioning", or "referring", is not something an expression does; it is something that someone can use the expression to do. Mentioning, or referring to, something is a characteristic of *a use* of an expression, just as "being about" something and truth-or-falsity, are characteristics of *a use* of a sentence. . . . We are apt to fancy we are talking about sentences and expressions when we are talking about the

uses of sentences and expressions. This is what Russell does. . . . The source of Russell's mistake was that he thought that referring or mentioning, if it occurred at all, must be meaning. . . . he confused expressions with their use in a particular context; and so confused meaning with mentioning, with referring. (Strawson 1971, 8–9)

Although it is true that (34) could be used in the situation roughly described by (35), (35) is of very limited use in arriving at the meaning of (34).

The same problem arises with (36).

(36)   Colorless green ideas sleep furiously.

Chomsky (1957) argued that (36) shows that there is a notion of syntactic well-formedness, which must be distinguished from semantic well-formedness, since the syntactically well-formed (36) has a status radically different from sentences that are both syntactically and semantically ill formed, like (37), for example:

(37)   sleep colorless furiously ideas green

But given current assumptions, the well-formedness of (36) cannot be strictly syntactic. Under the projection hypothesis, semantic properties of selection are crucially required to license syntactic structures. In fact, given a standard X-bar theory alone, without constraints from selection, there is no problem in attributing several well-formed structures to (37). Thus, it is no longer the case that structure is generated strictly by the geometric principles of Phrase Structure rules: geometric relations are licensed by the dynamic relations of selection. To account for the contrast between (36) and (37), in a framework in which syntax is dependent on dynamic lexical-semantic relations, one must assume that (36) is well formed as far as lexical semantics is concerned. That is, the elements combine in the appropriate way, the adjectives modify a noun, and a VP is predicated of an NP, following the canonical positions for such relations in the language. These requirements are not met in (37).

The reason that (36) sounds strange is that, at the level of S-semantics, we cannot find something that fits the descriptions we are given. It is difficult to conceive of a situation where a possible referent could be found for "colorless green ideas"—let alone sleeping ones—just as there is not a *conceivable* referent for a square circle, for example. The problem in (36) is therefore one of conceptualization and of reference, not of meaning: in our terms, it is a problem of Situational Semantics.[18] In other words, contrary to what Chomsky's analysis implies, the fact that something cannot be both green and colorless, or that ideas do not sleep, is not a linguistic phenomenon (see section 3.1.1.2 for more discussion of this point).

The fact that the well-formedness of (36), as opposed to (37), is due not to syntactic factors but to semantic factors and that (36) is *not* well formed in S-semantics confirms my position that there is a level of G-semantics, the level at which (36) is well formed. Conversely, the fact that (34) can refer to the situation in (35) is of little use, with respect to a semantic representation of the sentence that is relevant for syntax, because although (36) is referentially anomalous, it is grammatically well formed. If S-semantics has no import for the grammatical well-formedness of (36), it is hard to see why it would have any in (34).

Problems of reference failure and the violation of selectional restrictions have a long history in the literature, dating back to Aristotle. For example, Ewing (1937) argues that category mistakes (the traditional label for violations of selectional restriction), as in (38), are meaningful.

(38)   Quadratic equations do not go to race-meetings.

This is so, he says, because there are propositions that it entails (39a) and others that entail it (39b).

(39)a.   Quadratic equations do not watch the Newmarket horse-races.
   b.   Quadratic equations do not move in space.

The degree of anomaly of reference failure and category mistakes can be affected by negation (Horn 1989). Thus, many speakers find the following sentence much less anomalous than (36):

(40)   Colorless green ideas don't sleep furiously.

On the other hand, some word strings are not just anomalous: they are meaningless. Here are four examples:

(41) a.   Incomplete sentences: *Cambridge is between York
    b.   Combinatorially incorrect: *Are of fond not dogs cats.
    c.   Category violations: *I potatoed the of
    d.   Strict subcategorization   *I slept the armadillo

1.5.2.2.2 The Substantive Content of Theta Roles is Situational

When linguistic tests are proposed to determine when a specific theta role may be appropriately assigned, the results are inconclusive at best. For example, Jackendoff (1990a) observes that a test for Patients, namely, answering to the question "what happened to NP?" is not reliable because of the possibility of discourse Patients—elements that are considered "affected" by virtue of some surrounding context. Thus, the subject of *received* and the object of *entered* are discourse Patients in the following:

(42)a.   What happened to Bill was that he received this letter that said his girlfriend was breaking up with him, and so he got depressed.

    b.   What happened to the room was that a herd of elephants entered it and well, you can guess the rest.

Jackendoff contrasts these with *grammatical Patients* "whose role is assigned by the verb of the sentence itself, requires no surrounding story in order to be acceptable. Admittedly, the line is sometimes hard to draw" (1990a, 294). A typical example of such a grammatical Patient is *Fred* in (43).

(43)   Sue hit Fred.

In fact, it is never possible to draw the line. Typical examples are just that—they are based on typical situations in which the sentences can be used. In the absence of context, it is the prototypical situation of use that is attributed to the sentence and that determines the theta roles that are assigned; the prototypical situation constitutes the "surrounding story." But the factors that determine the prototypical, or central, use of the sentence are not grammatical factors, therefore, theta roles are always situational and never grammatical. In (43), *Fred* is not a Patient by virtue of some property of the verb: its theta role depends on the "real world" nature of the arguments involved. For example, if Fred is three times the size of Sue, or if he is a bully who clobbers whoever touches him, even accidentally, it might be much more appropriate to say "What happened to Sue is that she hit Fred" than the converse. Similarly, which argument in (44) is the Patient depends on the proportional size of the car and the tree, and in (45), on the situations described by the continuation of the sentence.

(44)   The car hit the tree.

(45)   John hit the wall

    a.   . . . and broke his nose.

    b.   . . . with a sledge hammer.

Theta roles are therefore not appropriate primitives to use in constructing Semantic Representations.[19] They are unsuitable to represent meaning because any slight change in the context can bring about a change in roles. The result will be an explosion of representations for the same verb that are impossible to relate in any revealing manner. Furthermore, theta roles do not fare any better for linking. This is because, even if the problem of polysemy just mentioned could be solved, theta roles could only be used to attribute labels. Linking on the basis of a list of theta labels obliterates the structural properties of the semantic representation. Nothing in the basic architecture of such an approach to linking leads us to expect any regularities, and the theory would have to depend on stipulations like UTAH to obtain the actual linking.[20]

1.5.2.2.3 The Paraphrase Methodology

The methodology behind the use of thematic roles also conflicts with a mentalist approach to language. The methodology is "situational," in that in most cases, choice of theta role is determined on the basis of paraphrase relationships with sentences where the roles are supposed to be more clearly identified. For example, in (46a), *the book* is said to be the THEME because it is the element moved to a GOAL in the paraphrase (46b).

(46)a.   John shelved the book
    b.   John put the book on the shelf

This paraphrase methodology is very much like that of logic-based approaches. One of the crucial factors in determining whether there is a relationship between two sentences is the relatively similar conditions of use of the sentences; in other words, truth conditions. So, with the paraphrase methodology, there is a reductive effect similar to one discussed earlier: two elements with the same use tend to receive the same semantic representation. But we saw that expressions that are equivalent in some of their uses are not conceptually equivalent. This paraphrase methodology is also surprisingly close to the one found in Generative Semantics, and it faces the same problems. As Chomsky (1971, 197) observes, substitution, even substitution of synonyms, cannot be carried out in intensional contexts in such a way as to preserve truth conditions. In other words, it is not possible for two paraphrases to be exactly equivalent.

Moreover, no clear criteria are given to determine whether or not a paraphrase is indicative of an underlying semantic representation. This reminds me of the longstanding debate about the semantic decomposition of words like *uncle, bachelor,* and *kill* and whether or not a word like *kill* should be decomposed into "deeper" semantic primitives, for example, as "cause to become not alive." Most generativists would now assume that a paraphrase of a word like this is irrelevant for its syntactic behavior. Why, then, should the paraphrase be relevant for attribution of thematic roles? Similarly, with converse expressions such as *to the left of* and *to right of,* are we to assume that one of the two is basic? Does productivity factor into it? Compare (46) with (47), or with (48):

(47)a. John put the teddy bear on the shelf.
   b. #John shelved the teddy bear.

(48)a. John put the book on the couch/car/ground . . .
   b. *John couched/carred/grounded the book

It could be argued that the paraphrase methodology is based on strategies that are well established in science. Assuming the very general methodological rule that one must admit a minimal number of principles in a theory—namely, only those that are necessary and sufficient to explain the relevant phenomena—one could propose as a second general rule that causes that induce similar effects are the same. Newton did this, for example, for the fall of bodies in Europe and in America, light in a kitchen fire and in the sun, and reflection of light on Earth and on the planets. The paraphrase strategy could be seen as an instance of the second rule in which similar effects are ascribed to the same causes. But one must be very careful to note that although the second rule follows from the first, all things being equal, it is rarely true that all things are equal, as example (47) shows (and, I would add, as the history of the discussions around this methodology also shows). As Ruwet (1982, 17) puts it, once one has a fairly sophisticated formal tool, there is a strong temptation to fall for what Leo Strauss calls the charm of competence and apply that tool to problems for which it was not made.

1.5.2.3 THE INADEQUACY OF THEORIES OF CENTRALITY OF SPACE

One way to try to solve the problem of polysemy is to appeal to a theory of metaphor (in a broad sense, not just "poetic effect"). One use of a given verb would correspond to its central meaning, and the other uses would be related to the central meaning metaphorically. What would such a theory of metaphor have to provide to relate these different uses? First, it would have to indicate how one determines the central meaning. I know of no proposals in theta analyses that have been made about this: it is usually taken for granted that we know what the central use is, with only a posteriori justification, when any justification is given. Second, a theory of metaphor would have to provide precise rules or principles to relate the central meaning to the other uses.

There are two criteria that are often proposed to determine whether a metaphorical relationship exists between two elements, similarity and substitution. But similarity is a vacuous predicate—it is always possible to find some kind of similarity between two elements—so we are left with substitution.[21] But what is substituted for what in noncentral uses in theta analyses? One possibility is to say that some expressions can be substituted for others, as we saw in the paraphrase cases like (46). However, we saw that this is not always true (see (47) and (48)), if ever, and no criteria are provided to determine which cases of syntactic paraphrase relationships are valid at the level of semantic representation.

Another possibility is to say that some primitives of a given conceptual domain can be substituted for those of another domain. Depending on how one deals with such domains, this could come very close to removing polysemy from the realm of linguistics, a move that I consider mistaken. As an example of this kind of substitution, it is usually argued that terms of spatial relations can be used to express temporal relations. For example, the prepositions and the verbs in (49) would each have a meaning, defined in terms of the conceptual domain of space. In (50), these spatial terms would be substituted for temporal terms.

(49) a.   in a box, at the restaurant, from New York to Philadelphia
     b.   Jean va à Montréal, Jean is going to Montréal

(50) a.   in an hour, at 5 o'clock, from 8 A.M. to 5 P.M.
     b.   Jean va partir, Jean is going to leave

But what is meant by substitution here? These spatial terms do not substitute for temporal terms; they are the only terms available. (This holds even for the future use of *aller*, which does not express the same thing as the morphological future of French; see the discussion in 3.1.2.4 below.) Moreover, this analysis will not work for cases like (43)–(45) above, unless we multiply the number of conceptual domains to a point where the analysis becomes a list with little explanatory appeal. Finally, some verbs allow multiple interpretations that are very difficult to relate in terms of conceptual domains or paraphrases. Here are a few examples of denominal verbs taken from Labelle (1989), where the interpretations, given in parentheses, do not seem to be relatable in terms of domain differences (N is the N from which the verb is derived):

(51) a.   écumer: from *écume* 'foam, scum' (produce N; remove N from st)
   b.   perler: from *perle* 'pearl, bead' (put N on st; be like N; render st like N)
   c.   fumer: from *fumée* 'smoke' (produce N; put st in N)
   d.   amorcer: from *amorce* 'starter, bait' (put N on st; put st in N)
   e.   clouer, boulonner, visser: from *clou* 'nail,' *boulon* 'bolt', *vis* 'screw' (put N in st or immobilize by means of N)

Note that assuming the centrality of space is of no help in distinguishing between subcases like these, which are all spatial. Another similar example is found in the discussion of the French verb *fermer* 'close' in Jongen (1985, 137, note 2), where the central meaning is also not clear. Is it that of acting on a container (*fermer une boîte* 'close a box') or acting on a closing device (*fermer une porte* 'close a door'), or is it an action of bringing together (*fermer un parapluie* 'close an umbrella')?

As we can see from the examples in (43)–(51), it is not at all obvious which meaning is central and how the different uses are related. It has long been recognized that it is not only difficult to provide criteria to determine which use is central but that it is also difficult to determine which of the uses actually is the central use. The following passage from Leisi (1973, 174–75) quoted in Nöth (1985) is illustrative:

> The word *foot* can be defined as "lowest portion of a human or animal leg (on which the creature stands)". In this case *foot of the mountain* is a metaphor. But it is not impossible to define *foot* from the very beginning as "lowest portion on which someone or something stands". In this case *foot of the mountain* would not be a metaphor. Depending on the definition of a word's normal meaning, a given usage will appear as within or outside it. Even when we clearly have two meanings before us, it may remain open, whether the case counts as metaphor or not. English *eye* means (1) "organ of sight" and (2) "hole in a tool". Is the second meaning a metaphor? Certainly the first use of the word *crane* for a machine with a lifting arm was metaphoric, but its status today is disputable.

If the notion of space is not central, as I claim, then we might wonder why space is so often claimed to be central. Given its frequent recurrence, there must be something to the idea that space is central. My answer is that there certainly is, but that it has nothing to do with I-language. There are two points that are relevant here, the ontological problem and the reasons why space is perceived as central.

Ontologically, to claim that spatial relations are basic and extend to other domains only postpones answering questions about the conceptualization capacity, since questions of this type will have to be asked about spatial relations eventually. Why not go directly to questions about conceptualization in general, and then ponder how it applies to all conceptual domains? Although Jackendoff seems to adopt a position in which spatial relations are basic and are used to express temporal and other relations in actually working out his analyses, he is more reserved when he elaborates on polysemy at a more general level. His position is actually quite close to the one I am advocating:

> ... [T]he theory of thematic relations claims not just that some fields are structured in terms of other fields, but that all fields have essentially the *same* structure. This structure is cognitively induced: one could not decide to abandon thematic structure for some other organization. It defines the terms in which any kind of discourse, literal or metaphorical, must be framed.
>
> I am inclined to think of thematic structure not as spatial metaphor but as an abstract organization that can be applied with suitable specialization to any field. If there is any primacy to the spatial field, it is because this field is so strongly supported by nonlinguistic cognition; it is the common ground for the essential faculties of vision, touch, and action. From an evolutionary perspective, spatial organization had to exist long before language. One can imagine the development of thematic structure in less concrete fields as a consequence of evolutionary conservatism in cognition—the adaptation of existing structure to new purposes rather than the development of entirely novel mechanisms. (1983, 209–210)

The development of linguistic cognition should be based on the same general cognition as spatial organization. It is of no use to have the intermediate step of appealing to the centrality of space in linguistic cognition. We should appeal directly to the conceptualization capacity. The only advantage of appealing to space is ease of exposition. This brings us back to the second issue: why is space perceived as central? One reason is that a spatial use of a word is generally much easier to illustrate than a more abstract use, so spatial uses are more frequent in examples of naive speakers (and linguists), but for purely expository reasons that have nothing to do with I-language.

A second reason for advocating centrality of space could be evolution, as mentioned by Jackendoff. But this raises the ontological question again: why should language tap into the conceptual system of spatial organization rather than into the general conceptualization capacity from which spatial organization arises? At first glance at least, the second option seems more "economical," since an I-language based on spatial relations would constantly have to undo or abstract away from purely spatial notions that are not present in language. I-language would still rely heavily on the conceptualization capacity. Moreover, although the primacy of spatial organization over language is very plausible from an evolutionary perspective, its primacy over temporal organization is much less obvious.

In any event, the centrality of space and the situational thematic analysis that derives from it work by analogy. For example, a thematic representation is, in a sense, analogous to the situation it describes; it corresponds only to the situation itself. But this does not seem to be the type of semantics employed by human beings at the level of language:

> Language derives essentially from the emergence, at the level of the human species, of a new form of representation, the semantic representation. The semantic representation superimposes itself on different perceptive representations evolved by mammals which, necessarily analogical in nature, mainly feed recognition memories. Semantic representation is not analogical because it is centrally autogenerated; it is eminently favourable for recall memories. More exactly, . . . the representation generator generates pre-representations, or potential representations, which become true representations only in as much as they correspond to something other than themselves. This happens when the products of the representation generator "meet" other data (Champagnol 1992, 8).[22]

A third reason for the centrality of space implicit in some discussions is that we intuitively feel it to be the case. Clearly, such a folk theory ought to have no place in linguistics. Yet, it is interesting to ask why such folk theories come about. I have the impression that it is due to the fourth reason for advocating the centrality of space: statistics. Spatial uses of words seem to be the ones to which we are most frequently exposed, especially at very early developmental stages. Thus, Jongen (1985) quotes the following passage from Bowerman (1978, 273), "the central referent for a word (. . . the prototype . . .) was, with a few exceptions, the first referent for which the word was used." He further comments, "This shows the importance, in the process of the child's identification of prototypical properties, of the initial referential situation and of its cultural frequency" (Jongen 1985, 137, note 2). Since as young children we apply our conceptualization system to spatial elements, we form the impression that the system itself is centrally spatial.

These four factors converge to produce the impression that there must be something to the idea that space is central. But this idea has nothing to do with I-language because none of these four factors are relevant for grammatical analysis.

1.5.2.4 THE PERVASIVENESS OF POLYSEMY

The examples of polysemy discussed above are not exceptional. On the contrary, most lexical items function like this, with many uses that, in thematic terms, must be given different representations. Moreover, the range of uses found across languages for closely related lexical items is quite regular. For example, in Part II, I will discuss six very common verbs in French that are generally analyzed as "movement" verbs: *aller* 'go,' *venir* 'come,' *arriver* 'arrive,' *partir* 'leave,' *entrer* 'enter,' and *sortir* 'go out'. I will argue that in order to account for the diversity of uses of these verbs, it is better to assume that they are not movement verbs and to abstract away from the features that might give the impression that they are. The many other uses of these French verbs are consistently found for their cognates in other languages. Thus, to the French *Max va partir demain,* we can relate the English *Max is going to leave tomorrow.* Several similar extensions of use from the spatial to other domains are discussed in Lichtenberk (1991) for a number of Austro-Melanasian languages. This must also be explained. If the six verbs above do not really belong to a class of movement verbs, but to a class defined at a more abstract level, we can begin to look for an explanation.

To abstract away from features of one particular use of a lexical item, a different method of approaching data must be used. Instead of basing our analysis on the prototypical use of a lexical item and trying to relate its other uses to this central one, we will look at a great variety of uses for that item. Then we will try to get to the essence of a verb's meaning by abstracting away from extralinguistic, situational factors and by factoring out what the arguments bring to the total computation.

Such a methodology, which involves studying a wide variety of examples, is contrary to the well-founded strategy of studying fairly impoverished, invented examples, so as not to overburden the linguistic intuition with facts that are irrelevant to the properties under study. But there is a risk to the latter strategy that we must avoid: instead of being guided purely by methodological concerns, the reduction of the variety of examples may be unconsciously biased by prototypicality. One could then concentrate too much on a very few prototypical examples and eliminate empirically relevant and crucial factors.[23] Examples must therefore be numerous and varied, using variation to try to determine what different factors could be involved; varying examples does not consist in replacing a [+human] NP by another one, for example (although the exact nature of these NPs could play a role in some cases, of course). Milner expresses this very nicely in the following passage:

> Examples should be numerous and varied for two reasons. On the one hand, so that their variety allows one to properly capture the property under study: each example is a combination of multiple linguistic properties; by multiplying the variations, one will reveal the independence of the property under study with respect to other properties with which it happens to be combined. Thus, if one wants to study Passive, one should give examples which show that passive is independent from the tense of the verb, from the relative or non relative, interrogative or non interrogative character of the sentence, etc.
>
> On the other hand, examples should be varied because they must take into account all the refutable consequences of the proposition under study, so that the whole set of possible refutabilities is being examined.[24] (1989, 116)

Even for highly purified and simplified sentences, there remain numerous situational factors at play. Hypersimplification of the data misses the fact that the ubiquity of polysemy is a central property of natural language. There is a price to pay for working with isolated and simplified sentences in laboratory-like conditions: "The laboratory and any closed system protects one from turbulences. Science is closed within. It goes, from its very beginning, from [Lucrecius'] *Meteors* to the oven, and will not come out from that enclosure again, which excludes chance and the uncontrolable, what today we would call hypercomplexity" (Serres 1977, 86).[25] Scientific research now being done on chaotic systems shows us that one cannot forever avoid hypercomplexity.

The position that I am advocating is that semantic representations should be purged of elements that do not belong in Grammar. The goal is not to eliminate hypercomplexity, but, on the contrary, to ascribe its full force to the web of shared knowledge, which is involved in the computation of the situations to which a sentence can refer. This will allow us to get a clearer view of the correspondence between semantics and syntax and of polysemy and metaphor. The position on basic abstract meanings that I propose on linguistic grounds—namely, that each lexical item shows deep similarities in all its uses—seems to be close to that of Claude Lévi-Strauss on metaphorical uses:

> When these myths, which were the starting point of our reflexion, depict a hero covered with dung and vermin or changed into stinking carrion, they do not embroider crudely on metaphors. . . . Because it is the opposite which is true: thanks to the myths, one discovers that metaphor lies in the intuition of logical relations between one domain and other domains, into the set of which it only reinstates the former [domain,] notwithstanding reflexive thinking which desperately tries to keep them separate. Far from being added to language as an embellishment, each metaphor purifies it and brings it back to its primal nature, by deleting, for an instant, one of the innumerable synecdoches of which speech is made.[26] (1964, 345)

1.5.2.5 THREE ARGUMENTS FOR THETA THEORY

In all fairness, if I intend to criticize theta theory as a valid semantic representation, I should look at cases brought up by proponents of theta roles. The three cases presented by Jackendoff (1983, 206–207) in favor of "the usefulness of thematic relations for explaining grammatical phenomena that lack a structural basis" provide illustrative examples. First, he discusses the case of reflexives in Psych constructions:

(52)a.   John is angry at himself.
    b.   John regards himself as stupid.

(53)a.   ?John is pleasing to himself.
    b.   ?John strikes himself as stupid.

Since (52) and (53) appear to have the same structure, we must appeal to the thematic hierarchy to explain the differences in acceptability, claims Jackendoff. The claim about similarity of structure has been challenged by Belletti and Rizzi (1988). We will see in chapter 4 that they are wrong, but we will also see that theta roles do not fare any better in accounting for these properties if more data are considered. I will argue that the source of the lesser acceptability of the sentences in (53) is a mismatch between the antecedent and the reflexive: the reflexive refers to an individual as a Substantive, but its antecedent, *John,* refers to an individual as a Concept.

A second phenomenon discussed by Jackendoff is control, as in (54), where the controller is determined by theta roles. For example, one could say that, since the one who receives an order is the one who carries it out, the Goal should be the one who is leaving in (a and b), and since the one who makes a promise is the one who carries it out, the Source of the promise should be leaving in (c and d).

(54) a. John gave Bill orders to leave. (Bill should leave)
     b. John got from Bill orders to leave. (John should leave)
     c. John gave Bill a promise to leave. (John should leave)
     d. John got from Bill a promise to leave. (Bill should leave)

But the distinction is really a pragmatic one, not a thematic one. Dowty (1991) discusses similar examples and argues that control in (55) is not determined by a thematic role hierarchy, but by pragmatic considerations about who would have what object at his or her disposal at what point in the action, as (56) shows:

(55) a. John bought a book to read to the children.
     b. John bought Mary a book to read to the children.

(56) Here is a bottle of wine. I brought it to drink with our/your/their dinner.

Jackendoff presents an intriguing puzzle from Gruber (1965) as a third argument in favor of thematic roles.

(57) a. Every oak grew out of an acorn.
     b. Every acorn grew into an oak.
     c. An oak grew out of every acorn.
     d. *An acorn grew into every oak.

(58) a. Bill carved every clown out of a piece of wood.
     b. Bill carved every piece of wood into a clown.
     c. Bill carved a clown out of every piece of wood.
     d. *Bill carved a piece of wood into every clown.

As Jackendoff comments,

Grammaticality in these sentences depends in part on the indefinite NP being included within the scope of the quantifier. Apparently, if the indefinite NP follows the quantifier, it can be within its scope, whatever the semantic relations. If the indefinite NP precedes the quantifier, though, thematic relations somehow come into play: when the quantified NP is source, as in the (c) cases, quantification is acceptable; but when the quantified NP is goal, as in the (d) cases, quantification is not possible. Thus appropriate scope of quantification can be achieved only if either the syntactic condition of ordering or the semantic condition on source-goal relations is satisfied. . . . What seems to be crucial in the semantic structure of these examples is that, because of the particular verbs used in these sentences, source-goal relations correspond to temporally dependent ascriptions of identity; first the objects in question were acorns and pieces of wood, then they became oaks and clowns. How this plays a principled role in quantification, however, is a mystery. (1983, 207)

A clue to the enigma lies in the fact that these examples are not as symmetric as the source-goal labeling leads us to believe. Thus if we change the arguments of (57b and 57c), as in (59), the asymmetry reveals itself.

(59)a.   Every young oak grew into a fine tall tree.
   b.   #A fine tall tree grew out of every young oak.

There is a subtle nuance in meaning between the INTO and the OUT OF sentences. The INTO sentences describe a process, a change from state X to state Y . On the other hand, the OUT OF sentences are more like a state. The latter is obscured by the fact that, in the "real world," there is usually a process that leads up to that state. However, it seems that the OUT OF sentences do not refer to the process, but only to the final state. Thus, the adverb *quickly,* with a reading where it modifies the process rather than the beginning of the event, is fine with INTO sentences, but odd with OUT OF sentences.[27]

(60)a.   The acorn grew into an oak quickly.
   b.   ?The oak grew out of an acorn quickly.

Similarly, there is a contrast when the sentences are in the progressive:

(61)a.   The acorn is growing into an oak.
   b.   ?The oak is growing out of an acorn.

Moreover, as Jackendoff himself observes, temporality seems to be the key to the mystery. Although one could relate the "temporally dependent ascriptions of identity" to notions like source and goal, it is also quite possible that the explanation lies directly in temporality, the theta correlate being totally parasitic. For example, given the looseness of assignment of theta roles, one could assign a source role to *an acorn* and a theme role to *every oak* in (62a) and a goal role to *an oak* and a theme role to *every acorn* in (62b), mimicking the temporality effects.

(62)a. Every oak was once an acorn.
    b. Every acorn will be an oak some day.

If temporally dependent ascription of identity and not thematic roles really is the key factor, we expect that there should be no contrast between quantified sources and quantified goals when temporally dependent ascription of identity is not a factor. This is borne out in (63).

(63)a. Every Canadian walked out of a room.
    b. Every Canadian walked into a room.
    c. A Canadian walked out of every room.
    d. A Canadian walked into every room.

In contrast with (57d) and (58d), there is apparently no problem with (63d). However, there are pragmatic restrictions on the situations to which (63d) can correspond: either (i) the same Canadian walked into every room ONE AFTER ANOTHER or (ii) different Canadian individuals walked into all the rooms, with various combinations. Both cases fall under a pragmatic restriction: no single Canadian can walk into two rooms at the same time. This might help us understand what is going on in (57d) and (58d). Ascriptions of identity in INTO sentences describe a change in the same individual from one state to another, whereas OUT OF sentences relate two individuals, one being presented as the origin of the other. If we assume that ascriptions of identity proscribe the distributive reading of indefinite NPs in which many individuals are involved, the equivalent of reading (ii) of (63d) would not be available in such cases. Thus, this reading is not possible in (57d) and (58d), although it is in (63d), because it is made unavailable by the fact that the indefinite NP has its identity ascribed temporally. As for the equivalent of reading (i), with a single acorn, for example, it cannot be temporally sequential because it is pragmatically impossible in ascription of identity of the type expressed by INTO sentences: the same acorn cannot become one oak, and then another oak, and so on. Nor is it possible for an acorn to grow simultaneously into more than one oak, let alone several. (To my knowledge, twin oaks in this sense are impossible.) But this is not pragmatically impossible for the example with the piece of wood: (58d) seems possible if one replaces *Bill* with *Picasso*. In this case, Picasso first carves a piece of wood into a clown, then goes on to modify it and carves it into a totally different clown, and so on. It is just that in (58d), we expect the byproduct "clown" to remain after the carving. Moreover, there is another situation where the same piece of wood could be used to carve several different clowns: the piece of wood could simply not be used in toto to make any single clown. This is of course impossible in the case of the acorn and oaks.

In summary, although some of the mystery about the quantification in (57) and (58) remains, the place to look for a solution seems to be in the direction of ascription of identity, not of thematic roles. A final attempt at saving thematic roles could be to acknowledge that there are indeed empirical and conceptual problems with determining the nature of specific theta roles in precise situational terms but that, in any event, the notion of thematic role relevant for Grammar is much more abstract; the relevant issue is simply their presence or absence in a given syntactic position. For example, whatever thematic roles are, the important assumption would be that there are no such roles assigned to the deep structure subject position in the following examples, which allows the movement of the lower clause subject:

(64)a.   John$_i$ was arrested t$_i$ by the FBI.
    b.   John$_i$ seems [t$_i$ to prefer red wine].
    c.   John$_i$ fell t$_i$ on his back.

But how can we be sure no role is assigned to a given position if we do not know what such a role might be? Intuitions about the presence or absence of theta roles will not do. Neither will the tests presented for absence of theta roles. Upon close scrutiny, they are quite weak (see, for example, Ruwet (1991) on the use of idioms and Ruwet (1990) on French clitic *en,* in this respect). Arguments that are based on selection also will not do. They take the following form. In (64b), we can tell that the subject position of *seems* is not a thematic position because no selectional restriction is imposed on that position. Thus, the selectional restrictions on the subject of *seems* are the sum of the restrictions on the subject of the infinitival complement, plus zero restrictions from *seems.* In contrast, in a control construction like (65), the fact that the subject of *wants* must be volitional is strictly because of the matrix verb, since *roll* can take nonvolitional subjects as in (66).

(65)a.   John wants to roll down the hill.
    b.   #The rock wants to roll down the hill.

(66)   The rock rolled down the hill.

There are two problems with this reasoning. First, as is well known, there are many cases where verbs that are analyzed as control verbs can behave like raising verbs (see Ruwet (1990, 1991), among others, for many examples):

(67)   This rock just doesn't want to roll down the hill.

Second, verbs vary significantly in the restrictiveness they impose on their arguments. A verb like *impeach,* for example, severely restricts both its arguments.[28] However, while the Experiencer of *please* is fairly restricted, the Subject may range over a variety of argument types.

(68)   John/that color/your coat/what you said pleased me a lot.

If verbs can vary so much in restrictiveness, a given thematic role could be associated with no selectional restrictions. For example, *seem* could assign a "Seemer" role, with no selectional restrictions—anything can seem. The only way to prevent this is to give more content to the notion of thematic role. But then we are back to the original problem of not being sure whether a thematic role is assigned to a given position, without looking into the nature of the content of thematic roles. And this, as I have argued, raises severe empirical and conceptual problems.

1.5.2.6 CONSEQUENCES FOR THE CHOICE OF PRIMITIVES

What are the consequences of the foregoing discussion for the topic of this section, namely determining the choice of primitives that are suitable for building semantic representations of lexical items? We have seen that thematic roles describe situations and that, as such, they are inadequate primitives to account for polysemous uses of lexical items. Moreover, in section 1.5.2.2.1, I showed, using the sentence *Colorless green ideas sleep furiously* as an example, that the level of semantics relevant for I-language is G-semantics. Theta roles, which are descriptions of situational properties, are therefore inherently inadequate as semantic primitives.[29]

What emerges from the discussion of the semantics relevant to Grammar is that there is an aspect of meaning that is strictly linguistic (what I call G-semantics) and that syntactic properties might follow almost entirely from this autonomous semantics. A shift is therefore desirable from autonomous syntax to autonomous grammar, which is the real issue in any event. In a way, this is not so distant from a recent position taken by Chomsky:

There is a distinction to be made between cognitively impenetrable systems that constitute what Pylyshyn (1984) calls "functional architecture" and systems that involve reference to goals, beliefs, and so forth, and perhaps inference of one or another sort. In Pylyshyn's terms, the distinction is between the "symbolic (or syntactic) level" and the "semantic (or intentional) level", each to be distinguished from a third level, the "biological (or physical) level" at which description and explanation are in terms of laws of physics, biochemistry, etc. (1985a, 262)

What is referred to here as the symbolic level could encompass both syntax and G-semantics; S-semantics would correspond to the "semantic (or intentional) level." [30]

The primitives of Grammar must be of a more abstract nature. Precise proposals can only come from detailed empirical studies, to which we will turn in Part II. But before doing so, I want to look at another aspect of the semantics relevant to Grammar.

1.5.3 FORMAL DIFFERENCES BETWEEN G-SEMANTICS AND S-SEMANTICS

An interesting question that arises under my proposal is whether the distinction between G-semantics and S-semantics corresponds to formal differences in their modes of representation. There are good reasons to believe that the formal representations of these two types of semantics are very different. An interesting and challenging problem, then, is to determine exactly how the formalism of G-semantics differs from that of S-semantics. A natural place to start is in exploring the hypothesis in (69):

(69) *Hypothesis:* All grammatical processes are dependent on constituent tree structure.

As a consequence of (69), we expect that if a semantic relation is not expressible in a tree structure, but only in a general graph, it will belong to S-semantics, not G-semantics. If this is the case, it will not be represented in the grammar. This is expressed in the following subhypothesis:

(70) *G-Semantics Hypothesis:* G-semantics representations have the form of tree structures.

In order to test this hypothesis, it will be useful to briefly review the basic properties of the formal object "tree." A tree is a restricted type of labeled graph. The basic restrictions on the kind of tree generally used in linguistic descriptions are the following (see Wall 1972; Partee, ter Meulen, and Wall 1990):

(71) (i) A tree is an oriented graph that expresses *dominance* relations: a node *x dominates* a node *y,* if there is a connected sequence of branches in the tree extending from *x* to *y.* The relations between nodes are therefore oriented from top to bottom, although the convention is not to actually indicate this by arrows in the tree graph.

(ii) *The Single Root Condition (Partee, ter Meulen, and Wall):* In every well-formed constituent structure tree, there is exactly one node that dominates every node

(iii) Precedence relations hold in a tree, so that two nodes are ordered left-to-right just in case they are not ordered by dominance.

(iv) Two nodes *x* and *y* cannot hold both a precedence and a dominance relation to one another (see Partee, ter Meulen, and Wall's *Exclusivity Condition*)

(v) Every node in a tree has at most one node immediately dominating it.

(vi) Lines in a tree must not cross.

Dynamic linguistic relations, such as Case assignment, subcategorization, and referential binding, for example, crucially depend on the geometric properties of the tree. What dynamic relations a given node can entertain with other nodes in a structure will be determined by the branching relations between that node and the other nodes. For example, given the basic properties of constituent trees, consider what branching relations node D has in the following tree:

(72)

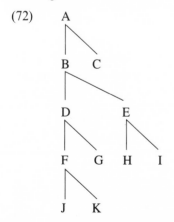

In (72), D has branching relations with the three nodes B, F, and G, since there is a branch connecting D with each of these nodes. Moreover, given the transitivity of dominance, this allows for branching relations to extend beyond the nodes with which D has an immediate branching relation. Thus, D has an extended branching relation with nodes J and K via node F, since D has a branching relation with F and F dominates J and K; similarly, D has an extended branching relation with E, H, and I, since D has a branching relation with B and B dominates E, H, and I. On the other hand, because of the orientation of the tree graph, no extended branching relation is established from D to A via B, since the branch relating A and B is not oriented from B to A, but in the opposite direction.

If grammatical processes are dependent on tree structure, an element in the position of D could have dynamic relations only with the nodes with which it has a branching relation—B, F, and G—and with the nodes with which it has an extended branching relation—E, H, I, J, and K. This seems to be the case, and it is pervasive in linguistic analysis. For example, feature percolation is generally dependent on direct branching, and many grammatical processes regulated by c-command and government fall under extended branching.[31] An instance of extended branching establishing a relation between two distant nodes is referential dependency.

(73)

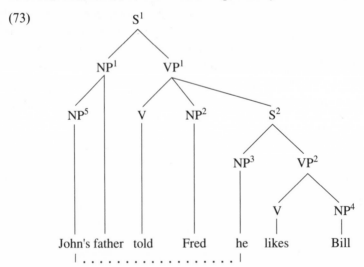

In (73), the grammar has something to say about the referential dependencies between NP^3 *he* and NP^4 *Bill* because the mother node of NP^3 *he* extends a branch down to NP^4 *Bill*. On the other hand, no grammatical condition is applicable from NP^3 *he* to NP^2 *Fred,* NP^1 *John's father,* or NP^5 *John,* since the orientation of the branch between S^2, the mother of NP^3 *he,* and VP^1 does not allow NP^3 *he* to extend a branching relation up to VP^1 or beyond. If (73) corresponded to a situation that actually involved co-reference between NP^3 *he* and NP^5 *John,* for example, this could not be expressed by a ranching relation extending from NP^3 *he* to NP^5 *John* in the tree graph, and this could only be expressed by a less constrained graph relation, like the one represented by the dotted line in (73). Now, given the hypothesis in (69) about the dependency of grammatical processes on tree structure, it follows that the co-reference relation between NP^3 *he* and NP^5 *John* in (73) could not be due to a grammatical process because it can only be represented as a general graph relation, not as a constituent tree relation. We therefore see a first effect of the hypothesis on the formal distinction between G-semantics and S-semantics: the situation alone will tell us whether a referential relation exists between NP^3 *he* and NP^5 *John,* not the grammar. In short, we see that obligatory *disjoint reference* between two NPs is a grammatical phenomenon, and it receives an analytical account based on tree relations. *Coreference* between a pronoun and a NP, on the other hand, is not a grammatical phenomenon, since it requires a formalism other than tree structures (although it does receive an analytical account based on general graph relations). Thus, on the basis of purely formal considerations, we have reached the same conclusion that Lasnik (1976) reached on empirical grounds.

We will use the formal distinction between G-semantics and S-semantics as a methodological tool: a semantic relationship will be part of a semantic representation only if it is expressible in terms of tree structures. If it cannot be so represented, we predict that it should have no effect on the Grammar. This assumption will influence the content and the form of the semantic representations, which will directly affect the form of the correspondence rules. For instance, as we saw in section 1.1.1 (see also section 2 below), a lexical-semantic representation that is structurally too poor or too rich requires argument linking to be *indexical,* in the sense that the relation between argument positions in the semantic representation and NP positions in syntax can only be represented as a general graph relation, not as a relation between two nodes in a constituent tree. If the hypothesis in (69) is correct, this would imply that argument linking has no effect on Grammar. Clearly, this is false. We therefore need another type of lexical semantic representation that has the formal properties required to represent such relations in tree structures.

1.5.4 THE MEANINGFUL CONTENT OF THE FORMALISM

The title of this section may appear to be a contradiction. If a formal system, in the technical sense, is defined as pure relations between abstract forms that are devoid of any conceptual content, it is impossible in principle for such systems to have meaningful content. But formal systems in the technical sense have never been used, either in linguistics or in mathematical studies in general. Moreover, such systems are not consistent with how the world is viewed in a mentalist approach.

The syntactic systems typically used in generative grammar are not formal, in the technical sense, because the very structures have meaningful content—the concept of orientation discussed in section 1.5.3, for example. The notion of projecting properties from lexical heads into the syntactic structure also means that the syntactic formalism is not devoid of meaning. In Chomsky (1981), semantic features of selection play a crucial role in the functioning of syntax, since they license the structures. This is explicitly integrated into the theory by the Projection Principle:

(74) Projection Principle:
    (i)   If β is an immediate constituent of γ at level L_i, and $\gamma = \alpha'$, then α θ-marks β in γ.
    (ii)   If α selects β in γ as a lexical property, then α selects β in γ at level L_i.
    (iii) If α selects β in γ at level L_i, then α selects β in γ at level L_j.

This means that the hypothesis of absolute autonomy of syntax, where no aspects of meaning affect the functioning of syntax, is abandoned. Does it mean that generative grammar in the technical sense is then abandoned, as claimed by Milner (1989), for example? In absolute terms, the answer seems to be yes. But there could be a relativized answer, where some aspects of grammar continue to function in a generative fashion, as a system of production rules in which arbitrary symbols are manipulated in an algorithmic fashion without regard to their meaning. The X-bar schema, notions like *government* and *c-command,* conditions such as the ECP and Subjacency, and the head initial/final parameter may be formal components, in this sense. Other possible candidates for autonomy include Case and Agreement, although these are more problematic. Thus, one could abandon the idea of a theory of generative linguistics in which a grammar is a formal system, in the technical sense, and still be left with a fairly large autonomous syntactic component.

However, history tells us that such a relativized approach to formal grammar should be abandoned. If grammars of natural languages are a subclass of formal grammars, they will have formal characteristics of this broader class. But this broader class of formal grammars has been shown *not* to be formal in the technical sense. Hence, to try to maintain or revive such a formal stance in grammars for natural languages would seem to be fruitless.

David Hilbert started a program to relate mathematical order to a purely formal system.[32] Hilbert's program, however, failed. It is now assumed that mathematics does not reduce to an abstract syntax. The relevance of the notion of formal content has been established: mathematical objects bear a certain semantic load, a certain notional content, that cannot be reduced to simple forms of organization.[33] Thus, Saunders MacLane (1981) observes that mathematical systems "codify deeper and nonobvious properties of the originating human activities [he gives examples of properties of motion like rotation and translation, symmetry, and algebraic manipulations]. In this view, mathematics is formal, but not simply "formalistic"—since the forms studied in mathematics are derived from human activities and are used to understand those activities" (464). So, to maintain a formal approach to natural languages in a strict sense would be going against the direction taken in the general class of formal grammars, of which grammars of natural languages are supposed to be a subclass.

If form has a certain notional content—meaning, in short—we must explore what that meaning is and how it relates to what linguists usually assume is part of meaning. Consider the notion of "constituent tree structure." In a purely formal approach, a tree expresses abstract relations between objects (the nodes); these relations and objects are part of the formal primitives. The tree is only a concrete, useful representation of the abstract primitives. As such, it is arbitrary and says nothing about the formal entities: it just provides a practical means of representing them so that the formal system can be communicated and commented on. In such an approach, X-bar is simply a construction procedure for trees. It abstracts away from any particular construction or part of a construction. Hence, an element constructed by X-bar can be identified only by its constitutive elements and their order. Therefore, such a constructed element is not a cohesive unit but an aggregate: it is analytic, not symbiotic.

But, on the other hand, if form has meaning and tree structures contain meaningful notions like orientation, relation, and dominance, the concept of "tree structure" is viewed quite differently. A tree is not just a useful tool, a representation, it is a schema that forms an integrated unit with a synthetic, symbiotic meaning of its own. Thus, in a simple tree schema like (75), there is much more than a concatenation of elements that will eventually be provided meaning by some other component. Such a schema already has meaning: the nodes VP and S correspond to relations between specific elements, and the respective positions of NP_1 and NP_2 say something about their orientation to one another.

(75)

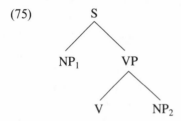

Besides the conceptual problems created by a hybrid system where some aspects of Grammar continue to function in a formal, generative fashion, under closer scrutiny, the subparts of Grammar that are supposed to exhibit such formal properties actually do not appear to be formal. Let us look at those we mentioned above.

(i) *X-bar:* The X-bar schema does not really generate structures in a purely formal fashion, since all of its processes are meaningful. Thus, its binary branching is an expression of the concept of association between the nodes involved. The trees produced by X-bar incorporate the meaningful notion of orientation. In a two level X-bar, each level is associated with a specific meaning: "close semantic association with the head" for the lowest level (COMPL) and more "remote semantic association" for the highest level (Spec). The very categories of the elements that X-bar relates are possibly partly determined by semantic considerations (see Grimshaw 1979 on canonical selection, Carter 1988 on concepts that are "more adjectival" than others).

(ii) *Government and c-command:* These notions express relations in a tree structure, which has meaningful content, as we just saw. Moreover, the two notions themselves are derivable from "orientation," as we saw in section 1.5.3.

(iii) *ECP and Subjacency:* If neither of these have any status in the Grammar, and both are derived from government and chains of selectional relations (Bouchard 1982, 1984a; Kayne 1983), then they also fail as purely formal notions.

(iv) *Head initial/final parameter:* This is, indeed, a good candidate for autonomy; but it is for low level reasons that have to do with articulatory (and gesticulatory) reasons that are somewhat accidental and do not constitute profound motivations for a formal Grammar of natural languages. We humans just cannot produce many sounds or signs simultaneously, and we must string them out. Therefore, they are ordered.

(v) *Case:* It is still an open question how and to what degree choice of Case assignment is dependent on selectional properties.

(vi) *Agreement:* There have been suggestions that agreement is dependent on the interpretation of indices and, hence, co-reference in many cases (see Fauconnier (1974), Bouchard (1987), among others, and section 3.3.2.2 below on past participle agreement and section 5.5 on subject-verb agreement). Although these are very sketchy discussions, they do indicate that the status of these elements as "formal" in nature and autonomous from semantic considerations is far from decided.

To assume that these elements could be formal is in opposition to a mentalist approach to language. In order for an approach to be formal, the well-formedness of a given sentence, S, must be determined on the basis of the application of the rules of a system, independent of the meaning of S. S is considered only as a concatenation of symbols. This is more akin to the metaphysics and epistemology of a logic-based approach than it is to a mentalist approach. Logic-based approaches postulate entities from an objective world that are related to abstract symbols of Language; it is of no importance that the symbols of Language are manipulated by human beings. In a mentalist approach, however, there is no direct connection between human language and the world as it exists outside of human experience. Natural languages are what they are because they take place in humans and are based on human concepts:

> A sign does not mean anything except to an intelligent being. If considerations of the well-formedness or internal structure of a sign could be totally sundered from the question of what it means to be intelligible, then semantics, however rigorous its mathematical format, would *have no meaning.* (Rosen 1980, 11)

Consider the concept of "orientation," to illustrate. "Orientation" is not an abstract symbol which is a representation, it is an organizing concept. It is in the formalism, in the tree structure, but not in the real world. We attribute it to the world as we understand the world, but it has no independent reality. Hence "orientation" does not get its meaning because it corresponds to entities or categories in the real world; "orientation," as a concept, has reality only in the structure of the mind.[34]

The formalism that I adopt has meaning, as all formalisms do: there is a semantics to syntax. I will take the meaning of the formalism into consideration in the computation of the meaning of lexical items and sentences. For Grammar, this assumption, in relation to the assumption that the semantics relevant for syntax does not include background knowledge, will allow us to elaborate simpler semantic representations. As we will see in the following chapters, these representations link directly and in a principled way with syntactic structures and allow a simplification of the base and the transformational components of the Grammar.

1.6 APPENDIX: NEWTON, THE ANCIENTS, AND GRAMMAR

There possibly is an additional reason not to integrate the web of background knowledge into grammar. Not only is situational semantics the wrong kind of semantics to be linked with grammar, because it is too concrete as I argued above, but it may also be the wrong kind of semantics in its choice of knowledge. The knowledge that is typically assumed to be expressed by language is roughly that of classical science. In this sense, its physics is basically Newtonian. Thus, it is generally assumed that the semantics of a sentence like (76) is such that at every moment t of that hour, John was walking (with well-known problems to which we return directly).

(76)   John went for a walk for an hour.

Now consider how a linguist deals with a very old written text, or the languages of hunter-gatherers. She or he assumes that the grammar of those languages and the grammar of a contemporary industrial society are essentially the same. As Pinker and Bloom (1990, 707) observe, "The grammars of industrial societies are no more complex than the grammars of hunter-gatherers. . . . [T]he ability to use a natural language belongs more to the study of human biology than human culture; it is a topic like echolocation in bats or stereopsis in monkeys, not like writing or the wheel." The assumption behind this is that language evolves at the pace of biological evolution, whereas knowledge—perception of the world, situational semantics—progresses more or less at the pace of scientific discoveries. Thus, language and knowledge are on two completely different time scales.

Because of its biological rhythm, today's language presumably has the same G-semantics as that of the languages of the Ancients or of primitive societies. Therefore, our G-semantics should still reflect a world view closer to the world view of humanity at the origin of language than at the dawn of classical science. If this is true, studies of the world view of the Ancients or of hunter-gatherers, whose social organizations are assumed to be more like those of prehistoric societies, and extrapolations from these should reveal something about the nature of the S-semantics of our forebears that has been grammaticized over time and hence, of today's G-semantics. This kind of study is not easy, and one must be very cautious about interpreting the results, but let me briefly present two cases that indicate that the world view of the past was indeed quite different from today's in some respects that are relevant to language, that is, to G-semantics.

First, as Prigogine and Stengers observe, "Modern science was born out of the breakdown of the animistic alliance with nature. Man seemed to possess a place in the Aristotelian world as both a living and a knowing creature. The world was made to his measure" (1984, 75). The world was not seen as an automaton as in classical science. The objects of the world were seen as active with human beings and similar to them, and people did not feel estranged from the world, as Pascal later would. We can see this in Aristotelian physics, which set out to explain phenomena like the fact that a stone "resists" a horse's efforts to pull it and that this resistance can be "overcome" by applying traction through a system of pulleys.

This view of things was dismissed by Galileo, for whom Nature never gives anything away, never does something for nothing, and can never be tricked. If all of Nature was viewed as much more active and humanlike, then it was normal to have the same predicates apply to people, animates, inanimates, time, and other mental entities, because all of these were on the same level, in an active universe. Thus, while we now see the notion of agentivity as centered on people, with animals perceived as close in a certain hierarchy, it was not the case for the Ancients. This is a possible explanation for the presence of "agents" in chemistry, for example, in our language. Classical science subsequently isolated humanity from nature, so we tend to see language as centered on us, and predicates as made for us. Metaphor and "anthropomorphism" are postulated for most of the rest. Simple examples like *le soleil se lève, se couche* 'the sun rises, sets,' which are now perceived as anthropomorphisms, originally were probably not. Nature and humanity were united and the same predicates applied to different types of entities from both sets. Originally, words (in particular, predicates), which are now perceived as having many uses that are very different from one another, were not necessarily perceived as polysemous. The perception of polysemy is due to our changed perception of the world, not to our grammar. Multiple uses are an omnipresent feature of language, and in chapter 2, I will propose a theory-internal explanation of *how* this is possible; the reflections above might explain *why* this phenomenon is recurrent in language.

A second aspect of the world view of the Ancients that is relevant to language has to do with the analysis of movement. One of the problems with a sentence expressing movement such as (76) above that is discussed by Dowty (1979), among many others, is that the semantic descriptions given for it usually imply that John should have been actually walking at every moment during that hour. But if he stopped to rest briefly or to do some window shopping, the sentence remains true, contrary to what is predicted. To solve the problem, Dowty introduces the notion of "psychologically relevant moment." So, in (76), John would have been walking at every psychologically relevant moment.

The problem is another instance where the wrong semantics was chosen. This time the problem arises from the conception that movement is uniform and identical at all points of the period of time being considered. Such a conception of uniformity of movement is only possible if a mathematical notion of movement is substituted for a physical one, as in classical science. Movement is said to obey the law of inertia—a body remains in a state of rest or of motion unless some force acts upon it—so it is seen as a state. The law of inertia presupposes an isotropic universe. The proponents of classical science—Newton himself was very clear about this—were aware that this conception of movement only applies in an idealized world, not in the actual physical world, where movement is much too complex to be subject to such laws.

As Koyré (1968) points out, this classical conception of movement in space is very different from the pre-Galilean or pre-Cartesian conceptions, with their finite universe and view of movement as a kind of becoming, a process of change affecting the bodies submitted to it. The notion was not mathematical but physical, the main source of inspiration being the organization and solidarity of biological functions. (It is correct to label it as a form of animism, but without the depreciatory connotation that comes from looking at it from our conception of things.) The Ancients saw the driving force, the "motor," as being internal to objects rather than external. The fact that a stone falls was seen as being caused by an internal property of the stone, a tendency or aim that the stone had. This differs greatly from the conception of an external force attracting the stone that appears in classical science.[35]

A mathematical conception of movement as being sequential, as in classical science, is not easily compatible with a nonisotropic space because what takes place between A and B is too complex if nonisotropic. The nonisotropic space of our immediate perception is more compatible with a conception of an object going from A to B being seen as aiming for B from A, without taking into consideration what takes place at the intermediate points.[36]

When Dowty introduced the notion of "psychologically relevant moment," he actually returned to a conception of movement that is very close to that of the Ancients. Movement of an object from A to B is not seen as a state in which all points between A and B are identical, but as a tendency or aim of the object in A to be at B. If this conception of movement is closer to the one grammaticized at the origin of language, we expect Grammar to express this kind of movement with a tendency or aim in its semantic representations rather than the uniform and sequential conception found in classical science. In chapters 2 and 3, I will argue that there is linguistic evidence that this is indeed the case: movement verbs express an aim from a point A to a point B, which is expressed by the orientation of the tree representation.

These reflections on the evolution of Grammar and the evolution of knowledge indicate that some elements of knowledge are unlikely to play an explanatory role in Grammar if we take into account their recent development, compared to the biological rhythm in which language evolves. When we look at a star that is thousands of light-years away, we see that star as it was thousands of years ago. When we look at our language, we see our conceptualization of the world as it was thousands of years ago. In this way, our language sets a certain frame to what we say about the world. Yet, we can still use our language to express our current conceptualization of the world. The fact that this is possible should not be viewed as a mystery, but as a challenge. In this book, I argue that this is possible because language does not say anything directly about events, but only about the contour of events. We fill in the rest with our shared background knowledge.

2 Selective Semantics and Syntactic Correspondence

In this chapter, I will present the details of my main hypothesis about the relationship between Conceptual Structure (CS), G-semantics, and Syntactic Structure. The main claim is that those properties of CS belonging to G-semantics map directly into syntactic structures. I thus adhere to Jackendoff's Grammatical Constraint on semantic theory:

(1)   One should prefer a semantic theory that explains otherwise arbitrary generalizations about the syntax and the lexicon. (Jackendoff 1983, 13; see Partee 1975 for a similar constraint, among others)

For Jackendoff, since language serves the purpose of transmitting information, "it would be perverse not to take as a working assumption that language is a relatively efficient and accurate encoding of the information it conveys" (1975, 14). If the lexical representations that he proposes are any indication, he seems to assume that "accurate encoding" of the information conveyed by language includes many situational elements. I depart from Jackendoff on this point. I assume that since the interlocutor is not ignorant of the context and has access to extralinguistic semantics of a general sort, the information conveyed by language does not have to be exhaustive. Language can ignore all details that are not necessary to its immediate means and maximally exploit knowledge common to participants in the discourse. In fact, it would be rather perverse not to take as a working assumption that language is relatively efficient; it does not redundantly encode massive amounts of information that are already accessible to the interlocutors from the context.[1]

Broadly considered, the problem is to determine how to link a strictly linguistic representation, Syntactic Structure (SS), to a nonlinguistic representation, CS. Frameworks that incorporate some form of projection principle usually assume an intermediate level, Lexical Structure (LS) (or some other such level), that takes from CS what is linguistically relevant and passes it on to SS. Two basic questions arise: (1) How much of the CS information is represented in LS? (2) How direct is the linking between LS and SS? The two questions are related, of course: an impoverished LS, as in (2), and a more complex one, as in (3), cannot be linked to SS by the same correspondence rules.

(2)   Sue hit Fred with a stick.
       LS: ((HIT (x, y)) WITH z)

(3)   Sue hit Fred with a stick. (Compare with Jackendoff 1987a)

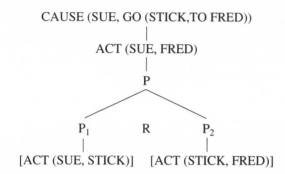

These two representations make quite different claims about the decomposition of *hit*. In (2), it is claimed that there is nothing linguistically relevant in further decomposing HIT, whereas in (3), HIT is not a linguistic primitive. On the other hand, the two representations make similar claims about argument linking, but for different reasons. In (2), structural properties are so poor that the correspondence between an argument position and an SS position could only be achieved by coindexation or a formally similar process such as an arc in a general graph; the correspondence is not representable as a constituent tree relation or as a mapping of one such tree into another. In (3), on the other hand, because the arguments occupy more than one position on more than one tier, there is also no way to have a direct linking between an argument and a grammatical function—an indexical procedure is needed here, too. Thus, Jackendoff (1990a) proposes a general correspondence rule of the form (4):

(4) | X^0 | | Entity |
       |__<YP<ZP≫ | corresponds to | F(<E_1>, <E_2, <E_3≫) |,
       where the YP corresponds to E_2, ZP corresponds to E_3, and the subject (if there is one) corresponds to E_1.

The representations in (2) and (3) both require a formalism that is more powerful and less constrained than constituent tree structure; thus, they are not compatible with the G-Semantics Hypothesis put forth in section 1.5.3. Moreover, there is a problem with these representations, since the hierarchical aspects of an LS like (2) or (3) could be almost totally irrelevant as far as argument linking with SS positions is concerned—there is nothing in the basic architecture of such approaches to lead us to expect any regularities in linking. Such regularities have to be stipulated, which causes numerous problems, as we will see below. In short, semantic representations that differ substantially from SS in their format, whether on the rich side or the poor side, are deficient in three ways: they do not allow for a direct linking of arguments with grammatical functions, they do not allow for any direct relation between nodes occuring in semantic representations and SS, and they do not express any direct relation between hierarchical aspects of the semantic representations and the SS.[2]

Considerations of the general empirical question of what is a possible word have led Richard Carter to propose lexical representations that are intermediate between (2) and (3). I will adopt a position along similar lines, with the added constraint that the representations be compatible with the G-Semantics Hypothesis. The semantic structures I propose are further supported by the fact that the linking with SS can be more direct. This makes interesting predictions for many syntactic constructions and therefore allows for precise claims about what is a (possible) sentence. Contrary to many proposals about argument linking, I assume that argument linking with syntactic positions is not uniform, but rather relativized, depending on structural properties of both SR and SS. As we will see, the latter turns out to produce a much simpler system. The motivation for the proposal is the one advocated by Chomsky from *Syntactic Structures* to *Knowledge of Language:* the entire question of interdependency of levels is one to be answered by empirical investigation rather than by methodological fiat. The structures and correspondence rules proposed will be justified by their role in explanation.

2.1 SYNTAX AND COMPOSITIONALITY

Before turning to examples of lexical representations and correspondence rules, let us clarify what properties are attributed to syntactic representations.[3] The syntactic and semantic components do essentially the same thing—organize meaningful elements into units. The properties of one of these, I argue, are almost entirely derived from the other—compositional properties of syntax are projected from compositional properties of semantics in a homomorphic fashion.[4]

This approach is similar to those of Stowell (1981) and Speas (1986), for example, in that one of its goals is to restrict the power of the grammar by eliminating much of the phrase structure component. It differs from them, however, in three important respects. First, I propose to derive all the properties of syntactic phrase structure formation, except for linearization and endocentricity value.[5] Second, I propose to derive these properties largely from factors external to syntax, namely structural properties of G-semantics representations. Thus, I do more than eliminate parochiality in phase structure (PS) rules—I have no PS component at all; nor rules, X-bar schemata, or node admissibility conditions. Third, my proposal affects not only the PS component, but also the transformational component, in that it restricts possible transformations. I will discuss this aspect of the proposal in Part III.

Speas (1988, 38) proposes "a theory of projection from the lexicon in which the only restriction imposed by X-bar theory is the restriction that sentences have hierarchical structure, and that all structure is projected from a head." I propose to go a step further and to derive the fact that sentences have hierarchical structure. This follows from the fact that sentences are related to a level of semantic representation that is itself hierarchically structured, and represented as constituent trees. This idea is implicit in Gruber (1965) and explicit in much subsequent work such as Jackendoff (1972), Carter (1988) and in Generative Semantics. Consequently, the correspondence rules that link these two levels are fairly trivial for hierarchical properties.

2.1.1 SYNTACTIC NODES AND COMPOSITIONALITY

Consider the problem of relating SS nodes and constituents to SR nodes and constituents. How directly are they related? The strong position is that correspondence between syntactic nodes and SR nodes is direct—every syntactic constituent in a sentence corresponds to an independent and identifiable contiguous piece of semantic structure. This is the position I will adopt. Jackendoff adopts a position that is not quite as strong: "every major phrasal constituent in a sentence corresponds to a conceptual constituent in the semantic structure of the sentence" (Jackendoff 1983, 76).

Jackendoff does not adopt the stronger position, where all syntactic nodes rather than just the major phrasal constituents are licensed by corresponding SR elements, because he believes that intermediate-level syntactic categories serve a strictly functional role; they have no semantic content. He conjectures that these nonmaximal syntactic categories exist because they help make up for the paucity of differentiation in syntactic dependency, compared to the variety of semantic dependencies. Syntax has a single dependency relation: a node is a daughter of another node. In semantics, on the other hand, there are at least five ways of embedding constituents, as shown in (5)–(9).

(5) Functional Argument:
John left Mary in the car.

(6) Restrictive Modifier:
a.   In NP: the red hat, the man who cracked the code
b.   In S: Max surprised everyone by arriving on time.
c.   In AP: quietly obnoxious
d.   In PP: straight down the hole

(7) Nonrestrictive Modifier:
a.   In NP: Albert, who was my friend, voted for Dubbs.
b.   In S: Cindy told the boss to buzz off, which I never could have done.
c.   In AP: Ron is fond of jelly beans, which I'll never be.

(8) Bounding Modifier:
a.   In NP: three tigers
b.   In S: They jumped in the snow five times/for three minutes.
c.   In AP: six feet long
d.   In PP: far into the night

(9) Logical Modifier:
a.   Definite Article: the mouse
b.   Sentential Negation: Alfred will not eat his meat.
c.   Quantifiers: Bill picked up something somewhere some way

According to Jackendoff, syntax fixes this problem by having intermediate levels—it tends to group modifiers of different types under different intermediate nodes.

This dichotomy in licensing of syntactic nodes, with some licensed by a dynamic (i.e., semantic) relation and others licensed by purely geometric (i.e., X-bar theoretic) factors, is pervasive in generative grammar. The shift has been more and more toward dynamic relations as licensers. For instance, in *Knowledge of Language,* Chomsky explicitly adheres to dynamic licensing for maximal projections:

We may, first of all, distinguish the licensing conditions for maximal and nonmaximal projections. The latter are licensed relative to the maximal projections in which they appear, by X-bar theory. For maximal projections, we might expect that each such phrase α must be licensed "externally" as either an argument or the trace of an argument, a predicate, or an operator. If an argument, α must be assigned a theta-role; if a predicate, α must assign a theta-role; and if an operator, α must bind a variable (which, furthermore, is an argument and must be strongly bound). Then the licensing conditions on LF representations are analogous to those on PF representations, except that the elements of the former are more complex: maximal projections with internal structure rather than phonetic segments. (Chomsky 1985a, 100–101)

The system proposed by Chomsky has the essential property that syntactic structure is a given, with some nodes, maximal projections, licensed by dynamic forces. Nonmaximal nodes are only licensed by geometric properties of the X-bar component. But could not the converse of the relation he proposes between dynamic forces and syntactic nodes also hold? Could it not be the case that the dynamic is the given and that syntactic positions are realized only if a dynamic relation holds between the elements that occupy those positions? This would correspond to the strong position presented at the beginning of this section, where each syntactic node has an SR equivalent. In the following subsection, I will discuss evidence that this is indeed the case.

2.1.1.1 No Vacuous Projection

If one adopts this strong position, there can be no vacuous projection in syntax. Intermediate nodes cannot be strictly functional: they must correspond to a semantic primitive; otherwise, no such node can be present in the syntactic structure.

In Jackendoff's discussion of the different types of semantic relations exemplified in (5)–(9), there is the implicit idea, made explicit by Carter, that "[n]ot only do linking relations involve constituents, but they form constituents, i.e. if X r Y is a linking relation between two constituents, then X + Y is a C [constituent]" (Carter 1988, 260). Therefore, even if his system is intended to be highly formal, with categories serving a strictly functional role, it is implicitly admitted that a node labeling a branching relation in syntax minimally means something—the combinatorial function that unifies two syntactic nodes is a concept, something like Strawson's associative function ASS (i,c). "Strawson claims that the combinatorial function is not a concept but a sign of general linguistic activity; if we take him at his word it must stand for the human capacity to create meanings rather than to refer to them, which is presumably unacceptable to Strawson. Furthermore, if phi-

losophy or rational thought is conceptual analysis, then since the combinatorial function is not a concept, 'general linguistic activity' must be inaccessible
to rational, i.e., analytical thinking" (Rosen 1980, 113). It is unlikely that any
linguist, generative or not, would accept such a conclusion. The only thing
that seems to stop Jackendoff from assuming that all nonmaximal nodes are
also licensed by SR correspondence is that there is not a "steady" correspondence between any given intermediate syntactic node and any particular semantic concept. That is, N' or V' or A' does not correspond to specific concepts or types of referents. But neither does any X^{max}, even for Jackendoff.
According to him, an NP, for example, can correspond to THING, PLACE,
EVENT, ACTION, MANNER, or AMOUNT. In fact, I will argue, there is
no reason why a given dynamic, semantic relation should ever be in a one-
to-one relation with any given geometric relation, be it syntactic or semantic.
Suppose we assume that the geometric properties of semantic representations
do not differ substantially from those generally assumed for syntactic representations. Under this assumption, there is then only one type of semantic
embedding; the differences in (5) through (9) are the results not of different
ways of embedding, but of the nature of the two elements that are related.
Thus, the dynamic relations differ, but not the geometric ones. The only requirement imposed on a geometric relation is that the elements that it puts
together are in a dynamic relation. This means that if no dynamic, semantic
relation is possible between two elements, they cannot enter into a syntactic
relation. For example, a verb and a noun cannot enter into a relation as
indicated by the labeling in (10a) because the dynamic relation implied is not
possible. The noun would have to be taken as functor and the verb as either
modifier or argument; and the semantics of nouns and verbs simply makes
this uninterpretable (cf. Bouchard 1979 about this relationship between dynamic and geometric relations). On the other hand, (10b) is potentially interpretable, even though it might not always be possible to find a situation to
which it refers (cf. the discussion of *Colorless green ideas* above).

(10)a. $[_{N'}$ V N]
    b. $[_{V'}$ V N]

With this in mind, consider the structure in (11) below. I assume, as does
Jackendoff, that an X^{max} corresponds to a conceptual constituent. I also assume, as discussed above, that an intermediate branching category corresponds to a conceptual constituent. Thus, in a tree like that in (11), Y' repre-

sents the relation established between the head Y and the conceptual constituent of the X^{max}. Y corresponds to the element that X^{max} is related to in SR, and Y' corresponds to an SR node representing that relation. All three, Y, X^{max}, and Y', thus correspond to SR elements.

(11)

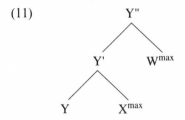

Interestingly, there is direct empirical support for the idea that nonmaximal syntactic nodes also correspond to SR nodes. I assume with Jackendoff (1983) that a conceptual constituent is a unitary piece of mental representation that is projectable. We will see directly that nonmaximal branching categories do correspond to such pieces of mental representation.

2.1.1.1.1 Testing Nodes for Content: Pragmatic Anaphora

One interesting way to test whether the mental representation involves both a conceptual constituent and a linguistic constituent comes from the interaction of language with another conceptual domain, as in the case of pragmatic anaphora:

> In order for a pragmatically controlled pronoun to be understood, its intended referent must emerge as a projected #entity# for the hearer. In turn, for such an #entity# to emerge, the hearer must have constructed from his visual field a projectable expression at the level of conceptual structure—that level where visual and linguistic information are compatible. Thus, there is an important connection between #thing#-perception and the use of pragmatic anaphora. (Jackendoff 1983, 48–49)

In other words, if a phrasal constituent is referred to by means of pragmatic anaphora, it corresponds to a projectable instance of a conceptual, ontological category. Therefore, pragmatic anaphora is one way to determine the existence of an independent conceptual constituent (see Jackendoff 1983 48ff). As Hankamer and Sag (1976) point out, there are many grammatically different types of pragmatic anaphora, which Jackendoff argues correspond to different kinds of conceptual structure primitives such as: THING, PLACE, EVENT, ACTION, MANNER, and AMOUNT. He gives the following types of examples for conceptual primitives that correspond to syntactic X^{max} projections.

(12)   (Cf. Jackendoff (1983))
    a.   *Pro-PP:*
        Your coat is here [pointing] and your hat is there [pointing].
        PLACE
        He went thataway [pointing]. DIRECTION
    b.   *Pro-VP* "do it/that":
        Can you do that [pointing]? ACTION
        Can you do this [demonstrating]? ACTION
    c.   *Pro-S* "that . . . happen":
        That [pointing] had better not happen again around here.
        EVENT
    d.   *Pro-manner Adverbial:*
        You shuffle cards thus/so/this way [demonstrating]. MANNER
    e.   *Pro-measure Expression:*
        The fish that got away was this/that [demonstrating] long.
        AMOUNT
    f.   *Pro-NP:*
        I hate that/those [pointing to spinach/carrots] THING TYPE or
        TOKEN

What is important for us is how nonmaximal projections behave with respect to pragmatic anaphora. If we can refer to a nonmaximal syntactic category by pragmatic anaphora, we can assume that such a category corresponds to a projectable node in Conceptual Structure. I will argue (in the next section) that intermediate level branching categories can be referred to with pragmatic anaphora and, hence, that they correspond to a node in Conceptual Structure, as all syntactic elements should.

2.1.1.1.2 Evidence for the Content of Intermediate Nodes

There are cases where a pragmatic anaphor refers to a nonmaximal projection. For example, many linguists would analyze the case of adjectival modification in (13) as involving at least one intermediate N-node (whether the topmost ADJ is attached to NP or lower is not directly relevant here). See, for example, Hornstein and Lightfoot (1981).

(13)

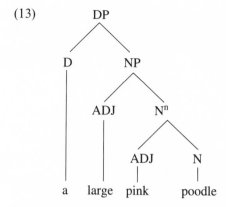

We know that the pronoun *one* can replace a nonmaximal N^n, as in *I want a large one,* where *one* is understood as *pink poodle.* This is also true of *en* in French. Each of these pronouns can be used in the context of pragmatic anaphora. In (14a), *one* refers to *pink poodle,* which shows that the nonmaximal node N^n in (13) corresponds to a projectable instance of an ontological category. In (14b), where *en* refers simply to *lions,* we see that N^0 also corresponds to a CS constituent.

(14) *Pragmatic anaphora with nonmaximal N projections:*
    a. A:[pointing to a group of large pink poodles and making sign with
        head meaning "Do you want one?"]
      B:Yes, but a small one.
      =Yes, I want a pink poodle, but a small one.
      #Yes, I want a large, pink poodle, but a small one.
    b. [Pointing to lions] J'en ai tué trois énormes hier.
       I-of-them have killed three huge yesterday
       "I killed three huge ones yesterday"

French also has pronouns that can stand for nonmaximal adjectival projections—*l'* stands for *fort* in (15)—and nonmaximal prepositional projections—*y* stands for the nonmaximal *dans la caverne* in (16).

(15) *Syntactic anaphora with nonmaximal A projection*
    Paul est fort, mais Jeanne l'est encore [$_A$ P plus [$_A$]].
    Paul is strong, but Jeanne it-is even more
    Paul is strong, but Jeanne is even stronger

(16) *Syntactic anaphora with nonmaximal P projection*
    Jean est dans la caverne et Paul y est [$_{PP}$ presque [$_P$]].
    Jean is in the cave and Paul there-is almost

Jean is in the cave and Paul is almost there

These pronouns can also be used in a context of pragmatic anaphora:

(17) *Pragmatic anaphora of nonmaximal A projection:*
   A: [pointing to Mary, who is lifting heavy bars, and pumping his bi-
        ceps to indicate he thinks Mary is very strong]
   B: Jeanne l'est encore plus.

(18) *Pragmatic anaphora of nonmaximal P projection:*
   A: [looking at a TV screen over B's shoulder to see if Max, the su-
        perhero, has been able to get into the cave]
   B: Il y est presque.

These examples show that many nonmaximal projections can be involved in pragmatic anaphora. Essentially, what we see is that if a constituent modified by another constituent Y can be projected as a certain kind of THING (or other CS primitive), it can also be projected as a (different) THING if it is not modified by Y. This directly reflects the dynamic nature of the endocentricity of the structures.[6]

We now have some evidence in support of the strong position taken at the outset of this section, that it is not just maximal constituents that correspond to an independent and identifiable contiguous piece of semantic structure—pragmatic anaphora tests show that branching nonmaximal projections also correspond to a constituent in Conceptual Structure.

2.1.1.1.3 Projection in Syntax

The question of the licensing of nonmaximal nodes revolves around the very notion of projection. Under the assumption that the geometric process of projection is essentially driven by the dynamic relationship that holds between the head and the nonhead, the geometry of X-bar has only two essential properties: (1) the projection is head initial or head final, and (2) the endocentricity value is one or more than one (see note 5). There is no need for explicit X-bar stipulations about the number of bar levels permitted, since that number is dependent on the number of constituents with which the head and its projections entertain dynamic relations. This means that there are two aspects to the licensing of intermediate syntactic nodes. When the node is branching and dominates the head and an argument or a modifier of the head, the node is licensed by the composing of its daughter nodes: the branching node corresponds to the semantic relation established between the semantic equivalents of its daughter nodes. However, if no dynamic relationship exists, there can be no syntactic relationship. So, for example, in a sentence such as *John left,* there can be no justification for nonbranching intermediate nodes in the V or N projections. This is contrary to standard assumptions. For example, under a Uniform Two-Level Hypothesis (Chomsky 1970), *John* and *left* have the structures shown in (19), although the nonbranching nodes, except for the preterminal nodes, have no semantic licenser (I abstract away from the DP hypothesis for expository purposes).

(19)

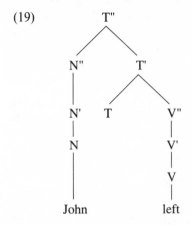

Here, there is no semantic justification from composition for intermediate nodes in the N and V projections. Nor does it seem that any grammatical process ever refers to nonbranching syntactic nodes like these. Consequently, there is no reason to believe that grammar gratuitously produces syntactic structures for their own sake—vacuous projection is unmotivated. I will assume that grammatical structures contain no superfluous material, such as nodes that neither branch nor dominate lexical material. In fact, nonbranching nodes that dominate lexical material, i.e., preterminal nodes, can also be dispensed with by assuming that all features of terminal nodes project, not just categorial features. Therefore, I will not assume a uniform level hypothesis, be it two or three or whatever number of bar levels, because nonbranching intermediate nodes are superfluous. Instead, I adopt the proposal of Bouchard (1979): heads project only to create a sister relation with another node, otherwise a head does not project.[7] The main assumption is that there is a Universal Bracketing Schema, as in (20), that expresses the associative function.

(20)   Universal Bracketing Schema: $[_{A'}$ A B] or $[_{B'}$ A B].

The Universal Bracketing Schema is based on the fact that one-element saturation is what is found in natural languages—a constituent that assigns a property to an element or modifies it, combines with only one such element. For example, predicates are saturated by only one element. A bracketing will be licensed only if there is a semantic relation between A and B, in which case it must take place or else there would be no saturation. The labeling of the brackets will be determined by the dynamic relation holding between the two elements. In the case of an argumental relation, in which the saturator's features are incorporated into the saturated element, it is the features of the saturated element that will percolate, thereby making it the head (see Flynn 1983; Speas 1984, 1986 on the idea that percolation of features follows from properties of the representations of lexical items).[8]

The binarity induced by one-element saturation is pervasive in linguistic analyses. For example, Dowty (1982, 84) assumes (21), which expresses the concept of binary combination.

(21)   A verb that ultimately takes n arguments is always treated as combining by a syntactic rule with exactly one argument to produce a phrase of the same category as a verb of $n - 1$ arguments.

Binarity is implicit in analyses of various linguistic phenomena, such as the following:[9]

(i) Compounding and affixation add one argument, if any (Selkirk's 1982 First Order Projection Condition, Baker's 1985 Mirror Principle, and Di Sciullo and Williams 1987);

(ii) An argument can compose with only one semantic role assigner and vice versa (the theta criterion)

(iii) An element bearing a semantic role or a Case must be adjacent to the role or Case assigner

(iv) Two elements bearing a semantic role cannot be equally closely related to a same semantic role assigner (the theta hierarchy)

(v) There is always an argument which is last to compose with the predicate (the external argument need not be indicated by a diacritic)

Note that the way binarity is introduced in the Grammar here differs from Kayne's (1984) approach. Kayne derives binarity from the need for unambiguous paths, whereas I derive binarity from one-element saturation. The approaches differ in that unambiguous paths are compatible with nonbranching intermediate nodes, whereas one-element saturation is not compatible with such superfluous nodes, as we saw in the discussion of (19). In short, the hypothesis is that bar levels have no grammatical reality because no syntactic process refers to such levels, per se.

2.1.1.2 A COMPARISON WITH STANDARD X-BAR

Let us briefly compare this proposal with more standard views of X-bar theory. For example, Stowell (1981) proposes the following five restrictions on X-bar:

(22) *Five restrictions on X-bar* (Stowell 1981):
  a. Every phrase is endocentric.
  b. The head always appears adjacent to one of the boundaries of X^1.
  c. The head term is one bar-level lower than the immediately dominating phrasal node.
  d. Only maximal projections may appear as non-head terms with a phrase.
  e. Specifiers appear at the X^2 level, subcategorized complements appear within X^1.

All the properties in (22) are either derived from the general assumptions or rejected.

Property (a): Even the fundamental property of endocentricity can be derived. By making the minimal assumptions in the general theory, we provide an answer to the question of why phrases should have to be headed. As Noam Chomsky observed in his class lectures of Fall 1993, in a minimal X-bar theory, primitives are only those taken from the lexicon—there are no independent categorial labels like N, V, A, or P. Such labels are just abbreviations for a shared collection of features by some lexical items. What would actually label nodes in a structure are lexical primitives, giving (simplified) structures as in (23):

(23)

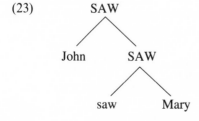

Since the only primitives available are those taken from the lexicon, when the computational system puts *saw* and *Mary* together, it must label the resulting structure with a lexical item. In the present case, the only interpretable choice is SAW. The fact that a phrase must be headed in such cases follows directly from the most stringent assumption of what can appear in a structure. Namely, only primitives taken from the lexicon. This is a very appealing proposal, since it relies on very salient elements of language—lexical items.[10]

Property (b) follows from the binarity produced by one-element saturation. Since a head can associate with only one element at a time, any given node can have only two daughters, and the one that is the head is then necessarily at one of the boundaries of that node.

Property (c) is a useful mnemonic convention, but it has no status in the theory. Whatever the number of bars on a node, it expresses the relation between its two daughters. For example, in (24), all the projections of *balloon* could simply be labeled N; given the hierarchy of the tree, plus the content of the daughter nodes, it is easy to determine what relation any of these N nodes represents. It is of course useful for a linguist discussing a particular tree structure to be able to refer to the nodes quickly and unambiguously— bars are useful for such expository purposes. But bars have no more status in the Grammar than indices such as the 1 and 2 used in (25) to distinguish between the N *John* and the N *hat*.

(24)

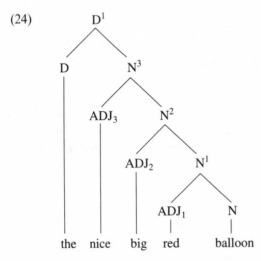

(25)

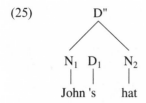

Property (d) is redundant. A head can have a dynamic relation only with an element that is an internally coherent and complete unit. Such a unit is an X^{max}, by definition. The highest node, whatever its number of bars, must constitute a coherent and complete combination of relations, and this is assured independently by dynamic (that is, semantic) requirements of the Grammar. For example, if a verb selects an argument, the selectional restrictions of the verb require the argument to have certain referential properties that will come from its internal organization: it is the computation of the combination of all the features required for argumenthood that corresponds to X^{max}. To attribute these semantic properties of coherence and completeness to a certain number of bar levels seems contrary to the spirit of X-bar theory, since it introduces semantic notions into a component that is specifically supposed to be devoid of such properties.

Property (e) is really three properties in one. It states that there are two levels, and it specifies what appears at each of these levels. There is no reason to require phrases to have two levels, nor is there any reason to prevent them from having more. The main argument for such a stipulation comes from the assumption that X^{max} should be a uniform level, with a fixed number of bars, so that subcategorization properties can be stated uniformly. For example, we want to be able to say that there is something common to the objects of *saw* in (26).

(26)a.   John saw [$_{D'}$ the dog]
    b.   John saw [$_{D''}$ Bill [$_{D'}$'s dog]]

What is common to the D^{max} complements of *saw* is not the number of bars they have. It is the fact that each of these D^{max}'s forms an internally coherent and complete unit with certain selectional features. What *saw* requires is such a complement. As we just saw in the discussion of property (d), it is not necessary to designate that this complement have a uniform level of bars; in fact, to do so is inconsistent with the spirit of X-bar.[11]

2.1.1.2.1 The Notion of Maximal Projection

In the present proposal, since structural relations are binary (and assuming for expository purposes that projection is successive, i.e., bar number increases at each instance of a combination with a projection of the head), the notion of maximal projection is not determined by a fixed number of bars. Rather, it is defined as the highest node of a given projection; no upper limit on bar number is determined by the theory. A noun like *John,* for example, which has no peripheral material in its projection, is both a N^0 and a N^{max}, since N^0 is the topmost projection in this case. On the other hand, *balloon,* in (24), projects to three bar levels to accomodate its three modifiers.

In an X-bar theory in which bar-levels are represented by two binary features, $[+/- \text{max}]$ and $[+/- \text{min}]$ (as in Muysken 1983, for example) it is possible to give essentially the same structure to a bare noun such as *John* as I do: this N would be $[+\text{max}, +\text{min}]$. However, the NP *the nice big red balloon* cannot be structured in the same way as suggested here. In Muysken's system, an intermediate node $[-\text{max}, -\text{min}]$ would iterate with the same bar value for two of the modifiers. A similar iteration of N^1 is often proposed for such cases by proponents of a Uniform Two-Level Hypothesis. Such a proposal weakens the system, since it comes down to stating that succession does not hold for a given level of X-bar. That is of little importance, if one considers bars to be only mnemonic devices. But in that case, it is not clear why one would want to distinguish between any of the levels, using a feature system. For example, if such features have any reality, the intermediate projections of N in (24) should actually count as the same node or similar nodes with respect to some property of Grammar, such as relative scope of the adjectives, for example, but that is not the case. The proposal is weak because of (22e), which attributes specific semantic properties to syntactic levels. In fact, to stipulate a fixed number of bars for X^{max} is more costly than simply to allow percolation with a bracketing schema, as in (20).

In any system that incorporates some notion of projection, percolation is constrained by the dynamic relations that hold between positions in the geometric tree. Thus, whether combinations like ADJ-N or V-NP are licit will be determined by dynamic principles that take into account lexical properties of the pair of nodes involved. This point is made by Chomsky (1981), who argues that the admissibility of combinations like ADJ-N or V-NP should not be accounted for by strictly geometric rules, such as Phrase Structure Rules (PSRs), because this needlessly complicates the grammar; the admissibility of such combinations is already determined, independently, by subcategorization properties of the lexical items. In fact, the system would then be too permissive, since, for example, PSRs could theoretically allow for a V to have a direct object in the geometrical tree, even if that V did not select a complement.

2.1.1.2.2 Specifiers, Complements, and Semantic Combination

Another way the present proposal differs from standard X-bar theory is in the appeal to the notions of specifier and complement. The use of labels like SPEC and COMPL can also lead to needless complication of the grammar. These labels are not part of X-bar theory, of course; they are used to indicate that the levels of X-bar sort out different peripheral material, with COMPLs appearing at a lower level than SPECs. This is to account for the fact that COMPLs combine with the head before SPECs do. But these restrictions on combination are dynamically determined, as the very labels SPEC and COMPL vaguely indicate. To have X-bar levels specifically sort out COMPLs from SPECs gives the impression that the geometric relations involved are somewhat independent of the dynamic relations involved and that the grammar must stipulate the universal relative position of SPEC and COMPL. Without this stipulation, one might expect parametric variation, with some languages having COMPLs higher than SPECs. But there is no need to attribute special properties to X-bar levels to ensure the relative positions of SPECs and COMPLs because dynamic relations already do this, as is true even in standard GB theory. In this sense, level differentiation of this sort has the same defect as PSRs. Consider the following simple example, to illustrate the dynamic rules involved. (Thematic notions are used strictly for expository purposes.) Suppose that the semantic combination of a PATH function, a GOAL argument, and a THEME argument can only be constructed dynamically by first combining PATH and GOAL and then combining this constituent with THEME. If all three elements have syntactic equivalents, as in *John entered the room,* for example, a simple linking rule will ensure that the constituent corresponding to the GOAL combines with the constituent corresponding to the PATH, in a geometric sister relation first, and that the node dominating these two then establishes a sister relation with the constituent corresponding to the THEME.

Examples in which the order of semantic combination determines the relative height at which elements can appear in the geometric tree are pervasive in the grammar. This is true not only for the relative positions of SPECs and

COMPLs, but also for the position of complements relative to each other. Multiple complements do not appear on the same level in syntax (technically, they have different scope or c-command domains). This is implicit in standard X-bar theory. But it poses a problem for Uniform Level Hypotheses, since they usually postulate only one level at which COMPLs can appear. A strategy frequently employed to get around this problem is to allow an intermediate level to iterate, as in (27) (see Hornstein & Lightfoot 1981).

(27)

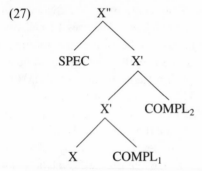

However, the order of the COMPLs is not free; the relative position of $COMPL_1$ and $COMPL_2$ is determined strictly on the basis of their dynamic relations in the structure.

A different strategy is found in Larson's (1988) analysis of Double Objects. He maintains both the Uniform Two Level Hypothesis and Succession by assuming dummy verbal heads that provide the necessary additional structure.

(28)

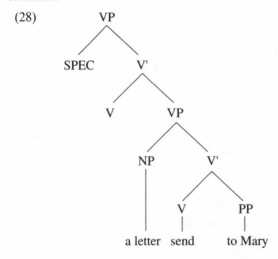

Note that the relative positions of *a letter* and *to Mary* are motivated by the dynamic relations that they hold with each other. The proliferation of semantically unwarranted nodes such as dummy V projections raises a host of problems, to which we will return below.

The relative position of noncomplements is also governed by dynamic relations. Thus, the difference in interpretation between the sentences in (29), in which there are two intentional knocks in (29a), but one intentional double knock in (29b), is attributed to the fact that the relative order of adverbs reflects their relative height in the structure. This, in turn, reflects the order in which they combine with what they modify (discussed in Andrews 1983; see section 4.4.5.1.1.3 for some discussion of combination inside NPs).

(29)a.   John [[[knocked on the door] intentionally] twice].
    b.   John [[[knocked on the door] twice] intentionally].

It is redundant to stipulate that X-bar levels have sorting properties, since, as we have seen, the relative positions of constituents are determined by dynamic relations in any case. Therefore, an X-bar system based on the bracketing schema in (20) is to be preferred. Such a system simplifies the grammar in a number of ways: (1) it makes the economy of statements about the possible number of bars; (2) it eliminates vacuous projections in cases like *John;* (3) it maintains Succession and does not lump together intermediate projections in cases like *the nice big red balloon;* and (4) it reduces the number of possible parameters pertaining to X-bar theory, since it disallows parametric variation in bar numbers across categories or across languages. In sum, the claim here is that the fact that a standard two-level X-bar system allows syntactic processes to refer to bar levels should count against such a system, both on conceptual and empirical grounds.[12]

I arrived at this X-bar system by investigating the hypothesis that every syntactic constituent in a sentence corresponds to an independent and identifiable contiguous piece of semantic structure, a hypothesis that was shown to be supported by data on pragmatic anaphora. In what follows, I will assume this hypothesis about syntactic node licensing to be correct. I turn next to the correspondence between the structure in which syntactic nodes appear and the structure in which their semantic licensers appear.

2.1.2 SYNTACTIC STRUCTURES AND COMPOSITIONALITY

In the preceding section, I propose that all syntactic nodes are licensed by correspondence with CS nodes. This is a strong version of compositionality of syntax, vis-à-vis semantic interpretation. However, one could think of an even stronger version of correspondence. Given what I have said so far, some node in syntax could correspond to some semantic constituent, and yet, the two representations could still be drastically different, since we have still seen no requirement that the overall structural organization of the two representations be similar. Although two syntactic nodes A and B could correspond to two nodes α and β in semantic representation, the structural relationship between the nodes in syntax could be very different from the one in SR; in fact, even the opposite could be the case. Thus, A could be higher than B in syntax as in (30a), while the opposite would hold in the corresponding SR (30b).

(30)a.   [A[. . . B . . .]]
     b.   [β[. . . α . . .]]

The only way to keep track of the correspondence between syntactic nodes and SR nodes in such a case is to have some common diacritic shared by the corresponding elements: the approach to linking is then forced to be indexical. But this kind of indexical approach to linking is too permissive on two counts. First, it goes against my general hypothesis about the representability of grammatically relevant processes, which states that all grammatical processes are dependent on constituent tree structure: the linking required in (30) is representable neither as a branching relation in a constituent tree structure nor as a mapping from one such structure to another. Second, even if every syntactic node had a corresponding node in semantic representation, the linking required fares no better than that required for an SR like (2) or (3) above, without some structural correspondence: there is nothing in the basic architecture of the approach that leads us to expect any regularities in linking, so that additional stipulations are required to account for the facts.

In order not to weaken the proposal by introducing indexical linking, we can radically depart from indexical approaches and instead rely squarely on the G-semantics Hypothesis: G-semantics representations have the form of tree structures. The advantage of the G-semantics Hypothesis is that it allows us to make claims about semantics that are directly testable on strictly linguistic grounds. If the structural organization of lexical representations is formally similar to that of syntactic structures, the correspondence between the two levels, SR and SS, need not be mediated through lists, as is often implicit in current proposals. Rather, that correspondence can be quite direct, through Homomorphic Mapping.

2.2 CORRESPONDENCE AND IDENTIFICATION

In order to give its strongest interpretation to the Grammatical Constraint (1), it is not sufficient to have syntactic constituents correspond to SR primitives; how the correspondence is established is crucial. It is a basic assumption of my approach that a lexical entry specifies the bare meaning of an item, that is, the meaning of the item cleared of any redundancies with S-semantics. There are three things more or less directly accessible to a speaker: the lexical items, the relations between the lexical items, and the context (analyzed with S-semantics rules and principles). The null assumption, the one that has to be refuted by argument if someone wishes to support an alternative view, is that the semantic formatives in the lexical representation of an item are all identified in some way in the sentence where the item occurs. Moreover, there are empirical reasons to favor this approach. As we saw in the discussion of *enfermer* 'to shut X up' in section 1.5.2.2, Boons (1985) has shown that situational notions like Agent, Theme, Goal, etc., which are not identified in the sentence by a specific element but rather attributed on the basis of contextual knowledge, are significantly unstable. Given the same sentence *Jean a enfermé le chat dans le salon* 'John shut up the cat in the living-room,' the notion of Agent, for example, may be present in some situations where the sentence is used, but not in others, with no syntactic change in the sentence. Such linguistically untraceable notions should not be part of the semantic formatives of the lexical representation of an item. In this approach, syntactically unmotivated elements will be ruled out by the Principle of Full Identification, introduced briefly in chapter 1.

(31) *Principle of Full Identification:* Every syntactic formative of a sentence must have a corresponding element in the semantic representation. Every formative of a semantic representation must be identified by a morphosyntactic element in the sentence with which that representation is associated.

To adopt Full Identification is essentially to adopt a strategy of minimalist economy toward Grammar, with accountability as a fundamental assumption that only linguistically traceable material is allowed.[13]

No doubt Full Identification will remind many linguists of Chomsky's (1985a) Full Interpretation, which states that every element of PF and LF must receive an appropriate interpretation. The two principles differ in that in Chomsky's Full Interpretation, it is only the syntactic formatives that must be licensed, whereas Full Identification is a constraint on both syntactic and semantic formatives. From (31) follows Carter's accountability requirement that "no semantic elements are allowed which are not given in the lexical entries of the formatives in the surface structure of the sentence" (Carter 1988, 49). Syntactic formatives, being more accessible than semantic formatives, are easier to test; if semantic formatives of lexical representations are closely related to syntactic formatives, as (31) suggests, then they, too, should be testable. Moreover, the Principle of Full Identification fits nicely with the hypothesis that G-semantics representations are dependent on constituent tree structure, since structural homomorphy between SR and SS representations greatly facilitates Full Identification.[14]

There are three ways to license semantic formatives: (1) a subpart of the SR tree can correspond to a lexical item by a mapping operation of chunking; (2) a node in SR can correspond to a syntactic node by linking; or (3) a node in SR can be identified by another node in SR via binding, a relation dependent on branching properties of the tree structure. In the next three sections, we will look at the details of these ways in which semantic formatives are identified.[15]

2.2.1 CHUNKING

We have seen that an indexical approach to linking is needed if the semantic representation of a lexical item is too poor (2), too rich (3), or structurally too different from the syntactic structure (30). But the basic architecture of an indexical approach would incorrectly lead us to expect that there are no linking regularities and that the relation between argument type and syntactic position is essentially arbitrary. Furthermore, indexical linking requires the formal power of a general graph representation, and this goes against the attempt to constrain grammatical processes to constituent tree representations. Moreover, most linking approaches are based on thematic roles, and as we have seen, the claims made by representations using thematic notions are about a certain use of the lexical items (or sentences) rather than their actual meaning.

Suppose we propose the simplest linking rule possible, isomorphic mapping, where all elements of semantic representations map directly into SS in a one-to-one fashion. Under this assumption, it would seem that the hypothesis that semantic and syntactic representations are alike cannot be correct, since it would mean that there is no semantic decomposition of words, and there are numerous arguments in favor of decomposition of lexical items. The arguments are of two types: arguments about possible words, and arguments about explaining syntactic differences between closely related words.[16] For example, Carter (1988, 296–97) argues that the entries for *go* and *come* should be as in (32) and (33).

(32)   LR (go):   ((A BE THERE) CHANGE)

(33)   LR (come): ((A BE HERE) CHANGE)

He proposes that the variable HERE in (33) is more informative than the variable THERE in (32). Thus, a sentence such as (34) requires a fair amount of context, otherwise there is a feeling of incompleteness. However, this is not the case in a sentence such as (35).

(34)   John went.

(35)   John came.

If one assumes some sort of decomposition, as in (32) and (33), the contrast between (34) and (35) can be easily captured (see Part II for a detailed analysis of French equivalents).

Since semantics is not just interpretive and crucially determines syntax, but since one-to-one correspondence between semantic and syntactic representations is untenable, let us consider the next best thing, namely, homomorphy. Dowty (1991, 567) gives the following description of a homomorphism: "Put simply, a homomorphism is a function, from its domain to its range, which preserves some structural relation defined on its domain in a similar relation defined on the range."[17]

For our purposes, a mapping of an SR to an SS will be homomorphic if it preserves the relative relations of the elements involved. For example, decomposition requires a process of "chunking" that maps some of the primitives into a single lexical item. If we assume Carter's representation of *go* in (32), the primitive functors BE and CHANGE and the constant THERE are all chunked into the lexical item *go*. Chunking can also affect an argument of the SR, which is then identified by the verb. This is the case for the argument FRIGHT, for example, in (36), assuming that 'frighten' is the result of the chunking of CAUSE-FRIGHT-TO (this decomposition of 'frighten' is purely for expository purpose; a detailed analysis of Psych verbs is presented in chapter 4).

(36)   LR (frighten): $[_A x [_B CAUSE [_C FRIGHT [_D TO y]]]]$

If both the domain and the range of the homomorphism are tree structures, SR and SS tree structures in the present case, then Homomorphic Mapping operates as in (37):

(37) *Homomorphic Mapping Principle:* In a mapping from SR to SS, dominance relations are preserved.

A corollary follows from this principle, the Endocentricity Principle, to which I return below.

(38) *Endocentricity Principle:* Given some mother nodes [A, B, . . . C] in a semantic representation, these may be collapsed into mother node K by chunking in a corresponding syntactic representation only if endocentricity is maintained, i.e., only if the heads of [A, B, . . . C] are chunked into the head of K.

Homomorphic Mapping actually follows from the Principle of Full Identification: syntactic and semantic formatives include the structural formatives of the tree structures, among which are the dominance relations.

Jackendoff (1987a, 1990a) argues that a lexical item is a correspondence rule—"a lexical item establishes a correspondence between well-formed fragments of phonological, syntactic, and conceptual structure; that is, the lexicon is a part of the correspondence rule component" (Jackendoff 1990a, 18). Assuming that a lexical item is a correspondence rule, there are two things that the rule must specify: (1) what semantic representation is an input to the rule and (2) what part of that semantic representation is identified by chunking, by the lexical item itself. Given Homomorphic Mapping, no other information needs to be conveyed by the lexical item. As we will see in the next two sections on linking (2.2.2) and binding (2.2.3), the fact that nonchunked arguments have to be linked to syntactic constituents or identified by a binder follows from Full Identification, and what they link to follows from the general linking convention expressed in the Homomorphic Mapping Principle, which itself follows from Full Identification, as we just saw. Note that the correspondence rule maps a semantic representation onto a syntactic representation. Crucially, since both of these are assumed to be tree structures, lexical items, like correspondence rules, are operations on tree structures.[18]

Thus, in the tree representation of (36) given in (39), the chunking operation of 'frighten' states that the part of the tree containing the nodes in bold are identified by 'frighten.'

(39)

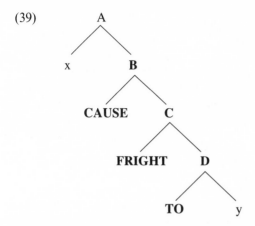

With (39) as input, the chunking rule 'frighten' states what nodes in the SR are collapsed into one node in the SS, and Homomorphic Mapping constrains the output, so that (39) maps into the syntactic structure (40).

(40)

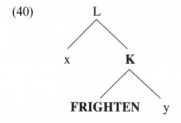

The chunking operation that maps (39) onto (40) obeys the Endocentricity Principle. The mother nodes B, C, and D are chunked into K, and CAUSE, FRIGHT, and TO—which are the heads of B, C, and D—are chunked into *frighten,* the head of K.

2.2.1.1 CONSTRAINTS ON CHUNKING

Chunking is not unconstrained, as has often been noted. McCawley (1968c) argued that lexical items must replace constituents. Ross (1972) and Jackendoff (1983) also proposed constraints on chunking.[19] Ross observes that the semantic structure of "try to find" can undergo chunking and be lexicalized

as "look for." But there could be no verb like "trentertain" that would correspond to the chunking of "try" and "entertainment" alone.

(41) (Ross's 88)
       a.   Fritz tried to find entertainment.
       b.   Fritz looked for entertainment.
       c.   *Fritz trentertained to find.

He argues from this example that if a verb lexicalizes multiple predicates
(event- or state-functions) that have been chunked, they must be adjacently
embedded in semantic structure. Jackendoff (1983) discusses similar examples and proposes a general principle of lexicalization:

(42) *Lexical Variable Principle:* A variable in the structure of a lexical
       item must be capable of being filled by a conceptual constituent.
       (Jackendoff 1983, 185)

He illustrates this principle as follows. Suppose we take a conceptual
structure like (43) which is lexicalized most transparently as "Joe put butter
on the bread".[20]

(43) (Jackendoff's 9.53) $[_{\text{Event}}$ CAUSE $([_{\text{Thing}}$ JOE$], [_{\text{Event}}$ GO $([_{\text{Thing}}$ BUT-
       TER$], [_{\text{Path}}$ TO $([_{\text{Place}}$ ON $([_{\text{Thing}}$ BREAD$])])])])]$

This CS can also be lexicalized as "Joe buttered the bread," in which the
verb incorporates the THEME, the PATH-function, and the PLACE-
function, but it cannot be lexicalized as "Joe breaded the butter on" with a
structure like (44) (Jackendoff's 9.54).

(44) "bread": $[_{\text{Event}}$ CAUSE $([_{\text{Thing}}$ x$], [_{\text{Event}}$ GO $([_{\text{Thing}}$ y$], [_{\text{Path}}$ z $([_{\text{Thing}}$
       BREAD$])])])]$

This would violate the Lexical Variable Principle because the variable z is
not a conceptual constituent, but a path-function whose argument has been
incorporated. Moreover, in order to express the argument z, such a verb
would have to subcategorize a transitive preposition occurring without its
object.

2.2.1.2 DERIVING THE CONSTRAINTS ON CHUNKING

In the present approach, there is no need to stipulate a particular condition
on chunking such as the Lexical Variable Principle, since its effects follow
from Homomorphic Mapping and the Endocentricity Principle. Chunking

allows a single terminal syntactic node, the lexical item, to correspond to several terminal nodes in the semantic representation, i.e., to several semantic primitives. Since the labeling of nonterminal nodes is determined by the head node in these structures, if a head node X is targeted for chunking, all nodes labelled X^n will be affected. Let us see how this accounts for the three cases presented above. In (39), chunking of the terminal nodes CAUSE, FRIGHT, and TO affects the nodes labeled by these heads (A and B for CAUSE, C and D for TO). After chunking, the node labeled FRIGHTEN determines the labeling of K and L. Moreover, the node immediately dominating FRIGHTEN represents the collapse of all the nodes that immediately dominated CAUSE, FRIGHT, and TO. All of this follows from the Endocentricity Principle. Essentially, this principle has a locality effect on composition: the argument of a primitive B can be collapsed with a primitive A only if primitive B is also collapsed with primitive A.

In addition, because chunking is homomorphic, all the nodes that were daughters of a node labeled by either CAUSE, FRIGHT, or TO in (39) are, in (40), daughters of a node labeled by the terminal node FRIGHTEN, into which CAUSE, FRIGHT, and TO are chunked. Respective dominance relations are maintained. Thus, x was a daughter of a projection of CAUSE and was higher than y, a daughter of a projection of TO; both are daughters of a projection of FRIGHTEN in (40), with relative height maintained.

Consider now Ross's example. The rough structure underlying (41) is given in (45).

(45)

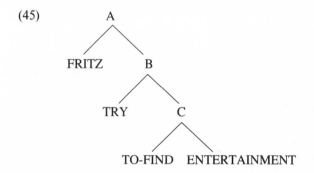

If we want to get something like "*Fritz trentertained to find" from (45), chunking would have to affect the terminals TRY and ENTERTAINMENT, as in (46).

(46)

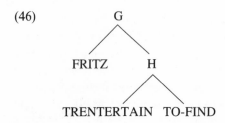

But (46) cannot be obtained, because the node immediately dominating TRENTERTAIN does not correspond to the collapsing of the nodes that immediately dominated TRY and ENTERTAINMENT. Node C of (45) is incorrectly collapsed into H, although the head node of C TO-FIND has not been collapsed by chunking into the head of H, TRENTERTAIN. One could argue that node C will not create an endocentricity problem if it is not collapsed into H, as in (47).

(47)

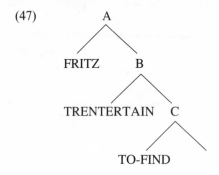

But node C is not legitimate here, since one of the branches under it has no node labeling it. This is not permitted in this system because a branch expresses a dominance relation between two nodes, and a relation with an empty position is uninterpretable.

The same reasoning applies to the derivation of Jackendoff's example: "Joe breaded the butter on" cannot be derived from (43) because the mother node labeled by the head node ON in the semantic representation would be collapsed into the mother node immediately dominating it and labeled by *breaded* in the syntactic representation, although ON has not been collapsed into *breaded* by chunking.

However, derivations which at first appear similar to this are possible. Given a rough semantic representation as in (48), then it is possible to derive "Fritz bottled the wine."

(48)

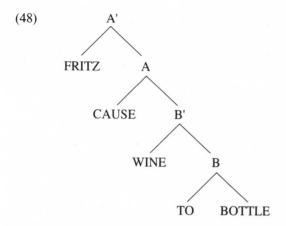

TO is the head of the B projection; CAUSE is the head of the A projection. The heads CAUSE, TO, and BOTTLE are collapsed into *bottled,* and the mother nodes A', B', and B are collapsed into the node H dominating *bottled* and *the wine.*

(49)

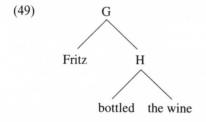

There is no endocentricity conflict in collapsing A, B', and B into H. H is labeled by *bottled,* which is the result of collapsing CAUSE, TO, and BOT-TLE. A is labeled by CAUSE, and B' and B are labeled by TO. Therefore, the heads of A, B', and B are collapsed into the head of H, which obeys Homomorphic Mapping and the Endocentricity Principle. WINE does not create problems like TO-FIND does in (45) because WINE does not head any of the nodes collapsed into H in (49). On the other hand, in (45) TO-FIND is the head of node C, which collapses into node H in (46); but TO-FIND does not collapse into the head of H; so the Endocentricity Principle is violated in (46), but not in (49).[21]

2.2.1.3 The Origins of Chunking

It is interesting to ponder why humans should have evolved with such chunking capacities. The answer is likely to be found in the advantages chunking provides in processing. It is well known that in processing, complex representations gain by being coded in simpler units. If this is correct, it follows that semantic representations stabilized by chunking as higher-level units should be much simpler to process; hence the evolutionary advantage of chunking (for additional discussion, see Jackendoff 1983, 125–26 and Champagnol 1992, among others). Of course, chunking is tempered by memory capacities. Thus, as Carter (1988, 115) observes, "English, etc., has prepositions because that allows us to get away with a smaller lexicon than we would need if for each complex notion expressed by a verb plus preposition combination we had a formally simple word."

2.2.2 REALIZATION AS SYNTACTIC CONSTITUENTS

What is left of the semantic representation after chunking has taken place is also subject to the Principle of Full Identification. One way for a constituent of the SR to satisfy this requirement is to be linked with a syntactic constituent, i.e., to be identified in syntax by corresponding to a syntactic constituent. Chunking operates with endocentric constituent structures as both input and output; endocentricity is preserved in the process, as required by the Endocentricity Principle (38). As a consequence, the structures at the output of chunking will determine the basic properties of linking. For example, *The dog frightens the cat* has a semantic representation as in (50), with the capitalized elements identified by the Verb itself, so that the output of chunking is as in (51).

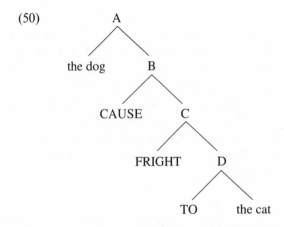

(50)

(51)

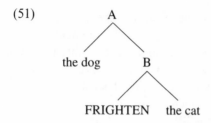

Since mapping is homomorphic, the relative positions of the arguments in syntax will reflect their relative positions at SR. That mapping is homomorphic derives from the fact that chunking is available (presumably due to its evolutionary advantages, as we saw above), and from the interaction of Full Identification and economy: Full Identification will force chunks and other non-chunked material to be identified in the syntax, and considerations of economy will ensure that as much of the SR as possible, including the dominance relations, is preserved. Therefore, there is no need for stipulative constraints on linking—relativized linking follows from the principles of the theory.[22]

2.2.3 BINDING IN SEMANTIC REPRESENTATIONS

A node in an SR can be identified by binding from another node in the SR. A typical example of this kind of identification is direct causation, as in inchoative (52a), which I will argue has the structure shown in (52b).

(52)a. The ice melted.
 b.

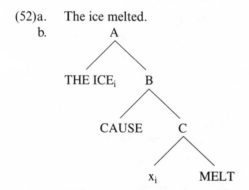

In (52), the argument THE ICE is identified by linking with the syntactic constituent *the ice*. The variable x_i is identified by being bound by THE ICE, so x_i is not linked to a syntactic node. CAUSE and MELT are identified by chunking into the V *melt*. THE ICE is in the position of the external argument, the position of the object of actualization in the sense of Voorst

(1988)—it is the entity that brings about the event. For the moment, I have represented this property of THE ICE by putting it in an argument position of the predicate CAUSE; but in section 3.2, we will see that the interpretation as object of actualization derives from structural properties of the position occupied by the external argument—its interpretation derives from its relation in the structure with the other elements, not from a predicate like CAUSE, which need not be present in the SR.

First, there is syntactic evidence that two argument positions are involved in the SR of *melt.* It comes from the fact that a transitive alternative in which the two positions are identified by linking with a syntactic constituent and no binding takes place is possible:

(53)a.   John melted the ice.

   b.

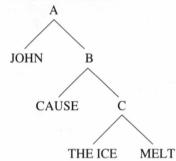

There is no binding in (53b), so the two argument positions in the SR are identified by linking with syntactic constituents—the topmost argument links with the highest syntactic constituent, which is the subject *John;* the lowest argument links with the lowest relevant syntactic constituent, which is the direct object *the ice.* Since I do not want to assume different representations for each use of *melt,* and since the transitive use of *melt* indicates that there are two argument positions in its SR, the inchoative use of *melt* receives the same two argument SR. The only difference between the two uses is whether the lower argument is identified by linking, as in the transitive use, or by binding, as in the intransitive use.

There is semantic evidence that the syntactic constituent *the ice* in (52) identifies two argument positions and that binding takes place. As we will see directly, the subject of an inchoative construction such as (52) both has properties of the entity that brings about the event and has properties of the entity that undergoes change. It has long been observed that lexical causatives like (53) contrast with syntactic causatives like (54), in that the former require more "direct causation" (Fodor 1970; Ruwet 1972; Shibatani 1976; McCawley 1978; Comrie 1985; Pinker 1989; Jackendoff 1990a). Ruwet (1972, 159) discusses the following contrast:[23]

(54)a. Le colonel a fait fondre trois sucres dans son café.
   The colonel has made melt three sugars in his coffee
   The colonel stirred three sugars into his coffee
   b. *Le colonel a fondu trois sucres dans son café
   The colonel has melted three sugars in his coffee

(55)a. Le chimiste (métallurgiste) a fait fondre le métal.
   The chemist (metallurgist) has made melt the metal
   The chemist (metallurgist) melted the metal.
   b. Le chimiste (métallurgiste) a fondu le métal.
   The chemist (metallurgist) has melted the metal.

He attributes the contrast between the (b) sentences to the fact that the melting of the sugar in (54) follows from causes that are not controlled by the colonel, whereas the chemist has a direct and continuous control over the melting of the metal in (59). Ruwet further observes that inanimate subjects in transitive causative constructions are also subject to this "direct responsibility" constraint, as illustrated in (56):[24]

(56)a. *La maladresse de Delphine a entré la voiture dans le garage.
   The clumsiness of Delphine has brought the car in the garage
   Delphine's clumsiness made the car end up in the garage.
   b. Le vent a cassé les branches.
   The wind has broken the branches.

The representation in (52b) predicts that the subject *the ice* should be understood as the entity that undergoes the change (by the position of *x*) as well as the entity responsible for the change (by the position of THE ICE). Therefore, the binding in (52) tells us that the ice—some property of the ice—is responsible for its own melting. As I will discuss below, this property of sentences that exhibit this kind of transitive/intransitive alternation constitutes evidence for the binding analysis.

Van Oosten states that "properties of the patient-subject are asserted to be responsible for the occurrence of the predicate" and that "properties of the patient-subject bear responsibility for the action of the predicate in a way that properties of the agent subject normally do" (1977, 68). Van Voorst has nice examples that illustrate this control or responsibility property of the subject of an inchoative (1992, 51). Consider the following examples (adapted from van Voorst 1992):

(57)a. She turned the page with the graphs, to go to the discussion part of the text.

   b. A gust of wind turned the page.

   c. The page turned.

Whereas (57c) is natural as a continuation to (57b), it is very odd in the context of (57a). This is because the inchoative (57c) implies responsibility on the part of the subject, so that the turning takes place because of something about the nature of pages. In the context of reading a book as in (57a), on the other hand, the reader controls the process of turning from beginning to end, and her input remains important throughout the event. This kind of external control is incompatible with the inchoative continuation. Voorst gives another set of examples that emphasize the point:

(58)a. He severely weakened your argument by pointing out the inadequacy of some of the assumptions it is based on.

   b. *The argument severely weakened during that discussion last night.

(59)a. The boxer severely weakened his opponent by giving him continued blows on the head.

   b. His opponent had severely weakened in the last round.

Support for the binding analysis of inchoatives can also be found in French. There is an interesting contrast in French between inchoatives and middle constructions with the reflexive clitic *se*. Whereas the subject is an active participant in the intransitive, as we just saw, the subject of the reflexive middle is a passive participant. As Labelle (1989, 10) puts it, "The intransitive construction in French is used when the entity in subject position has properties that are sufficient for bringing about the process, whereas the reflexive construction is used when the properties of the entity in subject position are insufficient for bringing about the process." Furthermore, consider the following contrasts, which have often been discussed (e.g., Junker 1987, Labelle 1989, Ruwet 1972, Zribi-Hertz 1987). A nice example is the following, from Rothemberg (1974):

(60)a. Jeanne rougit.
        Jeanne reddens
        Jeanne blushes

b. *Il vit le mouchoir rougir soudain.
   He saw the handkerchief redden suddenly
c. Il vit le mouchoir se rougir soudain.
   He saw the handkerchief self-redden suddenly
   He saw the handkerchief redden suddenly.

In (a), Jeanne becomes red (i.e., blushes) because of properties of a human being's skin: in a sense, she causes her own reddening. On the other hand, a handkerchief has no such property, so that the intransitive construction (b) is impossible. Note that *Jeanne se rougit* is possible if she is putting some rouge on her cheeks, for example, something that does not depend on her intrinsic properties and requires an external action.

Zribi-Hertz (1986) discusses the following two examples:

(61)a. Le cuisinier a mis le sucre à caraméliser.
       The cook put the sugar to caramelize
    b. *Le cuisinier a mis le sucre à se caraméliser.
       The cook put the sugar to self-caramelize

(62)a. Le ballon gonfle depuis cinq minutes.
       The balloon inflates since five minutes
       The balloon has been inflating for five minutes.
    b. *Le ballon se gonfle depuis cinq minutes.
       The balloon self-inflates since five minutes
    c. *Le ballon gonfle de gaz carbonique depuis cinq minutes.
       The balloon inflates of carbonic gas since five minutes
    d. Le ballon se gonfle de gaz carbonique depuis cinq minutes.
       The balloon self-inflates of carbonic gas since five minutes
       The balloon has been inflating with carbon dioxide for five minutes.

Once the cook puts the sugar over the heat, he does not intervene anymore, and caramelization takes place because of properties inherent to the sugar; that is why the *se* is not possible in (61). A sentence such as *Le sucre s'est caramélisé* is possible, but then it only describes the final state of the sugar. This is the type of example that leads Zribi-Hertz to observe that middle constructions with *se* are semantically oriented toward the end of the process. The contrast between (62a) and (62b) is based on the fact that the balloon becomes bigger because of properties inherent to it—perhaps, for example, lying in the heat of the sun will cause it to swell. As we have seen, *se* is not possible in such cases. On the other hand, in order for the balloon to inflate with carbon dioxide, external intervention is required, and as we see in (62c) and (62d), the *se* in (62d) is obligatory.

Why should we find these contrasts? If the intransitive construction is a case of binding as suggested here, then the rough overall schema of these constructions is something like [x_1 "actualizes" [x_2 PRED]], where x_1 is something inherent to x that is responsible for, or controls, or facilitates the realization of [x_2 PRED]. On the other hand, if *se* discharges the variable corresponding to the external argument (or "absorbs the external theta," see Bouchard 1984a), then the higher argument in (62d) is not identified by linking in (63), only the internal one is.

(63)

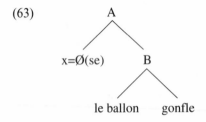

The *se* middle construction will therefore be oriented toward the end of the process, with an inactive subject; this will be the only option available, unless the subject has the appropriate properties to bring about the process itself.

In summary, there is evidence that two positions are involved in the SRs of verbs that undergo the transitive/inchoative alternation; the two positions available for the transitive use must also be present in the intransitive form. Moreover, in the intransitive sentences, the subjects are understood as the entity that undergoes the change, but they are also understood as being responsible for the change; they exhibit properties of active, direct causation. This follows directly in a binding analysis.

2.3 MINIMALISM AND G-SEMANTICS

To summarize, I am adopting a minimalist strategy toward Grammar in which accountability is fundamental; according to the principle of Full Identification, representations will include only linguistically traceable material. This minimalist approach has two major effects on syntax: first, the X-bar component is constrained so that X-bar categories are present only if they correspond to SR categories; and second, the class of transformations is highly constrained. In the following sections, I will indicate how the constraints on rule formulation that I propose significantly reduce the class of possible grammars, compared to more standard constraints on rule application, which do not.

2.3.1 A CONSTRAINED CLASS OF TRANSFORMATIONS

A transformation relates one structure to another. There are various types of operations that do this. *Type 1:* a transformation adds material to a structure to derive a second one. *Type 2:* a transformation deletes material. *Type 3:* a transformation collapses material by chunking. Movement transformations are a combination of adding and deleting—an element appears in a certain position in structure A, and then it appears in a new position in structure B, with subsequent deletion of the material in the original position. The new position either was already present in structure A as an open position introduced by the rules that are used to build the base, or that position is created by the transformation itself—this is typically the case for adjunction but is also possible for substitution when it is derived by Generalized Transformations (see Chomsky 1992), who returns to some of his earlier proposals from *The Logical Structure of Linguistic Theory*).

Movement transformations, as well as Type 1 and Type 2 transformations, are not minimal. They do not come for free, in the sense that they are not a virtual necessity. As Noam Chomsky observed in his class lectures (Fall 1993), we can imagine a Grammar that would not have movement transformations. On the other hand, chunking is within the domain of virtual necessity. Given the processing advantages of chunking, which codes complex representations into simpler units, I take chunking to be a defining property of natural language. Without chunking, natural languages would be practically unusable because of the complexity of the representations that would have to be processed. Moreover, chunking, regulated by Homomorphic Mapping, presupposes highly abstract representations of meaning. This makes for a diversely useful language, where sentences can refer to many differing situations. This diversity of use requires language to be heavily modulated by factors external to language. "If a species has the complex psychic capacity to develop a sufficiently rich cultural environment to provide highly complex modulations, it can have a communicational capacity that is highly abstract and remote from particulars: that is, highly underdetermining. A lesser species, with lesser endowment, would require more concrete communication, with much less underdetermining" (Ruhl 1989, 86). It is a defining property of users of natural languages that they belong to a species that has such a complex psychic capacity. Language is useful in an efficient way because it is abstract and versatile in modulation. This abstractness is processable because of chunking—hence the virtual necessity of chunking.

Endocentric chunking also has recoverability properties not found in copy and deletion; the former requires an additional position, and the latter goes directly counter to recoverability—that is why recoverability conditions are always added by its proponents to constrain its power. In contrast, endocentric chunking is the minimal structural change possible and allows full recoverability. In the spirit of the strong minimalist approach advocated in this book, I therefore propose to restrict the transformational component to the operation of chunking.

2.3.2 CONSTRAINING THE FORMULATION OF TS VERSUS THEIR APPLICATION

Note that it is the formulation of transformations, rather than the application, that is constrained. Recall Goldsmith's observation that "[o]nly constraints on rule formulation actively reduce the class of possible grammars" (1989, 153). Constraints on rule application, like those surrounding Move Alpha, do not reduce the class of possible grammars, in the absence of indications of what a possible restriction on Move Alpha is. It is often claimed that theta theory restricts the application of Move Alpha because theta theory constrains linking rules; but the restrictions on the *formulation* of linking rules allowed in theta theory are not outlined. Similarly, ECP and Subjacency, given appropriate structures, restrict the application of Move Alpha. But in the last few years we have seen a proliferation of escape hatches for Subjacency and of trace-licensers for ECP, by way of functional categories that are introduced in the structure. If no constraints are given on the formulation of what counts as a functional category and when it can be introduced in a structure, has the class of possible grammars been reduced?[25]

2.3.3 MODULARITY DOES NOT FURTHER CONSTRAIN RULE FORMULATION

Another instance where progress toward a reduction of the class of possible grammars is supposed to have occurred is the change from construction-specific rules to a more modular approach that began two decades ago. But this change does not reduce the class of possible grammars—the vocabulary has not changed, and all the operations that could be written in the old system can be performed in the new one. It is frequently claimed that the standard system of transformations was very rich, compared to the much simpler modular system of today and, hence, that the latter is preferable. But in order to evaluate the respective merits of the two approaches, one must compare the whole set of mechanisms of both approaches, not just one formal tool in one approach with one such tool in the other approach. To be of some value, a comparison must be systemic. Thus, in modular grammar, a number of simple principles interact, whereas the standard rule-based approach has a smaller number of complex rules. As Chomsky pointed out in *Aspects,* it is a very difficult task to determine whether a series of simple rules is preferable to a single more complex one (see also Bach 1977).

2.3.3.1 MOVE α AND WH-QUESTION FORMATION

A close look shows that the principles of the modular approach are not simpler than those of the rule-based approach. The difference between the two approaches is only in what they emphasize. In the modular approach, the emphasis is on general properties of the operations involved, whereas in the rule-based approach, it is on unifying rules that express the global effects of the interactions between the principles. This means that things are said in different ways, but the content is basically the same. For example, let us compare the rule of *move* α when it applies to a Wh-word, with the rules proposed to account for Wh-constructions in the standard approach. For example, consider Wh-Question Formation:

(64)   X - COMP - Y - Wh - Z
        1   2   3   4   5 $\Rightarrow$
        1   4+2   3   0   5

Although this rule is construction-specific, the vocabulary to write such a rule is not. Therefore, an account based on such a rule is not inherently more complex than one in the modular approach. In the modular approach, there is a single rule, move α. This formulation is but a metaphor, however, and it cannot be applied as such. In order to apply move α to a given structural description, the linguist interprets the metaphor and writes it in an appropriate form. Thus, since it "moves" α, this supposes that two positions are being related one to another as in (65).

(65)   A   B

Additionally, since move α is interpreted as relating A to B, regardless of what intervenes between A and B and regardless of what precedes A or follows B, three variables have to be present, as in (66).

(66)   X - A - Y - B - Z

Moreover, something has to indicate that, at the output, B appears in the position of A, as in (67).

(67)   X - A - T - B - Z
        1   2   3   4   5 $\Rightarrow$
        1 4+2 3 0   5

In modular grammar, the general formulation in (67) captures the idea that there are movement relations between phrase markers. But it is also clearly recognized in the standard theory that there is a unified class of operations called movement transformations—(67) merely summarizes the vocabulary common to the rules in that class.

The difference between the two approaches lies in the fact that the nature of the elements related to one another by the transformation is specified in each rule in the standard theory, but not in the modular approach. However, their nature must be specified elsewhere in the modular approach. Otherwise there would be wild overgeneration. Thus, it must be said in some way that a Wh-phrase is a trigger for movement. For example, one may assume that Wh-phrases are operator-like and therefore must bind a variable and that movement leaves behind a trace that can function as a variable under certain conditions. In terms of the standard theory, this is simply saying that a sub-class of movement transformations have that property in common; the theory can easily be extended to incorporate a device like a trace, as history shows. Similarly, the fact that COMP (or SPEC of COMP) is the landing site may be related to auxiliary assumptions, such as its X-bar status. All of this is perfectly compatible with the standard rules, which we could assume are triggered by the need to properly interpret their output. Therefore, the triggering may be the same in both approaches. Stating that there is a single movement rule is not a more significant generalization than stating that grammar has a class of operations consisting of movement transformations.

There are even cases where it seems to be an advantage to have more than one Wh-transformation. Thus, some Wh-words which may appear in Wh-Questions are not possible in relative clauses (see Ruwet 1982; Goldsmith 1989):

(68) a.   Comment fais-tu ça?
     a'.   How do you do that?
     b.   *Jean m'a montré la manière comment faire ça.
     b'.   John showed me the way how to do that.

(69) a. Pourquoi fais-tu ça?
  a'. Why do you do that?
  b. *Je connais la raison pourquoi tu fais ça.
  b'. I know the reason why you do that.

(70) a. Quand part-il?
  a'. When is he leaving?
  b. *Elle m'a dit le jour quand il part.
  b'. *She told me the day when he is leaving.

On the face of these examples, the multiple transformation approach seems to be at an advantage (although I suspect that a proper understanding of the relation between the head of a relative clause and a Wh-phrase will probably provide an explanation for the gaps in Relative Clause Formation).

2.3.3.2 TRACES DO NOT CONSTRAIN THE THEORY

One could argue that adding trace theory to the grammar has constrained the grammar, since derivations that involve lowering are now impossible. But if we consider the theory as it stands as a whole, the class of possible operations has not changed because the theory does not rule out in principle corrective devices that allow one to get around the effects of traces. For example, to avoid ill effects in cases where a displaced element appears to have been lowered so that it does not c-command its trace, it has at times been proposed that, in that particular instance, no trace is left behind, or that the trace can be deleted for some reason, or that the lowered element raises again at LF (LF is often used as a corrective to put in tune with the theory a surface structure that otherwise is underivable).

2.3.3.3 TRIGGERS IN MODULAR GRAMMAR ARE NOT MORE GENERAL

Nevertheless, one could claim that some triggers in the modular approach have a unifying effect and capture generalizations. For example, passives and raising constructions are unified by the single trigger of absence of Case. But in fact, the construction-particular triggers remain: all verbs with passive morphology trigger a passive-like movement, and the class of verbs listed as inherently non assigners of Case is the same as the class of raising verbs. Changing the label does not change the fact that the lists of members in these two classes must be specified in both approaches, so even parochiality of conditions is not removed—there is something construction-specific in both approaches.[26]

My goal is not to denigrate the modular approach, but simply to note that one must be very careful in evaluating and comparing alternative theories. If all the operations that could be written in the old system can be performed in the new one, as seems to be the case here, then the class of possible grammars has not been effectively reduced.

2.3.4 Minimalist Syntax, Semantics and Mapping

In contrast to constraints on the application of move α and to the aspects of modular grammar just presented, Homomorphic Mapping and endocentricity preservation are strong constraints on rule formulation, not rule application, as is indicated by the very fact that they follow from the architecture of the theory (as we saw in the discussion of (50) and (51)).

In short, not only is the level of semantic representation minimal (no material from situational background knowledge is allowed and no material that is not licensed by Full Identification) and the level of syntactic representation minimal (no vacuous projections and no vacuous categories), but the computational component that mediates between the two is also minimal (Homomorphic Mapping, in the form of chunking, is the only operation that relates semantic and syntactic representations).

The minimalist approach adopted here also has two strong effects on linking. First, given Full Identification, all elements of an SR must be identified, either by chunking, by binding, or by linking with an element in syntax. Thus, all that must be stated is what the SR of the lexical item is and what part of it is identified by chunking. The rest follows from Full Identification. Second, the specific linking relationship between a semantic formative and a syntactic element follows from Homomorphic Mapping.

Linking regularities follow from the architecture of the theory and are not arbitrary. The correspondence between semantic representations and syntactic representations is not mediated through lists, hence no specific linking conventions have to be given, and there is no need for stipulative constraints on linking like UAH or UTAH. Such a homomorphic correspondence is possible because of the more abstract nature of the semantic representations, a feature of the analysis that turns out to make for better representations of the meaning of lexical items, as we will see directly in Part II. Moreover, given that the regularities are more abstract than the ones described in terms of situational notions, like theta roles, the approach ascribes more autonomy to Grammar than situational approaches because linking does not depend on situational notions like Agent, Patient, etc.

In Part III, I discuss these assumptions and I present case studies of the effects they have on the analysis of basic types of syntactic constructions: NP movement in Psych constructions (chapter 4) and Head movement in V raising in French and English (chapter 5). I argue that there, too, the proposed mechanisms lead to more fruitful analyses.

PART II: SELECTIVE SEMANTICS AND THE LEXICON

3 A Case Study of Six French Verbs

In order to show what effects the selective semantics approach has on lexical analysis, I will present case studies of six basic French verbs: *venir* 'come,' *aller* 'go,' *arriver* 'arrive,' *partir* 'leave,' *entrer* 'enter,' and *sortir* 'go out.' I chose these particular verbs because they all exhibit a degree of polysemy that tends to be overlooked in standard analysis. In countless studies, these verbs (or their cognates) are considered to be standard examples of verbs of movement. The saliency of the movement use of these verbs is so overwhelming that it is regularly taken as part of their meaning. But to attribute properties of one use of a verb to its meaning proper constitutes a major obstacle to a systematic study of its behavior, since the analysis of all the other uses of that verb will be distorted. However, if we consider the different uses of these verbs, we will see that a great number of these uses do not involve movement at all. I will argue that, for each of these verbs, there is one abstract relation that is expressed in all of its uses. Once this level of abstraction is reached, none of the six verbs under study are movement verbs.

My goal is to explain why these verbs have such diversified uses (as do their cognates across languages) and why their spatial use is considered prototypical. Moreover, the primitives that a linguist uses delimit the object he is studying because these primitives are the expression of his explanatory principles. Use of spatial primitives suggests a centrality of space, hence reliance on situational properties. But we have seen in Part I that situational properties come under inadequate metaphysics and ontology for linguistic analysis.

In order to account for the common meaning in all the uses of any given verb and to account for the distributional similarities in these different uses, I will postulate abstract lexical entries for these six verbs, in the basic sense of the word "abstract"—"separated from matter, practice, or particular examples . . . free from representational qualities" (*The Concise Oxford Dictionary of Current English*). The specific organization of these lexical entries will allow us to "compute" the possible uses of these verbs, given the nature of their arguments and given the nature of the background knowledge on which the sentence is woven. It will then come as no surprise that these six pure expressions of relation can be used to refer to things other than movement, such as time, identity, implication, origin, and so on. These uses are predicted to be possible, with strict constraints on syntactic distribution holding across these fields, because of the unique abstract relation expressed by each of the verbs.

Given that three elements combine to determine the possible uses of a sentence—properties of the verb, its "actants" (i.e., arguments and adjuncts), and background knowledge—it would be incorrect to take a predicate-centrist approach and to attribute to the verb properties of the utterance from which it is arbitrarily isolated. We have already seen a glimpse of empirical evidence to this effect in section 1.3 concerning the verb *aller:* the rest of this chapter will be devoted to more detailed evidence of that type. We should also move away from situational notions in the study of "movement" verbs on general grounds of redundancy:

> The logic or topology of movement involves a starting point, an ending point, and a path of movement, and certain temporal-spatial constraints: for instance, if some entity E moves, then there are at least two times, t1 and t2, and two places, p1 and p2, such that at t1 E is at p1 and at t2 E is at p2. Since, by hypothesis, the existence of two end points and a line between them is innately specified, it is the case that whenever there is movement, the child in learning any particular verb of movement does not have to learn that it allows constituents in the sentence that indicate those points, any more than he/she has to learn that any sentence can have time and space adjuncts . . . the child knows that movement involves points and a path, among other things, and it is thus a bad idea to represent such knowledge in the lexical entry of each verb, which would imply that it could be otherwise. (Carter 1988, 285)

In other words, since knowledge of certain physical properties of movement is part of the general cognitive system, we do not need to include it in the lexical entry of each verb.

In the sections that follow, I will investigate numerous effects that the minimal tree structure representation of lexical entries has on the behavior of six French verbs—*venir, aller, arriver, partir, entrer, sortir.* I have chosen these six verbs because they fulfill all the conditions needed to present a thorough case for the necessity of the selective semantics approach over global approaches. Being highly polysemous, they involve a very large amount of recalcitrant data. The selective semantics approach will show how to make sense of that data, and at the same time, it will allow us to state all the relevant generalizations. As we go along, I will show why those generalizations cannot be stated in "situational" theories. The enterprise is long and difficult, but I believe it is the only way to get worthwhile results.

3.1 SIX VERBS OF MOVEMENT IN FRENCH
3.1.1 VENIR
3.1.1.1 USE 1 OF VENIR: MOVEMENT

Movement is generally considered to be the basic use of *venir*, with other uses derived from it

(1)   Max vient de Paris (demain).
       Max comes from Paris tomorrow.
       Max will come from Paris tomorrow.

The semantic representation that I propose for *venir* is given in (2):

(2)   Semantic Representation for *venir:*

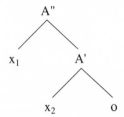

As discussed in section 2.1.1.1, a node labeling a branching relation in syntax minimally means something. The combinatorial function that combines two syntactic nodes is a concept, some sort of associative function. Therefore, minimally, A' in (2) indicates that x_2 "relates" with o, so that A' is a projection of o; A" indicates that x_1 "relates" with the relation A', so that A" is a projection of A'. Moreover, x_1 binds x_2, and x_1 is oriented toward x_2 because of the orientation properties of the tree. There is a constant value attributed to the element predicated of x_2, o, which stands for the deictic center. The deictic center is defined as the ME-HERE-NOW. This notion will become clearer as I go over the various uses of *venir;* as we will see, whether all three of the elements ME, HERE, and NOW are relevant in a particular use depends on the conceptual domain involved.

Venir is not represented as a verb of movement; it can readily be USED to express movement, but movement is not part of its meaning. Given the SR for *venir* in (2), Homomorphic Mapping and Full Identification work as follows: x_2 is identified by x_1 by binding; the fact that the deictic center o and the structural relations A' and A" of (2) are present in the SR of a given S will be indicated by *venir* itself; x_1 will be identified by linking with a phrasal element in syntax. For example, in (1) *Max,* the highest argument in syntax, is linked to x_1, the highest position in the SR of *venir; Max* also identifies x_2 via binding by x_1; *venir* indicates what kind of relationship is established between *Max* and the deictic center o. If a *de*-phrase adjunct is added to the sentence as in (1), then the complex SR for the sentence results from the combination of the SR of *venir* and the SR of its modifier, as in (3). I assume that the lexical definition of *de* specifies that its argument corresponds to the tail end of the orientation provided by the structure that it modifies, i.e., to the "source" of the orientation. Therefore, the meaning of (1) is represented as in (3) and can be captured in a nutshell as in (4):

(3)   Max vient de Paris:

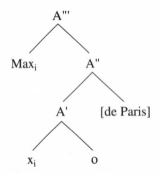

(4)   Max is oriented toward his being at the deictic center, with the
       tail end of the orientation being in Paris.

Since I propose a strictly compositional approach, let us see if the elements in the representation are sufficient to compute the movement use of *venir.* There is no primitive in the representation (3) that expresses movement. If we had a primitive for movement, then a new primitive would have to be introduced for each additional use of *venir,* resulting in an uncontrolled proliferation of primitives. Productive generalizations could not then be stated. What we have in (3) is the structural expression of the meaning of *venir,* with values attributed to the variables *Max,* o, and the adjunct *de Paris.*

All of this is set against a background of shared knowledge. The information we have from (3) is summarized in (5):

(5)a.   VENIR: relates variables, such that Max is oriented toward his being at o, with the tail-end of the orientation being in Paris.

  b.   MAX: since no specific context is given here, speakers assign to MAX a reference that is typical of the most frequent use of this proper name, namely that of a human being, a special type of spatio-temporal entity.

  c.   PARIS: again, no specific context is given, so speakers assign to PARIS the reference which is typical of the most frequent use of this proper name, namely that of a physical (spatio-temporal) place situated in France.

  d.   o: the deictic center o is the ME-HERE-NOW. The precise nature of the semantic domain in which the deictic center operates is determined by the nature of the arguments with which it interacts; here, it operates in the spatio-temporal domain because of the properties attributed to MAX and PARIS, when no specific context is given.

What kind of situation can we compute out of these pieces of information? If we combine the information in (5), we obtain something like (6):

(6)   The spatio-temporal entity *Max* is oriented toward his being at the spatio-temporal entity o, with the tail-end of the orientation being at the spatio-temporal entity Paris.

What does the notion of "orientation" used in (6) mean? Its presence in (6) is based on the orientation properties of the tree structure used to express the meaning of *venir*, but it is used here to relate entities that are ascribed spatio-temporal properties. We know that spatio-temporal entities are oriented with respect to one another in "real world" situations. Is this notion of "real world" spatial orientation different from that of orientation in tree structures? It is hard to see what it could possibly mean for the two notions of orientation to be different. I will therefore assume that "oriented with respect to one another" means the same thing in both the "real world" and semantic representation.

Of course, "orientation" can correspond to very different situations, given that the factors that determine orientation will differ greatly from one conceptual domain to another. To illustrate, I will discuss some factors that determine our interpretation of the notion of orientation in the most salient conceptual domain—space. We will see that, in the computation of spatial situations described by sentences, one must take into account extralinguistic factors that depend on the nature of the arguments in the conceptual domain involved, that is, on how we conceptualize and perceive objects in space. Moreover, these factors can change from one culture to another. However, the abstract relationship of orientation remains constant across cultures and conceptual domains. Once we begin to identify the relevant extralinguistic factors, we can compute the effects they will have on the use of a sentence, when combined with the orientation expressed by the tree structure, as in (3).

The different situations that a sentence can refer to result from differences in the nature of the elements combined, not from different notions of orientation. For example, Vandeloise (1986) showed that the prepositions of orientation *devant* 'in front of' and *derrière* 'behind' depend on the following functional properties of their object when used spatially (see also Clark 1973; Hill 1978, 1982; Traugott 1985; among others):

(7)a.   *Human beings* and *animals* are oriented "frontally," by the position of their organs of perception and interaction (eyes, mouth, ears, arms, legs, etc.).

   b.   *Furniture, tools, other "physical objects"* are oriented functionally, by the condition of their normal use (e.g., side with drawers for desk, normal direction of movement for car).

   c.   The orientation of *nonintrinsically oriented objects,* such as trees, columns, and the like, is determined by interaction with other actants.

It is these factors that will tell us what is the front or back of such objects as *Marie, l'auto* 'the car,' or *l'arbre* 'the tree,' so that we can compute the situations to which the sentences in (8) can correspond.

(8)a.   Jean est devant/derrière Marie.
        Jean is in front of/behind Marie.
   b.   Jean est devant/derrière l'auto.
        Jean is in front of/behind the car.
   c.   Jean est devant/derrière l'arbre.
        Jean is in front of/behind the tree.

In *Jean est devant Marie* (8a), Jean is on the side of Marie toward which her eyes, ears, mouth, and arms are directed. In *Jean est devant l'auto* (8b), Jean is placed in a position where the car would go if it went forward. The orientation of objects that are not intrinsically oriented, as in (8c), is particularly interesting. There are two ways to model the front-back orientation of nonintrinsically oriented objects. In the "closed-field" model, which is the basis of the French and English systems, canonical face-to-face interaction is the determining factor. So, in (9), *devant l'arbre* 'in front of the tree' will vary depending on the position of the French speaker (represented by the small human form):

(9)

Figure A   Figure B

In both figures, the speaker would say *le chien est devant l'arbre* 'the dog is in front of the tree,' although the situations described are very different; the dog is on the opposite side of the tree in Figure B, as compared to where it is in Figure A. The reason for this is that the side of the tree with which the speaker interacts face-to-face has changed, hence what constitutes *devant l'arbre* has also changed. An extralinguistic property of the argument *l'arbre*—it is not intrinsically oriented—is responsible for the fact that the very same sentence can be used to refer to two different situations. Such multiple uses can also arise for another reason: an intrinsically oriented element can also be considered without regard to its orientation and can be referred to as if it were an object without orientation. Thus, a sentence like (10) can correspond to both figures in (11), from the point of view of our French speaker: it all depends on whether *le chien* is viewed as intrinsically oriented (Figure B) or not (Figure A).

(10)   Le pistolet est devant le chien.
         The pistol is in-front-of the dog.

(11)

Figure A   Figure B

The second way to model the front-back orientation of nonintrinsically oriented objects is the "open-field" model, which is found in Hausa according to Hill (1978, 1982). Instead of face-to-face interaction, the determining factor is the frontal orientation of the speaker, which stretches out to infinity. Thus, in both Figures A and B of (12), a Hausa speaker would say something that would literally translate as 'the dog is in front of the tree,' since the front of the tree is in the continuation of the speaker's orientation (contrary to an English speaker who would say that the dog is behind the tree in both figures).

(12)

Figure A   Figure B

The fact that orientation is parametrized has other effects, as we will see in the discussion of other uses of the six verbs to be discussed in this chapter.

The point of these examples is that, in computing the situations described by sentences, extralinguistic factors must be taken into account. These factors depend on the nature of the arguments in the conceptual domain involved. Although a preposition like *devant* always makes the same semantic contribution to the computation of any sentence, the fact that it combines with these extralinguistic factors means that the same sentence can refer to different situations (cf. (9) and (10), for example).

Each preposition makes a uniform contribution to meaning across spatial uses, the same contribution to meaning it makes across conceptual domains. Of course, spatial factors play no role in other conceptual domains. Thus, front-oriented properties of *Jean,* like the position of his face, eyes, ears, etc., are totally irrelevant in the following sentences:

(13)a.   Jean est devant un problème de taille.
         Jean is in-front-of a problem of size.
         Jean is facing a sizeable problem.
    b.   Jean a tout son avenir devant lui.
         Jean has all his future ahead-of him.
    c.   Jean est courageux devant le danger.
         Jean is brave in the face of danger.
    d.   Ne t'inquiète pas, Jean, nous sommes derrière toi.
         Don't worry, Jean, we are behind you.

There are different factors at play in determining orientation in each conceptual field, some of which we return to in our discussion later in this chapter. This is because, in general, the factors that determine how we apply our conceptualization capacities are different in each conceptual domain, such as space, time, mental space, or other domains, partly because of important differences in how we are equipped to perceive objects in each of these domains. For example, physical factors such as those in (7) will have effects only on spatial uses of language. But the contribution of prepositions such as *devant* and *derrière* to orientation in any given sentence does not change from one conceptual domain to another—only the cognitive factors change. The notion of orientation is constant across semantic fields.

If the same notion of orientation at play in space or other semantic fields is involved in tree structures, we should be able to detect its effects in the computation of the meaning and use of sentences. In order to do so, we must proceed as we did for spatial orientation: we must identify the factors that determine orientation in tree structure. In keeping with the discussion of tree properties in 1.5.3, I propose the following factor:

(14)   x is ORIENTED toward y iff x has an extended branching relation with y, and y has no such relation with x.

If we combine the relation of orientation, in (14), with the other information obtained from the tree itself, given in (5), we obtain (6), repeated here as (15).

(15)   The spatio-temporal entity *Max* is oriented towards his being at
        the spatio-temporal entity o, with the tail-end of the orientation
        being at the spatio-temporal entity *Paris.*

The notion of orientation is present in (15) because of properties of the tree which is the semantic representation of *venir.* If the notion of orientation in tree structures is the same as the one in space, physical, spatio-temporal orientation holds between these elements, since referents with spatio-temporal properties are oriented with respect to one another in the movement use. This spatio-temporal relation between the actants of (1) can be schematized as follows:

(16)   PARIS   MAX   DEICTIC CENTER

In (16), the orientation of MAX is directed toward the point identified as the DEICTIC CENTER, and PARIS is a point at the origin of this orientation. We derive from the orientation of these spatio-temporal entities that there is an oriented axis that extends from PARIS to the DEICTIC CENTER.

Now we are ready to answer the question posed earlier: How does this analysis account for the movement use? Given the typical properties we attribute to the actants, in the absence of a specific context, movement is the most likely way for MAX to establish the relation schematized in (16), in a spatial domain. Therefore, I claim that movement is not grammatically expressed in a sentence like (1); there is no primitive that indicates that movement takes place. Rather, movement is deduced from prototypical, extralinguistic properties of the actants in the sentence. Language users do not refer to movement as a basic property that implies separation and distance; rather, movement is derived from an orientation and the property of having two spatio-temporal actants on the axis defined by this orientation.

The fact that multiple uses are possible for a sentence like (1) (Max vient de Paris) shows that movement is not a grammatical property of the sentence. Thus, note that MAX need not at all refer to a human being, it could just as well be a horse, a disease, a boat, a computer, or a laser beam. So although the prototypical MAX would have to move to establish the prototypical relation expressed by (1), MAX need not move at all to establish the relation if we depart from the prototypical case. Thus, MAX could *extend* between PARIS and HERE, if it were a laser beam, or if MAX were a giant, he could stretch between the two points. It could also be the case that we are not dealing with the prototypical referent for PARIS here. For example, PARIS could refer to a point on a map of the world, and MAX could be lying on the map. Similarly, PARIS could be used to refer to an ascription of origin rather than a spatio-temporal place, so that (1) could then mean that MAX is a Parisian or perhaps a computer made in Paris (only if *demain* 'tomorrow' is absent and the sentence is generic; see section 3.1.1.3 below). PARIS could even be used to refer to a period in the past, if we set the scene in a distant future in which Paris no longer exists. We could do this now with Atlantis (for those who believe it ever existed): *Max vient de l'Atlantide* 'Max comes from Atlantis' could be used to convey that MAX comes from a certain period of time.[1]

Examples like these, in which the same verb can be used to refer to different situations, can be generated at will. One simply has to depart from the prototypical case. The variations are not due to any grammatical changes, since as far as all the primitives of grammar are concerned here, nothing changes in the grammar.[2] As Jacques Lamarche was the first to point out to me, the differences in stativity and movement are essentially due to the "real world" nature of the arguments. This should not be surprising, since stativity and movement are not linguistic properties, but real world properties, properties of the web of background knowledge on which language is woven.

There is an observation made by Boons (1985) that also supports a more abstract analysis over situational ones: it appears that there are no "movement" verbs that express a movement on an axis without there being an orientation to that movement, so that no verb expresses back-and-forth movement on an axis. If the expression of movement is derived from orientation, as sketched here, this correlation is predicted, since there can be no movement without orientation and orientation is in a single direction.[3]

We now have an answer to the question of how and why *venir* is used to express movement in a sentence like (1). Strictly speaking, *venir* does not express movement, but it expresses an orientation relation between actants that is typically fulfilled by movement when the subject is an animate spatio-temporal element.

3.1.1.2 USE 2 OF VENIR: "PROGREDIENCE" WITH AN INFINITIVAL PHRASE

There is another construction with *venir* that is used to express movement:

(17)   Louis vient déjeuner.
        Louis is-coming to-lunch.

It differs syntactically from the movement use discussed in the preceding section in that there is an infinitive phrase instead of a PP following the verb. It is also semantically quite different. In sentences like those in (18), the PP expresses a source (a) or a goal (b):

(18)a.   Louis vient de Paris.
          Louis comes from Paris.
   b.   Louis vient à Montréal.
          Louis comes to Montreal.

But the infinitive here is neither of these. Moreover, although (17) is close in meaning to a sentence like (19),

(19)   Louis vient pour déjeuner.
        Louis is coming in-order-to lunch.

Lamiroy (1983) has argued convincingly that the two types of sentences differ significantly. For example, one of her arguments (following Gross 1968, 76) is that there is a restriction on the temporal interpretation of the infinitive in (17)—it must be the same as that of the higher verb—that does not hold in the *pour* phrase. Thus, in both examples in (20), the higher verb is in the present tense, whereas the lower verb is in the "passé composé," a tense expressing a past event, but only (20a), with "pour," is acceptable.

(20)a.   Jean vient tôt au bureau pour *avoir terminé* le travail avant samedi.
          Jean is coming early to the office in-order-to have finished the work before Saturday.

b. *Jean vient tôt au bureau *avoir terminé* le travail avant samedi.
Jean is coming early to the office to have finished the work before Saturday.

Damourette and Pichon (1911–1950) introduce the term "progrédience" to refer to the subtle semantics of constructions like (17):

> In *Louis vient déjeuner, déjeuner* is not only predicative, but also its verbal predicative value fuses with, is somewhat telescoped with, that of *vient,* of which it is the continuation as well as the justification. *Déjeuner* is not the end of Louis' coming, rather it is its psychological substance: the action of lunching is in a way already begun by the steps Louis takes towards the house where he is to eat. . . . What it [*venir*] needs as a complement, like all movement verbs, is a verbal virtuality which can "symphenomenalize" with its own phenomenon: which only an infinitive can do properly. That is the role of progrédience.[4]

In other words, in a progrédience use, the movement verb and the infinitival verb form a complex predicate. Progrédience is a broad phenomenon that can be found with infinitival complements of various movement verbs. Lamiroy gives the following list of cases where judgments are clear: *accourir* 'run up,' *aller* 'go,' *avoir été* (as a variant of *aller*), *s'en aller* 'go away,' *courir* 'run,' *descendre* 'go down,' *entrer* 'come in,' *monter* 'go up,' *partir* 'leave,' *passer* 'pass,' *redescendre* 'go down again,' *rentrer* 'come back in,' *remonter* 'go back up,' *repartir* 'leave again,' *ressortir* 'go out again,' *rester* 'stay,' *retourner* 'go back,' *revenir* 'come back,' *sortir* 'go out,' and *venir* 'come.' I will first discuss two constraints on the movement verb + infinitive construction, and then show how these properties of the construction can be accounted for in my analysis.

3.1.1.2.1 Two Constraints on Progrédience

Constraint 1: the subject must be animate (Lamiroy 1983):

(21)a.   Jean monte au grenier détruire les vieux journaux.
Jean is-going-up to the attic to destroy the old newspapers.
   b. *Les flammes montent au grenier détruire les vieux journaux.
The flames are-going-up to the attic to destroy the old newspapers.

(22)a.   Les flammes montent jusqu'au toit.
The flames are going up to the roof.
The flames rise up to the roof.
   b.   Les flammes ont détruit les documents.

The flames have destroyed the documents.

Since neither of these verbs obligatorily takes an animate subject, as we see in (22), Lamiroy concludes that the contrast in (21) must be due to a property of the construction movement verb+infinitive. A similar constraint holds of the subject of an infinitive psych verb in this construction. Thus, both sentences in (23) are acceptable only if Jean is fully aware of the effects he will have on Anne:

(23)a. Jean monte embêter Anne par son caractère égocentrique.
     Jean goes up to-bother Anne by his egocentric character.
     Jean is going upstairs to bother Anne with his egocentric character.
  b. Jean descend impressionner Anne par son intelligence.
     Jean goes down to-impress Anne by his intelligence.
     Jean is going downstairs to impress Anne with his intelligence.

Constraint 2: the infinitival verb can only be a stage-level predicate, not an individual-level predicate in the sense of Carlson (1977) or Milsark (1974):[5]

(24) a. Jean vient demander la nationalité française.
     Jean is-coming to-ask-for French nationality.
  a'. *Jean vient être de nationalité française.
     Jean is-coming to-be of French nationality.
  b. Jean monte parler à son frère.
     Jean is-going-upstairs to talk to his brother.
  b'. *Jean monte ressembler à son frère.[6]
     Jean is-going-upstairs to-look-like his brother.
  c. Jean entre louer une voiture.
     Jean is-going-in to-rent a car.
  c'. *Jean entre posséder une voiture.
     Jean is-going-in to-own a car.
  d. Jean retourne acheter un livre.
     Jean is-going-back to-buy a book.
  d'. *Jean retourne avoir un livre.
     Jean is-going-back to-have a book.

Thus, examples a, b, c, and d, in which the infinitive is a stage-level predicate, are fine, whereas a', b', c', and d', which have an individual-level infinitive, are unacceptable.

3.1.1.2.2 The Structure of the Progredience Construction

We will see below how my analysis of *venir* can help us understand these properties of the movement verb+infinitive construction. Given the meaning of *venir* in (2), repeated here as (25), the infinitival phrase of (17) ("Jean vient déjeuner") could potentially correspond to any of the three elements x_2, B″ or o (the deictic center).

(25)   Semantic Representation for *venir:*

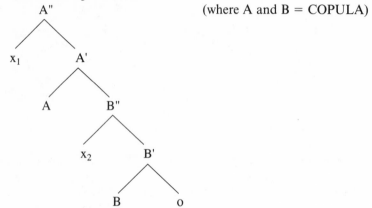

(where A and B = COPULA)

However, the infinitival clause in (17) is not interpreted as being the deictic center o; there is an unmentioned deictic center that is perceived in that sentence. Moreover, the deictic center can be made more precise by an *à*-adjunct phrase, as in (26):

(26)   Jean vient *à l'épicerie* acheter des fruits et légumes.
         Jean is-coming to the grocery-store to-buy fruits and vegetables.

The infinitive in these constructions does not occupy the position of the deictic center o in (25) because the constant o is already specified by the *à*-adjunct. If an element is introduced to further specify the nature of the deictic center, it can only do so as an adjunct, an *à*-adjunct in the present case because of the nature of the constant. If the infinitive were further specifying the deictic center, it would appear as an *à*-adjunct. Such *venir à* V_{inf} constructions do exist, and we will discuss them in section 3.1.1.6 below.

In the movement verb + infinitive construction, we have a bare infinitival clause in direct object position. Thus, the infinitival phrase does not correspond to the deictic center in (25). It cannot correspond to B″ in (25), either, since a phrase modifying a subpart of that constituent [*à l'épicerie* modifying the o] can appear independently of the infinitival clause as we see in (26). Given Homomorphic Mapping, the subject is linked to the highest position x_1 in (25). We are therefore left with a correspondence between the infinitival clause and x_2, which would give us (27) as the structure for (17).

(27)   Semantic Representation for *Louis vient déjeuner:*   (where A and B = COPULA)

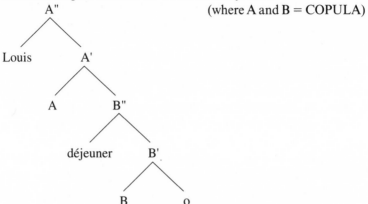

This means that in a sentence like *Louis vient déjeuner,* Louis is oriented toward the relation "déjeuner relates with o." If (27) expresses the meaning of such sentences, we can see why the notion of "progredience" has been proposed in relation to these sentences: the definition of progredience more or less paraphrases the content of (27). Thus, it is indeed the case in (27) that "*Déjeuner* is not the end of Louis' coming"—the deictic center o is that end. Moreover, if, as discussed in the previous section, the movement perceived in this use of *venir* is derived in part from the orientation in the tree representation of the meaning of *venir,* then *déjeuner* is involved in that orientation in a way that explains why Damourette and Pichon perceived that "the action of lunching is in a way already begun by the steps Louis takes towards the house where he is to eat": *Louis* in (27) is not oriented toward his being at o, as in the cases where x_1 binds x_2, but rather is oriented toward his having lunch at o. I will therefore take it that (27) appropriately expresses the progredience found in this construction.

3.1.1.2.3 Explaining the Constraints

Given (27), what can we make of the two constraints noted above? First, note that Constraint 1 requires the "animacy" of the subject. This is a situational notion and is not part of the information encoded in the Grammar. Thus, the fact that *the rock is sleeping* is odd is not due to the mismatch of grammatical features (for example, that *the rock* is [−Animate] and *sleeping* requires a [+Animate] subject). Rather, the oddness of the sentence is due to what rocks are in the world we live in; they could certainly be otherwise, as in cartoons, for example. The fact that rocks do not sleep is not a linguistic phenomenon, otherwise the fact that rocks do not float would also be a linguistic phenomenon and we could be led to the absurd conclusion that the theory of gravity is a linguistic theory.[7]

The fact that the feature [+/− Animate] is situational or contextual is acknowledged even in Chomsky (1965) (although he uses it as a syntactic feature). Discussing the adjective *sad,* he states that "it may well be assigned *contextual* features corresponding to various subfeatures of [−Animate], so as to characterize as deviant such sentences as 'the pencil is sad,' which cannot receive an interpretation analogous to that of 'the book was sad.' This matter has no relevance to the point at issue, though it raises nontrivial problems of a different sort" (Chomsky 1965, 235, note 39; my emphasis). The point at issue was the deviance of a sentence such as (28), which Chomsky analyzed as being derived by comparative deletion.

(28)   John is as sad as the book he read yesterday.

He attributed the deviance to the fact that *sad* has an animate argument in the matrix clause but an inanimate argument in the embedded clause, and this mismatch blocks the application of the transformation.

I think that it is inappropriate to have such situational features as [+/− Animate] directly play a role in the Grammar. Rather, the contrast in (28) is most likely due to how one refers to a human being like John when he is sad and how one refers to a book as being sad. The human being is referred to as an "individual," whereas it is the content of the book as perceived by a human being that is referred to, rather than the individuality of the book. It is this type mismatch in referential use that accounts for the oddness of (28).[8]

I think that the animacy contrast in (21), which illustrates Constraint 1, is also due to referential properties, namely how one views the relation expressed in B″ of the representation of the meaning of *venir.* For example, in the movement use of a sentence like *Jean vient de Paris,* the relation B″ toward which the subject is oriented is "Jean (= x_2) relates with o″. Now this relation can be seen as effective or noneffective. When seen as effective, Jean actually is traveling toward the deictic center. When noneffective, the relation of John's being here is seen as an "aim," we get a "schedule" interpretation in which the sentence is used to indicate that Jean is to come from Paris.[9] So, even under a basic movement use, the sentence can refer to two quite different situations.

This relationship between effective/noneffective reference and the notion of aim is borrowed from Franckel and Lebaud (1990), who use the notion to distinguish lexically between a verb like *entendre* 'hear,' which has an effective endpoint, and a verb like *vouloir* 'want,' which has a noneffective endpoint. Crucially, they assume that reference with an effective endpoint is always accompanied by an absence of both choice and agentivity on the part of the subject, whereas a noneffective endpoint reference is seen as the aim of the subject, which involves choice and agentivity.[10]

Now consider again the examples with infinitival phrases like (17). The "verbal virtuality" of the infinitival alluded to by Damourette and Pichon, which Stowell (1982) calls the "irrealis" of the event, is not the end point of the B″ relation in the entry of *venir*, but rather the "external argument" of that relation. I suggest that when a very concrete property is predicated of a "verbal virtuality," like the spatial aspect of the deictic center that is predicated of *déjeuner* in the B″ relation of (27), this necessarily causes the B″ relation to have a noneffective reference. Therefore, there is always aim in constructions with infinitival phrases in the position of x_2, since the subject is oriented toward an element with noneffective reference. Moreover, since we are considering a movement use of *venir*, what we have is the aim of the subject to establish a relation in space. I propose that such an aim can only be the attribute of animate entities, hence Constraint 1. To put it another way, since only animate entities have choice and agentivity, only they have the capacity for "aim" required by these constructions.

If we turn to constraint 2, namely that the infinitival verb cannot be an individual-level predicate, we can see why such a constraint holds, given the preceding discussion. The infinitival in the position of x_2 induces a noneffective reference. This is not compatible with individual-level predicates, since these express inherent, permanent properties and are thus effective by definition. We can now see that these seemingly unrelated constraints both follow from the structure we arrived at in (27), which is the only one possible in my analysis for a sentence with a bare infinitival complement of a movement verb.

Let me close this section with a brief remark. Sentences with *venir* that can be used to describe movement can usually also be used to describe extension (I will discuss this extension use more fully in 3.1.1.4):

(29)   Cette route vient de Montréal.
         That road comes from Montreal.

But extension and progredience are incompatible. Thus, although a sentence like (30) is ambiguous between a movement use and an extension use (as is made clear by the material in parentheses), sentence (31) has only a movement use.

(30)   Jean sort (à mi-corps) par la fenêtre.
         Jean leaves (to the waist) by the window.
         Jean is leaning out the window to the waist.

(31)   Jean sort voir Marie.
         Jean is-going-out to-see Marie.

As we will see in 3.1.1.4, the extension use comes from the binding of x_1 by x_2 in the representation of verbs like *venir.* X is thus in two positions at the same time. But since progredience comes from the linking of x_2 with an infinitival phrase, extension and progredience are incompatible.[11] X_2 cannot both be linked with an infinitival phrase and be bound by another variable at the same time.

3.1.1.3 USE 3 OF VENIR: ORIGIN

I have already discussed the origin use in (32a); the other examples in (32) are similar.

(32)a.   Max vient de Paris.
         Max comes from Paris.
    b.   Ce mot vient du latin.
         That word comes from Latin.
    c.   Le pouvoir vient du peuple.
         Power comes from the people.
    d.   Cette maladie vient de famille.
         That sickness comes from family.
         That sickness runs in the family.
    e.   La panne vient du carburateur.
         The breakdown comes from the carburator.

In (32a), instead of having a prototypical spatio-temporal reference, PARIS is used to refer to an ascription of origin: it is a place qua identity assigner, rather than a spatio-temporal place, so that MAX is a Parisian, or a computer made in Paris, or something else that "comes from" Paris. The fact that the sentence is in the present tense, yet is given a generic interpretation, is also an indication of the "distanciation" from the spatio-temporal (extending the use of the term coined by the school of Berthold Brecht). The moment of speech is usually anchored in the self of the speaker, but in the generic use, it is anchored in the self of the speaker crucially viewed as a self in a set of all selves. Similarly, the orientation in these examples is not toward a deictic center defined only with respect to the speaker's self, but again toward that self in a set of all selves, so that the statements are true across space and time. Essentially, given the meaning of *venir* in (2), we have here a centering orientation of the subject with respect to a property P, and this property is expressed by the *de* NP. For example, in (32a), the property PARIS is at the origin of the axis determined by the orientation of MAX toward the deictic center as set of all selves capable of defining a deictic center; so MAX is presented as a link that funnels the property PARIS toward all deictic centers at a moment that endures, since it is anchored on the set of all selves. MAX is attributed a permanent property—he is a Parisian. Therefore, in this use, (32a) says nothing about movement, per se. In fact, a sentence like *Mais je viens de Paris moi aussi* 'But I come from Paris me too' could perfectly well be uttered in Paris when used to express origin, although this would be an incongruous situation, if the intention was to express movement.

The other examples of (32) are very similar to (32a), except that the element used to ascribe a property is not a place. Moreover, the subject in (32b–e) is more like an event-name than a referent to an object in the world. Thus in (32e), discussed by Franckel and Lebaud (1990, 165–66), the event *la panne* is oriented toward the deictic center—therefore, it is relevant to the ME-HERE-NOW—with the source of the orientation being in the carburator: hence the perception that the carburator is somehow the cause of the event.

This use of *venir* is very close to the attribution of a property. Thus a corresponding sentence with *être* is possible in some of those cases, although the meaning is then slightly different.

(33)a. Max est de Paris.
         Max is from Paris.
    b. *Ce mot est du latin.
         That word is from Latin.
    c. *Le pouvoir est du peuple.
         Power is from the people.

    d.   Cette maladie est de famille.
         That sickness is from family.
    e. * La panne est du carburateur.
         The breakdown is from the carburator.

Among other things, there is a temporal connotation present in the sentences of (32) that is absent from those in (33). Conversely, not all attributions of a property may occur in the *venir* construction:[12]

(34)a.   Max est de langue anglaise.
        Max is of English language.
  b. * Max vient de langue anglaise.
        Max comes from English language.

We see that the origin use occurs when the entity of the *de NP* and the deictic center are referred to in a particular way. The sentences in (32) are further examples of the importance of making a distinction between the semantics which has some effect on the form and functioning of Grammar, and other semantics. Thus, whether one has a prototypical referent for PARIS or not has no effect on the form and functioning of Grammar, but it has an enormous effect on the situation being referred to.

3.1.1.4 USE 4 OF VENIR: EXTENSION

In addition, *venir* can be used to express extension.

(35)   Cette route vient de Montréal.
        That road comes from Montreal.

Assuming the semantic representation of *venir* as in (2), in (35), *cette route,* the highest argument in syntax, is linked to x_j, the highest position in the SR of *venir,* and the adjunct *de*-phrase corresponds to the tail end of the "orientation arrow" (by lexical specification). In effect, all that this sentence says is that "*Cette route* is oriented toward its being at the deictic center, with the tail end of the orientation in Montréal." If no context is given, we resort to what we generally know about roads and what is best known about Montréal. In such circumstances, the most likely way for *cette route* to establish the relation described by the sentence is by extending from Montréal to the deictic center. Essentially, the extension interpretation comes from the fact that sentence (35) says that *cette route* (= x) is in two positions at the same time. Again, that is not the only possible situation, but it is the prototypical one for the arguments involved here. There are cases where the multiplicity of uses of *venir* is more salient because no prototypical situation overshadows the others. For example, sentence (36) can refer to the three different situations in (37):

(36)   Ce pont vient de Paris.
         That bridge comes/is coming from Paris.

(37)a.   *Movement:* the bridge is on a truck and establishes a relation with
         HERE (deictic center) by moving from Paris.
    b.   *Extension:* the bridge extends across a river from Paris to HERE.
    c.   *Origin:* the sentence says we are dealing with a bridge made in
         Paris.

The following example is interesting because it shows that the abstract notion of orientation in tree structures must be in accord with "spatio-temporal" orientation:[13]

(38)   La rue Saint-Dominique est sûrement à sens unique, et je crois
         qu'elle vient par ici.
         Saint-Dominique street is surely a one-way, and I believe that it
         comes this way.

Venir tells us that *la rue Saint-Dominique* is oriented toward us (at the deictic center) in an abstract sense; with the information that it is a one-way street given in the first conjunct, this sentence can only be used if the flow of traffic on the street is also oriented toward the deictic center.

3.1.1.5 USE 5 OF VENIR: EXPRESSING TIME

Some of the uses of the verb *venir* raise interesting challenges for the study of polysemy. One of these certainly is that *venir* can express temporal relations. Even more challenging is the fact that *venir* can express both a "recent" past (39) and a future (40):

(39)a.   Max vient de partir.
         Max comes from leaving.
         Max has just left.
    b.   L'hiver vient de commencer.
         Winter comes from to-begin.
         Winter has just begun.

(40)a.   L'hiver vient vite cette année.
         Winter is coming quickly this year.
    b.   dans l'année qui vient

> *in the year that comes*
> in the coming year

But how can the same verb express both a past and a future?[14] One answer is to say that there are simply two verbs *venir.* This amounts to treating polysemy as homonymy. Another solution is to distinguish between *venir* and the expression *venir de,* and this is more interesting. The goal now is to see what it means to make this distinction. If we just list the two, we are not much better off than with the homonymy solution. A better approach to explore is to say that the two uses are different because their composition is different. Following this lead, we can break down the above question into two questions:

(41)(i)   Of all the elements that combine in the temporal uses of *venir* in
          (39) and (40), what makes these TEMPORAL uses?
   (ii)   Of all these elements, what makes these past/future uses?

The lexical representation of *venir* given in (2) expresses a relation that is neither spatial nor temporal nor of any other particular semantic field. It expresses an abstract relation paraphrasable as (42).

(42)   *Paraphrase of VENIR:* "x_1 is oriented toward its being at the deictic
       center (ME-HERE-NOW), with the tail end of the orientation op-
       tionally identified by a DE-phrase"

Therefore, the answer to these questions cannot come from *venir.* Rather, I will answer these questions along the following lines:

(43)   *Answer to (i):* these uses are temporal because one of the actants is
       temporal: (*partir, commencer* in (39) and *l'hiver, l'année,* in (40))[15]
       Answer to (ii): whether we have a past or future use depends on the
       interaction of Grammar and cognitive factors.

Expanding on the answer to (ii), we know that the Grammar indicates how the actants are oriented with respect to one another at an abstract level. That is the content of (2), paraphrased in (42) above. Recall that I am assuming a unique notion of orientation, so the same notion is involved in constituent trees and in the conceptual domains of time and space. Because the factors that determine orientation differ greatly from one conceptual domain to another, the notion of orientation actually corresponds to very different situations, depending on the conceptual domain involved. These different situations result from differences in the nature of the elements combined, not from different notions of orientation. This is where cognitive factors come into play. Since the only information in the Grammar about *venir* is the orientation of certain arguments with respect to one another, it is crucial to identify which extralinguistic factors determine orientation in a particular conceptual domain, in order to compute the actual effects of representations like (2).[16]

We have already seen that the cognitive factors that determine orientation in space are functional properties for objects intrinsically oriented in space and face-to-face interaction (in French and English) for nonintrinsically oriented objects (see the discussion of (9)–(12)). Since the situations in (39) and (40) are set in the temporal domain due to the nature of some of the actants (43i), the computation of the situations to which these sentences can correspond will depend on cognitive factors that determine TEMPORAL orientation. These factors are given in (44).

(44) *Cognitive factors that determine* TEMPORAL *orientation:*
    (i)   *Intrinsically oriented:* NOW (deictic center) is oriented toward the future; the past is oriented toward NOW.[17]
    (ii) *NOT intrinsically oriented:* all others actants in the temporal domain.

It is from these factors that we get the saying that "The past is behind us and the future lies ahead." Nonintrinsically oriented objects in the temporal conceptual domain are oriented according to the "closed-field" model in our examples—with canonical face-to-face interaction being the determining factor—since this is the basis of the French and English systems.

Now that all the Grammatical and cognitive factors are determined, we can see that computing the factors involved in (40) results in a FUTURE situation, whereas it results in a PAST situation in (39). First, consider the FUTURE interpretations in (40).

(45) Why do the examples in (40) refer to FUTURE situations?
    Grammatical factor:
    (a) Both *l'hiver* and *l'année* are subjects of VENIR, hence both are oriented toward the deictic center.
    Cognitive factors:
    (b) The deictic center is intrinsically oriented toward the future, in the temporal domain (44i).
    (c) The temporal elements *l'hiver* and *l'année* have no intrinsic orientation, so their orientation relative to other temporal actants is determined by canonical face-to-face interaction (44ii).

The orientation NOW⇒FUTURE (where the double arrow indicates the direction of an intrinsic orientation) follows from (44i); (45a) derives the orientation *l'hiver/l'année*→NOW; finally, (45c) produces NOW⇒←*l'hiver/l'année*. If we put all of these results together, we have the following, where the two instances of the arrow originating from NOW point in the same direction, since NOW has an intrinsic, invariable orientation:

> *Result:*   NOW⇒FUTURE
> NOW⇒←*l'hiver/l'année*
> Hence, we derive that *l'hiver/l'année* are in the future.[18]

Now, consider the PAST interpretation of the examples in (39).

(46) Why does *Max vient de partir* refer to a PAST situation?
    Grammatical factors:
    (a)   The semantic representation of VENIR indicates that there is orientation of MAX, the subject, toward the deictic center.
    (b)   The DE-phrase indicates that the temporal actant *partir* is at the tail end, the source, of that orientation.
    Cognitive factor:
    (c)   PAST is intrinsically oriented toward NOW (44i).

The grammatical factors in (46) tell us that MAX is oriented toward NOW and that PARTIR is at the tail end of that grammatically induced orientation; so we derive that MAX and PARTIR are oriented toward NOW, such that PARTIR→MAX→NOW.[19] The cognitive factors tell us that there is also an orientation toward NOW in the temporal domain, such that PAST⇒NOW. Lining up these two orientations, we get the following, where PARTIR is in the past because it must be at the tail end of the arrow pointing toward NOW:

> *Result:*   PAST⇒ NOW
> PARTIR→MAX →NOW

Before closing this section, I will make a few more observations on the past use of *venir.* It is often mentioned that the past described by *venir de,* as in (47), differs from that of a past form like (48), in that (47) expresses a "recent" past, as indicated by the translation.

(47) Jean vient de manger.
    Jean comes of to-eat.
    Jean has just eaten.

(48) Jean a mangé.
      Jean has eaten.

The analysis of *venir* presented here does not predict that there should be such a chronological difference: nothing in *venir de* indicates "recentness." Following Damourette and Pichon (1911–1950, #1766), I suggest that the distinction is not chronological, but rather it lies in the way of looking at the past. In (48), it is viewed as a "given that we can use," whereas in (47), it is viewed as something relevant to, and oriented toward, the present: "the past as the living source of the present." They give examples such as the following, which shows that the distinction cannot be chronological because the *a déchiré* event necessarily takes place in a more recent past than the *viens de* event in (49):

(49)   Ce que je viens de voir a déchiré mon coeur.
          This that I come of to-see has ripped my heart.
          What I have just seen has broken my heart.

As Damourette and Pichon note, "the wound is posterior to the fact of seeing. But, whereas the contemplation of the painful event is presented here as the beginning of a living succession of facts to which the present moment still belongs, the wound, however, is presented as a definitive acquisition of which the heart of the countess will always bear a sore or scar"[20] (Damourette et Pichon #1766). The more structural expression of their ornate description that I give, namely as an orientation toward the present, echoes the more formal distinction that Reichenbach (1947) proposed between simple past and present perfect in English, with the latter bearing some relevance for the present, as expressed in Reichenbach's association of the reference point R with the moment of speech S in his representation of the present perfect:[21]

(50)a.   Simple Past: E,R____S
    b.   Present Perfect: E____R,S

Reichenbach's analysis and the idea that the "recent past" reading is based on relevance to the present are supported by the fact that certain tenses are excluded for *venir* in the temporal uses discussed here:

(51)a.   *Max est venu de partir.
          Max is come from to-leave.
    b.   *Max sera venu de partir.
          Max will-be come of to-leave.

If *est venu* and *sera venu* already incorporate relevance to the moment of speech, as suggested in Bouchard (1984b), there is a redundancy that may account for the ungrammaticality of the sentences; the temporal use of *venir* also implies relevance to the moment of speech because of the orientation in the structure toward the deictic center, as we saw in (45) and (46). We will also see the effects of this "relevance by orientation" in the implicative uses of *venir* and *aller* below.[22]

Summing up, this discussion of the temporal uses of *venir* shows that once the factors are sorted out, the contribution of *venir* to the computation of situations to which sentences can refer is constant. That contribution is fairly abstract and is essentially as given in (2). The apparent multiplicity of meanings of *venir* that come from its multiple uses results from the computation of both grammatical and cognitive factors. Crucially, the latter have no effect on the form and functioning of Grammar, only on the computation of situations.[23]

3.1.1.6 USE 6 OF VENIR: END-REACHING (VENIR À)

Some sentences with *venir* have future connotations of a different type from the ones in the previous section.

(52)a.   Pierre en est venu à croire que Léa le trompait.
         Pierre has of-it come to believe that Lea cheated him.
         Pierre has come to believe that Lea cheated him.
    b.   Comment en es-tu venu à te casser la jambe?
         How of-it is you come to to-you break the leg?
         How did you happen to break your leg?
    c.   Si le directeur venait à mourir . . .
         If the director came to die . . .

For example, (52a) refers to a situation where first Pierre did not believe that Léa betrayed him and then was led to believe it. What all the sentences express is slightly different from a future, however. It is something like the temporal unfolding of an event that ends up precisely at the phenomenon expressed by the infinitive. If we look at the grammatical information provided by the sentences, this is exactly what we expect. If we compare this use to a spatial use of *venir,* such as *Jean vient à Montréal* 'John comes to Montreal,' we see that in both uses the constant o of (2) is further identified by an adjunct *à* phrase; the main difference between the two uses is that, here, the subject is oriented toward an event (expressed by *à*+infinitive) instead of a place (expressed by *à* + NP). Thus, given the meaning of *venir,* (52a) expresses something like "*Pierre* has been oriented toward his being at *croire que Léa le trompait*, with the tail end of the orientation identified by the clitic DE-phrase *en*." The clitic *en* here refers very generally to "circumstances" that have some bearing on the onset of the phenomenon of the infinitival clause; such a general referential *en* is quite frequently used to express the fact that an event took place with the main participant having no control over it. In short, nothing special need be said about this use of *venir*: given the nature of the elements involved—in particular the infinitival complement of *à* and circumstantial *en*—the computation of the information gives us exactly the right results.

3.1.1.7 USE 7 OF VENIR: INVOLVEMENT

In the following sentences, *venir* is used to convey the idea that the speaker feels somehow personally affected by, or deeply involved in, what is going on.

(53)a. Venir refroidir le monde pour rien! (V. Hugo, *Les Misérables*)
         To come and chill people for nothing!

   b. Ne venez pas me dire que Jean est malade!
       Don't come and tell me that Jean is sick!

   c. Mais ne voilà-t-il pas que notre si distingué collaborateur M. Allard vient faire de la minceur même de son oeuvre une raison pour qu'elle survive à jamais. (M. Proust. *Chroniques: A propos de Baudelaire*)
       But here it is that our so distinguished collaborator, M. Allard, comes and makes out of the very thinness of his work a reason for it to survive forever.

The construction is used quite frequently, yet it has received little attention. The comments that have been made about this use are nicely summarized in the following passage: "The only thing left to it [the verb] is to indicate the impulse which led to movement: an impulse which, in the absence of a real movement, is reduced to represent the spontaneity towards some activity, the personal psychic efficiency" (Damourette and Pichon (1911–1950: #1654)).[24]

We have a bare infinitival in object position here, so the syntax suggests that these sentences are structurally very similar to the examples of progredience discussed in 3.1.1.2. I will adopt the same structure for these examples of involvement: the infinitival phrase is linked to the position of x_2 in the lexical entry of *venir*, just as in the structure for progredience.

(54)   Semantic Representation for *Venir refroidir le monde pour rien:*
                                                     (where A and B = COPULA)

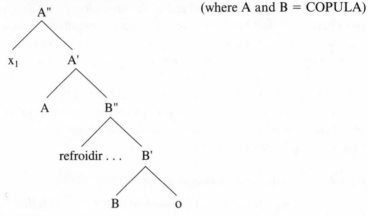

The difference between the involvement use and the progredience use of *venir* is not structural; rather, it is due to the referential use of the deictic center ME-HERE-NOW. We have seen uses of *venir* where reference is made to the spatial properties of the deictic center, expressed by HERE: the movement use, the progredience use, the extension use. Other uses refer to the temporal properties of the deictic center (expressed by NOW), giving past or future interpretations. In the involvement use, I suggest, reference is made to the third aspect of the deictic center, which is expressed by ME. ME does not refer to concrete properties of the speaker, such as spatio-temporal properties, but rather to identificational properties. These identificational properties of ME are also present in HERE and NOW: HERE refers to the place identified by the speaker ME, and NOW also makes a reference to the speaker, since it refers to the moment of speech.[25] When I say *Jean est venu à Montréal hier,* the adjunct *à Montréal* further specifies the deictic center. But I am not saying that Montreal = ME; rather, ME is functioning as an identifier, a reference point to determine what the deictic center is. The deictic center is identified with respect to ME, but it is not ME in spatio-temporal terms. By referring only to the ME aspect of the deictic center, one creates a centering effect not on a point in space or a moment in time, but on an "abstracted" speaker, something like the point of view of the speaker (see Lamiroy 1983, 139).

Now we can see why this use of *venir* has the effects described above. First, we get an aim because of the progredience induced by the position of the infinitival phrase—but without movement, since we are not referring to spatial properties of the deictic center. Thus, as in the progredience use, since the infinitival phrase is not the end point of the B″ relation in the representation of *venir,* it induces a noneffective reference of the B″ relation. Therefore, there is an aim in the sentence. However, since we are not considering a movement use, we have the aim of the subject to establish a relation on a "psychic" plane, as Damourette and Pichon (1911–1950, 1654) put it, namely with the ME as speaker and no more, without spatio-temporal properties—i.e., the ME as point of view. I propose that such an aim can only be the attribute of human entities, hence a constraint even stronger than the animacy constraint on progredience.

Second, since the centering is toward an entity that is abstracted from space and time, it is perceived as spontaneous; the sentences often express something that is unexpected (cf. Lamiroy 1983, 137).

Third, since the orientation is toward the ME with *venir,* we expect it to be similar to, but slightly different from, the involvement use of *aller:* "With auxiliary *venir,* one intervenes more in the expression, one suggests that one is somewhat personally touched by the disturbing action . . ." (Damourette and Pichon (1911–1950: #1667).[26] It this more personal involvement that distinguishes *venir* from *aller,* in this use.

3.1.1.8 USE 8 OF VENIR: AVAILABILITY

Venir can also be used to say that something is available.

(55)   Cette robe vient en trois tailles.
        That dress comes in three sizes.

Again what we have here is a variation in use due to a choice in how reference is being made. Not only is reference to the deictic center restricted to nonspatio-temporal ME, but additionally, the reference is generic. There is nothing very extraordinary about this, since other pronouns that refer to interlocutors like *nous/we* and *tu/vous/you* are also easily used generically. So (55) expresses that *cette robe* is oriented toward a generic nonspatio-temporal deictic center.

3.1.1.9 USE 9 OF VENIR: MEASURE, COMPARISON

Finally, *venir* can be used to compare or measure two elements with respect to each other.

(56)   Marie lui vient à l'épaule.
        Marie to-him comes to the shoulder.
        Marie comes to his shoulder.

This is really a subcase of extension. In addition to being a *venir* construction, this is also a case of inalienable possession, whereby the clitic *lui* is the "possessor" of the shoulder. Guéron (1991, p. 9) argues that in such constructions, "[T]he human body is interpreted as a geographic place where an event takes place which can be identified as the transition from one spatial configuration to another. . . . In order for the body to be interpretable as a place, the spatial transition can only affect a part of that same body: any other Theme would go beyond the limits of the place during its trajectory."[27] In other words, the body of the referent of the dative clitic defines the space within which the relation expressed by the verb will hold. This accounts for the contrast in (57), where (b) is impossible because *le fils* is out of bounds, beyond the limits of the body of *lui*.

(57)a.   Elle lui pince les fesses.
         She to-him pinches the buttocks.
         She pinches his buttocks.
    b. *Elle lui pince le fils.
         She to-him pinches the son.
         She pinches his son.

Coming back to (56), since it is an inalienable possession construction, the event must take place within the limits of the body of *lui*. If we put this together with the meaning of *venir*, then (56) expresses that "*Elle* is oriented toward o, which the *à*-adjunct further specifies as being *l'épaule*, all of this being delimited by the body of *lui*." Given the additional conceptual factor that, in the unmarked case, one pictures the human body in an upright position, with an orientation from the feet upward, we get the measure use of (56) (assuming a prototypical referent for *Marie*). In short, here we have a subcase of extension limited to a body because of inalienable possession.

3.1.1.10 CONCLUSION ON THE USES OF VENIR

In conclusion, *venir* is a verb with multiple uses, but only one meaning. Several factors combine to derive the various uses of *venir*, and the possible combinations of these factors constrain the situations that *venir* sentences can express. These factors are of different types. They may be strictly grammatical, like the tree representation of the meaning of *venir* in (2), with the orientation expressed in that tree, as well as the position of the elements in the structure, like the infinitival phrase in x_2 that induces the aim of the progredience use (27). They may also be reference factors, which bridge the relation between Grammar and general cognition, so that whether an element is referred to as an individual or a concept (28), as effective or noneffective (21) will affect the possible interpretations. Extralinguistic cognitive factors are also at play, such as the nature of an argument—whether it is a spatial, temporal, or animate entity. This affects how the element can realize the orientation and the two-point relation expressed by *venir*: as movement, extension, and so on. It is extralinguistic because, as we saw, otherwise the size of clouds would have to be a factor in the Grammar (see the discussion in section 1.3). Finally, other cognitive factors are needed to compute the possible situations to which a sentence can correspond, like the factors that determine frontal orientation in space and time—(7) and (44).

3.1.2 ALLER

Aller is another verb which is classified as a verb of movement. Like *venir,* it has multiple uses, but only one meaning.

3.1.2.1 USE 1 OF ALLER: MOVEMENT

As with *venir,* movement is considered by many to be the basic use of *aller,* with other uses being derived from it.

(58)   Max va à Québec (de Montréal).
          Max goes to Quebec City (from Montreal).

Traditionally and in most Case-thematic analyses (see Fillmore 1975; Gruber 1965; Jackendoff 1972, 1990a), *go,* the English cognate of *aller,* is analyzed as having three arguments: a Theme subject, a Source *from*-phrase and a Goal *to*-phrase. In addition, *go/aller* is often contrasted with *come/venir,* the former being located with respect to the point of departure and the latter being located with respect to the point of arrival. I depart from both of these assumptions. The semantic representation that I propose for *aller* is the following:

(59)   Semantic Representation for *aller:*

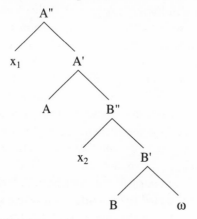

(where A and B = COPULA)

This means that in a sentence like (58), both the *à*-phrase and the *de*-phrase are adjuncts: the *de*-phrase is the same adjunct as the one we saw in some *venir* examples, and the *à*-phrase is an adjunct that further specifies the content of the constant ω. This constant ω is the antideictic center, that is, anything but the deictic center, or the complement of the deictic center. *Aller* is not opposed to *venir* as far as its orientation is concerned, since, just like *venir,* its orientation is toward a constant that can be further specified by an *à*-phrase. The difference between the two verbs lies in the nature of the constant, which is the deictic center o for *venir,* but the antideictic center ω for *aller.*[28]

All that (59) expresses is that x_2 "relates" with ω and that x_1 "relates" with this relation B″; also, x_1 is oriented toward x_2 because of the orientation properties of the tree. Additionally, I assume that x_1 binds x_2. Just as in the case of *venir,* there is no primitive in the representation (59) that expresses movement. So the question arises again: how does this representation allow for the movement use? The answer is the same as in the case of *venir:* if no specific context is given for a sentence such as (58), we draw on our shared knowledge background and attribute to Max, Québec, and Montréal proto-typical spatio-temporal references, including the fact that Max typically refers to an animate entity. Combining this extralinguistic information with the linking that the Grammar provides between the syntax of (58) and the semantic representation of *aller* in (59), we get something like (60)

(60)   The animate spatio-temporal entity *Max* is oriented toward his
            being at the spatio-temporal entity ω, which is further specified as

being the spatio-temporal entity *Québec;* the tail end of the orientation is at the spatio-temporal entity *Montréal.*

Because of the nature of the three actants in (58) in the prototypical case, the sentence takes place in a spatial domain. Movement is the most likely way in which the animate spatio-temporal entity MAX could establish the relation schematized in (60), given the normal size of a human being and the distance between these two cities. Here again, movement is deduced from prototypical, extralinguistic properties of the actants in the sentence.

There is a contrast between the movement use of *venir* and that of *aller:* the constant o need not be further specified (61a), but the constant ω must be specified by an adjunct (61b):

(61)a.   Max vient.
          Max is coming.
    b.   #Max va.
          Max is going.

As Carter (1988, 296) noted, there is a feeling of incompleteness in a sentence like (61b). It comes from the lack of information about the antideictic center; the only thing we know is that it is not "here." Such imprecision seems to be ruled out (presumably by discourse constraints) in spatio-temporal uses of *aller.* We will see that we must not make a sweeping generalization about *aller,* however, because some of its uses allow such imprecision (see the evaluative use of *aller* below).

3.1.2.2 USE 2 OF ALLER: PROGREDIENCE

We already saw in the discussion of progredience in 3.1.1.2 that *aller* is one of the "movement" verbs that appear in this construction. Thus, if we have an infinitival complement linked to the x_2 position of the semantic representation of *aller* in (59), and if *aller* has a movement interpretation, we get progredience as in (62).

(62)   Elle va courir un marathon à Montréal.
        She is going to run a marathon in Montreal.

Sentences like this, with a bare infinitival phrase complement of *aller,* are ambiguous between a progredience use and a temporal use. The two uses can be distinguished by the specific constraints that apply to each of them. We have already seen that the progredience use obeys an animacy constraint on the subject and a stage-level predicate constraint on the infinitival phrase. If either of these constraints is violated, only the temporal use is possible:

(63)   Les flammes vont détruire les vieux journaux. [temporal only]
         The flames go to-destroy the old newspapers.
         The flames are going to destroy the old newspapers.

(64)   Jean va ressembler à son frère. [temporal only]
         Jean goes to-look-like his brother.
         Jean is going to look like his brother.

The account of the constraints on progredience is the same as in the case of *venir* (see section 3.1.1.2). The infinitival phrase in the position of x_2 in (59) induces a noneffective reference of the B″ relation. Since we are considering a movement use here, only an animate subject is compatible with both the noneffective reference and the movement aspects of the sentence. As for individual-level predicates, they cannot be noneffective by definition.

3.1.2.3 USE 3 OF ALLER: EXTENSION

If movement is deduced from prototypical, extralinguistic properties of the actants in the sentence, then if we substitute elements with different spatio-temporal properties for one of the actants, we predict that the movement reading might not arise anymore. We saw in section 1.3 that this is indeed the case:

(65)a.   Jean va de Montréal à Québec.
         Jean goes/is going from Montréal to Québec.
    b.   Cette route va de Montréal à Québec.
         That road goes from Montréal to Québec.
    c.   Ce nuage va de Montréal à Longueuil.
         That cloud goes/is going from Montreal to Longueuil.

In (a), if *Jean* is not the prototypical human expected—but rather a giant, or a laser beam, for example, or if Québec and Montréal do not have the expected distance between them, as in the case of maps—the sentence is not used to express movement, but rather extension. In (b), extension is the unmarked interpretation, given the physical properties of *cette route*. As for (c), reference is made to a movement situation or an extension situation, depending on the size of the cloud. None of the determining factors for these differences are grammatical factors here.

3.1.2.4 USE 4 OF ALLER: EXPRESSING TIME

The verb *aller* also has a temporal use, which is often referred to as "near future":

(66)   Elle va courir le marathon (demain).
         She is-going to-run the marathon (tomorrow).

However, "near future" is not really an appropriate term. "Near" is not adequate because the temporal use of *aller* is not nearer to the present than the future, and "future" misses important differences between the temporal use of *aller* and the morphologically marked future tense.

Consider first "nearness." Just as Damourette and Pichon showed that the "recent past" use of *venir* is not really more recent than a 'passé composé' (see (49) above), it can be shown that temporal *aller* is no nearer to the present than the future tense. Thus, in (67), *va mourir* 'is-going to-die' is not nearer to the present than *aura l'apparence* 'will-have the appearance' but, in fact, more remote.

(67)   Il aura l'apparence d'un homme qui va mourir.
         He will-have the appearance of a man who is-going to-die.

The crucial notion is not nearness to the present but rather relevance to the present, as was the case for the "recent past" use of *venir.* The term "near" is thus inappropriate.

Second, a close comparison of temporal *aller* with the future tense reveals important differences in their uses. Damourette and Pichon (1911–1950: #1768) discuss two examples in which the future tense cannot replace temporal *aller.* First, the future tense in (68b) is odd, since all men are mortal; hence, the sentence is conversationally uninformative.

(68)a.   Il avait l'apparence d'un homme qui va mourir. (Maupassant, *Les soeurs Rondoli*)
         He had the appearance of a man who is-going to-die.
   b.   #Il avait l'apparence d'un homme qui mourra.
         He had the appearance of a man who will-die.

On the other hand, (68a) is used to indicate that the man shows some evidence that his death is imminent. A similar contrast is found in (69):

(69)a.   Quand tu vas te marier . . .
         When you go yourself marry . . .
         When you will get married . . .
   b.   Quand tu te marieras . . .
         *When you yourself marry-*FUTURE . . .
         When you will get married . . .

As Damourette and Pichon observe, (69a) could be used in talking to a young person who is already engaged, whereas it would be odd to use it in talking to someone with no wedding in sight. On the other hand, (69b) would be used in exactly the opposite contexts.

We can add the following contrast to their observations:

(70)a.　Jean ressemblera à son frère.
　　　　Jean will look like his brother.
　　b.　Jean va ressembler à son frère.
　　　　Jean is going to look like his brother.

(70a) is a bit odd. It expresses a kind of foresight, as if the speaker had some power to make Jean look like his brother and could throw a spell on Jean, for example. On the other hand, (70b) conveys that the speaker has some evidence NOW in Jean's looks that he will look like his brother. A similar contrast holds in (71):

(71)a.　Jean demandera la nationalité française.
　　　　Jean will ask for French nationality.
　　b.　Jean va demander la nationalité française.
　　　　Jean is going to ask for French nationality.

In (71a), the speaker is ordering or strongly suggesting that Jean ask for French citizenship. On the other hand, (71b) is a statement of a fact based on current evidence.

In all four sets of examples, temporal *aller* indicates that the present situation is somehow relevant to the future, which is not the case with the morphologically marked future. This then shows that the terms 'near' and 'future' are inappropriate as labels for this use of *aller.* We saw in section 3.1.2.2 that there are theory-internal reasons to assume that the bare infinitival phrase complement of *aller* must be in the position of x_2 in (59). We have just seen that an infinitival phrase in this position, with a movement use of *aller,* shows progredience effects. Given the syntax of the construction and the evidence for the relevance of the present that we found in temporal *aller* but not in the morphologically marked future, it seems that "temporal progredience" is a better term than "near future" to refer to temporal *aller.*

Why does temporal *aller* refer to a future, as opposed to a past, event? It depends on both grammatical and cognitive factors, as a close look at the semantic structure of a sentence like (66) reveals.

(72)   Semantic structure of *Elle va courir le marathon:*

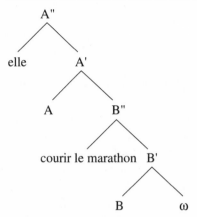

In (72), ω is predicated of *courir le marathon,* and *elle* is oriented toward that relation. In other words, *elle* is oriented toward the relation "*courir le marathon* relates with ω." In a temporal use, such as we have here, the B″ relation expresses the fact that *courir* and ω occur at the same time. Where in time could that be? Since the antideictic center ω is defined relative to the deictic center o (specifically, it is the complement of o), the temporal orientation of ω will also be determined with respect to the deictic center. Since ω is not intrinsically oriented, it is given a canonical face-to-face orientation with respect to o. We already know that o is intrinsically oriented toward the future (see (44) in 3.1.1.5). If we put all this information together, we get (73):

(73)   o⇒FUTURE   (by definition (44))
          o⇒ ←ω   (derived from the definition of ω)
          courir = at the same time as ω   (from the semantic structure (72))

> *Result:* If we line up the two instances of the arrow originating from NOW so that they point in the same direction, since NOW has an intrinsic, invariable orientation, the result is that ω is in the future and, therefore, so is *courir.*

So far, our analysis shows that temporal *aller* expresses "temporal progredience" in the future. But if temporal *aller* is analyzed as temporal progredience, several questions are raised:

(i) Why is there no aim, as in the spatial progredience reading of *venir* discussed in section 3.1.1.2 and of *aller* discussed in section 3.1.2.2.

(ii) Why are the two constraints of animacy and stage-level predicate that
     hold of spatial progredience not operative here?
(iii) Why does *venir* not also have both temporal and spatial progredience?
(iv) Why are there additional constraints on the tenses with which temporal
     progredience can appear?

The answer to the first two questions lies in the fact that what causes these
effects in spatial progredience is absent from the temporal progredience use.
First, recall from the discussion of *venir* in 3.1.1.2 that the "aim" found in
spatial progredience comes from the predication of a very concrete property
upon a "verbal virtuality"—the predication of the spatial aspect of the deictic or antideictic center upon the infinitival phrase. This predication necessarily induces a noneffective reference for the B″ relation, and noneffective reference induces "aim." But in the temporal use of *aller,* we do not have
predication of a very concrete property upon a "verbal virtuality." The antideictic center in this use refers not to a place, but to some point in time other
than NOW. This is still predicated of the "verbal virtuality," but it is not a
concrete property. Therefore, noneffective reference is not necessarily induced, and neither is aim. This answers question (i).

Question (ii) concerns the fact that neither the animacy constraint on the
subject nor the stage-level predicate constraint on the infinitival phrase holds
for temporal progredience, as we saw in (63) and (64), repeated here as (74)
and (75).

(74)   Les flammes vont détruire les vieux journaux. [temporal only]
         The flames are going to destroy the old newspapers.

(75)   Jean va ressembler à son frère. [temporal only]
         Jean is going to look like his brother.

The subject is not animate in (74), and the infinitival phrase in (75) is an
adjunct with an individual-level predicate. Why should there be such differences between spatial and temporal progredience? Again, it is in the causes
of these effects that we will find an answer. The animacy constraint on the
subject derives from the fact that only animate entities can have an aim to
establish a relation in space. But since there is neither aim nor spatial relation
in temporal progredience, the causes of the animacy constraint are not
present.

As for the stage-level predicate constraint on the infinitival phrase, it
arises from the incompatibility of individual-level predicates with noneffective reference. Individual-level predicates express inherent, permanent prop-

erties, and they are effective by definition. As we saw in the answer to question (i), temporal progredience, contrary to spatial progredience, does not necessarily induce noneffective reference, so individual-level predicates are just as possible as stage-level predicates here.

The answer to question (iii) is that a temporal progredience reading with *venir* is blocked because of its (semantic) similarity to the simple present. A temporal progredience use of *Louis vient déjeuner* 'Louis is coming to lunch' means that Louis is oriented toward the relation "*déjeuner* relates with NOW," hence *déjeuner* is NOW. But in terms of the information provided, this is only marginally distinct from what the simple present expresses, so the simple present is used, and the temporal progredience interpretation is blocked. An exception to this kind of semantic Blocking Principle (extending Aronoff 1976) is perhaps best illustrated in the very abstract interpretation of (76), close to the involvement use of *venir*.

(76)   Ce que tu dis là vient tout changer.
        This that you say there comes all change.
        What you are saying changes everything.

The temporal interpretation of (76) is slightly different from the simple present, so temporal progredience with *venir* might not be totally excluded by blocking: it is just extremely subtle and hard to pinpoint.

The answer to question (iv) is more complex. The temporal use of *aller* has a very restricted choice of tenses: it is not compatible with the past, future, perfect, or *aller* itself:

(77)a. Jean alla courir.   [spatial progredience only]
        Jean went to run.
    b. Jean est allé courir.   [spatial progredience only]
        Jean is gone to-run.
        Jean went running.
    c. Jean ira courir.   [spatial progredience only]
        Jean will go running.
    d. Jean va aller courir.   [spatial progredience only]
        Jean is going to go running.

The two most natural tenses found with temporal *aller* are the simple present and imperfect (the latter induces a conditional reading):

(78)   Jean va/allait courir.
        Jean is-going/was-going to run. (also *running*)

Note that the NOW that is part of the definition of the deictic center o and of its complement ω must not be confused with the moment of speech S of Reichenbach (1947). NOW does not necessarily correspond to S and can be shifted with respect to S, as in (79):

(79)a.   Jean viendra/ira chez Paul. (NOW shifted to the future)
         Jean will come/will go at Paul's.
    b.   Jean vint/alla chez Paul. (NOW shifted to the past)
         Jean came/went at Paul's.

Herein lies the answer to our question: temporal progredience, which involves a centering on o or ω with a purely temporal reference, is compatible with a sentence in the simple present, where no tense shifting has taken place, if we follow Reichenbach (1947) and assume a representation as in (80a). But centering on a point defined with respect to NOW, such as o or ω, and attributing to it a purely temporal reference is not compatible with a tense that shifts the NOW from the S, such as simple past (80b), future (80c), or present perfect (80d).

(80)a.   simple present: S,R,E
    b.   simple past: E,R____S
    c.   future: S____R,E
    d.   present perfect: E____R,S

A deictic or antideictic center with a purely temporal reference cannot be shifted from S. Therefore, the only tenses available with temporal progredience are nonshifting tenses like the simple present and imperfect (78).[29]

In summary, the peculiarities of the temporal use of *aller* follow from the interaction of the lexical structure assigned to *aller,* the nature of its arguments, properties of the tense system, and cognitive factors of temporal orientation. The properties of the temporal use of *aller* again argue in favor of the abstract representation proposed for the meaning of this verb.

3.1.2.5 USE 5 OF ALLER: INVOLVEMENT

I mentioned in the discussion of the involvement use of *venir* that *aller* also has such a use, where neither space nor time are relevant, but only the identificational properties of the ME of the deictic center, in the case of *venir,* or of its complement, in the case of *aller.* This difference (deictic center versus antideictic center) between *venir* and *aller* explains the subtle difference between the sentences in (81) and the same sentences with *venir* in (82).

(81)a. Et puis, vous allez dire qu'autrefois en France tous les hommes
        étoient sodomites (Tallemant des Réaux, *Historiettes*)
        *And then, you are going to say that in the past in France all men
        were sodomites.*

   b.   Il est bien évident que ce n'est pas un médecin qui ira nier l'in-
        fluence du physique sur le moral.
        *It is quite evident that it is not a doctor who will go and deny the in-
        fluence of the physical over the moral.*

(82)a. Et puis, vous venez dire qu'autrefois en France tous les hommes
        étaient sodomites.
        *And then, you come and say that in the past in France all men were
        sodomites.*

   b.   Il est bien évident que ce n'est pas un médecin qui viendra nier
        l'influence du physique sur le moral.
        *It is quite evident that it is not a doctor who will come and deny the
        influence of the physical over the moral.*

In the (b) sentence with *viendra,* the speaker is personally involved, presented
as a witness in some sense; with *ira,* it is instead the world that is presented
as a witness. Aside from this expected nuance, the effects are the same in
both involvement uses, and both uses are restricted to human subjects, due
to the "psychic" domain in which the relation takes place.

3.1.2.6 USE 6 OF ALLER: ATTRIBUTIVE

Another very frequent use of *aller* is attribution, as in (83).

(83)a. Le fauteuil va là et la bibliothèque va dans le coin.
        The armchair goes there and the bookcase goes in the corner.

   b.   Le prix Nobel de chimie est allé au docteur Smaltz.
        The Nobel prize in chemistry went to doctor Smaltz.

Although it is often the case that movement will result from attribution,
it is not true that it always does, so the two uses must be distinguished, as we
can see from the exchange in (84):

(84) A: Pourquoi est-ce que le chandail est sur cette tablette?
         Why is the sweater on that shelf?

     B: Parce que c'est là qu'il va.
         Because that is where it goes.

There is no movement implied in B's utterance here. The attributive interpretation of *aller* derives from the reference of the NP in the locative phrase in

these sentences. For example, *le docteur Smaltz* in (83) does not refer to any concrete properties of Dr. Smaltz, but rather to his identificational properties. Thus, the relation expressed by *aller* takes place in a conceptual domain other than the spatio-temporal one. I have called it "attributive" because the reference involved is to identificational properties, which are attributes.

3.1.2.7 USE 7 OF ALLER: EVALUATIVE

Some evaluative uses of *aller* are shown in (85), below.

(85)a.   Ça va bien/mal.
         It's going well/not well or *I'm well/not well* or *It fits well/badly.*
   b.   Jean va bien/mal.
         Jean is well/not well or *Jean fits in well.*
   c.   Cette voiture va bien.
         That car runs well or marginally *That car fits in well.*
   d.   La vente est bien allée jusqu'au 10 juin.
         The sale went well until June 10.
         (if *bien* has scope over the PP, *The sale indeed went on until June 10*).
   e.   Cette robe va bien à Marie.
         That dress fits Mary well or *That dress is indeed for Mary.*

Such evaluative uses of *aller* are extremely frequent. As with the other uses, the evaluative use of *aller* arises from the combination of several factors: the semantic structure of *aller,* the nature of the arguments and how they are referred to, the scope of the adverbs *bien* and *mal,* and what we know about the situation in which the sentence is uttered.

To illustrate, consider first sentence (85e). Setting aside the adverb, *aller* establishes a relation between *cette robe* and the relation $[x_2$ relates with $\omega]$, where x_2 is bound by *cette robe* and ω is further specified to be *Marie.* The adverb modifies the relation established by *aller.* Modification by *bien* is ambiguous in French: it can either confirm that the relation is the right one or mean that the relation is a good one according to the expectations of the speaker. The first case results in an attributive use of *aller* (The dress is indeed for Mary), whereas the second case results in the evaluative use of *aller* (The dress fits Mary well). The typical situation that the evaluative use of (85e) describes is one where Mary is wearing the dress. Given what a dress is, this is the most usual way to establish any relation with a dress, good or otherwise. But this does not mean that there is a second verb *aller* that is close in meaning to English *fit;* the 'fit' meaning really depends on the argument *la robe* here. If the subject is varied, then much more subtle situations emerge, as in (86), which are not "fitting" situations:

(86)   L'agressivité ne te va pas bien du tout.
         Agressivity does not befit you well at all.

Example (d) in (85) is similar to (e), except that (d) centers on a temporal element. Due to the different modifications that are possible with *bien,* either (d) expresses that the relation between the sale and 'until June 10' was a good one—many items were sold—or (d) says that the relation between the sale and 'until June 10'—i.e., the extension of the sale—was the right one.

Contrary to the examples in (d) and (e), in (85a–c), there is no adjunct that further specifies the antideictic center. This is interesting because, in the movement use of *aller,* there is a feeling of incompleteness when ω is left unspecified (see (61) above), but there is no such feeling here. Why should there be such a contrast between the movement use and the evaluative use of *aller?* In (c), *aller* establishes a relation between *cette voiture* and the relation $[x_2$ relates with ω], where x_2 is bound by *cette voiture* and *bien* tells us that the relation is a good one. Since ω is unspecified, the sentence tells us that the car establishes a good relation with everything or anything that is not the deictic center. What the car relates to will be determined by the situation. The sentence could be used when there is a good relation between the car and its unspecified driver—it drives well—where ω refers to the driver. Or there could be a good relation between the car and the race—the car is doing well in the race—where ω refers to the race.[30]

Whatever the subject, our shared background knowledge will tell us what counts as an element with which a relevant relation could be established. If the sentence is *Ce crayon va bien* 'This pencil writes well,' the unspecified user of the pencil is the most likely element (although not the only one). In other cases, it is very hard to know what the prototypical situation would be. For example, if I say *Le petit arbre va mieux* 'The small tree is better,' I could be referring to the health of the tree, or to some landscape I am working on, or to a drawing, or a set for a play.

On the whole, even if there are many choices, the possibilities here are fairly constrained compared to a movement use of *aller.* In a spatio-temporal use with no PP adjunct to specify the ω, as in #*Jean va,* there are simply too many possibilities, and the sentence is so uninformative that it is rejected by conversational conventions. On the other hand, in an evaluative use like (85b) *Jean va bien* 'John is well,' the possibilities are more restricted; it must be something about John that is able to "va bien." Furthermore, the relevant element can fairly easily be extracted from the context: health is often said to be the prototypical element here, although I think that when *Jean va bien* is used to answer a question like *Comment va Jean?* 'How is John?,' it is his life in general that is referred to, of which health is but one aspect. The good relation Jean has could also be with respect to a social group or a certain task he has to accomplish.

Sentences like (85a) introduce the additional problem of determining the reference of *ça*. In general, *ça* is used as a demonstrative pronoun as in *Donnez-moi ça* 'Give me that.' In (85a), *Ça va bien* 'It's going well,' *ça* does not deviate substantially from that general demonstrative use, except that its reference is much broader. If someone bends over my shoulder and asks *Comment ça va?* and I answer *Ça va bien, ça* refers to the activity I am engaged in, such as repairing a car, or painting a picture, or writing a book. In a situation where there is no activity that is prominent in the context, *ça* refers to the general activity I am engaged in, which is that of living, and the relevant relation could be established with things like my health, my job situation, or my family situation.

Note that *bien* is unmarked and *mal* is marked in the evaluative use. Thus, (87a) is less informative than (87b):

(87)a.   Ça va aussi bien que ça allait hier.
          It's going as well as it went yesterday or *I'm as well as I was yester-*
          day or *It fits as well as it did yesterday.*
     b.   Ça va aussi mal que ça allait hier.
          It's going as badly as it went yesterday or *I'm as not well as I was*
          yesterday or *It fits as badly as it did yesterday.*

In fact, (87a) could be used in a situation where both today's situation and yesterday's are not very good, whereas it would be odd to use (87b) if either situation was good. Given the unmarked status of *bien,* it comes as no surprise that it can be omitted in contexts where its meaning can be inferred.

(88) A: Ça va?
          It goes?
          Are you OK? or How are you?
     B: Ça va. Et vous?
          It goes. And you?
          I'm fine. And yourself?

An analysis based on the simple semantic representation of *aller* that I propose in (59) can account for the kind of variation in use discussed in this section. However, a sentence like (89) appears to be a counterexample to the claim that the representation of *aller* crucially includes the antideictic center ω and that the *à*-phrase is an adjunct that further specifies the content of ω.

(89)   Ce chapeau me va bien.
         That hat fits me well.

It should be impossible for a first person pronoun to correspond to the antideictic center. But a closer look at the sentence shows that, in fact, it supports my analysis. In (89), "I," the speaker, am evaluating myself "from outside" as a second instance of myself; I do not enter a self-to-self relation, but a self-to-other relation, seeing myself as other. Assuming, as is natural, that the deictic center is defined relative to the internal self, we then predict that any first person pronoun related to the antideictic center will obligatorily refer to a self-as-other, to a self as if from the exterior. This is what takes place in (89).

3.1.2.8 CONCLUSION ON THE USES OF ALLER

Damourette and Pichon (1911–1950: #1655) observe that there are uses of *aller* that are intermediate between a movement, temporal or involvement use. For example, they discuss (90), which hovers between a temporal and an involvement use:

(90)   Tu sais pourtant que vous couriez tous après ce garçon.—Voyons,
         père, tu ne *vas pas le défendre* (François Mauriac. Le noeud de
         vipère.)
         You know though that you all ran after that boy.—Come on, father,
         you are not going to defend him

This example illustrates part of the general problem of reference. When no context is given, it is very difficult to determine what aspect of an argument the speaker is referring to. For example, in (90), is it the temporal aspect of the (anti-) deictic center or its ME-identificational properties? Can one refer to both at the same time? In very many cases, we simply do not have enough information to answer the first question.

For Damourette and Pichon, each of these three uses of *aller* is "a specialization of its general possibilities." I do not agree with this assumption; we ought to determine what allows these uses. The answer for *aller*, just as for *venir*, seems to be that each interpretation depends on the interaction of many factors: the abstract meaning of the verb, the nature of the arguments, aspects of their referential properties, cognitive factors like those that determine orientation in space or in time, and general knowledge. The important thing is to sort out these various factors appropriately, otherwise the distinctions between the uses, as well as the links, are obscured. Moreover, the factors differ substantially in their nature. It is important to sort them out so that we do not include in the Grammar factors that do not belong there. Furthermore, understanding the various factors involved in each use will help to insure coherence in the conceptual approach. This sorting out of factors is also important for technical reasons of representability and accountability; if inappropriate primitives are included in the Grammar, the representations are likely to differ substantially from the "correct" ones and should be difficult to relate to the data in a revealing way.

To illustrate once again the difficulties that arise if the various factors are not sorted out but are introduced into the Grammar, consider the well-known phenomenon of using forms of *être* 'to be' as alternatives to forms of *aller*.

(91)a.   Jean est allé à Paris.
          Jean is gone to Paris.
          Jean went to Paris.
   b.   Jean a été à Paris.
          Jean has been to Paris.

(92)a.   Jean ira à Paris (demain).
          Jean will-go to Paris (tomorrow).
   b.   Jean sera à Paris (demain).
          Jean will-be in Paris (tomorrow).

If we analyze these sentences in thematic terms, *Jean* is a Theme-Agent, and *Paris* is a Goal in all four sentences. Is *être* now to be analyzed as a movement verb?

As I mentioned in 2.2, I assume that *être* does not correspond to the copula itself, but that it is a support for Tense when the sentence expresses only a copular relation.[31] The semantic structure for a sentence like (92b) is something like (93):

(93)

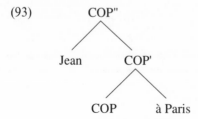

Another possibility, suggested to me by Louise Lavoie and Jacques La-marche, is to assume that COP is not a primitive of the Grammar. Rather, a lexical phrase can function as an actant or as a predicate; COP is just a useful abbreviation for "predicative use" and has no status in the Grammar. If two lexical phrases are sisters, as in (94), one of them will necessarily have to function as a predicate for the relation to be interpretable. A language spe-cific linearization parameter will indicate which is which:

(94)

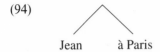

When some form of Tense is present, as in (92b), we get a semantic struc-ture, as in (95), with the consequence that *être* has to appear in syntax as a support for Tense.

(95)

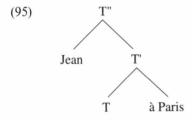

How does this representation allow a movement reading? The answer is simi-lar to the one given for *aller* and *venir* and was foreseen by Damourette and Pichon (1911–1950: #1642): "The accession of *être* to a movement use seems to have its roots in the fact that, when one has gone to some place, one necessarily has been there, in the ordinary sense of the verb *être,* for some period of time."[32] *Etre* is no more a movement verb than are *aller* or *venir.* Movement can be inferred from *Jean a été à Paris* 'Jean has been to Paris' because of the tense of *être:* if Jean was in Paris, by conversational implica-ture, he is not there anymore; and given that the prototypical referent for *Jean* is a man, the most likely way for him to no longer be in Paris is to move from Paris to some other place. The same holds for the future tense *Jean sera à Paris* 'Jean will be in Paris.' If the speaker uses a future, by conversational implicature, it is because Jean is not yet in Paris; given what he is, the most likely way for him to be in Paris at some later point in time is to move there.

If the nature of the subject changes, as in (96), for example, movement is not the only inference possible:

(96)   Le siège social de notre compagnie sera à Montréal.
         The headquarters of our company will-be in Montreal.

If the company is a new one, the headquarters are not moved to Montreal, they are established there. On the other hand, if I continue (96) with . . . *désormais* 'from now on,' one presumes that the company already existed and that a change took place and hence, that the headquarters moved.

Etre, therefore, does not express movement. In the case of *aller* and *venir,* movement is derived from two factors: the separation between the two argument positions in the semantic representation of these verbs, with one argument position binding the other, and the spatial nature of the arguments in the movement use. In the case of *être,* the separation in (91) and (92) is a temporal one—movement is not derived from a separation expressed by *être*—it does not express a separation. Rather, movement is derived from the separation in time expressed by the past and future tenses. The most likely way for Jean to be in Paris at one time and not to be in Paris at another time is to move to or from Paris between these two points in time. Given how movement is inferred in this use of *être,* we can see why it is much more difficult to infer movement in the simple present like in *Jean est à Paris:* in the present tense, there is no separation of the sort found in the past and future tenses. However, it is possible to introduce such a separation by adding a continuation like . . . *désormais* 'from now on.' The speaker then presumes that a change took place, and movement can be inferred.[33]

3.1.3 ARRIVER

The semantic structure for *arriver* is the same as the one for *venir* and *aller:*

(97)   Semantic Representation for *arriver:*

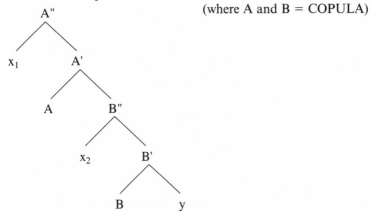

(where A and B = COPULA)

The distinguishing characteristic of *arriver* is that it has an open variable *y*, where *venir* has the constant o and *aller* has the constant ω. This means that the orientation induced by the tree structure is not directed toward a point defined in terms of deicticity, such as o and ω. We can see this contrast between the three verbs in the following example.

(98)a.   #Jean va venir à Montréal et à Melbourne.
          Jean is going to come to Montreal and to Melbourne.
   b.   #Jean va aller à Montréal et à Melbourne.
          Jean is going to go to Montreal and to Melbourne.
   c.   Jean va arriver à Montréal à 5 heures, ce qui fait qu'il n'arrivera
          pas à Melbourne avant 22 heures.
          *Jean will arrive in Montreal at 5 A.M., so that he will not arrive in
          Melbourne before 10 P.M.*

Suppose that the speaker is in Montreal, so that Montreal is related to the deictic center. (98a) is odd because both Montreal and Melbourne cannot be related to the deictic center (unless the speaker moves from one city to the other and Jean follows). On the other hand, we have the opposite situation in (98b). Montreal is assumed to be related to the deictic center in the context that is provided, yet *aller* is oriented toward the antideictic center. Montreal cannot be related to both at the same time, so the sentence is unacceptable in this context. In (98c), we see that *arriver* allows an orientation either toward the deictic center or toward some other element.

The fact that *arriver* has no specification of orientation at all with respect to the deictic center, either positive (o) or negative (ω), has a profound effect on its possible uses. Before discussing this effect, I will discuss the three elements we have seen that are localized, by definition, with respect to the speaker. These three elements, which I will refer to as deictically localized (D-LOC) elements, are the deictic center o, the antideictic center ω, and the moment of speech S. These elements establish a link between Grammar and "the real world" by referring to elements defined in terms of deicticity with respect to the speaker. What is important to the interpretation of *arriver* is the relationship between the D-LOC element S and the subject of a sentence.

An event (in a broad sense, including states) is a relationship between various actants. The sentence, on the other hand, is a relationship between an event and a point in time, a point in time that is defined with respect to the D-LOC element S. There is a conflict because the sentence requires a point, but the event is not a point, it is a relationship between "points"—the actants. The relation with a point in time, required by the sentence, can only be established by another point, so one of the points of the event, one of its actants, will have to be identified as the one that establishes a relationship with the temporal point. The subject is identified as the point of the event that is related to the temporal point of the sentence. By situating the subject with respect to the temporal point, the relationship that the subject entertains with the other actants is also situated; hence, indirectly, the event is situated in time. Because it ends up in the subject position, the highest actant in the Semantic Representation establishes the relationship with the temporal point; this is determined by the lexical specifications of the verb and the principle of Homomorphic Mapping. This actant has a privileged relationship with the D-LOC element S via the temporal point to which S is related, and therefore with the speaker, since S is defined in terms of the speaker.[34] Therefore, the choice of which actant appears as highest in a particular Semantic Representation gives rise to aspectual effects because the subject is the point of the event through which the whole event is related to time and the speaker; it is the position from which the speaker presents the event. In the case of *arriver,* there is an aspectual effect of suddenness, of spontaneity.

We have seen that in a tree structure such as the one in (97), the element x_1 is oriented toward the lowest actant. This constitutes a localization where x_1 is located with respect to a localizer. This localization, which I will refer to as grammatical localization (G-LOC), is internal to the grammar, in the sense that it does not depend on deicticity. Recall from the discussion in section 1.1.3 that logically converse relations such as above/under, in front of/behind, before/after, are never psychologically symmetric. Localizers are "stable" objects, whereas localized elements are "mutable" objects. In a localization by orientation, as in the semantic structures of the three verbs I am comparing, an element, x_1, is localized by being oriented toward a stable localizer (o, ω, y).

Suppose we make the natural assumption that localization in G-LOC is built on at least one D-LOC element in order for the sentence to refer to an event anchored in "reality." The important difference between *venir* and *aller*, on the one hand, and *arriver* on the other, is now clear. For the first two, the G-localizer of the orientation corresponds to a D-localizer, the D-LOC elements o and ω, respectively; in addition, in sentences with *venir* and *aller*, the subject is related to the D-LOC element S. In the case of *arriver*, however, the only element related to D-LOC properties is x_1, via its linking with the subject that relates to the D-LOC element S, as we just saw. Therefore, for *arriver*, it is not the G-localizer of the orientation that corresponds to a D-localizer; rather, it is the G-localized element corresponding to the subject that is related to the D-localizer S, and even then, only quite indirectly so. We can represent this schematically as follows:

	G-localized element	G-localizer	D-localizer
VENIR:	x_1	→	o	o
ALLER:	x_1	→	ω	ω
ARRIVER:	x_1	→	y	S (via x_1)

In other words, the Ground of the G-localization is a D-localizer with *venir* and *aller*, but with *arriver*, it is the Figure of the G-localization that corresponds to a D-localizer. When the Ground, the stable element, is D-localized, we may assume that it is possible to have subevents consisting of various mutable elements, Figures, that get D-localized. In that sense, a sentence built on a Ground D-localizer refers to an event with a potential for internal development; this is the case of *venir* and *aller*. On the other hand, when it is only the Figure that is D-localized, it is not possible to have mutations with respect to a Ground stabilized by D-localization, since the Ground is not D-localized and the Figure is "stabilized"; hence, the event can have no internal development. In other words, there is a G-localization waiting for a D-localizer; this is the case of *arriver*. Although a structure such as (97) expresses an orientation—and, therefore, a relation with a dynamic potential compared to a simple copular relation such as the one in *John is here*—this structure cannot express the internal development of this dynamic relation; this has for effect that the event is presented as sudden and punctual.

To illustrate this contrast in the expression of internal development, I will look at several uses of *arriver,* and briefly compare them with those of *venir* and *aller.* Some of the uses will involve movement, extension, etc. These aspects of *arriver* derive from the same combinations of factors as those discussed in relation to *venir* and *aller,* so I will not go over them here. I will instead concentrate on the differences.

3.1.3.1 USE 1 OF ARRIVER: MOVEMENT

The following sentences illustrate the difference between *arriver* and *venir* in the movement use:

(99)a.   Jean est arrivé en courant.
         Jean arrived running.
   b.   Jean est venu en courant.
         Jean came running.

In (99a), all we know is that Jean was running when he arrived. We do not know whether he was running before that because the event is expressed as sudden and global, with no internal development. In (99b), on the other hand, since *venir* expresses internal development, we know that Jean ran all the way. A similar contrast can be found in (100) (discussed by Jean-Jacques Franckel and Daniel Lebaud in a talk given at the University of Quebec in Montreal in 1992).

(100)a.   Je suis arrivé pour le voir mourir. (coincidence)
          I arrived to see him die.
    b.   Je suis venu pour le voir mourir. ("intention")
          I came to see him die.

In (100b), the internal development of the event, which leads to the witnessing of the death, gives the impression that I came with the intention of seeing him die. In contrast, if I want to convey that the only thing that matters to me is to move from a certain point and be by the side of the dying person, then I would avoid mentioning the internal development, as in (100a), where no intention is associated with the sentence, and simple temporal coincidence between the arrival and the death is all that is expressed.

3.1.3.2 USE 2 OF ARRIVER: HAPPENING

The following examples illustrate the same contrast.

(101)a.   Il lui est venu une idée/une tumeur.
          It to-him is come an idea/a tumor.
          He had an idea/got a tumor.
     b.   *Il lui est arrivé une idée/une tumeur.
          It to-him arrived an idea/a tumor.

(102)a.   *Il me vient un malheur.
          It to-me comes a misfortune.
     b.   Il m'arrive un malheur.
          It to-me arrives a misfortune.
          I'm in trouble.

A misfortune strikes suddenly (although its causes may have been developping over some time), whereas an idea or a tumor involves some kind of development. *Malheur* is thus compatible with *arriver,* whereas *idée* and *tumeur* appear with *venir.* Note also that these are impersonal constructions, which will be discussed in section 3.5.

3.1.3.3 USE 3 OF ARRIVER: CONTINUANCE

Arriver and *venir* also contrast with respect to the duration of the final state of the event.

(103)a.   André Breton est venu à Montréal en 1942.
          André Breton came to Montreal in 1942.
     b.   André Breton est arrivé à Montréal en 1942.
          André Breton arrived in Montreal in 1942.

With no further context, the impression given by (103a) is that Breton came through Montreal in 1942 and continued on, whereas (103b) implies that he stayed in Montreal and lived there for some time. The latter correlates with the fact that *arriver* expresses an event globally, without further development.

3.1.3.4 USE 4 OF ARRIVER: NO INTERNAL DEVELOPMENT

The following examples are also from Jean-Jacques Franckel and Daniel Lebaud:

(104)a.   Il faudrait appeler la police avant qu'ils n'en viennent/arrivent
          aux mains.

> *It needs to-call the police before that they of-it come/arrive to hands.*
>
> We should call the police before they come to blows.

b.   Au bout de cinq minutes, ils en sont venus/#arrivés aux mains.
After five minutes, they of-it come/arrived to hands.
After five minutes, they came to blows.

In (104b), the phrase *au bout de cinq minutes* refers to a development that is not compatible with the use of *arriver.*

3.1.3.5 USE 5 OF ARRIVER: EXISTENCE

In the following example, *arriver* has an existential reading, which is not possible with *venir.*

(105)a.   Ça arrive tous les jours.
It arrives every day.
It happens every day.

b.   *Ça vient tous les jour.   [* = for the existential reading]
It comes every day.

In the existential reading of *arriver* (105a), there is a global localization because the localizer y is identified as the set of all possibilities. This kind of holistic localization, on which the existential reading depends, is not compatible with *venir,* since, by definition, its localizer o is more restricted in scope.

Note that in the examples with *arriver* above, the variable y is often identified elliptically. This is in contrast with *aller,* even though its constant ω has almost as broad a domain of reference. So, for example, *Jeanne est arrivée* 'Jeanne arrived' is fine, but ??*Jeanne est allée* 'Jeanne went' is odd without significantly more context. It is likely that this contrast arises because a D-localization dependent on the G-localized element (the subject) allows a more freely elliptic localizer than a D-localization dependent on a G-localizer that itself supports the D-localization (unless the reference of this localizer is restricted enough to be uniquely identifiable, as in the case of the o of *venir*).

Related to (105) are the following sentences:

(106)a.   Il arrive/*vient qu'on n'y comprenne rien.
It arrives/comes that one of-it understands nothing.
It happens that one does not understand what's going on.

b.   ??Il n'arrive pas qu'on n'y comprenne rien.
It does not happen that one doesn't understand.

    c.   N'arrive-t-il pas qu'on n'y comprenne rien?
          Doesn't it happen that one doesn't understand?

The effect of combining the existential reading and the impersonal construction is that the event described by the embedded clause *qu'on n'y comprenne rien* is felt to be possible, but its D-localization cannot be predicted. Thus, we can continue (105a) with *je vais vous en donner trois exemples* 'I'll give you three examples,' but as a continuation of (106a), it is very odd. We cannot predict the D-localization because the G-localizer in the semantic representation is not linked to a D-localizer. In an impersonal construction such as (106a), the object *qu'on n'y comprenne rien* is linked to the position of x_2 in the semantic representation of *arriver,* and the impersonal *il* is linked to x_1. The subject *il* is related to the D-LOC elements, as are all subjects, but being the "ugly object" that it is (as Lauri Karttunnen refers to it), the localization of the event is still unpredictable.

Note, finally, that, as observed by Jean-Jacques Franckel and Daniel Lebaud (personal communication), negating the sentence, as in (106b), is odd because the absence (negation) of an unpredictable localization is uninterpretable. A rhetorical question of that negation, as in (106c), restores acceptability of the sentence because it implies the existence of instances of the unpredictable localization.

3.1.3.6 Use 6 of Arriver: Expectation and Accessibility

Arriver and *venir* also differ with respect to what is implied about the subject.

(107)a.   Jeanne n'arrive pas.
          Jeanne does not arrive.
    b.   Jeanne ne vient pas.
          Jeanne does not come.

The difference between (a) and (b) is as expected. Example (a), with *arriver,* is not localized, whereas (b), with *venir,* is. In (107a), we expect Jeanne, but we do not know where she is. The fact that *arriver* is negated tells us that Jeanne is not localized, that her localization has not (yet) taken place. In (107b), on the other hand, we do not expect Jeanne, and we (might) know where she is. The localization in which Jeanne is oriented toward the deictic center is negated.

There is also an interesting contrast when the sentences are not negated. Imagine a scene where I am at the window looking at Jeanne walking up the driveway. It would be fine for me to say (108a), but odd to say (108b).

(108)a.   Jeanne arrive.
   b. #Jeanne vient.

The crucial factor is "accessibility": if I see Jeanne coming, if she is accessible to my sight, then I must use *arriver,* as in (a), not *venir.* Conversely, if the newcomer is not accessible to me, I cannot use *arriver* and must use *venir.* We see this in (109), where some sign (a sound, a shadow) tells the speaker that someone is coming, although that person cannot be seen, and is thus not accessible:

(109)a.   Attention, on vient!
           Careful, someone is coming!
   b. #Attention, on arrive!
           Careful, someone is arriving!

This contrast again ties in with the fact that D-localization is handled differently with these two verbs. With *arriver,* the D-localization is based only on the subject, hence the subject is presumably accessible. With *venir,* the D-localization is based on the localizer, so by conversational implicature, the subject is not accessible.

3.1.3.7 USE 7 OF ARRIVER: STATIVITY

Arriver differs from both *aller* and *venir* in that a sentence like (110a) can have either an active or a stative reading, whereas in (110b and c), both *aller* and *venir* have only an active reading.

(110)a.   Jean est arrivé.
           Jean "is arrived" or *Jean has arrived.*
   b.   Jean est venu ici.
           Jean has come here.
   c.   Jean est allé là.
           Jean has gone there.

   Contexts are provided in (111) that make the contrast between the two readings of *arriver* clearer:

(111)a.   Jean est arrivé en coup de vent. (active use)
           Jean is arrived in a gust of wind.
           Jean dashed in.
   b.   Jean est arrivé depuis hier. (stative use)
           Jean is here since yesterday.
           Jean has been here since yesterday.

In section 3.4, I compare the six verbs studied in this chapter with respect to this nonactive use of the participle construction and conclude that this property correlates with the property of having a G-localizer that is not a D-localizer.

3.1.3.8 USE 8 OF ARRIVER: INCOMPATIBILITY WITH THE ORIGIN USE

The oddness of *arriver* with an origin use is illustrated below in (112b).

(112)a.   Mes yeux bleus me viennent de ma mère.
        My blue eyes come from my mother.
    b. #Mes yeux bleus m'arrivent de ma mère.
        My blue eyes arrive from my mother.

This oddness is probably due to the fact that the development of the event with *arriver* is perceived as sudden and spontaneous; this is incompatible with the lasting attribution characteristic of the origin use. Moreover, the origin use depends on a centering toward the NOW, which comes from the presence of the deictic center with *venir:* the deictic center is absent from the semantic representation of *arriver.*

3.1.3.9 SUMMARY OF ARRIVER

In contrast to the two verbs we have looked at so far, the D-localization of *arriver* is built on the G-localized element rather than on the G-localizer. This means that the G-localization expressed by *arriver* is a localization lacking a D-localizer, hence the event has no internal development and is perceived as sudden and/or punctual.

3.1.4 PARTIR

The verb *partir* is closely related to the verb *arriver.* Like *arriver,* it expresses an event with no internal development, which is sudden. However, whereas *arriver* is a sudden "being" somewhere, *partir* is a sudden "not-being" somewhere. *Partir* is not simply equivalent to the sentential negation of *arriver,* as we can see by comparing the two sentences in (113):

(113)a.   Jean n'arrive pas (à Montréal).
        Jean does not arrive/is not arriving (in Montreal).
    b.   Jean part (de Montréal).
        Jean leaves/is leaving (from Montreal).

As we saw in the discussion of (107a), with *Jean n'arrive pas* we expect Jean but we do not know where he is. The negation of *arriver* tells us that Jean is not localized, that his localization with respect to y has not (yet) taken place. On the other hand, with *Jean part,* we express that Jean has ended a localization at y to enter into a new localization relationship. This can be expressed by negating the lower part of the representation of *arriver,* which gives the following semantic representation for *partir:*

(114)   Semantic Representation for *partir:*

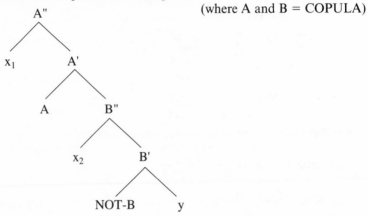

(where A and B = COPULA)

Since Jean is linked to x_1 in *Jean part,* and x_2 is bound by x_1, (114) tells us that the sentence expresses that "Jean is oriented toward his not being at y." *Partir* also shows an effect of "suddenness"; it is due, as with *arriver,* to the fact that the D-localization is not built on the G-localizer y, since y is not a D-LOC element. So although one can do things that prepare for (or lead to) a departure (or arrival), the departure itself has no internal development.

Absent from the representation of the meaning of *partir* is the primitive FROM; I claim that *partir* is not built on this primitive. The reason for this is that FROM marks the tail end of an axis. Although I assume that tree structures have an orientation, hence, derivatively, an axis, the tail end of this axis can be specified only by adjuncts, not by elements in the structure, since Homomorphic Mapping is violated otherwise. Thus, if one tried to express that the axis expressed by (114) had its origin in a point z by relating structure (114) with z by means of a FROM function, the result would be something like (115).

(115)

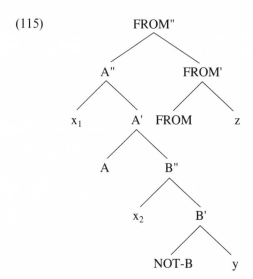

The problem with such a representation is that the orientation of the tree is not from the "source" z to A″ but rather from A″ toward z. This is the opposite of what we are trying to express.[35]

Many analyses use FROM to try to capture the "change from initial state" impression of *partir*. We cannot use such a primitive in our representation, as it provides the wrong interpretation. However, we must still account for this fact about *partir*. We must determine why we perceive *partir* as describing a change from an initial state to another state. The impression of change of state comes from the negation. *Arriver* expresses that x_1 is oriented toward its being at y, hence y is at the end point of the orientation. In the case of *partir*, x_1 is oriented toward its not being at y. If x_1 is oriented toward the absence of relation with y, in effect, toward a "nonrelation" with y, then x_1 does not already hold such a nonrelation with y (assuming that the notion of "orientation toward an A node" cannot be conceptualized as a loop, that is as "orientation toward an A node from this A node"; in other words, orientation cannot be both toward A and away from A). Therefore, x_1 must be at y at the tail end of its orientation—at its "origin"—so that it can be "not at y" at its conclusion. This is where the confusion between some instances of negation and FROM arises; the negation here implies that x_1 is at y at the tail end of the orientation, which is precisely what FROM would express. It is therefore not surprising that the primitive FROM has often been related to negation (see Carter 1988).[36]

With the semantic representation of *partir* in (114) now more firmly established on theory-internal grounds, consider the empirical consequences of the analysis. As we have now come to expect, *partir* has different uses, depending on the nature of the arguments and other factors. Sudden movements or events, like corks popping and gunshots, are expressed by *partir:*

(116)a.   Le bouchon est parti.
          The cork is gone or *The cork popped off.*
     b.   Le coup est parti.
          The shot went off.

Partir can also be used to express other spatial relations, such as extension (117) or a starting point without extension (118):

(117)a.   Trois routes partent du village.
          Three roads leave from the village.
     b.   La ligne part du coin supérieur de la page et descend en diagonale.
          The line starts from the upper corner of the page and comes down in a diagonal.

(118)   À partir de la route, il courut.
          Starting from the road, he ran.

As we see in the following examples, the starting point expressed by *partir* can be nonspatial and quite abstract:

(119)a.   Il faut partir de cette hypothèse.
          One must start from this hypothesis.
     b.   Cela part d'un bon coeur, de bonnes intentions.
          That starts from a good heart, from good intentions.
          It comes from a good heart, from good intentions.

The starting point can also be a value on an abstract scale, such as a price scale:

(120)   Voici des robes à partir de 200 dollars.
          Here are dresses starting at 200 dollars.

Partir also has an extension use in the temporal domain. In (121), *le spectacle* is referred to as a temporal extension and *partir* refers to the starting point of that extension.

(121)   Le spectacle part mal.
         The show starts badly.
         The show is off to a bad start.

Not only the starting point, but also the change of state, can be very abstract, as in (122), where y = existence and the stain is oriented toward non-existence. Thus, the change of state would be from existence to nonexistence.

(122)a. La tache part difficilement.
         The stain leaves with-difficulty.
         The stain doesn't come out easily.
    b.   La tache n'est pas partie.
         The stain didn't come out.

The change of state may be less radical, as in the case of a motor, which changes from a state of rest to an active state:

(123)   Le moteur est parti.
         The motor started.

This example is important because it also has a stative reading, meaning something like 'The motor is gone,' so that *partir* is similar to *arriver* in this respect. The contexts in (124) make the contrast clearer:

(124)a. Jean est parti en coup de vent. (active use)
         Jean is left in a gust of wind.
         Jean dashed out.
    b.   Jean est parti depuis hier. (stative use)
         Jean has been gone since yesterday.

Partir is also different from the other verbs in this study, in that in can take *avoir* as its auxiliary and be used transitively:

(125)a. Jean a parti le bal/une rumeur.
         John started the ball rolling/the rumor.
    b.   Jean a eu maille à partir avec Odile.
         Jean has had a stitch to start with Odile.
         Jean has had a bone to pick with Odile.

However, this transitive use of *partir* is restricted to a few idiomatic expressions like these and is not productive, so I will disregard it.[37]

In the interest of space, (and readability) I will not go into the details of the computation of the uses of *partir*. But from the lexical representation of *partir,* and its interaction with the factors that were presented in detail in the discussions of *venir, aller,* and *arriver,* I am confident that the reader can fill in many of the details.

3.1.5 ENTRER

The verb *entrer* has a semantic representation very similar to that of *arriver.* The difference between the two is that, in the case of *entrer,* the lower relation B″ has more content than the simple copular relation we have seen so far:

(126)   Semantic Representation for *entrer:*   (where A = COPULA)

```
            A"
           /  \
         x₁    A'
              /  \
            A     DANS"
                  /  \
                x₂    DANS'
                      /  \
                   DANS   y
```

In (126), the primitive DANS stands for the container/containee relation we saw in 1.1.3, in the discussion of the spatial use of the preposition *dans* 'in.' Recall that the container/containee relation is essentially one where the container controls the containee within boundaries determined by the container. In the case of objects that are spatial in nature, we saw that there are two factors at play:

A—The container controls the position of the containee and not vice versa.
B—The containee is included, at least partially, in the container.

Take a simple example like (127).

(127)   Le chat entre dans la boîte.
         The cat goes/is going into the box.

The sentence tells us that the cat is oriented toward "the cat having its position controlled by the box." Given the prototypical spatio-temporal properties that we assign to *le chat* and *la boîte* when no particular context is given, the most likely way for this relation to hold is for the cat to move into the box. Thus, movement is derived. Moreover, there is no internal development of the event with *entrer,* since the D-localization is not built on the localizer *y* because *y* is not a D-LOC element (see the discussion of *arriver*).

The fact that *entrer* is not restricted to three-dimensional containers indicates that the primitive DANS is part of its semantic representation. Recall that as long as an object is a potential container, regardless of how many dimensions it has, it can be an appropriate complement for *dans:* thus, containers may be three dimensional (128), two dimensional (129), or one dimensional (130).

(128)   Les bijoux sont dans la boîte.
         The jewels are in the box.

(129)   La vache est dans la prairie.
         The cow is in the prairie.

(130)   Le curé est dans la file.
         The priest is in the line.

The same possibilities are found with *entrer:*

(131)   Le chat est entré dans la boîte.
         The cat went into the box.

(132)   La vache est entrée dans la prairie.
         The cow went into the prairie.

(133)   Le curé est entré dans la file.
         The priest got into the line.

Since movement is derived from the nature of the elements that are in a relation of orientation toward a container/containee relation, we expect that changing the nature of the elements will affect the correspondence possibilities of the sentence. For example, still remaining in the realm of control within spatial boundaries by the container, we predict that the containee could extend between the two points x_1 and x_2 instead of moving: this is what we have in (134).

(134)   Cette route entre dans Québec par la porte Saint-Louis.
         This road enters Quebec City by the Saint Louis gateway.

The verb *entrer* can also have a measure use, as in (135), where no movement is expressed:

(135)   Vos quatre litres de peinture entrent trois fois dans ce contenant.
          Your four liters of paint fit three times in that container.

In fact, even a sentence like *le chat entre dans la boîte* can have a measure
use, in which the sentence expresses that the cat fits in the box.

The container/containee relation can be abstract rather than physical. For
example, the control and boundaries expressed by *entrer* in (136) are in the
domain of some social institution that has some form of power or authority
over the containee:

(136)   Jean est entré dans une maison de courtage/au collège/dans les
          forces armées.
          *Jean joined a brokerage firm/got into college/joined the armed
          forces.*

Another use of *entrer* is to express a belonging to some formula:

(137)   La crème entre dans beaucoup de recettes.
          Cream is used in many recipes.

The delimitations expressed by *entrer* can also be of a social nature:

(138)   Albertine est entrée dans une bonne famille/dans un parti poli-
          tique.
          Albertine joined a good family/a political party.

The delimitations can also be those of an activity:

(139)   Robert est entré en politique/en droit.
          Robert got into politics/into law.

There can also be control by emotional or physiological forces:

(140)   Il est entré en colère/en transe/dans le coma.
          He went into a fit/into a trance/into a coma.

Entrer can indicate a delimitedness of speech or thought:

(141)   Il est entré dans de longues explications/dans le vif du sujet.
          He went into long explanations/to the heart of the matter.

This diversity of uses is expected, since there are various ways in which a
container can control a containee within boundaries determined by the container, depending on the conceptual domain in which the relationship is established.

There is an important property that *entrer* shares with *partir* and *arriver:* its participle has either an active or stative use, as seen in (142). This property will be studied in detail in section 3.4 below.

(142)a.   Jean est entré en coup de vent. (active use)
           Jean is entered in a gust of wind.
           Jean dashed in.
   b.   Jean est entré depuis hier. (stative use)
           Jean has been in (here) since yesterday.

On the other hand, as shown in (143), *entrer* can be transitive, and this is fully productive.

(143)a.   Ils ont entré des marchandises illégalement au Brésil.
           They illegally introduced goods into Brazil.
   b.   Elle a entré les données dans l'ordinateur.
           She entered the data into the computer.

Transitivity will be the topic of section 3.2 below. As in the case of *partir,* I have left out the details of the computation of the uses of *entrer.* The methodology I propose should be fairly clear by now, and with the outline provided here, the reader should be able to fill the details.

3.1.6 SORTIR

Just as *partir* is built on the negation of the B" relation of *arriver, sortir* is built on the negation of the DANS relation of *entrer.* This assumption is motivated by the fact that, just as we saw in the comparison between *Jean n'arrive pas* 'Jean does not arrive' and *Jean part* 'Jean is leaving' in (113), *Jean est sorti* 'Jean went out' is not the sentential negation of its *entrer* counterpart *Jean n'est pas entré* 'Jean did not come in,' but rather negation at a lower level of the representation. In *Jean n'est pas entré,* we expect Jean to come in, but we do not know where he is. The negation of *entrer* tells us that Jean is not localized, that his localization with respect to container y has not (yet) taken place. On the other hand, *Jean est sorti* expresses that Jean has ended a localization delimited by container y to enter into a new localization relationship. This corresponds to the negation of the DANS relation, giving the following semantic representation for *sortir:*

(144)   Semantic Representation for *sortir:*

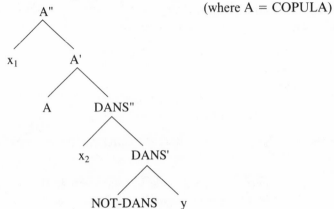

As in the case of *partir,* there is no primitive FROM in the representation of the meaning of *sortir.* Again, the impression of change of state, found in many uses of *sortir,* comes from the negation. In (144), x_1 is oriented toward not being controlled within the boundaries of *y,* in effect, toward its having a relation of noncontainment with *y.* In most cases, this orientation translates into a situation where *x* is first contained in *y* and then is not; this is why there is an impression of change of state. But neither a change of state nor even previous inclusion are always implied, as we will see below.

Another logically possible representation is one in which negation has scope only over *y,* so that the meaning of *sortir* would be represented as something like [x_1 COP [$_B x_2$ DANS NOT-y]. Besides the oddness of having a variable that is negated, there are two empirical reasons to reject this possibility. The first one has to do with the meaning of the word *dehors,* which can be roughly translated as 'outside.' Because of its meaning, *dehors* cannot function as a container; it has no boundaries within which to control a containee. We can see this by the fact that, contrary to a controller with boundaries, like *dans la cour* 'in the yard,' *dehors* cannot specify the container for *entrer:*

(145)a.   Jean est entré dans la cour.
           Jean came into the yard.
      b.   #Jean est entré dehors.
           Jean came into outside.

If *sortir* is like *entrer,* except that NOT negates only *y,* we would expect that *dehors* 'outside' should not be possible with *sortir* because *dehors* cannot be a container, and NOT-y implies that there is a container, y, that is not gone into. This is, in fact, not what we find. In (146a), if *dans la cour* specifies the content of NOT-y, we would expect (146b) to be bad because *dehors* would have to function as a container.

(146)a. Jean est sorti dans la cour.
          Jean went out into the yard.
      b. Jean est sorti dehors.
          Jean went outside.

The acceptability of (146b) is not compatible with negating the variable y, but it is compatible with the representation in (144), which states that *Jean* establishes a noncontainment relation with something that has boundaries adjacent to the referent of the adjunct modifier *dehors*. The representation of *sortir* says nothing about going into some place; there is not necessarily control by other boundaries, there is only noncontrol by y. Of course, in the "real world," almost every time people or objects escape the control of some container, they fall under the control of some other container. The one exception to this is "outside" itself, which seems to be conceptualized as having no controlling boundaries; this is not a linguistic phenomenon, but rather is dependent on our perception of the physical world.

The second argument against negating the variable comes from an observation by Boons (1985). A sentence like (147) is acceptable only in a situation where the house and the shed are connected, so that Max stepped directly into the shed. If there is no direct access between the two, and he has to walk through a yard, for example, then the sentence is odd.

(147)   Max est sorti de la maison dans la remise.
          Max went out of the house into the shed.

If it is the variable that is negated, this is unexpected because the sentence would then be supposed to mean that Max is oriented toward a container relation with something other than the tail end of the orientation. In this case, the house is the tail end of the orientation, so the sentence means that Max is oriented toward a relation with something other that the house; whether the shed is adjacent to the house or not should make no difference.

On the other hand, in the semantic representation of *sortir* in (144), x is oriented toward a state where x is not contained in y, so the axis of the orientation must cross the boundaries of y, going from inside them to outside them (assuming, as I did for *sortir*, that orientation cannot be conceptualized as a loop and, in the case of *sortir*, that the orientation cannot be both toward outside y and from outside y). As soon as x is not under the control of the boundaries of y, it is in a *sortir* state. This could explain the oddness of (147) when the two buildings are not connected—to go into the shed in such a situation involves more than escaping from the boundaries of the house. The effect may also be emphasized by the fact that *sortir* expresses an event with no internal development. Recall from the discussion of *arriver* and *partir* that for such verbs, the event is interpreted as "sudden." In the case of *sortir*, it is the break from the control by the container that is sudden.

Not only must the boundaries of the container whose control the subject is escaping and the boundaries of the "landing site" be contiguous, but if there are two containers, one inside the other, then they must share a boundary in order for the subject to "*sortir*" from both at once (Boons 1985). Thus, consider (148), where the bathroom is inside the house. The sentence is only possible if Max goes directly outside from the bathroom; otherwise there are two instances of going out.[38]

(148)   Max est sorti dehors de la salle de bain.
         Max went outside from the bathroom.

Although this "contiguity" is required in using *sortir*, there is not necessarily a passage from one place or state to another. For example, although the arm must touch the water in (149a), and the head must do so in (149b), there is no implication that there was a transition or that either the arm or head were underwater at any previous point in time.

(149)a. Son bras sort de l'eau.
         His arm sticks out of the water.
    b.   Il n'y a que sa tête qui sort de l'eau.
         There is only his head that sticks out of the water.

For example, (149a) could be used to describe a situation in which someone is keeping an arm out of the water, to keep something dry while crossing a river.

According to (144), the subject of *sortir* is oriented toward not being contained by y. Generally, as we have seen, this "noncontainment" will correspond to a situation in which the subject "escapes" from the boundaries of y. However, as we see in (149), physical movement is not necessary; resistance to a control of y will suffice. This is a form of orientation toward not being controlled, since it implies the potential for control of the subject within the boundaries of y. In order to use a verb such as *sortir*, potential control is needed by conversational implication since *sortir* expresses that x is oriented toward not being controlled within the boundaries of something; if that something had no potential control over x, it would be odd to talk about x escaping control.[39] In other words, in order for "escaping control" to be possible, at least potential control is required. More generally, the foregoing discussion indicates that, of the two factors at play in the use of DANS, both discussed in 1.1.3 and 3.1.5, the control of the position of the containee by the container is probably a property of DANS common to its uses across conceptual domains, whereas the partial inclusion of the containee is restricted to the domain of space. Therefore, noncontainment generally depends on noncontrol.

Most of the examples with *sortir* that we have seen so far involve movement. I assume that movement here derives from a combination of factors, as it did for the five previous verbs: orientation from x_1 to x_2 in the semantic representation of *sortir* and spatio-temporal properties of the elements to which the arguments refer. As expected, *sortir* also has an extension use when the nature of the arguments is appropriate, as in (150).

(150)   La route pour Montréal sort de Québec par la porte Saint-Jean.
          The road to Montreal leaves Quebec City by the Saint-Jean
          gateway.

The following are some other uses of *sortir*. In all these uses, the import of *sortir* is constant.

(151) *Escaping authority control:*
       a.   Jean est sorti de l'armée quand il a compris ce qu'on exigeait de
            lui.
            Jean left the army when he understood what was asked of him.
       b.   Jean sort de la Sorbonne.
            Jean comes out of the Sorbonne.
            Jean graduated from the Sorbonne.

(152) *Escaping emotional or physiological control:*
       Il est enfin sorti de sa rage/de sa transe/du coma.
       He finally came out of his rage/of his trance/of the coma.

(153) *Escaping delimitedness of speech or thought:*
       Vous êtes encore sorti de votre sujet, mon ami.
       You are again coming-out of your subject, my friend.
       You are departing from your subject again, my friend.

(154)   *Escaping boundaries of situations:*
   a.   Jean s'en est sorti, de ce foutu examen.
         Jean got himself out of it, that bloody exam.
   b.   Il est sorti grandi de cette situation.
         He came out taller from that situation.
         He came out of that situation a better person.

(155)   *Escaping boundaries of qualification:*
         Ça sort de l'ordinaire.
         It comes out of the ordinary.
         It is out of the ordinary.

All that varies in these examples is the nature of the arguments.

Sortir has two other interesting properties, to which we will return below: it has transitive uses (section 3.2), as we see in (156), and its participle can be used both actively and statively (section 3.4), as seen in (157).

(156)a.   Marie a sorti son cheval de l'écurie.
            Marie took her horse out of the stable.
      b.   Julie a sorti Paul de l'embarras.
            Julie pulled Paul out of embarrassment.
      c.   Les éditions Garamond vont sortir un autre livre sur l'ésotérisme.
            Garamond Publishing will put out another book on esotericism.

(157)a.   Jean est sorti en coup de vent. (active use)
            Jean dashed out.
      b.   Les tulipes sont sorties depuis hier. (stative use)
            The tulips have been out since yesterday.

Note that *sortir* is not a movement verb, even in its very "concrete" uses. Thus, in a way similar to that observed by Boons about *enfermer,* there is not necessarily movement in a sentence like *J'ai sorti le réfrigérateur de sa boîte de carton* 'I removed the refrigerator from its cardboard box.' In fact, given the nature and weight of a refrigerator, it is much more likely that the box was simply torn and the refrigerator was not moved at all.

Sortir has such a diversity of uses because there are various ways in which a containee can escape from the boundaries of a container; the nature of such boundaries varies greatly depending on the nature of the elements referred to by the arguments. What remains constant in all of these uses is the orientation of the subject toward noncontrol within boundaries that are determined by the container.

3.1.7 Strict Compositionality and Movement

I have assumed strict compositionality in the computation of the possible uses of a sentence. Whether a given sentence can refer to a certain situation depends on a combination of properties of the verb, properties of the actants that the verb relates to one another, and background knowledge about the actants and the situation being referred to. No meaning can be added to a sentence that does not come from these elements.

This position on strict compositionality has often been challenged. Before closing this section on the specific analyses of the six French verbs, I will look at a potential counterexample to strict compositionality, with respect to movement. Carter (1988) discusses the fact that the meaning of two combined lexical items may be different from the sum of their individual meanings. He illustrates this with the lexical items FLOAT and UNDER, which are neutral with respect to movement; they can be used both in static and in dynamic situations (Carter uses "static" to mean that only a three-dimensional (3-D) manner of motion is present, whereas "dynamic" implies a movement, in some direction, along a path). Strict compositionality predicts that they should be ambiguous when they are put together, and this is, indeed, the case in English. The sentence in (158) can describe either a situation where the bottle will remain afloat under the bridge (a "static" reading) or one where the bottle will come to be under the bridge by floating (a "dynamic" reading):

(158)   The bottle will float under the bridge.

But the word-for-word translation of this sentence in French can only refer to the static situation:[40]

(159)   La bouteille flottera sous le pont.

From this, it is tempting to conclude that languages can depart from strict compositionality, since the meaning "movement" can be added to the English example, but not the French one. I will argue that the contrast is much more subtle than is usually claimed and that strict compositionality, in fact, holds. In order to determine whether movement actually is added in English—and, if so, how and at what level of representation—we must look at these sentences in detail.

Consider some of the analyses of this contrast between French and English. Carter (1988, 181) proposes to account for the difference by an inference rule that, under certain circumstances, adds the meaning MOVEMENT to a sentence at the level of conceptual schemas, the rule applying in English but not in French. Talmy (1985) and Jackendoff (1990a) suggest a similar account based, instead, on correspondence rules, English having a rule that can add a GO-function to movement verbs, but such a rule lacking in French and Spanish. Emonds (1991) attributes the contrast to the simultaneous presence of path features and manner features in verb entries in English, such features being incompatible in French.[41] But the contrast is more complex than simply having movement added or not. It seems to be more of a lexical type of contrast. So it could be that FLOAT and FLOTTER are closely related verbs, but that they do not have exactly the same meaning; hence, the contrast. However, the contrast holds for a class of verbs, not just the two example verbs, FLOAT and FLOTTER. Therefore, we need a property that distinguishes the class of verbs like FLOAT from those like FLOTTER. There is such a property, I suggest, and its effects can be seen in a strict correlation between transitivity and dynamicity, which holds not only across languages but also internally to English: verbs that easily allow a dynamic reading like FLOAT have a transitive alternation, whereas more static verbs like FLOTTER have no transitive use. In view of this correlation, we must reconsider the relevant data. There are two claims that have been made about the data:

Claim 1: "Romance verbs which incorporate a feature of manner rather than of path are uniformly incompatible with directional PPs that express path and goal" (Emonds 1991, 388, after Talmy 1985).

Claim 2: "[S]imple intransitive 'manner-of-motion' verbs such as *wiggle, dance, spin, bounce,* and *jump . . .* can occur with Path-expressions —in English but not in Spanish or Japanese" (Jackendoff 1990a, 223)

Unfortunately, both claims are false, at least if French is representative of the class of languages that differ from English. The correct observations are in fact as follows:

Observation 1: French manner-of-motion verbs (MMV) are all compatible with a dynamic reading when combined with directional PPs; however, they are not compatible with a dynamic reading when combined with PPs that are neutral with respect to movement.[42]

Observation 2: English MMVs are all compatible with a dynamic reading
when combined with directional PPs; some, but not all, of
these verbs are compatible with a dynamic reading, even
when combined with PPs that are neutral with respect to
movement (the verbs that are so compatible appear to be
verbs that also have a "true" transitive use).

Let me illustrate with the sample of English MMVs used by Jackendoff
(1990a) (and their French equivalents). French MMVs prefer the static reading when combined with neutral PPs, as in (160), contrary to their English
equivalents in (161); however, the same French verbs are perfectly fine under
a dynamic reading when combined with directional PPs, as in (162), just like
their English equivalents in (163):

(160) *French MMV+neutral PP:*
    a.   Marie a flotté sous le pont.   (static)
    b.   Marie a valsé sous le lustre.   (static)

(161) *English MMV+neutral PP:*
    a.   Mary floated under the bridge.   (ambiguous)
    b.   Mary waltzed under the chandelier.   (ambiguous)

(162) *French MMV+directional PP:*
    a.   Ophélie a flotté vers/jusqu'à Hamlet.   (dynamic only)
    b.   Marie a flotté jusque dans la grotte.   (dynamic only)
    c.   Cendrillon a valsé jusqu'au prince.   (dynamic only)

(163) *English MMV+directional PP:*
    a.   Ophelia floated toward/up to Hamlet.   (dynamic only)
    b.   Mary floated as far as the cave.   (dynamic only)
    c.   Cinderella waltzed up to the prince.   (dynamic only)

We see, therefore, that English and French MMVs do not differ when
combined with directional PPs (cf. (162) and (163)): as expected under strict
compositionality, they then allow only a dynamic reading. A contrast between the two languages does exist when the PPs are neutral with respect to
movement, however. We could account for this by assuming that there is a
parameterization in the way to interpret "neutrality":

(164)a.   *The French way (restrictive interpretation):* if a PP is not specified
        for movement, movement did not occur (static only).
   b.   *The English way (loose interpretation):* if a PP is not specified for

movement, we do not know whether movement occurred (ambiguous).

But any account that includes something like (164b) fails because, contrary to what we found in (161), some English MMVs are *not* compatible with a dynamic reading when combined with neutral PPs:

(165) *Class-2 English MMV*
   a.   Mary wiggled in the bed.   (static only)
   b.   Mary wiggled up to Paul.   (dynamic only)
   c.   Mary danced under the chandelier.   (static only)
   d.   Mary danced toward Paul.   (dynamic only)

An account like (164) is also inadequate because if the verb is itself a directional verb, then even with a neutral PP, we get a dynamic situation, as expected under strict compositionality:

(166)a.   Marie est entrée dans le lac.
          'Mary entered the lake.'
     b.   La voiture est descendue en bas de la colline.
          'The car went down the hill.'

Note that the neutral PP need not be dynamic at all: it could be the static locus where the dynamic event expressed by the verb took place, as is clear in (167):

(167)   La voiture est descendue du camion en bas de la colline.
        The car came off the truck at the bottom of the hill.

Summing up the observations, strict compositionality correctly predicts the output of the combinations in (168a–c) (where N = neutral; D = directional):

(168)a.   V(N) + PP(D) = D
     b.   V(D) + PP(N) = D
     c.   V(D) + PP(D) = D
     d.   V(N) + PP(N) = N (except for a class of English MMVs =
          N or D)

We are left with (168d), which obeys strict compositionality in French and for some English MMVs (cf. (165)) but appears to violate compositionality in the FLOAT class. This is where the additional correlation noted above comes in: the English MMVs that are compatible with a dynamic reading, when combined with neutral PPs, also have a "true" transitive use. This could be a key to the contrast between French and English, as well as to the contrast between the two kinds of English MMVs—there is a relationship between transitivity and orientation. Thus, I argued above that a verb like *entrer* has a representation that comprises the structural relations in (169), where x_2 "relates" to y and x_1 "relates" to the relation B":[43]

(169)

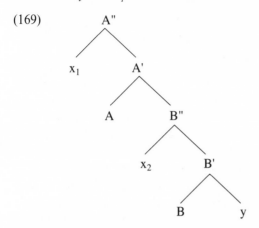

So, in a sentence like (170), *Jean* is oriented toward *dans la maison* because *Jean* is linked to x_1, which binds x_2, and x_1 is oriented toward x_2 because of the orientation properties of the tree structure.

(170)   Jean est entré dans la maison.
         Jean is entered in the house.
         Jean came in the house.

It is the presence of the two positions x_1 and x_2 in the lexical entry that gives us the orientation. As we saw in the discussion of *melt* in section 2.2.3, the availability of two argument positions also allows both positions to be filled (under certain conditions; see section 3.2 on transitivity below). When the higher position binds the lower one, we get an intransitive sentence; otherwise, the two positions are identified in syntax; hence, the transitive sentence as in (171):

(171)   Jean a entré la voiture dans le garage.
         Jean has brought the car in the garage.

Therefore, transitivity and orientation are related—a structure with two argument positions such as (169) can result in a transitive sentence, and because of the two positions, the subject is necessarily oriented in a certain direction. Now we can see the link with transitivity for some English MMVs—they have a transitive alternate, which means they have two positions available in their entries, so they are "oriented" predicates. Thus, the following MMVs, which are all compatible with a dynamic reading when combined with neutral PPs, have a transitive use:

(172) a.   Mary floated the box under the bridge.
      b.   Henry waltzed Harriet under the chandelier.
      c.   Bill bounced the ball against the board.

Since the intransitivization of these MMVs is the result of binding between two positions, the subject is always oriented in these sentences, as I argued for the French example (170): x_1, which is linked to the syntactic subject, is oriented toward x_2 because of the orientation properties of the tree in the lexical representation. It is now clear why verbs like *float, waltz,* and *bounce* differ both from other English MMVs and from French MMVs— verbs such as these three have two positions in their representations, so they are directional verbs. Therefore, it is no surprise that they behave like other directional verbs, both in French and English: given strict compositionality, that is exactly what is expected. Since FLOAT is directional, the combination FLOAT + neutral PP is not of the type (168d)—V(N) + PP(N) = N—but instead as in (168b)—V(D) + PP(N) = D.[44]

We can verify this correlation with transitivity by comparing the transitive verbs in (172) with other English MMVs that we saw in (165) do not allow a dynamic reading when combined with neutral PPs. There is a problem, since some of them do have transitive alternates:

(173) a.   Mary wiggled her nose/her tongue.
      a'. *Mary wiggled Bill into a corner.
      b.   Mary danced a waltz/a rumba.
      b'. *She danced him into a corner.

As (173) shows, these MMVs are not "true" transitives, in the sense that the second position does not allow the same type of argument as the first one, so that x_1 cannot bind x_2. The second position is restricted to inalienables in (173a) and to cognate objects in (173b). However, I have found some speakers who accept sentences like (173a') and (173b'). Interestingly, they also accepted a dynamic reading for the combination with a neutral PP, as in (165c), as anticipated by my analysis.

Some MMVs raise another problem. Like the verbs in (173), they are extremely restricted in their transitivity—their direct object can only be a measure phrase or some animal over which the subject has total control.

(174) a. John jumped the fence.
    a'. John jumped the horse/*goat over the fence.
    b. John swam the Channel.
    b'. John swam his dog/#Mary across the river.

Yet these MMVs do get a dynamic reading with neutral PPs:

(175)a. John jumped under the bridge.
    b. She swam under the bridge.

If these verbs are not "true" transitives, as defined above, they do not get their direction from the Grammar, from the orientation in the lexical structure. However, the orientation in the tree of the lexical structure is not the only means by which a verb can get to express a sense of direction, and these verbs are examples of just that. The verbs in question could be labeled Directional-Manner-of-Motion verbs. One way to encode this is by means of 3-D features, as suggested by Jackendoff in several of his works. Verbs like *jump* and *swim,* I suggest, can be directional because of their 3-D properties, that is, their representation at the 3-D level is itself directional.[45]

In summary, we can conclude from this discussion that the result of combining elements like FLOAT and UNDER does not constitute a counterargument to strict compositionality. On the contrary, compositional meaning predicts when an MMV can have a dynamic or a static interpretation, and strict compositionality holds in all the cases discussed: a sentence has a dynamic reading when either the MMV or the PP is directional; it is static only if both are nondirectional. An MMV can be directional either because of the orientation expressed by the very format of its lexical structure or because of its 3-D properties. The former holds when we have "true" transitive verbs. These observations are valid for both English and French types of languages. The difference between the two types of languages does not reside in a parameter like (164), after all, which appealed to a restrictive versus a loose interpretation of 'neutrality.' Rather, the difference resides in greater possibilities of transitivity in English compared to French. Why there should be such a difference between the two languages will be the topic of section 3.2.[46] In order to arrive at this conclusion, it is crucial to take into consideration the direction that derives from the orientation of the tree structure representations of the lexical entries presented in the previous sections.

3.1.7.1 SUMMARY OF STRICT COMPOSITIONALITY AND MOVEMENT

First, it should be clear that this study of six basic verbs of French and a few manner of motion verbs is far from exhaustive, either in the range of examples of these verbs or in extending the analysis to other verbs. For example, how the verb *study* differs from the six verbs analyzed here, I do not yet know, and much work would be needed to answer such a question. Nevertheless, a sufficient number of uses of these six verbs has been analyzed to make it clear that Grammar is concerned only with the semantics of syntax, not with the whole of conceptual structure, and hence to give a direction to lexical studies like these.

The purpose of this section was to see how the behavior of *venir, aller, arriver, partir, entrer,* and *sortir* could be explained, to look into the reasons for the diversity of uses for these verbs. The answers I provided are based on two central points: (1) Grammatical representations *exclude* situational and background knowledge; (2) Grammar *includes* tree representations and makes use of their meaning content.

This approach allows us to account for the fact that each of the six verbs is monosemic: each verb expresses the same relation in all of its uses. The single relation of each verb can be expressed, once a proper level of abstraction is reached. At that level, none of the six verbs are movement verbs. The way the abstract entities in their semantic representations are organized allows us to compute the possible uses of the verbs, as long as we also consider the nature of their arguments and the nature of the background knowledge on which the sentence depends. It is precisely because these verbs express fairly abstract relations that they can be used in domains that are far removed from the domain of space, such as time, identity, implication, origin, and so on. These uses are predicted to be possible, subject to strict constraints derived from the abstract organization of the verbs. Purging the semantic representations of situational material also offers a solution to the linking problem faced by cluttered representations, since Homomorphic Mapping is possible between these abstract semantic representations and syntactic representations.

The approach outlined here is also highly modular, not just internal to the Grammar but also in computing the possible interpretations of sentences. Very often, these interpretations are said to depend almost entirely on the verb: such predicate-centrist approaches tend to attribute to the verb properties of the utterance from which it is arbitrarily isolated. Such a conflation of meaning and use can lead to a very confusing use of paraphrasability and interchangeability. For example, the verb *être* is interchangeable with the verb *venir* in an Origin use, as in (176), and it is interchangeable with the verb *aller* in a Movement use, as in (177):

(176)a.   Jean vient de Paris.
        Jean comes from Paris.
   b.   Jean est de Paris.
        Jean is from Paris.

(177)a.   Jean est déjà allé à Paris.
        Jean has gone to Paris before.
   b.   Jean a déjà été à Paris.
        Jean has been to Paris before.

But we would not want to conclude that *être, aller,* and *venir* all have the same meaning. These examples simply show that there are contexts in which the relation that *être* establishes between actants and the relation that *venir* establishes between actants can refer to the same situation and that this also holds for *être* and *aller.* We can conclude that context is important in the computation of a situation and that, crucially, it must be kept separate from the meaning of the verb.

Instead of a predicate-centrist approach, I have, therefore, argued for a more modular approach that is based on the fact that there are many elements that combine to determine the possible uses of a sentence: properties of the verb, such as the kinds of relations it establishes between the actants, as well as the presence of particular constants; properties of the actants, such as the nature of the elements they refer to; and properties of background knowledge, such as prototypical properties of humans, for example, how they may establish a relation between two points at a certain distance, as well as factors that determine the orientation of objects in space or in time.

Such an approach is more in line with a mentalist approach to language, since it uses the cognitive knowledge shared by speakers. Thus, the analysis is not symbolic because language is not assumed to be the manipulation of abstract symbols that get their meaning via correspondences to entities and categories in the world. Consider the concept of orientation used extensively in the analyses: it is not an abstract symbol which is a representation, rather it is an organizing concept. It is part of the formalism in the tree structure but not in the real world: speakers attribute it to the world as they conceptualize the world. It does not get its meaning through correspondence to entities or categories in the real world. This is an important point: "orientation" is truly in the structure of the mind, so the tree structures that express the meaning of the six verbs studied are more like conceptual schemata than representations.

Although I believe, along with Lakoff (1987, 206), that there is no direct connection between human language and the world as it exists outside human experience and that human language is based on human concepts, I do not believe that human concepts are motivated by human experience. On the contrary, rules of conceptualization must exist before experience, in order for experience to be conceptualized. So, for example, there is no advantage in having the notion of "orientation" based on space because even to perceive space as oriented, one needs a concept of orientation. Given this assumption, we can explain abstract uses of language without recourse to metaphor and mental imagery. In this approach, those concepts that are not directly grounded in experience are, in fact, not any more abstract than spatial notions like orientation. I do not believe that all thought is grounded in experience. We make use of pre-existing structures of the mind to comprehend things, and thoughts do not grow out of experience without preliminary ground to grow on. These preexisting structures crucially determine all aspects of conceptualization. There is no need to postulate a special "imaginative capacity that allows for 'abstract' thought and takes the mind beyond what we can see and feel" (Lakoff 1987, xiv). The mind is already beyond what we can see and feel, and it organizes our perceptions according to its conceptualizing capacities.

A point that should be clear by now is that the choice of primitives is loaded. Primitives affect the form and the conception of Grammar and its place in cognition. If one assumes a mentalist approach to language, as most linguists now profess, the choice of primitives should be compatible with a mentalist view of the world. One conclusion we can draw from the study of these six verbs is that theta roles are too situational to be appropriate primitives of Grammar in a mentalist approach: they include both Grammar and background knowledge and obscure the autonomy of linguistic semantics.

Technically, the approach presented here is "transformational" because it maps a semantic tree structure into a syntactic tree structure. However, it differs from other more familiar transformational approaches. This approach is different from Generative Semantics because it crucially relies on background knowledge (so Grammar has much less to express); and it has a much more constrained transformational component, since only Homomorphic Mapping is assumed. Similarly, the approach differs from the Government and Binding analysis in what counts as semantically relevant for Grammar—the use of situational theta roles in GB being a clear example of that difference—and in the fact that homomorphy severely restricts rule formulation, as discussed in section 2.3.

The study of the six verbs presented above is an indication of the type of analysis that such an approach requires. In the remainder of this chapter, I will explore some syntactic consequences that follow from the lexical properties attributed to the six verbs.

3.2 TRANSITIVITY

A central point of the lexical analyses of section 3.1 is that the orientation in tree structures is not just formal, but plays a role in determining the semantics of lexical items. The appropriate direction of orientation was provided by binding between variables; the additional level of structure introduced thus ensures that x_1 is oriented toward x_2. We saw some evidence for these two positions in the contrast between *float* and *flotter* and also between *waltz* and *dance* (section 3.1.7). Verbs that have a transitive use are directional, in the sense that combined with a neutral PP they have a dynamic reading, whereas the others only have a static reading. There is also syntactic evidence for two positions in the semantic representation of the verbs *entrer* and *sortir,* since these verbs may be used transitively, as mentioned in 3.1.5 and 3.1.6.

(178)a. Ils ont entré des marchandises illégalement au Brésil.
         They illegally introduced goods into Brazil.

    b.   Elle a entré les données dans l'ordinateur.
         She entered the data into the computer.

(179)a. Marie a sorti son cheval de l'écurie.
         Marie took her horse out of the stable.

    b.   Julie a sorti Paul de l'embarras.
         Julie pulled Paul out of embarrassment.

    c.   Les éditions Garamond vont sortir un autre livre sur l'ésotérisme.
         Garamond publishing will put out another book on esoterism.

These verbs may be used both transitively and intransitively because there are two ways for the second variable in their semantic representations to be identified: either the second variable (x_2) is bound by the first variable (x_1), which results in the intransitive use, or the second variable (x_2) is linked to an argument in syntax, which results in the transitive use.

This account of the transitive/intransitive alternation of the verbs *entrer* and *sortir* is the same as the account of the transitive/intransitive alternation of lexical causatives, discussed in section 2.2.3. We saw, for the lexical causatives, that the analysis of the alternation based on variable binding not only accounted for the syntactic facts, but also correlated nicely with subtle nuances in meaning in the intransitive use. If the transitive/intransitive alternation of *entrer* and *sortir* is accounted for by variable binding, we expect to find similar nuances in meaning. Below, I will briefly review the discussion of the lexical causatives and show how the same subtleties of meaning are, in fact, present in the intransitive use of *entrer* and *sortir*.

Recall from section 2.2.3 that in the inchoative use of a lexical causative (*the ice melted,* for example), the subject (here, *the ice*) is understood as both the entity that undergoes the change (because it is associated with the position of x_2) and the entity responsible for the change (because it is associated with the position of x_1); the ice (or, at least, some property of it) is responsible for its own melting. To repeat van Oosten's (1977, 68) observation, "[P]roperties of the patient-subject bear responsibility for the action of the predicate in a way that properties of the agent subject normally do."

We saw further support for the binding account in the contrast, in French, between such inchoative constructions and middle constructions with the clitic *se.* The subject in the inchoative is an active participant, as we just saw, whereas the subject of the reflexive middle is a passive participant. Recall Labelle's (1989, 10) observation that "[t]he intransitive construction in French is used when the entity in subject position has properties that are sufficient for bringing about the process, whereas the reflexive construction is used when the properties of the entity in subject position are insufficient for bringing about the process." I can illustrate this point with the examples in (180), where Jeanne blushes because of properties intrinsic to her, whereas the handkerchief requires an external actualizer to cause it to redden.

(180) a. Jeanne rougit.
          Jeanne reddened.
          Jeanne blushed.
     b. *Il vit le mouchoir rougir soudain.
          He saw the handkerchief redden suddenly.

c.   Il vit le mouchoir se rougir soudain.
     He saw the handkerchief self redden suddenly.

I accounted for this distinction by assuming the schema [x_1 "actualizes" [x_2 PRED]] for these constructions. In the intransitive construction, x_1 is something inherent to x that is responsible for, controls, allows [x, PRED].[47] On the other hand, the clitic *se* discharges the variable corresponding to the external argument so that the higher argument is not identified by linking to an argument in syntax. Furthermore, it does not bind the lower argument. The subject of the *se* middle construction is thus "inactive," and the construction is oriented only toward the end of the process.

Now if we consider the intransitive use of *entrer* and *sortir*, which I also accounted for by variable binding, we find similar effects. Ruwet (1991, 292) notes that the first observation about inchoatives holds of the intransitive use of *entrer* and *sortir* (an observation that he attributes to Jean-Paul Boons): "[T]he animate subject of *partir* 'leave', *entrer* 'enter', etc., is in a sense both an 'agent' and a 'theme': it both originates and undergoes the process denoted by the verb and is in control of the process from beginning to end" (see also Ruwet 1991, 259, note 33). In fact, this point about animate subjects holds of the intransitive use of all six verbs studied here, since they all involve binding. As for the distinction between intransitives and middle constructions with clitic *se*, it also holds of *entrer* and *sortir*, as is well illustrated by the sentences in (181):

(181)a.   Le fusil se sort facilement de l'armoire avec cette clé.
          The gun self comes-out easily of the cupboard with this key.
          One can easily take the gun out of the cupboard with this key.
     b.   *Le fusil sort facilement de l'armoire avec cette clé.
          The gun comes-out easily of the cupboard with this key.

In (181a), the presence of *se* indicates that there is an unmentioned external argument that acts on the gun. The manner modifiers *facilement* and *avec cette clé* are possible because they are of a type that requires a form of manipulation, and the unmentioned external argument is of a nature that is compatible with this. On the other hand, intransitivity in (181b) arises from variable binding; 'le fusil' both undergoes the change (because it is associated with x_2) and is responsible for the change (because it is associated with x_1). The manner modifiers are not acceptable, since there is no unmentioned external argument and 'le fusil' is not compatible with the manipulation implied by the modifiers (*Le fusil sort de l'armoire* is acceptable and simply means 'The gun is sticking out of the cupboard').

There is therefore good evidence, both from syntactic constructions and interpretations, for the binding analysis of the six verbs discussed in section 3.1. However, this analysis raises a problem: if all six verbs involve two positions, why do only two of them have transitive uses? As we can see in (182), *aller, venir, arriver,* and *partir* cannot be transitive (except for a handful of exceptions in the case of *partir,* as shown in (125) above).

(182)a. *Jean a allé/venu/arrivé Marie.
      Jean has gone/come/arrived Marie.
   b. *Jean a parti son fusil.
      Jean has gone-off his gun.

Under this analysis, the transitive reading is possible when x_1 does not bind x_2. Since these verbs cannot be transitive, there must be something in their semantic representations that forces the binding of x_2 by x_1, thus forcing them to be intransitive. Let us compare the structures of the six verbs in question:

(183)a. *Venir:* $[x_1 \text{ COP } [x_2 \text{ COP } o]$
   b. Aller: $[x_1 \text{ COP } [x_2 \text{ COP } \omega]$
   c. Arriver: $[x_1 \text{ COP } [x_2 \text{ COP } y]$
   d. Partir: $[x_1 \text{ COP } [x_2 \text{ NOT-COP } y]$
   e. Entrer: $[x_1 \text{ COP } [x_2 \text{ DANS } y]$
   f. Sortir: $[x_1 \text{ COP } [x_2 \text{ NOT-DANS } y]$

There is an obvious difference between the first four verbs and the last two verbs. In the case of the first four verbs, the higher and the lower relations involve the same functor COP with maximally simple semantics. The variables x_1 and x_2 may have the same value, and binding can take place. On the other hand, in the case of the last two verbs, although the higher relation also involves the maximally simple functor COP, and the same value for the variables x_1 and x_2 is also possible, the lower relation is different. In both cases, the lower relation involves the more complex functor DANS. As a result, the two classes of verbs differ in their potential for recoverability of content. For the first four verbs, the content of x_2 can be recovered from x_1, and the content of the lower relation R_2 can be recovered from the higher relation R_1, since both R_1 and R_2 are COP; so this is a case of double recoverability. For the last two verbs, however, only the content of x_2 can be recovered from x_1. The content of R_2 (DANS) is different from the content of R_1 (COP), so it cannot be recovered from it; this is a case of single recoverability.

I will show that this difference in recoverability correlates with the difference in transitivity. In the case of double recoverability, the lower variable always satisfies Full Identification without having to resort to linking with a direct object; by general considerations of economy, these verbs are never transitive. On the other hand, in the case of single recoverability, what Full Identification requires of the lower variable is not always fully recoverable, so linking with a direct object is possible; hence a transitive use.

We can schematize the content common to the semantic representations of the six verbs being discussed as in (184), where R stands for a predicative relation.

(184) $[x_1 \; R_1 \; [x_2 \; R_2]]$

In the case of double recoverability, R_1 and R_2 are both COP (183a–d). The head of the corresponding syntactic structure is therefore the result of chunking COP_1 and COP_2; we can assume that the result of this chunking cannot be distinguished from COP at the level of syntax.[48] Additionally, x_2 is bound by x_1. The fact that binding is obligatory in this case may be traceable to the fact that the two relations involved are COP relations. We can assume that an element that can have the COP_2 relation can also have the more general COP_1 relation. This means that x_2 can always be identified by x_1 by binding, without an additional element to which x_2 is linked; by considerations of economy, binding is obligatory. The schema of the content common to the semantic representations of double recoverability verbs, after chunking and binding, is as in (185).

(185)   *Conflation of Double Recoverability:* $[x_1 \; COP_1 \; [x_2 \; COP_2]] \Leftrightarrow [x_1 \; COP]$

This schema is a conflation of schema (184), conflation being an analogue of chunking that operates on schemas rather than on tree structures.

In the case of single recoverability, R_1 and R_2 are not identical, but rather COP and DANS (183e and f). The head of the corresponding syntactic structure is therefore the result of chunking COP and DANS. Additionally, x_2 can, but need not, be bound by x_1. If there is binding, the schema of the content common to the semantic representations of the two single recoverability verbs *entrer* and *sortir,* after chunking, is as in (186).

(186) *Conflation of Single Recoverability:* $[x_1 \; COP \; [x_2 \; DANS]] \Leftrightarrow [x_1 \; COP + DANS]$

The principle of Full Identification states that the presence and content of every element in the semantic representation of a sentence must be recoverable from its morphosyntactic elements. So, for example, something not identified by chunking or binding will have to be linked to a morphosyntactic element. In the case of single recoverability, schematically represented as (186), the presence of the lower variable of the semantic representation is "detectable" in syntax because the head verb transmits to syntax lexical features that indicate two different relations are involved, hence two arguments. Moreover, this detectability is enhanced by the fact that binding in the semantic representation is not obligatory. So linking of the lower variable is a possibility, hence transitivity is possible. But with double recoverability, no indication remains in syntax that two relations are involved, since the chunking of COP_1 and COP_2 cannot be distinguished from COP, at that level. Moreover, binding is obligatory. So the presence of the variable x_2 is completely obliterated. Everything required of the lower variable by Full Identification is always fully recoverable, without linking it to a morphosyntactic element. Therefore, economy dictates that this variable is not linked to a syntactic argument, and these verbs are not used transitively.

Under this analysis of the transitive/intransitive alternation, we must reconsider the contrast between English Manner of Movement Verbs (MMVs) and French MMVs discussed in 3.1.7. Recall that many MMVs in English may be both transitive and intransitive, but their French equivalents can only be intransitive (*float/flotter, waltz/valser, bounce/rebondir*). I claimed in 3.1.7 that transitivity is related to orientation. For example, the fact that an English verb such as *float* has a transitive use indicates that there are two argument positions, x_1 and x_2, in its semantic representation. When *float* is intransitive, it is because x_1 binds x_2, and this binding makes the verb inherently oriented because, as I argued, one way in which orientation is expressed in languages is via tree structures in Grammar. I will call this G-orientation.

Differences in transitivity may well follow from differences in how orientation is expressed in English and French. Thus, I have also alluded to another way to express orientation, one which plays a very large role in Jackendoff's work, namely, 3-D orientation (Jackendoff 1987b, chapter 10) and Jackendoff (1990a)). He assumes, following Marr (1982), that the 3-D model structure is a form of visual representation that encodes geometric and topological properties of physical objects.[49] He suggests that the lexical entry for some words includes a 3-D model representation, in addition to its phonological, syntactic, and semantic structures.

Since there are two ways to express orientation, languages might differ in the emphasis they give to one or another of them. One language might emphasize G-orientation: if some or all of the orientation in a given lexical item can be expressed by G-orientation, then it must be expressed by G-orientation. Another language might focus on 3-D orientation: any orientation that could be represented in terms of 3-D primitives would have to be represented that way. The semantic representation of some lexical items expressing direction would be less complex in a language that emphasizes 3-D orientation, because direction would be represented by a 3-D concept that would be decomposed only at the visual-conceptual level, not at the level of Grammar. A language that opts for G-orientation will have more semantic representations with two variable positions and will therefore be likely to have a greater number of intransitive verbs with transitive variants. On the other hand, a language that favors 3-D orientation should have the opposite tendency. That is precisely what we found in comparing English and French—English allows transitive forms of some intransitive verbs that are strictly intransitive in French. If we assume that English favors G-orientation, whereas French opts for 3-D orientation, this difference is expected. Ultimately, semantic representations with two positions should be found in this second type of language only when the orientation is so minimal that it cannot be expressed in 3-D form. Conversely, 3-D representations would be possible in English-like languages only when the lexical item expresses properties that cannot be expressed using Grammatical tools, such as tree structures. Thus, I am not saying that English has no 3-D representations (the difference between *wiggle* and *wriggle* is probably 3-D), I am claiming that an orientation that *can* be expressed by G-orientation *must* be expressed that way in English.

There are independent reasons to believe that there is such a difference in type of orientation between French and English. If a relational element does not function as such for some reason, something will be missing to express orientation by a relation in the semantic structure; the language will favor the use of 3-D orientation instead of G-orientation. There are contrasts between French and English that indicate that the use of 3-D in French may come from a loss of relational strength. We saw in note 22, in this chapter, that French, but not English, allows either a point or an interval to function as the temporal point S. If we make the assumption that a point is to an actant what an interval is to a relation, then relations should function as actants in French since intervals function as points. On the other hand, relations should not function as actants in English, since intervals do not function as points in that language.

Besides the different treatment of S, how French and English differ in their analysis of intervals and relations correlates with another difference between the two languages. In Double Object constructions, such as (187), the second NP object is predicated of the first one:

(187) a.   John gave Mary a headache.
      a'. *John gave a headache to Mary.
      b.   John gave Mary a book.
      b'. John gave a book to Mary.

This holds even in the second example (187b), where "possession" is not a special thematic relation but an inference from the predication.[50] When the second NP can have only a predicative interpretation in the sentence, as in (187a and a'), English must have a Double Object construction, because a relational element like a predicative NP cannot function as a point or actant in English. Therefore, this NP cannot be the complement of a preposition such as *to*. In French, however, whether an NP is purely predicative or not, it can appear in an actant position, since a relational element can function as actant in this language; thus, a predicative NP is the complement of the preposition *à* in (188).

(188)a.   Jean a donné mal à la tête à Marie.
          Jean has given a headache to Mary.
          Jean gave Mary a headache.
      b.   Jean a donné un livre à Marie.
          Jean gave a book to Mary.

These two observations relate to G-orientation and 3-D orientation in the following way. Since an interval or a relation can function as a point or actant in French, a COP relation embedded in a structure can function as a point in French. Such a COP-as-point has a lower relational "strength," since it is not relational at the level(s) where it is seen as a point: this obviates G-orientation at that level, and this would favor the use of 3-D orientation.

Summing up, in this section, we saw that four of six of the verbs studied do not have transitive alternations because they are subject to double recoverability, both of the lower variable and lower relation. So the presence of the lower variable is completely obliterated, and it is not linked to a syntactic argument. That is why these verbs are not used transitively. As for the difference between French and English, with respect to transitive uses of MMVs, it is due to a choice between 3-D orientation and G-orientation, this choice relating to a general difference between the two languages as to whether relational elements are allowed to function as actants or not.

3.3 CHOICE OF AUX

In order to further evaluate the theory of lexical representations that I am adopting, I will now compare its explanatory and predictive power with that of other current theories with regard to another syntactic property—the choice of auxiliary verbs (AUX). I will discuss the extent to which the lexical properties I attributed to the six French verbs being discussed are confirmed by evidence. Specifically, in 3.3.1, I will show that, where other theories only stipulate what class of constructions a particular AUX is compatible with, my theory explains why BE is compatible with a certain class of constructions and HAVE with another and not the converse. The theory also provides an account of the peculiarities found in different languages; this is illustrated in ten basic constructions in 3.3.1.3. Since there is a correlation between AUX choice and past participle agreement in Romance languages, I will then present, in 3.3.2, a theory of agreement that accounts for that correlation, while it satisfies the criteria of strict minimalism I have adopted. The analysis does not depend on movement transformations or on contentless functional categories, such as AGR, but rather on indexation; this allows it to generalize to all types of agreement, including cross-sentential agreement as in *John$_i$ came in. He$_i$ looked happy.*

3.3.1 GENERAL PROPERTIES OF CHOICE OF AUX
3.3.1.1 PREVIOUS ANALYSES

In French, the choice of auxiliary varies from one class of verbs to another. This variation is found in the six verbs discussed above: when intransitive (189a), they take *être* 'be' as AUX; when transitive (189b), the AUX is *avoir* 'have':

(189)a.   Jean est/*a venu/allé/arrivé/parti/entré/sorti chez Marie.
          Jean is/has come/gone/arrived/left/entered/gone-out of Marie's.
      b.   Jean a/*est entré/sorti les données dans l'ordinateur.
          Jean has/is entered/taken-out the data in the computer.

The SR of these verbs always has two variable positions, whether they are used transitively or intransitively. One could try to account for the choice of

TABLE 1 Binding of the Object by the Subject and Choice of AUX

Language	Transitive	Unaccusative	Raising Verb	ETRE	Passive
French	avoir	être	avoir	avoir	être
Italian	avere	essere	essere	essere	essere
Spanish	haber	haber	haber	haber	ser
English	have	have	have	have	be

AUX by adapting the proposition of Burzio (1985), which is based on syntactic binding—BE is the AUX when the subject binds the object—and transpose it to lexical binding. The AUX *être* would be used when binding takes place at the level of lexical semantic representation and there is only one position in syntax. The AUX *avoir* would be used when no binding occurs in the semantic representation and two positions are present in syntax. However, this approach will not work. First, the generalization does not hold across all verbs within a single language. So in French, for example, some intransitive verbs take *avoir* yet seem to involve only one variable, in both semantics and syntax (*Jean a marché* 'Jean has walked'); some intransitives that usually take *être* sometimes take *avoir* (*Elle a monté à cheval pendant trois ans* 'She rode horses for three years'); and reflexive constructions that involve two variables and should therefore take *avoir,* actually take *être* (*Il s'est regardé* 'He looked at himself'). Second, the generalization does not hold across languages. French with English, as well as two closely related Romance languages, are compared in table 1.

Another possibility one could explore is an account of this distribution, based on thematic properties of the subject, along the lines of Perlmutter (1978), Burzio (1985) and Lois (1990), for example. However, such an analysis would be inappropriate on general grounds, since, as I have argued, thematic properties are not relevant to grammatical analysis. Moreover, if enough different constructions are considered, thematic analyses fail on empirical grounds: the choice of AUX should not be determined by one particular use of a given verb, and if all uses are taken into account, the number of different theta roles that are required for the same verb make an enlightening generalization impossible.

Kayne (1993b, 2) criticizes the type of auxiliary selection found in Perlmutter (1978) and Burzio (1985) as being "akin to the rich and specific transformations of the sixties (and early seventies, as in Kayne (1975))." He proposes an analysis that is modular and that crucially assumes that auxiliary *have* and main verb (i.e. "possessive") *have* should be thought of in parallel fashion. It is easy to see that an approach that attributes significance to the similarity between the two uses of *have* is less likely to be led to propose a rule specific to the "auxiliary + past participle" construction, or even any property of *have* itself that makes specific reference to past participles. (Kayne 1993b, 2)

First, following recent work on Hungarian by Anna Szabolcsi, which assumes that a possessive construction like *John has a sister* derives from a copular construction, he assumes that possessive *have* must derive from the structure in (190):[51]

(190)   BE [$_{DP}$ SPEC D/P$_e^0$ [DP$_{poss}$ [AGR^0 QP/NP]]]

For Kayne, the crucial element here is D/P$_e^0$, "an empty prepositional D^0." For Case reasons, the DP$_{poss}$ must raise to the SPEC of the copula BE. From (190), we would expect to incorrectly derive *John is a sister*, instead of the desired *John has a sister*. But Kayne (1993b, 6) suggests that "it is plausible to take the SPEC of D/P$_e^0$ to be an A-bar position, following Szabolcsi's idea that this DP is significantly similar to CP." But then movement of DP$_{poss}$ through this position and into the SPEC of BE, an A-position, is illicit. Because of this, he assumes that D/P$_e^0$ must incorporate into BE, so that the SPEC of D/P$_e^0$ "becomes, as a result of incorporation, a derived SPEC of D/P$_e^0$ + BE, and hence counts as an A-position." The result of the incorporation of D/P$_e^0$ with BE (D/P$_e^0$ + BE) surfaces as *have*.

As for auxiliary *have*, it shares the initial part of the possessive structure and is only distinguished from possessive *have* by the fact that the possessor DP and possessed QP/NP are replaced by a substructure appropriate for participles, as in (191). Incorporation is again obligatory, for the same reasons as in the analysis of possessive *have*.

(191)   BE [$_{DP}$ SPEC D/P$_e^0$ . . . [$_{VP}$ DP$_{subj}$ [V DP$_{obj}$]]]

In short, this analysis is based on a diacritic use of functional categories: D/P$_e^0$ is simply used to label some structures so that we get *have* instead of BE when the empty prepositional D/P$_e^0$ is present in the structure. We can tell that this element is present because BE surfaces as *have*. This throws no light on the distribution of *have*. As Kayne himself notes (1993b, 8), "the distribution of auxiliary *have* becomes partly a question of what kind of verbal structures can be embedded in a DP sister of BE, and partly a question of what DP can move into the Spec of the larger DP, and when." But the answers, again, are diacritic. For example, in the discussion of the difference between standard Italian, which takes *avere* for transitives, and some dialects, which take *essere* instead, the analysis is based on the assumption that there is a participial AGR_S that is "inert" in standard Italian, whereas this AGR_S is "not inert" in the dialects. When the AGR_S is inert, the analysis is similar to the account of English above; when the AGR_S is "not inert," the offending A-bar position is converted into an A-position via the incorporation of this active AGR_S. This use of $+/-$ inert AGR_S is just an unrevealing diacritic label for the construction. Moreover, such a use of the notions of A versus A-bar position is problematic, as Noam Chomsky pointed out in lectures at the University of California, Irvine, in the spring of 1993, since one can determine whether a given position is A or A-bar only by comparing constructions. Thus, in the Lectures on Government and Binding (LGB) framework, the subject position is an A position, even in raising constructions where no theta role is assigned because a theta role can be assigned to that position in other constructions.[52] Paraphrasing what Kayne says about the analyses of Perlmutter and Burzio, we could say that his own analysis is akin to the rich and specific functional categories of the eighties and early nineties.

Another avenue to explore is an aspectual account of the variation in the choice of AUX. For example, Guillaume (1970) suggests that *être* is the AUX for verbs like *sortir,* which "contain a limit of tension"—once one is *sorti* (gone out), one cannot continue to *sortir* (to go out/exit). On the other hand, *avoir* would be the AUX for verbs that "open up on a perspective of continuation," such as *marcher* (to walk)—if one stops walking, nothing prevents one from immediately walking again. It is not clear to me how such an analysis would apply when there is a different AUX for different uses of the same verb. The analysis seems to hold only for a restricted set of uses, those involving movement. But does a verb like *sortir* still "contain a limit of tension" in its extension use or in a stative use such as *une île qui sort de l'eau* 'an island that sticks out of the water'? Furthermore, since aspect is a property of a construction rather than of a verb alone, as Vendler (1967) and Dowty (1979) have shown in detail, is a verb like *marcher* still "open" in constructions with a delimiting phrase, such as *Jean a marché jusqu'à la gare* 'Jean walked to the train station?'

In Bouchard (1992b), I propose an aspectual account of the choice of AUX based on the notions of "Object of Actualization" and "Object of Termination," which I adopted from Voorst (1988). In that analysis, each AUX in each language is specified for the aspectual role it allows a verb to assign to its subject. But there are constructions where the analysis fails. For example, French unaccusatives take *être* as AUX (192a), whereas inchoatives take *avoir* (192b), yet both have a subject that is both Object of Actualization and Object of Termination, via variable binding, under the analyses presented in sections 2.2.3 and 3.1.

(192)a.   Jean est venu hier.
           Jean is come yesterday.
           Jean has come/came yesterday.
       b.   La corde a cassé.
           The rope has broken.

In any event, all these approaches to AUX choice raise a general question: why should ETRE (standing for *être, be, essere, ser,* etc) and AVOIR (standing for *avoir, have, avere, haber,* etc) have the particular distribution that we find? Why should ETRE go with one-variable verbs, or verbs with derived subjects, or verbs with Theme subjects, or verbs with a limit of tension, or verbs with any other such specification? Is it possible for some languages to have just the opposite pattern, with AVOIR being associated with these specifications? Is there some deeper and more general principle involved here?

3.3.1.2 A General Account of the Distribution of ETRE and AVOIR

I will argue that there is in fact a generalization that is being missed that these questions make evident. One should not consider the distribution of ETRE or AVOIR only in their use as AUX verbs, but in general. If ETRE is the manifestation of the copula, as I suggested earlier in sections 2.2 and 3.1.2.8, then the question of the distribution of ETRE as an AUX can be phrased more generally (as with Kayne's discussion of the two verbs *have*): under what conditions does ETRE, the manifestation of the copula, appear? We have already seen that ETRE is present if two conditions are met: there is a Tense that requires ETRE as a support, and the semantic representation involves a simplex copula relation (if more content was present, it would have to be identified, and ETRE cannot express content). A simplex copula relation is a singular predication, that is, a relation of predication that directly involves a single actant, in contrast with other relations of predication that relate actants one to another.

So ETRE will be found in constructions like those shown in (193), but not in constructions like that shown in (194), since in (194) R_2 is not a bare predicate for x because R_2 has the external argument y.

(193)a. $[x \ R_1]$
   b. $[x \ R_1[R_2]]$
(194) $[x \ R_1[y \ R_2]]$

Examples of simplex copula relations are given in (195). In (195a), *Jean* is the actant, and *heureux* is the simplex predicate; in (195b), *Marie* is the actant and *la meilleure candidate* is the simplex predicate.[53]

(195)a.   Jean est heureux.
         Jean is happy.
   b.   Marie est la meilleure candidate.
         Marie is the best candidate.

I will argue that the reason AUX ETRE is present in constructions is that those constructions are instances of simplex copular relations. As for AUX AVOIR, it occurs when the semantic representation of the verb expresses more than a simplex copular relation. Even though the relation expressed by AVOIR is relatively simple, we know from its nonauxiliary uses that AVOIR expresses a more complex relation than the simplex copula relation expressed by ETRE. This can be seen in the contrasts in (196) and in (197), as well as in the uses in (198).

(196)a.   Marie a la meilleure étudiante dans son cours.
         Mary has the best student in her class.
   b.   Marie est la meilleure étudiante dans son cours.
         Mary is the best student in her class.

(197)a.   Marie a eu un bébé hier.
         Mary has had a baby yesterday.
         Mary had a baby yesterday.
   b.   Marie a été un bébé hier.
         Mary has been a baby yesterday.
         Mary was a baby yesterday.

(198)a.   Jean a une belle maison.
         John has a nice house.
   b.   Je l'ai vraiment eu cette fois.
         I him-have really had this time.
         I really had him this time.
   c.   Février n'a que 28 jours.
         February only has 28 days.

AVOIR expresses that the subject has some form of control over the object, as has often been noted (cf., for example, Damourette and Pichon 1911–1950; Benveniste 1966, for French; Pinker 1989; Jackendoff 1990a, for English).[54]

Given that ETRE can express only a simplex copula relation, and that AVOIR expresses that the subject has some control over the object, certain facts about the distribution of these auxiliaries are predicted. For example, it should be impossible for any language to have ETRE for transitive verbs and AVOIR for unaccusatives. In the next section, I will look at ten constructions that involve choice of AUX. French examples will be the basis for the discussion, with examples from Italian and English added to illustrate some particular points. I will show that this analysis of the distribution of ETRE and AVOIR is supported in a wide variety of constructions.

3.3.1.3 AUX CHOICE IN TEN CONSTRUCTIONS

An AUX is lexically selected by the main predicative element of the sentence (generally the verb). In the present analysis, the choice depends on properties of the Semantic Structure of that main predicative element.

Construction 1: Simple predicative sentences

(199) a. Jean est heureux.
          Jean is happy.
     b.   John is happy.

(200) a. Jean est un bon étudiant.
          Jean is a good student.
     b.   Jean a un bon étudiant.
          Jean has a good student.

Analysis: In (199a, b) and (200a), there is a copular relation between actants and bare predicates, so AUX = ETRE. In (200b), the relation is not a pure copular relation, but a control relation, so AUX = AVOIR.

Construction 2: Transitives

(201) a. Jean a cassé une branche.
          Jean has broken a branch.
     b.   John has broken a branch.

Analysis: There is a relation between the point x and the embedded predication-relation [y BREAK]. Since [y BREAK] is not a bare predicate, this is not a simplex copula relation, so AUX = AVOIR.

Discussion: In these examples, the main predicate has the following Semantic Structure: [x [y BREAK]], which can be paraphrased as "*x* is oriented toward *y*'s breaking."[55]

Construction 3: Passives

(202)a.   Paul sera renvoyé.
    b.   Paul will be fired.

Analysis: We do not have the whole structure [x R_1 [y R_2]] here, since *x* is suppressed by passive morphology (see below). The subject is *y,* and we have a simplex relation between *y* and R_2, so AUX = ETRE.

Discussion: Given Full Identification and Homomorphic Mapping, vacuous projection is strictly impossible in the present model. This means that syntactic structures with "open" positions as landing sites for transformations are not possible, since such positions can never be licensed. Every analysis of passive in Government and Binding theory and in Relational Grammar states, in some way or other, that passive morphology suppresses one of the arguments (see Chomsky 1981; Jaeggli 1986; Baker et al. 1989; Rosen 1984; Perlmutter and Postal 1984). In my analysis, as argued in Bouchard (1991), that is all that has to be said: the passive morpheme suppresses an argument. Both why it is the external argument that is suppressed and why there are promotion effects follow from the general architecture of the theory. The external argument is suppressed because it is the highest argument in semantic structure. If a lower argument were suppressed, the result would not be interpretable. Since semantic composition, which is assumed here, is built up hierarchically, each higher argument depends on lower composition for its interpretation: a gap in the lower part of the structure would render all the higher structure uninterpretable. As for the promotion effects, they follow from Homomorphic Mapping: if the highest argument position in semantic representation is suppressed, then the next highest position becomes the highest, and so it is mapped onto the highest syntactic position, i.e., the subject position. Instead of stipulating that the Grammar contains some promoting device that operates under special conditions, the architecture of this theory predicts that promotion effects like those in passive should be found.

Construction 4: Unaccusatives

We saw in 3.2 that there are two types of unaccusatives: those that do not have a transitive use, because their SR undergoes a conflation of double recoverability (203), and those that have a transitive use, because their SR undergoes a conflation of single recoverability (204).

(203) *Conflation of a Double Recoverability:* $[x_1 \text{ COP}_1 [x_2 \text{ COP}_2]] \Leftrightarrow [x_1 \text{ COP}_2]$
Jean est venu/arrivé/allé . . .
John has come/arrived/gone . . .

(204) *Conflation of a Single Recoverability:* $[x_1 \text{ COP } [x_2 \text{ DANS}]] \Leftrightarrow [x_1 \text{ COP}$
$+ \text{ DANS}]$
Jean est sorti/monté . . .
John has gone out/gone up . . .

Analysis: In either type of conflation, we have a simplex copula relation, since the elements with which x_1 relates are bare predicates. So in French, AUX = *être*. On the other hand, we saw in the discussion of (188) above that English does not allow a relation to function as an actant. Since conflation is an instance of a relation functioning as an actant, it does not take place in English. Without conflation, R_2 is not a bare predicate in the English equivalents of (203) and (204), and since *y* remains, in English, AUX = *have*.

Discussion: Interestingly, conflation is not always possible in French. If a verb that usually takes *être* as AUX contains some expression of manner, and if an emphasis is given to that manner, then the AUX is *avoir*. Damourette and Pichon discuss two examples that nicely illustrate this. First, the verbs *demeurer* and *rester* can be used to describe two kinds of situations, and this correlates with the choice of AUX:

(205)a. J'ai demeuré/resté dans cet immeuble (pendant cinq ans/#minutes).
I lived in that building for five years/#minutes.

   b. Je suis demeuré/resté dans cet immeuble pendant cinq minutes/#ans).
I remained in that building for five minutes/#years.

They comment: "[W]hen these verbs take *être,* they draw our attention to the end of the phenomenon as being identical to the beginning of the phenomenon, whereas when, with *avoir,* they express dwelling, they only indicate the duration of the fact of dwelling in such a place" (Damourette and Pichon 1911–1950: #1639).[56] I would also claim that there is an indication of manner with *avoir* which distinguishes 'dwelling' from simply 'remaining there.'

The second case discussed by Damourette and Pichon involves the verb *monter.* It is a verb that usually takes ETRE as its AUX in its intransitive uses, as in (206).

(206)   Je suis monté chez moi.
         I am raised at me.
         I went upstairs to my place.

They discuss sentence (207), which was uttered by a woman who was short of breath from climbing a few flights of stairs:

(207)   C'est que j'ai monté.
         It is that I have raised.
         It's because I climbed.

There is clearly an emphasis on the manner of moving here, just as there is in the following use of *monter:*

(208)   J'ai monté à cheval pendant trois ans.
         I have raised at horse during three years.
         I rode a horse for three years.

It is possible to explain why the AUX is *avoir* when there is emphasis on the expression of manner in the following way. Consider Jackendoff's (1987b, 1990a) idea that a 3-D model representation may be introduced into the lexical entry of some words discussed in 3.1 and 3.2, and suppose that we adapt it to verbs that express the kind of manner shown in (205)–(208). Eventually, we have to ask ourselves exactly how the 3-D representation is introduced into the lexical entry. It could be that there is more than one way to relate 3-D expressions of manner to Semantic Structures. The two most likely possibilities are that the 3-D expression of manner may be introduced alongside the phonological, syntactic, and semantic structures or that it may be introduced as a feature inside the semantic structure. In the latter case, we may assume that the 3-D element is attached to an element in the Semantic Structure, such as COP_1 in a structure like $[x_1 \ COP_1 \ [x_2 \ COP_2]]$. Suppose that, when the 3-D expression of manner is a feature inside the semantic representation in this way, this affects the emphasis on the expression of manner. So (209) would be the structure for the uses of *monter (rester)* in (205a) and in (207) and (208).

(209) $[x_1 \ 3\text{-}D + COP_1 \ [x_2 \ COP_2]]$

But then COP_1 is no longer a "simplex" COP, which could explain why conflation is not possible and why the AUX is *avoir.* Since nothing is yet known about the details of how 3-D representations interact with Semantic Representations, I will not speculate any more.

Construction 5: Intransitives

(210)a.   Jean a marché.
    b.   John has walked.

Analysis: As we saw at the end of 3.2, there is a difference between English and French, in that English intransitive verbs have a much greater likelihood of having transitive uses than their French counterparts. I attributed this to the fact that English tends to use G-orientation, whereas French tends to use 3-D orientation. This means that the two sentences in (210) have different Semantic Representations. Since 3-D specifications are always strong with this class of verb, and since French favors 3-D orientation, there is not a simplex copula relation in the semantic representation of (210a); instead, the structure is $[x_1 \; 3\text{-D} + \text{COP}_1 \; [x_2 \; \text{COP}_2]]$, as in (209), and therefore the AUX is *avoir*. In English, 3-D manner is not primary, so the structure is $[x_1 \; R_1 \; [x_2 \; R_2]]$. However, conflation does not take place because that would be an instance of a relation functioning as an actant, something which is not allowed in English; therefore, x_1 does not have a simplex relation with $[x_2 \; R_2]$, since this relation does not involve a single actant, so the AUX is *have*.[57]

Construction 6: Inchoatives

(211)a.   La corde a cassé.
    b.   The rope has broken.

Analysis: We saw in 3.2 that inchoatives and unaccusatives are quite similar. Both constructions fall under the general schema $[x_1 \; R_1 \; [x_2 \; R_2]]$, with binding between the two variables; in both constructions, the subject undergoes a change (because it is related to x_2) and is responsible for the change (because it is related to x_1). Yet despite this similarity, the constructions have a different AUX in French: *être* for unaccusatives but *avoir* for inchoatives. This is because of an important difference between the two constructions: whereas the two variables x_1 and x_2 are identical in an unaccusative sentence like *Jean est venu* 'Jean came,' with x_1 oriented toward its being at the deictic center, that is not the case in inchoatives. In inchoatives such as those in (211), x_1 "actualizes" $[x_2 \; \text{PRED}]$, where x_1 is something inherent to x, which is responsible for or controls or allows $[x_2 \; \text{PRED}]$, so that in (211), the rope is responsible for its own breaking. Thus, the two variables are not identical in inchoatives; they have the same referent but not the same way of referring to it—x_1 is a metonym of x_2.

Conflation is defined on identical variables. The variables x_1 and x_2 are not identical in the inchoative construction, so conflation does not take place in $[x_1 \ R_1 \ [x_2 \ R_2]]$ and x_1 does not have a simplex relation with $[x_2 \ R_2]$, since two actants are involved. Therefore, the AUX is *avoir* in French. In English, conflation is not even an option.[58]

Discussion: Before continuing with these constructions, I will briefly discuss a generalization that cuts across lexical causatives, unaccusatives, and inchoatives:

(212)   *Lexical Causatives, Unaccusatives and Inchoatives Generalization:* In these three constructions, the subject is responsible for the change of state.

In unaccusatives and inchoatives, this comes from the binding between x_1 and x_2; the subject is responsible for the change and undergoes it. Ruwet (1972, 158ff) made some observations that relate to this generalization. He says that all lexical causatives have a corresponding intransitive construction of the form NP *être* V-*é*, where the participle V-*é* can be either stative or not, depending on the V. Thus, the participial constructions in (214) correspond to the lexical causatives in (213):

(213)a.   Le chimiste a fondu le métal.
            The chemist has melted the metal.
      b.   Alice a monté Humpty Dumpty sur son mur.
            Alice has put Humpty Dumpty up on his wall.

(214)a.   Le métal est fondu.   [stative]
            The metal is melted.
      b.   A huit heures moins le quart, Humpty Dumpty est monté sur son
            mur.   [nonstative]
            At quarter to eight, Humpty Dumpty went up on his wall.

On the other hand, if only a syntactic causative is possible, because of properties of the subject as in (215), only a corresponding intransitive construction of the form NP *avoir* V-*é* is possible (216a). The corresponding intransitive construction of the form NP *être* V-*é* is not possible, as we see in (216b).

(215)a.   Les pluies ont fait monter le niveau de la rivière.
            The rainwater made the level of the river go up.
      b.   *Les pluies ont monté le niveau de la rivière.
            The rainwater raised the level of the river.

(216)a.   Le niveau de la rivière a monté.
            The level of the river went up.

b. *Le niveau de la rivière est monté. (*if nonstative)
   The level of the river is gone up.

However, I think it is incorrect to say that some lexical causatives, like (213b), must have a corresponding nonstative construction, like (214b), and cannot have a corresponding stative construction, like (217).

(217)   Donc, pour l'instant, Humpty Dumpty est monté sur son
        mur.   [stative]
        So for now, Humpty Dumpty is up on his wall.

In fact, it seems to me that only stative (217) is possible as a continuation to the lexical causative (213b) and that nonstative (214b) is not possible in that context. This is because the lexical causative implies control over the direct object *Humpty Dumpty* by the subject *Alice:* this is compatible with the stative (217), which would be an adjectival passive of (213b), but it is not compatible with nonstative (214b), since the nonstative is an unaccusative that implies "self-control"—some form of responsibility for the change on the part of the subject, as stated in the Generalization in (212). On the other hand, the situation is reversed in the context of a syntactic causative like (218):

(218)   Alice a fait remonter Humpty Dumpty sur son mur (par les
        gardes du roi).
        *Alice made Humpty Dumpty be put back up on his wall by the
        guards.*
        Alice made the guards put Humpty Dumpty back up on his wall.

Note that (218) is ambiguous: the embedded clause could be a passive, with *les gardes du roi* being the external argument of *remonter;* or, if one omits the material in parentheses, the embedded clause could be an active (unaccusative) construction, with *Humpty Dumpty* as the external argument (the sentence then means "Alice made Humpty Dumpty go back up on his wall"). With an embedded active verb, nonstative (214b) is fine as a continuation. With an embedded passive verb, (217) is fine as a continuation. The correlation between causatives and intransitive constructions is as follows:

(i) If a lexical causative has a corresponding *être* + V *é,* which is stative
    [(213) + (217)], the result is fine, because the subject, x_1, has full control
    over the object, x_2, in the lexical causative, and x_2 has no control in
    the stative.

(ii) If a lexical causative has a corresponding *être* + V *é,* which is nonstative (i.e., unaccusative) [(213) + (214b)], the result is bad, because the subject, x_1, has full control over the object, x_2, in the lexical causative, and x_2 has some control in the unaccusative.

(iii) If a syntactic causative has a corresponding intransitive (inchoative) *avoir* + V *é* [(215) + (216a)], the result is fine, because the subject, x_1, does not have full control over the object, x_2, in the syntactic causative, and x_2 has some control in the inchoative.

(iv) If a syntactic causative has a corresponding *être* + V *é,* which is nonstative [(218) + (214b)], the result is fine only if the embedded infinitival is active, because the subject, x_1, does not have full control over the object, x_2, in the syntactic causative, and x_2 has some control in the nonstative.

(v) If a syntactic causative has a corresponding *être* + V *é,* which is stative [(218) + (217)], the result is fine only if the embedded infinitival is passive, in which case x_2 has no control in the causative because of the passive and x_2 has no control in the stative.

Summarizing, in a lexical causative, the subject, x_1, has full control over the object, x_2; when a lexical causative has a corresponding intransitive construction where the subject is equivalent to x_2, this intransitive construction must be stative because x_2 has no control over itself. On the other hand, in a syntactic causative, the subject, x_1, does not have full control over the object, x_2, so x_2 has some degree of autonomy; when a syntactic causative has a corresponding intransitive construction where the subject is equivalent to x_2, this intransitive construction may be nonstative because x_2 has some control over itself.

Why there should be such correlations is clear, given the generalization in (212): it is the subject, x_1, that is in control in a lexical causative, not the object, x_2; so an equivalent of x_2 cannot appear as subject of an unaccusative or an inchoative because it is then attributed some control, which contradicts the information provided by the lexical causative.[59]

Construction 7: Reflexives

(219)a.   Tu ne t'es pas regardé.
     b.   You haven't looked at yourself.

Analysis: With respect to AUX choice, the French reflexive construction is like passive; the whole structure [x R_1 [y R_2]] is not available because *x* is suppressed by *se.* The subject corresponds to *y,* so there is a simplex relation between *y* and R_2, and the AUX is *être.* In English, cliticization of this sort is not possible, so the construction is just like a transitive construction. Therefore, the AUX is *have*.[60]

Discussion: As I mentioned in 2.2.3, I assume, as in Bouchard (1984a), that *se* discharges the variable corresponding to the external argument ("absorbs the external theta"). Therefore, the higher argument in the Semantic Representation of *regarder* is not identified by linking in (219a): only the internal argument is linked with a syntactic position, and the neutralizing of the highest argument by *se* has the effect of promoting the internal argument, which is linked to the subject position. Therefore, the French reflexive construction is similar to the passive, in that the syntactic subject is linked to the internal argument. The difference between the two is that while the passive completely neutralizes the external argument, *se* identifies the external argument according to the agreement index it receives in syntax. What *se* does is represent in the syntax an indexation similar to the one that takes place in the Semantic Representation in inchoatives.[61]

Construction 8: se-middle

(220)a.   La corde s'est cassée.
   b.   The rope has broken.

Analysis: In French, this construction is exactly like the reflexive, as far as AUX choice is concerned. In English, the construction is not possible because of the lack of cliticization. The closest option possible is the inchoative, as in (220b), with binding between two positions, but since there is no possibility of conflation in English, a simplex relation is impossible and the AUX is *have*.[62]

Discussion: The *se*-middle is exactly like the reflexive *se*, with neutralization of the external argument, except that in the middle, the *se* does not identify the external argument according to the index it receives in syntax; the *se* middle construction is oriented only toward the end of the process, with an inactive subject. As we saw in 2.2.3, this will be the only option possible if the subject does not have sufficient properties to bring about the process as in *Il vit le mouchoir se rougir soudain* 'He saw the handkerchief redden suddenly.'

Construction 9: SEMBLER

(221)a.   Jean a semblé avoir mieux compris.
   b.   John has seemed to have better understood.

Analysis: Examples with *sembler* do not involve *x* binding *y* in [x R_1 [y R_2]] with R_1 a "pure" COP; R_1 is not COP, it is SEMBLER, so the conditions for conflation are not met. Therefore, SEMBLER acts like a transitive verb with a subject and direct object (the embedded clause), with no simplex relation, so the AUX is AVOIR. This holds for both French and English. It is interesting to note that the AUX in this construction is *essere* (ETRE) in Italian. Conflation seems to obey less restrictive conditions in Italian than it does in French. In French, conflation will take place in [x R_1 [y R_2]] only if R_1 is a "pure" COP. In Italian, conflation will occur as long as R_1 does not impose specific selectional restrictions, even for binding in syntax.

Discussion: In order to link *Jean* to the lower predicate, it must be assumed either that *Jean* binds a trace in the subject position of the infinitive or that *Jean* directly binds the embedded VP. I assume direct binding with no trace, since I do not allow open subject positions; a raising-type analysis is thus not possible. The fact that the subject of SEMBLER appears to bear only the selectional restrictions of the embedded verb is not due to raising but to the fact that verbs vary greatly in the degree of restrictiveness they impose on their subject. SEMBLER imposes no restrictions whatsoever, as discussed in 1.5.2.5.

Construction 10: ETRE

The verb *être* takes *avoir* as its auxiliary, and *be* takes *have*.

(222)a.   Jean a été heureux.
      b.   John has been happy.

I assume a structure like (223) for (222a):

(223)

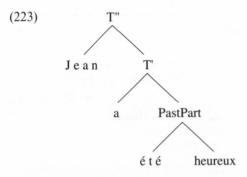

Analysis: The topmost relation is not a simplex one, so the topmost AUX is AVOIR. Note that, once again, Italian differs from French and English

and uses *essere* here. The reason is that, as we saw in the discussion of SEM-
BLER, Italian allows syntactic conflation, which derives a simplex relation,
hence the AUX is *essere*.[63] The relation between *Jean* and *heureux* is simplex,
as we saw in *Construction 1* above, so *été* is a sister to *heureux*. However, the
relation between *Jean* and PastPart is not simplex, since PastPart is a complex relation in which *été* takes *heureux* as a complement.

3.3.2 CHOICE OF AUX AND PAST PARTICIPLE AGREEMENT

I have been quite critical of AUX selection based on thematic properties
and of movement in constructions like passive, since this requires an "open"
subject position that is not compatible with Full Identification and Homomorphic Mapping. I have also criticized contentless functional categories
such as AGR, which are also incompatible with Full Identification. Nevertheless, all three have been used in recent analyses of past participle agreement,
in particular in Kayne (1985). If I wish to reject the elements at the basis of
such analyses, I should propose an alternative analysis of past participle
agreement.

I will briefly discuss the proposals on past participle agreement by Kayne
(1985) and the proposals about agreement based on functional categories by
Pollock (1989) and Chomsky (1991) (based in part on an idea by Emonds
1978). I will argue that they should be rejected because they are incapable in
principle of accounting for some types of agreement (section 3.3.2.1). Instead, I will put forth a theory of agreement based on coherent interpretation
of coindexed elements, which can generalize to all the types of agreement
(section 3.3.2.2). Then I will show how the theory accounts for past participle
agreement (section 3.3.2.3). Section 3.3.2.4 presents data from sylleptic
agreement (agreement based on meaning instead of form) that supports the
analysis. Finally, I will show how the analysis explains a correlation noted by
Lois (1990) between choice of AUX and past participle agreement.

3.3.2.1 SPEC-HEAD AGREEMENT AND SCIENTIFIC REDUCTIONISM

Kayne (1985) proposes a generalization whereby both complement-participle
agreement in French and subject-verb agreement reduce to a Spec-Head relation. For example, in (224a), the participle *écrites* agrees with *les* because *les*
rises from object position and passes through the Spec of the participle before adjoining to the auxiliary verb, as indicated by the traces in (224b); at
an intermediate step, *les* has a Spec-Head relation with *écrites,* and Kayne
assumes that this is what triggers agreement.

(224)a.   Je les ai écrites.
          I them have written + FEM + PLUR.
          I have written them.
     b.   [je [les$_i$ + ai [t$_i$ [écrites t$_i$]]]]

Pollock (1989) introduced the node AGR and Chomsky (1991, 1992) used that node in an attempt to extend the generalization: all instances of agreement could fall under such a Spec-Head relation with a node AGR. To say that past participle agreement involves a Spec-Head relation between the moved direct object and an AGR node, at some level of representation, distorts the problem in two ways. First, the label AGR refers to a process of agreement: the node itself only bears the features that are relevant to agreement, just as the direct object NP bears features that are relevant to agreement. Therefore, AGR, if AGR is a node at all, is really a node [$+\alpha$ features], features that could just as well be directly on the participle itself (as assumed in Kayne 1985). Labeling a node "AGR" gives the impression that one has a theory of agreement, when, in fact, nothing is said about the mechanisms of agreement theory, how it occurs, or why.

Second, having an AGR node gives the impression of a unified analysis of different types of agreement, since AGR can be postulated in other constructions where agreement phenomena are found. Aside from the fact that the actual features that agree vary from one construction to another, so that AGRO and AGRS, for example, really have to be distinct categories, adding a category AGR to all constructions where agreement is found is an artificial unification: the constructions could just as well be put in a list to which an agreement process applies or attributed a diacritic of a totally different nature. A much deeper understanding of why agreement takes place in the constructions where it does, and not elsewhere, is achieved if the agreement can be explained on the basis of elements independently motivated for each construction.

Consider the motivation for the functional category AGR with respect to agreement phenomena. If we look back at how this category was introduced in the theory, we see that, first, Kayne (1985) argued that it was possible to reduce complement-participle agreement in French to a process similar to subject-verb agreement: both would depend on a Spec-Head mediation. This is legitimate scientific reductionism. Note, however, that no AGR category is yet motivated, since Kayne had the Spec-Head relation established directly between the two agreeing elements. Introducing an AGR node for other purposes, as Pollock (1989) did, and saying that it could be used to mediate agreement does not make the node AGR motivated, with respect to agreement, since we can make do without it, as in Kayne's original analysis. Of course, one could object that the position of AGR in a structure receives independent motivation from the analysis of other phenomena, like the placement of adverbs in surface structure (see in particular Pollock 1989; Chomsky 1991; and much work that has followed). However, there are many problems with these analyses of adverb placement, including the danger of multiplication of functional nodes with the falsification problem that this creates. This will be the topic of chapter 5.

In any event, the question is whether different types of agreement can be reduced to Spec-Head relations. It is often claimed that all types of agreement reduce to Spec-Head relations. But a moment's thought immediately shows that there are problematic cases like the ones in (225):

(225)a.   John$_i$ showed Mary a picture of *his$_i$/*her$_i$ uncle.
     b.   John$_i$ came in. *He$_i$ looked very happy.
     c.   A pointing to B who is trying to catch up with a woman who is skating very fast on the river:
           "You'll never be able to catch up with *her.*"

It is hard to see how these cases of agreement between a pronoun and its antecedent could be mediated by a Spec-Head relation. In fact, Spec-Head agreement being restricted to sentence grammar, it is *in principle* incapable of accounting for extra-sentential agreement, as in (225b), and for agreement that depends on pragmatic anaphora, as in (225c). One will have to say that antecedent-pronoun agreement is a different kind of agreement.

But should not a strong adherent to scientific reductionism turn the question around? If Spec-Head agreement cannot generalize to these cases, can the analysis of these cases generalize to Spec-Head agreement, thereby potentially rendering the use of AGR superfluous? And should not the scientific reductionist worry about the fact that reductionism has not been carried to its logical conclusion *before* going on to use categories like AGR in a wide variety of constructions? Even more so, if an attempt has been made at generalizing an analysis of antecedent-pronoun agreement and if it has been shown to be possible?

3.3.2.2 AGREEMENT AS A DERIVATIVE PROPERTY OF COINDEXATION

I will now propose an analysis that can generalize to all cases, including those in (225). The basic points of the analysis I will adopt have already been proposed elsewhere (Bouchard 1987; 1992b). Although the spirit of the analysis will remain the same, the details are different. In Bouchard (1987), I argued that an agreement theory based on coindexation does have that potential as a unified theory of agreement phenomena. We can assume the following natural principle:

> *Coherence Condition on Coindexation:* Coindexed elements must be interpreted coherently.

This means that there can be no clash in the features that coindexed elements share. For example, an index must have a single value for features of person, number, and gender. Agreement follows from this condition on coindexation. To have agreement depend on properties of the indices is not new, of course. I have proposed it myself (Bouchard 1984a; 1987), and it is also found in some form or other in the works of numerous authors (see Baker and Brame 1972; Jackendoff 1972; Fauconnier 1974; Lapointe 1980; Hoeksema 1983; Chierchia 1987; Pollard and Sag 1992, to name a few).

The Coherence Condition on Coindexation accounts for agreement of the type illustrated in (225), where coindexation derives from the theory of reference. Subject-verb agreement also follows from this condition. Recall from the discussion in 3.1.3 that a subject is the privileged actant of the event expressed by a verb, the actant that establishes a relationship with the temporal point. The subject is therefore the link between the event and T. If we assume that this link is established by coindexation, we straightforwardly explain why agreement takes place between subject and T, by means of the very general mechanism of agreement under coindexation. Some data from Aissen (1989) favor this indexation account of agreement over an AGR analysis. She gives examples from several languages where the verb agrees not with the subject but instead with the combination of the subject and a comitative:

(226)a.   Elindultunk a vezetömmel. (Hungarian)
        we-left the my-guide-with.
        I left with my guide. (also: We left with my guide.)

    b.   Ka ra bow Tamag. (Yapese)
        PAST *they come*-DUAL *Tamag.*
        He came with Tamag.

    c.   Libatotikotik xchi?uk li Xune. (Tzotzil)
        we-went with DEF *Xun.*
        I went with Xun. (also: We went with Xun.)

    d.   Hasan-la gittik. (Turkish)

Hasan-with we-went.
I went with Hasan. (also: We went with Hasan.)

Aissen says that the comitative marker in the Hungarian, Yapese, and Turkish examples is distinct from the general marker of conjunction. A structural analysis by means of an AGRS has no direct way to account for this kind of agreement. In a coindexation analysis of agreement, one simply has to assume that the index of both the subject and the comitative determine verbal agreement in these languages.

The analysis also extends naturally to another instance of agreement where it is hard to see how it could be mediated by a Spec-Head relation: agreement in sign languages. In sign languages, reference is expressed by assigning a 3-D locus in the space in front of the speaker to each referent and then pointing back to these loci to refer to these entities. Some directional verbs agree with their subject and, for some of them, also with an object. Desouvrey (1994), expanding on an idea by Lee (1994), discusses the subject and object agreement in the equivalent of (227) in the Langue des signes québécoise (LSQ) 'Québec Sign Language.'

(227)   John gave Mary a book.

Simplifying, the speaker starts signing the verb GIVE on the same axis as the locus of the referent for JOHN (subject agreement) and ends signing the verb on the same axis as the locus of the referent for MARY (object agreement). Therefore, spatial indexing is used for the expression both of reference and of agreement, exactly as expected in an analysis of agreement based on indices. On the other hand, to build anything like Spec-Head relations to account for agreement expressed in this 3-D manner would be highly artificial, if possible at all.

Therefore, this analysis has the advantage of treating in a unified way agreement due to coreference, as in (225), subject-verb agreement, and subject-/object-verb agreement in LSQ. In the next subsection, I will show that it also accounts for past participle agreement, because that agreement also involves a relation of coindexation between the direct object and the participle, a coindexation which in this case depends on the formalism of the theory of assignment of semantic roles.

3.3.2.3 PAST PARTICIPLE AGREEMENT AND COINDEXATION

There are two ways for a verb to assign a semantic role to a direct object in syntax:

Option 1: The direct object and the V can be related by government, a relation which can be minimal (sisterhood) or extended (by Connectedness, as in Kayne 1983, or V Chain, as in Bouchard 1984a); or

Option 2: The direct object and the V can be related by coindexation, thus
creating a chain closer to the usual notion (see McCawley 1970
and Stowell 1981 on coindexation between V and direct object).

Essentially, Connectedness and V-Chain formation are formal means of
extending the government relation by transitivity, so that a given V can
"reach up" to assign its semantic role to an argument that is far from the
position where such assignment is "normally" done. There are structural conditions on such extensions, which have been extensively studied and of which
Kayne (1983) gives the essential details. There are also lexical and contextual
conditions on the possibility of such extensions. Everything that falls under
the topic of "bridge verbs" can be counted among the conditions that determine some kind of transparency of the verbs involved. Erteschik-Shir (1973),
and subsequent work of hers, explores this question in detail and I discuss it
in 4.4.11.

The two options above have been proposed to account for Semantic Role
assignment, and each has been defended by various authors. There seem to
be good arguments in favor of each of them. However, there is no need to
use both options at the same time for the same construction, since they do
the same work, i.e., assign a semantic role. Suppose, therefore, that a language chooses between Option 1 and Option 2 as its primary means of assigning a semantic role, the other option being used only "Elsewhere," that
is, where the primary option cannot apply. It is natural to expect that a language that opts for a coindexation relation will also opt for simplex relations
that result from conflation, since indices are presumably attributed to actant-
like elements, such as conflated relations. Therefore, from the analysis of
choice of AUX in 3.3.1, we can deduce that French and Italian choose coindexation Option 2 because they exhibit conflation effects in their AUX selection, whereas English and Spanish choose government Option 1.

Consider the consequences this difference in semantic role assignment has
for past participle agreement. If the direct object is in situ, as in (228), a
problem immediately arises for a language, such as French, that has chosen
the coindexation option:

(228)   Jean a repeint les tables.
           Jean has repainted the tables.

If the Semantic Role is assigned by coindexation between *repeint* and *les tables,* there should be agreement between the two (which there is not here), and there should also be binding of *les tables* by *repeint.* This binding would violate binding theory in a strict sense, since binding theory is a theory about indexation not reference, as argued in Bouchard (1987).[64] Thus, this indexation cannot take place. French must therefore revert to the government option for (228): since no coindexation can take place here, we correctly predict that there will be no agreement. On the other hand, if the direct object is cliticized as in (229), then coindexation between *les* and *repeintes* poses no problem for the binding theory: the past participle is bound by *les* and functions as its trace for all practical purposes. There is no need for an NP trace in direct object position to the right of the participle; in fact, there cannot be such a trace, since it would create a binding theory problem just like *les tables* in (228).

(229)   Je les$_i$ ai repeintes$_i$.
          I have repainted them.

French therefore exercises its unmarked option in (229). Since there is coindexation between *les* and *repeintes,* there is agreement between the two elements, as expected; the features they share will have to bear the same values, because of the coherence requirement on the index that they share.

Contrary to French, Spanish opts for government and Connectedness, so there is no coindexation between *las* and *escrito* in (230).

(230)   Las he escrito.
          Them have written.
          I have written them.

Since the relation between V and its object is established by extended government via Connectedness, not coindexation, here, there is no agreement.

In Wh-constructions, French will again use the coindexation strategy; *repeintes* is coindexed with *quelles tables* and functions as its trace, so there is agreement in (231). In Spanish, Connectedness is used, and no agreement takes place in (232).

(231)   Quelles sont les tables$_i$ que tu as repeintes$_i$?
          Which are the tables that you have repainted [FEM PLUR]?

(232)   ¿Quales son las mesas que has repintado?
          ¿Which are the tables that you have repainted [MASC SING]?

Similarly, the agreement that takes place between the subject and the participle in French unaccusatives, as in (233), is an indication that they are coindexed according to my analysis of agreement. It is likely that this coindexation results from the fact that conflation creates a simplex relation, assuming that a simplex relation resulting from conflated relations is more actant-like than complex relations. On the other hand, Spanish unaccusatives do not undergo COP conflation, since Spanish selects Option 1 and the Semantic Role is assigned via Connectedness, which results in the absence of agreement, as in (234).

(233)   Ces tables$_i$ sont arrivées$_i$ par bateau.
         These tables have come [FEM PLUR] *by boat.*

(234)   Estas mesas han llegado por barco.
         These tables have come [MASC SING] *by boat*

However, both languages exhibit participle agreement in passive constructions, since it is a property of passive morphology to create a simplex relation:[65]

(235)   Ces tables$_i$ ont été repeintes$_i$.
         These tables have been repainted   [FEM PLUR].

(236)   Estas mesas han sido repintadas.
         These tables have been repainted   [FEM PLUR].

3.3.2.4 Sylleptic Agreement as Empirical Support for a Coindexation Analysis

In this section, I present an additional argument for analyzing past participle agreement as a result of long-distance coindexation rather than as a local Spec-Head relation similar to the local relation found in subject-verb agreement. The argument comes from the facts of sylleptic agreement, which is based on reference rather than morphology. Nonlocal sylleptic agreement, which depends on coreferential indexation, is quite frequent in French (see *Le trésor de la langue française* for many examples).

(237) *Nonlocal Sylleptic Agreement:*
       a. *Le castor* est l'emblème du Canada. *Ils* se retrouvent dans tous les cours d'eau.
           The beaver is the emblem of Canada. They are found in all the waterways.
       b. C'est *la sentinelle* qui *le premier* s'inquiète.
           It is the sentry (FEM) *who the first* (MASC) *becomes anxious*

    c.   *On* est *tous loyaux* envers la couronne.
         We (SING) *are all loyal* (PLUR) *to the crown.*

On the other hand, sylleptic agreement in a Spec-Head configuration, such as adjective-noun or subject-verb, seems to be impossible:[66]

(238)a.   Le pauvre loyal/*loyaux
         The poor loyal (SING)/*loyal* (PLUR)
         The loyal poor
    b. *Les pauvre loyal
         The (PLUR) *poor* (SING) *loyal*
    c. *Le pauvre subissent tous les coups.
         The poor (SING) *endure* (PLUR) *all the hardship.*
    d. *On sommes/sont tous loyaux envers la couronne.
         PRO-3SING BE-1PLUR/BE-3PLUR *all loyal to the crown.*
         We are all loyal to the crown.

The pronoun *on* has a sylleptic use in many French dialects. It receives morphologically third person singular, but it refers to a plurality of individuals, including the speaker: it then has the same reference as first person plural *nous*. It is therefore a rare case of mismatch between morphological features of person and number and referential features. When it has this use, we could attributed to *on* the simplified lexical entry in (239):

(239)   *On* = N;
        Morphology: third person singular;
        Reference: plurality of individuals, including the speaker.

Given the observations above about (237) and (238), we expect *on* to agree sylleptically (as a first person plural) when agreement is nonlocal and depends on coreferential coindexation. This is what we find, as shown in (240).

(240)   C'est vrai, on$_i$ ne pense qu'à nous$_i$/*lui$_i$/*eux$_i$ Et alors?
        It is true, PRO-3SING only think about us/him/them. So what?

Here, although *on* is morphologically third person singular, a pronoun coreferential with *on* can only be first person plural (*nous*), not third person singular (*lui*) or third person plural (*eux*). It is possible to have third person singular *soi* in (240), but only when *on* is used generically, not when it has the plural reference we are concerned with here. On the other hand, if we compare (238d) and (240), we see that sylleptic agreement is not possible between the subject *on* and the verb. This confirms that there is an important difference between nonlocal agreement, which depends on coreferential coindexing, and local agreement, such as subject-verb agreement: only the former can be sylleptic.

Now that we know that *on* does not allow sylleptic agreement in local Spec-Head relations such as Subject-Verb, we can use this to determine whether past participle agreement is dependent on a Spec-Head (i.e., local) relation. If past participle agreement is dependent on a Spec-Head relation, we expect not to find sylleptic agreement with a past participle. However, if past participle agreement depends on nonlocal coindexation, then we expect sylleptic agreement to be possible. The following examples show that there is sylleptic agreement of the past participle. (Many more examples can be found under the entries 'syllepse' and 'sylleptique' in various French dictionaries and encyclopedias.)

(241)a. Hier, *on* alla ensemble à Versailles, accompagn*és* de quelques dames. (Madame de Sévigné, *Lettres*)
         Yesterday, PRO-3SING *went together to Versailles, accompanied* (PLUR) *by a few ladies.*
         Yesterday, we went together to Versailles, accompanied by a few ladies.

     b. Grouille, je te dis, quand tu es de corvée, *on* est toujours serv*is* les derniers. (Sartre, *La mort dans l'âme*)
         Hurry up, I tell you, when you are on duty, PRO-3SING BE-3SING *always served* (PLUR) *the last.*
         Hurry up, will you, when you are on duty, we are always served last.

     c. *On* dort entass*és* dans une niche. (Pierre Loti, *Vers Ispahan*)
         PRO-3SING SLEEP-3SING *piled* (PLUR) *in a doghouse.*
         We sleep crammed together in a doghouse.

These examples show that past participle agreement with *on* is sylleptic. Therefore, we know that past participle agreement is different from subject-verb agreement; the two should not be unified under a Spec-Head analysis.

  These data also seem problematic for my analysis, since I unify subject-verb agreement, past participle agreement, and coreferential coindexation agreement as coindexation agreement, where agreement follows from a coherent interpretation of the shared index. How then can I explain the lack of sylleptic agreement in the subject-verb coindexation of *on* and the verb in (240), since sylleptic agreement occurs with *on* in the other types of agreement? The answer lies in the particular relation a subject holds with Tense that triggers agreement. Recall from sections 3.1.3 and 3.3.2.2 that the agreement on the verb does not come from a direct coindexation between subject and verb, but rather between subject and Tense (T). This coindexation is triggered by the fact that the subject is the privileged point of the event through which the whole event is situated, with respect to a temporal point. The coindexation of the subject with T is not dependent in any way on the reference of the subject, but rather strictly on its status as the privileged actant of the event. We saw in the discussion above that sylleptic agreement occurs when referential properties of an element take over its morphological properties. Since referential properties are not involved in the coindexation of the subject with T, no sylleptic agreement effects appear on T. Thus, an analysis of agreement based on coindexation is to be preferred because it allows a unified account of several types of agreement, including sylleptic agreement.

3.3.2.5 A CORRELATION BETWEEN CHOICE OF AUX AND PARTICIPLE AGREEMENT

Lois (1990) notes an interesting correlation between choice of AUX and past participle agreement, which ties in with the discussion of the previous sections:

(242)   In Romance languages, agreement of the past participle, when the auxiliary is AVOIR, is found only in those languages where there is an alternation of auxiliary between AVOIR and ETRE in the complex tenses.

We saw in table 1 that Spanish uses only *haber* 'have' to form its complex tenses, whereas in French and Italian, the AUX varies, depending on the verb class. As Lois observed, only French and Italian have past participle agreement when AVOIR is the AUX. She proposes an analysis of AUX choice based on thematic properties of the constructions, which is close to Burzio's (1985) proposal, and claims that the interaction of her analysis with Kayne's (1985) analysis of past participle agreement can account for the correlation in (242). I will show that Lois' analysis runs into problems but that my coindexation analysis avoids them and that it explains the correlation in (242).

Under her analysis, all auxiliaries are assigned a specification as to their capacity to transmit a thematic role to the subject and to assign a Case. The specifications she proposes for the French and Spanish auxiliaries are given in (243) (where u is an unspecified value).

(243)   *avoir* = [+theta role subject], [+objective Case]
         haber =[u theta role subject], [−objective Case]
         être = [−theta role subject]
         ser =   [−theta role subject]

To account for the correlation, she adopts the following hypothesis:

(244)   If the Participial Suffix bears features (of number), it must have a
         Case.

Now consider the data in (245):

(245)a. Je les ai écrites.
         I them have written+FEM+PLUR.
         I have written them.
    b. *Las he escritas.
         Them have written.
         I have written them.
    c. Les enfants sont arrivés.
         The children are arrived+PLUR.
         The children have arrived.

For (245a), Lois assumes that *les* gets Case from *ai* and that the suffix *-es* gets
Case from the V.[67] In (245b), there are two elements that must get a Case, *las*
and the suffix *-as,* but since *haber* is not a Case-assigning AUX, only one
Case can be assigned (by the V), and the sentence is not well formed. To
account for (245c), Lois adopts a suggestion by Pollock (1984) (see also
Belletti 1988), according to which an unaccusative V assigns a Case; *-s* can
then get its Case from V.

Note that the way in which the Participial Suffix gets its agreement features in this analysis is not directly relevant; that the features are present, and
obey (244), is sufficient for the analysis. Thus, the features could come from
Spec-Head agreement between the moved object and the participle, as in
Kayne (1985), by Spec-Head agreement between the moved object and an
AGR node, as in Chomsky (1991), or any other agreement mechanism, including coindexation, as I propose. Therefore, the analysis is compatible on
this point with Kayne's proposal and those of Pollock and Chomsky, as well
as mine, and as it is presented, it cannot be used as an argument in favor of
adopting one way of accounting for agreement over another. In fact, as Lois
herself notes (her note 11), her analysis is not directly compatible with an
analysis that the direct object moves through an intermediate position between the AUX and the participle, which can be taken as an indication that

the analysis I propose is to be preferred over these others, since they all assume such an intermediate position.

There are three empirical problems with her analysis. First, she has AUX *avoir* assigning Case, thus losing the explanation Kayne (1985) gave for the ungrammaticality of *J'ai les lettres écrites*. Second, the analysis allows *haber* to be the AUX of unaccusatives, but it does not prevent *ser* from being selected. In other words, she explains why *haber* is possible with unaccusatives, but does not explain why it is required. Finally, in her analysis, unaccusatives assign Case. This incorrectly predicts the possibility of agreement of an unaccusative past participle in Spanish, with *haber* as AUX. Moreover, she leaves aside the fact that, in French, the AUX of *sembler* and of *être* is *avoir,* but in Italian, the AUX of *sembrare* and of *essere* is *essere*.

The analysis is crucially based on the possibility of having no theta roles assigned to some subject positions with certain verbs whose subjects are derived. Earlier, I argued against such a proposal on general grounds, and Ruwet (1991) has questioned many of the arguments proposed to determine the derived status of subjects. I will, therefore, try to show that an account of AUX choice based on conflation and simplex relations, as presented in 3.3.1.2 above, can account for the correlation in (242) under an analysis of past participle agreement based on coindexation between the "displaced" object and the participle, rather than a local Spec-Head relation.

The reason for the correlation in (242) between past participle agreement and AUX alternation in complex tenses is clear in the analysis of agreement based on coindexation: both past participle agreement and selection of AUX ETRE depend on simplex relations. If a language has conflation into simplex relations as the unmarked option, i.e., if the language adopts Option 2, that language has both past participle agreement and AUX ETRE in certain constructions; if Option 1 is selected, the language has neither.[68]

The analysis proposed here does not suffer from the three empirical problems outlined above. First, a sentence like *J'ai les lettres écrites* is impossible because, contrary to Kayne (1985), there is no movement through an intermediate position between the AUX and the participle in my analysis: there simply is no position available for the direct object there. Second, *ser* cannot be the AUX of unaccusatives in Spanish because Spanish does not have conflation since it selects Option 1. Finally, there is no agreement of an unaccusative past participle in Spanish with *haber* as AUX, because when semantic roles are assigned via Connectedness, there is no coindexation and therefore no agreement (see the discussion of (234)). Thus, this analysis of agreement based on coindexation avoids the problems raised by Lois' analysis and explains the correlation between choice of AUX and participle agreement in Romance languages.

3.3.2.6 CONCLUSION OF CHOICE OF AUX AND PAST PARTICIPLE AGREEMENT

Six different cases of agreement were discussed: (1) subject-verb, (2) object-verb, (3) pronoun-antecedent, (4) agreement in LSQ, (5) object-past participle, and (6) sylleptic agreement. We saw that, in principle, Spec-Head agreement cannot account for extrasentential cases of pronoun-antecedent agreement and would be highly artificial for agreement in LSQ and sylleptic agreement. On the other hand, agreement based on the Coherence Condition on Coindexation generalizes naturally to all six cases.[69] Therefore, the coindexation analysis of agreement should be selected on the basis of scientific reductionism.

3.3.3 SUMMARY OF CHOICE OF AUX

In this section, I argued that we find ETRE as the AUX in certain constructions for the same reasons that we find it elsewhere. ETRE is the realization of the copula; it is found whenever there is a simplex relation. This is in keeping with the claims made about the semantic structures of the six verbs studied and was discussed with relation to ten different constructions. I argued that the correlation noted by Lois (1990) between past participle agreement and AUX alternation in complex tenses is due to the fact that both past participle agreement and selection of AUX ETRE depend on simplex relations. Such an analysis of agreement, based on coindexation, allows for a unified account of apparently diverse agreement phenomena.

3.4 STATIVE READING OF THE PARTICIPLE

We saw above that four of the six verbs we are concerned with allow both an active and a stative reading of the past participle (that is, a reading with internal development of the event and one without such an internal development), whereas the other two allow only an active reading:

(246)a.   Active (nonstative) use:
          Jean est venu/allé/arrivé/parti/entré/sorti en coup de vent.
          Jean is come/gone/arrived/left/entered/go-out in a gust of wind.
          Jean came/went/arrived/left/came in/went out in a hurry.

b. Stative use:
Pour l'instant, Jean est #venu/#allé/arrivé/parti/entré/sorti.
For now, Jean is come/gone/arrived/left/come-in/gone-out.

Two questions arise. (1) Why is a stative reading possible for *arriver, partir, entrer,* and *sortir?* (2) What is different in *venir* and *aller* that prevents them from having a stative reading? It is tempting to correlate this difference in stativity with the distinction between verbal and adjectival passive. However, I will discuss the influential analysis of adjectival passive proposed by Levin and Rappaport (1986) and use it as a preliminary argument that the distinction between verbal and adjectival passive is not well founded. In fact, passive formation is of no help in accounting for the difference in stativity. I will then argue that the reason for the difference is that statives have no internal development and that this is only compatible with the semantic representations of *arriver, partir, entrer,* and *sortir,* not with those of *venir* and *aller,* as already discussed in 3.1.3.

Suppose we approach the problem by assuming that these stative uses are adjectival passives. We could try to relate these facts to an analysis of adjectival passives, such as that in Levin and Rappaport (1986). There are four main points to their analysis:

(247)a.   *-ed* in verbal passivization suppresses the external theta role.[70]
b.   Adjectival Passive Formation (APF) externalizes the direct argument.
c.   APF affects only monotransitive verbs;
d.   APF changes the category of the lexical item from verbal to adjectival.

If the stative uses in (246b) are indeed cases of APF, this contradicts property (a), at least in those analyses where unaccusatives do not have an external argument (see section 4.4.3 for more examples). As for property (b), it follows directly from property (a) in the present approach. As we have already seen, when the external argument is suppressed, the Homomorphic Mapping creates a promotion effect by linking the next highest semantic argument with the highest position in syntax.

Property (c) could provide us a clue to the contrast in (246b): maybe there is something about *arriver, partir, entrer,* and *sortir* that makes them similar to monotransitive verbs, but this is missing in *venir* and *aller.* Unfortunately, property (c) will not be of any help in accounting for the contrast, because, in fact, it does not actually hold for adjectival passives. Levin and Rappaport (1986, 631) state the generalization as follows:

(248) *Sole Complement Generalization:* An argument that may stand as a sole NP complement to a verb can be externalized by APF.

They argue that this is supported by the following facts. When a dative verb, like *feed,* takes either a theme argument or a goal argument as an internal argument, but only the goal may stand as sole NP complement, only the goal may be externalized by APF.

(249)a. feed a hamburger to the children
     b. feed the children a hamburger
     c. *feed a hamburger
     d. feed the children

(250)a. *unfed hamburger
     b. unfed children

However, when a verb has two internal arguments, neither of which can stand alone, it is impossible to externalize either of these arguments. *Hand* and *slip* illustrate this.

(251)a. hand a knife to Jim
     b. hand Jim a knife
     c. *hand a knife
     d. *hand Jim

(252)a. slip a message to the spy
     b. slip the spy a message
     c. *slip a message
     d. *slip the spy

(253) *a recently handed knife; *a recently handed person

(254) *a furtively slipped message; *a furtively slipped spy

All the examples Levin and Rappaport give in support of their generalization are with prenominal adjectives. The generalization in (248) predicts that any participle used as an adjective, whether prenominal or postnominal, should be ungrammatical. As the following examples show, this is not the case. Adjectival participles of verbs that do not obey generalization (248) are as acceptable as the participles of verbs that obey the generalization, when in postnominal position.

(255)a.   The food fed to the children was tainted.
   b.   The knife handed to Jim wasn't sharp enough.
   c.   The message slipped to the spy caused her demise.

It makes sense that adjectival participles used prenominally must be able to have a Sole Complement; if another complement was obligatorily present, it would produce a phrasal prenominal adjectival passive, and this is ruled out on independent grounds for all adjectives in English. (See section 4.4.5.1.1.3 for a possible explanation.) Therefore, it comes as no surprise that the examples in (256) are as bad as *a proud of his son father.

(256)a.   *the fed to the children food
   b.   *the handed to Jim knife
   c.   *the slipped to the spy message

The problem with participles like *handed* and *slipped* is that they cannot be stripped of their additional complement, as *fed* can, so it is impossible to have them prenominally at all. The restrictions Levin and Rappaport observe are not about APF, but about prenominal modifiers in general. They are right that a thematic approach does not work here, but, unfortunately their structural approach does not work, either. In any event, the Sole Complement Generalization is an odd one. There is no obvious reason why adjectival passives should be restricted in this way, since adjectives in general are not prevented from having internal arguments in addition to their external argument: *a woman proud of her son, something impossible to do,* etc.

In fact, even the arguments to the effect that these passives are adjectival, rather than verbal, are not convincing. For example, consider the three most frequently used diagnostics for adjectivehood reviewed by Levin and Rappaport. The first claim, that *un-* attaches to adjectives but not to verbs, is simply false. As Levin and Rappaport themselves point out, there are negative verbs like *unload* and *unbutton.* They say that this is a different *un-* from the one that attaches to adjectives. This verbal, "reversative," *un-* is different, in that "*John unloaded the truck* does not exhibit the meaning that would be linked to negative *un-,* that John did not load the truck. Rather, it means that someone first loaded the truck and John then undid this action." (Levin and Rappaport 1986, 625, note 6). What their comparison between *unload* and *did not load* illustrates is that "reversative" *un-* exhibits properties of contrary negation rather than of contradictory negation. Is the *un-* attached to adjectives really any different in this respect? As Horn (1989) shows, following a long tradition going back to Aristotle, "Predicate denial—in which the entire predicate is negated—results in contradictory negation. Predicate term negation—in which a negative verb is affirmed of the subject—results in a contrary affirmation" (Horn 1989, 21). Now *un-*, whether attached to an adjective or a verb, typically has the meaning of contrary negation. Thus, as discussed in Sproat (1992), a predicate denial, i.e., sentential negation, like *not happy* is merely contradictory, so that (257a) "is consistent with a state of affairs where Freddie is sad, neither happy nor sad, or indeed ecstatic" (Sproat 1992, 349) as in (257b) (see also note 36 above on the scope of negation):

(257)a.   Freddie is not happy.
      b.   Freddie is not (merely) *happy,* he's overjoyed.

On the other hand, a negative adjective like *unhappy* has a contrary, opposite meaning, so that (258a) is only consistent with a situation where Freddie is the opposite of happy: it cannot be that he is "neither happy nor sad," nor that he is ecstatic (as indicated by the unacceptability of (258b)).

(258)a.   Freddie is unhappy.
      b.   #Freddie is un*happy,* he's overjoyed.

There is no reason to assume that there are two different morphemes *un-*; whether attached to an adjective or a verb, *un-* is term negation, therefore contrary negation. Because of this, many adjectives—such as color adjectives and shape adjectives, for example—are not compatible with *un-*, since they do not have contraries (**unred, *unflat*). On the other hand, the verbs that do take *un-* have a contrary, opposite reading: *unload* is the opposite of the action of loading; *unbutton* is the opposite of *button;* and so on. In short, when the semantics of the two uses of *un-* are compared, they turn out to be the same, namely contrary negation. Therefore, there is only one *un-* morpheme, and it cannot be used as a test to distinguish between verbal and adjectival passives.

The second diagnostic for adjectivehood is based on the ability of the element to be embedded under certain verbs in English; verbs like *seem, re-*

main, sound, and *look* are supposed to select only adjectival—but not verbal—complements. It may indeed be the case that there is such a restriction
on the selection properties of these verbs, but there are other factors involved,
since not all adjectives may appear under all of these verbs. Even *fed,* which
should be potentially adjectival, can only appear under these verbs if modified by an adverb:

(259)a.   The children seemed *(well) fed.
     b.   The children remained *(well) fed.
     c.   #The children sounded (well) fed.
     d.   The children looked *(well) fed.

Thus, there is an additional semantic constraint on elements appearing under
these verbs, which could rule out the so-called verbal passives on independent grounds. The third test involves prenominal modifiers; only adjectives
(and not verbs) may occur in this position. Fabb (1984) provides clear arguments which challenge this evidence.

The three main arguments that these participles are adjectival, rather than
verbal, do not hold; there are semantic factors involved that indicate it might
not be necessary to postulate a category change in passive constructions,
after all. Whether some passives appear to be more adjectival than others is
not due to a change in category, but rather to the fact that the semantics of
the participle involved is closer to that of an adjective than the semantics of
other participles considered to be "verbal." Such an "adjectival" participle
would be allowed in contexts governed by semantic properties of adjectives,
but not because they are labeled "adjective."[71] Under this analysis, there is
no need to distinguish between the two types of passive participles in terms
of their category (which is more in tune with the hypothesis sketched in note
70). This means that, of all the properties attributed to Adjectival Passive
Formation shown in (260), only the affixation of the morpheme *-ed* would
remain. This is a positive result, since it reduces the rule to a more coherent
process.

(260) Properties of Adjectival Passive Formation:
     a.   Affixation of the passive morpheme -ed
     b.   Change of category: $[+V, -N] \rightarrow [+V, +N]$
     c.   Suppression of the external role of the base verb
     d.   Externalization of an internal role of the base verb

    e.   Absorption of Case
    f.   Elimination of the [NP, VP] position

Unfortunately, for the six verbs noted in (246b), even with the modifications outlined above, passive formation cannot distinguish between those that have both an active and stative uses and those that have only active use. We are back to the original observation that four of these verbs can be stative and the other two cannot. Let us therefore consider the properties of statives themselves, to see if any distinctions between the six verbs could stem from these properties.

    Essentially, statives are not delimited. They have neither beginning nor end, neither object of actualization nor object of termination (see Smith 1978; van Voorst 1988; Tenny 1987; among many others). Hence, statives do not take place as events do and have no internal development. We saw in section 3.1.3 that *venir* and *aller* contrast with the four other verbs in precisely this respect. Verbs like *arriver, partir, entrer,* and *sortir* are perceived as sudden, spontaneous, with no internal development, whereas *venir* and *aller* express internal development of an event. I attributed this to the fact that the Ground of the G-localization (the localization established by relationships in the semantic representation) is localized deictically (D-localized) by the deictic center o and the antideictic center ω in the case of *venir* and *aller.* Since subevents consisting of various mutable elements—Figures—may get D-localized in that case, a sentence built on a Ground that is a D-localizer, as in the case of *venir* and *aller,* refers to an event with an internal development. But in the case of *arriver, partir, entrer,* and *sortir,* it is only the Figure of the G-localization that is D-localized (by being the subject that is related to the moment of speech S); so it is not possible to have mutations with respect to the Ground of the G-localization stabilized by D-localization, since the Ground is not D-localized and the Figure is "stabilized"; hence, the event can have no internal development for *arriver, partir, entrer,* and *sortir* because the G-localization of these four verbs is not based on a D-LOC element, such as the deictic center o or the antideictic center ω, as we can see in (183), repeated here as (261).

(261)   *Venir:* $[x_1 \text{ COP } [x_2 \text{ COP o}]$
             Aller: $[x_1 \text{ COP } [x_2 \text{ COP } \omega]$
             Arriver: $[x_1 \text{ COP } [x_2 \text{ COP y}]$
             Partir: $[x_1 \text{ COP } [x_2 \text{ NOT-COP y}]$
             Entrer: $[x_1 \text{ COP } [x_2 \text{ DANS y}]$

Sortir: [x₁ COP [x₂ NOT-DANS y]]

Therefore, I propose the generalization in (262) to account for the availability of the stative use with a given participle:

(262) *Stative Participle Generalization:* A (passive) participle can have a stative use only if it is possible for the event associated with it not to have an internal development.

We may assume that the correlation in (262) is deduced from the definition of stativity itself. Since *venir* and *aller* obligatorily have an internal development, because they are built with the D-localizers o and ω respectively, the participle of these verbs cannot be used statively.

3.5 IMPERSONAL CONSTRUCTIONS

All six verbs studied here can be used in impersonal constructions fairly freely, as shown in (263), except for *aller,* which requires particular contexts, in particular the presence of a locative, as we see in (264).

(263)   Il est venu/*allé/arrivé/parti/entré/sorti quelqu'un.
          It is come/gone/arrived/left/entered/gone-out someone
          There came/went/arrived/left/entered/went-out someone

(264)a.   Il est venu plus de gens *(ici) qu'il n'en est allé *(chez Jean).
          There came more people (here) than there went to Jean's place.
          More people came here than went to Jean's place.
      b. Il y va plein de touristes à chaque année.
          It there goes full of tourists at every year.
          Many tourists go there every year.
      c. Il y va de ma vie.
          It there goes of my life.
          My life depends on it.

Given Homomorphic Mapping, the impersonal construction will be possible when there are two positions available in the semantic representation of the verb, since in order to get the correct linking for a sentence such as *il est venu quelqu'un,* two positions are required: one for *quelqu'un* and one for *il.* Since all six verbs have two positions in their semantic representation, they are compatible with the impersonal construction. The structure of an impersonal construction, such as *il est venu quelqu'un,* is as in (265):

(265)

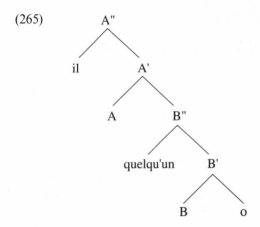

The idea that two positions are required in impersonal constructions is similar to the position taken by Burzio (1985) and Belletti (1988), who use impersonal constructions as a test for unaccusativity (although their position differs crucially from mine in that they assume the syntactic promotion of a direct object to a subject position, and I do not).

However, the data are extremely complex, and I am not sure that it is possible to give a full account of it at present, or that it will ever be possible, given the nature of the factors involved. For example, as Labelle (1989) and Willems (1985) show, two positions are not necessary for a verb to be used in the impersonal construction; some unergatives, which are one-position verbs, appear in this construction.[72] Here are a few examples of such unergatives:

(266)a. Il a dormi dans ce lit plusieurs monarques. (Zribi-Hertz 1982)
         There slept in that bed many monarchs.
         Many monarchs (have) slept in that bed.

   b. Il y dîne une clientèle choisie. (Willems 1985)
       There eats there a select clientele.

   c. Il en a couru des chevaux, ce matin! (Labelle 1989)
       It of-them have run horses, this morning!
       There are lots of horses that ran this morning!

   d. Des gratte-ciels, il en jaillit à tous les coins de rue depuis dix ans.
       (Labelle 1989)
       Skyscrapers, it of-them spring-up at every street corner since ten years.

Skyscrapers, there have been some springing up at every street corner for the last ten years.

e. Il en a coulé de l'eau sous les ponts.
    It of-it has run of the water under the bridges.
    There has been lots of water going under the bridges.

f. Il en a téléphoné du monde aujourd'hui! (Labelle 1989)
    It of-them has phoned of-the people today!
    There are so many people who phoned today!

On the other hand, inchoatives, which I analyze as having two positions, are generally not very good in impersonal constructions, as in (267), although there are some exceptions, as shown in (268).

(267)a. * Il a cassé trois branches.
         There have broken three branches.

    b. * Il a rougi quelqu'un.
        There blushed someone.

    c. * Il a tourné une page.
        There turned a page.

(268)a. ? Il en a roulé des billots sur cette pente! (Labelle 1989)
         There are quite a few logs that rolled on that slope!

    b. Il en a roulé des têtes pendant la révolution! (Labelle 1989)
        There are quite a few heads that rolled during the revolution!

So we have three sets of data: (1) unaccusatives, which are two-position constructions that appear quite freely in the impersonal construction, as in (263) and (264); (2) unergatives, which are one-position constructions for which the impersonal construction is much more restricted, with unclear felicity conditions, as in (266); and (3) inchoatives, which are two-position constructions that generally do not admit the impersonal construction, as in (267), although there are exceptions here, too, as in (268). I will sketch an analysis that offers a uniform account of these facts. However, as many details remain to be worked out, it is only intended to suggest a direction for future research.

In short, I propose the minimal hypothesis that impersonal constructions are indeed found only with two-position constructions, as predicted by Homomorphic Mapping. In the case of the six verbs studied here, the analysis is straightforward, given a semantic structure as in (265). Impersonal *il* is in the highest argument position in the Semantic Representation, so it is linked with the subject position. This raises the question of why *venir, aller, arriver,* and *partir* can participate in this construction at all. We saw in section 3.2 that these verbs do not have a transitive use because conflation applies, transforming the complex relation $[x_1 \ R_1 \ [x_2 \ R_2]]$ into the simplex $[x_1 \ COP]$. The variable x_2 is obliterated and is thus not available for interlevel processes such as linking with a syntactic argument. In the impersonal construction, the direct object links with x_2. Since these verbs occur in the impersonal construction, we can assume that x_2 must be available and that conflation has not taken place.

What could cause the lack of conflation in (265)? I will argue that it has to do with the nature of impersonal *il*. "Ugly objects" such as impersonal *il* have few features; just enough to function as a pivot to situate the event with respect to the temporal point. Impersonal *il* can only be in the argumental position that links to the subject position. It cannot be a direct object, since it cannot function as an actant that is involved in the delimitation of the event. This is why there are no direct object impersonal pronouns. Since the value of impersonal *il* can only be attributed to the variable in the highest argument position, impersonal *il* cannot bind an internal argument. Therefore, there can be no binding between x_1 and x_2 in $[x_1 \ R_1 \ [x_2 \ R_2]]$ when the highest argument is impersonal *il*. Binding of x_2 by x_1 is usually obligatory for these four verbs, as we saw in the discussion of transitivity in 3.2 because the upper and lower relations in their semantic representations are both COP, and, usually, an element that can have the COP_2 relation can also have the more general COP_1 relation. In that case, x_2 can be identified by x_1 by binding, without an additional element to which x_2 is linked, and considerations of economy make binding obligatory. But impersonal *il* can only have the more general relation, not the more specific relations that COP_2 induces with various elements.

For these reasons, the conditions for conflation are not satisfied and conflation does not take place when impersonal *il* is the subject. Since x_2 cannot be bound by x_1, it must link to a syntactic phrase in order to satisfy Full Identification. This phrase will have to be the direct object, because of Homomorphic Mapping, which is the source of the "demotion of the subject" effect in these constructions.

The possibility of linking x_2 to the object means that, in these constructions, there is no "oriented axis," and therefore predicts that no phrases that modify such an axis should be possible. Recall that an oriented axis is created when there is binding between two variables in the semantic representation of a verb. As I argued in 3.1.1.1, an adjunct *de*-phrase can modify the tail end of such an oriented axis, as in (269), where Jean is oriented toward his being at the deictic center, with the tail end of the orientation being in Québec.

(269)   Jean vient de Québec.
         Jean comes from Quebec City.

But in impersonal constructions, as in (265), no binding takes place, so no oriented axis can be derived from the structure. This predicts that *de*-phrases should be incompatible with impersonal constructions. The prediction is borne out: the sentences in (270), with *de*-phrases, are fine, but their impersonal counterparts, in (271), are ungrammatical.

(270)a.   C'est de ses mauvaises habitudes alimentaires que lui est venue
           cette tumeur.
           It is from his bad eating habits that this tumor came to him.
           It is from his bad eating habits that he got this tumor.
     b.   C'est de ce livre que lui est venue l'idée de simuler un suicide.
           It is from this book that came to him the idea of simulating a
           suicide.
           It is from this book that he got the idea of faking suicide.

(271)a.   #Il lui est venu une tumeur de ses mauvaises habitudes ali-
           mentaires.
           There came to him a tumor from his bad eating habits.
     b.   #Il lui est venu une idée de ce livre/ de ce que tu as dit.
           There came to him an idea from that book/from what you said.

The analysis of unaccusative impersonal constructions is straightforward, if one assumes that they have a semantic representation, as in (265), with *il* occupying the highest argument position and the direct object linking with x_2. But the analysis of the other impersonal constructions is much less obvious. If we turn to the second case, we can explain why unergatives, which have one-position constructions, can appear in impersonal constructions by assuming that, under as yet unclear conditions, *il* + COP may be added to an unergative. So, [TROIS PERSONNES TELEPHONER] would become *Il a téléphoné trois personnes* 'Three people phoned,' with the semantic structure in (272):

(272)a.   Il a téléphoné trois personnes:
   b.   COP"

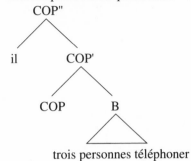

trois personnes téléphoner

Given Homomorphic Mapping, there is no difficulty in accounting for the presence of an "Agent" in direct object position in (272a). Since *trois personnes* is not the highest argument in the semantic structure, but the second highest, it maps onto the second highest syntactic position. Zubizarreta (1987, 154) generates the postverbal subject of impersonal constructions in a position adjoined to VP. But as Labelle (1989) argues, we would expect these subjects to agree with the verb in French, since other subjects right-adjoined to VP agree with the verb:

(273)a.   Dans le jardin couraient Paul et Marie.
            In the garden ran-PLUR Paul and Marie.
   b.   N'ont été exécutés que quelques prisonniers.
            Have-PLUR been executed-PLUR only a few prisoners.

Labelle gives four other arguments in favor of the hypothesis that these subjects are direct objects, rather than adjoined to VP. (1) The postverbal NP regularly appears before a PP complement, rather than after, as would be predicted under the adjunction analysis:

(274)   Il roule des milliers de voitures comme celles-là sur les routes.
            There runs thousands of cars like those on the roads.

(2) There is a definiteness effect in impersonals—the "demoted" subject must not be a specific definite NP; but this effect is not found when the subject is right-adjoined to VP, as in locative inversions. Compare (275) with (273a).

(275)   *Il a mangé Paul et Marie dans ce restaurant.
            There ate Paul and Marie in that restaurant.

(3) In the impersonal construction, a postverbal indefinite or partitive object NP must be introduced by *de,* and not *des,* in the presence of a negative marker, as in (276a and b). This is the same as a direct object (276c and d),

but unlike the postverbal NP of locative inversion, which need not be introduced by *de* (276e).

(276)a.   Il n'a jamais dormi *de* malades dans cette chambre.
        There never slept sick-people in that room.
    b.   * Il n'a jamais dormi *des* malades dans cette chambre.
    c.   Je n'attends pas *d'*invités.
        I do not expect any guests.
    d.   * Je n'attends pas *des* invités.
    e.   On a déjà dit qu'à l'analyse syntaxique ne correspondait pas *d'*analyse/*une* analyse . . .
        We have already said that to the syntactic analysis did not correspond an analysis..

(4) Finally, *en*-cliticization is restricted to direct object NPs, not VP-adjoined NPs.

(277)   J'en ai vu trois.
        I of-them have seen three.
        I saw three (of them).

The postverbal NP of the impersonal construction allows *en*-cliticization, whereas the postverbal NP of the locative inversion, which is VP-adjoined, does not:

(278)a.   Il en courait plusieurs dans le jardin.
        There of-them ran many in the garden.
        Many of them were running in the garden.
    b.   * Dans le jardin en couraient plusieurs.
        In the garden of-them ran many.

Further support for the assumption that locative inversion postverbal NPs are adjoined, whereas impersonal construction postverbal NPs are in object position, comes from the fact that direct objects cannot agree with the participle under my analysis of participle agreement in 3.3.2.3. Thus, the fact that postverbal NPs in locatives trigger agreement, as in (273b), suggests that they cannot be in object position, and the fact that postverbal NPs in the impersonal construction do not trigger agreement, as in *Il a été exécuté quelques prisonniers* 'A few prisoners have been executed,' suggests that they might be in object position.

Labelle makes another observation of a different nature, which directly relates to the structure proposed in (272). She notes that when the subject of an unergative verb appears VP-internally, "the event denoted by the verb is not presented as being the result of the activity of the 'logical subject,' which is therefore denied part of its responsibility for bringing the event into existence" (Labelle 1989, 30). For example in (279), what is important is not the action of the three people but rather the fact that, of the possibly large number of people who could have called, three did.

(279)   Il a téléphoné trois personnes ce matin. (adapted from Labelle)
         There phoned three people this morning.

However, this implication, that the subject is denied responsibility for bringing about the event, is exactly what we expect, given a structure like (272). If the fact that x_j "actualizes" the event is expressed by its orientation toward [x_2 PRED], as suggested in note 47, then indeed the argument *trois personnes* no longer is in a position to actualize the event in a structure like (272), since it is not oriented toward [x_2 PRED] but is itself [x_2]. A better understanding of what it means for an argument to be an "actualizer," to be responsible for bringing about the event, will no doubt help us understand the conditions under which this responsibility can be denied.

Finally, consider the third case, that of inchoatives, which are two-position constructions, but allow the impersonal construction only marginally. Why is it so difficult to introduce *il* + COP with an inchoative, as in (280) (= (267a)), where the structure of the inchoative itself is [trois branches$_i$ R$_1$ [x_i CASSER]]?

(280)   *Il a cassé trois branches.

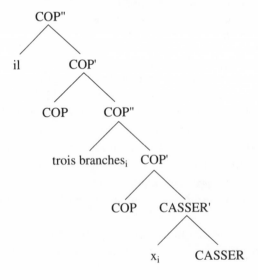

There are two reasons, one functional, the other more formal. First, as we just saw, the effect of constructing an impersonal by introducing *il* + COP is to deny the subject responsibility for bringing about the event. On the other hand, we saw in 3.2 and 3.3.1.3 that constructing an inchoative has exactly the opposite effect and emphasizes the responsibility of the subject. For example, in *La branche a cassé* 'The branch broke,' x_1 "actualizes" $[x_2$ PRED], where x_1 is something inherent to x that is responsible for, controls, or allows $[x_2$ PRED], the branch is responsible for its own breaking. This clash in the respective functions of the impersonal and inchoative constructions makes them incompatible.

Second, inchoativization affects transitive constructions, that is, constructions with two distinct argument delimiters not subject to conflation. But the addition of *il* + COP, as in (280), would create a verb with three arguments, all nonprepositional. This is not possible because nonprepositional, or "bare," arguments are delimiters, and there can be at most two delimiters for an event—an actualizer and an endpoint. Apparent counterexamples, like double-object constructions, actually have only two bare arguments, since one of the NPs is not argumental but predicative (see the discussion of (187) in 3.2).

Given these two observations, inchoatives cannot appear in impersonal constructions. But why then are some inchoatives possible in the impersonal, as in (268) repeated here?

(268)a.   ?Il en a roulé des billots sur cette pente! (Labelle 1989)
             There are quite a few logs that rolled on that slope!
      b.   Il en a roulé des têtes pendant la révolution! (Labelle 1989)
             There are quite a few heads that rolled during the revolution!

The reason, I think, is that *rouler* does not function as a transitive verb here, presumably because its 3-D specifications overshadow its semantic structure specifications in this use (see the first option in the discussion of *monter* 'go up' in 3.3.1.3, in which the 3-D expression of manner is introduced alongside the phonological, syntactic, and semantic structures). The emphasis is on the 3-D aspects of the rolling action of the logs and heads, not on some actualizer, external as in the transitive construction, or internal as in the inchoative construction. Thus, although there is a nonimpersonal inchoative (281a) corresponding to (268b), there is no transitive (lexical causative) equivalent to (268b), only a syntactic causative (281b). A transitive sentence with *rouler* is possible (281c), but it has a different, even more gruesome use, in which the heads are physically rolled.

(281)a. Plusieurs têtes de nobles ont roulé pendant la révolution.
         Many heads of the nobility have rolled during the revolution.
     b. Les révolutionnaires ont fait rouler plusieurs têtes pendant la révolution.
         The revolutionaries made many heads of the nobility roll during the revolution.
     c. Les révolutionnaires ont roulé plusieurs têtes de nobles pendant la révolution.
         The revolutionaries rolled many heads of the nobility during the revolution.

(268a) also implies the nonmanipulative use of *rouler:* if it is acceptable at all, it is only if *rouler* is used in the same "indirect" way it is used in (268b). The question mark reflects the fact that the transitive, "manipulative" use of *rouler* is more likely in the case of logs, which should make the impersonal more difficult to get.

We saw that there are three kinds of impersonal constructions. Some are built on unaccusative verbs, others on unergative verbs, and some on inchoative verbs. I assume that impersonal *il* occurs with two-position verbs, in the highest argument position, as indicated in (265). The construction is subject to certain conditions, which the six verbs studied seem to satisfy.

3.6 THE RESIDUE OF TIER THEORY

The simple representations that I adopt contrast with those in approaches that assume multiple tiers in semantic representations, such as Jackendoff (1987a, 1990a), for example, with thematic tiers dealing with motion and location, action tiers dealing with Agent-Patient relations, and temporal tiers that correlate the first two.[73] One could object that my representations are too simplified and cannot express what these other theories can. There are two major arguments in favor of such multitier representations: (1) they provide an account of arguments that have more than one theta role by having them bear different roles on different tiers; and (2) thematic and action tiers being related to one another by temporal tiers, this provides an account of temporal relations between subevents of the event expressed by a sentence.

Consider first multiple theta role assignment. Multiple theta constructions do not require multiple tiers: some roles can be assigned by binding; others are not linguistically relevant; hence they are not really present in the Grammar. For instance, in (282), Jackendoff assumes that *the ball* gets three thematic roles: it is the Goal of [STICK [GO TO BALL]], the Patient of [FRED ACT BALL], and the Theme of [BALL [GO TO CENTER FIELD]].

(282)   Fred hit the ball into center field with a stick.

Although I do not think that thematic notions of this sort are part of grammar, assignment of two more abstract semantic roles corresponding to Goal and Theme does not require multiple tiers. The former can be assigned directly by *hit* and the latter by the PP, via binding, a process already present both in Jackendoff's analysis and in the present one. As for the Patient role, we have already seen in section 1.5.2.2.2 that it is not a grammatical but rather a discourse notion that depends on contextual factors like relative size of the arguments, whether one has a violent character or not, etc.

As for the ordering of subevents, such as the fact that Fred acts on the stick before the stick acts on the ball in (282), this is beside the point, since these notions are contextual, not grammatical. Lastly, Jackendoff proposes a final temporal point to account for the inference of termination whereby, if X goes to Y, then X is at Y at the termination of that event of going. But given the decomposition of *aller* that I proposed, that inference is easily derived. Thus, in *Jean va à Québec,* all that the sentence means is something like "Jean is oriented toward the relation 'Jean relates with Québec.'" It is clear why the inference of termination obtains: the termination state corresponds to the lower relation 'Jean relates with Québec,' the A′ of (59) above. I conclude that there are no compelling arguments for tiered representations of semantic properties.

3.7 CONCLUSION

Six French verbs, prototypical cases of "movement verbs," were discussed in this chapter. Many uses of these verbs were considered, and it was shown that labeling them as "movement verbs" is misguided. Instead of disregarding these other uses, or introducing excessive polysemy and metaphor, it proved useful to abstract away from the situational properties of the movement uses of these verbs, to make a sharp distinction between 'use' and 'meaning.' The more abstract representation of the meaning of these verbs presented here was shown to account for constraints that hold across their different uses. In particular, linking properties were shown to follow from two simple, general, and highly constraining principles: Full Identification and Homomorphic Mapping. Crucial in achieving the abstraction was the fact that tree structures have meaning that is available to semantics; in particular, we saw the importance of the orientation inherent in tree structures. Although highly abstract, the proposed meaning representations proved to be adequate; since language is not used in a vacuum, but rather makes extensive use of the wealth of background knowledge shared by speakers, it is possible to compute from the abstract representations, the actual situations to which sentences can refer. As well as producing interesting empirical results, this more abstract approach confirms that a better mentalist model of Grammar is achieved when situational properties are excluded from the Grammar.

This does not mean that the linguist should disregard situational primitives. On the contrary, situational primitives must be studied, so that their effects on Grammar can be understood. But they only interact with Grammar, they do not belong in Grammar, and incorporating them into grammatical representations profoundly obscures the facts. Therefore, the linguist must be keenly aware of situational factors and not include them in his grammatical analyses but rather make sure that no such factors slip in.

PART III. SELECTIVE SEMANTICS AND SYNTAX

This part of the book deals with the effects on the syntax of adopting Selective Semantics, in particular the effects of Full Identification and Homomorphic Mapping. These two principles severely constrain X-bar theory, and this, in turn, constrains what can be a possible transformation.

The effect of Homomorphic Mapping is that the linking of arguments and grammatical functions is more direct, from structure to structure, without intermediate levels consisting of lists or multiple tiers. This more direct linking allows for a more constrained X-bar theory: there need not be a fixed number of bar levels in a projection; in fact, there cannot be. The number of levels is fixed in each particular case by the number of arguments or modifiers in the semantic structure and with which a syntactic correspondence is established. Moreover, given Full Identification, all syntactic nodes must correspond to a node in the semantic structure. This prohibits both vacuous projection and the proliferation of categories that function strictly as escape hatches, or landing sites, for moved elements (such as AGR). Consequently, the transformational component is also highly constrained: no rule can move an element to a node whose sole role in the grammar is to serve as a landing site, since such "open" positions cannot exist. Most "promotion" constructions will therefore have to be reconsidered.[1]

Within this more constrained theory of transformations, the only type of transformation that is allowed is chunking under Homomorphic Mapping because it is the only type of transformation that comes for free, in the sense that it is a virtual necessity; movement transformations, which are not minimal in this sense, are disallowed (see section 2.3.1). Where in principles and parameters theory, a movement transformation might be postulated to relate two positions, in this theory, there is no such transformation.

Movement transformations fall into three general types: A-movement, A-bar movement and Head movement. Since the more constrained theory of transformations that I adopt does not allow movement transformations, all the standard cases of movement have to be reexamined and given alternative analyses. There are three ways to do this. First, if there is a promotion effect, one may argue that the effect derives from Homomorphic Mapping rather than a movement transformation. Second, one may show that the elements in the two positions being related are both independently licensed by a corresponding node in semantic representation, so that the relation between the two positions is not transformational but rather a case of binding in a single phrase marker. Third, one may argue that the postulated relation does not actually exist and that no relation at all holds between the two positions.

I have already discussed a few examples of these three strategies. For example, in *Construction 3* of section 3.3.1.3, I argued that the promotion effect observed in a case of A-movement, such as passive, derives from Homomorphic Mapping. I showed that binding between two positions may account for properties of unaccusatives, in chapter 3, and for properties of inchoatives, in 3.2 and *Construction 6* of 3.3.1.3. As for the raising relation in constructions with verbs such as *sembler* 'seem,' I argued, in the discussion of *Construction 9* of 3.3.1.3, that the theta-to-nontheta relation does not exist and that the construction is better analyzed as a case of binding between two "theta" positions.

A case of A-bar movement was discussed in section 3.3.2.3 on participle agreement. I argued that Wh-movement should be analyzed either as a case of binding, where the S-internal position of the Wh-phrase is licensed by the relation to the verb (as argument or adjunct) and the SPEC of COMP position is licensed by the relation with a [+Wh] COMP, or as a case of extension of the government relation by Connectedness.

I cannot go into the details of all the constructions claimed to fall under the three types of movement transformation. It will be more fruitful to look at typical cases in detail than to give a cursory glance to all the possible cases. In this way, the reader will at least have a precise idea of the kind of arguments I would make and can extrapolate to other cases using a similar strategy.

Since I have only discussed cases of phrasal movement so far, a case of Head movement will be the topic of Chapter 5. Verb-to-Tense head movement (V to T) has been proposed to account for the positions of the verb and adverbs with respect to one another. I will argue that when two positions are involved, both V and T are licensed with respect to the semantic structure so that head binding, not movement, takes place; moreover, in many instances where movement has been postulated to account for the placement of ADV and V, different structures are involved because the meanings are different, so the sentences cannot be transformationally related, in any event. The analysis proposed makes no use of unlicensed AGR or of movement.

But, first, a construction inappropriately analyzed as phrasal movement is examined in chapter 4. Psych-verb constructions exhibit peculiar properties, but a unified analysis of these properties cannot be achieved by means of a phrasal A-movement transformation or a binding account. Rather, I will show that the relation claimed to hold between two positions in some Psych constructions does not exist and that a semantic/pragmatic account of the peculiar properties of the construction is to be preferred.

4 Psych Verbs

In this chapter, I will examine Psych verbs because sentences in which some classes of these verbs appear exhibit an apparent crossing of thematic roles, which has led many linguists to analyze them as being transformationally related. This has led to analyses in which several peculiar properties of these classes of verbs have been related to the transformational analysis. I will claim that previous analyses were wrong in this respect and that no such crossing is found; as for the other properties, they come from the referential peculiarities of the arguments in these constructions, which take place in the conceptual domain of "mental space."

4.1 PSYCH VERBS AND CONSTRAINED MOVEMENT: THE PROBLEM

The effect of Homomorphic Mapping is that the structural organization of syntactic structure reflects semantic structure. In this more direct correspondence, the linking of argument positions to syntactic Grammatical Function positions is not indexical; rather, the relative relations between arguments in semantic structure are carried over to syntactic structure, and linking is straightforward. As we saw in chapter 2, one syntactic effect of this direct correspondence is that any syntactic node must be justified by its corresponding to a node in the semantic structure. This means that both positions involved in any movement must be independently justified, by corresponding to a node in semantic structure; there can be no movement to an "open" syntactic position, and movement to a licensed position is not a transformation but binding within a single phrase marker. Thus, movement transformations are not possible in this theory.

I examine Psych verb constructions because the widely-accepted analysis of these constructions, revived recently by Belletti and Rizzi (1988), derives one class of Psych verb constructions by a promotion of an object to an "open" subject position. Such a movement analysis is not available in my framework, so I will propose another analysis of these constructions.

Recall what the facts are. There is a contrast between two classes of Psych verbs, the Fear-type (*mépriser,* in French) and the Frighten-type (*dégoûter,* in French), illustrated by (1) and (2), respectively.

(1)   John fears Mary/your decision/the storm.

(2)   Mary/your decision/the storm frightens John.

It was noted very early on (see Postal 1971; Jackendoff 1972; and references therein) that the selectional restrictions on the subject of Fear-verbs and those on the object of Frighten-verbs are essentially the same, and, similarly, that the selectional restrictions on the object of Fear-verbs and those on the subject of Frighten-verbs are also essentially the same. Jackendoff (1972) identifies the subject of Frighten-verbs as a Theme and the object as a Goal, and Ruwet (1972) notes that the opposite pattern occurs in (1), although Ruwet talked about a Place role instead of a Goal role. In short, the theta roles seem to be crossed. I will use Pesetsky's (1990) terminology and refer to Fear-verbs as Experiencer-Subject (ES) verbs and to Frighten-verbs as Experiencer-Object (EO) verbs.

For an analysis in which selectional properties are analyzed in thematic terms, the apparent crossing of selectional restrictions is problematic, since, in such an analysis, it is assumed that GF positions in Deep Structure (DS) should correspond in a fairly regular way to thematic roles (see Fillmore 1968 for an early proposal to this effect; for more recent proposals, see Perlmutter and Postal's 1984 Universal Alignment Hypothesis and Baker's 1988 Uniformity of Theta Assignment Hypothesis).[2] To avoid having two very different Deep Structures for sentences like (1) and (2), as their Surface Structures suggest, there were a number of early proposals to derive (2) from a DS similar to (1) (Rosenbaum 1967; Chapin 1967; Chomsky 1970; Lakoff 1970a; Postal 1971).[3] I illustrate this in (3) with Postal's (1971) PSYCH MVT transformation.

(3)   DS: John frightens Mary/your decision/the storm. ⇒
        SS: Mary/your decision/the storm frightens John.

EO verbs (the "frighten" class) were marked [+PSYCH MVT], whereas ES (the "fear" class) verbs were [−PSYCH MVT]. This was in the spirit of early Transformational Grammar, where regular correlations of this type were said to be accounted for in a more economical way if analyzed transformationally. Details of this analysis will render it no longer tenable in a GB framework—it violates the theta criterion, and marking of lexical items for specific transformational rules is not possible, since all such rules have been replaced by move α—but the motivation behind the analysis is still being used.

Belletti and Rizzi, assuming that theta roles of Psych verbs must be assigned in a rigid way, according to (4), and using the same logic, propose to derive (2) in a manner compatible with present assumptions, as in (5).

(4) *Linking Principle of Experiencer Verbs:* Given a Theta-grid [Experiencer, Theme], the Experiencer is projected to a higher position than the Theme. (Belletti and Rizzi's (119) 1988).

(5) *DS: [[frightens Mary* $_{VP}$] John $_{VP}$] ⇒
SS: Mary [[frightens *t* $_{VP}$] John $_{VP}$]

In (5), using their terminology, the Theme is assigned to the Direct Object position, just as it is in (1), so that this theta role can be said to be assigned uniformly to the Direct Object position. Since it is impossible, given current assumptions, to mark EO verbs as [+RAISE−OBJECT-TO-SUBJECT], they are assumed to trigger the movement for another reason; EO verbs are assumed to be deficient Case assigners, so the NP object is forced to raise. Note, however, that this does only half of the job. The role of Experiencer, although it is now assigned higher than the Theme in both (1) and (5), is not assigned uniformly to the same position: it is assigned to the subject position in (1), but to a VP-adjoined position in (5).

Another analysis that tries to preserve the uniformity of theta role assignments is found in Grimshaw (1990). She proposes that the lexical entry of a verb contains not only a thematic tier, but also an aspectual tier. On the thematic tier, ES verbs and EO verbs do not differ: the Experiencer, the highest of the two thematic roles in the thematic hierarchy, is always assigned higher than the Theme in the syntactic structure. Under her analysis, it is on the aspectual tier that the two classes of verbs differ. ES verbs like *fear* are stative, as in (6), whereas EO verbs like *frighten* are causative and so are analyzed, as in (7), with a first subevent that is a CAUSE.

(6)   Fear: Experiencer   Theme   (Thematic tier)

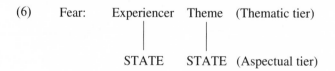

          STATE   STATE   (Aspectual tier)

(7)   Frighten: Experiencer   Theme   (Thematic tier)

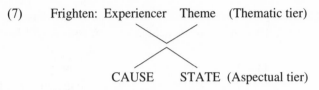

          CAUSE   STATE (Aspectual tier)

In the ES class of verbs, the first position in the aspectual tier is associated with the first position in the thematic tier, and there is also a correspondence between the second positions of both tiers. But Grimshaw claims that the situation is different for EO verbs: the first position in the thematic tier does not correspond to the first position in the aspectual tier; instead, the second argument in the thematic tier is associated with the first element in the aspectual tier, and the first element in the thematic tier corresponds to the second position in the aspectual tier. "The special character of the non-agentive *frighten* class has its source, according to this proposal, in a conflict between the two hierarchies, the subject being most prominent in the causal hierarchy but not in the thematic hierarchy" (Grimshaw 1990, 25). Thus, the lines of association cross in (7), but not in (6). Since aspectual properties govern the Deep Structure realization of arguments, in Grimshaw's analysis, we can expect differences at D-structure between these two verb classes.

Pesetsky (1988, 1990) proposes yet another analysis of Psych constructions. He notes that, in large part, the problem in analyzing these constructions comes from the assumption that the theta role of the object in ES verbs is the same as that of the subject in EO verbs. He assumes that there is no crossing of roles, since the roles are, in fact, distinct. He notes that this assumption is commonplace in the philosophical literature on this topic (see Kenny 1963).

In Pesetsky's analysis, the Subject of EO verbs bears a CAUSE role, whereas the Object of ES verbs bears the role of TARGET OF EMOTION or SUBJECT MATTER OF EMOTION (which, he notes, are often lumped together as "object of emotion," but should not be) (1990, 34). His classification is given in (8).

(8) *Class 1.a:* Subject = EXPERIENCER, Object/P-Object = TARGET OF EMOTION: angry at, like, love, satisfied with, content with;
Class 1.b: Subject = EXPERIENCER, Object = SUBJECT MATTER OF EMOTION: worry about, bored with, concerned about, fear, afraid of.
Class 2: Subject = CAUSE, Object = EXPERIENCER: anger, please, delight, satisfy, content, worry, bore, concern, frighten.

In Pesetsky (1990), the alignment of theta roles and GFs is governed by the following principles:

(9) *Linking Principles (Pesetsky's (239))*:
   a. A Cause argument is the highest argument of its predicate.
   b. An Experiencer is the highest argument of its predicate.

For ES verbs, which have no Cause argument, linking is simple—the Experiencer appears in subject position. But in the case of EO verbs, which have both a Cause and an Experiencer, the linking principles force the construction to be biclausal. He assumes that EO verbs are derived from ES bases by a zero morpheme CAUS; the Experiencer is the highest argument of the ES Psych-verb base, and the Cause is the highest argument of CAUS.[4]

Pesetsky shows that the assumption that different theta roles are assigned to the Subject of EO verbs, and the Object of ES verbs is substantiated by the fact that their truth conditions differ. First, consider the distinction between CAUSE and TARGET OF EMOTION illustrated in (10) (Pesetsky 1992, 17), based on an observation by Kenny 1963).

(10)a. Bill was very angry at the article in the Times. (Object = TARGET)
    b. The article in the Times angered Bill. (Subject = CAUSE)

In (a), Bill has evaluated the article and formed a bad opinion of it: he finds it objectionable in some respect. In (b), the situation could be as (a), but it could also be the case that Bill thinks that the article is splendid, but its subject causes Bill to be angry. For Pesetsky, this contrast is due to the following difference: "A CAUSE argument must simply be causally connected to the emotion described by the predicate and borne by the EXPERIENCER. The TARGET argument, however, is *evaluated* by the EXPERIENCER as part of what the philosopher Nissenbaum calls "the emotional episode": in general, a negative emotion (like *angry*) entails a negative evaluation, a positive emotion (like *loves*) entails a positive evaluation" (Pesetsky 1988, 11).

A distinction should also be made between CAUSE and SUBJECT MATTER OF EMOTION, as we see in (11).

(11)a. John worried about Mary's poor health. (SUBJECT MATTER OF EMOTION)
    b. Mary's poor health worried John. (CAUSE)

"[In (a)], whenever John was experiencing the worry described in the example, he was thinking in some way about Mary's health. [. . . In (b), . . .]

it is sufficient that Mary's poor health causes John to experience worry, but the subject matter of his thoughts while experiencing worry could have nothing to do with Mary's health." (Pesetsky 1988, 13)

All three of the above analyses—Belletti and Rizzi's, Grimshaw's, and Pesetsky's—are forced to use unconstrained indexical linking because they rely on thematic notions. In addition, Pesetsky's use of special theta role labels like EXPERIENCER, TARGET OF EMOTION, and SUBJECT MATTER OF EMOTION is not very explanatory and raises further problems, as we will see below. Grimshaw's use of multiple tiers further weakens the possibility of constraining the correspondence between arguments and syntactic positions. Raising analyses like Belletti and Rizzi's in which EO verbs are assumed to have a derived subject, also face a problem in the choice of AUX and past participle agreement of these verbs: they do not select the AUX usually found with derived subjects, nor is past participle agreement with the subject triggered, as it usually is in cases of derived subjects such as passives and unaccusatives. Also, as it stands, Belletti and Rizzi's analysis leaves unexplained the fact that double-object Psych verbs are always deficient Case assigners, so that the two arguments never surface as double objects with an expletive subject, for example.

In addition, these analyses are all subject to an observation made by Dowty (1991) about the raising analysis: "[N]o matter how compelling the arguments may be that Stimulus (= Theme) subjects of Psych verbs behave like 'derived subjects' (e.g., raised, passivized and nonthematic NPs) in English and Italian, while Experiencer objects are like underlying subjects, the deeper question which these accounts do not answer is why THIS particular class of lexical predicates should occur in these abstract underlying structures and appear in this surface alternation, while other classes of verbs (prototypical transitives like *kill,* statives, motion verbs, three-place verbs, etc.) never do" (Dowty 1991, 580, note 23). In other words, these analyses are subject to the same problems as any analysis that links the properties of certain verbs with their ability to govern rules: the main criticism of such analyses, leveled against analyses as early as Lakoff (1970b), is that they lack deep explanatory power, since too much is simply listed.

Given my position that situational notions such as thematic roles do not participate in Grammatical processes, I must reject these analyses on principle. As we will see in the next section, these analyses have two serious empirical problems that independently suggest that they should be abandoned, as should any analysis that gives a special status to EO verbs, whether in their thematic organization, aspectual organization, or DS configuration. I will respond to Dowty's objection by proposing that Psych verbs are not grammatically "special," after all, and that their peculiarities do not depend on grammatical factors but on the distinct referential nature of mental entities such as feelings.

4.2 Two Problems with Treating EO Verbs as Special

The first problem for analyses that treat EO verbs as special in the ways just discussed is that EO-type Psych constructions, with similar syntactic and aspectual properties, can occur with verbs that do not seem to have any inherent "psychological" content. In fact, contrary to what these analyses predict, this construction is very productive, with verbs switching fairly freely from a "normal" use to a Psych use. The second problem is that the thematic analysis is not just incorrect in its basic premises, as I argued in chapter 1, but also that the versions of such an analysis generally assumed are incorrect in their details. I will show that there is no crossing of theta roles and that each of these "Psych" roles can be assigned in several different positions, so that the motivation for these analyses stemming from an attempt to assign thematic roles uniformly at Deep Structure is not substantiated. Moreover, in the analysis that I propose, factors emerge that are obscured by thematic notions, and this provides an analysis that is empirically more adequate.

4.2.1 Productivity

The first problem was noted by Ruwet (1972). In his discussion of Postal's transformational account, he noted that there is a third class of Psych Verbs that have to be accounted for: the *frapper* (*strike*) verbs, as in (12).

(12)a. Paul a frappé/ébloui/empoisonné Marie par son discours.
        Paul struck/blinded/poisoned Mary with his talk.
     b. Paul strikes Mary as intelligent.

Ruwet shows that this class of verbs is very productive in French. He lists dozens of verbs, and adds that almost any causative action verb can become a "Psych verb." I believe that this productivity is even more general: verbs traditionally labeled "Psych verbs" are but a subcase of a very productive class of "Psych constructions." For a vast class of verbs, if one of their argument positions is filled by a *psy-chose*—a psychological object, found only in mental space, such as an emotion—the construction is a Psych construction.[5] This is possible with just about any change-of-state verb with two or more arguments, as we will see below. Psych verbs always form Psych constructions because the psy-chose argument is incorporated into the verb (fright, fear, disgust, love, or hate, for example), but that is all that is special about them. As far as most other properties are concerned, I will show that Psych verbs are like ordinary verbs. They have no special Deep Structure, special thematic structure, or thematic roles. All verbs, when used as Psych predicates, whether with an incorporated psychose argument or not, do have a special aspectual status, but it differs from the one Grimshaw attributes to them; instead, it has to do with the "mental" nature of the arguments involved (see the discussion under (36) below and section 4.4.5.2 on Affectedness).

Consider the following sets of examples, which illustrate the productivity of the construction. The examples in (13)–(18) are instances of Psych constructions without incorporation of the psy-chose argument, whereas in examples (19) and (20) the psy-chose argument is incorporated into the verb so that the verb is always Psych. In all the examples, I indicate the standard thematic role with which the psy-chose and the Experiencer correspond, for further comparisons below. The psy-chose is in bold when not incorporated; the Experiencer is underlined and its corresponding role indicated at the end of the example.

(13) THEME psy-chose, without incorporation:

    a.   Jean fait **peur** à <u>Marie</u>   [Exp. = Goal]
         Jean makes scare to Marie.
         Jean scares Marie.

    b.   <u>Paul</u> a **peur** de Marie.[6]   [Exp. = Place]
         Paul has scare of Marie.
         Jean is afraid of Marie.

    c.   Jean donne du **soucis** à <u>Marie.</u>   [Exp. = Goal]
         Jean gives some worry to Marie.
         Jean worries Marie.

    d.   Il y a en <u>Pierre</u> un profond **mépris** de l'argent.   [Exp. = Place]
         There is in Pierre a deep contempt for money.

    e.   <u>Paul</u> voue une **haine** féroce à
         Virginie.   [Exp. = Agent and Source]
         Paul vows a ferocious hate to Virginie.

    f.   Ce **désir** de vengeance <u>me</u> vient de Paul.   [Exp. = Goal]
         This desire for vengeance comes to me from Paul.

    g.   <u>Il</u> ne pouvait plus contenir sa **rage.**   [Exp. = Place?]
         He could no longer contain his rage.

(14) PLACE psy-chose, without incorporation:
    a.   Cela a mis <u>Marie</u> en **colère.**   [Exp. = Theme]
        That put Marie in anger.
        That angered Marie.
    b.   <u>Paul</u> est tombé **amoureux** de Marie.   [Exp. = Theme]
        Paul fell in love with Marie.
    c.   <u>Paul</u> est tombé de désespoir en **désespoir.**   [Exp. = Theme]
        Paul fell from despair into despair.

(15) GOAL psy-chose, without incorporation:
    a.   Paul a poussé <u>Marie</u> à la **haine**/au **désespoir.**   [Exp. = Theme]
        Paul pushed Marie to hatred/to despair.
    b.   Le vieux moine a poussé <u>Paul</u> au **dégoût** de soi. [Exp. = Theme]
        The old monk pushed Paul to self-disgust.
    c.   <u>Paul</u> a donné libre cours à sa **colère.**   [Exp. = Agent]
        Paul gave free rein to his anger.

(16) SOURCE psy-chose, without incorporation:
    <u>Marie</u> ne revient pas de **l'horreur** de ce spectacle.   [Exp. = Theme]
    Marie does not come over the horror of that scene.
    Marie cannot get over the horror of that scene.

(17) INSTIGATOR ("Agent") psy-chose, without incorporation (Whole
    class of action verbs like *frapper*):
    a.   Jean a frappé/empoisonné <u>Marie</u> par son
        discours.   [Exp. = Theme]
        Jean struck/poisoned Marie by his talk.
    b.   Ces nuages <u>me</u> disent qu'il va pleuvoir.   [Exp. = Goal]
        These clouds tell me that it will rain.
    c.   Une **peur** bleue <u>le</u> gagna/ s'empara de *lui.*   [Exp. = Theme?]
        A blue (=towering) fright won him/came over him.
    d.   Paul a fait tomber <u>Marie</u> à la renverse par son intelligence.
        Paul made Marie fall head over heels with his
        intelligence.   [Exp. = Agent/Theme]
        (Psy-chose and EXP not coarguments here)
    e.   La **rage** l'étouffe.   [EXP = Theme]
        Anger chokes him.
    f.   La **jalousie** <u>le</u> mine.   [EXP = Theme]
        Jealousy saps him.

(18) INSTRUMENT (?) psy-chose, without incorporation:
    a.   <u>Il</u> était rempli **d'amertume.**   [Exp. = Place?]

He was filled with bitterness.
b.   Elle débordait de **joie.**   [Exp. = Place?]
     She overflowed with joy.

(19) THEME psy-chose, with incorporation (numerous):
      a.   Pierre méprise l'argent.   [EXP = Agent and Source/Goal?]
           Pierre despises money.
      b.   L'argent/cette idée dégoûte Pierre.   [EXP = Goal]
           Money/that idea disgusts Pierre.
      c.   Paul a dégoûté Marie de cela.   [Exp. = Goal]
           Paul disgusted Marie of that.
           Marie is disgusted with that, because of Paul.
      d.   Merckx a profité/bénéficié de l'abandon d'Ocana.
           Merckx profited/benefitted from Ocana's
           withdrawal.   [EXP = Agent + Goal]
      e.   L'abandon d'Ocana a profité/bénéficié à
           Merckx.   [EXP = Goal/Place]
           Ocana's withdrawal was of profit to/benefitted Merckx.
      f.   Jean aime Marie.   [Exp. = Source or Goal?]
           Jean loves Marie.
      g.   Jean a intéressé Marie à la philosophie. [EXP = Theme/Source?]
           Jean interested Marie in philosophy.

(20) PLACE (or GOAL or THEME?) psy-chose, with incorporation:
      a.   Cet article/ Marie a enragé Paul.   [Exp. = Theme/Goal?]
           That article/Marie angered Paul.
      b.   Paul a emmerdé Julie toute la soirée.   [EXP = Theme/Goal?]
           Paul plagued Julie all evening long.

To these we could add a substantial number of cases of metonymy such as, for example, the signs of anger used to refer to anger discussed in Lakoff (1987 p. 380 ff), such as *He lost his cool, He was foaming at the mouth, You make my blood boil, She was scarlet/blind with rage, She was shaking with anger, He was hopping mad.*

What problem does this extensive productivity of Psych constructions raise for the three types of analyses discussed in section 4.1? The problem is essentially the same as the one observed by Ruwet (1972), with respect to Postal's (1971) analysis, and already seen in the context of the thematic analyses of the six verbs studied in chapter 3: these analyses require a proliferation of homonymous verbs, which raises the concern that language would suffer from generalized homonymy. For example, a verb like *frapper* would have to have two lexical entries, depending on whether it is used "normally" or with a Psych interpretation.[7] This means that in an analysis that attributes the peculiar syntactic properties of Psych verbs to a particular Deep Structure, as do Belletti and Rizzi, the two sentences in (21) and (22) would have radically different Deep Structures, with the two arguments occupying different underlying syntactic positions.

(21)   Marie frappe Paul (avec un marteau).
        Marie strikes Paul (with a hammer)
        DS [$_{IP}$ Marie [$_{VP}$ frappe Paul]]

(22)   Marie frappe Paul (par son intelligence).
        Marie strikes Paul (with her intelligence).
        DS [$_{IP}$—[$_{VP}$ [$_{VP}$ frappe Marie] Paul]]

As we will see in section 4.4, the *frapper* class of Psych verbs, as well as other Psych verbs without incorporation, exhibit syntactic properties that Belletti and Rizzi attribute to this kind of unaccusative Deep Structure.

The same problem arises in an analysis that attributes these syntactic peculiarities to a difference in aspectual structure: *frapper,* and all of these other verbs, would have to have two different lexical entries, each with a different aspectual structure. Similarly, in an analysis that proposes to account for these peculiar properties by means of different thematic roles, *frapper,* and all of these other verbs, would have to have entries with special theta roles like EXPERIENCER and TARGET OF EMOTION, when used in a Psych construction, but regular roles otherwise.

Moreover, as Ruwet (1972, 232) noted, the homonymy here is not at all perceived as similar to the one in *voler* (to fly) and *voler* (to rob). The two uses of *frapper,* and these other verbs, are not pure coincidence: speakers perceive a systematic semantic correspondence between the two uses. This is not captured by the three types of analyses discussed above.

4.2.2 THE THEMATIC ANALYSIS OF PSYCH PREDICATES

As the data in (13)–(20) show, if the theta roles assigned in Psych constructions are constant—perhaps EXPERIENCER and TRIGGER (i.e., that which triggers the emotion)—a systematic alignment of these theta roles with GFs is impossible (I use TRIGGER instead of THEME because this element does not have the properties of a Theme, as defined in Gruber (1965), where Theme is the element being situated on a Path or in a Place). The EXPERIENCER and the TRIGGER can be in just about any syntactic position, as (23) and (24) show.[8]

(23)a. EXP = subject: (13b,e,g), (14b,c), (15c), (17), (17d), (19a,d,f), (21a,b)

   b. EXP = direct object: (14a), (15a,b), (17a,c,e,f), (19b,c,g), (20a,b)

   c. EXP = dative object: (13a,c,f) (17b), (19e)

   d. EXP = P-object: (13d), (17c)

(24)a. TRIGGER = subject: (13a,c), (14a), (15a,b), (17a,b,c,d), (19b,c,e,g), (20a,b)

   b. TRIGGER = direct object: (19a,f)

   c. TRIGGER = dative object: (13e)

   d. TRIGGER = P-object: (13b,f), (14b), (19d)

   e. NO TRIGGER: (13d), (14c), (15c), (16), (17e,f)

A similar attempt to align the EXPERIENCER and TRIGGER roles with the "standard" thematic roles, AGENT and THEME, in cases where the verbs can alternate between a Psych use and a normal use will also fail, as a cursory look at the data makes clear. Moreover, if we consider the psychose argument, which is the emotion that the TRIGGER induces in the EXPERIENCER, we see that this element can also appear in any syntactic position and with any "standard" theta role.

In terms of situational primitives like theta roles, selectional restrictions of ES and EO verbs do seem to cross, as we saw in (1) and (2) above, repeated here as (25) and (26).

(25)   John fears Mary / your decision / the storm.

(26)   Mary / your decision / the storm frightens John.

Thus it is tempting in such an approach to revert to a paraphrase methodology, as discussed in section 1.5.2.2.3, in which one of the crucial factors in determining whether there is a relationship between two sentences is the relatively similar conditions of use of the sentences (that is, truth conditions). But we saw in 1.1.3 that expressions that are equivalent in some of their uses are not conceptually equivalent.

Moreover, true minimal pairs of EO and ES constructions are extremely hard to find, as Ruwet (1972) amply illustrated; he showed that minor differences exist between nearly every potential minimal pair. I will not repeat all his examples here, since the material would cover several dozen pages and is easily available elsewhere, in any event, but it should be pointed out that, even for the verbs used as typical examples of ES and EO verbs in French and English, the selectional restrictions are not exactly the same, and crossing does not hold ((27 a and b) from Ruwet 1972):[9]

(27)a.   La couleur verte/que Paul ait pu dire une chose pareille dégoûte
         Pierre.
         The color green/that Paul could have said such a thing disgusts
         Pierre.
    b.   #Pierre méprise la couleur verte/que Paul ait pu dire une chose par-
         eille.
         Pierre despises the color green/that Paul could have said such a
         thing.
    c.   The brown spots on Ronald's skin frighten Nancy.
    d.   #Nancy fears the brown spots on Ronald's skin.

Another problem in the thematic analysis of EO verbs is that some Triggers can be "agentive," in some cases.

(28)   John amuses/frightens the children.

Here John may or may not be amusing/frightening the children voluntarily,
and he might (or might not) be aware of his effect on the children. One could
not simply say that sentences like (28) are just "vague," in that respect, because, in thematic analyses, many syntactic properties depend on whether a
sentence is agentive or not. For example, only if the sentence is agentive can
it be in the progressive or imperative or have the subject bind a reflexive
object. Is this then another case of homonymy, with two entries for *amuse,*
frighten, and the like? Why couldn't verbs of the *frapper* class also sometimes
be agentive in their Psych use?[10]

(29)   Jean a frappé (*volontairement) Marie par son intelligence.
         *Jean (*voluntarily) struck Marie with her intelligence.*

In the three types of analyses discussed above, it is very difficult to predict
when agentivity is possible and when it is not.
    From the two problems discussed in this section 4.2, we are forced to
conclude that an account of the peculiar syntactic phenomena found in
Psych constructions based on special structures stemming from thematic
properties is empirically untenable. Psych constructions are the same as "normal" constructions, with respect to the productivity of the syntactic configu-
rations involved. The availability of agentivity, the productivity of Psych constructions, and the fact that their thematic properties are not different from
"normal" thematic properties will follow directly from my analysis of Psych
constructions.

4.3 WHAT A PSYCH CONSTRUCTION IS

In this section, I argue that a Psych interpretation results from the contact of a psy-chose with an Intentional Subject. Since there are different ways for the elements of such a relation in semantic representation to correspond with elements in a syntactic representation, various classes of Psych constructions surface; but they are all based on the elementary contact relation. I also discuss Psych constructions in which the psychological object—the psy-chose— is not an emotion or feeling, but an entity being referred to as a Concept. This leads me to a discussion of intentionality and, in particular, of how intentionality supersedes agentivity in Psych constructions.

4.3.1 A PSY-CHOSE IN CONTACT WITH AN INTENTIONAL SUBJECT

We saw that Psych constructions, like other constructions, may involve a variety of "thematic" relations. What sets Psych constructions apart from other constructions is that one of their arguments is a psy-chose and that another argument is "affected" by the psy-chose. When a verb expresses physical contact between two objects, that contact induces a change of state in one or the other of these objects, hence one of them is affected. Similarly, I assume, in mental space, the psy-chose is somehow put in contact with the argument it affects. This argument must be an entity capable of hosting the emotion or feeling that the psy-chose refers to. In other words, the psy-chose affects an Intentional Subject (henceforth, I-Subject). So affectedness is derived from an abstract notion of contact between arguments in a semantic representation. Note that the Subject of Consciousness, who is aware that such a Psych contact has taken place, is not necessarily the affected I-Subject. Thus, for some EO Psych verbs, such as *humilier/humiliate,* the I-Subject is not necessarily conscious of being affected, as is the case in the following example in which Jean is unaware that he is being humiliated.

(30)   Sa patronne humilie constamment Jean et il ne s'en rend même pas compte.
         His boss constantly humiliates John, and he does not even realize it.

I propose that the difference between a Psych construction and a "normal" construction is that, since the psy-chose is a mental object, it establishes contact with an I-Subject at the level of mental space rather than at the level of physical space. Ruwet (1972) expresses this intuition very clearly in his discussion of the *frapper* class of verbs:

It is clear that we are dealing here with a very productive, very general phenomenon and that there is a systematic relation between the A and B classes of verbs; a grammar of French which did not take this into account would be inadequate. Moreover, in most cases, any native speaker of French has the intuition of a semantic relation between the two homonymous verbs. On the whole, and from an impressionistic point of view, this relation can be expressed as follows. In the (a) examples as well as the (b) examples, the verbs describe a process of which the subject NP is the cause, and this process, in one way or another, affects, or has an effect on, the being or object referred to by the object NP. The difference is that, in the (a) examples, the effect in question is of a purely physical nature, whereas, in the (b) examples, it is a case of a psychological, mental effect." (Ruwet 1972, 231)[11]

I assume that physical affectedness and mental affectedness are represented in the same way—contact. *Frapper* expresses affectedness of its direct object in both its physical and psychological uses because *frapper* expresses a contact in its abstract semantic representation.

One way to account for the fact that the same relations can hold between psychological elements as hold between spatio-temporal elements, and to provide a unified analysis of the two phenomena, is to assume that basic spatial relations extend to other domains. That is the position taken by Gruber (1976) and Jackendoff (1983, 1990a), who postulate that functions in other fields—for example, time, possession, and temperature—use essentially spatial functions: "In the spatial field, a Thing is located spatially; in possessional, a Thing belongs to someone; in ascriptional, a Thing has a property; in scheduling, an Event is located in a time period" (Jackendoff 1990a, 26).[12] Elaborating on these examples, Gruber says that the pair *from . . . to* expresses a transition of position, as in (31a), but that it can also be found in various other semantic fields:

(31)a. Positional: John went from New York to Paris.
    b. Temporal: She stayed from 4 o'clock to midnight.
    c. Meteorological: The temperature rose from 15° to 20° in 5 minutes.
    d. Activity: The circle suddenly switched from turning clockwise to counterclockwise.
    e. Identificational: Bill converted from a Republican to a Democrat.
    f. Possessional: He bought a book from her. He sold a book to Mary.

g.   Abstract: He reported to Mary from Bill that he wished to see
      her.

In thematic terms, one could say that the basic distinction between a
Psych construction and a non-Psych construction is a difference in thematic
roles, just as there is no thematic distinction between the examples in (31):
the distinction is one of semantic field. But we saw in section 1.5.2 that this
kind of metaphorical approach, where spatial relations are basic and extend
to other domains, only postpones answering the relevant questions about the
conceptualization capacity itself. Since these questions will have to be asked
about spatial relations in any event, I argued, why not first consider conceptualization in general and then ask how it applies to all semantic domains. In
such an approach, Psych constructions and "normal" constructions are similar because the same abstract relations hold between Psych elements and
between spatial elements. These abstract relations are stripped of situational
thematic attributes because such situational thematic notions are too context
dependent. (See the discussion of the role "Patient" in 1.5.2.2).

If we assume that a psy-chose must affect an I-Subject, and that it does
this by making contact with it in mental space, then a Psych construction
can be built on any verb expressing an abstract relation of contact. For example, this includes verbs based on the two abstract relations in (32).

(32)   a.   b.

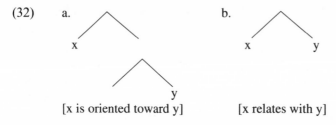

[x is oriented toward y]   [x relates with y]

Psych constructions can be classified, roughly, as follows. First, a distinction can be made on the basis of incorporation: if the psy-chose argument is
incorporated by chunking, the verb is "inherently" Psych, in the sense that
it will always be in a Psych construction because of the very nature of the
incorporated argument (this is the class usually referred to as Psych verbs).[13]
Second, a Psych construction could be built on relations like the ones in (32),
but with the psy-chose identified by linking with a syntactic position rather
than by incorporation. Finally, another distinction can be made: a Psych
construction involves both a psy-chose and an I-Subject, but it is of no relevance which of the two is the Figure and which is the Ground (or Theme and

Goal). So, for example, within the verbs that appear in either (32a) or (32b), the psy-chose could be x and the I-Subject y, or the converse, the psy-chose could be y and the I-Subject x. Thus, the psy-chose *peur* seems to correspond to the x and the I-Subject *Marie* to the y of (32b) in example (33), but we seem to get the opposite in (34), with the psy-chose *colère* being the y and the I-Subject *Marie* being the x (with the addition of yet another factor here, that of 'container').

(33)   Pierre fait peur à Marie.
        Pierre makes fright to Marie.
        Pierre frightens Marie.

(34)   Pierre met Marie en colère.
        Pierre puts Marie in anger.
        Pierre angers Marie.

I am not making any claims here about the specific semantic structure that should be attributed to these verbs; a much more detailed study of all of the uses of these verbs would be needed for that, and it exceeds the scope of this work. However, I do claim that, whatever representations Psych uses of verbs have, they are identical to the regular representations of those verbs.

4.3.2 CLASSES OF PSYCH CONSTRUCTIONS

I now turn to the different classes of Psych constructions that surface in syntax. The fact that there can be so many different types of Psych constructions, and that they should be so productive, comes as no surprise, if one assumes that their abstract semantic organization is like that of any "normal" physical spatial relation. It is not always easy to determine to which particular class of Psych construction a given verb belongs. The first distinction, whether or not incorporation has taken place, is fairly easy to determine.

(35)a. Cela a enragé Pierre.   [+incorporated]
        That enraged Pierre.
   b.   Cela a mis Pierre dans une rage terrible.   [−incorporated]
        That put Pierre into a terrible rage.
   c.   Cela a éveillé en Pierre une rage terrible.   [−incorporated]
        That awoke in Pierre a terrible rage.

If there is no incorporation, it should be possible to determine which position the psy-chose or the I-Subject correspond to in the semantic representation, once we have a proper understanding of the abstract representations involved. Nonincorporated structures, such as the prepositional phrases in (35b and c) are more accessible than the incorporated structures.

When incorporation has taken place, as in (35a), however, classification is more difficult. We can rule out some possibilities, given endocentricity restrictions on the process of chunking (see the discussion of the Endocentricity Principle in section 2.2), but the exact classification of incorporated Psych verbs remains difficult to determine. In some cases, morphological evidence may help. For example, Boons (1987) argues that certain prefixes in French determine the aspectual value of a verb: *ex-* is initial, so in *expatrier* 'expatriate,' *patrie* 'homeland' is the initial location; *trans-* is bipolar, so in *transvaser* 'decant,' both the initial and the final location are a 'vase' (container of some sort); *a-*, *en-*, and *in-* are final, so the final location is a 'coast' in *accoster* 'come alongside,' a prison in *emprisonner* 'imprison,' and a liquid in *immerger* 'immerse.' Examples such as those in (36) would therefore be cases where the location is incorporated.

(36)a. Jean a affolé Marie.
         Jean put Marie in madness.
         Jean made Marie go mad.
    b.   Jean a ensorcelé Marie.
         Jean put Marie in a spell.
         Jean captivated Marie.

In the incorporated cases, it is also very difficult to determine whether the Psych construction is based on orientation (32a) or simple "relating" (32b) because clues like prepositions are missing. Other clues, such as the adverbs that are compatible with movement uses of verbs, are also of little use in Psych constructions because they also require certain aspectual features of measurement that are absent from Psych constructions. As Voorst (1992) observes, psychological events are unmeasurable: either a feeling exists or it does not, and there is no process leading up to a final state. Thus, I cannot be half-struck by John's behavior or half-admire that scientist, and someone cannot half-frighten me. This contrasts with physical events: when someone is making a chair, at different stages of the event, subparts of the chair gradually go together. But when someone is making me angry, or breaking my spirit, this implies that I am already angry, or that my spirit is broken (see also section 4.4.4 on Progressive and section 4.4.5.2 on Affectedness). Such observations about the measurability of psychological events can be found as far back as Aristotle, who said that pleasure is an activity and a whole, in the sense that it is complete at every moment (*Nicomachean Ethics* K 4).

Despite the fact that classifying particular Psych verbs is not always easy, we can nevertheless consider how the classification that I propose—based on the four factors of (1) incorporation or nonincorporation, (2) oriented or simplex relation, (3) SUBJ, OBJ or PP psy-chose, and (4) SUBJ, OBJ or PP I-Subject, as in (37)—relates to the four classes of Psych constructions we started with, shown schematically in (38).

(37)

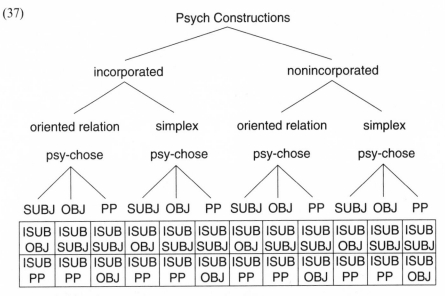

(38)a.   Class 1: Fear, Mépriser   EXPERIENCER Verb TRIGGER
  b.   Class 2: Frighten, dégoûter   TRIGGER Verb EXPERIENCER
  c.   Class 3: Strike, Frapper   TRIGGER Verb EXPERIENCER
  d.   Class 4: all other nonincorporated constructions

Class 4 is the easiest to identify, since it is the most transparent. The absence of incorporation is obvious, so the psy-chose is easily identified by its lexical properties, for example, anger, fear, joy; and the surface prepositions are helpful in determining what semantic relation is involved.

Class 1 verbs and Class 2 verbs are both the result of incorporating a psy-chose, but it is difficult, at this stage, to make any strong generalizations about their semantic properties, as we just saw. Of course, a clear distinction between these two classes lies where the I-Subject argument appears: the I-Subject is the syntactic subject in class 1, the direct object in class 2.

Class 3 verbs do not involve incorporation of a psy-chose, since, unlike verbs in classes 1 and 2, they are not always Psych in nature. The I-Subject argument is the direct object. But where is the psy-chose? There is no element in sentences like (39) which has the inherent lexical properties, such as anger, fear, or disgust, of a psy-chose.

(39)a.   Mary strikes me as intelligent.
    b.   Marie me frappe (par son intelligence).

It is the external argument, the Actualizer of the event in the sense of Voorst (1988), that is the psy-chose. The ability of the Instigator to function as psy-chose has been noted in various frameworks (although, of course, it is not couched in these terms). For example, in type theory, an Actualizer NP can refer either to an individual or to the properties of an individual (Grimshaw 1990; Partee and Rooth 1983; Kenny 1963).[14] When interpreted as properties of an individual, the Actualizer is a psy-chose, since it is in the realm of mental space.

4.3.3 An Intentional Concept as a Psy-Chose

Another way to look at the Actualizer (the external argument) as the psy-chose is in terms of intentionality, meaning whether or not a referent in the sentence is presented by the speaker as capable of intent or of hosting an emotion or feeling. I will argue that, when the Actualizer is not referred to as an entity capable of intent—i.e., as a Concept rather than an I-Subject—it is a psy-chose. Thus, it is the Actualizer-as-Concept that is the psy-chose in the *frapper*-class of Psych constructions.

As has often been noted (see Coppieters 1982, 1990, and references therein), an entity can be seen from either an external, neutral, point of view or from an internal point of view. If viewed externally, the entity is treated as a Concept; if viewed internally, it is treated as a "Substantive," that is, an entity that can be a participant in an event. Furthermore, there is a subclass of Substantives that can themselves be viewed as I-Subjects, since they are capable of intentionality. These three notions, Concept, Substantive, and I-Subject, are roughly defined in (40) and exemplified in (41), where John is a Concept in (41a), a Substantive in (41b), and an I-Subject in (41c).

(40) *Concept:*   1. external point of view, neutral with respect to the entity

2. objective judgment of speaker, omniscient narrator

Substantive: 1. internal point of view
2. entity as participant

I-Subject: 1. internal point of view, feelings of the entity
2. entity is conscious of event (attributed by speaker)

(41)a.   John is a guy who is very confident. (Concept)
   b.   John caught a cold. (Substantive)
   c.   John is not sure if he wants to talk to Mary. (I-Subject)

The distinction between Concept, Substantive, and I-Subject is involved in determining the choice of some pronouns in French. Coppieters (1982, 1990) discusses how the choice between pronouns *il* and *ce/ça* in French correlates with different ways of refering to an Instigator (subject) NP. Thus, in using *ce,* speakers are giving their opinion on the state of the entity from an external point of view and without indicating whether that entity is aware of it or not. In other words, the entity is treated as a Concept. On the other hand, *il* is used to refer to the entity as a Substantive. The following examples from Coppieters (1982) further illustrate his analysis.

(42)   Jean se rendait enfin compte qu'il avait tout essayé et tout raté. Il/ C'était un homme pauvre désormais. Pourquoi avait-il eu tant de malchance?
Jean finally realized that he had tried everything and failed at everything. Henceforth he would be a poor man. Why on earth had he been so unlucky?

The use of *il* in (42) implies that *Jean* is aware of his situation and that he realizes he is a poor man. Under this interpretation, the question *Pourquoi avait-il eu tant de malchance?* expresses his anger and despair. On the other hand, when *ce* is used, the opinion of the speaker about Jean's misfortune is expressed, and the question *Pourquoi avait-il eu tant de malchance?* is rhetorical. This becomes even clearer if one forces an external point of view, that is, forces the reading in which the speaker is judging the event as in (43): the use of *il* then becomes unacceptable.

(43)   Jean se rendait compte qu'il avait tout essayé et tout raté. *Il/C'était un homme pauvre désormais, et je me sentais plein de pitié pour lui.
Jean realized that he had tried everything and failed at everything. Henceforth, he would be a poor man, and I was full of pity for him.

On the other hand, forcing an interpretation from an internal point of view expressing Jean's feelings, as in (44), renders the use of *ce* unacceptable:

(44)   Jean se rendait compte qu'il avait tout essayé et tout raté. Il/*C'ét-
         ait un homme pauvre désormais, et il en voulait amèrement à sa
         malchance.
         Jean realized that he had tried everything and failed at everything.
         Henceforth, he would be a poor man, and he was bitterly angry at
         his bad luck.

Thus, the distinction between Substantive, I-Subject, and Concept determines the choice of some pronouns in French. This provides independent motivation for the use of such notions in linguistic analysis, such as the analysis of the class 3 verbs, exemplified in (39) above.[15] We are now in a position to answer the question: Where is the psy-chose in the *frapper*-class of Psych constructions?

We have seen that an Instigator can be referred to either as a Concept or a Substantive (which can be an I-Subject). We can assume that when interpreted as a Concept, the Instigator is a psy-chose, since it is within the realm of mental space. In a sentence like *Jean a frappé Paul* 'Jean hit Paul,' the Instigator *Jean* can be interpreted as a Concept, if he struck Paul as a nice person; as a Substantive, if he inadvertently struck Paul when he walked by; or as an I-Subject, if he struck Paul with a bat (see Coppieters 1990, 15). Interpreting *Jean* as an I-Subject gives the "agentive" reading, whereas interpreting *Jean* as a Concept gives the reading where *Jean* is a psy-chose, that is, an element in the semantic field of mental space.

Note that in order for this class of verbs to have a Psych interpretation, it must be the case that the subject be interpreted as a Concept. Otherwise, the construction will not have a psy-chose, since there is none present, either as a surface argument or as an incorporated argument. Furthermore, if the entity in subject position of these verbs can be interpreted only as a Concept, such as *The beauty of Ava Gardner* or *The flaw in the argument,* a Psych reading is necessarily induced. As we will see in 4.4 below, the fact that the Psych use of *frapper* class verbs requires the subject to have a Concept interpretation accounts for their peculiar syntactic properties.

4.3.4 AGENTIVITY IN TERMS OF INTENTIONALITY

This way of looking at the "agentive" reading of Psych sentences as dependent on the distinction between Concept and I-Subject is supported by an observation in Ruwet (1991). He notes that the type of sentential complementation found in a given sentence depends in part on the way of referring to the matrix and embedded subjects. If both subjects are referred to as I-Subjects, the complement is infinitival; if only the matrix subject is an I-Subject, the complement is not infinitival because of the need for an overt subject in this kind of "mismatch." I will show that the behavior of complements headed by a Psych verb is accounted for, if their agentive uses are analyzed as cases where the subjects are referred to as I-Subjects and their nonagentive uses as cases of subjects viewed as Concepts.

Ruwet considered verbs that allow a finite complement, if the matrix subject and the embedded subject are disjoint in reference. These verbs divide into three classes on the basis of their behavior when the matrix and embedded subjects are coreferential: (A) verbs like *croire* 'believe,' *estimer* 'believe,' and *penser* 'think,' which allow both infinitival and finite complements; (B) verbs like *vouloir* 'want,' *souhaiter* 'wish,' and *désirer* 'desire,' which generally allow only infinitival complements; and (C) verbs like *remarquer* 'notice,' *comprendre* 'understand,' and *voir* 'see,' which allow only finite complements.

(45) *Class A:*
       a.   Je crois que je peux résoudre cette question.
            I think that I can resolve this question.
       b.   Je crois pouvoir résoudre cette question.
            I think to-be-able to-resolve this question.

(46) *Class B:*
       a.   *Je veux que je parte.
            I want that I leave.
       b.   Je veux partir.
            I want to leave.

(47) *Class C:*
       a.   Pierre$_i$ remarque qu'il$_i$ a les traits tirés.
            Pierre notices that he has haggard features.
       b.   *Pierre remarque avoir les traits tirés.
            **Pierre notices to-have haggard features.*

One could simply conclude that class (C) is a matter of subcategorization. As for classes (A) and (B), they could be distinguished on the basis of mood: class (B) verbs take subjunctive complements. One could argue that these complements are transparent with respect to binding theory; they would not define a distinct binding domain, so a pronoun bound by the matrix subject could not appear in them without violating the binding theory (see, among

others, Picallo 1984; Raposo 1987; and Suñer 1987). Instead, Ruwet hypothe-
sizes that this distribution is not random. His hypothesis is that "there exists
an **iconic** link between the (superficial) form of the sentence—simple or complex, compact or articulated—and the content, experienced as relatively simple or relatively complex, perceived as a unitary process or else as being decomposable into separate moments" (Ruwet 1991, 8).

Although I have some reservations about adopting an analysis based on
iconicity, the observations themselves are important. The elements of the
content that bear primarily on the choice of sentential complement are the
referent of the matrix subject and the referent of the subordinate subject and
whether these referents are identical, in which case the relation is of self-to-
self, or distinct, in which case the relation is of self-to-other. Ruwet discusses
many examples that show that with verbs of class (C), even when the matrix
and embedded subjects refer to the same individual, they do not refer to it in
an identical way, and the relation tends to be like a self-to-other relation. For
example, in (47a), Pierre notices something about himself, as he would about
someone else: he is distancing himself from his own self. On the other hand,
class (B) exhibits a self-to-self relation, where the matrix and embedded subjects refer to the same individual in an identical way, so that there is continu-
ity in the will and acts of the referent, which is quite different from the internal articulation present when the relation is self-to-other. This difference,
according to Ruwet, explains why there are two overt coreferential subjects
that appear in class (C) constructions, but only one such overt element in
class (B).

What is important for our discussion is that, to further support his analysis, Ruwet then discusses ten syntactic effects that facilitate distancing and
that do indeed make subjunctive clauses more acceptable in class (B). One of
these effects is using a class-2 Psych verb in the sentential complement. Thus,
while (48a) is not as good as (48b), it is certainly more acceptable than the
paradigmatic Equi cases, as in (46).

(48)a.   ?Je veux que j'amuse ces enfants.
         *_I want that I amuse those children._
     b.   Je veux amuser ces enfants.
         I want to amuse those children.

Ruwet comments: "Insofar as the (a)-examples are acceptable at all, they are
interpreted as nonagentive; when the subject is repeated, I tend to see, as if
from the exterior, a second instance of myself, the one denoted by the embed-

ded subject, and this encourages the nonagentive interpretation" (Ruwet 1991, 27). But why should this distancing correlate with a nonagentive interpretation? It seems that it is not just self-to-other relations, as in his other examples, that induce distancing and render class (B) sentences acceptable. The nonagentive reading of subjects of class 2 Psych verbs is the result of interpreting them as Concepts. When they are embedded under verbs like *vouloir,* which have I-Subjects, distancing is induced, and sentences like (48a) are rendered more acceptable.

Further support for the analysis comes from another observation by Ruwet. He notes that the passive of a class-2 Psych verb is worse embedded under *je veux que . . .* 'I want that,' which is rather surprising in his analysis, since passive of action verbs is one of the ten effects he claims facilitate distancing.

(49)a.   Je veux qu'on m'étonne. (Diaghilev)
          I want that people surprise me.
   b. ?*Je veux que je sois étonné.
          I want that I be surprised.

As Ruwet notes, in (49b), the subject of the passive is the Experiencer, and he says there is a "minimal distance" between the *je* subject of *vouloir* and the *je* Experiencer in the lower clause. In my terms, passivization brings the I-Subject of *étonner* into the subject position; since both this Experiencer *je* and the *je* subject of *vouloir* are I-Subjects, there is no distancing, and a sentence with two overt pronouns such as (49b) is not good. On the other hand, it is the subject of the active form of class-1 Psych verbs that is an I-Subject; this correctly predicts that I-Subject/Concept distancing should also be impossible with the active form of class-1 Psych verbs:[16]

(50)a. ?*Je veux que j'aime Marie.
          I want that I love Marie.
   b.   Je veux aimer Marie.
          I want to love Marie.

The distancing between matrix and embedded subjects, which correlates with noninfinitival complements, is in terms of notions of intentionality, such as I-Subject and Concept. The fact that the variation in "agentivity" of Psych verbs interacts with this distancing process indicates that this agentivity is better analyzed in terms of intentionality.

4.3.5 Summary of the Psych Construction

To briefly sum up, I assume that a Psych construction is not different from other constructions, in that the basic semantic relations are the same as in other constructions. Any syntactic construction can be a Psych construction. What distinguishes a Psych construction from other constructions is not a particular syntactic or semantic relationship between arguments, but rather the nature of the elements that are related. Psych constructions must have a psy-chose, and that psy-chose must be in an appropriate relationship with an I-Subject. This relationship may be an orientation, as in (32a), or a simple relation, as in (32b). A psy-chose can be inserted as a syntactic argument or incorporated into the verb. In the latter case, the verb is inherently "psychological"; these verbs are the ones referred to as Psych verbs. An element interpreted as a Concept can function as a psy-chose, allowing a verb which is not "normally" a Psych verb to have a Psych interpretation. Although I will continue to use the term 'Psych construction,' it should be clear that what is really meant by the term is the Psych use of any construction.

This analysis predicts that Psych constructions are dependent only on the presence of a psy-chose: any construction that has a psy-chose in it is a Psych construction, no matter what the semantic relations involved in that construction are. Thus, a verb like *frapper* does not undergo radical changes in its semantic representation in its Psych use. Just as in the case of movement verbs in the previous chapter, the basic semantics of *frapper* remains the same in its various uses. A Psych situation is computed through several factors, including the manner in which reference is made to some arguments. This predicts that Psych constructions should be productive, and the examples presented in (13) to (20) confirm that this is indeed the case. On the other hand, this productivity makes analyses with special deep structures, special aspectual linkings, or special theta roles essentially untenable. I will now argue that attributing special properties like these to Psych constructions also fails to account for many syntactic properties attributed to these constructions.

4.4 Syntactic Properties of Psych Constructions

It has often been noted that "standard" Psych constructions (i.e., those with an incorporated psy-chose in my analysis) behave peculiarly, with respect to a number of syntactic processes (there is an extensive list of references on the subject that extends over the last 30 years; I will give those relevant for each property below). In the next subsections, we will look at the behavior of Psych constructions in general (including the nonincorporated ones), with respect to the following properties:

(i) Binding of an anaphor by the subject
(ii) Backward reflexivization
(iii) Passivization
(iv) Progressive verb form
(v) Nominalization
(vi) Compounding
(vii) Imperative verb form
(viii) Pro$_{arb}$ as subject
(ix) Embedding in a causative construction
(x) Interaction with adverbs like *personally*
(xi) Extraction from within the direct object

I will evaluate how the different types of analyses discussed in section 4.1 handle the data. I will refer to these analyses as (1) the Deep Structure analysis, which attributes special Deep Structures to a class of Psych constructions (as in Postal 1971; Belletti and Rizzi 1988); (2) the Aspectual Structure analysis (as in Grimshaw 1990); (3) the Thematic Structure analysis (as in Pesetsky 1988, 1990); and (4) the Psy-chose analysis, which I proposed above. It will become clear from this discussion that there are no structural, aspectual, or thematic differences between Experiencer Object and Experiencer Subject verbs. I will show that the special properties that have been attributed to Psych constructions all derive essentially from the fact that, in Psych constructions, the method of reference to certain arguments is different from the one in "normal" constructions.

4.4.1 BINDING OF DIRECT OBJECT ANAPHORS

It is often mentioned (Postal 1971; Ruwet 1972; Belletti and Rizzi 1988; Pesetsky 1988, 1990; Grimshaw 1990, among others) that ES and EO Psych verbs are distinguished by the binding properties of their subjects: the subject of an ES verb like *fear* or *hate* can bind an anaphor, but not the subject of an EO verb like *frighten* or *worry* (note that the latter holds only for the nonagentive reading of *frighten*).

(51)a.　They fear/hate themselves.
　　 b. ?*They frighten/worry themselves.

For Belletti and Rizzi, the contrast is due to a difference in chain formation. They assume structures as in (52).

(52)a.   [They$_i$ [fear themselves$_i$]]
   b.   DS [$_{VP}$ [$_{VP}$ frighten they] themselves] $\Rightarrow$ SS They [$_{VP}$ [$_{VP}$ frighten t]
        themselves]

The reflexive is properly bound in (a); in (b), however, the trace of the derived
subject is not locally bound by *they*, but by *themselves*, resulting in the ill-
formed chain (*they, themselves*, t) which contains two arguments.

Grimshaw (1990) has a different analysis, which is based on type theory
and on the assumption that with non-agentive psychological predicates, the
subject is actually not an individual but belongs rather to the type "properties
of individuals." She attributes the ungrammaticality of (51b) to a mismatch
between the type of the antecedent ("properties") and the type of the reflexive ("individual").

This account of the facts in (51) does not relate directly to other aspects
of her analysis of Psych constructions, however. As she noted, it raises the
question of why these verbs have both peculiar anaphora-binding properties
and peculiar argument structure. For Grimshaw, "the answer is that the subjects (Themes) of the *frighten* verbs are not individuals, despite appearances.
Agentive predicates never have this kind of subject—Agents are *always* of
the individual type" (Grimshaw 1990, 161). This is rather stipulative and
unrevealing. Why is the Theme of *fear* in (51a) not also restricted to the
"properties of individuals" type, which would then trigger a type mismatch
in binding? Moreover, in order to account for the fact that the subject of
frighten can bind a reflexive when it is agentive, it must be assumed that
frighten can undergo a major argument structure switch, from agentive to
nonagentive.

Analyses that attribute special syntactic or aspectual structures to Psych
verbs, such as the ones in Belletti and Rizzi (1988) and Grimshaw (1990), are
not compatible with the minimalist approach that I propose. I will now show
that they also make wrong predictions. They predict that only a special class
of Psych verbs should block binding of a reflexive by the subject, but in fact
a vast class of "normal" verbs have this property in their Psych uses; some
Psych verbs that should disallow this binding allow it in many contexts. Psych
verbs in English and in Romance languages should exhibit the same behavior,
yet there are important differences between them. To account for these facts,

I borrow Grimshaw's idea of a mismatch, but I reset it in terms of notions of intentionality rather than type.

In an earlier version of this work, published as Bouchard (1994), I used type theory to account for the impossibility of a sentence like (53a). I assumed, along the lines of Grimshaw (1990), that *d'Artagnan* is referred to as "properties of an individual" rather than as an "individual" here. The sentence is bad, I concluded, because the reflexive refers to an individual, so there is a mismatch.

(53)a. ?* D'Artagnan s'impressionne par son audace.
   D'Artagnan impresses himself with his audacity.
   b.   D'Artagnan impressionne Athos par son audace.
   D'Artagnan impresses Athos with his audacity.

Ruwet (1993) points out that under this analysis, I would be forced to make the bizarre assumption that *son audace* in (53b) signals a property of the properties of (the individual) d'Artagnan. Furthermore, Ruwet observes that a central property of Psych constructions is that the subject of Psych verbs like *fear* and the object of Psych verbs like *frighten* is an I-Subject. A theory of intentionality is therefore better suited than type theory to explain the peculiarities of Psych constructions.

Independent motivation for the use of intentional notions in the account of properties of reflexives can be found in an observation by Cantrall (1974), exemplified by sentence (54).

(54)   The women$_i$ were standing in the background, with the children behind themselves$_i$/them$_i$.

Cantrall asks us to imagine a situation where the sentence describes a picture where the women are seen with their back to us. He notes that the use of *themselves* is possible only if the children are situated behind the women *from the women's point of view,* that is, at the forefront of the picture. On the other hand, the pronoun *them* suggests that the children are situated behind the women, from the point of view of the speaker, hence in the background of the picture and, in fact, in front of the women from their perspective.

In order to understand the effect of notions of intentionality in the interpretation of reflexives, in terms of the approach that I propose, I must clarify what I assume a reflexive is and what is anaphoric dependency. First, let us follow Pica's (1987) assumption that a reflexive is analyzed as an inalienable of the self as a whole. In our terms, we could say that the reflexive is a Sub-

stantive, as defined above. If we put this together with what we saw above—
a matching effect, the relevance of intentional notions in the interpretation
of reflexives, and the reflexive as a Substantive—then we have an account of
Cantrall's example. The anaphorically dependent reflexive is a Substantive;
the matching effect forces its antecedent to be interpreted as a Substantive,
as well, and not as a Concept. This matching effect finds an explanation if
anaphoric dependency is understood in the context of Wasow's (1972) Novelty Condition:

(55) *Novelty Condition:* An anaphorically dependent element cannot have
more determinate reference than its antecedent.

Wasow proposes this condition to account for facts like the following.

(56)a.   A captain$_i$ walked into the room. The officer$_i$ at first said nothing.
   b.   *An officer$_i$ walked into the room. The captain$_i$ at first said
        nothing.

Since reference as a Concept is more limitative than reference as a Substantive, it follows that the antecedent of the reflexive in Cantrall's example
(54) must be a Substantive; otherwise, the antecedent would be less determinate in reference, in violation of the Novelty Condition. Hence, the antecedent of the reflexive is forced to be a Substantive, and that is why the presence
of the reflexive has the effect of expressing the internal point of view of the
protagonist: by definition, referring to an element as a Substantive is viewing
it internally.[17]

Therefore, I will assume that an anaphorically dependent reflexive, referring to a Substantive, cannot be bound by an element interpreted as a Concept; such a binding constitutes a violation of the Novelty Condition, resulting in an unacceptable sentence. The matching effect derived from this
state of affairs will account for numerous properties of Psych verbs. For example, consider again the sentences in (51). In (51a), the subject is necessarily
an I-Subject, since it is a subject of perception, an "Experiencer," and there
is no problem in matching with the Substantive *themselves,* since an I-Subject
is a Substantive with intentionality. In (51b), on the other hand, the subject is not a subject of perception, so it need not be a Substantive. If it is an
I-Subject, we get the "agentive" reading and there is no mismatch, since both
they and *themselves* are Substantives. However, if the subject is not interpreted as an I-Subject, but rather as a Concept, there is a mismatch with the
Substantive reflexive, and the sentence is unacceptable.

Given my analysis, one might expect to get a sentence like (57), with core-reference between *John* and *him,* since *him* does not have more determinate reference that its antecedent.[18]

(57)   *John$_i$ amuses him$_i$.

However, such a sentence is not possible, given the nature of the Novelty Condition. The Novelty Condition does not supercede the binding theory; the Novelty Condition is a condition on the reference of elements that become anaphorically dependent by the procedures of a binding theory (the specific nature of which is immaterial). In other words, if a reflexive is bound properly, as far such a binding theory is concerned, the Novelty Condition can overrule the binding, but if, as in (57), no binding is allowed by the binding theory, the Novelty Condition is not active.

Additional data on binding in Psych constructions reveal three basic problems for analyses that treat Psych verbs as special: (1) the binding mismatches are more widespread than these analyses would predict; (2) not all verbs in the EO class show these peculiarities; and (3) there are some unexpected differences between Romance languages and English.

Problem 1: Underdetermination

It is not just a small class of Psych verbs that do not allow the subject to bind a direct object reflexive, as in (51b). This restriction also holds for two highly productive classes of Psych constructions, as illustrated by the example with *frapper* in (58a) and the example of non-incorporation in (58b) (recall that Ruwet 1972 gives a very long list of such alternating verbs in French).

(58)a.   *Jean se frappe par son intelligence.[19]
          Jean strikes himself by his intelligence
     b.   *Paul s'est poussé au désespoir.
          Paul pushed himself to despair

In a chain formation analysis such as Belletti and Rizzi's, this means that all such verbs must have two entries: one that corresponds to a derivation where there is an argument directly generated in subject position, and the Psych one, where there is a derived subject. Double entries would also be required in Aspectual Structure and Thematic Structure analyses. In any of these analyses, the result is a grammar with a great degree of homonymy; from the point of view of learnability, it would be odd for UG to favor homonymy on such a grand scale. As Milner (1989, 348) points out, we expect meaning differences to be reflected in phonological form. Moreover, as Ruwet (1972, 233) notes, a double-entry approach would leave unexplained why homonyms have developed only with verbs of the EO class, and not with verbs of the ES class.[20]

Problem 2: Overdetermination

The sentence in (58a) is different from the one in (51b). In (51b), the sentence is fine with an agentive reading in which the entities denoted by the subject intentionally frighten themselves (by telling ghosts stories, for example). Such an "agentive" reading, where the reflexive would be properly bound, is impossible in (58a). This is because verbs of the *frapper* class do not have an incorporated psy-chose, nor is there an overt argument with inherent psychose properties like *colère* 'anger' or *amour* 'love' here. In the absence of such an argument, the Psych interpretation for a *frapper* class verb, is only possible when the external argument is interpreted as a Concept and thus becomes the psy-chose. The internal argument must be an I-Subject, since it is the entity affected by the Psych relation. A mismatch occurs when the external argument (a Concept) binds the internal argument (an I-Subject), and the sentence is unacceptable.[21] On the other hand, an EO verb like *frighten* always has a Psych interpretation, whether its external argument gets a Substantive or a Concept interpretation, since it has an incorporated psychose; its Instigator need not get a Concept interpretation for the construction to be Psych, and no mismatch need arise. Therefore, we expect that there may be some variation among EO verbs as to whether their subject can bind a reflexive. Those verbs, which allow a Substantive reading for their external argument, should allow reflexives, whereas those verbs with only a Concept reading should not. This prediction is borne out: some verbs, such as *frighten* and *dégoûter* 'disgust,' shown in (59), quite freely take an external argument that is a Substantive, whereas others, such as *depress* and *préoccuper* 'worry,' do not, as shown in (60).

(59)a.   They frighten themselves.   OK if Substantive, ?* if Concept.
     b.   Jean se dégoûte.   OK if Substantive, ?* if Concept.
          Jean disgusts himself.

(60)a.   ?* John depresses himself.
     b.   * Jean se préoccupe.
          John worries himself.

However, the analysis predicts that the reflexive pronoun should be possible with verbs such as the ones in (59) only if the subject is a Substantive; this is verified by the test with *il/ce* in French:

(61)a. Jean dégoûte Marie, et pourtant il/c'est ce qu'elle a de plus cher.
        Jean disgust Marie, and yet he/it is what she has that is dearest.
    b. Jean se dégoûte, et pourtant il/*c'est ce qu'il a de plus cher.
        *Jean disgust himself, and yet he/*it is what he has that is dearest.*

In (61a), we can see that the subject of *dégoûter* indeed can be a Substantive or a Concept, since one can refer to it with *il* or *ce*. On the other hand, (61b) shows that the reflexive is only compatible with a subject that is referred to with *il* and hence that is a Substantive.

Whether the external argument may be a Substantive or a Concept seems to be a lexical property of these verbs. Why should there be such a difference in the possible referential interpretation of the external argument of verbs? The answer is related to observations in Kenny (1963) (see also note 51 below). He observes that some emotions are necessarily accompanied by external manifestations of the feelings on the part of the one who experiences the emotion, whereas other emotions can be concealed more easily. This variation in external manifestation is also true for the trigger of the emotion. A person triggering the emotions conveyed by *dégoûter* and *frighten* may be very expressive, and one can talk of a disgusting or frightening gesture. In fact, emphasis on the expressiveness of the trigger may be so strong, with *dégoûter* and *frighten,* that only this 3-D aspect of the emotion is conveyed: a gesture can be judged disgusting or frightening by a bystander without it actually disgusting or frightening the person at whom it is directed. On the other hand, the emotions conveyed by verbs like *depress* and *préoccuper* are more centered on the Experiencer—they are not externally manifested by the trigger. Thus, one cannot refer to the expressiveness of the trigger, and it is odd to talk of a preoccupying gesture or depressing gesture.

The availability of a Substantive external argument is directly related to the expressiveness of the trigger. *Frighten/dégoûter* verbs can have a Substantive as their external argument because, with these verbs, the trigger is very expressive and such expressiveness is the property of a person viewed globally, with all its attributes, as a Substantive. On the other hand, just the opposite holds for verbs like *depress/préoccuper:* there is no expressiveness of the trigger, which is viewed from a much more limitative, abstract perspective, as a Concept.

Besides lexical properties, another factor that governs the interpretation possibilities of the external argument of EO verbs is the context in which the verb appears. As Belletti and Rizzi note, the sentence in (62), in which the reflexive is stressed, is better than the ones in (60). Adverbs that indicate volition or intention also make such sentences more acceptable. In our terms, these are factors that make the I-Subject interpretation more likely (Ruwet 1991 gives a variety of examples where this can be observed).

(62)   Ultimamente, Gianni preoccupa perfino se stesso.
         Lately, Gianni worries even himself.

To say that the subject of these verbs can switch role from Theme to Agent, and hence from derived to nonderived subject when the reflexive is stressed, would not be very revealing and just creates another problem of homonymy. If "agentivity" switches are instead analyzed as options involving either an I-Subject or a Concept interpretation for the subject, we can correlate these options with factors such as expressiveness, as we saw above. Moreover, we can predict why the I-Subject interpretation is not possible for the *frapper* class of verbs in their Psych use. This interpretation is not possible, because the external argument must be a Concept—a psy-chose—to derive the Psych use.[22]

Van Voorst (1992) also points out that this kind of switch is not found only with verbs of emotion or feeling, but in general with any verb that can refer to an event taking place in "mental space." This is expected under my analysis, since the Concept interpretation is a strictly mental attribute.

(63)a.   John helped me better understand the life of a linguist.
    b.   Socrates changed my life.
    c.   Chomsky convinced me to become a linguist.
    d.   Sartre showed me the way.

In these examples, the subjects can receive two interpretations: one in which the individual referred to actually interacted with me and did something to me—I am referring to it as an I-Subject—and another in which it is properties of the individual that affected me, such as the individual's writings, or way of life—I am referring to it as a Concept. As expected in the analysis proposed here, only when the subject is referred to as an I-Subject can it bind a reflexive: the sentences in (64) are not ambiguous.

(64)a.   John helped himself better understand the life of a linguist.
    b.   Socrates changed himself.

     c.   Chomsky convinced himself to become a linguist.

     d.   Sartre showed himself the way.

In sum, whereas the Deep Structure, Aspectual Structure and Thematic Structure analyses predict that verbs of the EO class should be consistent with respect to the binding of a reflexive object, we found that they actually vary markedly. The factors involved are not syntactic, aspectual, or thematic, but have to do with the way of referring to certain arguments, with intentionality.

Problem 3: Differences between Romance Languages and English

Grimshaw (1990) notes that Romance examples of EO reflexive binding are much worse than English examples.

(65)a. ?*John strikes himself as pompous.

     b.   *Jean se frappe par son intelligence.

This is another problem for the Deep Structure, Aspectual Structure, and Thematic Structure analyses, since they predict that verbs of the EO class should be consistent across languages, with respect to the binding of a reflexive object. For example, the contrast in (65) is unexpected in a chain formation analysis such as Belletti and Rizzi, since the chain is ill formed in both cases. The crucial difference lies in the fact that the reflexive is a clitic in the French example. I assume, along the lines of Bouchard (1984a), that the reflexive clitic *se* neutralizes the external argument so that there is a single syntactic argument chain involved here (see sections 2.2.3 and 3.3.1.3 above). The sentences in (65) are then very different from each other: in (65a), *John* is linked to the Actualizer and *himself* is linked to the internal argument. In order for a verb of this class to be used as a Psych verb, its Actualizer must have a Concept interpretation, which provides the construction with a psychose. In (65a), *John,* interpreted as a Concept, binds the I-Subject reflexive *himself,* and the Novelty Condition is violated, as we saw above. In (65b), however, there is a single syntactic argument chain, so not only is the Novelty Condition violated, but, additionally, there is a mismatch, since the same argument is interpreted as both an I-Subject and a Concept. Therefore, (65b) is a stronger violation than (65a).

This mismatch analysis of the French facts predicts that, if we can construct an example where there is a mismatch on the same element in English, even when principles of chain formation and the like are not violated, the sentence should be deviant. For example, a reflexive in the subject position of the verb *depress* is predicted to be strongly deviant, since it would involve a mismatch, for that element: being a reflexive, it must be an I-Subject; being the subject of *depress,* it must be interpreted as a Concept (see the discussion of (60a)). The prediction is borne out in (66).

(66)   *They expect themselves to depress Mary.

The data presented above lead us to conclude that the peculiarities of the distribution of reflexives in Psych constructions turn out not to be dependent on structural, aspectual, or thematic properties, but rather on the method of reference in sentences having to do with mental space. A reflexive interpreted as a Substantive or an I-Subject must be bound by an antecedent interpreted as a Substantive or I-Subject. If a Psych reading requires that the antecedent of such a reflexive be interpreted as a Concept, the sentence is deviant.

One possible objection to the analysis proposed here is that appealing to the manner of reference is introducing metaphysics into linguistic analysis. For example, James Higginbotham (personal communication) suggested to me that one would be better off dealing with the problem in terms of notions more widely used in generative linguistics. In terms of the type theory that I used when he made his suggestion (I assume that he would hold a similar position with respect to the intentional notions I am now using), one could say that (67a) is bad, because when *John* does not refer to an individual but to properties of an individual, the syntactic structure is actually different. Instead of having the usual structure (67b) for the subject *John,* there would be an empty category head expressing something like "properties," as in (67c) (presumably similar to the structure for [$_{NP}$ properties of [$_{NP}$ John]]).

(67)a. ?*John frightens himself.
    b.   [$_{NP}$ John]
    c.   [$_{NP}$e [$_{NP}$ John]]

Because of the extra structure in the NP, *John* does not c-command the reflexive in (67a), hence the ungrammaticality. Aside from the fact that no one knows what the boundaries of linguistics are or whether ways of making reference have a place in linguistic theory, this type of alternative raises serious difficulties.

If the analysis of sentences such as *Colorless green ideas sleep furiously* requires considerations of reference rather than strictly algorithmic manipulations, as we saw in 1.5.2, it is also certainly possible to appeal to referential properties in the analysis of Psych constructions and reflexives. In fact, it would be rather odd to discuss binding theory without ever talking about reference. One can postpone it, as the use of *e* in (67c) does, but one cannot avoid it—at some point, one has to explain what the *e* means.[23] Whether referential properties actually are instrumental in the analysis of the property under scrutiny in (67) is another question, of course. I think there are problems with a syntactic analysis like the one in (67), which show that, in fact, an analysis based more directly on referential properties is more adequate. First, how are we to account for the subtle differences between French and English noted in the discussion of (60)? Then there is the problem of the content of *e* in (67): what is it, and how can we differentiate it from other empty categories in a revealing way? More importantly, one still has to explain why the reflexive cannot be bound by the whole [$_{NP}$e [$_{NP}$ John]]. Is it that a reflexive cannot be bound by an element with the referential properties of *e?* But, once that assumption is made, one is appealing to referential properties, so why not do without the *e* and go directly to the referential properties of *John,* since the additional structure helps in no way. One can certainly postulate abstract entities, but by considerations of minimality, abstract entities should be introduced only when strictly necessary.

4.4.2 BACKWARD BINDING OF A REFLEXIVE

Another binding property often mentioned in the discussion of Psych verbs is that, for EO verbs, the direct object can bind a reflexive inside the subject.

(68)a. That book about herself struck Mary as embarrassing.
   b. *That book about herself struck Mary on the head.

This binding property would be evidence for the derived status of the subject of an EO verb, since the c-command relation, which is assumed to be a crucial factor in the binding of anaphors, seems to be established in some way from object to subject in (68a), contrary to what is found with nonderived subjects. I will show that such an analysis cannot be maintained. First, backward binding is not found only in EO constructions, but also in constructions where derived subjects are unlikely or impossible. Second, contrary to what is expected, backward binding does not extend to other phenomena dependent on c-command. I will argue that one can account for the facts if long distance binding of a reflexive is not viewed as binding of an anaphor, but rather as binding of a logophoric pronoun, subject to discourse conditions. In the particular case of backward binding, this means that the initial phrase is part of the Content of Consciousness of the antecedent.

In Belletti and Rizzi's analysis, the backward binding follows from their assumption that a sentence like (68a) has a DS quite different from (68b): the subject is derived in (a) and c-commanded by *Mary* at DS, and they assume that c-command at DS is sufficient for a reflexive to be properly bound. But this structural account fails empirically.

First, note that things are not as simple as the data in (68) would lead one to believe. Contrary to what is predicted, some backward reflexivization examples can be constructed that are not as bad as (68b) and where the subject is not derived. In (69a), the sentence is not a Psych construction; in (69b), which is a complex Psych construction, the derived status of the subject is hard to maintain, and in (69c), the antecedent of the reflexive would not c-command it, even assuming a derived subject analysis.[24]

(69)a. ?These stories about himself don't describe John very well.
   b. ?These stories about himself made John anxious to the extreme.
   c. ?These nasty stories about himself broke John's resistance.

Pesetsky (1990) gives several examples of this type, which he attributes to Martin (1986), and which also argue against an unaccusative account of backward binding. In (70), the antecedent of the anaphor is not a direct object, but the subject of a small clause; in (71a and b), the antecedent is the object of a causative verb and the subject of an infinitival complement in (71c and d); in (72), the antecedent is the object of an apparently "normal" verb, but used figuratively.

(70)a. Each other's remarks made John and Mary angry.
   b. Pictures of each other make us happy.
   c. These stories about herself made Mary nervous.
   d. Pictures of himself give John the creeps.

(71)a. Each other's criticisms forced John and Mary to confront their problems.
   b. Pictures of each other caused John and Mary to start crying.
   c. Those rumors about himself made John behave more carefully.
   d. Pictures of herself used to make Sue blush.

(72)a. ?Each other's stupid remarks eventually killed John and Mary.
   b. ?Each other's criticism harmed John and Mary.
   c. ?Rumors about herself always plunge Mary into a deep depression.
   d. ?Those pictures of himself ultimately destroyed Bill.

As Pesetsky notes, the examples are much worse if the verbs in (72) are used nonfiguratively.

(73)a. *Each other's stupid friends eventually killed John and Mary.
    b. *Each other's parents harmed John and Mary.
    c. *Each other's teachers insulted John and Mary.
    d. *Each other's swimming coaches plunged John and Mary into the pool.

Pesetsky gives no explanation for these facts, he simply provides the following descriptive generalization (his (96)):

(74)   A Cause argument of a predicate π behaves as if c-commanded by the phrase governed by π.

But (74) is inaccurate. It is not always the argument governed by the predicate that counts as the antecedent, as in (69c), where "John" is the antecedent for "himself," but "John's resistance" is the phrase governed by the predicate "broke." Pesetsky himself, in his note 28, provides the following counterexamples to his generalization.

(75)a.   These rumors about himself$_i$ caught John$_i$'s attention.
    b.   The jokes about herself$_i$ got Mary$_i$'s goat.
    c.   Each other$_i$'s nasty remarks really ruffled [John and Mary]$_i$'s feathers.
    d.   Each other$_i$'s teasing really got their$_i$ dander up.

(76)a.   The photos of himself$_i$ made John$_i$'s face turn red.
    b.   The rumors about herself$_i$ made Mary$_i$'s hair stand up.
    c.   Each other$_i$'s threats made [John and Bill]$_i$'s skin crawl.

The antecedent of the reflexive is not governed by the predicate in any of the examples in (75) and (76). This shows that generalization (74) is inaccurate. These examples also add to the evidence against Belletti and Rizzi's analysis, since the antecedent here would not c-command the subject at DS if it were derived because the antecedent is embedded in a complement. This kind of data is also a problem for Grimshaw's aspectual analysis. She assumes that long-distance anaphors must have an antecedent that is maximally prominent in the event structure (assuming that an argument which participates in the first subevent in an event structure is more prominent than an argument which participates in the second subevent). But the antecedents in (69)–(72) and (75) and (76) are not more prominent than the complements in which they are embedded.

A second objection to Belletti and Rizzi's analysis, as well as Pesetsky's generalization, is that it leads us to expect that other cases of binding involving c-command should also behave in a special way in constructions with an EO verb. For example, a pronoun backward bound by a Quantified NP might be expected to be okay. But as the following example from Jackendoff (1990b, 435) shows, backward binding of QNP-bound pronouns is not possible in an EO Psych construction.

(77)   *Those pictures of his$_i$ mother embarrassed every boy$_i$.

The converse problem is faced by the Deep Structure analysis of (78a). If the Deep Structure for (78a) is as in (78b), then pronominal *le* c-commands *Jean* at that level (along the same lines as Belletti and Rizzi's account of (68)), which may incorrectly predict that they cannot be coreferential.

(78)a.   L'oncle de Jean$_i$ le$_i$ dégoûte.
           Jean's uncle disgusts him.
     b.   [$_S$ Δ [$_{VP}$ [$_{VP}$ le dégoûte] l'oncle de Jean]

Another type of problem for these analyses is a constraint that seems to hold of the subject NP and which appears not to be related to structure at all. Consider the following examples:

(79)a.   That picture of Mary is funny because it has an odd shape/frame.
     b.   That picture of Mary is funny because of what she looks like
           in it.

As is well known, in order for backward reflexivization to take place, the subject must be a picture NP. But the interpretation of the picture NP is further constrained. Normally, a picture NP can have two possible interpretations: one in which we are referring to the object itself, as in (79a), and one in which we refer to what the picture represents, as in (79b). Yet in backward reflexivization contexts, only the representational interpretation is possible. Thus, an objective interpretation of the picture NP is not possible in (80).

(80)   That picture of herself struck Mary as funny.
         OK = . . . because of what she looked like in it.
         ?? = . . . because it had an odd frame.

There is no explanation for these facts in a structural analysis such as Belletti and Rizzi's or Pesetsky's, since the strictly structural conditions on binding should be met in (80), whether or not the NP is interpreted as representational. Similarly, there is no reason to believe that the prominence in event structure assumed by Grimshaw should vary according to the representational status of the NP.

In addition to the above observations, there are other, nonstructural, conditions on long-distance reflexives. I am not talking about proposals that theta hierarchy plays a role in binding and similar claims (see Jackendoff 1972; Giorgi 1984; Hellan 1985; among others). The conditions I have in mind have to do with the nature of the bound element itself and the point of view from which the sentence is seen, notions that have been discussed at length in the literature.[25] These factors are crucial for the analysis of reflexives, since long-distance reflexives might not be anaphors in the strict sense, after all, and might depend on conditions other than structural ones for their interpretation. More precisely, these long-distance reflexives seem to behave in many respects like logophoric pronouns. Broadly speaking, a logophoric pronoun is one that takes as antecedent elements that bear certain discourse roles. For example, Zribi-Hertz (1989) states that a reflexive pronoun may be logophoric and thus occur nonlocally bound, if and only if it refers back to the minimal Subject of Consciousness.

Suppose we assume that a condition of this sort also governs the distribution of backward reflexivization. Since it is based on the notion of 'Subject of Consciousness,' it is natural to assume that it is sensitive to the interpretation of an argument as I-Subject or as Concept; presumably, a Subject of Consciousness is always an I-Subject. I, therefore, propose the following condition:

(81) *Long Distance Anaphor Binding:* A long distance anaphor can be bound by a Subject of Consciousness, if the Anaphor is in the Content of Consciousness of that Subject of Consciousness.

A Subject of Consciousness is an entity to which the speaker attributes consciousness (including himself and the person he is talking to). A Content of Consciousness is what the speaker presents as being part of an entity's consciousness. Therefore, a long-distance anaphor is bound by a Subject of Consciousness, if the anaphor is in a part of the sentence, the meaning of which part is presented by the speaker as being in the consciousness of that Subject of Consciousness. I will refer to this as logophoric binding. This condition accounts for the data above. For example, consider (68), repeated below as (82). In (82a), *that book about herself* is a Concept in the Content of Consciousness of the I-Subject *Mary,* because Mary is crucially aware that the book is about herself; hence, *Mary* can be the antecedent for the reflexive.

In (82b), *that book about herself* is a Substantive, a concrete object, and its content is not presented as being part of Mary's consciousness; so *Mary* cannot be the antecedent for the reflexive.

(82)a.   That book about herself struck Mary as embarrassing.
   b.   *That book about herself struck Mary on the head.

The sentences in (75) involve expressions in which the subject expresses a Content of Consciousness of the antecedent of the reflexive, so the I-Subject antecedent is available for logophoric binding. In (76), the antecedents are presented as crucially aware that the "content" of the photos, rumors, or threats, concerns them, hence the logophoric binding here also.

The binding condition in (81) may well be more general. It may account for other cases of "connectivity" between a reflexive and its distant antecedent, discussed in Higgins (1979), such as those in (83).

(83)a.   Pictures of himself, John knows Bill likes.
   b.   Which pictures of herself did Mary buy?

The general condition on connectivity holds for reflexives that are embedded in NPs that do not have an "objective reading," such as picture NPs when they are representational, as in (82a), and delimiting operators, as in (83). Since *himself* can be bound by either *John* or *Bill* in (83a), both of these potential antecedents must be Subjects of Consciousness, if condition (81) is correct. The external arguments of *know* and *like* are indeed Subjects of Consciousness. We can verify that the condition is correct by replacing one of these verbs by a verb whose external argument is not a Subject of Consciousness; in this case, the external argument should not be a potential antecedent for the reflexive. This is borne out. Consider the verb *require.*

(84)   That old man requires a lot of care.

In (84), the subject can either be an I-Subject, in which case, for example, the old man actually asks for care, or the subject can be a Concept, in which case, in one possible scenario, it is a doctor who actually requested that the old man be taken care of, and the old man might not even be aware of this. Now note that if we replace *knows* in (83a) with *requires,* as in *Pictures of himself, John requires that Bill likes,* the interpretation of the subject of *requires* is not ambiguous: only the I-Subject interpretation of *John* is possible if *John* is the antecedent of the reflexive, since a Concept is not a potential antecedent here, according to (81), because a Concept is not a Subject of Consciousness.[26]

It is not just backward binding of a reflexive that is governed by Subject of Consciousness conditions. Kuno (1972) discusses a set of phenomena under the heading of Direct Discourse Analysis for the complements of verbs of saying, feeling, knowing, and the like. His Direct Discourse representations allow him to account for the contrast in (85) and (86) on the basis of the contrast in (87) and (88).

(85)   *That Mary$_i$ was a millionnaire is one of the things that was told by her$_i$.

(86)   That Mary$_i$ was a millionnaire is one of the things that was told about her$_i$.

(87)   *Mary$_i$ told (someone) "Mary$_i$ is a millionnaire."

(88)   (Someone) told about Mary$_i$ "Mary$_i$ is a millionnaire."

It would require quite a reconstruction in (85) and (86) to get the facts right in any of the structural analyses we have seen. On the other hand, an analysis based on intentional notions is straightforward. As Coppieters (1982) observes, all these complements of verbs of saying, feeling, and knowing correspond to a class of referentially opaque environments, complements of verbs of propositional attitude.

A verb of propositional attitude attributes its complement to the consciousness of its agent/Experiencer. This is precisely the reason why such complements have to be considered as propositions rather than sentences. Thus, the parallel between the communicative act, involving a speaker addressing an audience, the reflective situation involving a thinker, and the experiencing situation in which an Experiencer feels a certain emotion, is that all involve individuals conceived as intrinsic beings-as-subjects ("I" and "you" in D.D.A. terminology) [I-Subject in my terminology.]. Let us remember that a being-as-subject is a consciousness presented directly from the inside, as if the speaker let that consciousness express itself without his intervening in the process. If such beings-as-subjects are named from the speaker's perspective, through a proper name or a definite description for instance, in a clause that is supposed to convey the internal content of their consciousness [as in (85)], it will form an explicit denial by the speaker of their being-as-subject status, a status which is a prerequisite for the interpretation of the sentence. No such clash will arise in connection with individuals conceived of extrinsically, as beings-as-concepts [as in (86)], since the extrinsic attitude does present an individual from an external perspective. (Coppieters 1982, 15)

In other words, (85) is bad because Mary is named by her proper name in her own Content of Consciousness, and (86) is good because the part of the sentence where the NP *Mary* appears is not part of Mary's Content of Consciousness.

To illustrate with just one more example, consider the contrast between (89) and (90), discussed in Jackendoff (1975) and Reinhart (1983):

(89)   *In John's picture of Mary, she found a scratch.

(90)   In John's picture of Mary, she looks sick.

In (89), *she* is an I-Subject; hence, as discussed by Coppieters, the sentence is bad because Mary is named from the speaker's perspective in a clause that conveys the Content of her Consciousness. But in (90), *she* is not an I-Subject, so *she* is not viewed as having a Content of Consciousness containing a reference to herself through the proper name *Mary;* hence there is no clash in the referential interpretation of the sentence. Coppieters' explanation is in line with my proposal in (81), and together they suggest that many (if not all) cases of peculiar behavior in backward binding depend on the initial phrase being a Content of Consciousness of the potential antecedent.

4.4.3 PASSIVIZATION

Both Belletti and Rizzi (1988) and Grimshaw (1990) predict that passivization of EO verbs is impossible. For Belletti and Rizzi, this should be impossible because EO verbs have a derived subject and derived subjects do not passivize. They say the contrast in (91) is because *venir* 'come' is an unaccusative verb (and thus has a derived subject).

(91)a.   Il a été discuté de la question.
          It was discussed of the question.
   b.   *Il a été venu chez moi.
          It was come to my place.

For Grimshaw, passivization of EO verbs should be impossible because passive can suppress only an external argument. She defines 'external argument' as an element most prominent on both the aspectual and thematic tiers; EO verbs have no external argument because none of their arguments are "most prominent" on both tiers, since their association is crossed. Pesetsky's analysis, and the one presented here, make no such prediction about passivization of EO verbs.

The 'no passivization' prediction is, in fact, false; passives of EO verbs are possible.

(92)   Mary was frightened/amused by the clown.

Belletti and Rizzi's and Grimshaw's response to such examples is that these are not verbal passives but rather adjectival passives. Pesetsky (1990) reviews their arguments for the adjectival nature of these passives and shows that they are not convincing; I will briefly discuss their arguments below. Moreover, the standard tests used to distinguish between verbs and adjectives seem to go directly against their claims. Regardless of the validity of their hypothesis, they still fail to explain why adjectival passives should be any better than verbal passives here. Is it that adjectival passive can apply to derived subjects or to arguments that are not external? This does not seem to be correct because, although it is possible to find some unaccusative participles functioning as NP-internal adjectives, as in (93), it seems impossible to get them as sentential predicates, as we saw in (91b).

(93)   The Captain welcomed aboard the newly arrived passengers.

This means that both the unacceptability of (91b) as an adjectival passive and the acceptability of (92) as an adjectival passive require additional explanation. Moreover, as Pesetsky points out, examples like the one in (93), where the unaccusative participle is an NP-internal adjective, are rather sporadic. We find examples like those in (94) (Pesetsky's (32), many based on Bresnan 1978), but other unaccusatives cannot be used as adjectival passives, as we see in (95) (Pesetsky's (33)).[27]

(94)a.   elapsed time
    b.   newly appeared book
    c.   newly arrived packages
    d.   capsized boat
    e.   fallen arches
    f.   blistered paint
    g.   departed travelers
    h.   a fallen leaf
    i.   a widely traveled man
    j.   an undescended testicle
    k.   a risen Christ
    l.   a struck window
    m.   drifted snow
    n.   a lapsed Catholic
    o.   a collapsed lung
    p.   a failed writer

q. faded wallpaper
r. well-rested children

(95)a. *an (already) occurred event
  b. *(recently) grown weeds
  c. *(newly) come packages
  d. *(recently) floated leaves
  e. *(recently) peeled skin (if skin that has peeled naturally)
  f. *(often) smelled paint (if paint that smelled); *bad-smelled paint
  g. *(recently) left travelers
  h. *a (recently) surfaced problem
  i. *a (widely) toured violinist
  j. *a (recently) died celebrity
  k. *a (brightly) glistened paint
  l. *a (visibly) trembled orator
  m. *the (regularly) twinkled star
  n. *the (already) stumbled horse
  o. *the (sharply) pulsated organ
  p. *a (recently) succeeded writer
  q. *a (seldom) trembled house
  r. *(well-)slept children

Pesetsky concludes that unaccusatives seem to generally resist adjectival passivization as much as verbal passivization, which calls into question Belletti and Rizzi's and Grimshaw's suggestion concerning EO passives.

Let us now turn to Belletti and Rizzi's arguments for the adjectival status of sentences like (92). Their two main arguments are based on specific aspects of Italian syntax. First, cliticization in reduced relative clauses in Italian is possible only if the clause is verbal (96a), not if it is adjectival (96b).

(96)a. la notizia communicatagli
        the news communicated-to him
  b. *la notizia ignotagli.
        the news unknown-to him

They note that *ne*-cliticization is impossible with EO verbs and conclude that the passives of these verbs are adjectival:

(97)a. La sola persona affascinata da questa prospettiva
        the only person fascinated by this perspective
  b. *La sola persona affascinatane
        the only person fascinated-ne (by it)

But Pesetsky (1988) argues that the ungrammaticality of (97b) is because of an additional constraint that generally prohibits the *ne* of the passive from cliticizing to the participle in a reduced relative clause, whether it is verbal or adjectival, as shown in (98).

(98)a. *la sola persona uccisane
  the only person killed-ne by him
 b. *la sola persona colpitane
  the only person struck-ne by him
 c. *la sola persona arrestane
  the only person arrested-ne by him
 d. *la sola persona toccatane
  the only person touched-ne by him

Belletti and Rizzi's second argument is based on the fact that Italian can form passives with auxiliary verb *venire* 'come' instead of *essere* 'be.' These passives can only be verbal passives, not adjectival passives, so that (99a) has only an eventive reading, whereas (99b) can be either eventive or stative.

(99)a. La porta viene chiusa alle cinque.
  The door comes closed at five.
  The door is closed at five.
 b. La porta è chiusa alle cinque.
  The door is closed at five.
  The door is closed at five.

Passives of EO verbs formed with auxiliary *venire* are impossible (100), so Belletti and Rizzi conclude that passive of EO verbs must be adjectival.

(100) *Gianni viene preoccupato da tutti.
  Gianni comes worried by everybody.

But again Pesetsky argues that the test is flawed. He says that *venire* is possible only with "eventive" predicates. Adjectival passives are noneventive, and EO verbs also often have a similar aspectual property. However, such sentences can be made acceptable if placed in an eventive context:

(101)a. Il publico venne affascinato dalla conclusione di quel concerto.
  The public came fascinated by the conclusion of that concert(o).
 b. Gianni venne spaventato da questa prospettiva alle cinque.
  Gianni came frightened by this perspective at five.

Thus, it seems that the two arguments put forward by Belletti and Rizzi for the adjectival nature of the passive of EO verbs do not hold.

Grimshaw (1990) also advances two arguments for the adjectival nature of the passive of EO verbs. First, she says that "these cases consistently pass all the tests for adjectivehood with flying colors. They allow negative *un*-prefixation, they occur as complements to the verbs which select APs (*remain*, etc.), and they are relatively unfussy about prepositions: *frightened*, for example, can occur with *about, by,* or *at*" (Grimshaw 1990, 113). But this only shows that these can be adjectival passives, not that they cannot be verbal passives. Moreover, a quick check of a list of verbs of the EO class shows that Grimshaw's sweeping statement is too strong: many of these verbs fail some of the tests.[28]

(102) a. *undisgusted, ?unpreoccupied, *unbored, *unshocked, *unstruck.
 b. bothered by/*at/about/with
   struck by/*at/*about/with
   depressed by/*at/about/with
   interested by/*at/*about/*with
   annoyed by/?at/?*about/with
   bored by/*at/*about/with
   shocked by/at/about/?*with
   preoccupied by/*at/*about/with
   scared by/*at/*about/*with
   fascinated by/?*at/about/with
   worried by/?at/about/with
   impressed by/?*at/?*about/with

Her second argument goes as follows: EO verbs can take the progressive in the active, (103a), but not in the passive, (103b):

(103) a. The situation was depressing Mary.
 b. *Mary was being depressed by the situation.

Since the progressive is incompatible with stativity, she argues that this shows that EO verbs are stative when in the passive, hence adjectival.

However, Pesetsky argues that a closer look at the data leads to a quite different conclusion, in fact, just the opposite of what Grimshaw claims. He suggests that there are two classes of EO verbs. First, some EO verbs are essentially stative, even in their active use: they resist the progressive form with the meaning of iterated action and are odd with the punctual use of the simple past tense, as we see in (104) and (105) (Pesetsky's 52 and 53).

(104)a. ??Odd noises were continually depressing Sue.

    b. ??Bill was sitting around happy as a lark, when an unexpected groan from the next room suddenly depressed him.

(105)a. ??Sue was continually being depressed by odd noises.

    b. ??Bill was sitting around happy as a lark, when suddenly he was depressed by an unexpected groan from the next room.

A second kind of EO verb is not exclusively stative: these verbs are quite acceptable in the progressive form or the punctual past, in the active as well as the passive.

(106)a.   Odd noises were continually scaring Sue.

    b.   Bill was sitting around, calm as could be, when an unexpected groan from the next room scared him.

(107)a.   Sue was continually being scared by odd noises.

    b.   Bill was sitting around, calm as could be, when suddenly he was scared by an unexpected groan from the next room.

Since the verbs in (104) and (105) and in (106) and (107) would belong to the same class in Grimshaw's (and Belletti and Rizzi's) analysis, the oddness of the passive progressive (104) and of the punctual past tense (105) cannot be taken as evidence that the passive of *depress* is adjectival.

This brings us back to (103): we expect the ungrammaticality of (103b), given that *depress* is stative, but the acceptability of (103a) is then surprising. Pesetsky argues that this is not the "iterative" use of the progressive, but rather a special use of the progressive, also found with other stative verbs, as Baker (1989) notes. For Pesetsky, the acceptability of (103a) recalls the acceptability of the progressive with other statives:

(108)a.   Karen is finally understanding the proof.

    b.   Donald is finding your accusations ludicrous.

    c.   I think Bill is really liking this performance.

    d.   Sue is truly hating the sea-urchin sushi.

    e.   Harry is clearly fearing an outbreak of the flu.

Baker's comments on some of these sentences give us a flavor of what the special interpretation is: "Sentence [(108a)] would typically be used if Karen was only partly done going through the proof, [(108c)] would be appropriate at an intermediate point in the performance, [(108b)] would be used if Donald had heard only some of the accusations" (Baker 1989, 489) For Pesetsky, (103a) has a similar flavor to it: "If someone says that 'the situation is de-

pressing Mary,' we naturally infer that this person is making a judgment . . .
about some situation which has not played itself out at the time of the utterance." (Pesetsky 1990, 18).

Interestingly, none of the verbs that take this special reading in the progressive (*understand, find, like, hate, fear*) allow progressive passives (109)
(Pesetsky's (58)), although their nonprogressive passives are unproblematic
(110) (Pesetsky's (59)); yet none are unaccusative in Belletti and Rizzi's
analysis.

(109)a. ?? This proof is finally being understood by Karen.
      b. * Your accusations are being found ludicrous by Donald.
      c. * I think this performance is really being liked by Bill.
      d. * The sea-urchin sushi is truly being hated by Sue.
      e. * An outbreak of the flu is clearly being feared by Harry.

(110)a.   This proof is understood by Karen.
      b.   Your accusations were found ludicrous by Donald.
      c.   I think this performance was really liked by Bill.
      d.   The sea-urchin sushi was truly hated by Sue.
      e.   An outbreak of the flu is feared by Harry.

Pesetsky concludes that the data do not show that EO verbs have an adjectival passive but rather that "progressive forms of stative predicates require
a particular interpretation which is for some reason incompatible with the
passive. Crucially, unaccusativity is not diagnosed." (Pesetsky 1990, 19).

Moreover, Pesetsky shows that this fact can be used to argue specifically
against an analysis of EO passives as being strictly adjectival. The argument
goes as follows: the adverb *much* can modify an adjectival passive, but not a
verbal passive, as we can see in (111) (Pesetsky's (51)).

(111)a.   This idea was (much) discussed in the 70's.
      b.   This idea was (much) talked about in the 70's.
      c.   This idea was (*much) considered important in the 70's.
      d.   This idea was being (*much) talked about in the 70's.

As expected, progressive aspect is incompatible with a passive form modified
by *much,* as in (111d). If we assume that the presence of *much* (and similar
adverbs, such as *extremely*) is a test for adjectival passives, the fact that EO
verbs like *scare* or *frighten* are incompatible with the progressive aspect only
when modified by *much,* but acceptable otherwise, would indicate that they
do not have an adjectival passive, but in fact have a verbal passive, contrary

to Belletti and Rizzi's and Grimshaw's claim. This can be seen in (112) (Peset-sky's (60b and 61b))

(112)a.   In those days, Bill was often being (*much) frightened by one
          thing or another when I would come home from work.
      b.   In those days, Bill was often being (*extremely) annoyed by Bill's
          [*sic*] behavior.

Moreover, if only adjectival passives, and not verbal passives, are sup-posed to allow idiosyncratic prepositions, the contrasts in (113) (Pesetsky's (62–65)) noted by Postal (1971, 43) would again indicate that a verbal passive of EO verbs is indeed possible.

(113)a.   Sue was continually being scared by/*at sudden noises.
      b.   Bill was often being enraged by/*at totally innocent remarks.
      c.   Sue was continually being annoyed by/*with mysterious sounds
          from the cellar.
      d.   John was always being deeply impressed by/*with things that left
          the rest of us cold.

To this we could add that other standard tests that are assumed to distinguish between adjectives and verbs also indicate that EO passives can be verbal. I will mention two of these here. First, adverbial modification of verbs differs from modification of adjectives: for instance, in French, verbs can be modi-fied by *beaucoup* and adjectives by *très,* but not vice versa.

(114)a.   Jean a *beaucoup/*très* lu cette semaine.
          *Jean read a lot/*very this week.*
      b.   Jean est *très/*beaucoup* heureux.
          *Jean is very/*much happy.*

EO passives generally allow both modifiers (with some minor variation), im-plying that both an adjectival and a verbal passive are possible.

(115)a.   Jean a été *beaucoup* dégoûté/impressionné par Paul. (verbal)
          Jean was much disgusted/impressed by Paul.
      b.   Jean a été *très* dégoûté/impressionné par Paul. (adjectival)
          Jean was very disgusted/impressed by Paul.

Similarly, verbs enter into the *tant . . . que* construction, whereas adjec-tives enter into the *si . . . que* construction instead.

(116)a.   Jean a *tant/*si* lu cette semaine qu'il n'a pas pu voir Zoé.
          *Jean read so much/*so this week that he couldn't see Zoé.*

b.   Jean est *si/*tant* distrait qu'il a oublié sa canne à pêche.
      *Jean is so/*so much absentminded that he forgot his fishing rod.*

As with the preceding test, this test shows that EO passives are capable of deriving either adjectival or verbal passives.

(117)a.   Jean a été *tant* dégoûté/ impressionné par Paul qu'il a immédi-
           atement rejeté/adopté sa théorie. (verbal)
           Jean was disgusted/impressed by Paul so much that he immediately
           rejected/adopted his theory.
      b.   Jean a été *si* dégoûté/ impressionné par Paul qu'il a immédi-
           atement rejeté/adopté sa théorie. (adjectival)
           Jean was so disgusted/impressed by Paul that he immediately re-
           jected/adopted his theory.

The fact that there are two classes of EO verbs with respect to stativity correlates with the fact that there are also two classes of EO verbs with respect to expressiveness—expressive verbs such as *frighten* and nonexpressive verbs such as *depress,* discussed in section 4.4.1 (see (59) and (60) above). I pointed out that the emotions conveyed by verbs like *depress* are more centered on the Experiencer, so the trigger argument in subject position is restricted to a Concept interpretation; since a Concept subject can only have a stative property attributed to it, the nonexpressiveness of a verb such as *depress* has the effect that the verb is "essentially stative even in its active use" in Pesetsky's terms.

To summarize this section on passivization, I conclude that the analysis of EO passives as strictly adjectival is incorrect: the passives of EO verbs are not different from other passives; they may be either verbal or adjectival. This raises serious problems for Belletti and Rizzi's and Grimshaw's analyses. On the other hand, Pesetsky's analysis is compatible with these results. In the psy-chose analysis, where EO verbs are not syntactically different from other verbs, these are, in fact, the expected results.

4.4.4 PROGRESSIVE

Grimshaw's argument for the adjectival nature of EO passives is crucially based on the assumption that the progressive is incompatible with stative predicates. Although there is some truth to that assumption, and much has been written about it (including Vendler 1967 and Lakoff 1970a), the assumption is known to have its share of problems. In his careful study of aspect, Dowty (1979) noted some systematic counterexamples, such as *lying, sitting, standing, resting, perching,* and *sprawling,* which are all aspectually stative in one of their interpretations and yet allow the progressive in that interpretation. Voorst (1988) also noted that *missing* and perception verbs do not fit the generalization: *missing* is stative and allows the progressive, while perception verbs are not stative yet disallow it. Dowty notes that the restriction on the progressive seems to be, instead, in terms of interval semantics. Noninterval (or momentary) predicates disallow the progressive, but interval predicates, including some statives, allow it.

Roughly, an interval predicate is one that defines a complex change-of-state that is true of a precise interval. The interval is bounded at one end by one particular state of affairs and at the other end by another state of affairs. The progressive aspect is compatible only with an interval predicate because the progressive is used to "freeze" one time frame within the interval that the predicate defines. In *John is building a house,* the speaker focuses on an intermediate frame in an interval. At the end of the interval, as far as the speaker can tell, a house is likely to have been built. Stative predicates, on the other hand, are true at interval *I,* just in case the state they describe is true at all moments within *I:* in a sense, a stative is not decomposable into subevents. Therefore, statives are generally incompatible with the progressive; because it cannot freeze one time frame in the interval of the stative, a stative has no interval time frames.

However, some stative verbs do take the progressive: *lying, sitting, standing, resting, perching,* and *sprawling.* Dowty suggests that this may be because we cannot determine whether the subject of these verbs is stationary with only one time frame. The meaning of these verbs requires that the subject is stationary and we need to compare two time frames to determine it. Since an interval is present, the progressive may refer to one time frame within it. On the other hand, we might expect certain verbs like *know* and *love* to occur freely with the progressive in such an approach, but Dowty counters the possibility:

> *John knows French* is made true not by John's doing anything at that moment, but by past occasions of John-stages having stage-properties of speaking French, and *John loves Mary* is somehow or other made true by past (and presumably future) instances of John-stages bearing certain relations to Mary-stages. To the extent that an interval of time could be said to be "the" interval of their truth, it would seem to be (in most cases) only a large and vaguely defined interval including a vague number of past instances of the truth of certain stage-predicates,

and presumably including a vague number of future instances of certain stage-predicates. . . . Therefore it seems not surprising that our language should treat them as true of an individual (as opposed to its stages) at any moment within this vague interval, rather than make us somehow try to indicate the large interval we have in mind. (Dowty 1979, 179)

In other words, a vague number of stages over a long and vaguely defined interval in the "real world" is not treated as defining a linguistically relevant interval. We can relate this to the discussion of Baker's sentences (108), repeated here as (118).

(118)a.   Karen is finally understanding the proof.
     b.   Donald is finding your accusations ludicrous.
     c.   I think Bill is really liking this performance.
     d.   Sue is truly hating the sea-urchin sushi.
     e.   Harry is clearly fearing an outbreak of the flu.

These verbs also seem to involve a "vague interval," which would explain their relative compatibility with the progressive form. What seems to be going on in (118), however, is that the use of the progressive with these verbs brings about a particular reading where the interval is no longer very large and vague, but rather is interpreted as the type of interval usually compatible with the progressive. This explains the special interpretations for these sentences noted by Baker; for example, he says (118c) would be appropriate at an intermediate point in the performance. In fact, it appears that the progressive has forced a change in the interval usually attributed to *like* from "vague" to more precise and restricted.

We can also understand, in these terms, the difference between the two classes of EO verbs: the "statives"—which strongly resist the progressive form and only get a special interpretation similar to the ones in (118), such as *depress*—and the "expressives"—which allow the progressive form fairly freely, such as *scare* and *frighten*. Pesetsky comments that "It is quite likely that the relevant distinction has to do with the nature of the onset of the emotion referenced by the EO verb. I guess that emotions which typically come on suddenly and consciously (e.g., frights and surprises) allow iterative progressive, while emotions which typically grow imperceptibly (e.g., boredom and depression) do not" (Pesetsky 1990, 17–18). In terms of interval semantics, frights and surprises would be interval predicates, whereas boredom and depression would fall into the "vague interval" category and thus would be analyzed as noninterval predicates.

Mufwene (1984) proposes to redefine stativity in terms of the potential for permanence or nontransient duration. The constraint on the progressive is then that it is compatible with nonpermanence, but not with permanence. Statives are highly marked for permanence and do not allow the progressive easily, whereas activities are low on permanence and make the use of the progressive necessary in most instances to describe an event. Van Voorst (1990), following on Mufwene's idea that permanence is not absolute but scalar, suggests that Psych verbs might be neutral with respect to permanence. "A psychological verb without the progressive form can describe a more permanent, non-generic, feeling. When the progressive form is present, a less permanent feeling is involved or an interpretation emerges under which the subject is somehow active" (van Voorst 1990, 5). He gives (119) as examples where the use of the progressive implies that the subjects are "somehow active." In these examples, they actively show that they like the wine and admire the painting.

(119)a.   The gourmets are adoring the wine at today's banquet.
   b.   They are admiring the beautiful Van Gogh.

The examples in (119) are very similar to Baker's examples (118) above: here, too, the judgment is an intermediate one, based on only part of the available evidence. Thus, in (119a), we do not have confirmation that the gourmets actually adore the wine, but the evidence we have, given their present behavior, is that we will eventually be able to make such a judgment.

A common point to all these observations is that the use of the progressive seems to be dependent on the potential for activity of the subject. In my terms, this means that it depends on the Substantive versus Concept interpretation of the subject; the former has a strong potential for activity, while the latter has a very low potential for activity.[29] As for Pesetsky's observation that "progressive forms of stative predicates require a particular interpretation which is for some reason incompatible with the passive" (1990, 19), it could be attributed to the prototypically very low potential for activity of the subject in a passive construction. I leave these matters for further investigation.

4.4.5 NOMINALIZATION

Grimshaw (1990) gives another argument for her analysis of EO verbs as aspectually different from other verbs. She notes that these verbs do not nominalize to give event nominals, only result nominals. She proposes an account of this fact, based on the peculiar aspectual properties she attributes to EO verbs. She assumes that event nominalization adds an external argument *Ev* (event), which forces the former external argument to be suppressed; since EO verbs do not have an external argument, because of the crossing of their aspectual linking, they cannot be nominalized in this way. Pesetsky (1990) proposes an alternative analysis of the nominalization of EO verbs, based on the assumption that these verbs are causatives of ES verbs, derived by zero affixation; EO verbs cannot be nominalized because zero-derived words do not permit the affixation of further derivational morphemes.

In the next two sections, I will show that there are problems with these analyses and that they cannot be maintained. I will then propose in 4.4.5.2 an analysis of Psych verb nominalization in terms of intentionality.

4.4.5.1 TWO UNSATISFACTORY ANALYSES OF PSYCH VERB NOMINALIZATION

4.4.5.1.1 Grimshaw's Analysis and External Argument R

Grimshaw (1990) assumes that the reason EO verbs do not nominalize to give event nominals, but only result nominals, is that event nominals have an argument structure, whereas other nominals do not. In the spirit of analyses in which nonevent nominals are assumed to have a referential external argument, *R*, and verbs have an event, *E*, variable in their lexical conceptual structure, Grimshaw assumes that creating an event nominal adds an external argument, *Ev*, (the eventive counterpart of *R*) to the verbal base and forces the former external argument to be suppressed, that is, removed from the argument structure of the predicate. Because EO verbs never have an external argument in her analysis because of the crossing of their aspectual linking, they cannot undergo this kind of nominalization, since there is no external argument to suppress. However, we will see below that the elements *R* and *E* are not linguistically motivated. Therefore, an analysis based on these elements such as Grimshaw's cannot be correct.

Before we turn to these problems, note that, at first blush, the restriction on the nominalization of EO verbs seems incorrect, given examples as in (120), all of which appear to be event nominals formed from EO verbs.

(120) a. the entertainment of the children
      b. the embarrassment/humiliation of the audience
      c. the depression of the patients

But Grimshaw warns us that, just as in the case of passives, we must evaluate the evidence more carefully. First, EO verbs often have agentive counterparts: these will undergo nominalization in the usual way, just as they undergo passivization, since they have an external argument (note that this assumption entails multiple entries for these verbs). Second, it is only argument-taking event nominals that are derived by suppression of the external argument, not result nominals. The prediction made by her analysis, therefore, is that nominalizations of EO verbs will have either a result or an agentive interpretation. This is illustrated in (121).

(121)a.   John's public embarrassment/humiliation of Mary
    b.   Mary's embarrassment/humiliation
    c.   the embarrassment/humiliation of the bystanders

(121a) is an agentive process nominal. (121b) is a result nominal, and (121c) can be interpreted as a result nominal or an agentive process nominal, but (121c) cannot have a nonagentive process reading.

Grimshaw proposes several tests to distinguish event nominals from other nominals.[30]

Test 1: Modifiers like *frequent* and *constant* force the event interpretation of singular nouns:

(104)a.   The assignment is to be avoided.
    b.   *The constant assignment is to be avoided.
    c.   The constant assignment of unsolvable problems is to be avoided.
    d.   We constantly assign *(unsolvable problems).

Test 2: A possessive gets a clear subject interpretation, such as "agent," only if the N has an argument structure, hence only in event nominals: the possessive is clearly a subject if an agent-oriented adjective like *intentional/deliberate* is present:

(122)a.   *The instructor's intentional/deliberate examination took a long time.
    b.   The instructor's intentional/deliberate examination of the papers took a long time.

Test 3: A *by*-phrase is also an argument-adjunct; it must be licensed by an argument structure, so it must be in an event nominal:

(123)   the destruction *(of the city) by the enemy

Test 4: The indefinite determiner, the numeral *one,* and demonstratives such as *that* occur only with result nominals, not event nominals:

(124)   They observed the/*an/*one/*that assignment of the problem.

Test 5: Result nominals pluralize, but event nominals do not:

(125)   *The assignments of the problems took a long time.

Test 6: Event nominals do not occur predicatively or with equational *be:*

(126)   *That was the/an assignment of the problem.

Test 7: Spanish has unambiguous modifiers corresponding to English *by: por* is found only in event nominals, while *de* is found in other nominals:

(127)a.   la destruccion de la ciudad por el ejercito
           the destruction of the city by the army
     b.   *un libro por Chomsky
           a book by Chomsky
     c.   un libro de Chomsky
           a book of Chomsky
           a book by Chomsky

Similarly, in English, postnominal genitives are unambiguously modifiers and occur only with result nominals: *an examination of Bill's* can only be a result nominal, not an event nominal.

Test 8: Some possessives cannot be interpreted as related to an argument structure, like temporals (*this year, this week, this semester*), so they are not found with event nominals.

(128)   *This semester's constant assignment of unsolvable problems led
           to disaster.

Test 9: Event control is possible only with event nominals (129a); unambiguous result nominals never allow event control (129b):

(129)a.   The examination of the patient in order to determine whether
           . . .
     b.   *The exam in order to determine whether . . .

Test 10: Only event nominals license aspectual modifiers, like *in an hour, for six weeks:*

(130)a.   The total destruction of the city in only two days appalled ev-
           eryone.
     b.   Only observation of the patient for several weeks can determine
           the most likely . . .

Grimshaw's claim, therefore, is that nominalizations of EO verbs should systematically pass these tests as nonevent nominals. Unaccusative predicates, which also lack external arguments, are also expected not to form event nominals. But Grimshaw observes that -*ing* nominals, which she assumes are event nominals, are found with unaccusative verbs:[31]

(131)a. the (rapid) melting of the ice
    b. the (rapid) freezing of the lake

For her, this shows that -*ing* nominalization is possible for certain verb classes with no suppression. She, therefore, revises her analysis: "The principle governing nominalization will now be that if there is an external argument it must suppress. If the base has no external argument, suppression is not necessary" (Grimshaw 1990, 123). But this appears to undermine her argument about EO verbs: even if they do not have an external argument, they should be able to form nominals without suppression, as in (132).

(132)a. *the movie's depressing of the audience
    b. *the audience's depressing by the movie
    c. *the depressing of the audience by the movie

Grimshaw argues that (132a and b) are ungrammatical because the possessive is not an argument. It, therefore, cannot satisfy an argument position in the predicate, but only a suppressed position; there is no suppressed position in EO nominalizations because there is no external argument to suppress. As for (132c), it is ungrammatical because *the movie* is the Theme and *the audience* is the Experiencer, but *by* does not assign a Theme role, and *of* does not assign an Experiencer role.

The two central aspects of this analysis, the suppression of an external argument and the addition of *Ev,* are problematic. First, the stipulation that the addition of a new external argument by nominalization forces the former external argument to suppress seems to be unique among processes that add an argument: the external argument is usually simply demoted, not suppressed. A typical case of this is causativization, as in (133).

(133)a. Albert lit *A la recherche du temps perdu.*
       Albert reads *"A la recherche du temps perdu."*
    b. Marie a fait lire "A la recherche du temps perdu" à Albert.
       Marie made Albert read "A la recherche du temps perdu."

The second problem has to do with the theoretical status of the argument that nominalization adds to the base predicate. Independent motivation for

Ev is said to come from its similarity to *R,* which itself is closely related to *E.* The original motivation for *R* and *E* was to analyze some linguistic data with the tools of logic, such as variable-like elements. The central claim that I will make is that, in the cases where the observations are valid, phrase structure is sufficient to account for the facts, and there is no need of such variable-like elements; in other cases, I will show that *E* and *R* lead to incorrect analyses of the data.

Following work by Williams (1981), Di Sciullo and Williams (1987), and Higginbotham (1985), Grimshaw assumes that the external argument added in event nominals is the nonthematic argument *Ev,* which is essentially an eventive counterpart of the argument *R.* This argument *R* is quite different from other arguments, in that it is not the realization of a participant in the lexical conceptual structure of the head nominal. Grimshaw's *Ev* is similar to *R* in that respect, so it is not clear why it should have any "suppression" effects on true thematic roles. It seems that positing this special kind of argument is generally motivated only by an a priori assumption that syntactic representations should resemble logic-like formalisms involving quantifiers and variables.[32]

4.4.5.1.1.1 *R and Nonthematic Argument E*

Since much of the independent motivation for *Ev* is supposed to come from its being an eventive counterpart of the argument *R,* let us examine the motivations proposed for *R.* First, there would be some indirect motivation: there are existing arguments for the nonthematic argument *E.* Since we have one such nonthematic argument, why not assume another one? This reasoning presupposes that there is strong independent motivation for *E.* I will now show that this is not the case.

The nonthematic argument *E* is assumed to correspond to an event position in the argument structure of verbs: verbs of action for Davidson (1966) and all verbs for Higginbotham (1985). In his original discussion of *E,* Davidson, following work by Reichenbach (1947), proposes that the verb *kick* in a sentence like *Shem kicked Shaun* is a three-place predicate, as in (134).

(134)   (Ex)(Kicked (Shem, Shaun, x)).

Davidson proposes such structures in an attempt to solve the problem of variable polyadicity for verbs when they combine with adverbials. Thus, to most philosophers, a sentence such as (135) contains a five-place predicate (Kenny 1963).

(135)   Jones buttered the toast in the bathroom with a knife at mid-
         night.

There is a problem with this reasoning: if *Jones buttered the toast* is analyzed as containing a two-place predicate, *Jones buttered the toast in the bathroom* as containing a three-place predicate, and so on, the logical relations
between these sentences, namely that (135) entails the others, are obliterated.
Davidson says that "[t]he problem is solved in the natural way, by introducing
events as entities about which an indefinite number of things can be said"
(91). In his terms, (135) would be represented as something like (136):

(136)   There is an action x such that Jones did x in the bathroom and
         Jones did x with a knife and Jones did x at midnight (where x cor-
         responds to "buttered the toast").

But, as Davidson himself notes, the intuition behind (134) is not very natural:
"If we try for an English sentence that directly reflects this form, we run into
difficulties. 'There is an event x such that x is a kicking of Shaun by Shem' is
about the best I can do, but we must remember 'a kicking' is not a singular
term" (Davidson 1966, 92). Intuitively, the event consists of the relationship
expressed by the verb, which is established between the two arguments. It is
difficult to see how this event could be an argument of the very same verb.
This problem becomes clear in the fact that the postulated E argument is
generally described as being different from other arguments: it is not the
realization of a participant in the LCS of the verb.

It is important to note that the only representations considered by Kenny
(1963) and Davidson (1966) are of the type used by logicians. But, at its roots,
the problem discussed is a linguistic problem, and, from a purely linguistic
point of view, the choice of representation for a sentence should be based on
strictly linguistic factors. An a priori desire to represent linguistic knowledge
with variable-like elements, as a logician would, is not justified, unless it can
be shown that it is grounded in independent linguistic data. Otherwise, as
Jackendoff (1983) observed when he introduced his Grammatical Constraint,
there would be very little constraint on the content of semantic representations or on how they relate to syntactic representations.[33]

Therefore, our search for a semantic representation that can account for
the variable polyadicity of verbs should first and foremost consider the syntactic representations of these sentences. If we assume that an adverbial
phrase modifies its sister node, then a constituent structure representation,

as in (137), accounts for the facts without resort to translation into a logic-like formalism with an E variable.

(137)

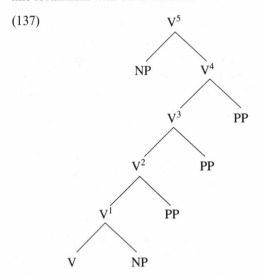

In (137), the verb first combines with its direct argument into V^1; then V^1 combines with *in the bathroom* into V^2; then *with a knife* combines with V^2 into V^3; then *at midnight* combines with V^3 into V^4. The entailments follow directly: predicating V^4 of Jones entails predicating V^3 of Jones, since V^3 is the predicative head of V^4; predicating V^3 of Jones entails predicating V^2 of Jones, since V^2 is the predicative head of V^3; and so forth. A syntactic structure like (137) does not deny that actions are represented in linguistic structure; (137) is based on the assumption that the action corresponds to a V, plus its internal arguments, and that it is predicated of the subject. Arguments are the phrases that are obligatory in the verb's lexical representation because they refer to an entity involved in the event or state, whose participation is necessarily implied by the nature of the event or state denoted by the predicate (see Rochette 1988 and Long 1974 for a similar assumption, among others). In this example, only *the toast* is an obligatory internal argument. The action is represented by the constituent V', and there is no need for an additional element like Davidson's E. Note that the x in (136) corresponds to the action depicted by the V', not to the event, since this x and the V' do not include the external argument *Jones*. It is, therefore, incorrect to call this element the event E.

Furthermore, as Carter (1988, 269) points out, Davidson's approach is quite limited. It correctly predicts that (139) entails (138), but there are many other entailments it should derive but cannot, such as those in (140).

(138)   John destroyed a document.

(139)   John destroyed a document at noon.

(140)a.   Until noon, a document existed.
  b.   After noon, the document did not exist.
  c.   A document ceased to exist at noon.
  d.   John caused a document to cease to exist at noon.

In fact, an analysis based on representations like (137) is to be preferred on empirical grounds. For example, it makes the correct predictions, with respect to the possible interpretation of a sentence like (141), whereas an analysis based on E does not.

(141)   Jones buttered the toast in the bathroom at midnight and at five.

An analysis based on the constituent structure of (141) predicts that *at five* can be conjoined either with the PP *at midnight* or with the constituent *buttered the toast in the bathroom at midnight*. This second reading is ruled out because it is contradictory. In the first reading, the implication is that the buttering at five also took place in the bathroom. But a representation à la Davidson incorrectly predicts one interpretation where there is a first event— "There is an action x such that Jones did x in the bathroom and Jones did x at midnight"—and then a second event—"There is an action x such that Jones did x at five"—with x being replaced by "buttered the toast" in both cases. This is incorrect, since the second event of the conjunct must also have taken place in the bathroom in (141).

Moreover, an analysis involving an E variable cannot correctly predict the interpretation of stacked adverbials, as in (142).

(142)a.   John [[[knocked on the door] intentionally] twice].
  b.   John [[[knocked on the door] twice] intentionally].

As we saw in 2.1.1, stacked adverbials are not interpreted as if they all modify the same E variable. Rather, the highest adverbial modifies an event modified by a more internal adverbial. Thus, there is a difference in adverbial scope between (142a) and (142b) (see Andrews 1983). In (142a), there are two instances of intentional knocking by John, whereas in (142b), there is only one instance of intentional double knocking by John.

An analysis involving an E variable would represent both (142a) and (142b) as in (143).[34]

(143)   (intentionally (E)) & (twice (E)) & (knock (John, on door, E))

Such a representation would lead us to believe, incorrectly, that the sentences in (142) are synonymous, whereas an analysis based on constituent structure, as in (137), directly accounts for the two interpretations.

Davidson argues that proposing an E variable also allows him to account for the inferences in (146) (among others), derived from the sentences in (144) and (145).

(144)   I flew my spaceship to the Morning Star.

(145)   The Morning Star is the Evening Star.

(146)a. (Ex)(Flew (I, my spaceship, x) & To (the Morning Star, x))
     b. (Ex)(Flew (I, my spaceship, x))
     c. (Ex)(To (the Morning Star, x))
     d. (Ex)(Flew (I, my spaceship, x) & To (the Evening Star, x))

A constituent structure representation, as in (147), also allows one to make the proper inferences without resorting to a representation with an E variable.

(147) $[_{v_3}$ I $[_{v_2} [_{v_1}$ flew my spaceship$]$ $[_{pp}$ to the Morning Star$]]]$

The first inference, (146a), is straightforward; it is simply the direct interpretation of the structure in (147). The second inference, (146b), can be captured by a general rule of "modifier stripping": *flew my spaceship* is a constituent modified by the directional phrase *to the Morning Star*, this combination being predicated of *I*; we can infer from this that *flew my spaceship*, without its modifying phrase, is predicated of *I*. Inference (146c) follows, since the *to*-phrase corresponds to an orientation terminating at *the Morning Star*, and it modifies *flew my spaceship*: the latter is predicated of *I*, so we get this inference. The last inference, (146d), is derived as follows: a statement like (145) tells us that we have two names for the same Place, hence we can use either name to identify that place as the termination point of an orientation. None of these inferences require the presence of an E variable to be properly stated.

Proposing an E variable is also supposed to account for the reference of *it* in (148).

(148)   Strange goings on! Jones did it slowly, deliberately, in the bathroom, with a knife, at midnight.

"We are too familiar with the language of action to notice at first an anomaly: the 'it' of 'Jones did it slowly, deliberately, . . .' seems to refer to some entity, presumably an action, that is then characterized in a number of ways" (Davidson 1980, 105). Davidson says that the problem is solved by assuming that the *it* refers to *E*. In a constituent structure analysis, this presents no anomaly. Pronouns generally refer to constituents, and so does *it;* it refers to a syntactic constituent that corresponds to the V^1 of (137).

A constituent structure representation can solve the three problems that led Davidson to introduce *E:* there is no variable polyadicity, per se, in linguistic terms, since the added elements are adjuncts, not arguments; inferences like those in (146) and the reference of *it* in (148) depend on the syntactic structure. Since assuming an *E* variable in the representation of verbs is, in fact, inadequate, as we saw above, it cannot be used as indirect motivation for positing an *R* or *Ev* variable in the representation of nouns.

4.4.5.1.1.2 *R and NPs as Predicates*

A more direct motivation for *R* comes from NPs used predicatively. Consider (149). The assumption is that *fond* is a two-place relation and that its external argument is satisfied by predication. Under this assumption, what is to be said about *a man* in (150)?

(149)   John is fond of Bill.

(150)   John is a man.

A possibility suggested by Williams (1981) is to treat (150) in a way very similar to (149). He suggests that *John* is assigned the external role of the NP, *a man,* just as it is assigned the external role of *fond.* Williams assumes that this is possible because all NPs have an open argument position, or *R* role. This position can be satisfied from outside the NP by predication, or internally to the NP, which produces a referential NP. For example, the *R* role of *a man* in (150) is satisfied externally, by *John,* whereas the *R* role of *a man* in *A man came in* is satisfied internally.

Another way to account for the predication between *John* and *a man* in (150), without the additional apparatus of an *R* role, is to assume that *John* and *a man* are coindexed. This indexing would be part of a general indexing procedure; all nodes are indexed, and the index is interpreted on the basis of the properties of the node. Thus, coindexation is interpreted as coreference, if the elements bearing the identical indices are referential, but coindexation will be interpreted differently, if the elements are not both referential. There are several proposals along these lines in the literature. For example, Chomsky (1981) proposes coindexation between the subject of S and AGR, which he assumes is not interpreted as coreference, because AGR has no reference. Similarly, a trace and its antecedent are coindexed, but they are not coreferential. Williams (1980) proposes that a predication relation is formally expressed by coindexing an NP and a VP. In Bouchard (1987), extending an idea from Bouchard (1984a), I argued that the theory of agreement can be replaced by a condition on indices, namely, that indices must be interpreted coherently. For example, if a DET, an adjective, and a noun are coindexed as in le_i $beau_i$ $livre_i$ 'the beautiful book,' or la_i $bonne_i$ $solution_i$ 'the good solution,' the three elements must have identical features of number and gender. Otherwise, the index they have in common could not be interpreted coherently. Coindexing *la, bonne,* and *solution* is not interpreted as coreference, however, since none of these elements are referential on their own. A similar argument was made in 3.3.2.3 for past participle agreement.

To account for (150), we can assume that the basic principles relevant to the interpretation of the index of an NP are the following: if the NP bearing the index is in an argument position, a position linked to a variable in the semantic representation, as *John* is in (150), then the index is interpreted referentially; if the NP bearing the index is not in an argument position, which is the case for *a man* in (150), then the index is interpreted predicationally. Because of these properties of the two NP nodes, (that one is in an argument position and the other is not), the coindexation of the two NPs formally expresses a predication relation in a way similar to that proposed in Williams (1980), without the presence of an *R* role. I conclude that NP predication, as in (150), does not motivate the use of *R.*

4.4.5.1.1.3 *R and Adjectival Modification*

The final motivation for *R* I will discuss comes from Higginbotham's (1985) analysis of NP internal adjectival modification. He assumes that nonthematic argument-structure is involved in modification, as well as predication. Modification is accomplished by "identification" of the external argument of the modifier with the *R* argument of the noun. For example, for him, in the expression *long dissertation,* the adjective *long* has an external argument, as does *dissertation,* and the two arguments are identified and then jointly satisfied. I will show that, again, the additional assumption is unnecessary and is, in fact, in some cases inadequate.

The first problem with Higginbotham's proposal is that θ-marking internal to the noun relates two roles that are quite different from one another. The role assigned by the adjective is fairly close to what is usually understood by *thematic role,* but the *R* role of the noun is not, since it is not a participant in the lexical conceptual structure of the noun. Relating these two kinds of elements seems to require a very strong interpretative input on part of the linguist.[35]

Higginbotham discusses the nominal expressions *white wall, good violonist,* and *big butterfly.* He says that *white wall* is unambiguously interpreted as "white and wall," *good violonist* is unambiguously interpreted as "good as a violonist," and *big butterfly* is ambiguous between "big and butterfly" and "big for a butterfly."

Based on these different interpretation possibilities, he claims that there are different kinds of θ-licensing and that adjectives must specify what kind of licensing they allow. I disagree with him about the interpretation of the first two examples—they are as ambiguous as *big butterfly.* This ambiguity is transparent in the case of *good violinist* (see Lumsden 1987 and the discussion below). *White wall* is also ambiguous, but it cannot be related to two different situations, for independent reasons, which I will discuss shortly.

Before discussing the interpretation possibilities of Adj + N combinations, I will briefly outline the structure I am assuming. There are two types of elements that concatenate in syntax: heads (H) and phrases (P). The three possibilities for concatenation (disregarding order) are: head-to-phrase, phrase-to-phrase, and head-to-head. I assume, as does Lamarche (1990, 1992), that an adjective can have two kinds of syntactic relations with an N that it modifies: a head-to-head relation or a head-to-phrase relation.[36] A head-to-head relation is established when two X^0 elements join to form an endocentric constituent labeled, as usual, according to the features of one of the daughter nodes. What is different about this relation is that the resulting constituent is itself a selectional head. A head-to-phrase relation is the more familiar $Y^0 - XP$ situation. This difference could be represented structurally as in (151), where (a) is a head-to-head relation and (b) is a head-to-phrase relation.[37]

(151)   a. X^0 b. X'

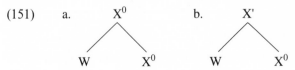

W X^0 W X^0

Clitics typically exhibit the relationship in (151a), which is generally referred to as adjunction in the base (although I assume adjunction is only possible for X^0 heads).

Following Lamarche (1990, 1992), I assume that a head must be in absolute left position in the NP in English and French (see note 41 for a generalization). This assumption is apparently violated by any phrase with a prenominal adjective, as in (152):

(152)   the big boat, le gros bateau

I will argue that such examples are not counter-evidence to this claim: If *big* and *boat* do not have a head-to-phrase relation, but a head-to-head relation, the complex head [$_N$ big boat] is in the absolute left position of the projection of N (assuming the DP hypothesis, in which the determiner has its own projection and takes the projection of N as its complement):

(153)

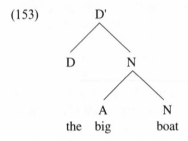

Assuming that a prenominal adjective and the noun it modifies form a complex noun head immediately accounts for the fact that, while English only allows N-N compounding and not compounding of NPs, it is possible for prenominal adjectives to appear in compounds, such as *a rare-book collector.* Under my assumptions, [$_N$ rare book] forms a complex noun head, which compounds with the noun *collector.*

If we also assume that a head must be in absolute left position, this correctly predicts that adjectival phrases should not appear to the left of the N head, which is a well-known fact:[38]

(154)a. *a fond of her son mother
     b.   a mother fond of her son
     c. *une fière de son fils mère
     d.   une mère fière de son fils

Examples like these show that prenominal and postnominal adjectives do not have the same syntactic relations with the head noun: a noun and a postnominal adjective have a head-to-phrase relation. We, therefore, expect prenominal and postnominal adjectives to have a different semantic relation with the head noun, since structure affects interpretation. This prediction is borne out. In French, as is well known, adjectives are interpreted differently, depending on whether they precede or follow the noun head.[39]

(155)a.   une ancienne église
          an old church or *a building that used to be a church*
    b.   une église ancienne
          an old building which is a church

I assume, along the lines of Milner (1989, 336), that the lexical meaning of a noun is its virtual reference. The virtual reference of a noun is a set of conditions or features that an object in the world must satisfy in order to be picked out, in actual reference, by a syntactic phrase headed by that noun. The virtual reference of *église* 'church,' for example, might include [used for worship of god(s)]. We can account for the differences in meaning in (155) by assuming that an element in a head-to-head relation with a noun, such as a prenominal adjective, can modify a subset of this set of conditions or features of the head N, since a prenominal adjective becomes part of a complex nominal head, hence part of its virtual reference. On the other hand, a postnominal adjective, which is in a head-to-phrase relation with the noun, modifies the whole set of features of the head N. Prenominal adjectives are expected to be potentially ambiguous in their modification; they modify either the whole set of features or a subset of those features. Consider the examples in (155). Suppose that *ancienne* means something like 'of times past.' Since it is postnominal in (155b), it must modify the whole set of the features of *église,* so all of those features are interpreted as being "of times past." This gives the reading "an old building which is a church." But in (155a), two readings are possible. First, there is a reading where only a subset of the features of *église* is modified by *ancienne.* In this reading, the feature [used for worship of god(s)] is considered "of times past," which gives "a building that used to be a church." The second reading for (155a), which is identical to the reading of (155b), arises when the subset of features modified by the adjective happens to be identical to the whole set of features.

Under this approach, a modification relation involves setting up a relation between elements on the basis of the syntactic structure and defining the relation by means of the semantics of the modifier. I claim that all adjectives have the potential to modify either the whole set or only a subset of the features of the head N, depending on the syntactic structure involved. What modification relation can be defined crucially depends on the meaning of the adjective—what kind of feature it can modify, and the meaning of the N— what features it has. Each ADJ-N pair must therefore be studied to see what its possible interpretations are, and cross-referring between pairs will help to determine what kinds of features a particular N has and what kinds of features a particular ADJ can modify. In fact, a pattern emerges, as is clear in the studies that give an extensive list of such pairs in French with a description of their semantics (see Forsgren 1977; Waugh 1977; and Lamarche 1990; among many others). The pattern is harder to detect in English, because the obligatory prenominal position of the adjective obscures some of the effects. But if we consider French examples corresponding to the English ones discussed above, the position of the adjective should highlight the two interpretations mentioned above. This is indeed the case.

(156)a.   un gros papillon: 'big for a butterfly' or 'big and butterfly'
      b.   un papillon gros: 'big and butterfly'

(157)a.   un bon violoniste: 'good as a violonist' or 'a violonist who is a good man'
      b.   un violoniste bon: 'a violonist who is a good man'

(158)a.   un mur blanc: 'white and wall'
      b.   un blanc mur (stilted): very subtle difference, hard to describe.

The combination *mur* and *blanc* appears to have a very similar reading, regardless of the position of the adjective, because of the semantics of the adjective—the meaning of a color adjective cannot be attached to a subset of the features of a N like *mur*, or of any noun, presumably because the 3-D features of color adjectives are more readily associated with the actual reference of a noun and make it difficult for these adjectives to be part of the virtual reference. This is probably why color adjectives are highly preferred in the postnominal position in French.[40]

The French data confirm the hypothesis that the different possible interpretations of ADJ-N pairs correspond to a difference in syntactic structure.[41] All adjectives are potentially subject to the alternation in interpretation; when one of the interpretations appears to be difficult, there is presumably a difficulty in the semantics induced by the syntactic combination, not just in the semantics of the adjective. Adjectives do not need to lexically specify what kind of θ-licensing they allow, as Higginbotham (1985) proposed. In fact, since the differences in interpretation can be correlated with different syntactic structures, different kinds of θ-marking are not necessary at all. Moreover, if the interpretation of *gros papillon* depends on the modification by *gros* of a subset of the features of *papillon,* this is not compatible with an *R* role analysis, since *R* corresponds to the referent of *papillon,* not to subfeatures of the referent.

We have discussed three possible motivations for *R:* the parallel with *E;* the existence of predicate NPs; and adjectival modification. There seems to be no compelling reason to adopt an argument position like *R* on the basis of linguistic facts. I, therefore, reject an analysis of nominalization that is based on the notion that there exists a non-thematic argument *R* that serves as the external argument of nouns.[42]

4.4.5.1.2 Pesetsky's Analysis—Zero-Affix CAUS

Having rejected an analysis of nominalization based on *R* and, thus, Grimshaw's proposal that EO verbs do not nominalize as event nominals because of aspectual properties, I now turn to Pesetsky's (1990) analysis of EO verbs as derived by a zero-CAUS morpheme. I will show that, although zero morphology may be a factor in the analysis of EO verbs, it does not seem to be of any help in accounting for the peculiarities of Psych verbs, with respect to nominalization.

Pesetsky assumes that EO verbs are causatives of ES verbs, derived by zero affixation (159a), and that the nominalization of an EO verb has the structure in (159b), where *!annoy* is a root that does not occur except when combined with some other morpheme:

(159)a. $[[!\text{annoy}] \, \varnothing_{\text{CAUS}}]$
    b. $[[[!\text{annoy} \, _v] \, \varnothing_{\text{CAUS}}] \, \text{ance} \, _N]$

However, this kind of word formation, in which overt morphemes follow null morphemes, is never found, as expressed by the following generalization (Myers 1984):

(160)   *Myers' Generalization:* Zero-derived words do not permit the affixation of further derivational morphemes.

This means that *annoyance* can be derived only by adding the nominalizing morpheme directly to the root, as in (161).

(161) $[[\text{annoy} \, _v] \, \text{ance} \, _N]$

This correctly accounts for the fact that these nominals lack all causative force, as was first observed by Lakoff (1970a).

Pesetsky attributes the effects of Myers' Generalization in a noun like (161) to an interaction of two conditions. First, he assumes that zero morphemes are subject to the following filter:

(162) *Empty Morpheme Filter (EMF) (Pesetsky's (209)):* A phonologically zero morpheme μ is licensed either by (i) or (ii):
        (i) μ projects lexical features (licensing by X-bar theory)
        (ii) μ is head-governed.

Second, he assumes the following condition:

(163) *Affectedness Condition (Pesetsky's (235)):* Where α assigns a [−affected] θ-role and is dominated by β, treat α as the head of β whenever possible.

Recall that Pesetsky assumes that ES verbs assign the θ-roles Target of Emotion or Subject Matter of Emotion to their objects; he assumes that these roles are [−affected] roles. This means that the internal θ-role assigned by ES *!annoy* in (159) is [−affected], and, by the Affectedness Condition, *!annoy* is the head of [[!annoy] $\varnothing_{CAUS}$]. The EMF, in conjunction with (163), will then rule out a form like (159b), because (i) in (162) is not satisfied since *!annoy* is the head that projects lexical features, not $\varnothing_{CAUS}$, and (ii) is not satisfied since the structure prevents *!annoy* from governing $\varnothing_{CAUS}$. As Pesetsky says, "[w]henever a zero morpheme combines with a predicate π that assigns a [−affected] role, and this combination is non-category changing, [the Affectedness Condition] forces π to be chosen as the head. This causes the zero morpheme to violate the EMF" (1990, 69).[43] The interaction of the EMF with the Affectedness Condition is assumed to account for the absence of a causative reading with EO nominals like *annoyance* and for the fact that EO verbs do not assign [−affected] roles such as Target or Subject Matter of Emotion, as in (164).

(164)   Mary worried John (*about the TV set).

In fact, however, the analysis does not work. It actually predicts that no EO verb should exist in the form that Pesetsky presents it. He assumes that EO verbs are formed by zero-causativization of ES predicates, as in (165).

(165)a.   ES verb: John worried about the TV set.
           John = Experiencer; *worried* = ES; *the TV set* = Subject Matter
      b.   EO verb: The TV set worried John.
           The TV set = Cause; *worried* = ES + CAUS; *John* = Experiencer

This means that the zero-CAUS morpheme is attaching to a predicate that assigns a [−affected] role, without changing the category of that predicate. This violates the EMF, so all EO verbs should be ruled out. Although Pesetsky does not directly address this issue, it seems that he would be forced to assume that in (165b), the ES *worry* does not assign its [−affected] role, for some reason. The ES would then not be forced to be the head of the ES+ CAUS complex, and the zero morpheme CAUS could pass the EMF.

However, this raises a serious question about linking of arguments and conventions like UAH and UTAH. Under what conditions can a θ-role fail to be assigned? Why can not the [−affected] argument drop in the nominal, thus allowing it to have a causative interpretation? If assigning the [−affected] role is optional, we would expect a nominal parallel to the verbal construction in (165), as in (166) (Pesetsky's (157b) and (166b)).[44]

(166)a.   Mary's constant annoyance about/at/with us got on our nerves.
          [$_{NP}$Experiencer ES+*ance* Subject Matter]
     b.   *Our constant annoyance of Mary got on our nerves.
          [$_{NP}$Cause ES+CAUS+*ance* Experiencer]

In (166b), *annoy* is assumed to have no [−affected] Subject Matter role, yet the construction is not grammatical. To say that the Experiencer in (166b) is [−affected] will not help, because this would also rule out (165b). It seems that Pesetsky is forced to assume that the [−affected] role is optionally assigned in the verb but obligatorily assigned in the nominalized form. This is not very satisfying.

Another problem for Pesetsky's analysis is that it seems to rule out some constructions that are supposedly grammatical. Thus, commenting on examples like the one in (166b), he says: "Alongside structures of the form in [(167a)], we do not find structures that we would analyse as [(167b)]" (Pesetsky 1990, 48).

(167)a.   [[ES-predicate V] nominalizer]
     b.   *[[[ES-predicate V] $\varnothing_{CAUS}$] nominalizer]

But recall that such examples are possible, at least for Grimshaw, who gives (168), repeated from (121a), as an instance of an EO nominalization with an agentive reading.

(168)   John's public embarrassment/humiliation of Mary

Embarrassment and *humiliation* here have a structure like (167b). The ES verb *!embarrass* is made EO by attaching zero-CAUS and then nominalized by adding *-ment*. Forms such as these are problematic for Pesetsky's analysis, which predicts that they should not exist.

If Pesetsky's analysis is to be extended beyond Psych verbs, it will face the problem of accounting for the fact, noted by Grimshaw (1990), that unaccusatives generally resist nominalization with a process interpretation.

(169)   * the train's frequent arriving[45]

In this case, there seems to be no motivation to propose a zero morpheme to account for the ungrammaticality of (169).

Pesetsky's analysis is attractive, and it might be the case that zero morphology is a factor in analyzing EO verbs, as we will see in section 4.4.6 on compounding. However, these problems indicate that there are additional factors involved and that Pesetsky's analysis cannot be adopted as he formulated it.

4.4.5.2 A BETTER ANALYSIS: THE STATUS OF AFFECTEDNESS IN THE GRAMMAR

In this section, I will discuss the four cases outlined above that are problematic in Pesetsky's analysis. I will show that an account of these cases in terms of aspects of intentionality specific to Psych constructions extends to all cases of nominalization of Psych verbs. What constrains the event nominalization of EO verbs is that the nature of a Genitive NP forces it to be a Substantive with very strong agentivity: so the nominalization of an EO verb, and of an ES verb for that matter, will be strongly agentive.

The four types of constructions which are problematic for Pesetsky all involve affectedness. They are shown in (170).

(170)a.   John worried Mary (*about the TV set). (see (164))
      b.   * Our constant annoyance of Mary got on our nerves. (see (166b))
      c.   John's public embarrassment/humiliation of Mary. (see (121a))
      d.   * The train's frequent arriving. (see (169))

In (170a), some [−affected] θ-roles, Target and Subject Matter, must be inactive in order for the construction to be possible. However, in (170b), dropping the same [−affected] θ-roles does not save the corresponding nominal constructions. Strangely, dropping the same [−affected] θ-roles can save the corresponding nominals if they are "agentive," as in (170c). Nominalizations of unaccusatives as in (170d) share the bad fate of the constructions with [−affected] θ-roles, although they do not seem to depend on affectedness of an argument in this case since no zero morpheme is involved.

Consider first (170a). I will argue that affectedness is not involved in such examples at all. First, Pesetsky's Target/Subject matter of Emotion "argument" (in this case, *about the TV set*) are not arguments, but adjuncts. The *about* phrase in *Mary worried about the TV set* is a modifier, not an argument. All that a Psych construction need contain is a psy-chose (the incorporated WORRY), an I-Subject (Mary), and a relation putting the two in contact; the *about* phrase is not necessary. As a modifier, the *about* phrase is not an integral part of the Psych nature of the construction; whether or not *the TV set* has a [−affected] θ-role is irrelevant.[46] Second, these modifiers are prohibited from appearing in these constructions not because a [−affected] θ-role of the verb is no longer available, but because of a general condition on certain types of adjuncts. Specifically, these adjuncts are only possible when the subject is sufficiently "agentive" to control what is going on. Three sets of data illustrate this. First, note that it is possible, in fact, to have causative EO constructions where these modifiers are present (in Pesetsky's terms, the [−affected] θ-roles Target and Subject Matter have not dropped).

(171)a. Mary satisfied Bill with her trip to Beijing.
   b. ?Albert worried John about the adequacy of his insurance coverage.
   c. Mary bores John with her/*his life as a linguist.
   d. Bill constantly bothered Mary about her future.

These sentences are constructed on the model of the sentences in (172), given in Pesetsky (1990) to illustrate that a Cause, an Experiencer, and a Target of Emotion/Subject Matter of Emotion may not occur in the same sentence.

(172)a. *The Chinese dinner satisfied Bill with his trip to Beijing.
   b. *Bill driving at night always worries John about the adequacy of his insurance coverage.
   c. *The problem of lexical entries bores John with his life as a linguist.
   d. *Something Bill had said bothered Mary about her future.

The difference between (171) and (172) is that the subjects in (171) are potentially agentive.

Pesetsky's analysis correctly predicts that the nonagentive readings will be impossible, as we saw above. However, under this analysis, the agentive readings should also be ungrammatical. In fact, they appear to be much better than their nonagentive counterparts. The sentences in (171) are presumably causative under an agentive reading, since the more simple related examples in (173) are.

(173)a.   John satisfied Bill.
    b.   Albert worried John.
    c.   Mary bores John.
    d.   Bill bothered Mary.

This means that Pesetsky would have to assume that the three roles—Cause, Experiencer, and Target of Emotion/Subject Matter of Emotion—are present in the same sentence, in (171).

Note, however, that in order to be acceptable, the sentences in (171) must receive an interpretation in which the 'individual' referred to by the subject is strongly in control. Thus, (171a) will be acceptable if, for example, Bill has been nagging Mary to go to Beijing, although she does not want to go, and she finally says to him, "OK, to satisfy you, I'll go to Beijing." (171b) would be acceptable if Albert, John's insurance agent, was constantly reminding John that his insurance coverage was inadequate. (171c) describes a situation in which Mary is talking on and on to John about her life as a linguist, so that, exasperated, he finally says, "Mary, you're boring me." (Note that with *his life* instead of *her life,* Mary has less control over the adjunct and the sentence is not as good.) (171d) requires a context in which Bill is always talking to Mary about her future. The sentences in (171) do not describe something taking place in mental space. They refer, rather, to the external behavior that typically produces the emotions or feelings described by the verbs, not to the actual state of mind. Thus, if Bill, or some behavior of Bill's, bothers Mary in a Psych sense (his driving at night, for example), it is inappropriate for her to tell him, "Stop bothering me"; Bill must be literally doing something *to* her for this to be appropriate.

The sentences in (171) involve a more 3-D use of these verbs and allow the modification by the PP, whereas those in (172) involve a purely Psych use and do not allow this modification. Why should there be such a contrast in modification in these two uses? The answer lies in a property of the PP modifiers: they can be related only to an argument that has some control over what is happening, as can be shown by their behavior in two other constructions, causatives and inchoatives.

As discussed in 3.3.1.3, syntactic causatives differ from lexical causatives in that the latter require total, direct control of the situation on the part of the subject. The contrast is illustrated in (174), in which the subordinate clause in (a) is a syntactic causative, whereas in (b), it is a lexical causative.

(174)a.   Alice a fait remonter Humpty Dumpty sur son mur mais elle ne
           l'a pas fait remonter elle-même sur son mur.
           *Alice made Humpty Dumpty climb back onto his wall but she did
           not make him climb back onto his wall herself.*

   b.   Alice a fait remonter Humpty Dumpty sur son mur mais elle ne
           l'a pas remonté elle-même sur son mur.
           *Alice made Humpty Dumpty climb back onto his wall but she did
           not put him back onto his wall herself.*

The examples are from Ruwet (1972, 37) who comments: "[(174a)] is contradictory, but [(174b)] is not; thus, in order for Alice to put Humpty Dumpty back on his wall, she must act on him directly, physically, by taking him in her arms, for example, and placing him on the wall; whereas she can make him climb back simply by persuasion, without herself acting directly."[47] If the causer cannot have such strong control over the causee, then lexical causation is not possible, as shown in the following contrast:

(175)a.   Delphine a fait entrer la voiture dans le garage.
           Delphine made the car enter into the garage.

   b.   Delphine a entré la voiture dans le garage.
           Delphine entered the car into the garage.

(176)a.   Delphine a fait entrer les invités au salon.
           Delphine made the guests enter into the living room.

   b.   *Delphine a entré les invités au salon.
           Delphine entered the guests into the living room.

Delphine can directly control the car in (175), but not the guests in (176). In lexical causation, the causer is in complete control, and the causee has no control over what is going on. As shown in (177), modification of the "weak" causee argument is not possible:

(177)a.   Alice a fait remonter Humpty Dumpty sur son mur avec tristesse.
           Alice made Humpty Dumpty climb back onto his wall with sadness.

   b.   Alice a remonté Humpty Dumpty sur son mur avec tristesse.
           Alice put Humpty Dumpty back onto his wall with sadness.

In (177a), *avec tristesse* 'with sadness' can modify either *Alice* or *Humpty Dumpty.* In (177b), however, it can only modify *Alice,* since only she is sufficiently "in control."

Given that I analyze inchoatives as lexical causatives in which the causer argument binds the causee argument, I also expect these constructions to exhibit control effects. Recall that in inchoatives, the causer is not seen as a complete self, but rather as a subpart of the self. Thus, in an inchoative like *la corde a cassé* 'the rope broke,' some property of the rope is responsible for the rope's own breaking. Control by such a causer should be limited. Compare the inchoative in (178a) and the reflexive in (178b). In (178a), the physical person *Marie* becomes pale because of physical properties intrinsic to her. The causer binds the causee at the level of Semantic Structure, and there is only one syntactic argument, although there are two argument positions in Semantic Structure. In (178b), there are two syntactic arguments, and Marie becomes pale because she acts on herself as a whole person (by using some powder for example).

(178)a. Marie pâlit.
         Marie pales/becomes pale.
     b. Marie se pâlit.
         Marie pales herself/makes herself become pale.

If control by the causer is more limited in inchoatives than in the reflexive constructions, this should have effects on the presence of PP modifiers, since they require strong control by the causer. Interestingly, a modifier like *à la poudre* 'with powder,' which requires strong control, is compatible only with a causer that can exert such control, as shown by the following contrast (see Junker 1987).[48]

(179)a. *Elle pâlit à la poudre.
         She pales with powder.
     b. Elle se pâlit à la poudre.
         She pales herself with powder.

On the other hand, if the modifier is not controllable, as, for example, *d'énervement* 'with nervousness,' it is not compatible with a construction with a subject that is "in control," such as the reflexive, but may appear in the inchoative:

(180)a. Elle pâlit d'énervement.
         She pales with nervousness.
     b. *Elle se pâlit d'énervement.
         She pales herself with nervousness.

Thus, we see that the presence of certain modifiers depends on the control of the subject. Let us now return to the examples in (171) and (172). In both sets of examples, the direct object has no control over what is going on, as is usually the case with internal arguments. Modifiers that require control, such as *with her trip to Beijing* and *about her future,* cannot relate to this argument, and interpretations involving this relation are ruled out. In (172), the referent of the subject does not have the proper attributes to control the modifier. In these examples, the subject does not even have a Substantive interpretation, but rather a Concept interpretation. The examples in (172) are unacceptable because the subject is not "agentive" enough to control the modifier. On the other hand, in order to be acceptable, the sentences in (171) must receive a particular interpretation in which the subject is even more agentive and in control than usual. Under that interpretation, the modifier can be controlled by the subject. This is possible only if the subject is interpreted as actively physically involved. For example, if Mary bores John in purely mental space, just because of what she is to him, no argument has any control over this. John has no control over his being bored, and Mary, as a psy-chose, could be boring him quite unwillingly and unknowingly. Under a more 3-D interpretation of "boring," where a physical action of Mary's is involved, there is potential control by both protagonists. Thus, John could say to Mary "Stop boring me," or he could walk away. In the purely mental space interpretation of boring, neither action is appropriate; one can not just walk away from the fact that someone causes one to be bored. Thus, the examples in (171) allow the modifiers because the Psych verbs are given a more 3-D interpretation in which the subject controls the action. The examples in (172) do not allow the modifiers because neither the subject or the object sufficiently control the event.

This analysis predicts that syntactic causatives, which behave differently from lexical causatives, in that the causee argument has some control over the event, should allow the PP modifiers. As Pesetsky (1990) observes, the syntactic causatives corresponding to the examples in (172) are acceptable, as in (181).

(181) a.   The Chinese dinner made Bill satisfied with his trip to Beijing.
     b.   Bill driving at night always makes John worry about the ade-
        quacy of his insurance coverage.
     c.   The problem of lexical entries made John bored with his life as a
        linguist.
     d.   ?Something Bill had said made Mary bothered about her future.

To summarize the discussion of (170a), it is not necessary to assume that [−affected] θ-roles like Target and Subject Matter become inactive to account for constructions like *John worried Mary (*about the TV set);* their behavior can be accounted for by assuming that what Pesetsky refers to as Target/ Subject Matter of Emotion in these cases are not arguments but adjuncts. The presence of these modifiers is subject to a general condition of control. This analysis explains why examples that appear to violate Pesetsky's Target/ Subject Matter of Emotion restriction, like those in (171), are actually acceptable in contexts in which the subject is highly "agentive." Contrary to what Pesetsky assumes, affectedness is not involved in this case.[49]

Now consider (170b), repeated below.

(170)b.   *Our constant annoyance of Mary got on our nerves.

The problem for Pesetsky is to explain why dropping a PP containing a [−affected] θ-role makes a sentence like (170a) acceptable, but does not do the same for (170b). Since I assume that a dropped PP like *about the TV set* is a modifier in (170a), not an argument, I do not need to assume that a [−affected] θ-role has become inactive in (170b).

Sentence (170b) is ungrammatical because of the nature of one of its arguments: the Genitive *our.* The Genitive frequently corresponds to a situation of possession (hence the label of Possessor that situationalists often use for the Genitive), but it does not have to. For example, in *John's book, John* can be the owner, author, editor, printer, designer, person who likes the book, or person who suggested reading it. I assume that the Genitive is an argument that establishes an abstract relation in the semantic domain of 'Identity.' This relation of 'Identity' with the head N (in this case, *annoyance*), can correspond to various situations.[50]

I make the natural assumption that identification is done with respect to a whole self, a Substantive, otherwise the subpart identifier would be mentioned instead. Because of its identificational role, the Genitive *our* in (170b) must, therefore, be a Substantive. However, the nonagentive interpretation of a Psych construction requires that the Actualizer *our* in (170b) be interpreted as a Concept rather than as a Substantive. This aspect of the nonagentive interpretation clashes with the identificational requirement of the Genitive, causing the unacceptability of (170b). As expected, if the Genitive *our* is interpreted as "agentive," the sentence is much better, as noted in the discussion of (166b) above.

Under this analysis, it is clear why the "agentive" reading makes (170c) acceptable.

(170) c   John's public embarrassment/humiliation of Mary.

In the agentive reading of this Psych construction, the Genitive *John's* is interpreted as a Substantive. There is no conflict with the identificational requirement of the Genitive. All that changes in the construction is the referential interpretation of the Genitive.

Finally, consider (170d).

(170) d   *the train's frequent arriving

In order to understand what is going on in this type of example, consider what happens when the Genitive is a "preposed" direct object. Grimshaw (1990) notes that the examples are not as acceptable as is generally assumed. The most famous example, (182), is also the most felicitous.

(182)   the city's destruction by the enemy

But other cases are much less acceptable:

(183)a. ??the tree's removal by Mary
      b. ??during the course of the food's ingestion by worms
      c. ??the book's publication by MIT Press
      d. ??the politician's nomination by the senate

A possible explanation for this fact is that Genitive identification requires not only that the Genitive NP be a Substantive but also that it be an Actualizer rather than an Object of Termination when "event" roles like these are present in the semantic representation. This is a natural assumption, given the analysis of the subject Actualizer outlined in section 3.1.3. The external argument Actualizer already has an identificational function similar to that of the Genitive, since it is the pivot for the relationship between the event and the temporal point of the sentence. Process nominals like those in (183) have both an Actualizer and an Object of Termination. Because the Actualizer is expressed in the *by*-phrase, the Genitive can be linked to the Object of Termination only. This clashes with the requirement that the Genitive identifier be linked to the Actualizer, the element with an identificational function at the level of the event.

This gives us a clue to the problem with (170d). *Arriving* is a process nominal; its argument functions like the argument of the corresponding "unaccusative" verb *arrive*. I assume for unaccusative verbs that the Actualizer binds the position of the Object of Termination in the semantic representation. The NP *the train* cannot be in the Genitive in (170d) because it is linked to both the Actualizer and the Object of Termination; this clashes with the identificational requirements of the Genitive, which, as we saw above, cannot be related to an Object of Termination.

An example like (184), on the other hand, is much better.

(184)   the train's arrival

Arrival is not a process nominal, so *the train* is not an Actualizer here. There is no clash since the Genitive *the train's* only holds a loose 'Identity' link with the N.

In this section, I have shown that a unified analysis of the four types of examples in (170) is possible, without the problematic assumption that a thematic role may sometimes be inactive. The crucial factor at play in these nominalizations of Psych verbs, I argue, is the intentionality properties of the Genitive identifier, which must be a Substantive and which can be linked to no other event role except the role of Actualizer.

4.4.5.3 ZERO MORPHEME SUG

Before closing this section on nominalization, I would like to make a few remarks about another interesting construction that Pesetsky (1990) discusses. In support of his analysis based on the interaction of zero morphology and affectedness, Pesetsky argues that it accounts for another construction, not related to EO verbs and zero-CAUS. This "manner" construction was first discussed in Higgins (1979).

(185)a.   John's manner was proud (*of his son).
     b.   Bill's remarks were angry (*at the government).
     c.   Sue's behavior was nervous (*about the exam).
     d.   Mary's expression was optimistic (*about the results).
     e.   Bill's words were sad (*about John).
     f.   Tom's attitude was fearful (*of an earthquake).
     g.   John's behavior is over-eager (*to leave).

Pesetsky remarks that the adjectives in (185), predicated of NPs that express properties of a person, are interpreted differently from how they are interpreted when predicated of a person, as in *Tom was proud*. For example, *"John's manner was proud* means something like *John's manner suggested that he was proud"* (41). To account for this, he posits a zero morpheme SUG (for "suggest") that attaches to an adjective and allows it to be predicated of an NP whose head is a word like *manner,* with the additional meaning illustrated above. In his analysis, the sentences in (185) are ungrammatical when the material in parentheses is included, because this material contains a [−affected] θ-role. His Empty Morpheme Filter and Affectedness Condition together account for this ungrammaticality in the same way these conditions account for the examples in (186).

(186)a. *The article angered Bill at the government.
    b. *John worried Mary about the TV set.

I will argue below that there is another way to analyze the data and that it should be preferred. The interpretation of a sentence like *John's manner was proud* is not really that *John's manner suggested that he was proud,* but rather that John's behavior had some typical exterior signs of a person who is proud; the speaker as Subject of Consciousness is making a 3-D assessment of John's manner. This, I believe, is the special use being made of the adjectives here: *John's manner was proud* is not a predication of pride but of behavior showing the typical signs of pride. Similarly, *Bill's words were sad* does not mean that *Bill's words suggested that he was sad;* it means that he said them with an intonation that is typical of a sad person. The sentence expresses a purely 3-D evaluation (I am assuming 3-D to include sound propagation as well as light, of course). In the unmarked case, these exterior signs of sadness will suggest that Bill is sad. However, contrary to what Pesetsky's analysis would lead us to believe, this is not necessarily the case. For example, if Bill tells us that he is sad in a normal voice, a voice that does not have a "typically sad" pattern, then although Bill's words (more than) suggested that he was sad, it would be inappropriate to say that *Bill's words were sad.* The SUG morpheme analysis would give the wrong interpretation in this case.

In fact, there is no need for any zero morpheme to account for the inter- pretation: all we have to say is that some adjectives that express emotions that have typical external signs can also be used to express the typical 3-D manner of their "normal" use, in which case they are predicated of NPs headed by *manner, remark,* and the like, which refer to some of these external signs.[51] On the other hand, if one includes the material in parentheses in (185), *manner* or *remark* cannot head the subject because the predication is no longer 3-D. *Proud of his son, proud of his fish,* and *proud of his results* are not 3-D. The man's external behavior indicates pride and would count as 3-D predication, but we need more than this to determine what he is proud of.

One fact that Pesetsky presents in support of his analysis is that it predicts nominalization of these SUG constructions to be impossible because they would have the general pattern in (187), which is ruled out by the EMF and the Affectedness Condition.

(187)   *[[X + SUG] + nominalizer]

(188)a.   His bearing was proud.
       b.   *his bearing's pride *[[PROUD + SUG] + nominalizer]

(189)a.   Your remarks were angry.
       b.   *your remark's anger *[[ANGRY + SUG] + nominalizer]

(190)a.   Her expression was optimistic.
       b.   *her expression's optimism *[[OPTIMIS + SUG] + nominalizer]

In Pesetsky's analysis, the bases PROUD, ANGRY and OPTIMIS assign a [−affected] theta role (which is certainly not obvious in these cases), and therefore must be the head, by his Affectedness Condition. On the other hand, the zero morpheme SUG must also be the head of the word, by his Empty Morpheme Filter. This results in a clash, and the word is not well formed. This analysis is subject to the same criticism as the zero-CAUS morpheme: why is the [−affected] role inactive in the sentences to resolve the conflict between the two conditions, and why is that impossible in the case of nominalizations?

My analysis of the Genitive explains the ungrammaticality of the (b) examples, without recourse to a zero morpheme. Recall that I assume that the Genitive is an argument that establishes an abstract relation in the semantic domain of 'Identity.' On the other hand, I have just argued that Higgins' manner constructions are strictly 3-D, hence strictly spatial. Therefore, this construction is not compatible with the Genitive. If this account is correct, it is not the nominalization of the "manner" examples that is a problem here, as Pesetsky's analysis suggests, but simply the presence of a Genitive in these examples. A nominalization of the construction without a Genitive is predicted to be possible. This is indeed the case; a 3-D interpretation of the nominalization is possible in the following examples:

(191)a.   the pride of his bearing
       b.   the anger of your remarks
       c.   the optimism of her expression
       d.   the irritability of his comments

    e. the sadness of his words
    f. the fearfulness of your behavior

(192)a. There was sadness in Bill's words.
     b. There was pride in John's manner.
     c. There was optimism in her expression.

(193)a. John's manner had pride in it.
     b. Bill's remarks had anger in them.

An analysis of nominalization on the basis of 'Identity' properties of the Genitive accounts for the facts, without recourse to a zero morpheme SUG.

4.4.5.4 SUMMARY

We have seen that EO verbs have peculiar properties, with respect to nominalization. To account for these properties, Grimshaw attributes a special status to the subject of EO verbs, assuming that it is not an external argument. Since event nominalization requires that an external argument be suppressed by adding a new external argument Ev (event), similar to R, event nominals cannot be derived from EO verbs. We saw, however, that the status of nonthematic arguments like R is problematic. Pesetsky (1990) proposes to account for these peculiarities by assuming that EO verbs are derived by a zero-affix CAUS, and that this zero affix has special properties. But his analysis relies on a notion of affectedness that is not well defined and that must be stipulated about EO verbs; a serious problem also arises in the suppression of some [−affected] arguments. Although zero affixation might be involved in the derivation of EO verbs, this does not seem to be enough to account for all that is going on. Both analyses run into a problem with a productive alternation pattern in EO verbs. The behavior of EO verbs in nominalization is unusual only when they are nonagentive. Switching from a nonagentive to an agentive interpretation dramatically affects grammaticality, but it is not clear in either analysis precisely why this switch has any effects on nominalization.

I suggested, instead, that the nominalization of EO verbs is like that of other verbs. As usual, the referent of the Actualizer of an EO verb may alternate between a Substantive and a Concept. The agentivity effects arise when the referent is a Substantive. The reference of a Genitive is obligatorily Substantive because of the very nature of the relation the Genitive establishes with the head noun. This means that a Genitive Actualizer of an EO verb cannot have the Concept interpretation and must be a Substantive. Coming back to the basic cases in (132), we immediately see why (a) and (b) are bad— it is difficult to interpret the Genitive NP here as strongly agentive, as the Substantive interpretation requires.

(132)a. *the movie's depressing of the audience
    b. *the audience's depressing by the movie
    c. *the depressing of the audience by the movie

As for (c), a more comprehensive study of the meaning of *by* will be necessary to account for its ungrammaticality. My impression is that, just as the Genitive must be a Substantive because it serves as a reference point for an Identity relation, *by* might also require its object to be a Substantive because *by* also determines a reference point, as shown in (194).

(194)a. Come here by me.
    b. I will travel by Paris.
    c. I will travel by train.
    d. She did it by day.
    e. This room is 2 meters by 4 meters.
    f. He knows it by heart.

Finally, this analysis makes an interesting prediction about ES verbs. Since the Actualizer of ES verbs such as *fear* and *love* is a person perceiving passions, emotions, or desires, its reference is an I-Subject and, therefore, is a Substantive. We expect a nominalization of these verbs with a Genitive (or *by*-phrase) to be acceptable, since there is no clash with the Identity requirement of the Genitive. Thus, event nominals with *-ing* are fine:

(195)   John's fearing/loving of Mary

However, if reference must be to the whole self in an Identity relation, the Genitive in (195) should be more "agentive" than the subject of a sentence like (196), since here reference could be only to the individual as a person perceiving passions, emotions, or desires.

(196)   John fears/loves Mary.

It must be the case, therefore, that there are some external signs of John's feelings in (195), since the global person includes that aspect of John, signs which are not necessarily present in the context of use of the sentence. Indeed there is such a contrast, as can be seen in (197), where (a) is odd, since it should have been apparent that John feared/loved Mary.

(197)a. #John's fearing/loving of Mary certainly came as a surprise.
    b. That John feared/loved Mary certainly came as a surprise.

This property of the Genitive Actualizer of nominalizations of ES verbs reinforces my analysis of the nominalization of EO verbs: in both cases, the Genitive Actualizer must be a Substantive.

4.4.6 COMPOUNDING

Grimshaw (1990) gives another argument in favor of her aspectual analysis of Psych verbs. She notes the following asymmetry between ES verbs and EO verbs, with respect to compounding.

(198)a. Man fears god.
    b. A god-fearing man.

(199)a. God frightens man.
    b. *A man-frightening god.

While the object of *fear* can form a compound with *fearing,* this is not possible for the object of *frighten.* She argues that this follows from general constraints on synthetic compounding and the particular argument structure that she assigns to each of the classes of Psych verbs. She makes two general assumptions about synthetic compounding: (1) the nonhead is theta-marked by the head; (2) elements inside a compound are theta-marked "before" elements outside a compound, that is, an element inside a compound must have a θ-role lower in the hierarchy than one outside the compound. For example, consider (200).

(200)a. Gift-giving to children.
    b. *Child-giving of gifts.

Assuming the theta hierarchy Agent > Experiencer > Goal > Theme, (200a) is fine because the least prominent argument, the Theme *gift,* is inside the compound, while the more prominent Goal argument *children* is outside. On the other hand, (200b) is ill-formed because the least prominent argument is outside the compound, while a more prominent argument is inside. The same conditions will account for the contrasts in (201) and (202).

(201)a. Flower-arranging in vases.
    b. *Vase-arranging of flowers.

(202)a. Cookie-baking for children.
    b. *Child-baking of cookies.

This way of restricting the assignment of θ-roles inside a compound is similar to Roeper and Siegel's (1978) First Sister Principle.

Returning to (199), the problem with *man-frightening god, according to Grimshaw, is that the Theme *god* is theta-marked outside the compound, "after" the Experiencer *man*. She notes, however, that (203) is just as bad as (199b), even though the least-prominent Theme is internal to the compound.

(203)   *a storm-frightening child

Capitalizing on the distinction between theta tier and aspectual tier, Grimshaw suggests that compounding requires that the least-prominent argument on both the theta tier and the aspectual tier must be internal to the compound. In (203), *child* is the least-prominent argument on the aspectual tier, but *storm* is the least prominent in the theta tier. Given her analysis of EO verbs, each of the two arguments is the least prominent on one of the tiers; compounding is impossible, because both arguments cannot be internal to the compound at the same time. "Since there is no way to theta mark without violating one or the other of the two sets of prominence relations, there is no well-formed compound corresponding to non-agentive *frighten*" (Grimshaw 1990, 25).[52]

There are three empirical problems with this analysis. First, the analysis predicts that compounding of an EO verb should greatly improve with an agentive interpretation. For example, in (199b), *god* is prominent on the aspectual tier, since it is a Cause and *man* is a State; if *god* is an Agent, then it is also prominent on the thematic tier, *man* being an Experiencer. The compound is predicted to be good, since the less prominent argument *man* is inside the compound; but compounds as in (199b) are bad even under an agentive interpretation.

Second, it seems that this kind of compounding is not very productive, even with the ES class for which it is supposed to be possible. *A god-fearing man* seems to be an exception: it is an expression with biblical connotations, meaning something like 'a man who reveres god.' Thus, the grammaticality judgments for the examples in (204) and (205) vary considerably.

(204) *ES class:* a god-fearing man, a child-despising man, a cookie-loving man, a food-adoring man, a linguist-admiring man, a politician-detesting man, a police-dreading man.

(205) *EO class:* a man-frightening god, a child-disgusting food, a child-amusing clown, a boss-worrying secretary, a journalist-terrifying ter-

rorist, politician-humiliating results, a man-horrifying accident, a husband-surprising wife.

Third, there are two -*ing* morphemes: one is a nominalizer, and the other forms adjectives. With both classes of Psych verbs, compounds in which -*ing* is used as a nominalizer are often better than when -*ing* is used to form an adjective. For example, *linguist-admiring* can be used as a prenominal adjective, as in *a linguist-admiring man,* meaning "a man who admires linguists," or as a nominal, as in *He's all for linguist-admiring.* Similarly, *husband-surprising* can be used either prenominally as an adjective, as in *a husband-surprising wife* (very marginal) or as a nominal, as in *She's all for husband surprising.*

On the whole, it seems that there is a contrast between the two classes of Psych verbs as predicted by Grimshaw's analysis, but it is often fairly weak. If we wish to reject this analysis because of the special status it gives to EO verbs as discussed earlier, we need to find another explanation for the compounding facts. First, for the data in (200)–(202), another explanation immediately comes to mind. In all of these cases, a preposition is lost in the derivation and a condition akin to recoverability of deletion, which says that no element can be deleted if its existence cannot be "recovered" from the remaining elements, could explain the ill-formedness of these examples.[53] Second, cases involving external arguments (206) and unaccusative predicates (207) can also be accounted.

(206)   *The hours for girl-swimming at this pool are quite restricted.

(207)   *Leaf-falling makes a big mess.

Grimshaw assumes that compounds have two theta domains, one internal to the compound and one external to it. Thus, in (200)–(202), the Agent external argument of the head is assigned outside the compound. In (206) and (207), the head of the compound has only one argument: the argument structure of the head is saturated internally (by *girl* and *leaf*), and there is no argument for the external theta domain of the compound. Grimshaw assumes that this is ruled out by a general theory of predicates and arguments.

Another way to explain these facts is to modify slightly the condition on synthetic compounding. Instead of assuming that it is the least prominent argument that is compounded, we could assume that the argument compounded with the head must be the Object of Termination. This is not the case in (206), where *girl* is the Object of Actualization, nor is it the case in (207), where *leaf* is both the Object of Termination and the Object of Actualization.

Finally, we must account for the Psych verbs, and the contrast between (198) and (199). First, we will consider the possibility that Myers' Generalization, as captured by Pesetsky's EMF ((162) above), can explain the contrast. Although I will not espouse the whole analysis, for reasons discussed in 4.4.5.1.2, I agree that the presence of a zero-causative affix may play a role here. Recall that the EMF rules out nominalizations of the form in (208).

(208)   *[[[ES − predicate $_V$] $\varnothing_{CAUS}$] nominalizer]

(209)   shows the structure of "annoyance," which is ruled out by the
         EMF.

(209)   *[[[annoy $_V$] $\varnothing_{CAUS}$] ance $_N$]

This explains why *annoyance,* for example, is not a causative nominalization: the nominalizer must be attached directly to the base because a zero causative morpheme would not pass the EMF.

To account for the ill-formedness of compounding with EO verbs, as in (210), we could assume that an adjective-forming suffix in the position of the nominalizer in (208) is also ruled out by the EMF.

(210)   *tourist − [annoy + CAUS + ing $_{ADJ}$] attraction

But this cannot be the explanation for the fact that these forms are not acceptable because affixing *-ing* to an EO verb is fine when there is no compounding, as in (211).

(211)   annoying attraction

Crucially, (211) has a causative interpretation, so in Pesetsky's terms, the internal structure of *annoying* contains a causative zero morpheme.

(212)   [[[annoy V] $\varnothing_{CAUS}$] ing $_{ADJ}$]

We, thus, expect (212) to be ruled out by the EMF. However, Pesetsky reports Myers' observation that

> wherever a phonological string like *support* is assigned to two syntactic categories (here, verb and noun), only one of its categorizations (here, the verb) allows the affixation of derivational morphemes. Thus, the verb *support* yields *supportive,* but the noun *support* yields nothing like *supportial*$_{adj}$ or *supportious.* Myers interprets these data as arguing

that one member of the pair is always zero-derived from the root represented by the other member. The derived member shows the restriction
against further derivational affixation (Pesetsky 1990, 49).

But Pesetsky noted that there are systematic exceptions to Myers' observation. He searched the entries from A to C in *Webster's Seventh Collegiate
Dictionary,* looking for noun-verb pairs of identical spelling. He then looked
at the listed derivatives of these words, searching for words ending in unambiguously denominal suffixes and words ending in unambiguously deverbal
suffixes. He found two systematic exceptions: *-able* and *-er.* It is to account
for these exceptions that he introduced the second clause of the EMF, repeated here as (213).

(213) *Empty Morpheme Filter (EMF):* A phonologically zero morpheme μ
         is licensed either by (i) or (ii):
         (i) μ projects lexical features (licensing by X-bar theory)
         (ii) μ is head-governed.

He assumes that *-able* and *-er* are head-governors. If *-able* and *-er* can be
head-governors, perhaps *-ing*$_{adj}$ could also be a head-governor? But then, why
did not *-ing* turn up in Pesetsky's search? Pesetsky searched only *listed* derivatives of noun-verb pairs of identical spelling. Derivatives with *-ing* are fairly
productive and so are not usually listed in dictionaries. So the fact that Pesetsky's search did not come across *-ing* as an exception could be because of
dictionary writing choices rather than linguistic factors (although, of course,
the latter often do influence the former). In fact, a quick look at Myers'
list of noun-verb pairs with identical spelling allows one to construct many
derivatives with *-ing* that are well-formed, as in (214).[54]

(214)a.   *N bases:* accenting colors, functioning car, influencing person, lim-
             iting rules, orbiting satellite
       b.   *V bases:* caressing hand, commanding advantage, protesting jour-
             nalists, reversing effect, supporting cast

I will extend Pesetsky's speculation about *-er* and *-able* to *-ing* and assume
that *-ing* has features that allow it to license a zero morpheme under clause
(ii) of the EMF. The grammaticality of (211) and of the examples in (214)
then follows.

Now let us return to our original problem, namely the ill-formedness of
synthetic compounding based on EO verbs, such as **tourist-annoying attraction.* In order to solve the problem, the nature of synthetic compounding

must be understood. Synthetic compounds are exceptional in that a predicate-argument relation is established between the head and the non-head. Generally, nouns only take arguments that are combined with prepositions, as in (215).

(215)a. *gift money
     b.   gift of money

To account for this, Emonds (1985) proposes that nouns have no direct theta-marking capacity. The fact that even deverbal nouns do not take arguments without prepositions is likely because of morphological structure. A verbal base, which normally takes an argument, can no longer establish the relevant semantic relation with an argument, once it is embedded under a nominal affix, since it can no longer govern the argument, as (216) illustrates.

(216)

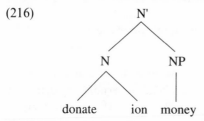

In (216), the nominalizer -*ion* is the head of N and prevents the verbal base *donate* from entering a semantic relation with an argument. Without the help of a preposition, *of* in this case, the structure is ill formed.[55]

Root compounding, as in (217), is possible with nouns, however.

(217)

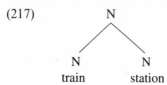

Root compounds cannot be eventive, since events require a predicate-argument relation, and we assume that nouns do not take arguments. A compound noun, such as (217), can only have a result interpretation. Moreover, no condition based on Event structure can hold of such a compound. For example, there can be no requirement that the compounded nonhead be an Object of Termination, since such a notion depends on Event structure. That is why, in root compounds, elements other than the Object of Termination can be the nonhead; *train* in (217) is an Identifier.

If these speculations about semantic role assignment in nominals are correct, then the structure of synthetic compounds must not be as in (216) or as in (217). Rather, the structure must be such that the base can govern and assign a semantic role to the nonhead argument. Suppose we assume the structure in (218), in which synthetic compounding takes place before affixation of the nominalizing (or adjectivizing) affix.

(218)

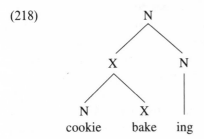

First, *cookie* and *bake* are compounded, and then *-ing* is affixed. A predicate-argument relation can be established between *bake* and *cookie* in (218), since *bake* governs *cookie*.[56]

We now have an explanation for the ill-formedness of adjectival synthetic compounds with EO verbs, as in **tourist-annoying attraction,* as compared with the well-formedness of adjectives derived from EO verbs by affixation, as in *annoying attraction.* The structure of the synthetic compound is as in (219), that of the adjective as in (220) (see (212) above).[57]

(219)

(220)

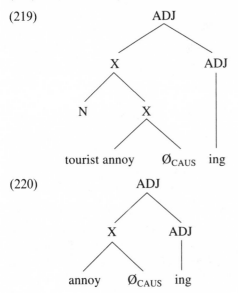

In the discussion of (212), which corresponds to (220), I assumed that *-ing,* just like *-er* and *-able,* is a proper head-governor. The zero morpheme CAUS thus satisfies clause (ii) of the EMF, and the adjective is acceptable. The reason for the ill-formedness of (219) is now clear: because of the compounding of *tourist* and *annoy*+CAUS, the zero morpheme is too deeply embedded to be governed by *-ing,* and, hence, it does not pass the EMF.[58]

In this section, I examined Grimshaw's analysis of Psych verbs and showed that the distinction between EO and ES Psych verbs in terms of their behavior in compounds, is not clear-cut. I offered a morphologically based analysis of the inacceptability of synthetic compounds, using Pesetsky's zero causative morpheme. However, I am not at all convinced that all EO verbs are causative, nor am I convinced that all ES verbs are not. Given that there are problems with the data, as noted in the discussion of (204) and (205), there are good reasons to be careful in proposing too powerful and sweeping an analysis here. While the above discussion is highly speculative, it does at least suggest that an account of the compounding facts is possible without assigning a highly special status to EO verbs.

4.4.7 Imperative

Ruwet (1972) noted that verbs of the *frapper* class (EO verbs) are incompatible with the imperative:

(221)   ?? Frappe-le par ton intelligence!
         Strike him with your intelligence!

The same holds for EO verbs with a nonagentive subject.

(222)   Dégoûte-le! (good only if agentive subject)
             Disgust him!

The claim seems to be falsified by examples like those in (223).

(223)a.   Frappe-le par ton intelligence et tout ira bien.
           Strike him with your intelligence and all will go well.
      b.   Dégoûte-le de la viande et il se fera végétarien.
            Disgust him with meat and he will make himself a vegetarian.

We must be careful to distinguish between imperative *form* and imperative *force.* Although all the sentences in (221) to (223) are in the imperative form, only those in (221) and (222) have imperative force. The imperative forms in (223) do not have imperative force, but are rather interpreted as conditionals; they can be paraphrased as in (224).

(224)a.   Si tu le frappes par ton intelligence, tout ira bien.
            If you strike him with your intelligence, all will go well.
    b.   Si tu le dégoûtes de la viande, il se fera végétarien.
            If you disgust him with meat, he will make himself a vegetarian.

Imperative force holds when a command or request is addressed to an individual, usually an individual in the immediate surroundings of the speaker. This can be seen in the case of third-person imperatives, such as (225), which is a request that one of the individuals present fixes the typewriter (Susan Schmerling, personal communication).

(225)   Someone fix this typewriter!

It seems that verbs like Psych *frapper* and nonagentive *dégoûter* are incompatible with imperative force. Because the addressee in a sentence with imperative force is an individual in the immediate surroundings of the speaker, it cannot be a Concept. Psych *frapper* is not compatible with this use, since its Psych reading depends on the interpretation of its subject as a Concept. Similarly, I assume that nonagentive EO verbs such as *dégoûter* require that their external argument be interpreted as a Concept. They are, therefore, incompatible with imperative force.

That these two types of Psych verbs are incompatible with imperative force follows directly from the analysis presented here. On the other hand, there is no obvious way to explain this in the other analyses we have looked at. For example, although some constructions with derived subjects cannot be imperative, (226a), others can be, (226b). This seems to be due to a constraint on imperatives that requires that the addressee be capable of some control over the action or state. If the addressee is not capable of such control, the command or request is impossible (227).

(226)a. ?? Be arrested!
    b.   Get arrested!

(227)a. ?? Be tall!
    b.   Be nice!

Furthermore, some constructions that pass standard tests for unaccusativity, and so are commonly analyzed as having derived subjects, are fine in the imperative, as long as these conditions of control hold:

(228)a.   Viens ici!
            Come here!

b.   Va chez Paul!
     Go to Paul's!

Thus, an analysis of Psych verbs on the basis of derived versus nonderived subject will not account for the imperative facts because not all derived subjects behave the same way. Trying to account for the imperative facts in terms of aspectual structure, by stating that addressees must be most prominent on both the aspectual and thematic tiers, would just be an unrevealing restatement of the problem. Finally, an analysis on the basis of special thematic roles fares no better, since it would have to state explicitly that a Cause cannot be an addressee—in a nonagentive Psych construction. A more simple restriction, that no Cause can be an addressee, would not suffice because a volitional Cause can be an addressee in Psych (see (222)) or other constructions:

(229)   Roll down the hill!

There is a definite advantage for an analysis that is based on the reference possibilities of the argument, since all we need to claim is that a Concept cannot be given orders because it cannot control the action or state.

4.4.8 PRO$_{ARB}$ AS SUBJECT

Following unpublished work by Alfredo Hurtado (personal communication) (and Jaeggli 1986), Belletti and Rizzi (1988) propose an additional test for an analysis of EO verbs on the basis of unaccusativity. They note that there is a use of third person plural *pro,* in Italian, in which the plural specification does not imply semantic plurality.

(230)   *pro* ti stanno chiamando. Deve essere Gianni.
          They you are calling. Must be Gianni.
          Someone is calling you. It must be Gianni.

Belletti and Rizzi make the claim in (231):

(231)   *Arb* interpretation can be assigned to deep subject *pro*'s only; it is incompatible with unaccusative structures.   [NP-movement structures]

The reason for the claim is illustrated in the contrast between the unergative and transitive examples in (232) and the examples of NP-movement in (233).

(232)a.   *pro* hanno telefonato a casa mia.
          Somebody telephoned my place.

b. *pro* mi hanno mandato un telegramma.
 Somebody sent me a telegram.
c. *pro* hanno visto Gianni in giardino.
 Somebody saw Gianni in the garden.

(233)a. **pro* sono arrivati a casa mia.
 Somebody arrived at my place.
b. * *pro* mi sono sembrati matti.
 Somebody seemed to me to be crazy.
c. * *pro* sono stati visti in giardino.
 Somebody has been seen in the garden.

The *arb* interpretation for third person plural *pro* subjects of EO verbs is impossible:

(234)a. * Evidentemente, in questo paese per anni *pro* hanno preoccupato il governo.
 Evidently, in this country somebody worried the government for years.
b. * *pro* hanno colpito il giornalista per la gentilezza.
 Somebody struck the journalist with his kindness.
c. ?? Qui *pro* hanno sempre entusiasmato/commosso gli americani.
 Here, someone always excited/moved the American people.

Belletti and Rizzi conclude that these subjects are underlying objects. But Pesetsky (1990) questions the diagnostic and the generalization. First, he argues that a distinction must be made between the "Corporate" use of the third person plural and the "Generic" use. Once this is done, it becomes clear that the generalizations involved are semantic, not syntactic.

The Corporate plural pronoun (3pl) "seems to pick out some socially designated group of people, prototypically governments, bosses, criminals or shopkeepers" (Pesetsky 1990, 29). As Belletti and Rizzi note, the referent of the pronoun need not be plural. This can be seen in the English-Corporate-3pl use also; for example, there could be a single cashier in (235c).

(235)a. They robbed Mrs. Johnson.
b. They're making us fill out our income tax forms early this year.
c. They accepted our check at the supermarket.
d. They sell cigarettes on Melrose Street.

Pesetsky argues that the proper description of these data is not syntactic, as in (231), but rather semantic, as in (236) (Pesetsky's (104)).

(236)   *"Corporate" interpretation can be assigned to agentive-third person
        pronouns (pro in Italian) only; it is incompatible with non-agentive
        θ-roles.*

He says that this is a better generalization because it correctly predicts
that deep subjects that are non-agentive should not get this interpretation:[59]

(237)a.   *They received a punch in the nose at the supermarket.
    b.   *Al mercato hanno preso un pugno sul naso.

(238)a.   *They got a phone call yesterday.
    b.   *Ieri hanno ricevuto una telefonata.

It also predicts that agentive unaccusatives should be fine:

(239)   Sono venuti riparare il lavandino.
          Somebody came to fix the sink.
          [One repairman came from the shop]

If we now turn to the Generic use of the third person plural, we see that
it has a distribution that differs from the Corporate-3pl use. Pesetsky says
that it also fails to diagnose unaccusatives, since deep objects can be third
person plural Generics.

(240)a.   In America, they're required to fill out income tax forms every
          year.
    b.   In America, sono ?costretti/obbligati a fare la dichiarazione dei
          redditi tutti gli anni.
          *In America, they are constrained/obliged to make a declaration of
          their income every year.*

The Generic 3pl also differs from the Corporate 3pl because the generic 3pl
can occur as the Experiencer subject of ES predicates.

(241)   Evidentemente, in questo paese per anni *pro* hanno temuto il ter-
          remoto.
          Evidently, in this country people feared the earthquake for years.

In contrast, sentences with EO verbs and their periphrastic counterparts
resist Generic 3pl:

(242)a.   *In France, they worry you.
    b.   *In France, they make you worried.
    c.   *In Francia, ti preoccupano.
    d.   *In Francia, ti rendono preoccupato.

Pesetsky suggests a generalization for 3pl Generics that is similar to the one that Rizzi (1986) proposed for direct object *pro:* 3pl Generics must be "affected by the event in which they occur, either by being changed or being conscious participants in the event" (Pesetsky 1990, 31).

I agree with Pesetsky's general conclusion that the distribution of 3pl Generics depends on semantic factors and is not a diagnostic for unaccusativity, although it is not clear to me exactly what these semantic factors are. Given that the Corporate pronoun refers to groups of people metonomically through individuals and that 3pl Generics are conscious participants in the event, according to Pesetsky, it might be that these kinds of pronouns cannot refer to Concepts. Note that the unacceptable examples in (234) and (242) all have subjects that are referred to as Concepts.

4.4.9 EMBEDDING IN A CAUSATIVE

Another construction in which ES and EO verbs behave differently is the causative construction. As Belletti and Rizzi note, ES verbs in Italian can be embedded as an infinitival complement of the causative *fare,* but EO verbs cannot.

(243)a. Questo lo ha fatto apprezzare/temere/ammimare ancora di più a Mario.
This made Mario appreciate/fear/admire him even more.

b. *Questo lo ha fatto preoccupare/commuovere/attrarre ancora di più a Mario.
This made Mario worry/move/attract him even more.

Belletti and Rizzi argue that this provides an additional argument for their unaccusative analysis. They relate (243) to the following facts observed by Burzio (1985):

(244)a. Gianni ha fatto telefonare (a) Mario.
Gianni made Mario call.

b. *Gianni ha fatto essere licenziato (a) Mario.
Gianni made Mario be fired.

Under Burzio's analysis, in the causative, the embedded VP is raised. The following structures are assigned to the sentences in (244).

(245)a. Gianni ha fatto [$_{VP}$ telefonare] [(a) Mario $_{VP}$].

b. *Gianni ha fatto [$_{VP}$ essere licenziato t$_i$] [(a) Mario$_i$ $_{VP}$].

The ungrammatical (245b) is excluded because the trace in object position is not bound by its antecedent at S-structure. Belletti and Rizzi assume the following structures for the sentences in (243).

(246)a.   Questo lo ha fatto [$_{VP}$ apprezzare] [a Mario $_{VP}$].
  b.   *Questo lo ha fatto [$_{VP}$ preoccupare t$_i$] [a Mario$_i$ $_{VP}$].

They assume that the surface subject of the EO verbs is an underlyingly object and claim that (246b) is ruled out for the same reason as (245b).

Given this configuration, we might expect reconstruction of the moved VP to "save" the ungrammatical examples, since binding through reconstruction of traces moved under VP-raising is possible, as in (247).

(247)   John was sure that Mary would be arrested, and [$_{VPk}$ arrested t$_i$] [she$_i$ was t$_k$].

Such a structural analysis is not required, in any case, since there are other ways to account for the facts. First, note that the ungrammaticality of the passive embedded under *fare* in (246b) could just as well depend on a constraint against having any AUX embedded under causative verbs *fare* and *faire*, as in the French example with AUX *avoir* below.

(248)a.   Jean a fait manger la tarte aux enfants.
         Jean made the kids eat the pie.
  b.   *Jean a fait avoir mangé la tarte aux enfants.
         Jean made the kids have eaten the pie.

On the other hand, an infinitival unaccusative verb embedded under *faire* is fine, as in (249).

(249)   Le directeur a fait [$_{VPk}$ venir t$_i$] Mario$_i$ t$_k$ à son bureau.
         The director made Mario come to his office.

This is problematic for Belletti and Rizzi (and Burzio), because the subject of the unaccusative is assumed to be underlyingly an object; the structure of (249) should be the same as (245b) and (246b), with an unbound trace.

Second, the ungrammaticality of embedding an EO verb under *fare* as in (243b) can be related to an independent condition on causatives. The Causee, the subject of the embedded infinitival complement, must be an individual over which the Causer may have some control, and the Causee itself must have the potential to control the course of events described by the infinitival VP; otherwise, the causative is inappropriate.[60] Thus, compare (250) with (251). (To my ear, the examples in (250) are not perfect, presumably because of the presence of *être* and *avoir*, although they are not auxiliary verbs to other verbs here.)

(250)a. ?Paul l'a fait être gentil.
  Paul made him be nice.
  b. ?Paul a fait avoir plus de patience aux enfants.
  Paul made the children have more patience.

(251)a. *Paul l'a fait être grand.
  Paul made him be tall.
  b. *Paul l'a fait avoir de grands yeux.
  Paul made him have big eyes.

Clearly, a constraint based on derived versus underived subjects is not appropriate, because "derived" subjects can appear under *faire*, as in (252).

(252) Dans son film, Paul l'a fait sembler être grand/avoir de grands yeux.[61]
  In his movie, Paul made her seem to be tall/to have big eyes.

I will argue that the relevant notion is 'controllable Substantive.' The subject of a clause embedded under *fare/faire* must be a controllable Substantive. Under this analysis, the unacceptability of (243b) is straightforwardly derived. As we have seen, the subject of EO verbs like *preoccupare* 'worry,' *commuovere* 'move,' and *attrarre* 'attract,' is typically not interpreted as a Substantive, but as a Concept. This is incompatible with the requirement of *fare/faire*. On the other hand, some EO verbs quite freely allow a Substantive interpretation of their subject, so it should be possible to embed these verbs under *fare/faire* with an "agentive" interpretation. This is indeed the case:

(253) Jean a fait dégoûter/amuser Marie à Paul.
  John made Paul disgust/amuse Marie.

Similarly, verbs of the *frapper* class (EO verbs) should only allow a non-Psych interpretation when embedded under *fare/faire*, since the Psych interpretation of these verbs is dependent on the interpretation of their subject as a Concept, rather than a Substantive. The following facts noted by Belletti and Rizzi corroborate this.

(254)a. Questo ha fatto sì che io lo colpissi.
  This has made such that I him-struck.
  This made me strike him.
  b.(*)Questo me lo ha fatto colpire.

This me him-have made strike.
This made me strike him.

Belletti and Rizzi observe that (b) allows only the physical (non-Psych) inter-pretation of *colpire* 'strike.'

I conclude that the fact that EO verbs cannot be embedded under caus-ative *fare/faire* is not an argument for assigning them an unaccusative struc-ture. An unaccusative analysis fails to account for the grammaticality of embedded-raising sentences, as in (252), or of typical unaccusatives, as in (249).[62] The independently motivated condition on causatives that I propose, namely that the Causee must be controlable and have control over the event of the infinitival VP, accounts for the embedding facts discussed by Belletti and Rizzi, as well as the problematic examples discussed above.

4.4.10 INTERACTION WITH ADVERBS LIKE "PERSONALLY"

Postal (1971) noted that the distribution of sentence-initial *personally* is not the same with EO verbs as it is with ES verbs.

(255)a.   Personally, I fear Mary.
    b.   *Personally, Mary fears me.

(256)a.   *Personally, I frighten Mary.
    b.   Personally, Mary frightens me.

He proposes to account for these facts with a condition on *personally* that states that this adverb can only be related to a deep structure subject. Since the subject of an EO verb is derived, *personally* cannot be related to it (256a); on the other hand, since the object of an EO verb is a subject in deep struc-ture in Postal's analysis, *personally* can be related to it (256b).

However, Ruwet (1972) showed that there are problems with this claim. He gives several examples from French that show that adverbs like *personally* can relate to NPs that are not analyzed as deep subjects. Here are a few of his examples (his (126 and 127)):

(257)a.   "Personnellement," dit Cécile, "j'ai été complètement pervertie
        par Valmont."
        Personally, said Cécile, I was completely perverted by Valmont.
    b.   Personnellement, la lecture de Chomsky m'a beaucoup aidé.
        Personally, the reading of Chomsky helped me a lot.

c. Personnellement, cette fille a conquis mon coeur.
   Personally, that girl won my heart.
d. Personnellement, ceci a retenu/éveillé/attiré mon attention.
   Personally, this held/awoke/drew my attention.
e. Personnellement, ces faits répondent à mon attente.
   Personally, these facts answer my expectations.
f. Personnellement, ceci ne me dit rien qui vaille.
   Personally, this tells me nothing of worth.
g. Personnellement, mon foie me donne du soucis.
   Personally, my liver gives me some worry.
h. Personnellement, la révolution est le cadet de mes soucis.
   Personally, revolution is the least of my worries.

Consistant with the assumptions made in this book, I propose the following (descriptive) condition on the distribution of *personally/personnellement.*

(258)   When left dislocated and expressing the speaker's opinion, *personally/personnellement* relates to the first person singular NP, which is the most prominent I-Subject in the sentence.

This will account for the contrast between EO and ES verbs. Since the subject of an EO verb can be a Concept, as in (256b), the object is the designated NP, according to (258). The subject itself can be an I-Subject, as in (256a), in which case the sentence tends to be "agentive." With an ES verb, as in (274), the subject is always an I-Subject, since it is the Experiencer; so it is the designated NP, according to (258), and *personally* can only appear with a first person subject (255a), not with a first person object (255b).

Condition (258) also accounts for all the cases in (257). For example, (257c) is possible because neither the subject *cette fille* nor the idiomatic direct object *mon coeur* is an I-Subject in a Psych reading of *conquis.* Thus, *mon* is the highest I-Subject and can be related to *personnellement.* Note that if the idiomatic *mon coeur* is replaced by the nonidiomatic *mon frère* 'my brother,' *mon frère* is the highest I-Subject, and *personnellement* can no longer be related to *mon*—the sentence **Personnellement, cette fille a conquis mon frère* is unacceptable.

The two uses of *frapper* should contrast, according to (258), since the Psych use of *frapper* requires a Concept interpretation of the subject.

(259)a. ?Personnellement, Pierre m'a frappé au visage.
   Personally, Pierre struck me in the face.

b.   Personnellement, Pierre me frappe par son intelligence.
     Personally, Pierre strikes me with his intelligence.

Note that the contrasts above can appear weak in some cases because there are at least two uses of sentence-initial *personnellement* in French: one in which the content of the sentence expresses the speaker's opinion and one in which the speaker is contrasted with some other group. The first interpretation is the most salient one in the examples given above. The following example is a case of the second interpretation:

(260)   Marie a embrassé tout le monde sur le front, mais, personnelle-
        ment, elle m'a embrassé sur la joue.
        *Marie kissed everyone on the forehead but, personally, she kissed
        me on the cheek.*

As (260) shows, contrastive *personnellement* does not observe the condition in (258). This is also true for EO and ES verbs: contrary to *personally* and *personnellement* expressing an opinion, contrastive *personnellement* can be related to the object of ES verbs (261a) and to the subject of EO verbs (261b):

(261)a.   Les enfants aiment et respectent Marie, Robert et Jean. Mais per-
          sonnellement, ils me craignent.
          *The children love and respect Marie, Robert and Jean. But person-
          ally, they fear me.*
     b.   Tous les autres professeurs s'entendent bien avec les étudiants.
          Mais personnellement, je les effraie.
          *All the other professors get along with the students. But personally,
          I frighten them.*

Why should there be such a contrast between the two uses of the adverbials? When *personally* and *personnellement* express an opinion, they are related to an I-Subject, as stated in (258), for reasons that are intuitively fairly clear: I-Subjects have opinions, Concepts do not. On the other hand, a contrast between an individual and another group does not have to be established on the basis of the whole self; it can be established on the basis of an individual's actions or on the basis of some properties of an individual. Therefore, contrastive *personnellement* can be related to a first person NP viewed either as an I-Subject or a Concept. An analysis on the basis of intentional properties like I-Subject and Concept can account for the behavior of *personally* and the differences in the two uses of *personnellement*.[63]

4.4.11 EXTRACTION FROM THE DIRECT OBJECT

Belletti and Rizzi observe that, given the structure they propose for EO verbs in which the Experiencer is adjoined to VP, as in (262), the Experiencer is expected to lack properties typically associated with canonical direct objects.

(262)

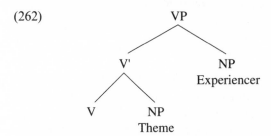

It does indeed, say Belletti and Rizzi: the Experiencer object differs from direct objects with respect to extraction processes, it is possible to extract out of a direct object, as in the (a) examples, but not out of an Experiencer, as in the (b) examples. They give the following data to support their claim Belletti and Rizzi's (83–87) and (96b and c):

(263)a.   la compagnia *di cui* tutti ammirano [il presidente *t*]
          the company of which everybody admires the president
    b. *la compagnia *di cui* questo spaventa [il presidente *t*]
          the company of which this frightens the president

(264)a.   la ragazza *di cui* Gianni teme [il padre *t*]
          the girl of whom Gianni fears the father
    b. *la ragazza *di cui* Gianni preoccupa [il padre *t*]
          the girl of whom Gianni worries the father

(265)a.   il libro *di cui* molta gente disprezza [l'autore *t*]
          the book of which many people despise the author
    b. *il libro *di cui* molta gente disgusta [l'autore *t*]
          the book of which many people disgust the author

(266)a.   il candidato *di cui* questa ragazza apprezza [i sostenitori *t*]
          the candidate of whom this girl likes the supporters
    b. *il candidato *di cui* questa prospettiva impaurisce [i sostenitori *t*]
          the candidate of whom this perspective frightens the supporters

(267)a.   la persona *di cui* la tua segretaria conosce [la sorella *t*]
          the person of whom your secretary knows the sister

b. *la persona *di cui* la mia macchina entusiasma [la sorella *t*]
    the person of whom my car excites the sister

(268)a. Gianni *ne* teme [molti *t*]
         Gianni of-them fears many.
     b. *?Questo fatto *ne* preoccupa [il presidente *t*].
         This fact of-it worries the president.
     c. ??Questo fatto *ne* preoccupa [molti *t*].
         This fact of-them worries many.

Belletti and Rizzi (1988) claim that extraction out of the direct object of
a verb of the *fear* class (the (a) examples) is fine because this is extraction out
of the Theme NP and this position "is lexically θ-marked by V, hence it does
not qualify as a barrier and is fully transparent to extraction" (329). Extraction out of the Experiencer object of a verb of the *frighten* class (the (b)
examples) is not possible, since this is extraction out of the Experiencer NP in
(262), and this position "is not lexically θ-marked, hence it is a barrier" (329).

The facts are not as simple as Belletti and Rizzi's analysis would lead us to
believe, however, and the system must be further refined; there are important
nuances that can be observed here, which are unexpected given their analysis.

First, Belletti and Rizzi say that the examples of Wh-extraction out of the
Experiencer position in (263)–(267) are worse than extraction out of another
VP-adjoined position, the postverbal non-unaccusative subject as in (269)
(Belletti and Rizzi's (94b)).

(269)   ??il diplomatico *di cui* ti ha telefonato [la segretaria *t*]
         the diplomat of whom called you the secretary

Second, Belletti and Rizzi say that *ne*-extraction out of the Experiencer,
as in (268b and c), is a weaker violation than Wh-extraction out of the Experiencer.

Third, contrary to what Belletti and Rizzi imply, the contrasts in (263)–
(267) are not sharp but vary, depending on the choice of verb, among other
things. Thus, Pesetsky (1990, 74) remarks that "[(264b)], for example, is reported by L. Burzio (personal communication) to be 'basically OK' if *preoccupa* is replaced by *offese* 'offends' or *spaventò* 'frightened'." These judgments
definitely hold for French, where the examples equivalent to the Italian examples in (263)-(268) exhibit at most rather weak contrasts.

(270)a. la compagnie dont tous admirent le président
     b. ?la compagnie dont ceci effraie le président

(271)a. la fille dont Jean craint le père
 b. ?la fille dont Jean préoccupe le père

(272)a. le livre dont plusieurs personnes méprisent l'auteur
 b. ?le livre dont plusieurs personnes dégoûtent l'auteur

(273)a. le candidat dont cette fille aime les partisans
 b. le candidat dont cette fille effraie les partisans

(274)a. la personne dont ta secrétaire connaît la soeur
 b. ?la personne dont mon auto excite la soeur

(275)a. Jean en craint plusieurs.
 b. ?Ce fait en inquiète le président.
 c. Ce fait en préoccupe plusieurs.

Moreover, the weakly deviant examples are fine in some particular contexts. For example, (271b) is improved when embedded as follows:

(276)a. Voici la fille dont Jean préoccupe tant le père.
 Here is the girl of whom Jean worries so much the father.
 b. La fille dont Jean préoccupe le plus le père, c'est Marie.
 The girl of whom Jean worries most the father, it's Mary.
 c. La fille dont Jean a préoccupé le père pendant des années . . .
 The girl of whom Jean worried the father for years . . .

In (277), I list the three observations about extraction out of the object of EO verbs that must be accounted for:

(277) *Observations about extraction out of the object of EO verbs:*
 a. Wh-extraction out of the Experiencer object is worse than extraction out of a VP-adjoined postverbal non-unaccusative subject
 b. *Ne*-extraction out of the Experiencer object is a weaker violation than Wh-extraction out of the Experiencer object.
 c. The contrast between extraction out of the object of an EO verb and out of the object of an ES verb is not sharp, but varies depending on the choice of verb.

Belletti and Rizzi account for the first observation (277a) by assuming that the two VP adjunctions do not have the same structure. The structure of sentence (269), with an inverted subject, is not (262), but rather (278).

(278)

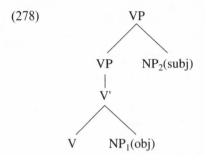

In (262), the Experiencer is under the lowest segment of an adjunction structure, whereas in (278) the postverbal subject NP$_2$ is under the highest segment
of VP. Belletti and Rizzi (1988) speculate that this higher segment may be a
weaker barrier, but they do not give the details of this aspect of the analysis.

In the case of the second observation (277b), Belletti and Rizzi make the
following suggestion:

> If the clitic *ne* is moved directly from NP to INFL, then subjacency is
> violated in all the cases, with both NP and VP barriers crossed. Then
> the deviance of these structures is accounted for, but the gradation is
> not captured by bounding theory. If the clitic is first moved to the verb
> inside the VP, then only one barrier is crossed, i.e., NP, hence subja-
> cency would be violated in [a sentence like (264b)], but not in [(268b
> and c)]. (330)

They say that the weak deviance that remains under cliticization as in (268b
and c) could be accounted for by a different module, namely binding theory.
Here *ne* would c-command its trace "only in the weak sense of Aoun &
Sportiche (1983), not in the strong sense of Reinhart (1976) which seems to
be required for binding purposes" (Belletti and Rizzi, 1988 330–31, note 25).
Belletti and Rizzi seem to assume that the binding theory violation would be
a weak one here, but we are not told why it is only a weak violation; binding
theory violations are generally assumed to be "strong" (ungrammatical).

Pesetsky (1990) tackles the third observation (277c). First, he says, the
difficulty in extracting out of the Experiencer NP follows, in his analysis,
from the fact that with causative EO verbs, this NP is syntactically special.
In his biclausal analysis, this NP is the subject of a small clause embedded
under a causative verb. Extraction out of that subject position is difficult, just
as extraction out of periphrastic causative constructions involving experi-
encers is difficult, as in (279) (his (242)), because of Connectedness (Kayne
1984) or Path Containment (Pesetsky 1982).

(279)a. la compagnia *di cui* questo renderà [il presidente *t*]
?*preoccupato/?*spavento/(?)felice
the company of which this made the president worried/frightened/
happy

b.?(?)Il fallimento della compagnia *ne* ha reso [il presidente *t*] preoccupato.
The failure of the company of-it made the president worried.

Pesetsky (1990) seems to attribute the variations in acceptability noted in
the discussion of (263)–(268) to the fact that EO verbs may not all necessarily
be biclausal: "[T]here may be cases in which more than one solution is possible. In this connection, I should stress once again that the theory of Lexical
Semantics does not dictate syntactic structures; it merely constrains these
forms. Thus, the fact that *annoy* must receive a complex syntactic analysis
consisting of a causative predicate and an ES predicate does not entail anything about other verbs whose semantics are consistent with similar analyses" (Pesetsky 1990, 75). Allowing such variation in the linking between semantics and syntax requires correspondence rules that are so highly
unconstrained that they are almost impossible to falsify. Moreover, we are
not told how this variation would affect other aspects of the syntax of these
nonbiclausal causative verbs, nor are we told what properties actually account for the choice of one linking solution over another, for a given verb.

Belletti and Rizzi and Pesetsky propose structural accounts for the three
observations above. But much is left open in those proposals: notions like
"weak barrier" and "weak binding" are not well defined, and the reference
to "other solutions" for linking of EO verbs when they are not biclausal
is quite vague. Given the data in (276), a purely structural account seems
inappropriate, since a change of context or emphasis affects the appropriateness of the extraction.[64]

There have been proposals in generative grammar to account for some
extraction facts by means other than structural conditions. Erteschik-Shir
(1973 and subsequent work) is a notable example of such an attempt.
Erteschik-Shir (1981) discusses cases where the opacity of an NP, with respect to Wh-extraction, varies depending on subtle contextual differences.
She gives the following data from Cattel (1979), who asks whether there could
be a generalization that covers both (280) and (281), and (282) and (283).[65]

(280)a. John wrote a book about Nixon.
b. Whom did John write a book about?

(281)a.   John destroyed a book about Nixon.
　　 b.   #Whom did John destroy a book about?

(282)a.   I like the gears in that car.
　　 b.   Which car do you like the gears in?

(283)a.   I like the girl in that car.
　　 b.   #Which car do you like the girl in?

Erteschik-Shir argues that Wh-extraction is constrained by a Dominance condition that can account for these contrasts: a constituent can be extracted only out of an environment in which it can be interpreted as dominant.

(284) *Dominance (Erteschik-Shir 1981):* A constituent c of a sentence S is dominant in S if and only if the speaker intends to direct the hearer's attention to the intension of c, by uttering S.

Erteschik-Shir and Lappin (1979) propose an operational test for establishing the possibility of a dominant reading of a constituent c_i in a sentence S—the lie test. It involves "constructing a discourse sequence in which a speaker asserts S and his hearer denies S by denying c_i in an appropriate manner. If the denial is possible, then c_i admits of a dominant reading. If the discourse is unnatural, this indicates that a dominant reading of c_i is excluded" (Lappin 1982, 139). If we apply the test to *Nixon* in (280) and (281) and to *that car* in (282) and (283), we see that *Nixon* is dominant only in (281) and *that car* only in (283), hence the extraction possibilities.

(285)   Sam said: John wrote a book about Nixon.
　　　　 Which is a lie—it was about a rhinoceros.

(286)   Sam said: John destroyed a book about Nixon.
　　　　 #Which is a lie—it was about a rhinoceros.

(287)   Sam said: John likes the gears in that car.
　　 a.   Which is a lie—he never saw the car.
　　 b.   Which is a lie—he never tried the gears.

(288)   Sam said: John likes the girl in that car.
　　 a.   #Which is a lie—he never saw the car.
　　 b.   Which is a lie—he never saw the girl.

The contrast between (280) and (281) is verb governed. The fact that *Nixon* is not dominant in (281) can be explained in terms of the semantic force of the verb *destroy:* the speaker "intends to focus the hearer's attention on the act of destruction rather than on the content of the quasi-NP" (Erteschik-Shir 1981, 667). On the other hand, the contrast between (282) and (283) is governed by the relationship between the NPs. "Only those cases where the items can be interpreted as being integral parts of the car allow extraction because it is only in those cases that *that car* can be interpreted dominantly" (Erteschik-Shir 1981, 668–69). *That car* is not dominant in (283) because *the girl* is not an integral part of the car.[66]

The Dominance condition is very natural as a condition on Wh-extraction, since questioning or relativizing a constituent focuses the attention of the hearer on that constituent. Another way to express the condition is in terms of Subject of Consciousness (SC) and Content of Consciousness (CC). As Ruwet (1990) observes, any sentence expresses a Content of Consciousness, which presupposes a Subject of Consciousness. There can be more than one Subject of Consciousness of the Content of Consciousness for a given sentence. Generally, the speaker is one of them, and so is the hearer, assuming that if one reads or hears a sentence, one immediately absorbs its Content of Consciousness (whether one understands it or not or believes in it or not is another matter). What the lie test shows is that, in order for speaker and hearer to disagree about the truthfulness of an assertion, they must first agree about what is being asserted. If the assertion is not part of the Content of Consciousness of both the speaker and the hearer, it is unnatural for the hearer to deny what the speaker said; the lie test is about their shared Content of Consciousness. A cannot accuse B of lying about a situation unless A believes that B knows whether that situation is true or false (unless A is accusing B maliciously). One way to make this clear is by considering the transparency of the NPs involved. As is well known, an NP can be "transparent" or "opaque." Thus, in (289), John might be aware that the Mr. Smith he met is Mary's father, in which case the NP *Mary's father* is transparent for John; or John might not be aware of this, in which case the NP *Mary's father* is opaque for John.

(289)   John met Mary's father.

Consider the exchange in (290).

(290)a. A: Mary's father was elected president.
   b. B: That's a lie—it was Mr. Smith.
   c. B: That's false—it was Mr. Smith.

If A utters (290a), B can reply as in (290b) only if *Mary's father* is opaque for B, so that B believes that Mr. Smith is not Mary's father and B believes that A knows that Mr. Smith is not Mary's father and A is trying to deceive B; if B believes that A does not know anything about the identity of the individuals involved—that there is no intention to deceive on A's part—then only the weaker (289c) is an appropriate reply. In sum, if the speaker thinks that a Subject of Consciousness knows something to be true but says or implies the opposite, the speaker may say "That's a lie" because the SC intends to deceive the speaker; if the speaker does not think that the SC intends to deceive anyone but is wrong, the speaker says "That's false."

Similar contrasts between transparency and opaqueness arise with some verbs, as can be seen in the following exchanges:

(291) A: You just destroyed a book.
     B: That's a lie—it was a painting.

(292) A: You just destroyed a book without realizing it (i.e., without realizing that there was a book among the things you destroyed)
     B: #That's a lie—it was a painting.

The sequence in (292) is inappropriate because it is contradictory: A asserts that B was unaware of the nature of an object B has destroyed, hence this is not part of B's Content of Consciousness, but B comments on the nature of that object as if it were part of his Content of Consciousness.

On the other hand, certain verbs strongly imply that their subjects are fully aware of the nature of the object:

(293) A: You just wrote a novel.
     B: That's a lie—it was an autobiography.

(294) A: You just wrote a novel without realizing it
     B: That's a lie—it was an autobiography.

In (294), B was aware of the nature of what he was writing; it is just that A and B disagree about the nature of the book (as often happens).

We saw above that Ersteschik-Shir observed that Dominance can be verb governed, as in the contrast between (280) and (281), or governed by the relationship between the NPs involved, as in the contrast between (282) and (283). In terms of Content of Consciousness, we can say that the transparency of the V and the transparency of the relationship between the NPs are relevant for the lie test because they determine whether some element of the sentence is part of the Content of Consciousness of both the speaker and the hearer. If an element is not part of the Content of Consciousness of both of these Subjects of Consciousness (SC_0—the speaker, and SC_1—the hearer), then that element can never be dominant, since attention cannot be drawn to it.

Many sentences express the Content of Consciousness of an argument, in addition to that of SC_0 and SC_1: thus *Max* is also a Subject of Consciousness in (295) and (296).

(295)a. A: Max thinks that god is dead.
    b. B: That's a lie—I know Max is a true believer. (A is a liar)
    c. B: #That's a lie—we see manifestations of god all around us. (Max is a liar)
    d. B: That's false—we see manifestations of god all around us.

(296)a. A: Max said that god is dead.
    b. B: That's a lie—I know Max is a true believer. (A is a liar)
    c. B: That's a lie—we see manifestations of god all around us. (Max is a liar)
    d. B: That's false—he said people behave as if God was dead.

As can be seen, verbs differ in transparency for an additional SC like *Max*. How does such an additional SC count with respect to Dominance? To see this, let us return to the examples discussed by Erteschik-Shir.

(297)a. John wrote a book about Nixon.
    b. # . . . although he was unaware that it was about Nixon.
    c. That's a lie—it was about a rhinoceros.
    d. Whom did John write a book about?

(298)a. John typed a book about Nixon.
    b. ? . . . although he was unaware that it was about Nixon.
    c. ?That's a lie—it was about a rhinoceros.
    d. ?Whom did John type a book about?

(299)a. John destroyed a book about Nixon.
    b. . . . although he was unaware that it was about Nixon.
    c. #That's a lie—it was about a rhinoceros.
    d. #Whom did John destroy a book about?

The (b) clauses, as continuations of the (a) clauses in these examples, show that the degree of awareness of the SC *John* about the topic of the book is directly correlated with the degree of Dominance exhibited by the lie test and Wh-extraction. Thus, John could hardly write a book about Nixon without being aware that it was about Nixon, but he could possibly type the book without knowing that it was about Nixon (if he is a typist, for example), and he could certainly destroy a book without knowing its subject matter. The judgments given in (297)-(299) are the unmarked ones, but given appropriate contexts, they might vary. The key point is that it is the degree of awareness of *John* that would vary, depending on lexical properties of the verb.

Similarly, the transparency of the relationship between gears and cars contrasts with the relative opacity of the relationship between girls and cars (see note 66) in examples like (287) and (288), repeated here:

(287)   Sam said: John likes the gears in that car.
   a.   Which is a lie—he never saw the car.
   b.   Which is a lie—he never tried the gears.

(288)   Sam said: John likes the girl in that car.
   a.   #Which is a lie—he never saw the car.
   b   Which is a lie—he never saw the girl.

The first relationship, between gears and cars, is part of the CC of all SCs: the presence of gears in cars is part of the general knowledge shared by speakers. The degree of an SC's awareness of the second relationship, between girls and cars, will vary according to context.

Thus, both verb governed Dominance, as in (297)-(299), and Dominance governed by the relationship between parts of the NP, as in (287) and (288), are related to the CC of the SCs involved. This relation between Dominance and Content of Consciousness can be expressed as follows:

(300)   A constituent c of a sentence S can be dominant only if it is transparent for all the Subjects of Consciousness in S.

Let us now return to the sentences involving Wh-extraction and Psych verbs. If we apply the lie test to these constructions, we see that there is also a Dominance contrast. For example, let us apply the lie test to English sentences similar to the unrelativized forms of (265), as in (301) and (302):

(301)   Jane said: Mary despises the author of that book.
   a.   Which is a lie—she doesn't know him.
   b.   Which is a lie—she hasn't read it.
   c.   #Which is a lie—he doesn't know her.

(302)   Jane said: Mary disgusts the author of that book.
   a. #Which is a lie—she doesn't know him (Okay, if Mary is
       "agentive")
   b. #Which is a lie—she hasn't read it.
   c. Which is a lie—he doesn't know her.

The judgments given here are those of a neutral context. In (301), since one can despise an author as an individual (a) or because of his work (b), either *that book* or the whole NP can potentially be dominant. The subject *Mary* is an SC, since it is an Experiencer, and both *that book* and the whole NP are in her CC, so both are dominant. Given Erteshik-Shir's condition that a constituent can only be Wh-extracted if it can be interpreted as dominant, Wh-extraction out of a direct object of an ES verb as in this case should be possible, and it is, as we saw in the Italian (a) examples of (263)–(267) and the French (a) examples of (270)–(274) above.

In the case of EO verbs, as in (302), the object *the author of that book* is the Experiencer, so it is a SC. On the other hand, the subject *Mary* is not an SC here, if she is viewed as a Concept (nonagentive), so Mary's knowledge about the author or his work is not relevant to determine whether he is disgusted. It seems that because *the author of that book* is an SC, no subpart of it can be dominant. Presumably because of condition (300), and the fact that a definite description describing a Subject of Consciousness cannot be part of its own Content of Consciousness, as discussed in section 4.4.2. Therefore, since an NP inside the direct object of an EO verb is generally not dominant, Wh-extraction of this NP should be impossible, given the Dominance condition on Wh-extraction; this is what we found in the Italian (b) examples of (263)–(267) and the French (b) examples of (270)–(274) above.

Extraction depends on Dominance, which depends on the Subjects of Consciousness and the Contents of Consciousness of a sentence. Since the object of an ES verb is a CC, whereas the object of an EO verb is a SC, we may expect this to correlate with extraction possibilities. We now have an alternative to the structural account of extraction out of the object of EO verbs. I will briefly evaluate the two proposals by comparing how they deal with the three observations on extraction noted in (277).

We have seen in discussing non-Psych constructions that what is part of a CC is determined by two basic factors: the semantics of the verb and the transparency of the NP. This brings us to observation (277c): EO verbs vary in the acceptability of extraction out of their objects. It is likely that the semantics of these verbs could explain this variation, just as it does for non-

Psych verbs. Thus, if there is a contrast in extraction possibilities between the object of *preoccupare* 'worry' as opposed to *offese* 'offends' or *spavento* 'frightened,' we expect this to correlate with the lie test.

(303)   Sam said: Jane worries the author of *The Horse's Mouth*.
         That's a lie—he wrote *Lucky Jim*.
         Which book does Jane worry the author of?

(304)   Sam said: Jane offended the author of *The Horse's Mouth*.
         That's a lie—he wrote *Lucky Jim*.
         Which book did Jane offend the author of?

(305)   Sam said: Jane frightened the author of *The Horse's Mouth*.
         That's a lie—he wrote *Lucky Jim*.
         Which book did Jane frighten the author of?

It seems to be impossible to give definitive judgments about these examples: the judgments depend very highly on the context, and there are too many factors involved. In a Psych construction, the speaker intends to direct the hearer's attention to the feelings of the Experiencer. The nature of some properties of the Experiencer can affect whether a given element triggers a feeling or not. For example, if the Experiencer is the author of a book, then knowledge of the book might indicate to the speaker or hearer exactly what elements are likely to trigger a feeling in the author. The speaker could potentially be directing the attention of the hearer to that fact. The title of the book would then be mentioned to refer metonomically to the Content of Consciousness of the author, that is, to some opinion of his, given the content of the book. Thus, in all three examples above, if we know that the author expresses certain political views in the book in question, this might partly determine how we expect him to react to Jane. Thus, one can know whether Jane would disgust the author either by reading his book or by deducing it from his behavior when confronted with Jane. Note that this means that the nature of the trigger *Jane* is also important. Jane could be a terrorist, a pacifist, or a fascist: in each case, she would have a quite different effect on a pacifist author than she would have on the author of a book about the inevitability of war. This, combined with the semantics of the verbs, creates a host of possible variations. For example, because the relationship between a certain kind of person and what an author has written in a given book might trigger very predictible reactions, the following extractions are fairly acceptable.

(306)a.   Which book does that kind of person worry the author of?
          Fascists like him worry the author of *Struggle for Democracy.*
    b.   Which kind of book does Nixon worry the authors of?
          He worries the authors of books about the infallability of democracy.

Note that this kind of interaction between NPs has similar effects with ES verbs. Thus, while an extraction like (307a) is fairly acceptable in a neutral context, a much more elaborate context is needed to make (b) and (c) acceptable, because of the nature of the NPs.

(307)a.   Which book does Mary despise the author of?
    b.   Which book does Mary despise the readers of?
    c.   Which book does Mary despise the printer of?

It is fairly clear why the author of a book could give rise to certain feelings, since the book expresses her thoughts, but it is less obvious for its readers, and even less so for its printer.

Similar effect holds of non-Psych verbs. To take one example, in *John destroyed a book about Nixon,* what the book is about is generally not important as far as the destruction is concerned; it could be that it is not even part of the destroyer's CC. But in some contexts, such as *John destroyed all books about Nixon,* the content of the book can be crucial. As expected, since the *about*-NP is dominant in this context, extraction is much better:

(308)   Who did John destroy all books about?

To sum up the discussion of observation (277c), the nature of the verb and of the NPs involved in a sentence allow for a variation in the degree of Dominance of the NP internal to the direct object of a verb. As a result, extraction out of the object of an EO verb is more difficult than that of an ES verb, since the object of an EO verb is a Subject of Consciousness, and a definite description describing a Subject of Consciousness can be part of its own Content of Consciousness only under very particular conditions. Extraction out of the object of an EO verb can become acceptable, given a proper context (see (303)–(306)), whereas extraction out of the object of an ES verb is made less acceptable in a context where the extracted NP is less dominant (see (307)). This kind of variation in extractability is unexpected under a strictly structural account.

Observation (277c), about the fact that the contrast in extraction out of objects of EO verbs as opposed to ES verbs is weak, stemmed from the obser-

vation by L. Burzio (reported by Pesetsky) that some EO verbs, such as *offend*
and *frighten,* allow extraction more easily than others, such as *worry.* He
reports a contrast between (309a), which is not very good (I would add "out
of context," because, in French, it may be better in some contexts or if the
relationship between the NPs is changed), and the (b) and (c) examples,
which are "basically OK."

(309)a. #la ragazza *di cui* Gianni preoccupa [il padre *t*]
         the girl of whom Gianni worries the father
     b. la ragazza *di cui* Gianni offese [il padre *t*]
         the girl of whom Gianni offends the father
     c. la ragazza *di cui* Gianni spaventò [il padre *t*]
         the girl of whom Gianni frightened the father

This contrast correlates with one often observed between the two sets of
verbs (with various effects, as we saw in previous sections), namely that the
subject of verbs like *offese* and *spaventò* can have an "agentive" interpretation, whereas it is difficult to interpret the subject of *preoccupa* as "agentive."
I argued that the distinction should be stated in terms of intentionality of
reference—I-Subject versus Concept—and depends on the expressiveness of
the trigger. The expressive triggering NP of verbs like *offese* and *spaventò* is
potentially a whole self, hence an I-Subject.

The difference in extraction possibilities correlates with the expressiveness
of the triggering NP as follows. Under the 3-D use of these verbs, where
emphasis is put on the expressiveness of the triggering NP, the examples in
(b) and (c) above emphasize the external manifestations, by the subject trigger, of offending or frightening the Experiencer *il padre.* These sentences do
not express the internal feelings of the Experiencer *il padre,* which is possibly
not even a Subject of Consciousness under the 3-D use. Therefore, Dominance of the NP internal to the direct object does not violate condition (300),
and extraction is possible. In the case of *preoccupare* in (a), however, the fact
that it is centered on the Experiencer makes it impossible for *il padre* not to
be a Subject of Consciousness, and extraction is impossible.[67]

There is a second difference between the two types of EO verbs that correlates with the first distinction: only those EO verbs that can take an I-Subject
as external argument can also appear in an impersonal passive construction.
Thus, we have a contrast between (310) (examples from N. Ruwet, personal
communication) and (311):

(310)a.   Il a été amusé beaucoup d'enfants.
          It has been amused many of children.
          Many children have been amused.
     b.   Il a été dégoûté du tabac une bonne partie de la population.
          It has been disgusted of tobacco a good part of the population.
          A good part of the population has been disgusted of tobacco.
     c.   Il a été séduit un grand nombre de bonnes d'enfants.
          It has been seduced a big number of nannies.
          Numerous nannies have been seduced.
     d.   Il a été surpris (en flagrant délit) une quantité de couples ad-
          ultères.
          It has been caught in the act a quantity of adulterous couples.
          There have been numerous adulterous couples caught in the act.

(311)a.   *Il a été préoccupé une bonne partie de la population.
          It has been preoccupied a good part of the population.
     b.   *Il a été frappé une bonne partie de l'auditoire.
          It has been struck a good part of the audience.

In an unaccusative analysis of EO verbs, this contrast is unexpected. In fact, just the opposite is predicted. If EO constructions have the same structure as unaccusative verbs, they should freely appear in impersonal constructions, as unaccusatives generally do, since they are assumed to have a non-theta-marked subject position in which impersonal *il* could appear. However, like unaccusatives, they should not passivize, since they have no external argument. In fact, all the verbs above can passivize; but there is some difference between the two types because the Actualizer argument cannot be implicit, and must appear in a *by*-phrase, for the verbs in (311) (here (313)):

(312)a.   Beaucoup d'enfants ont été amusés.
          Many children were amused.
     b.   Une bonne partie de la population a été dégoûtée du tabac.
          A good part of the population was disgusted by tobacco.
     c.   Un grand nombre de bonnes d'enfants ont été séduites.
          A great number of nannies have been seduced.
     d.   Une quantité de couples adultères ont été surpris (en flagrant
          délit).
          A quantity of adulterous couples have been caught in the act.

(313)a.   Une bonne partie de la population a été préoccupée *(par cette
          affaire).

A good part of the population has been preoccupied (by that event).
b.   Une bonne partie de l'auditoire a été frappée *(par l'attitude du président).
A good part of the audience has been struck (by the attitude of the president).

There is yet another difference between the two types of EO verbs. Only those verbs that can have an I-Subject as their external argument (and thus appear in the impersonal passive construction) can have generic *on* as a subject.

(314)a.   On a amusé beaucoup d'enfants.
          PRO-GENERIC has amused many children.
     b.   On a dégoûté du tabac une bonne partie de la population.
          PRO-GENERIC has disgusted of tobacco a good part of the population.
     c.   On a séduit un grand nombre de bonnes d'enfants.
          PRO-GENERIC has seduced a great number of nannies.
     d.   On a surpris (en flagrant délit) une quantité de couples adultères.
          PRO-GENERIC has caught in the act a quantity of adulterous couples.

(315)a.   *On a préoccupé une bonne partie de la population.
          PRO-GENERIC has preoccupied a good part of the population.
     b.   *On a frappé une bonne partie de l'auditoire.
          PRO-GENERIC has struck a good part of the audience.

It seems that EO verbs can appear in either both of these constructions (impersonal passive and generic *on*) or neither of them. One way to account for this patterning is to assume that an argument that has a generic reading, whether it be by lexical specification like *on* or because of the impersonal passive, cannot be a Concept (see the discussion in section 4.4.8). Given that the external argument of "inexpressive" EO verbs such as *préoccuper* 'worry' and of verbs such as Psych *frapper* must be a Concept, these verbs can appear neither with *on* nor in impersonal passives.

We can begin to understand the variation among EO verbs, with respect to extraction and other phenomena, when we take into account the fact that these verbs vary in the expressiveness of both the Experiencer and the Trigger. It is this variation in expressiveness that affects the I-Subject versus Concept status of the arguments and, therefore, affects their status as a Subject of Consciousness. Given the relation between Dominance and Subject of Consciousness expressed in (300), the variation with respect to extraction follows. Only dominant NPs may be extracted. Since arguments of EO verbs vary in their status as Subject of Consciousness and Content of Consciousness, an NP inside one of these arguments may be dominant or not, and may be extracted or not, depending on the verb and the context.

The fact that the Experiencer might not count as an SC under certain conditions, with related effects on Dominance and extraction, is also at the root of the observation that context may improve some deviant examples, such as those in (276), repeated below as (316).

(316)a. Voici la fille dont Jean préoccupe tant le père.
Here is the girl of whom Jean worries so much the father.

b. La fille dont Jean préoccupe le plus le père, c'est Marie.
The girl of whom Jean worries most the father, it's Mary.

c. la fille dont Jean a préoccupé le père pendant des années
the girl of whom Jean worried the father for years.

The addition of modifiers like *tant, le plus,* or *pendant des années* makes the reporting of the event much more speaker oriented. It is the speaker's opinion about how the father, the Experiencer object, feels that is emphasized rather than the Experiencer object's actual feelings. This centering on the speaker has an effect similar to the 3-D use of the verbs in (309). The status of the direct object Experiencer as a Subject of Consciousness is lessened; the definite description describing the Experiencer is no longer presented as part of the Experiencer's Content of Consciousness, but only as part of the Content of Consciousness of the speaker and hearer. This means that the NP inside the direct object Experiencer may be dominant and that Wh-extraction of this NP is possible.

Consider now observation (277b), namely that *ne*-extraction out of the Experiencer object is a weaker violation than Wh-extraction. As we saw above, Belletti and Rizzi proposed that *ne*-extraction, contrary to Wh-extraction, does not trigger Subjacency effects. For them, the fact that *ne*-extraction is not perfect is because of the binding theory: *ne* only weakly c-commands its trace in (317) (see the discussion of (268)).

(317)a. *?Questo fatto ne_i preoccupa [il presidente t_i].
This fact of-it worries the president.

b. ??Questo fatto ne_i preoccupa [molti t_i].
This fact of-them worries many.

I have already pointed out that the notion of weak c-command is problematic. Note, furthermore, that Belletti and Rizzi have no account of the fact that (317b) is better than (317a) (the French equivalent of (317b) is perfect, whereas the French equivalent of (317a) is odd). This casts further doubt on their analysis.

Under my analysis, the difference between Wh-extraction and *ne*-extraction is that the latter is not subject to Dominance conditions: in *ne*-extraction, as opposed to Wh-constructions, the speaker does not intend to direct the attention of the hearer to the intension of *ne*. Therefore, regardless of whether a direct object NP is transparent or not, *ne* can be freely extracted out of it. The exception, of course, is the object of an EO verb. As we see in (317), *ne* cannot be freely extracted out of the object when it has the form in (317a), but *ne* can be extracted out of the Experiencer object with the form in (317b). To explain this difference, I will appeal to another condition on the distribution of *ne,* which was proposed by Ruwet (1990) for French *en* (and *y*). Ruwet, responding to work by Lamiroy (1988), argues that *en* is an antilogophoric pronoun, in the sense that it is subject to the negative discourse condition in (318).

(318)   In a proposition that expresses a Content of Consciousness CC_i, neither *en* nor *y* can be coreferential with an N'' that represents the Subject of Consciousness SC_i of that CC_i.[68]

This accounts for the following contrast, where *en* is in the CC of the SC *Emile* in (319a), but not in (319b).

(319)a.   * *Emile* espère/souhaite que Sophie *en* tombera amoureuse.
           Emile wishes/hopes that Sophie will fall in love with him.
       b.   *Emile* mérite que Sophie *en* tombe amoureuse.
           Emile deserves that Sophie fall in love with him.

Ruwet gives several other kinds of examples where the condition makes the right predictions. For example, first and second person pronouns are always SCs of the CCs of a sentence with a verb like *mériter* 'deserve.' As expected, (320) contrasts with (319b).[69]

(320)   * Je mérite que cette jeune fille en tombe amoureuse.
           I deserve that that young girl fall in love with me.

The sentence in (321) shows that the relevant notion for Ruwet's condition (318) is actually disjoint reference, rather than noncoreference, since all these possibilities are equally bad.

(321)   *Max$_i$ et Marie$_k$ espèrent qu'on en$_{i/k/i+k}$ parlera à "Apostrophes."
          Max and Marie hope that they will talk about him/her/them on
          "Apostrophes."

En cannot be used to refer to an SC (319) and (320), or a part of an SC (321).
This can be expressed by the notion of "distantiation"—*en* cannot be used
by an SC to "distantiate" itself from itself, that is, to see itself or part of itself
"from outside." This is expressed in (322), which follows from (318):[70]

(322)   Pronoun *en* (and presumably *y*) cannot be used to distantiate from
        an SC.

The three cases of distantiation are schematized in (323).

(323)a.   SC$_i$——————— en$_i$ coreference (319)
   b.   [SC$_k$ . . . NP$_i$ . . .] —— en$_i$ disjoint reference (321)
   c.   [SC$_k$ . . . t$_i$ . . .] ——————— en$_i$ extraction of subpart of SC (317a)

Distantiation occurs when *en* functions as an argument distinct from the SC.
In (a), *en* and the SC corefer, so there is distantiation, since these are two
distinct arguments. In (b), *en* corefers with a subpart of the SC (an NP inside
the SC), so again there is distantiation. In (c), we have the same configuration
as in (b), except that *en* does not corefer with a subpart of the SC, but rather
binds a trace that corresponds to a subpart of the SC; *en* is not an argument
distinct from this subpart of the SC, since it forms a single chain with the
trace; however, since the chain [*en,* t] is only a subpart of the SC, this chain
is distinct from the SC, and there is distantiation.[71]

Given (322), it is clear what is wrong with (317a) (= (323c)). Extracting
ne out of the SC headed by *presidente* means that *ne* is being used to distantiate from a part of the SC, which is disallowed (assuming that *ne* functions
like *en* with respect to distantiation).

On the other hand, as argued in Milner (1978), Haïk (1982), and Bouchard (1988a), the status of *en/ne* in constructions like (317b) is quite different.
In (317b), *en/ne* is the head of the direct object SC. This can be represented
schematically, as in (324).

(324)   [SC$_i$ . . . t$_i$ . . .]——en$_i$ extraction of the head of the SC (317b)

In (324), there is no distantiation between the SC and *en* because they
form a single chain, since *en* binds a trace that is the head of the whole SC.
This contrasts with the cases in (323), where *en* is in a chain distinct from the
SC. This difference explains the contrast in acceptability between (317b),

which is fine because there is no distantiation, and these other cases, which are not possible because there is distantiation.[72]

Finally, consider the observation (277a), that Wh-extraction out of the Experiencer object is worse than extraction out of a VP-adjoined postverbal nonunaccusative subject. First, the observation is not correct: as we have seen, Wh-extraction out of the Experiencer object is fine in many contexts. This kind of extraction is governed by a condition based on notions like Dominance, Subject of Consciousness, and Content of Consciousness. Experiencer objects, because of their status as potential SC, have some peculiar properties with respect to extraction, as we have seen. We expect Wh-extraction out of a VP-adjoined postverbal nonunaccusative subject to be governed by the same Dominance condition. However, this VP-adjoined position has a different status from the Experiencer object, with respect to its SC and CC potential, so differences in extraction possibilities are likely to exist.[73] Thus, contrasts in extraction possibilities between Experiencer object and postverbal, nonunaccusative subject are not problematic in the approach taken here, since these two elements interact with the relevant factors (SC and CC) in potentially quite different ways.

To conclude this section, I agree with Belletti and Rizzi that the Experiencer object lacks properties of canonical direct objects, with respect to extraction. However, a structural account of the data fails in many respects. To equate the Experiencer object with a postverbal subject (in that it is not θ-marked directly by the verb) makes too strong a prediction, since extraction out of the EO is fairly acceptable in many contexts. Moreover, nonstructural notions like weak barriers, weak violation of the binding theory, and variations in linking of different EO verbs are required to account for variations not predicted by the structural account proposed. We observed that many of the subtle variations can be accounted for with notions like Dominance, Subject of Consciousness, and Content of Consciousness. These notions can be readily correlated with the semantic properties that I attributed to the Experiencer object.

4.5. CONCLUSION

I turned to Psych verbs in this chapter because of the analysis proposed by Belletti and Rizzi, in which a certain class of Psych constructions (those with EO verbs) are derived by raising an object into an "open" subject position. Such an analysis is not compatible with my attempt to construct a grammar in which all parts of a Syntactic Structure must correspond to some constituent in Semantic Structure—in such a grammar, no vacuous syntactic structures can exist. Belletti and Rizzi's analysis is based on a general hypothesis about theta assignment and some syntactic peculiarities of EO verbs. I argued that the fundamental observation on which their theta analysis is based, namely that there is crossing of theta roles with EO verbs, as compared to ES verbs, is incorrect. Moreover, the productivity of Psych constructions, with "regular" verbs easily entering Psych uses, makes a structural analysis unlikely, since a great number of verbs would have to be assigned different lexical entries just for their Psych use. The productivity of the construction argues against any analysis that treats it as marked, or special, be it because of its syntactic structure (Belletti and Rizzi 1988), aspectual structure (Grimshaw 1990), or thematic structure (Pesetsky 1990).

A detailed study of the syntactic peculiarities of EO verbs revealed that such a structural analysis cannot account for their behavior. Instead, I proposed an account where these syntactic peculiarities are because of the specific referential properties of some arguments in Psych constructions. In all other respects, there is nothing special about Psych constructions.

The particular referential properties of some arguments in a Psych construction come from the very nature of the construction. The "event" takes place in mental space, a psy-chose establishing a contact with an I-Subject, a Subject of Consciousness. Therefore, the reference of these arguments is different from the manner in which reference is made to entities in the physical world.

I argued that this method of reference is a crucial factor in accounting for the special properties found in Psych constructions. Thus, (1) *binding of direct object anaphors* is different with EO verbs because a reflexive is a Substantive, so its antecedent must be a Substantive, not a Concept, since an antecedent cannot have a more limitative reference than the reflexive (as stated in the Novelty Condition); some triggers of emotions and feelings, which are the subjects of EO verbs, are Concepts, so they cannot be antecedents for a reflexive and cannot themselves be a reflexive. (2) *Backward binding of a reflexive* is more widespread than just in EO sentences and involves binding of a logophoric pronoun, subject to discourse conditions; such a pronoun can be bound by a Subject of Consciousness only if it is in the Content of Consciousness of that SC. (3) EO verbs were seen not to be different from other verbs, with respect to *passivization*—they can undergo both verbal and adjectival passivization, so are not structurally different. (4) EO verbs resist the *progressive* because it depends on the subject's potential for activity—since EO verbs often have a subject referred to as a Concept, this is not compatible with the progressive. (5) The fact that *EO verbs do not nominalize as event nominals* does not depend on the presence of elements like *R, E,* and *Ev,* since these are unmotivated; the identificational nature of a Genitive NP forces it to be a Substantive, and, since it cannot be a Concept, this constrains the nominalization of EO verbs—if the Genitive subject is a Concept, it is not eventive, and if the Genitive subject is a Substantive, it is eventive and "agentive." (6) The constraints on *compounding* of EO verbs are basically morphological: assuming that EO verbs are causatives derived by zero affixation, and synthetic compounding as in **tourist annoying attraction* first involves compounding [tourist [annoy+$\emptyset$]], to which the nominalizer *-ing* is then added, the derivation breaks down because the zero morpheme is too deeply embedded to be properly licensed. (7) The incompatibility of some EO verbs with the *imperative* comes from the fact that the addressee is an individual in the immediate surroundings of the speaker, hence it cannot be a Concept. (8) As for the impossibility for EO verbs to have *pro$_{arb}$ as a subject,* I presented Pesetsky's arguments, which show that this restriction depends on semantic factors and is not a test for unaccusativity; given that the Corporate pronoun refers to groups of people metonomically through individuals, and that 3pl Generics are conscious participants in the event, it is likely that these kinds of pronouns cannot refer to Concepts. (9) The difficulty for EO verbs to be *embedded under a causative verb* such as *fare/faire* derives from the fact that the causee (the subject of the infinitive) must be controllable by the matrix subject and must itself have some control over the event of the infinitival VP, so it cannot be a Concept. (10) EO and ES verbs interact differently with *personally* when it is used to express an opinion because opinions are attributed to I-Subjects (Substantives) not to Concepts; when used contrastively, *personally* is compatible with EO verbs as well as with ES verbs. (11) Finally, *extraction out of the direct object* is not a straightforward yes/no phenomenon, but varies according to the context, such as whether the reporting is speaker oriented and according to the expressiveness of the EO verb; these factors affect the status of arguments as Subjects of Consciousness, which is already peculiar with Psych verbs, and it, therefore, affects extraction, since extraction is governed by a Dominance condition, which is based on the notions of Subject of Consciousness and Content of Consciousness.

4.6 Appendix: Lexical Redundancy Rules

There is a possible objection to my productivity argument: one could ask why I have disregarded an alternative solution compatible with the three other types of analyses. Why is the fact that there are many verbs that have syntactic properties similar to those of EO verbs a problem? Could we not just say that there is a lexical redundancy rule which relates *frapper$_a$* and *frapper$_b$*, for example?

(325) a.   Jean a frappé$_a$ Marie sur le nez.
           Jean struck Mary on the nose.
      b.   Jean a frappé$_b$ Marie par son intelligence.
           Jean struck Mary as intelligent.

Of course, any systematic relation can always be captured artificially by stipulation. But, in such approaches, the systematicity does not follow from anything, whereas I have argued that it follows from overall properties of the Grammar in the approach that I propose. Moreover, it is not at all obvious what such a redundancy rule would look like, given that there does not seem to be any systematic relation between the "Psych roles" and "normal" thematic roles or grammatical functions, as we saw in the discussion of examples (13) through (20).

There are also several arguments against such a redundancy rule solution, which I made throughout the text, and I will summarize them here. First, it would be odd for UG to favor homonymy on such a grand scale from a learnability point of view. Second, an additional redundancy rule would have to be stated for "agentivity" switches, with restrictions on which class of Psych verb allows an "agentive" subject. Third, general constraints would have to be proposed on the redundancy rule that forms Psych verbs, to exclude verbs of creation like *bake,* 3-D verbs, and verbs that are very specific about the nature of their arguments, such as *expatrier* and *transborder.* All of these are excluded naturally in the present analysis because of intrinsic measurability properties of their arguments; the type of arguments that they can take is restricted to "concrete" elements, which are not compatible with Psych relations that take place in mental space. Fourth, there are numerous subtleties in the syntactic behavior of these constructions that must be taken into account, such as the fact that the possibility of binding a reflexive complement varies among EO verbs or even for the same EO verb, depending on the context. This kind of variation also holds for other syntactic properties, such as extraction out of the direct object.

The general redundancy rule could be supplemented in such a way that some of these problems could be circumvented. But the additional proposals needed would essentially have to restate what I proposed on the basis of referential properties of arguments, and the relationship between such proposals and the redundancy rule would be somewhat ad hoc. Moreover, since the effects of the redundancy rule are captured by my proposal, on the basis of referential properties of arguments, and since such a concept is needed even in a redundancy rule approach, the redundancy rule solution should be abandoned for reasons of economy. The essence of the approach I propose is summarized in Carter's (1988, 238) statement that "[t]he simplest criterion for polysemy is Occam's razor: never posit two senses for a lexeme when one will do the work. But the implementation of this principle is theory-bound. A theory of semantic description must provide a metalanguage description, and thus the question will arise of whether it is possible to represent a posited sense or pair of senses in the metavocabulary our theory provides."

5 Verb Movement

5.0 INTRODUCTION: VERB MOVEMENT AND SELECTIVE SEMANTICS

Pollock (1989) and Chomsky (1991, 1992), following an idea by Emonds (1978), propose an analysis of the distribution of adverbs and negation in French and English on the basis of head movement of V to T. A head-movement analysis cannot be maintained within the theory I am proposing because Homomorphic Mapping is the only transformational process allowed. Their analyses require a contentless Functional Category, Agr (several such categories for Chomsky). This category cannot exist in my theory, since it corresponds to no element in Semantic Structure and cannot be licensed by Full Identification. That the Agr node is intended to be totally devoid of semantic content in Chomsky's proposal is quite clear: he assumes that the trace of Agr, but not the trace of a V, for example, can be freely deleted, precisely because Agr plays no role at LF.[1]

There are two ways to solve the problem of licensing Agr: either we attribute some kind of semantic content to Agr (and adjust Chomsky's proposal accordingly), or we show that Agr is not necessary. I will opt for the second alternative and argue that there is no motivation for an Agr node; the problem of licensing Agr then disappears with the node itself.

There are two main motivations given for postulating an Agr node: agreement facts and the position of the verb with respect to adverbs and negation. As we saw in 3.3.2, the first motivation for the Agr node, namely, its putative usefulness in accounting for agreement facts, simply does not hold. In what follows, I will argue that the second motivation for Agr, namely, that it serves as a landing site for the verb between negation and an adverb, also fails. Postulating Agr to account for the data is not necessary, since all the positions needed to derive the proper results are already available (see also Iatridou 1990). Furthermore, in some cases, the "short Verb movement" analysis makes the wrong predictions.

In section 5.1, I present the core of the data used to motivate verb movement in Pollock (1989) and Chomsky (1991, 1992). Section 5.2 discusses numerous problems with the Agr node analysis. In 5.3, I propose an alternative analysis that is based on the assumption that French and English differ morphosyntactically. I argue that Tense in French is a strong morpheme, and so it licenses an independent syntactic node. The complex of features $V+T$ occupies two nodes in syntax, one licensed by the features of T, one licensed by V. Since both the lower position of the $V+T$ complex (the verbal position) and the higher position of the $V+T$ complex (the Tense position) are licensed with respect to the semantic representation, and since the elements in these two positions are identical, the analysis is based on head *binding* rather than head movement.[2] In English, on the other hand, Tense is weak, so the $V+T$ complex licenses only one node in syntax. The distribution of adverbs and negation in these two languages is then shown to follow. Section 5.4 extends the analysis to inversion constructions.

5.1 THE DATA: THE AGR ACCOUNT

The Agr analysis tries to answer very interesting questions about the data, questions raised in the most part by Emonds (1978). The first question has to do with the position of manner adverbs:

Question (A): Why do adverbs precede tensed verbs in English but follow them in French?

(1)a.   John often kisses Mary.
   b.   *John kisses often Mary.

(2)a.   *Jean souvent embrasse Marie.
   b.   Jean embrasse souvent Marie.

To answer this question, Pollock assumes that the deep structures for these sentences are alike, with the ADV adjoined in a pre-VP position as in (3), but that the two languages differ with respect to Agr.

(3)
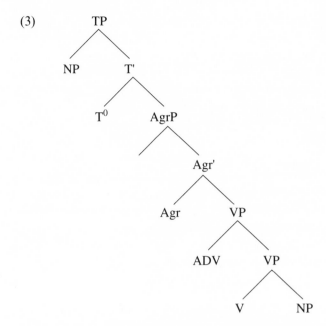

Pollock assumes, for both languages, that the tensed verb must raise to T, because T is a Tense operator that must bind the event variable E of the verb. Because of locality conditions (notably the ECP), the V must raise through the intermediate Agr head in order to reach the position T. This is possible in French because Agr is assumed to be strong. A strong functional category is assumed to be transparent to theta-role assignment, so a theta-assigning verb raising through it can still assign a theta role appropriately. Therefore, *embrasse* raises to T, a position that precedes the adverb, as in (2b). This movement is obligatory because the Tense operator must bind a variable; (2a), where there is no movement, is ungrammatical. In English, Agr is assumed to be weak. A theta-assigning verb thus cannot raise through Agr because theta theory would prohibit it, since the verb could no longer assign a theta role; the verb cannot raise directly to T, skipping Agr, because of locality conditions. Pollock assumes that in this case, there is a 0-*do*, a verb similar to the one in *do*-support, but with no phonetic content, that is generated in Agr, copies the theta grid of *kisses*, and raises to T to satisfy the requirement of the Tense operator. Affix hopping then puts the inflection on the verb. Since *kisses* does not move, it follows the adverb (as in (1a)).

Chomsky (1991) proposes the slightly different structure (4):

(4)

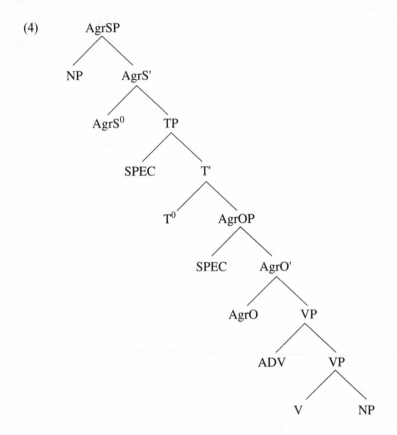

   Chomsky has two Agr nodes, AgrS and AgrO, to account for subject and
object agreement, respectively. The verb raises to AgrS in French for the
same reasons as in Pollock's analysis: Agr is strong in French. In English, on
the other hand, AgrS moves down to T^0, to which it adjoins, and then this
combination moves down to AgrO. Finally, the whole combination moves
down to V, which creates a surface structure with the adverb preceding the
verb. (It must be assumed here that a weak Agr adjoined to V does not block
theta marking, because V, not Agr, is the head.) But requirements of the
Tense operator are not satisfied in this way, says Chomsky, so the V+AgrO+
T+AgrS complex must raise back to T at LF. This down-and-up derivation
is the only one available in English. In French, both the short-raising derivation and the longer down-and-up derivation are possible, but by a principle
of economy, the shortest derivation must be chosen. It is left unexplained

in this analysis why the V+AgrO+T+AgrS complex must wait until LF to raise back to T. Why can it not raise to T at SS, deriving the French order for English?

Chomsky (1992) provides an answer to this question. The down-and-up derivation is no longer required. He assumes that, in all languages, verbs are inserted with their full inflectional features, which must be checked against the inflectional element I at PF and removed by a matching operation at LF. In French, since the inflectional features are strong, they must be dealt with in PF. But in English, they are weak and not visible at PF, so LF movement is sufficient. Since LF-movement is possible in English, it is selected because it is more economical than overt movement. The reason that LF-movement is less costly is as follows: "The intuitive idea is that LF-operations are a kind of "wired-in" reflex, operating mechanically beyond any directly observable effects. They are less costly than overt operations. The system tries to reach PF "as fast as possible," minimizing overt syntax. In English-type languages, overt raising is not forced for convergence; therefore it is barred by economy principles" (Chomsky 1992, 43).

Question (B): Why can the adverb follow an auxiliary in both languages?

(5)a. *John completely has lost his mind.
  b. John has completely lost his mind.

(6)a. *Jean complètement a perdu la tête.
  b. Jean a complètement perdu la tête.

There is no difference between French and English here; the auxiliary starts off in the lower VP and raises to Agr and then to T without creating a problem because AUX is not a theta-assigning element. Whether Agr is transparent to theta-role assignment or not, an auxiliary can move through it. As for the requirement that the Tense operator must bind a variable, Pollock assumes that it is satisfied, because the auxiliary is generated in a Spec of VP position, inherits the theta grid of the verb, and carries it to T; this inheriting of theta grid is assumed not to be affected by an opaque Agr. Chomsky (1992, 43) adopts this analysis in slightly different terms: he assumes that auxiliaries, lacking semantically relevant features, are not visible to LF rules, so "if they have not raised overtly, they will not be able to raise by LF rules and the derivation will crash." Chomsky's statement is stronger than Pollock's, since auxiliaries would have to lack all features relevant to LF. It is not at all obvious that this hypothesis is tenable.

Question (C): Why is there *do*-support in negative sentences in English but nothing like it in French?

(7)a. *John likes not Mary.
  b.   John does not like Mary.

(8)   Jean n'aime pas Marie.

Both Pollock (1989) and Chomsky (1991) assume that NEG is the head of a phrase that is generated as a complement of Tense. Pollock's structure is as follows (He assumes that *ne* is the head of NEG, and *pas* is in its Spec.):

(9)

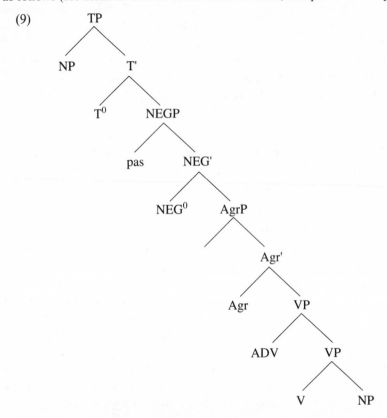

The two analyses differ substantially in their accounts here. For Pollock, raising in French is no problem. First, Agr is strong, so the verb can raise through it. Secondly, the trace left in NEG[0] by *aime* (which picks up the negation clitic *ne*) is properly governed across NEGP, because there is the lexical element *aime* in T that can L-mark NEGP, making it not a barrier. In

English however, it is a 0-*do* that raises through NEG^0. It cannot properly govern the trace left in NEG^0 from the head of TP because 0-*do* is not lexical and cannot L-mark NEGP, which remains a barrier. English, therefore, reverts to lexical *do*-support, so the trace in NEG^0 is L-marked and thus saved from the ECP.

Chomsky's account is quite different. In French, the V raises to AgrO and adjoins to it (creating a complex Agr head); then this complex raises to NEG^0, and so on. Since the trace in the position of AgrO is an Agr trace, not a V trace, it can delete at LF because it has no content (after having properly γ-marked the trace of V, in the sense of Lasnik and Saito 1984). It, therefore, creates no problem with respect to the ECP. In English, however, because Agr is weak, it is not the verb that raises and adjoins to Agr, but rather Agr that lowers and adjoins to the verb. This means that when this combination raises at LF, the trace it leaves behind is a trace labeled V, not Agr, and such a trace cannot be deleted at LF. This trace is not properly governed, because of the presence of the barrier NEGP, and the sentence is ruled out by the ECP. *Do*-support is required to get a proper derivation.

Do-support does not apply in affirmative sentences, even though that would mean a shorter derivation, because the least effort demanded by the principle of economy involves more than simply counting steps in a derivation: UG principles are assumed to be less costly than language-specific rules. So UG principles are applied whenever possible, with language-particular rules used only to "save" a D-structure yielding no output. Since there is a derivation for affirmative sentences that relies only on UG principles, as we saw for (1a), it must be chosen over the language-specific *do*-support derivation, even though the latter is shorter.

Question (D): Why is there *do*-support in question inversion in English and nothing like it in French?

(10)a. *Likes-he Mary?
    b.   Does he like Mary?

(11)   Aime-t-il Marie?

Pollock's answer is based on the idea that this inversion is the result of raising from T to COMP. If it were 0-*do* that raised from T to COMP, it would be unable to L-mark TP, since it is not lexical. TP would then be a barrier to 0-*do*'s government of its own trace in T. Therefore, lexical *do* is required. Chomsky assumes that an interrogative construction has a complementizer Q ([+wh]) which is an affix. Because it is an affix, a phonological base must raise to it. In French, this would be the V, but in English, the V cannot raise through the weak Agr. To allow an output, dummy *do* is inserted and then raised to COMP to bear the Q affix.

Question (E): How do verbs get their Tense and agreement affixes?

Neither Chomsky nor Pollock give a specific answer as to how affixation takes place, but both assume that affixation is dependent on syntax, either because the verb and its affixes are put together by syntactic movement (Pollock 1989; Chomsky 1991) or because they are brought into the appropriate structural relationship for checking (Chomsky 1992). Syntax also determines the order of morphemes for Chomsky (1991).

Question (F): How does subject-verb agreement take place?

Again, we are not told much about the actual process of agreement. The claim made is that agreement is syntactically conditioned: agreement with an NP is always the reflection of a government relation between the head of Agr and that NP; the element that moves into Agr^0 agrees with the NP in SPEC of Agr.

5.2 PROBLEMS WITH AGR

There are deep-rooted problems in an analysis that is based on Agr. I will start by looking at the list of the main tools that do the work in the two Agr analyses discussed above.

  (i) The structures (as in (3), (4) and (9)) are crucial, as is the fact that heads can adjoin to one another by movement.
 (ii) The presence of Agr nodes, as well as the distinction between strong and weak Agr nodes, which has effects on theta-assignment, is central.
(iii) It is crucial that there be only one main position for the adverb, with an extra secondary pre-INFL position for English.
 (iv) It is crucial that there be only one main position for NEG.
  (v) The presence of a Tense operator binding an E variable is an important trigger for movement for Pollock; the trigger is of a morphophonological nature for Chomsky.
 (vi) *Do* (and its non-lexical counterpart, 0-*do*) must copy theta grids; moreover, *do*-support must be a marked, language-particular rule.
(vii) Auxiliary verbs must inherit theta grids.

Unfortunately, all of these proposals are problematic, as we will see in the next subsections. I will look at each in detail because this will help to show what assumptions need to be changed in the search for a more satisfactory analysis.[3] I will then propose an analysis that is also based on the idea that the syntactic nature of some inflectional morphemes is different in French and in English, but with a major change in implementation.

5.2.1 THE STRUCTURE

The major problem here is how structures like those in (3), (4), and (9) are generated. Given X-bar theory, it cannot be stipulated in Phrase Structure rules that these are the relative positions of T, Agr, NEG, VP. Rather, this must follow from the selectional properties of the heads. Following Grimshaw (1979, 1981), Pesetsky (1982), and Rochette (1988), constituent selection is now generally assumed to be derived from semantic selection. This means that the semantic properties of these heads should determine their relative positions. But since Agr is crucially assumed by Chomsky not to have semantic content, so that its trace can delete at LF, there is an obvious problem here. Even T is problematic in that respect. To account for the two possibilities in (12), Chomsky assumes that *être* raises only to Agr in (a), but up to T in (b).

(12)a.   Ne pas être heureux
          Not to be happy
   b.   N'être pas heureux
          To be not happy

To get the correct inflection in (a), T is assumed to lower to *être,* and its trace is said to be deletable since it plays no role at LF. But if T and Agr are contentless, how can they have the semantic properties of selection required to derive the structures without appealing to Phrase Structure rules?

Deletion in itself also creates a problem for the structures. Chomsky (1991, 11) assumes that deletion leaves behind both e^0 and eP. This is not a category, it is just a position, he says. But this position is not an X-bar projection of anything, and it is not licensed by dynamic selectional relations. So specific X-bar-theoretic principles are needed: "by X-bar-theoretic principles, the dominating category AgrP is now eP, an XP with no features." Since this position is not licensed by a dynamic relation, a rule system is reintroduced, with all the power and redundancy that we know such systems to have.

Adjunction creates additional structural problems. Chomsky (1991) assumes that the trace of elements adjoined as in (13a) is deletable at LF because it is the trace of Agr and has no substantive content, whereas the trace of elements adjoined as in (13b) cannot be deleted because it is a V trace, which is visible at LF.

(13)a. $[_{Agr}$ V [Agr]]
    b. $[_V$ V [Agr]]

It is hard to see why the substantive content of these elements should differ so significantly at LF, since, after all, they simply represent a different structural organization of the very same heads.

A final structural problem comes from the motivation given for adopting structure (4). Chomsky adopts the structure in (4) rather than (3) because, according to Belletti (1988), in languages where the tense morpheme can be distinguished from the subject agreement morpheme, T is closer to the stem than is AgrS. This follows in Chomsky's structure since, on its way up, the verb picks up first T and then AgrS. However, there is an empirical problem pointed out by Iatridou:

> According to Ken Hale (personal communication), both orders of morphemes are found in languages. This might be answered by a parametric variation in the order in which the two constituents can occur cross-linguistically. However, this has at least one obvious problem. If the relationship between Tense and AgrP is taken to be one of semantic selection or subcategorization, then what could be said about those two elements if Tense can subcategorize for AgrP and AgrP can subcategorize for Tense as well? The cases of word order parameterization that I know of involve linear, not structural ordering. For example, comparison of VO and OV languages does not lead one to the conclusion that in some languages the verb subcategorizes for the object, and in others the object subcategorizes for the verb. The hierarchical order is taken to be the same in both language types. (1990, 565, note 3)

This problem does not arise in the analysis of agreement on the basis of indexing that I presented in 3.3.2.2. The subject agrees with the verb because it is coindexed with the Tense inflection on the verb, since the subject is the privileged actant of the event that establishes a link with Tense. The analysis does not predict that there should be a set order between the agreement morpheme and Tense, since this morpheme has no selectional relation with

Tense. Their order, with respect to one another, depends on low-level parameters of linearity.

As for the cases where there is a selectional relation between morphemes,
such as Tense and the verb, and also some of the combinations of morphemes
discussed in Baker (1985), the very idea of having syntactic movement generate the surface order of these morphemes is an odd one. As Di Sciullo and
Williams (1987) point out, the relationships between these morphemes reflects selectional semantics. There is no point in deriving the surface order
from syntactic or morphological processes: it is ultimately dependent on semantic properties.[4]

5.2.2 THE AGR NODE

We saw above the problems created by the absence of selectional properties
for Agr: it forces one to reintroduce into the grammar a mechanism that has
the power of Phrase Structure rules. One could try to solve this problem by
ascribing selectional properties to Agr, namely, aspectual properties. But until we are shown in what way having such a node explains any aspectual
properties of sentences, the proposal is empty. Does the presence of such a
node make any verifiable predictions about different aspectual classes of
verbs, for example? And if one could find some motivation for a node with
aspectual properties, it would remain to be explained why it should have
the properties attributed to Agr nodes, that is, why an Aspect node should
trigger agreement.

In any event, as I already pointed out in the discussion of past participle
agreement in 3.3.2, to claim that agreement with an NP is always the reflection of a SPEC-Head relation inside an Agr projection is very problematic.
Even in the local cases discussed by Pollock and Chomsky, postulating an
Agr node makes the wrong predictions in many cases. Thus, if agreement
with the past participle in (14) is the result of raising the participle into the
head of AgrO, with the clitic going through the Spec of AgrP, then the sentence in (15a) is problematic.

(14)   Jean les$_i$ a [AgrOP t$_i$ [AgrO repeintes$_v$] [VP t$_v$ t$_i$]].
        Jean them has repainted + FEM + PLUR.

(15)a. Jean les a souvent repeintes.
        Jean them has often repainted + FEM + PLUR.
   b.   Jean les a repeintes souvent.

Chomsky (1991) assumes that the order ADV-V in (15a) is the result of optionally not moving the participle, but this sentence is then predicted to be ungrammatical. The position of the past participle with respect to the adverb indicates that the participle did not raise to Agr-O, so there should not be agreement, but there is. One way around this problem is to say that the adverb *souvent* is attached to AgrP instead of VP here, but there is no semantic basis to assume that an adverb can modify an AgrP node.

There is also an inconsistency with the way that the strong/weak Agr distinction is made. The proposal that strong Agr allows the verb to assign its theta role, but that a weak Agr does not, goes counter to the feature percolation convention generally held (see Lieber 1980, for example), which states that features of a nonhead can percolate up in a morphological structure only if they are absent from the head. So the weaker the head, the more features from nonheads should be able to percolate, according to this convention. When V adjoins to Agr, the resulting structure is $[_{Agr} V \, Agr]$, with Agr as the head. Therefore, an Agr with more features, like the French Agr, should be more opaque than an Agr with fewer features, like the English Agr, but the opposite assumption is required.

Finally, if weak Agr is not visible at PF, how can an English AUX move to it at PF? And if Agr has no content at LF, how can an English V move to it at LF?

5.2.3 THE POSITION OF THE ADVERB

It is crucial for both Agr analyses above that the adverb appear only in one VP-initial position. If the adverb could appear in several positions, there would be no motivation for any of these movements. But most previous studies on adverbs (in generative grammar or other frameworks) recognize that there are many positions in the sentence where an adverb can appear (Keyser 1968; Kuroda 1970; Jackendoff 1972; McConnell-Ginet 1982; Ernst 1984; and Travis 1988, to name but a few). Not all adverbs can appear in all the available positions, but quite a few adverbs have a high degree of "transportability." For example, manner adverbs like *cleverly* and *clumsily* are fairly free: they can appear sentence-initially (16a), between the subject and the VP (16b), or sentence-finally (16c) (see Jackendoff (1972)).

(16) a.   *Cleverly/clumsily,* John dropped his cup of coffee.
     b.   John *cleverly/clumsily* dropped his cup of coffee.
     c.   John dropped his cup of coffee *cleverly/clumsily.*

The adverbs receive a different interpretation depending on where they appear in the sentence. This can be very subtle, but it is nevertheless real. For example, in (16a), the adverbs do not describe the manner in which John dropped his cup, but rather the opinion of the speaker that this was done at the right moment (*cleverly*) or wrong moment (*clumsily*). On the other hand, (16b and c) both refer strictly to the manner in which the cup was dropped. That the two types of modification—opinion and manner—are different is clear in an example like (17), which could be uttered in a situation where John's pretending to be clumsy in the presence of a criminal turned out to save the situation:

(17)   Cleverly, John clumsily dropped his cup of coffee on the thief's lap.

Examples of adverbs in various positions abound in the literature. The problem with the Agr analysis is that it claims that the adverb is always in the same position and that it is the verb that moved. Thus, in (18a and b), the adverb *souvent* would be in the same position, adjoined to the VP, in both sentences. The difference in order would come from the raising of the participle above the adverb in (18b).

(18)a.   Pierre a souvent embrassé toutes ses nièces.
           Pierre has often kissed all his nieces.
     b.   Pierre a embrassé souvent toutes ses nièces.

This predicts that the scope of *souvent* with respect to the direct object *toutes ses nièces* should be the same in both sentences. In fact, this is not the case. With a neutral intonation, there is a strong preference for *souvent* to have wide scope over the quantified *toutes ses nièces* in (a) and narrow scope in (b).

Another problem with adverbs for the Agr analysis is that an extra pre-INFL position must be postulated for English, to account for sentences like (19a):

(19)a.   My friends rarely are unhappy.
     b.   My friends are rarely unhappy.
     c.   *Mes amis rarement sont malheureux.
     d.   Mes amis sont rarement malheureux.

As Pollock points out in his note 8, since English aspectual verbs are assumed to raise in English as in French (since they have no theta-assignment properties affected by weak Agr), we would expect *be* to precede the adverb as in (b), as *être* does, in (d), if the adverb is generated in VP-initial position.

Since (19a) is possible, French and English must differ in the number of base positions for adverbs: English, but not French, must have an adverb position between NP and INFL. Since not all adverbs are possible in that position, as shown in (20), Pollock assumes that the meaning of the adverb governs in part where it can appear.

(20)a. *My friends completely are unhappy.
    b. My friends are completely unhappy.

It is certainly broadly assumed that the meaning of an adverb determines what node it can attach to and modify, and hence in what position it can appear (see the references at the beginning of this section). But if the difference in possible positions between French and English is based on meaning, it implies that there is a whole class of adverbs that do not exist in French, namely, the ones that can appear in that pre-INFL position in English. This is hard to believe. If the difference between the two languages cannot be attributed to a dynamic semantic property in this way, the Agr analysis must stipulate that there are two positions for adverbs in English, but not in French. But such a purely geometric stipulation is equivalent to a Phrase Structure rule, with the problems of power and redundancy that ensue.

Another problem, pointed out to me by Jacques Lamarche, is that true manner adverbs like *carefully* do not behave as expected. When the verb is not followed by additional material, these adverbs must follow, not precede, the verb. Thus, we have the following contrast:

(21)a. John carefully spoke to Mary.
    b. *John carefully spoke.
    c. John spoke carefully.

5.2.4 THE POSITION OF NEG

Just as there is more than one position for adverbs, with a change in the scope of their modification possibilities, according to what node they are attached to, there is also more than one position for NEG and its scope differs accordingly (see Horn 1989 and the discussion in section 3.4 above). The position given to NEG by Pollock and Chomsky (as in structure (9) above) corresponds to sentential negation, as in (22). For them, a sentence like (23) is derived by raising *have* above the NEG. But as Iatridou (1990) argues, a sentence like (23) is a case of constituent negation rather than sentential negation.[5]

(22)   Not to have played football for many years is a disadvantage in a major game.

(23)   To have not played football for many years is a disadvantage in a major game.

This distinction is important; if (23) is indeed a case of constituent negation, there is no reason to postulate a rule raising *have* above NEG for this sentence, since the *not* is generated below *have,* when its scope is only over the VP constituent. I assume that, in the case of constituent negation, the NEG is adjoined to the constituent it modifies. If all the cases of alternations of the position of NEG fall under such a contrast between sentential negation and constituent negation, the empirical support for a movement analysis of these alternations is greatly weakened, since the sentential NEG and the constituent NEG are not generated in the same position.

Iatridou gives two tests that show that (23) is a case of constituent negation. First, as is well known, if a quantifier is inside the c-command domain of negation, it can be interpreted as being inside the scope of negation or as having wider scope than negation. For example, (24) can mean either (25a) or (25b).

(24)   John has not been playing football for many years.

(25)a. John used to play football but he hasn't played in the last fifteen years. (*many* has scope over *not*)

   b. John started playing football only one year ago. (*not* has scope over *many*)

If a sentence has constituent negation on the VP, an adjunct outside VP cannot be in the scope of the negation. Thus, (26) can only be interpreted as in (25a).

(26)   John has been not playing football for many years.

If we return to (22) and (23), we see that sentence negation as in (22) can have either of the two readings in (25), but that constituent negation as in (23) only allows wide scope of the quantifier as in (25a).

The second test she proposes is based on *because*-adjunct clauses (Linebarger 1987). When NEG c-commands the *because* clause, there is a scope ambiguity. Thus, (27) is consistent with either (28a) or (28b).

(27)   John didn't grow corn because he wanted to make money.

(28)a. John grew not corn but rice, because the latter's market price is better.

   b.   John did grow corn, not out of monetary considerations, but because the government ordered him to.

Consider the two infinitival versions of (27) in (29) and (30):

(29)   Not to have grown corn because he wanted to make money . . .

(30)   To have not grown corn because he wanted to make money . . .

We find the same contrast as above: here too sentential negation in (29) is
ambiguous between (28a) and (28b), whereas (30) can be interpreted only
with NEG having narrow scope, as in (28a).

In addition to these two tests provided by Iatridou, I will give two more
that demonstrate the same point, namely, that postauxiliary NEG in infinitives is a case of constituent negation rather than sentential negation.

The first test is based on a long-standing observation discussed in detail in
Horn (1989) (briefly alluded to in note 36 of chapter 3). Constituent negation
consists in affirming a negative predicate of the subject, which presupposes
the existence of the subject. Sentential negation, on the other hand, is a denial
of a predicate. In this case, the existence of the subject is not presupposed;
denying a predicate of a nonexistent subject results in a true statement. In
other words, contrary (=constituent) negation presupposes the existence of
the subject, whereas contradictory (=sentential) negation does not. As the
following examples show, sequences such as *to be not happy* and *n'être pas
heureux* seem to be cases of constituent negation, since the existence of the
subject is presupposed. This is parallel to clear cases of constituent negation,
such as morphological negation.

(31)a.   It is normal for Socrates not to be happy, since he is dead (and
        dead people have no feelings).
     b.   Il est normal pour Socrate de ne pas être heureux puisqu'il est
        mort (et les morts n'ont aucun sentiments).

(32)a.   #It is normal for Socrates to be unhappy, since he is dead.
     b.   #Il est normal pour Socrate d'être malheureux puisqu'il est mort.

(33)a.   #It is normal for Socrates to be not happy, since he is dead.
     b.   #Il est normal pour Socrate de n'être pas heureux puisqu'il est
        mort.

This contrast is unexplained in an analysis where the different orders are
obtained simply by raising *be* and *être* above NEG, since NEG should then
have the same scope irrespective of the position of the auxiliary.

Second, an argument can be made using contraction facts. In sentences like (34)–(36), contraction of *not* is possible only if there is sentential negation, not if there is constituent negation.

(34)a. I can not go.
    b. I cannot/can't go.

(35)a. I have not seen Mary in five weeks.
    b. I haven't seen Mary in five weeks.

(36)a. I will have not seen Mary in five weeks.
    b. *I will haven't seen Mary in five weeks.

In both (34) and (35), the (a) sentence is ambiguous between a sentential negation reading, "I am unable to go"/"I have been unable to see Mary," and a constituent negation, "I have the possibility of not going"/"I had the possibility of not seeing Mary." The (b) sentence has only the sentential negation reading. In (36), on the other hand, only constituent negation is possible, because of the low position of NEG relative to the tensed auxiliary verb, so contraction is totally out.

This is predicted in an analysis of contraction along the lines of Bouchard (1986) (based in part on an idea by Postal and Pullum 1982). I argued that contraction (including cases like *wanna*) is subject to a government condition: an element A can contract with an element B only if B governs A.[6] So in (34) and (35), *not* can contract with the verb to its left when there is sentential negation because the structure is as in (9) above (but, I assume, without the AgrP). *Can* and *have* are generated in T and take NEGP as a complement and, hence, govern the head *not* of NEGP (along the lines of Belletti and Rizzi 1981). In the case of constituent negation, the NEG is internal to the lower VP, as in (37), so the government condition is not met and contraction is not possible.[7]

(37)

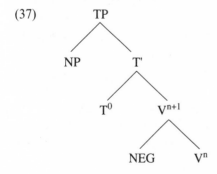

If we now turn to a case where the auxiliary precedes the NEG in an infinitival clause as in (38), an analysis based on a single position for NEG would have to claim that the AUX raised above the NEG into T. But this incorrectly predicts that contraction should be possible, since *have* would then govern the NEG.

(38)   *To haven't eaten for three days made him grouchy.

Example (38) shows two things: (1) raising to T does not occur in infinitival clauses, and (2) at least some instances of NEG placement in sequences like AUX NEG V are because of constituent negation and not sentential negation with raising.

5.2.5 THE BINDING OF THE E VARIABLE BY A TENSE OPERATOR

The proposal that a Tense operator binds an *E* variable immediately raises the problem of the highly dubious theoretical status of elements like the *E* variable. I discussed this at length in section 4.4.5.1.1.1 and will not repeat the arguments against *E* here.

There are also important technical problems with this aspect of Pollock's (1989) analysis. I said above that I would not dwell on technical problems, but I must briefly discuss those related to binding by a Tense operator, since they seriously undermine the falsifiability of the analysis. The main problem is that there are so many ways for this binding to take place that it is difficult to see how any sentences could be ruled out on any principled basis. There are four ways in which a Tense operator can be related to an *E* variable in Pollock. First, French theta-assigning verbs raise through Agr to T, carrying along the *E* variable in their theta grid. Second, *do* and 0-*do* in English are generated in Agr, copy *E* along with the theta grid from the V, and raise to T like the French V. Third, AUX in French and English is generated in Spec of VP, inherits the *E* variable along with the theta grid from the theta-assigning V, and raises to T. Finally, English Modals are generated under T and bind the empty [e] of Agr, some sort of 0-*do* which presumably copied *E* along with the theta grid from V. This is summarized in (39).

(39)   *Relations between the Tense operator and the E variable* (Pollock 1989):
   a.   Theta verbs in French: Adjoin the bearer of *E* to operator T
   b.   *Do* and 0-*do* in English: Adjoin the copier of *E* to Operator T
   c.   AUX in French and English: Adjoin the inheriter of *E* to Operator T

    d.   English Modals: Inflect by operator T the binder of the copier
        of E.

This raises several questions. First, what is the unified notion of 'binding' here? Second, why does an opaque Agr have negative effects on a V bearing a theta grid that adjoins to it, but no such effects on an element generated in it that copies or inherits such a theta grid? Third, why cannot *do* appear with an AUX, as in **I do be happy?* Pollock's answer to this question is that *do* cannot occur with Aux, because then the Tense operator would have a variable that would not have a restricted range of variation, and so would fail to denote anything (Pollock 1989, 400). But as he points out in his note 33, in *John is happy,* the variable must denote a state of happiness, so he says *be/ have* inherit the theta grid of the predicate. Because of this difference, where "*do* copies the T-grid of a V(P), whereas *be, have,* and modals inherit one by (a form of) specifier-head agreement," he must assume that *do* cannot copy from an inheriter (*be, have*) or from a binder of an inheriter (modals). Nor can an inheriter inherit from a copier, since we do not have sentences like those in (40):

(40)a.   *John has done go. (John has gone)
    b.   *John is doing go. (John is going)
    c.   *John will do go. (John will go)

On the other hand, he must assume that an AUX can inherit from another inheriter, since we do get AUX-AUX and modal-AUX sequences as in (41).

(41)a.   He has been serious about it all along.
    b.   I must have seen you somewhere before.

All of this is very obscure and will remain so until the difference between the two processes of copying and inheriting is clarified. The problem is compounded by the fact that Pollock assumes that AUX is sometimes introduced in Agr in Deep Structure (see his structure (129) in note 4 above) so that AUX is then not in a SPEC-head relation with V but in the same position as copier *do.*

5.2.6 Do-Support as a Language-Specific Rule

(42)a.   *John likes not Mary.
    b.   John does not like Mary.

(43)   Jean n'aime pas Marie.

Recall from the discussion of (7) and (8) (repeated here as (42) and (43)) that, in Chomsky's (1991) analysis, *do*-support does not apply in affirmative sentences, even if that means a shorter derivation, since UG principles are assumed to be less costly than language-specific rules. They are "wired-in" and distinguished from acquired elements of language, which bear greater cost. Since there is a derivation for affirmative sentences, which relies only on UG principles, it must be chosen over the shorter *do*-support derivation because *do*-support is assumed to be language specific.

But is that assumption well founded? In a theory that assumes empty slots, to have a dummy element fill an empty slot is not language specific, it is a general UG strategy. If something creates an empty slot in a language, there is a UG strategy that says that the slot is filled by a dummy element of the appropriate category. If the empty slot is verbal, a dummy verb like English *do* fills the slot.[8] If the empty slot is nominal, as when Nominative Case is assigned to a subject position with no argument present, then a dummy nominal element such as impersonal *it* or *il* fills the slot.

What is language specific is just the choice of element that is used as a dummy in any given language for any given category. For English to choose *do* as a dummy–verbal element in this way is no more language specific and no more costly than the choice of lexical element for the semantic structure corresponding to HIT (*hit* in English, *frapper* in French), for third person singular ($-s$ in English, $-t$ in French), and so on. In note 22, Chomsky (1991) acknowledges that *do*-support is not, strictly speaking, language specific, though he says he will "continue to use this term for expository purposes." If *do*-support is not language specific and hence not of a higher cost, we are left with no good reason for the absence of *do*-support in simple affirmative sentences in English or in French.

5.3 STRONG/WEAK: A MORPHO-SYNTACTIC DISTINCTION
5.3.1 A PROPOSAL

In line with the discussion in the previous chapters, the analysis that I will present relies heavily on general principles of economy. In accord with the general proposals of this book, I adopt the following hypotheses:

(1) A node like Agr cannot be present in the structure because the very nature of such a node is incompatible with Full Identification and Homomorphic Mapping.

(2) The structure cannot contain a special pre-VP position for adverbs: whether an adverb can appear there, or in any other position, will depend on whether a dynamic modification relation can be established between the adverb and its sister node.

(3) The fact that there appears to be an additional position in the structure for pre-INFL adverbs in English but not in French cannot be stipulated on the structure itself and must be derived from other properties of the two languages.

(4) The NEG phrase between T and VP in the structure is strictly restricted to sentential negation.

(5) The fact that Tense appears as the highest head in the sentence must be motivated.

(6) *Do*-support should be just that and should follow from the general analysis; when T has to stand on its own, a dummy verb will be inserted as a morphological support for the Tense affix.

Assuming that sentential negation must be as high as possible in the structure so that it has scope over categories expressing predicative content, without having scope over Tense, and assuming that Tense must be in the most prominent head position in the sentence, I propose (44) as the basic structure of a sentence (where the NEGP is present only in negative sentences, of course):

(44)

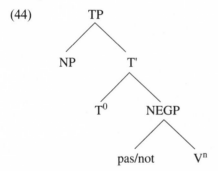

Contrary to Pollock, I assume that *pas* is the actual negator and *ne* only a scope marker. This is supported by the fact that *ne* is not obligatory in negatives in many dialects of French and the fact that *ne* appears as a scope marker in nonnegative constructions as in (45).

(45) Il ne chante que des chansons d'amour.
He NE *sings* CONJ *songs of love*
He only sings love songs.

5.3.1.1 TENSE AS THE MOST PROMINENT PROJECTION OF THE SENTENCE

Before turning to the details of the analysis, I would like to motivate the presence of Tense in the structure and its prominent position. The idea that a proposition is made up of a subject, a predicate, and a Tense dates back to Aristotle. Tense is not necessarily found in a single element in the sentence, but it can consist of a combination of morphosyntactic elements. For example, the fact that a present perfect tense expresses a centering of a past event onto the present is because of the combination of present tense *have* and the past participle. As we saw in section 3.1.2.4, I argued in Bouchard (1984b) that a tense representation is not a label, but a structured representation that maps homomorphically with the morphosyntactic structure of a sentence. Thus, the positions of the elements S (Moment of Speech), R (Reference Point), and E (Event) in the tense structure for the present perfect in (46) match with the relative positions of the elements they correspond to in (47): *has,* which expresses the anchoring on present, takes a projection of *lived* as its complement because the past expressed by *lived* is dependent on the S,R label corresponding to *has.*

(46)   S,R
          E_____|

(47)   Albert has lived in Princeton for thirty years.

It is a general requirement that every tense structure must be anchored onto the Moment of Speech S and that the other elements in the tense structure are "complements" of the Moment of Speech (or complements of its complement). By Homomorphic Mapping, the morphosyntactic element expressing the Moment of Speech S will have to appear as the most prominent head in the syntactic structure. Therefore, T must head the sentence, since T expresses the Moment of Speech S. It is important to bear in mind that, strictly speaking, T is not Tense, but the anchor of Tense onto the Moment of Speech.

5.3.1.2 TWO FACTORS THAT DETERMINE THE POSITION OF ADVERBS AND NEGATION

There are two factors that determine the position of adverbs and negation in French and English.

Factor 1: The meaning of an adverb determines what nodes it can attach to and modify, hence what position it can appear in.

The same holds for constituent negation; sentential negation depends on the relation of NEG with V^n and T, as expressed in (44). Factor 1 is a very generally accepted idea, as I mentioned in 5.2.3. It follows from this that adverbs receive a different interpretation, depending on where they appear in the sentence, because where they appear is determined by what they are modifying (see the discussion of (16)). Depending on its meaning, an adverb can combine with different types of elements: manner adverbs typically combine with a V projection (VADV); adverbs expressing the point of view of the speaker combine with an E-projection, where E here stands for Banfield's (1982) "énoncé" ('statement') (EADV); finally, sentential adverbs (SADV) have a range of modification in between these two. Some French examples are given in (48).

(48) VADV (manner): complètement 'completely,' facilement 'easily,' avec fracas 'with a crash,' tous 'all,' beaucoup 'a lot,' presque 'almost,' à peine 'hardly,' souvent 'often,' rapidement 'fast,' brusquement 'abruptly,' . . .

SADV: rarement 'seldom,' probablement 'probably,' toujours 'always,' hier 'yesterday,' demain 'tomorrow,' aujourd'hui 'today,' maintenant 'now,' souvent 'often,' rapidement 'quickly,' . . .

EADV: brusquement 'abruptly,' clairement 'clearly,' rapidement 'quickly,' de toute évidence 'quite obviously,' . . .

Of course, the meaning of some adverbs allows them to combine with more than one category of elements, in which case they can occupy more than one position. Moreover, I assume, along with Travis (1988), that adverbs are not constrained to attach only to the maximal projection of a given category; she assumes that feature percolation allows an adverb head to "appear anywhere along the projection line of the licensing head" (293). As discussed at length in 4.4.5.1.1.3, I assume a slightly more restricted distribution of adverbs (and adjectives): in a head-initial language such as French and English, an adverb to the left of a projection X^n, which it modifies, can attach only to the head X of that projection in a head-to-head relation, with the semantic effects that this kind of head-to-head relation induces.

Factor 1 is not specific to any language. The fact that the meaning of an adverb determines what it can combine with holds in every language. Furthermore, it would be surprising to find important differences between languages, with respect to the possible classes of adverbs, at least between languages as closely related as French and English. The differences in adverb placement must be because of another factor that distinguishes between these two languages and that interacts with Factor 1 and the Tense-dominated structure in (44) to derive these effects.

Factor 2: T is strong in French, but it is weak in English.

This is similar to Iatridou's (1990) position, except that I have a very different idea of what it means and what effects it has. Iatridou uses strong/weak T in the same way that Pollock (1989) and Chomsky (1991) use strong/weak Agr: only strong T is transparent to assignment of theta roles by a verb. But as we saw in 5.2.2, this is problematic, since it goes counter to what is generally held in morphological analyses, namely, the weaker a head is, the more transparent it is.

I propose that Factor 2 has a more straightforward effect. A strong-T morpheme licenses an independent syntactic node, but a weak-T morpheme does not. In a French sentence such as (49), the strong V+T *mange* licenses two nodes in syntax. The higher node, licensed by the T part of *mange,* binds the lower one, licensed by its V part. The lower node V is not phonetically realized, because its content is already identified by its binder *mange.* In English, on the other hand, the weak V+T *eats* only licenses one node in syntax as in (50).

(49)   Il mange des pommes.

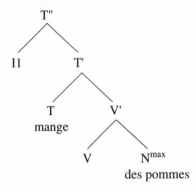

(50)   He eats apples.

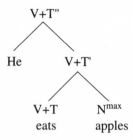

Note that in both cases, the relation between T and V is essentially the same. The requirement that the morphosyntactic element expressing the Moment of Speech—namely, T—must appear as the most prominent head in the syntactic structure is satisfied in both cases; T is a head that takes a V projection as its complement. The only difference between French and English is in the level at which the relation is established—either in syntactic structure for strong T or in morphological structure for weak T. Nothing is added to the theory, since the distinction between the levels of morphology and syntax is already motivated. Moreover, no vagueness is introduced in the Grammar—an element is inserted at the syntactic or the morphological level. This contrasts with how the notion of strong/weak morpheme interacts with theta assignment in the Agr analyses—not only are all sorts of transfers of strength possible, as we saw in 5.2.5 (copying, binding, and inheriting), but there is also nothing to prevent one from postulating different degrees of strength. For example, one could postulate an even stronger Agr than the French one, which would allow a V+NP combination to raise through it, for example, or an Agr of intermediate strength between French and English, which would allow only verbs that are "weak" theta role assigners to go through it (a "weak" theta verb could be defined as a verb with no external role, such as a raising verb or a passive verb). From the point of view of constraining the Grammar, an approach based on levels of insertion is at a definite advantage (provided one does not introduce a host of otherwise unmotivated levels, of course).

5.3.2 ADVERBS IN TENSED CLAUSES

If a VADV is inserted, it will combine with a V projection. In a French sentence such as (51), surface *mange* only realizes the T part of V+T, so a VADV in a head-to-head relationship combines with the lower V, with the result that *mange* precedes the VADV *souvent*.

(51)   Il mange souvent des pommes.

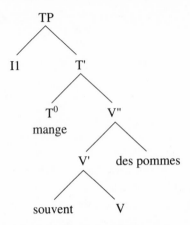

In an English sentence such as (52), surface *eats* realizes the whole of V+T. The combination *eat+s* is the morphosyntactic element expressing the Moment of Speech since it has the T element −*s* as its head. Therefore, *eats* will have to appear as the most prominent head in the syntactic structure in order for its morphological head to head the sentence by transitivity of headedness. A VADV in a head-to-head relationship, such as *often* here, will combine with the V projection V+T, with the result that *eats* follows *often*.

(52)   He often eats apples.

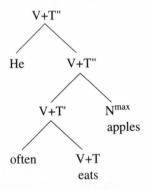

The respective orders V+ADV and ADV+V follow directly from the way of expressing the strong/weak distinction—as a syntactic versus morphological realization of T.[9]

Since Factor 2 is the only language-particular statement in this analysis, it should be responsible for all the differences between French and English, with respect to adverb and NEG placement. For example, by Factor 1, adverbs are able to appear in many positions. Given the head-initial parametric choice of English and French, an adverb can potentially attach to the right of any projection of the category it modifies and to the left of the head in a head-to-head relation, if the result is a possible semantic combination (if it is not incoherent or contradictory). It is indeed the case that there are many positions in the sentence where an adverb can appear (Keyser 1968; Kuroda 1970; Jackendoff 1972; McConnell-Ginet 1982; Ernst 1984; Travis 1988). Thus, a SADV like *probably* or *probablement* can attach to different projections of T and a VADV like *completely* or *complètement* can attach to different projections of V:

(53)a. The tornado probably ruined George.
   b. The tornado probably has ruined George.
   c. The tornado has probably ruined George.
   d. *The tornado has ruined probably George.
   e. The tornado has ruined George, probably.

(54)a. *Jean probablement perd la tête.
     Jean probably loses his mind.
   b. *Jean probablement a perdu la tête.
     Jean probably has lost his mind.
   c. Jean a probablement perdu la tête.
   d. *Jean a perdu probablement la tête.
   e. Jean a perdu la tête, probablement.

(55)a. The tornado completely ruined George.
   b. *The tornado completely has ruined George.
   c. The tornado has completely ruined George.
   d. *The tornado has ruined completely George.
   e. The tornado has ruined George completely.

(56)a. *Jean complètement perd la tête.
     Jean completely loses his mind.
   b. *Jean complètement a perdu la tête.
   c. Jean a complètement perdu la tête.
   d. Jean a perdu complètement la tête.
   e. Jean a perdu la tête complètement.

The contrast between (55a) and (56a), involving VADVs, is expected, given the difference in the strength of T in the two languages, as we saw in

(51) and (52). So is the contrast between (53a) and (54a) and the one between (53b) and (54b). In (53a and b), the SADV *probably* is in a head-to-head relation with the V+T elements *ruined* and *has,* respectively, and everything is fine because these are temporal elements, the kind of elements a SADV combines with. But in (54a and b), the only way to have the SADV *probablement* precede the verb or the auxiliary on the surface is to have the ADV generated in a head-to-head relation with *perd* or *a,* the realizations of T alone. For (54b), for example, this gives us a structure like (57).

(57)   *Jean probablement a perdu la tête.

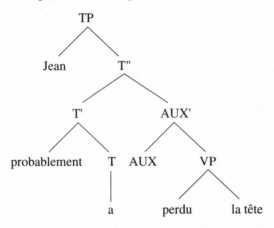

The reason for the ungrammaticality of this sentence is that "pure" T cannot be modified by an adverb in a head-to-head fashion (Recall from the discussion in section 4.4.5.1.1.3 that head-to-head modification implies modification of a subpart of an element, not a whole element). An adverb in this position would have to be modifying a subpart of T, which seems to be impossible. This is presumably because T, the Moment of Speech, is defined with respect to the speaker, and such an element cannot be modified. In this analysis, the contrast between the two languages, with respect to adverbs that precede T, comes from the fact that the adverb in a head-to-head relation modifies T alone in French—which is impossible—whereas it modifies V+T in English. We thus avoid the problem of having to stipulate that English has an extra, pre-INFL position. French cannot put an adverb in that position because T licenses a syntactic node on its own in French and so cannot be modified in a head-to-head relation. That means that, in French, a SADV can only appear as a right-sister to T, as in (58).

(58)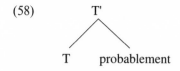

Most of the other cases are fairly straightforward. Both (53d) and (54d) are impossible because the SADV can only be combined with a V-projection in that position, not a T-projection. On the other hand, in (53e) and (54e), the SADV is fine, because it is generated to the right of the T-projection. In (55b) and (56b), the VADV cannot appear to the left of the auxiliary, because it would have to be in a head-to-head relation with AUX+T in English and T in French; since it is a VADV, temporal elements are not the kind of elements it can combine with. Both (55c) and (56c) are fine, because the VADV is in a head-to-head relation with the V; (55e) and (56e) are also fine, since the VADV is generated to the right of the V-projection.

However, things are not as simple in the remaining cases—(53c), (54c), (55d), and (56d). In (53c) and (54c), the SADV is between the auxiliary and the participle. How can that be? One solution is to assume, along the lines of Travis (1988), that the SADV is generated to the right of the X^0 projection of T in French and of V+T in English. The SADV would then be a right sister to T in French and not in a head-to-head relation with it. This combination is not rejected, as was the head-to-head relation in (54a and b), because it is the whole T, not a subpart of it, that is modified.

But this raises the question of why it is that both English and French have such a slot to the right of T ((53c) and (54c)), but only French has one to the right of V ((55d) and (56d)). We could adopt a proposal by Iatridou (1990); discussing the contrast in (59), she suggests, following Di Sciullo and Williams (1987), that one can stipulate that French (and Italian) share the structure in (60), with an extra slot for the adverb, because "the morphological component provides [V Adv] words" (Iatridou 1990, 563).

(59) a.   A peine comprendre l'italien . . .
     a′. To hardly understand Italian . . .
     b.   Comprendre à peine l'italien . . .
     b′. *To understand hardly Italian . . .

(60)

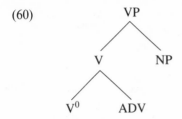

Yet another possibility, she says, is to adopt the idea of Travis (1988) that "some adverbs are heads without maximal projections and can be sisters to the verb. This would imply that *comprendre à peine* in [(59b)] is a sort of complex verb" (Iatridou 1990, 563). But these two options are stipulatory. Moreover, to assume that the sequence VADV forms a verbal complex predicts exactly the opposite of what we found with respect to scope assignment in (18).

Instead of stipulating a different structure, we can derive these effects from the distinction that exists between French and English, with respect to how they generate T. As Lamarche (1990, 1992) observed, given that French has a syntactic T, as in (51), this element will canonically govern or c-command to the right, like all syntactic heads in French. If we assume that, in addition to the requirement that it must establish a semantic relation with the verb, a VADV can attach to V only if it will be within the scope of an element of the tense structure (such as S, R, or E), both sequences VADV + V and V + VADV will be licensed in French. The syntactic head T canonically c-commands the elements in the VP to its right, which will satisfy the scope requirement of the adverb. In English, however, T is only a morphological head, and like all morphological heads in English, it canonically establishes relations toward its left rather than its right. Only the sequence [VADV + V + T] is licensed in English.[10] In both languages, the sequence VADV + PARTICIPLE may be acceptable because the VADV is in the scope of the tense element of the participle (the E____| of (46), which expresses PAST). The reason there is such a temporal scope condition on VADVs may be that such manner adverbs are never exhaustively related to the V alone; "manner of doing" involves tense. Therefore, a VADV must be related to both V and a temporal element—the adverb is related to V by being in a sister relation with it, whereas it is related to a temporal element by being in its scope.

Summarizing, the distribution of adverbs in tensed clauses is highly complex because of the nature of the factors involved. However, there are regularities that do emerge because of the fact that prehead positions are licensed by a head-to-head relation. There is a structural effect to this condition: there is greater transportability of an ADV⁰ than of an adverbial phrase because a head has an additional position that is not accessible to phrasal elements. Only heads can appear in pre-X positions in a head-to-head relation.

(61)a. Paul a retiré sa main prudemment.
         Paul has removed his hand carefully.
    b.   Paul a prudemment retiré sa main.
    c.   Paul a retiré sa main avec précaution.
         Paul has removed his hand with care.
    d.   *Paul a avec précaution retiré sa main.

(62)a. Bill dropped the bananas noisily.
    b.   Bill noisily dropped the bananas.
    c.   Bill dropped the bananas with a crash.
    d.   *Bill with a crash dropped the bananas. (Travis 1988)

There are also semantic effects of two types. First, given that an ADV that appears as a left-sister to a node enters into a head-to-head relation with that node, the semantic combination that results is different from the one obtained when the ADV is a right-sister to the node, since the latter relation is phrase-to-phrase. The differences are often subtle, as we saw in the discussion of parallel adjectival cases in 4.4.5.1.1.3, but tangible, as the contrast in (63) shows.

(63)a. He carefully fixed the car.
    b.   He fixed the car carefully.

In (a), the meaning is that he was careful to fix the car; in (b), the interpretation is that the manner in which he fixed the car was careful.

A second semantic effect is that, since a pre-X position can be occupied only when the ADV enters in a head-to-head relation with the X, such a position is not accessible to an SADV or a VADV whose semantics does not allow it to modify a subpart of X (see 4.4.5.1.1.3 for a similar observation about adjectives). Such an adverb has the distribution of a phrasal adverbial, even though it is alone in its projection. Thus, adverbs like *hier* and *demain,* which cannot modify a subpart of an event, cannot appear in a head-to-head relation with the V expressing the event. That is why they cannot appear in a pre-V position as shown in (64) and (65).

(64)a. *Jean hier a perdu la tête.
         Jean yesterday has lost his mind.

  b. *Jean a hier perdu la tête.
  c. Jean a perdu la tête hier.

(65)a. *Jean demain va rencontrer son patron à la Sorbonne.
      Jean is-going-to tomorrow meet his boss at the Sorbonne.
   b. *Jean va demain rencontrer son patron à la Sorbonne.
   c. Jean va rencontrer son patron à la Sorbonne demain.

The counterpart to such adverbs are adverbs whose semantics allows them to compose only in a head-to-head relation. Thus, whereas a VADV generally appears freely in a pre-V or a VP-final position, as we saw in (55) and (56), some adverbs like *presque, bien, mal,* and *tous* seem to appear only in a Pre-V head-to-head relation. Although one cannot tell whether they were generated in a pre- or post-verbal position in (66a), since the lower V is phonetically empty in French (see (51)), the contrast in (66b and c) indicates that a position other than pre-V head-to-head is not natural for these adverbs.[11]

(66)a. Mes amis comprennent tous/?presque/bien/mal l'explication.
       My friends understand all/almost/well/badly.
   b. Mes amis ont tous/presque/bien/mal compris l'explication.
       My friends have all/almost/well/badly understood.
   c. *Mes amis ont compris tous/presque/bien/mal l'explication.
       My friends have understood all/almost/well/badly.

Why an adverb like *presque* 'almost' must be in a head-to-head relation is fairly clear—its semantics requires it to modify only a subpart of whatever it composes with. Note that *presque* is particularly difficult to get in any position but preparticiple on the surface, as in (66b). There is a sharp contrast between (66b) and the sentences in (67a and b):

(67)a. *Jean presque aime ses voisins.
       Jean almost likes his neighbors.
   b. ??Jean aime presque ses voisins.
       Jean likes almost his neighbors.
   c. Jean aime presque tous ses voisins.
       Jean likes almost all his neighbors.

To understand why (c) is better than (b), we must look beyond the linear order here. In (c), the post-V *presque* is structurally related to *tous,* which it modifies, and is not a VADV. Example (a) is ungrammatical because the VADV *presque* combines with T in that position, but this is an impossible modification. The reason (b) is even marginally acceptable is possibly because, given the ungrammaticality of (a), this is the only way to express a meaning in which *presque* modifies the V. The marginality of the sentence comes from the fact that *presque* must be a head-to-head adverb.

Note, finally, that the possibility of having two adverbs, one on each side of the participle, as in (68) (discussed in note 4 above), does not create problems in the present analysis:

(68)   Marie a été souvent soumise outrageusement à ce genre d'humiliation.
       Marie has been often submitted outrageously to that kind of humiliation.

Here, *outrageusement* is licensed just like the VADV in (56d), whereas *souvent* is licensed as in (56c). On the other hand, an adverb that can only be a SADV like *probablement* cannot appear separated from a T projection:

(69)a.   Marie a probablement été soumise à ce genre d'humiliation.
         Marie has probably been submitted to that kind of humiliation.
    b.   ?*Marie a été probablement soumise à ce genre d'humiliation.

5.3.3 ADVERBS IN INFINITIVAL CLAUSES

Expanding an idea in Chomsky (1957, 1991), who assumes that INFL in infinitival clauses is not an affix, let us assume that there is no T in infinitival clauses, since they are not anchored with respect to the Moment of Speech. Instead of T, I will assume that infinitival clauses contain an element INF (see Kayne 1990, 1991; Hirschbühler and Labelle 1993). Assuming that INF is strong in French (V+INF licenses two nodes in syntax), and weak in English, the structures for infinitival clauses are similar to the ones for tensed claused in (49) and (50) above.

(70)   manger des pommes.

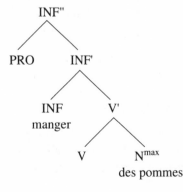

(71)   V+INF"

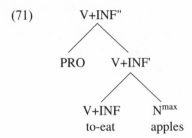

We expect manner adverbs to behave like VADVs in tensed clauses, and indeed they tend not to appear to the left of the infinitival verb or auxiliary in French and tend not to appear to the left of the auxiliary or to the right of the infinitival verb in English:[12]

(72) a. ?*Attentivement lire ce texte vous préparera pour l'examen.
    a'. ?To carefully read this text will prepare you for the exam.
    b. Lire attentivement ce texte vous préparera pour l'examen.
    b'. *To read carefully this text will prepare you for the exam.
    c. *Attentivement avoir lu ce texte vous préparera pour l'examen.
    c'. *To carefully have read this text will prepare you for the exam.
    d. Avoir attentivement lu ce texte vous préparera pour l'examen.
    d'. To have carefully read this text will prepare you for the exam.
    e. Avoir lu attentivement ce texte vous préparera pour l'examen.
    e'. *To have read carefully this text will prepare you for the exam.

This distribution represents a serious problem for Pollock's (1989) analysis. He postulates an Agr node specifically to allow the V in infinitives in French to raise freely above the ADV, which he generates in a position adjoined to VP but not higher than NEG. He attributes the optionality of the V-raising to the fact that there is no T in infinitives, hence, no trigger forcing the movement to a higher position. However, the fact that the infinitival verb must precede the adverb (compare (72a) with (72b)) contradicts this hypothesis. Pollock gives (73) as evidence for the optional raising of the V above *tous.*

(73)a.   On imagine mal les députés *tous* démissionner en même temps.
       One imagines with-difficulty the members-of-parliament ALL resign
       at the same time.
   b.   On imagine mal les députés démissionner *tous* en même temps.

My impression is that *tous* in (73b) forms a constituent with *en même temps,* as in the English *all at the same time.* If so, the relative positioning of the verb and adverb is not free here, either. When *tous* follows the verb, as in

(73b), it does not modify the verb, but what follows *tous*. When *tous* is a VADV, it has to precede the infinitival verb. Recall from the discussion of (66) that adverbs like *tous, presque,* and *bien* are adverbs that must enter into a head-to-head relationship, hence, they must appear to the left of the head they modify. This is confirmed by the following sentences.

(74)a. *Presque* oublier son nom . . .
    To almost forget one's name . . .
  b. ??Oublier *presque* son nom . . .
    To forget almost one's name . . .

(75)a. Ils ne veulent pas *tous* manger de la tarte.
    They do not want all to eat the pie.
  b. ??Ils ne veulent pas manger *tous* de la tarte.
    They do not want to eat all the pie.

(76)a. *Bien* faire ses leçons prépare pour l'avenir.
    Well to-do one's homework prepares for the future.
    To do one's homework well prepare for the future.
  b. *Faire *bien* ses leçons prépare pour l'avenir.

Again, the optionality predicted by Pollock's analysis does not hold here.[13]

However, these sentences also raise a problem for my analysis. Since these VADVs can precede INF in French, we could conclude that the INF of neither the verb nor the auxiliary licenses a separate syntactic node. If it did, a VADV should not be able to attach to it, just as a VADV could not attach to T in French (see the discussion of (51) above). That would mean that INF is weak in French. But then we would lose the account of the sentences in (72). To solve this paradox, recall the reason why these head-to-head adverbs are ruled out in pre-T position in French: it is not possible to modify a subpart of T. But if the nature of INF is different from that of T, maybe it is possible to modify a subpart of INF, in which case, we expect head-to-head adverbs like those in (74)–(76) to appear in pre-INF position.

There are indications that this is indeed the case. If the nature of INF is different from that of T, we do not expect to find exactly the same ADVs combining with INF. Moreover, when an adverb can combine with either T or INF, the meaning of the combination should be slightly different. The latter is extremely difficult to demonstrate, but it is relatively easy to show that the former is correct. For example, it is indeed difficult to combine the adverbs *probably* and *probablement* with INF, whereas we saw it is easy to combine them with T, (53) and (54).

(77)a. *For the tornado to probably ruin John is likely.
   b. *For the tornado to probably have ruined John is likely.
   c. *Ce sera une joie de probablement ruiner Jean.
      It will be a pleasure to probably ruin Jean.

On the other hand, other elements that behave like SADVs in tensed clauses can be combined with INF (Compare these examples with (51) and (52).):

(78)a. ?To often have eaten apples does not guarantee good health.
   b. To have often eaten apples does not guarantee good health.
   c. ?Souvent avoir réussi des examens n'est pas nécessairement un signe de grande intelligence.
   d. Avoir souvent réussi des examens n'est pas nécessairement un signe de grande intelligence.

On the whole, SADVs preceding INF are marginally acceptable. What is interesting is that they seem to be equally acceptable in French as in English, whereas the judgments for pre-T position differed in the two languages. It was absolutely impossible to have an adverb precede a tensed verb or auxiliary in French (54a and b), but it is possible in infinitives, as in (78c). Therefore, it is not surprising that some head-to-head adverbs are fine before infinitival verbs.

Summarizing, the only difference between infinitival clauses and tensed clauses is the presence of INF instead of T. Otherwise, nothing else changes in the analysis. V+INF licenses two syntactic nodes in French, but only one in English. The small differences between infinitives and tensed clauses in French are because of the different nature of INF and T; it is possible to modify INF, but not T, with head-to-head adverbs.

5.3.4 NEGATION IN TENSED CLAUSES

Recall from the discussion of (44) that I assume that sentential negation must have as wide a scope as possible over elements that express predicative content in the structure, except for T, which must be in the highest head position in the sentence. Along the lines of Pollock (1989), I assume that the NEGP of sentential negation must be a complement of T and that sentential NEG must have the PREDVP (the "content" VP) as its complement. The morphosyntactic analysis of strong/weak T predicts that French and English should differ in how they can satisfy the requirements of T and of sentential negation. French can easily satisfy the requirements, since T is generated on its own as sister to NEGP, as in the structure in (79). As indicated, a sentence like (80a) is generated straightforwardly, with the scope marker *ne* inserted as a clitic to the V+T *aime*.

(79)

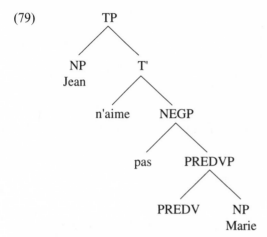

(80)a.   Jean n'aime pas Marie.
    b. *John (not) likes (not) Mary.

(81)a.   Jean n'a pas compris Marie.
    b.   John has not understood Mary.

The V+T in the position of T can bind the V+T in the position of PREDV across the head of NEGP *pas,* assuming some form of relativized minimality where an element like *pas* does not count as a proper binder of such elements.

Sentence (81a) is also derived straightforwardly by generating the AUX+T *a* in the position of T, with a lower AUX projection as its complement (this lower AUX is licensed by the minimal semantic content of the auxiliary. See sections 3.3.1.2 and 3.3.1.3). The lower AUX takes the PREDVP headed by the verb *compris* as its complement. Therefore, the PREDVP is in the scope of NEG.

(82)

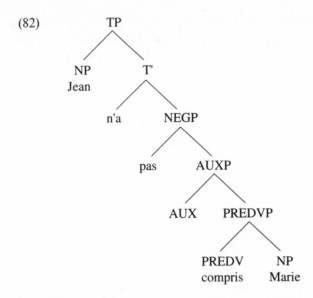

In tensed sentences, one cannot tell whether the NEGP dominates both the AUXP and the PREDVP or just the lower PREDVP, since both options would derive the same surface order. However, we will see in the discussion of negation in infinitives that the former is the appropriate assumption for modern French.

In English, sentence (81b) is even more straightforward. The tense-bearing element *has* licenses a single node and is directly inserted into the T position; the PREDVP headed by *understood* is inserted into the VP slot, so that the requirements of both NEG and T are directly satisfied.

Sentence (80b) with a simple verb in English cannot satisfy the two requirements, however. Since V+T licenses a single node in this case, it is impossible for the PREDV+T to both take NEGP as a complement—as is required of T—and be a complement of NEG—as is required of PREDV. This is why there is *do*-support.

When something forces T to be separated from PREDV in a language where V and T normally are inserted as a unit in syntax, Dummy Verb Support operates as a means of separating T from V, to create an extra node. Thus, in English, the two requirements on NEG and T are satisfied as in (83), where *does* is inserted directly into the position of T and *like* into the head of the PREDVP in structure (79):

(83)   John does not like Mary.

If we look at the whole paradigm of negation in French and in English, shown in (84)–(87), we see that this analysis captures the facts.

(84)a. *Les enfants ne pas lisent cette page.
   b.   Les enfants ne lisent pas cette page.

(85)a. *The kids not read that page.
   b.   The kids did not read that page.
   c. *The kids read not that page.

(86)a. *Les enfants ne pas ont lu cette page.
   b.   Les enfants n'ont pas lu cette page.
   c. *Les enfants n'ont lu pas cette page.

(87)a. *The kids not have read that page.
   b.   The kids have not read that page.
   c. *The kids have read not that page.

The fact that only the (b) sentences are acceptable directly follows from the two requirements on NEG and T: only in the (b) sentences is the element bearing T (or T itself) the head of the sentence, while sentential NEG has the PREDV as its complement. Of course, as the discussion in section 5.2.4 made clear, the judgments given here are for sentential negation. Some of the sentences labeled ungrammatical above ((85b), (86c), and (87c)) are in fact acceptable under an interpretation as constituent negation. This interpretation can be emphasized by the following continuations:

(88)a.   The kids read not that page, but the following one.
   b.   ?Les enfants n'ont lu pas cette page, mais la suivante.
   c.   The kids have read not that page, but the following one.

5.3.5 NEGATION IN INFINITIVAL CLAUSES

Since the scope of sentential negation must be as wide as possible in the sentence, excluding T, and since there is no T in infinitives, sentential negation will always be the most prominent projection, when it appears in infinitives.

(89)

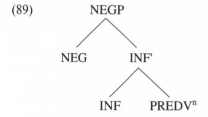

This directly explains why sentences (90b) and (91c) are ungrammatical under sentential negation.

(90)a. Ne pas lire cette page.
   b. *Ne lire pas cette page.

(91)a. Not to read that page.
   b. To not read that page.
   c. *To read not that page.
   d. *To do not read that page.

(92)a. Ne pas avoir lu cette page.
   b. N'avoir pas lu cette page.
   c. N'avoir lu pas cette page.

(93)a. Not to have read that page.
   b. To have not read that page.
   c. To have read not that page.

The analysis predicts that if the negative element is not in the most prominent projection, it will be constituent negation, not sentential negation. This is borne out in English, as we saw in section 5.2.4. First, *not*-contraction is impossible in such cases (see (36) and (38)). Second, everytime an auxiliary precedes (hence, is higher than) NEG in infinitives—as in (93b and c) and even (91b), if one assumes *to* is an auxiliary, as in Postal and Pullum (1982)—the interpretation is that of constituent negation, not sentential negation, as we saw in the discussion of (23), (30), and (33). This also holds for the French sentences with AUX in (92b and c), which are instances of constituent negation.

This analysis also explains why there is no *do*-support in negative infinitives, as in (91d). As discussed in 5.3.4, when a language has V+T licensing only one node, as English does, *do*-support is needed to split T from V. Otherwise, it is impossible to satisfy both the requirement that T be the head of the most-prominent projection in S and the requirement that sentential NEG have scope over categories expressing predicative content. Since there is no T in infinitives, only one of the two requirements has to be satisfied—the one concerning PREDV—so there is no need for a *do*.

With this analysis in mind, consider the following examples from Pollock (1989):

(94)a. Ne pas être heureux est une condition pour écrire des romans.
   Not to be happy is a requirement to write novels.

b. N'être pas heureux est une condition pour écrire des romans.
To be not happy is a requirement to write novels.

(95)a. Ne pas avoir de voiture en banlieue rend la vie difficile.
Not to have a car in the suburbs makes life difficult.
b. *N'avoir pas de voiture en banlieue rend la vie difficile.
To have not a car in the suburbs makes life difficult.

(96)a. Ne pas posséder de voiture en banlieue rend la vie difficile.
Not to own a car in the suburbs makes life difficult.
b. *Ne posséder pas de voiture en banlieue rend la vie difficile.
To own not a car in the suburbs makes life difficult.

Pollock offers (95b) as good, but I have found no one who considers it nearly as good as the auxiliary use of *avoir,* in (92b), or *être,* as in (94b); most speakers judge it closer to (96b). The fact that both orders NEG−AUX and AUX−NEG can be found in French in infinitives, but for lexical verbs, only the order NEG−V is possible, is presented by Pollock as evidence for a distinction between theta-assigning verbs and non-theta-assigning verbs. He argues that, since the functional node above NEG in infinitives is opaque to theta assignment in French, lexical verbs cannot move there, whereas auxiliary verbs are free to raise to that position because they do not assign any theta roles. There are two problems with this "free-raising" analysis of AUX: one is dialectal, the other historical.

5.3.5.1 DIALECTAL VARIATION IN THE DISTRIBUTION OF FRENCH PAS

For some speakers of French, including myself, the NEG can follow the auxiliary, as in (94b), only if it represents constituent negation; here NEG is associated with the following adjective *heureux.* Constituent negation associated with the element to the right of NEG in (95b) and (96b) is much less natural, so the sentences are less acceptable. It is not altogether impossible in a contrastive context, as in (97):

(97)a. N'avoir pas une, mais deux ou trois voitures devrait être l'ambition de tout bon consommateur.
To have not one, but two or three, cars should be the ambition of all good consumers.
b. Ne posséder pas une, mais deux ou trois voitures devrait être l'ambition de tout bon consommateur.
To own not one, but two or three, cars should be the ambition of all good consumers.

We can also see that the NEG is associated with the ADJ in (94b), by the fact that the acceptability of such sentences degrades considerably if the element with which NEG is associated does not allow constituent negation in the absence of a contrastive context (98) or morphophonological reasons, as with the clitic in (99).

(98)a. Je voudrais ne pas être dans cette auto.
        I would like not to be in that car.
   b. *Je voudrais n'être pas dans cette auto.
        I would like to be not in that car.
   c. ?Je voudrais n'être pas dans cette auto, mais sous cette auto.
        I would like to be not in that car, but under that car.

(99)a. Etre heureux ou ne pas l'être, voilà la question.
        To be happy or not to it-be, that is the question.
   b. *Etre heureux ou ne l'être pas, voilà la question.
        To be happy or to it-be not, that is the question.

A NEG that follows an infinitival verb, and that has nothing to its right to allow constituent negation, is also impossible, as the following examples from Pollock (1989) show (his (119)):

(100)a. Les choses que je croyais ne pas exister existent.
         *The things that I thought **ne** not to-exist exist.*
         The things that I thought didn't exist, exist.
    b. *Les choses [que je croyais n'exister pas] existent.
         *The things that I thought **ne** to-exist not exist.*

Note that resorting to the theta nature of the verb will not do here, since a pair of sentences with *être* exhibits the same contrast:

(101)a. Les choses que je croyais ne pas être sont.
         *The things that I thought **ne** not to be are.*
         The things that I thought were not, are.
    b. *Les choses [que je croyais n'être pas] sont.
         *The things that I thought **ne** be not are.*

What all of this means is that some speakers cannot interpret the sequence AUX_{inf} NEG, as in (92b) and (94b), as sentential negation. To maintain Pollock's analysis, we would have to assume that the INF node above NEG must be "super"-opaque: it cannot be the landing site of either theta-assigning lexical verbs or non-theta-assigning auxiliary verbs (or perhaps possibly the node is absent altogether). In my analysis, where sentential negation NEG is assumed to appear as the highest head in infinitives, all these facts follow directly. Since any NEG not in that highest position is an instance of constituent negation, it must have something to its right that it can combine with, to modify.

5.3.5.2 DIACHRONIC CHANGE IN THE STATUS OF NE AND PAS

Pollock's analysis, based on the opacity of Agr, also faces a problem with the diachronic data of French. Until about the end of the seventeenth century, lexical verbs used to appear before or after negative particles freely, as in (102) (see Hirschbühler and Labelle 1993 and references therein).

(102)a.   Ce qui est difficile, c'est de *ne s'abandonner pas* au plaisir de les suivre. (Mme de la Fayette, *La princesse de Clèves* [1678], 94)
          What is difficult is not to abandon oneself to the pleasure of following them.

    b.   . . . , nous fûmes bien malheureux de *ne pas t'emmener.*. (Bergerac, *Voyage* [1655], 127)
          . . . *,we were very unhappy to not take you with us . . .*

One could propose that a change has occurred between the two stages of French: the functional node above NEG in infinitives was transparent to theta-marking in the earlier period and then became opaque (I will henceforth refer to that functional node as the F-node, since there is no consensus on what that node is: T, AgrS, or INF). One would hope to find other changes in the language that correlate with this shift in opacity, otherwise the notion is used as a mere diacritic to identify the stages; this has been attempted by Martineau (1990), Pearce (1991), Roberts (1992), and Dupuis et al. (1992). They all assume that the gradual shift in opacity is related to pronominal features of French verbal inflection and that it has effects on the acceptability of pro-drop and clitic climbing. Assuming that, at the pro-drop stage, the F-node has strong pronominal features, it could be accessible to lexical verbs, if such strong pronominal features allow theta assignment by the verb (although it is still unclear to me why such features should have that effect on theta-role assignment).

But Hirschbühler and Labelle, who analyzed the historical data in detail, observe that the chronological facts do not fit with this proposal:

"[T]he chronology of the changes regarding (1) null subjects, (2) non-finite lexical V to the left vs right of *pas,* (3) the possibility for *pas* to occur or not in between the clitics and the infinitival verb, and (4) clitic climbing with modals, raises real doubts as to the claim that the phenomena just mentioned are related in the sense of being dependent on a unique parameter. By and large, null subjects are gone by the end of the sixteenth century, the *ne V$_{inf}$pas* construction with lexical verbs is out of use by the middle of the eighteenth century, the *ne cl pas V$_{inf}$* construction is still well represented in most of the eighteenth century, with a strong decrease in the last quarter of the century . . . clitic climbing with modals is still found in the eighteenth century, much less so in the nineteenth century. . . . (Hirschbühler and Labelle 1993, 9)

Since pro-drop disappeared well before the *ne V$_{inf}$pas* construction, there is no independent motivation for an analysis on the basis of the assumption that pronominal features determine theta opacity.

In any event, there is good evidence that another change occurred between the two stages of French, and I will argue that this independently motivated property is sufficient to account for the shift from *ne V$_{inf}$pas* to *ne pas V$_{inf}$*. The theta-opacity property is therefore not needed to account for the facts, a good result given the problems with that analysis.

The additional change that took place lies in the status of both *ne* and *pas*. It is not the degree of opacity of the F-node that changed, but rather the very nature of *ne* and *pas*. I argued in 5.3.4 that *ne* is a scope marker in modern French and that *pas* is the negative element. But at an earlier period, *ne* was the negative element and *pas* (along with *point*) was not a negator, but rather a quantifier of a minimal quantity (a very common view in the French grammatical tradition), so that *pas* was able to function as a negative polarity item quantifying on the bare verb (Hirschbühler and Labelle 1993, 17; Muller 1991, 219–20). Hirschbühler and Labelle provide three arguments to that effect. First, up to the end of the sixteenth century, *pas/point* behaved in some respects like other adverbs: for one thing, they could be fronted to clause-initial position.

(103) . . . pas ne travailler, poinct ne me soucier (Rabelais, *Gargantua:* 22)
     p-neg not to work, p-neg not to worry

As they observe, this ability to move suggests that their syntactic status was distinct from what it is in contemporary French.

Second, until the end of the sixteenth century, *ne* was the negator, since it did not need to be associated with an additional element like *pas* or *point* to express negation, as it now does.

(104)a. ce que je ne croy, dit la vieille (Habanc, *Nouvelles Histoires* [1585], 82)
         which I NE believe, said the old+FEM
         which I do not believe, said the old lady

   b.   Tyron . . . lui disoit qu'il avoit grand tort de ne s'accoster d'Angélique (Habanc, 117)
        Tyron . . . him+told that he had great fault to NE get involved with Angélique
        Tyron . . . was telling him that he was wrong not to get involved with Angélique

Third, *pas/point* could occur in questions without *ne* and, hence, were not dependent on its presence:

(105)   Et moy, suis-je dans un bain? suis-je pas plus à mon ayse que toy? (Montaigne, *Essais,* III, 6, in Muller 1991, 225)
        And me, Am I in a bath? Am I in the least more at ease than you?

Here, the form of the question (translated by Muller as 'Suis-je si peu que ce soit plus à mon aise que toi' 'Am I in the slightest amount more at ease than you?'), makes it clear that the expected answer was negative, which shows that *pas* (similarly with *point*) functioned, at the time, as a negative polarity item (Muller 1991: 225). (Hirschbühler and Labelle, 17)

It seems clear, therefore, that, while *ne* is a scope marker and *pas* is a negator in contemporary French, *ne* was a negator and *pas* a quantifier of minimal quantity at this earlier period of French. Since the status of *ne* and *pas* is so different at the two stages of French, their position in the structure can also be assumed to be different. They do not have the same dynamic relations: *ne* heads the NEGP and the adverb *pas* modifies either the PREDVP or the INF in Middle French, but *ne* is a scope marker and *pas* heads the NEGP in contemporary French.[14]

(106)   *Middle French:*

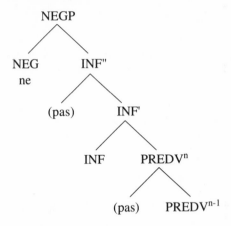

(107)   *Contemporary French:*

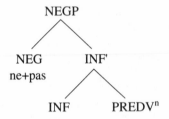

There are two possible orders in structure (106): the order *ne V_{inf} pas* is derived if adverbial *pas* is attached to PREDV, and the order *ne pas V_{inf}* is derived if *pas* is attached to INF. Both were found in Middle French. The *ne pas V_{inf}* order of contemporary French derives from the structure in (107). The switch from one order to the other results from the change in status of *ne* and *pas,* which causes a change in their positions.

This solves the problem of accounting for the distribution of lexical infinitival verbs with respect to *ne* and *pas.* We are left with the problem of modals and the auxiliary verbs *avoir* and *être.* As we can see in figure 5.1 (from Hirschbühler and Labelle, 8), at about the end of the seventeenth century, lexical verbs were appearing nearly 85% of the time in the modern construction *ne pas V_{inf}.* But there is a time lag of two centuries between lexical verbs and modals. "In contemporary spoken French, as well as non-archaic writing styles, modals are assimilated to main verbs, i.e., they do not appear to the left of *pas* in infinitival clauses. From figure 1, it can also be seen that in 1950,

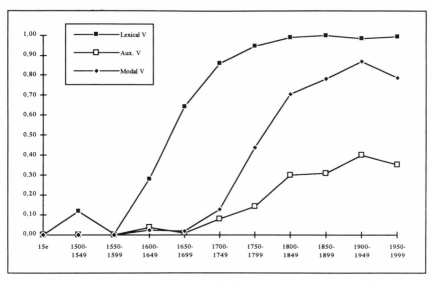

FIGURE 5.1 Evolution of the modern construction. Source: Hirschbühler and
Labelle 1993, 8.

the 85% level had not been reached for auxiliaries, more or less a century
after a similar level has been reached for modals" (Hirschbühler and Labelle
1993, 4). Since the shift for auxiliaries has only recently approached comple-
tion, it is expected that there will be some discrepancies among speakers.
Thus, we saw in the discussion of (94)–(96) above that while Pollock gives the
order *ne AUX$_{inf}$pas* and *ne pas AUX$_{inf}$* as relatively free, many speakers, including myself, only accept the order *ne pas AUX$_{inf}$* for sentential negation.

How could the lag between lexical verbs, modals and auxiliary verbs have
arisen? In the present analysis, the position of *ne* and *pas* with respect to
these three verbal elements depends on two things: the position of *ne* and *pas*
themselves; and the condition on sentential negation, which says that the
element marking sentential negation must have scope over categories expressing predicative content, but not over T.

In the stage of French that has the structure as in (106), where *ne* is the
head of NEGP and *pas* is an adverb, the condition on sentential negation is
satisfied whenever *ne* precedes V, modal and AUX. The order of these elements with *pas* does not depend on the condition on sentential negation,
since *pas* is not a negator at that stage of French. With the shift from structure (106) to structure (107), lexical infinitival verbs, which clearly have predi-

cative content, must follow *pas* in order to be in its scope. Modals did not shift at the same time as lexical verbs because modals did not originally count as having the relevant kind of content. They gradually came to have the kind of content that forced them to be under the scope of NEG, presumably because the notion of "content" in the condition on sentential negation was gradually relaxed. As for auxiliary verbs, it is natural to assume that their gradual alignment with the other classes of verbs, with respect to the condition on sentential negation, was slower, because they are less contentful.

Summarizing, the analysis put forward here is based mainly on a shift in the nature and position of *ne,* from NEG to scope marker, and of *pas,* from quantifier of minimal quantity to negator. A second factor, which accounts for the slower change of modals and AUXs in figure 1, is the nature of the "content" in the condition on sentential negation. Over time, this notion became more and more relaxed and encompassing, going from the content of lexical verbs to that of modals, to that of AUXs, thereby gradually extending the elements over which NEG must have scope.[15]

5.3.6 SUMMARY OF THE MORPHO-SYNTACTIC ANALYSIS

In this section, I have argued that under the morpho-syntactic account of the distribution of adverbs and negation in French and English that I propose, four basic assumptions are sufficient to account for the data. Two of these assumptions are not new, they have been defended by other people and are practically inescapable in any analysis, since they depend on very basic properties of adverbs and sentential negation. (1) First, it is the semantics of an adverb that determines what it can modify and therefore what it can attach to and whether head-to-head relations are possible; this explains why there is so much variation in their distribution. (2) The NEG of sentential negation must be under the scope of T and must take "content" VPs in its scope. I added the third assumption that T is the head of the sentence because it corresponds to the Moment of Speech that anchors the Tense of a sentence. These assumptions are so basic that it would be surprising to see any parametric variation at that level. Therefore, to account for the variation between English and French, I made a fourth assumption: V+T (and V+INF) is either strong and licenses two nodes in syntax, or it is weak and licenses only one syntactic node. French has a strong T, whereas English has a weak T.

Given these assumptions, we get the following answers to the four questions about the distribution of adverbs and negation in French and English, raised in section 5.1.

Question (A): Why do adverbs precede tensed verbs in English but follow them in French?

Answer: SADVs and VADVs modify the T or the V, respectively, in a head-to-head relation when they precede them. In English, since V+T is only one syntactic head, these adverbs will precede it. In French, V+T licenses two syntactic nodes: the upper node is a T-node, the lower one a V-node. The VADV may appear in a head-to-head relation with the V-node, thus following V+T. An SADV cannot enter into a head-to-head relation with "pure" T, so it will be in a phrase-to-phrase relation with a projection of T, and follow V+T.

Question (B): Why can the adverb follow an AUX in both languages?

Answer: In both languages, a VADV can appear in pre-VP position in the scope of the tense element of the participle; additionally, in French, a VADV can appear as a right-sister of the participle because the VADV is in the scope of a syntactic T-node. An SADV is generated to the right of the AUX+T in French; since it cannot enter into a head-to-head relationship with a T-node, the SADV cannot precede the AUX in French. In English, the SADV may be generated to the right of the temporal complex AUX+T. There is no need to postulate an additional position in the structure for pre-AUX adverbs in English: an SADV in that position is in a head-to-head relation with the complex AUX+T. The position is there in French, but it is not usable, since it requires an ungrammatical head-to-head modification of "pure" T.

Question (C): Why is there *do*-support in negative sentences in English but nothing like it in French?

Answer: Dummy verb support takes place when something forces weak T to be separated from the V; a dummy verb is then inserted as a morphological support for the Tense affix. Since V+T licenses a T-node, in addition to a V-projection in French, no dummy verb support is required. In English, the conflicting requirements of NEG and T force morphological T to be separated from the V. The answer to Question (D), which is about *do*-support in interrogatives, is the subject of the next subsection.

5.4 INVERSION IN INTERROGATIVES

In order to determine why *do*-support sometimes occurs in interrogatives, we have to understand precisely the structure and meaning of those sentences. Before turning to the English data in section 5.4.2, I will discuss the assumptions I make about what triggers inversion in interrogatives (section 5.4.1). In section 5.4.3, I apply the analysis to inversion in French.

5.4.1 SOME THEORETICAL ASSUMPTIONS

I make two basic assumptions that are fairly uncontroversial and that account for the inversion data when coupled with the morpho-syntactic analysis presented in the previous sections.

5.4.1.1 INVERSION AS T IN COMP

First, I assume that inversion in interrogatives is akin to having movement to COMP. This immediately explains the observation of Goldsmith (1981) that this kind of inversion takes place only in matrix clauses, since COMP is filled in embedded clauses. Goldsmith gives a list of contexts where inversion takes place (The French sentences, except for (109c), translate fairly directly into the English ones):[16]

(108) *Contexts for Inversion in English:*
    a.   Yes/no: Did Mary see it?
    b.   Wh-Q: Where did John go?
    c.   NEG-like ADVs: Seldom/never did John go.
    d.   *If*-like: Had John five minutes to himself, he would rush to the pool.
    e.   Exclamations: Is she ever pretty!

(109) *Contexts for Inversion in French:*
    a.   Yes/no: Marie l'a-t-elle vu?
    b.   Wh-Q: Où Jean est-il allé?
    c.   Matrix-initial ADVs: Aussi/peut-être Jean y est-il allé.
                        Thus/maybe Jean went there.
    d.   *If*-like: Jean avait-il cinq minutes de libre qu'il filait à la piscine.
    e.   Exclamations: Est-elle belle!

It is standardly assumed, following Baker (1970), that in yes/no and Wh-questions there is a CP dominating the sentence, with a Q element in its COMP⁰ head; the Wh-phrase is in the Spec of this Q-COMP. Under this view, inversion could be seen as T-to-COMP movement because of some need of T (some counterpart of my assumption that it needs to be the highest head). To account for the other inversion contexts, it would be easy, under this analysis, to posit a different COMP element, perhaps CONDI (a conditional element) for (108d) and (109d) and EXCL (an exclamation element) for (108e) and (109e). In each case, the presence of the CP would then force

T to move. I will not adopt such an analysis, for two reasons. First, the content of such elements as Q (and CONDI and EXCL, which I just suggested) is entirely undefined. Second, this analysis ignores the fact that structure includes meaning. The very fact that T precedes the rest of the sentence in the inverted forms means that it is in a different position structurally. This structural difference may well be responsible for the different illocutionary force of the inversion sentences.

I will assume that this is the case. A structure with a T that has greater scope than usual, dominating even the subject, has a special illocutionary force. Since T anchors the sentence to the speaker, because the Moment of Speech in T is defined with respect to the speaker, giving broader scope to T is like focusing on that relation. I assume that this very focusing is what induces the special illocutionary force of these sentences.

The structure in these constructions, therefore, must minimally have a T-node generated in a position external to the noninverted sentence, abbreviated here as S, as shown in (110).

(110)

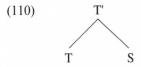

5.4.1.2 COMPLEX INVERSION AS DOUBLE CASE MARKING

Complex Inversion, as in (111), occurs when a clitic pronoun appears postverbally and copies the features of the preverbal subject. It shares properties with Spanish clitic doubling, as in (112).

(111)   Jean vient-il?
         Jean comes-he?
         Is Jean coming?

(112)   La vio a Maria.
         Her saw to Maria.
         I saw Maria.

In both (111) and (112), there is double Case-marking. In the Spanish example, Kayne (1984) assumes that a "doubling" clitic is possible because Spanish has the preposition *a,* which can be inserted to assign a second Case to the NP *Maria.* I will assume instead that it is the other way around. Spanish marks its animate complements with the Case assigning preposition *a.* The V does not assign its Case to this NP complement, and the "doubling" clitic must be inserted to realize the Case of the verb. I assume that something very similar takes place in French Complex Inversion. Because there is a T in a position external to S that binds a T in its regular position internal to S, there are two positions from which Case is assigned by T. The postverbal clitic is inserted to realize the additional Case.

In the next two sections, I examine the inversion data in both languages, although I do not look at all the contexts in (108) where inversion is found. In English, I use Wh-questions to illustrate the analysis of inversion, but I use yes/no questions in French, to avoid interference from Stylistic Inversion.

5.4.2 INVERSION IN ENGLISH

(113)a.   What did he leave?
     b.   What did John leave?

(114)a. *What left he?
     b. *What left John?

(115)a.   What has he left?
     b.   What has John left?

(116)a. *What does he have left?
     b. *What does John have left?

First, we see that whether or not the subject is pronominal makes no difference in the inversion facts, in English. Thus, (114a) is as bad as (114b). Moreover, as shown in (117), English has nothing equivalent to the Complex Inversion of French (111); it is ungrammatical to have a postverbal pronominal copy of the subject as an alternative to the inversion of the subject.

(117)a. *What John did he/it/there leave?
     b. *What John has he/it/there left?

As the examples in (114) show, focusing of a V+T complex is ungrammatical. I assume that this is because the external T-node must be a pure T-node, with no predicative content; presumably, only focusing of pure T provides the desired illocutionary force. Therefore, *do* must be inserted, as in (113), to separate the content of V from T.[17] Moreover, since *did* is the element bearing T, it must appear in the highest head position, external to the regular sentence, to obtain the proper illocutionary force.

From these assumptions, we derive (118) as the structure for (113b).

(118)

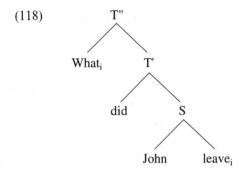

The Wh-phrase *what* appears in the highest Spec because it must be related to the highest T, the one expressing the proper illocutionary force (reinterpreting Baker's (1970) use of the Q-morpheme). *John* can appropriately receive Case from the sole nominative Case assigner, *did,* since this T element has a phonological base and can govern *John,* by minimality.[18] All of this is achieved directly, without movement.

The same analysis can be assumed for sentences with an auxiliary, such as (115). Since the auxiliary itself separates T from the PRED-V, there is no need for *do.* Everything follows as above, with the auxiliary playing the role that *do* assumed in (113). The AUX provides a base for T, and no dummy verb needs to be inserted; the examples in (116) are ungrammatical. Finally, Complex Inversion, as in (117), is not possible, because it requires a double assignment of Nominative Case, but there is only one Nominative-Case marker in the sentence.

An interesting question is why there is no *do*-support in a sentence where the subject is Wh-questioned:

(119)a.   Who went to New York?
   b.   *Who did go to New York? (with nonemphatic *did*)
   c.   Who has gone broke?

I will adopt a solution along the lines of George (1980) and Chomsky (1985b, 48), who assume that, in constructions with "vacuous movement," the Wh-subject appears in subject position rather than in Spec of COMP. Under my analysis, this means that Wh-phrases are not required to be in Spec of the external T-node, presumably because they have sufficient features to indicate the illocutionary force on their own. Suppose the requirement is that a Wh-phrase with interrogative illocutionary force must be in the highest Spec of the sentence. A Wh-phrase in subject position already satisfies this requirement; on the other hand, Wh-phrases other than the subject will need the extra structure created by an external T-node, in order to satisfy the requirement. When the Wh-phrase is in subject position, there is neither an external T-node nor the additional structure that comes with it. Therefore, there is no need to have the AUX in a position other than its usual one or to have T separated from the PREDV by *do* support. This explains the contrast between the subject Wh-questions in (119) and the object Wh-questions in (113)–(116).[19]

5.4.3 INVERSION IN FRENCH

Turning to French, we see that there are two kinds of inversion (again, setting aside Stylistic Inversion)—Clitic Inversion, where a clitic subject is inverted with the T-bearing element, as in (120a) and (122a); and Complex Inversion, where nonpronominal subject NPs are not inverted, but rather a pronominal clitic with the same person and number features as the subject appears post-verbally, as in (121a) and (123a).

(120)a.   Part-il?
          Leaves he?
     b.   *Part Jean?
          Leaves Jean?

(121)a.   Jean part-il?
          Jean leaves he?
     b.   *Il part-il?
          He leaves he?
     c.   *Il part Jean?
          He leaves Jean?

(122)a.   Est-il parti?
          Is he left?
          Has he left?
     b.   *Est Jean parti?
          Is Jean left?

(123)a.   Jean est-il parti?
          Jean is he left?
          Has Jean left?
     b.   *Il est-il parti?
          He is he left?
     c.   *Il est Jean parti?
          He is Jean left?

   In French, T is a strong morpheme, so V+T licenses two nodes in syntax.
The higher one is a pure T-node, and the lower one is a PREDV node. In
order to obtain the desired illocutionary force, there must be a way for T to
have greater scope than usual. A pure T-node is therefore introduced, which
takes the regular sentential structure as its complement, just as in English. If
we simply add this external T-node to the regular sentence structure of
French, we get the structure in (124), where T_1 is the added external T-node
and T_2 is the regular T-node internal to the sentence.

(124)

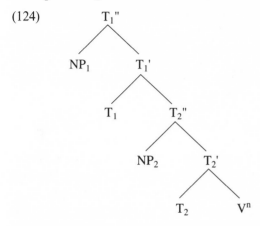

However, this structure is not quite correct, as we will see directly.
   As discussed in 3.1.3, the external argument must be related to T. Since
there are two T-nodes in (124), there are two positions in which an external
argument could possibly appear, indicated by NP_1 and NP_2. Since there is
only one subject argument in the semantic representation, only one subject-
NP position can be licensed in the syntax, by Homomorphic Mapping. I
assume that the subject is base-generated in NP_1 and that the position labeled
NP_2 is absent from the structure. The reason for this is that the positions of
NP_1 and NP_2 are not equal; NP_2 cannot be assigned Case. The external
T-node (T_1) cannot assign Case to NP_2 because the lower T_2 is a more local
Case marking element for NP_2. The other potential Case marking element is
the internal T-node (T_2). But if we assume that the external and internal
T-nodes form a chain, by binding (since only one Tense is present in the
semantics of the sentence), and that canonical Case assignment can only
involve an element that is the specifier of the whole T-chain (where "specifier" is seen as a relation with the chain, not as a position, since, in a positional view of the specifier, it cannot be a specifier of a chain, but rather of

a particular node), then NP_2 cannot get Case because the presence of the external T-node means that NP_2 is not the Spec of the whole chain.[20] On the other hand, the subject may appear in NP_1, since that position specifies the whole T-chain. I therefore adopt the structure in (125).

(125)

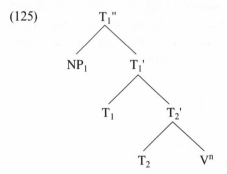

An NP in the position of NP_1 gets Case from the external T-node, satisfying its Case requirements. But a problem remains: there are two Case markers in (125), the external and internal T-nodes. Therefore, there must be an element that realizes the Case of the second Case marker, the internal T-node. However, we just saw that there is no position that can be licensed in which to put a Case-bearing NP. This is why the clitic appears; a clitic is a Case-bearing element that does not occupy an NP position. It is realized in the position of T and is cliticized to the phonetic realization of T in the external T-node. This is similar to the case of Spanish clitic doubling discussed in (112).

I assume that clitic pronouns in French never occupy an NP position, even when the clitic is argumental, as in *Il part* 'He leaves' or *Jean le regarde* 'Jean looks at him.' Full Identification and Homomorphic Mapping do not require the clitic to be related to a position. Combining CL+V essentially has the effect of chunking as in 2.2.1. In this case, too, a position present in the Semantic Representation is absent from syntax because it is recoverable from the lexical specifications of an element in the sentence—the verb in the cases we looked at in 2.2.1, the combination CL+V in the present case.

A sentence like (126) might seem to cause a problem because the Wh-phrase *quand* will also have to appear in the Spec of Q+T in (125) (see Kayne 1983; Rizzi and Roberts 1989).

(126)   Quand Jean part-il?
          When Jean leaves-he?
          When is Jean leaving?

But in the present approach, nothing restricts the number of complements or specifiers of a given head, except semantic combination (again, if we view these as relations, not positions). Since an argument subject and a Wh-phrase have very different relations with the head, there is no problem in having both there. The Wh-phrase presumably must have scope over the whole sentence because of the properties of illocutionary force that it has when in sentence-initial position, so it appears higher than the subject.

We now have an account of the placement of *Jean* in initial position in a sentence like (121a) and of the need for clitic doubling. The same account will hold for (123a), the only difference being that it is the AUX+T that appears in T_1 instead of V+T. Examples (120b), (121c), (122b), and (123c), with an inverted nonpronominal NP *Jean,* are ungrammatical because no Case can be assigned to *Jean* in that position.

Now consider subject clitics. As we saw above, a post-V or post-AUX clitic, as in (120a) and (122a), gets Case from T_2. However, (121b) and (123b), where there are two clitics, are both ungrammatical. Why should this be? Why should not the initial *il* in these sentences be licensed in the same way as *Jean* is in (121a) and (123a)? Kayne (1984, 216) accounts for the impossibility of two clitics here by assuming that a chain can bear only one overt morphological Case. However, it seems a bit odd that the Case on the clitic *il* counts for this constraint but not the Case on an NP like *Jean.* Kayne seems to be on the right track, but he misses one critical point—clitics and NPs are licensed differently. A clitic has to be attached to a head, and an NP does not. Capitalizing on this distinction, I propose to account for the data with the Two-Identical-Clitic constraint:

(127) *Two-Identical-Clitic Constraint (TIC):* A verb cannot bear two clitics which are identical in syntactic features.

This constraint precludes two clitics *il* from appearing on the same verb. Independent facts supporting the TIC are given in (128).

(128)a. Jean me lui a fait raconter cette histoire.
         Jean me to-him has made tell that story.
         Jean made me tell him that story.
     b. *Jean lui lui a fait raconter cette histoire (*nous nous, *me me
         . . .)[21]
         Jean him to-him has made tell that story (us to-us, me to-me)
     c. Nous nous voyons souvent.

We us see often.
We see each other often.

While it is possible to have two dative clitics on the same verb as long as they are not of the same person as in (128a), two identical clitics are out in (128b). Two phonologically identical clitics of the same person can appear on the same verb, provided they do not bear the same Case (128c).

Given the evidence for the TIC, we have an explanation for the absence of clitic doubling when the subject is a clitic. On the other hand, this means that, in sentences (120a) and (122a) where a single clitic appears, this clitic must bear two cases. Since the clitic does not occupy a NP position, but simply realizes the Case on the verb, this might not be so problematic, after all.[22]

As for sentences where the subject is Wh-questioned, the *in situ* analysis of these "vacuous movement" constructions proposed for the English examples in (119) above correctly predicts that there should be no inversion of the clitic subject or doubling of the full NP in French; the Wh-phrase is in the "normal" subject position, there is no external T-node, and Case is assigned only once.

(129)a. Qui part?
         Who leaves?
     b. *Qui part-il?
     c. Qui est parti?
         Who is left?
         Who has left?
     d. *Qui est-il parti?

On the other hand, nothing I have said so far explains why, when there is a full-NP subject and the direct object is questioned, clitic doubling, as in (130b), is not possible and Stylistic Inversion is required, as in (130c).

(130)a. Que fait-il?
         What does he?
         What is he doing?
     b. *Que Jean fait-il?
     c. Que fait Jean?

In fact, the problem only arises when the direct object is *que*. When the Wh-phrase is a full, nonpronominal NP, as in (131), Complex Inversion is fine:

(131)   Quel travail Jean fait-il?
         What work Jean does he?
         What work does Jean do?

This suggests that the problem with (130b) is not caused by clitic doubling, but by *que*. *Que* here is a pronominal clitic, the clitic counterpart of *quoi*, and following the same pattern as *me/moi* and *te/toi*, the clitic and strong forms of the first and second person pronouns (as argued by Goldsmith 1978; Hirschbühler 1979; and Bouchard and Hirschbühler 1986; and contrary to Obenauer 1976 and Koopman 1982, who claim that it is a complementizer). As a clitic, it must be next to the verb, so the subject *Jean* is generated postverbally under Stylistic Inversion.

Given my analysis of clitic doubling in Complex Inversion, the postverbal clitic in (132) is only a realization of Case, not some kind of agreement element. But each of the clitics appears to be manifesting the same person and number features as the subject.

(132) a. Jean part-*il?*
Jean leaves he?
Is Jean leaving?

    b. Jean est-*il* venu?
Jean is he come?
Did Jean come?

    c. Toi et moi allons-*nous* enfin finir ce travail?
You and I go we finally to-finish that work?
Are you and I finally going to finish that work?

Following the analysis of Bouchard (1984a), I would say that the only reason the clitics in (132) have features of person, number, and gender is that this is forced upon them by the Principle of Lexicalization:

(133) *Principle of Lexicalization:* A noun N will be lexicalized if and only if φ-features are present in the entry of N at PF, where φ = person, number, gender, Case.

"Informally, what this principle says is that a lexical noun must have all φ-features at PF, i.e., person, number, gender, Case, whereas a non-lexical noun, i.e., an empty category, must not have any of these features at PF" (Bouchard 1984a, 41). Therefore, since the nominal clitic is a realization of Case in the examples in (132), it must also bear the other minimal φ-features required by the Principle of Lexicalization. I assume that the clitic is coindexed with T_2, because it is the realization of the nominative Case of T_2, and that the full NP is coindexed with T_1 to get its Case. Since T_1 and T_2 are coindexed, all four elements (T_1, T_2, the clitic, and the full NP) share an index. For reasons of coherence in interpretation of the indices, agreement takes place, as discussed in section 3.1.3. However, the coherent interpretation of the indices here is not induced by coreference, because the clitic is not in an argument position—it is only a realization of Case and is not referential. That is why the agreement in inversion involves only the minimal φ-features of person, number, and gender required by (133), in addition to Case, and not some additional features found with some NPs when agreement is because of coreference. For example, (134) shows that it is the clitic *ce,* not the clitic *il,* that pronominalizes *cela,* yet *il,* not *ce,* is the clitic in Complex Inversion (135). This is because agreement due to coherence under coreference requires the presence of demonstrative feature of *ce,* whereas agreement in inversion only requires the minimal features of *il.*

(134) a. Cela, c'est très important.
        That, that is very important.
     b. *Cela, il est très important.
        That, it is very important.

(135) a. Cela est-il très important?
        That is it very important?
        Is that very important?
     b. *Cela est-ce très important?
        That is that very important?
        Is that very important?

A similar argument can be made with *personne* 'no one.' *Personne* cannot be pronominalized by *il* (136a), yet *il* doubles *personne* in Complex Inversion (136b).

(136) a. *Personne, il ne voudrait m'aider.
        No-one, he would like to help me.
     b. Personne ne voudrait-il m'aider?
        No-one would-want he me help?
        Would anyone want to help me?

Data from vernacular French support aspects of the analysis of inversion in standard French presented here. For instance, many idioms of French have developed a totally unmarked form *ti* or *tu* that replaces the agreeing clitic of the Complex Inversion of standard French. *Ti* or *tu* is used as a question marker and derives diachronically from *t-il.* This element *ti* or *tu* does not agree with the subject and can appear even with clitic subjects, since this does not constitute a case of identical clitics on the verb; this supports the analysis on the basis of the TIC. The following examples from Quebec French illustrate this:

(137)a. Marie a-tu vu ce film-là?
　　　 Marie has INTERROG *seen that movie there*
　　　 Has Marie seen that movie?
　 b. Elle a-tu mangé?
　　　 She has INTERROG *eaten*
　　　 Has she eaten?

In this dialect, the complementizer *que* is present in Wh-questions, and there is no inversion in interrogatives:

(138)a. Quand que Jean vient?
　　　 When that Jean comes
　　　 When is Jean coming?
　 b. *Quand que Jean vient-il?
　 c. Quand qu'il vient?
　　　 When that he comes
　　　 When is he coming?
　 d. *Quand que vient-il?

In this case, interrogative illocutionary force is not expressed by an external T-node, but by a particle on T (137) or by the Wh-phrase itself in a Spec external to S (138). This supports my "vacuous movement" analysis of subject Wh-questions in (119): Wh-phrases are not required to be in Spec of an external T-node, because they have sufficient features to indicate the illocutionary force on their own. Neither Complex Inversion nor Clitic Inversion are well formed, as in (138b) and (138d), because they both require an external T-node, which is absent in this construction.

Summarizing this section on inversion, I assume that a pure T-node, external to S, is introduced to express interrogative illocutionary force in standard French and in English. The effects are different in the two languages because the initial structure is different. In English, this means that weak T must be separated from V, which accounts for the existence of *do*-support. In French, interrogatives end up with two T-nodes; therefore, there are two Nominative Case assigners and an extra clitic pronoun is present to realize the additional Case.

5.5 CONCLUSION

At the outset of this chapter, I indicated that recent analyses of the distribution of adverbs and NEG are incompatible with two central tenets of the theory developed in this book. First, since I am trying to restrict the transformational component to Homomorphic Mapping, an alternative had to be found to head movement of V to T because it is not a sufficiently restricted operation. Second, a contentless Functional Category such as Agr is not licensed by Full Identification, so I argued that we must make do without such categories. In the course of developing an alternative analysis, I showed that an analysis on the basis of Agr is, in fact, descriptively inadequate. Crucial to the discussion was the fact that it is not linear or structural positions that license such elements as adverbs and NEG, but the relation that they hold with other elements. Positions only predict where an element can appear, not what relation it holds or what its interpretation is, so an analysis on the basis of positions only is inadequate from a descriptive point of view. For example, I showed that it is not sufficient to predict where NEG can appear; whether it receives a sentential or constituent interpretation must also be determined. Similarly, an adverb receives different interpretations, depending on what it relates to.

To account for the difference between French and English, with respect to adverb and NEG placement, I proposed a different interpretation of the notion of strong/weak morpheme. A strong morpheme licenses a syntactic node on its own, so French V+T licenses two syntactic nodes because T is strong; a weak morpheme, such as English T, does not license its own node, so V+T in English licenses only one syntactic node. The differences in adverb and NEG placement between the two languages follow from the fact that the element with which an adverb or NEG can establish a relation is not the same in French and in English because the strong and weak morphemes derive different structures. Since the relations are different, the distribution is predicted to differ.

Afterword

This work is a study of the relation between syntax and semantics. The central point is that one cannot study syntax without looking deeply into semantics, and vice versa. The problem with avoiding semantics is that one is liable to be doing a disguised form of semantics in syntax, with the risk that the results will be unsatisfactory, because the semantics is not directly addressed.

As for studying semantics without syntax, the danger is that one will not focus on strictly linguistic facts, for example, in borrowing from nonlinguistic systems, like logic. This can be especially counterproductive when the system adopted is fundamentally different from the task of linguistics. For example, if this other system is not mentalist and does not recognize the importance for the language capacity, of the interaction with general cognition, there is a danger that nonlinguistic notions, such as the size of trees or clouds or the fact that rocks do not sleep, will find their way into the theory. A similar problem arises if the approach is mentalist, but also global, in the sense that it incorporates into Grammar elements from background knowledge. Theories that require such information are far too concrete and "involve elements that are really playing no explanatory role and that we should try to eliminate as we seek to discover what is really doing the work of explanation" (Chomsky 1985a, 255–56).

If one does take into account the shared knowledge on which language is built and purges Grammar of these notions, a more abstract theory emerges, uncluttered by situational notions. Such a theory can better capture the meaning of lexical elements and the constraints that hold across their uses (Chapter 3). As well, a much simpler linking on the basis of homomorphy, Full Identification, and endocentricity can be assumed, one that is not stipulated, but rather derives from the architecture of the theory. Such a theory also makes for a more restrictive Grammar, where all nodes in syntax and in semantics are subject to accountability. This means that movement analyses making use of "open" positions must be rejected because such positions are not licensed. Only the chunking transformation is maintained, because it is in the domain of virtual necessity.

In the first case study, on NP movement in Psych constructions (chapter 4), I found that Psych constructions are not structurally special in any way, and no movement transformation is required. The peculiar properties that they do have derive from the special nature of their "mental" arguments. In the second case study, on verb raising (chapter 5), I found that the Agr node was unlicensed and had to be dropped. The notion of strong/weak was also too vague. Instead, I proposed an analysis that makes use of a more central aspect of the Grammar, namely the distinction between the levels of syntax and morphology. The analysis provides a more accurate account of the placement of adverbs and negation; agreement facts of various sorts are also brought into line, including some cases of agreement that an Agr analysis is incapable of accounting for, in principle.

The search for an alternative analysis forced me to look at the data in more detail and under a different light in both cases. This proved to be worthwhile, since the analyses that emerge are more comprehensive and less stipulatory than the existing analyses, which do not obey the stringent constraints set on the Grammar by the abstract theory adopted here. Of course, much work still remains: there are numerous constructions that, under the conditions proposed here, would be given a different analysis from that of standard generative grammar. Whether this abstract theory can deal with these constructions appropriately remains to be seen, but the results of the case studies presented in this book convince me that it is a worthwhile task to carry on with the work and that the enterprise will prove to have been useful in the end.

Notes

Chapter One

1. One of the rare examples in recent studies where this distinction between knowledge and meaning is carefully taken into account is Franckel and Lebaud (1990). However, they do not study the effects of this distinction on the correspondence with syntactic form, which is the main preoccupation of this book.

2. Moreover, many linguists who study semantic matters in depth have also been critical of a logic-based approach to semantic theory because it requires a kind of intellectual boot-strapping. For example, Richard Carter comments: "People tend to use expressions like "two-place predicate" as if their meaning was clear, and as if these were inevitable notions in any system of semantic description, in any semantic theory. I don't see why we should assume this. This notion, and most others familiar from logic and philosophy, are in fact rather transparently derived from syntactic notions of natural language. We understand them at all, I think, only in that we can analogize to constructions from our own language as we read them: they are essentially parasitic" (Carter 1988, 236). The idea that notations in formal logic are essentially parasitic and boil down to translations of superficial structures of natural languages is also found in Fauconnier (1977) and Ruwet (1982).

3. Many examples of logic-based analyses of linguistic phenomena illustrate the danger of falling prey to the trappings of a rigorous and powerful formalism. One can get caught in the internal details of the theory and lose contact with what it is a theory of, namely, linguistic reality. The following comment from Serres (1977, 57), is very apropos: "The so-called experimental sciences were rigorous before being exact. They did not suffer from a lack of mathematics, but an excess" (Les sciences dites expérimentales ont été rigoureuses avant que d'être exactes. Elles ne souffraient pas d'un défaut de mathématiques, mais d'un excès).

4. "Contrairement à ces sciences exactes qui aspirent à offrir une information exhaustive et autonome à un interlocuteur ignorant du contexte, le langage ignore tout détail inutile à ses fins immédiates et exploite au maximum la connaissance commune aux participants du discours. Ce savoir partagé, dont la logique aussi bien que la géométrie refusent l'aide, représente la trame indispensable sur laquelle s'inscrit le langage" (Vandeloise 1986, 22).

5. These judgments are for "normal" life. If, for example, the elephant had just been inside the matchbox, then (17) would be fine (it is either a *very* small elephant or a *very* big matchbox). The Grammar does not depend on the size of elephants, nor does it depend on the size of clouds, as we will see in the discussion of (23) in section 1.3 below.

6. For a classification and comparison of the different types of analyses of DANS and its close equivalents in German and English, see Vandeloise (1992).

7. Marantz (1984, 302–303) argues that lambda notation negates much of the force of Montague's projection principle, the final effect being that semantics is not directly reflected in syntax. However, as Ratté (1991) points out, for Montague, intensional logic was intended only as a transitory support. He actually envisioned a direct interpretation of natural language: intensional logic was but an intermediate step, it was part of the technical explication. See Montague (1974) and Lewis (1970) for an attempt at eliminating intensional logic.

8. Even verbs that require highly complex representations in conceptual or thematic terms, like *buy* and *sell,* for example, do not require this complexity to be expressed in their Grammatical representations, if we accept the notion of web of shared knowledge and if we include in it a faculty of "Social Cognition" (see Jackendoff, "Is There a Faculty of Social Cognition," talk presented at McGill University, February 1992). Jackendoff suggests that humans might share an internalized social organization that would contain modes of social interaction, such as 'Market Pricing,' which would contain notions of linearized value of an object and agreement between individuals, and so on. Set against such a background, the crisscrossing of an object with an appropriate amount of money, after agreement, and so on, may very well not have to be present in the strictly linguistic representations of these verbs.

9. This Homomorphic-Mapping approach echoes Freidin's (1978) observation that a construction derived by a rule of NP preposing that is structure preserving, with movement into an independently generable empty NP position, might as well be base generated.

10. However, Carter (1988, 102–103) observed that it is probably not an accident that *have* and *avoir* and *contain* and *contenir* are exceptions to passivization and *tough-*movement. This could be attributed to semantic properties of these verbs, in which case the motivation for Prohibitions A and B is weakened.

11. See Lakoff's (1987, 332–33) discussion the Kay-Kempton color experiment. As far as I can tell, the experiment does not show that fuzziness is an inherent part of grammar: it only shows that having a name for something can help in deciding difficult cases of conceptualization.

12. See also Simatos (1986) for an in-depth study of the nonreferentiality of idiomatic expressions.

13. It is more complicated than I suggested in the text. Not all nouns that are not referentially autonomous can be modified by *très.* While *faim* is not referentially autonomous (for example, it cannot passivize **Faim a été eue par Jean* 'Hunger has been had by Jean'), we saw in (8) that *part* is not referentially autonomous, yet it cannot take a degree adverb *Glaucon a pris (*très) part à cette discussion* 'Glaucon has taken very part to that discussion.' There are certainly other factors involved.

14. The grammatical system itself is not required to have a relation with reality. In fact, if it projects at all, it seems to project to a different world, where objects have gender, for example. See Tasmovski-De Rijk and Verluyten (1981) and Bouchard (1984a).

15. That conceptual structures are crucial in understanding language use does not mean that *all* aspects of these structures have effects on language use. For example, we saw in 1.5.1 that category fuzziness has no effect on use, at least not if we mean effects on use found only in language. For example, a speaker might hesitate in using a word like *vase, cup* or *bowl,* because of the difficulty in some cases of classifying such objects properly in our perceptual system. But this kind of hesitation could arise in nonlinguistic contexts, like picture experiments, hence are not in the realm of linguistic use strictly defined as above. Note that if there is fuzziness in our conceptualization of objects, and if I am right in claiming that Grammar is different and exhibits no such fuzziness, the relationship between language and the world cannot be very direct. For instance, it cannot be the case that there is a "real" objective world out there and that thought consists essentially in the manipulation of abstract symbols which get their meaning via correspondences to entities and categories in the world, with linguistic expressions getting their meaning via their capacity to correspond to the real world or some possible world. On the contrary, Grammar is different in crucial ways from our perception of the world. In that sense, the approach requires Internalized concepts rather than Externalized concepts.

16. Dowty (1991, 586, note 29) makes a similar observation about some movement verbs:

(i)   All the students gathered in the hall.

(ii)   The crowd dispersed.

In (i), some students could have been there already; similarly in (ii), some people could remain, as long as they were not enough of them to be considered 'a crowd.'

17. It should be clear that here I am talking about the traditional notions of truth and falsity of sentences in natural language. Modern logic has developed a different approach to truth, which is roughly equivalent to "well formed": a proposition is true in a given system S if one can apply the rules of S and derive that proposition as acceptable by those rules.

18. The idea that there is a crucial relation between selection and reference; hence, Situational Semantics, in my terms, is already present in McCawley (1968a, 1968b). He showed that the reference of a NP, not properties of its head, is the important factor for its selection, as can be seen in (i):

(i)a.   My buxom neighbor is pregnant.
   b.   #My virile neighbor is pregnant.

19. A similar criticism is leveled against Generative Semantics by Kempson (1975), who argues that semantics loses its predictive power if any speaker-relative concepts like intentions or assumptions are included in a grammatical statement.

20. Other roles, Agent, Actor, and the like, do not fare any better. See Catlin and Catlin (1972), Dowty (1979), Verkuyl (1989), and particularly Voorst (1992, 1993) on the problem of attributing any linguistic effects to such notions as Agentivity. For example, *John* is not a prototypical Actor in (i); it does not fit easily into the frame "What X did

was. . . ." Yet it is easily possible to depart from prototypicality and set the scene in a society where receiving letters is prohibited and results in imprisonment, in which case (ii) becomes natural (unfortunately for John).

(i)   John received a letter.

(ii)a.   What did John do to get arrested?
   b.   What he did was receive a letter.

21. On the vacuity of similarity, see Chomsky (1959, 50), among many others. It makes the notion of *motivation* of Lakoff (1987) quite dubious, since it is based on similarity: for Lakoff, a noncentral member of a radial category is "motivated" by the central member "in the sense that they bear family resemblances to it" (65). Degrees of similarity—which do not appear to be forthcoming—will have to be provided to make his theory falsifiable. Umberto Eco's *Foucault's Pendulum,* particularly section 63, is a vivid illustration of the claim that it is always possible to find some kind of similarity between two elements.

22. "Le langage découle essentiellement de l'apparition, au niveau de l'espèce humaine, d'une nouvelle forme de représentation, la représentation sémantique. La représentation sémantique se superpose aux différentes représentations perceptives développées par les mammifères qui, de caractère nécessairement analogique, alimentent principalement des mémoires de reconnaissance. La représentation sémantique n'est pas de caractère analogique parce que centralement autogénérée; elle est éminemment propice aux mémoires de rappel. Plus exactement, . . . le générateur de représentations génère des pré-représentations, ou représentations potentielles, qui ne deviendront de vraies représentations que dans la mesure où elles correspondront à autre chose qu'à elles-mêmes. Ceci est réalisé lorsque les produits du générateur de représentations "rencontrent" d'autres données."

23. This is essentially what Ruwet (1991) refers to as the Swallow Fallacy (One swallow does not a summer make), which "consists of finding an example sentence—a single example sentence—and drawing a sweeping generalization, based on the conviction . . . that what makes that example sentence Good or Bad will hold across a large range of formally similar structures" (xviii).

24. "Les exemples doivent être nombreux et variés pour deux raisons. D'une part, pour que leur variété permette de bien cerner la propriété soumise à examen: chaque exemple est une combinaison de propriétés linguistiques multiples; en multipliant les variétés, on fera apparaître l'indépendance de la propriété qu'on examine à l'égard d'autres propriétés avec lesquelles elle se trouve combinée. Ainsi, si l'on veut examiner le Passif, on devra donner des exemples qui manifestent que le passif est indépendant du temps du verbe, du caractère relatif ou non relatif, interrogatif ou non interrogatif de la phrase, etc.

D'autre part, les exemples doivent être variés parce qu'ils doivent prendre en compte toutes les conséquences réfutables de la proposition soumise à examen, afin que l'ensemble des réfutabilités possibles se trouve parcouru."

25. "Le laboratoire et tout système clos protègent des turbulences. La science est fermée dedans. Elle va, dès son départ, des *Météores* au poêle, et ne sortira plus de cette clôture, qui exclut le hasard et l'incontrôlable, nous dirions aujourd'hui l'hypercomplexité."

26. "Quand ces mythes, qui ont servi de point de départ à nos réflexions, dépeignent un héros couvert de fiente et de vermine ou changé en charogne puante, ils ne brodent pas "crûment" sur des métaphores. . . . Car c'est l'inverse qui est vrai: grâce aux mythes, on découvre que la métaphore repose sur l'intuition de rapports logiques entre un domaine et d'autres domaines, dans l'ensemble desquels elle réintègre seulement le premier nonobstant la pensée réflexive qui s'acharne à les séparer. Loin de s'ajouter au langage à la façon d'un embellissement, chaque métaphore le purifie et le ramène à sa nature première, en effaçant, pour un instant, une des innombrables synecdoques de quoi le discours est fait."

27. The discussion of these sentences is another illustration of the kind of problem raised by thematic notions such as Source. A Source sometimes refers to situations in which there is a process, such as movement, and sometimes only to stative situations, in which case it corresponds to 'origin.' I am focusing on the stative "origin" use of the OUT OF sentences here. There is also a processive reading that is possible as in (i):

(i)   A small oak is growing out of the pile of leaves.

This is again different from the change of state described by the INTO sentences:

(ii)   #The pile of leaves grew into a small oak.

See Part II for a discussion of the origin use of sentences like (iii):

(iii)   Jean vient de Paris.
        Jean comes from Paris.

28. The subject must denote a body with the power to impeach (such as Congress) and the object must denote someone in high office (such as the President).

29. To these deep problems with thematic roles as primitives of the Grammar, we could add traditional problems in identifying thematic roles and using them to distinguish arguments. See Dowty (1991), who nicely summarizes these problems in his section 3.

30. The position I am advocating is also very close to the one taken by Chomsky (1975a), who proposes two levels of semantic interpretation: SI-1, which is connected to the operation of the language faculty, and SI-2, which relates to other cognitive faculties. I depart from his position with respect to where the boundary between the two levels is set. In his writings since then, Chomsky has located many elements in SI-1—theta roles, for example—which I put outside of Grammar altogether. Another important difference lies in the fact that Chomsky's position tends to be syntactico-centrist; for him, semantics is mainly interpretive. I suggest that, in fact, a great deal of the organization of elements in syntax depends on how things are organized in semantics.

31. The notion of extended branching corresponds to Pullum's (1985) notion of IDC-command: a IDC-commands b if and only if a's mother dominates b. But there is no need to stipulate that such a condition holds of some grammatical process or, for that matter, to stipulate any notion of command in any of its guises. If we assume tree representations, "command" conditions follow from the transitivity of dominance and the orientation of trees, as we just saw. The same holds for a notion that stipulates the *first branching node* to be the minimal upper bound for some grammatical processes. In (72), for example, the

first restriction follows from the fact that D has a branching relation with B, so B can be the minimal upper bound for D's relations, but D has no direct branching relation with A, nor does D's branching relation with B extend to A, because of the orientation of trees from top to bottom.

As for the *branching* restriction, we will see in section 2.1.1.1 that it could not be otherwise, since nonbranching nonterminal nodes are excluded from the grammar (assuming preterminal and terminals to form one node).

32. Hilbert's original impetus came from a problem posed by non-Euclidian geometry: although spherical and hyperbolic geometry differed from Euclidian geometry with respect to the parallel postulate, they shared other postulates with Euclidian geometry. One way to make sense out of this was to assume that the shared postulates were of a more abstract nature, with formal elements assigned a different meaning in different geometries. In this way, the formulas shared by the various geometries would be the same not because they contained the same concepts, but because they consisted of the same strings of symbols. For example, depending on which geometry one is dealing with, the symbol L could be either a line or a great circle; the symbol PN could be either a plane or the surface of a sphere; and so on. Mathematics, in such a program, is the study of meaningless symbols, and mathematical proofs are sequences of strings of uninterpreted symbols, with the lines of a proof related to one another by regular rules. For more discussion, see Kleene (1967, chapter 4), Lakoff (1987, chapter 14), and references therein.

33. See Piotrowski (1991) for some discussion.

34. The foregoing discussion explains why situational notions like thematic roles are found in formalist approaches. At first, it appears to be incoherent to have such concrete, referential notions in a formal system. But, in fact, they are not so unexpected, since symbolists will eventually want to relate their representations to the objective world out there. The main objection to such a situational system is that all possible meanings would then be contained in the inventory of the natural partitions of the environment. This means that individuals could learn new meanings but could not produce new ones, only recover them. This seems in contradiction with the semantic productivity observed, and in particular with the creation of abstract mental objects. See Champagnol (1992) for a very perceptive discussion.

35. Conceptual shifts such as the one of classical science are extremely difficult to formulate for those who are used to thinking according to the established model. Koyré (1968) attributes Kepler's failure to come up with the classical theory of physics to the difficulty of going from one conceptual system to another, even though he had all the results required to reach Newton's conclusions. Newton's genius was in being able to make such a conceptual shift.

36. There is another difference between the classical and preclassical conceptions of movement. For the Ancients, initial point A and final point B were very important in rectilinear movement, as compared to circular movement (see Aristotle's *Physics* 265a). The aim of the object moving from point A to point B because of an internal force was crucial in their conception of rectilinear movement, whereas circular movement had no such aim and so was said to be a purer, more abstract form of movement. But in classical

science, there is no such distinction between the two types of movement, because all points are of equal importance in both types of movement.

Chapter Two

1. It must be noted that, although constraints such as the Grammatical Constraint have a strong methodological appeal, their status cannot be raised to that of an absolute constraint on the construction of semantic theories, since their suitability eventually depends on how the brain processes information. Unfortunately, we know too little about this to be able to evaluate this organic component at this time. For example, it is possible that relating two formally different representations is not a problem for the brain, given some kind of compiler that mediates between the two. However, taken as a subcase of Occam's principle, the Grammatical Constraint remains valid until proven empirically untenable.

2. This indexical problem is not restricted to generative approaches: it is also found in apparently radically different approaches to the pairing of syntax and semantics. For example, Lakoff (1987, 489) proposes a form-meaning pairing which is literally indexical: the syntactic element is represented by i, the semantic element by i'.

3. A preliminary discussion of the material found in this section is presented in Bouchard (1991).

4. Morphology also puts meaningful elements together. Although I believe that there are some important differences between the two, they have many properties in common (for example, compare Di Sciullo and Williams (1987) for arguments). This is because many of their essential properties are projected from the same deeper level—Semantic Representation. I will return to some of these properties of morphology.

5. Endocentricity value is a language specific parameter that determines whether a node allows only one or more than one head, to percolate features to it. See Bouchard (1984a, chapter 4) for the relevance of this parameter to the analysis of nonconfigurational languages, which I argue are ambiguously structured rather than nonconfigurational. It is quite likely that even endocentricity value is set in semantic representations.

As for linearization, my position is similar to the one taken in Kayne (1993a), who proposes to derive the basic properties of X-bar theory from properties of linearization. However, his analysis is based on the presence of numerous contentless functional categories, which goes directly against the position taken here. In Bouchard (unpublished manuscript), I argue that this proliferation of functional categories makes his theory impossible to falsify.

6. One difference between maximal and nonmaximal projections is that a maximal projection seems to be able to correspond to either a TYPE or a TOKEN, whereas a lower projection can only correspond to a TYPE. The distinction is clear for the N projections in (14). This fact has often been noted (see, for example, Milner's (1982) discussion of actual and virtual reference) and can perhaps be attributed to the fact that the TOKEN reading requires a relation with a determiner that the nonmaximal N projection does not have.

7. This relates to ideas expressed in Tesnière (1976, 42): "[The] structural plane and

the semantic plane are independent from one another. But this independence is but a theoretical view of the mind. . . . Between the two, there is no identity, but there is parallelism. On the structural connections are superimposed . . . semantic connections . . . one can formulate the parallelism by saying that the structural expresses the semantic." Thanks to Sylvie Ratté for pointing out this passage. ("[Le] plan structural et le plan sémantique sont indépendants l'un de l'autre. Mais cette indépendance n'est qu'une vue théorique de l'esprit. . . . Entre les deux, il n'y a pas identité, mais il y a parallélisme. Aux connexions structurales se superposent . . . des connexions sémantiques. . . . On peut formuler le parallélisme en disant que le structural exprime la sémantique.")

8. A Universal Binary Bracketing principle was proposed in Bouchard (1979). It differed from the present proposal in that the principle was postulated to apply directly to syntactic structures. The approach adopted there was, in some respects, very similar to the one outlined here: it was highly modular, and, crucially, the main component responsible for accepting or rejecting the structures generated by the universal binary bracketing principle was the interpretive component via grammatical functions: "Fusion into constituents is free, but if the resulting constituents are not functionally interpretable, then the sentence is filtered out" ("La fusion en constituants est libre, mais si les constituants qui en résultent ne sont pas fonctionnellement interprétables, alors la phrase est filtrée") (Bouchard 1979, 24). However, it lacked a proper semantic theory to draw from.

9. The fact that binarity is pervasive in grammar may be related to more general considerations. Since, by analysis, all distinctions can be reduced to a system of dichotomy, binarity can be seen as a logical consequence of distinctiveness in the Platonic sense (see Milner 1989, 329). Such considerations about distinctiveness are pervasive in Roman Jakobson's work in phonology. A branching node determines two things. It defines a domain in which elements combine, and the number of branches the node immediately dominates indicates how many elements combine. In the absence of any means in a particular language to get further information about which elements combine, distinctiveness forces the structural relation to be binary. If, however, information can be garnered from other means than the syntactic structure, such as rich morphology, for example, the structure need not be binary. This is what takes place in a more freely ordered language such as Latin. In an extreme case, such as a so-called nonconfigurational language like Warlpiri, the additional information is so rich that one node may be sufficient to determine the domain of the sentence, all other relations being identifiable independently of the structure. As discussed in note 5, the endocentricity value in such a language is set so that more than one head can percolate features to a node and "use" it to establish a relationship with complements, specifiers, modifiers. In this book, I only discuss languages like English and French, where binarity is forced upon the structure.

10. In compounds like French *ouvre-boîte* (*open-can* = 'can-opener'), it seems that neither *ouvre* nor *boîte* labels the structure, but rather a third lexical item meaning 'can-opener.' Chomsky's minimal approach to labeling directly accounts for the fact that combining two words without labeling the result by one of these elements necessarily takes on a new lexical meaning: the combination is a new lexical item, since the label can only be some other lexical item.

11. Recall that, in GB, subcategorization is assumed to follow in most part from selection, with possibly a purely syntactic residue, Case assignment, to distinguish between certain constructions (although I suspect that further studies into the intricate details of the meaning of verbs like *ask* and *inquire* are very likely to explain the contrasts observed between such verbs independently from Case theory).

12. In light of these considerations, the fact that reference is made to bar levels in *Barriers* should not be seen as an argument in favor of bar levels, but rather as an indication of where to begin reformulating that approach, with the hope that such information will further our understanding of the constructions involved.

13. In this sense, I share the concerns of Emonds (1991) about approaches to natural language semantics that depart from the available syntactic evidence, preferring logico-analytical constructs based on "the anti-theoretical research method of common sense" (375). I fully agree with him that "[i]n our present state of knowledge, fruitful study of the rational mind must be rooted in the study of syntax" (426). However, I depart from his approach where it makes use of thematic situational notions to represent the meaning of sentences. His position is also situational and nonsyntactic, in that he uses truth conditions to determine that sentences like those in (i) are semantically alike:

(i)a.   John bought the book from Bill.
  b.   Bill sold the book to John.

Furthermore, I disagree with his assumption that "with *drink,* the direct object (the theme and patient) is obligatory in the semantics but optional in the syntax, while an understood complement of place (meaning for Jackendoff roughly "into the mouth of NP_i," where NP_i is the subject of *drink*) is obligatory in the semantics but absent in the syntax" (402), and with his assumption that *go,* when used statively to express "be compatible," is a different verb from activity *go,* since it has a totally different theta grid. To me, these positions are in contradiction with his own stated goals because they suppose that, independent of the syntax of a sentence S_j, "we already have a good idea about what is in SR_j," something that like him "I flatly deny" (373).

14. Chomsky (1985a, 1991) discusses some consequences of Full Interpretation. On the whole, Full Interpretation disallows superfluous steps in derivations and superfluous symbols in syntactic representations. It follows, for example, that there can be no vacuous quantification or free variables in natural languages. In short, Full Interpretation states the strong position that syntactic elements must be interpreted in order to be licensed. However, auxiliary hypotheses that are made weaken this strong claim. For example, since it is assumed that an element like existential *there* receives no interpretation, and therefore is not licensed as a legitimate LF object (Chomsky 1991), such an element must either be eliminated in the mapping from SS to LF (Chomsky 1985a) or it must have an associated element that licenses its presence at LF (Chomsky 1991). The latter solution seems to me to be contradictory, since the associate will be licensed, but *there* itself still will not be. Functional elements like AGR might also not be present at LF. Intermediate A-bar traces in movement originating from an A-position and traces of AGR must be eliminated at LF (Chomsky 1991). Hence, several syntactic elements receive no semantic interpretation.

Another weakness of Full Interpretation is that it sets no constraints on what can appear in a semantic representation. No accountability is required, so any number of elements could potentially appear in the semantics without ever having a syntactic equivalent. Comparatively, the homomorphic approach taken here is a stronger claim, since it not only disallows the presence of uninterpreted syntactic elements, it also disallows unascribed semantic elements. Moreover, Chomsky notes that Full Interpretation is not a logically necessary property of any possible language: it is not observed in standard notations of quantification theory in logic, for example. But since Full Interpretation is a property of natural language, it is stipulated to be part of UG. Such a stipulation is not necessary in the approach presented here, since Full Identification follows from homomorphic correspondence between semantic representation and syntactic representation; it is built in the architecture of the framework. Moreover, homomorphic correspondence does not allow "corrections," such as deleting elements in the mapping from one level of syntactic representation to another, and hence, it is more constrained than Full Interpretation. Furthermore, it leads us to the interesting conclusion that expletives and functional elements will have to have some kind of semantic content because syntactic structure is strictly determined by its relation with semantic representations. Finally, while Chomsky does, in fact, allow elements at LF that are, strictly speaking, superfluous for semantic interpretation, namely non-branching non-maximal projections, such intermediate nodes are not allowed in a homomorphic correspondence approach as we saw above. On the whole, the Full Identification approach is more restrictive than one based on Full Interpretation and less stipulative.

15. An element in SR can also be identified by being "obvious" and hence not require an "outside" identifier: this might be the case for the copula, which would never be realized in syntax (*be* corresponding not to the copula itself but being a support for Tense). This fourth type of identification will be discussed briefly in Part II.

16. I must emphasize that, for our purposes, an argument for decomposition will be valid only if it has linguistic effects. Thus, the fact that the meaning of an item can be further decomposed into subparts is not sufficient to assume that it is so represented in its lexical entry. Furthermore, paraphrasability is neither an argument for semantic decomposition nor an argument for selecting among semantic representations.

17. On the notion of homomorphy in a linguistic context, see Montague (1970), Keenan and Faltz (1985), Partee et al. (1990). There is also an echo of the position I am advocating in Carter (1988). Discussing the fact that two expressions with the same use conditions such as *to the left of* and *to the right of, uncle,* and *father's brother* are usually assigned the same SRs, Carter says that they should be assigned distinct SRs corresponding point by point to the distinct syntactic forms. "It eliminates the general problem . . . of why human languages make available in so many cases such widely differing forms for the expression of what the first position claims to be identical meanings. That additional explanatory burden seems to put the burden of proof on those who claim that languages, in this respect, do not wear their semantic hearts on their formal sleeves." (31)

18. Therefore, technically, chunking is a transformation, since it maps one tree structure into another. Because the mapping is from a semantic representation onto a syntactic

representation, this raises the question of whether this approach is subject to the same criticisms as Generative Semantics. For example, recall Fodor's (1970) argument against McCawley's (1968c) proposal to derive KILL from CAUSE-TO-DIE: while two adverbials are possible in (i a), one with the higher clause and one with the lower clause, this is not possible in the lexical causative (i b).

(i)a.   Bill caused Fred to die on Tuesday by shooting him on Monday.
   b.   #Bill killed Fred on Tuesday by shooting him on Monday.

But this kind of criticism holds only against an analysis where the relation between *kill* and *cause to die* is a syntactic one. If *cause to die* is only in the lexical representation of *kill*, not in the syntactic representation of the sentence, its structure is not accessible in syntax: the contrast in (i) is not a problem in such an analysis. In (a), *on Tuesday* modifies *die*, and *by shooting him on Monday* modifies *caused Fred to die on Tuesday*. But this splitting of the modification is not possible in (b) because modification holds between two constituents: the result is that in (b), *on Tuesday* cannot modify *die*, since *die* is not a syntactic constituent to which *on Tuesday* could be a sister. So the two modifiers are related to *killed Fred*, hence the oddness.

   What about the cases where adverbials do seem to exhibit scope ambiguities like *almost* in (ii) (cf. Morgan 1969)?

(ii)   John almost killed Mary.

As Zwicky & Sadock (1975) argue, this seems to be a case of vagueness rather than ambiguity. It would be on the same level as *John has a shirt*, which is open between *John has a red shirt* and *John has a blue shirt*, in the sense that one can imagine distinct situations to which the sentence can be applied with equal appropriateness. Thus, "x almost VERBs" means simply "there is a possible world very similar to the actual world in which 'x VERBs' is true." Another important difference between Generative Semantics and the approach presented here has to do with what aspects of semantics are relevant to Grammar. The proposal here is that the notion of semantics relevant to linguistics is a relatively narrow one. Generative Semantics, on the contrary, came to consider more and more of situational semantics as part of the domain of linguistics, to such a degree in fact that linguistic theory itself became so encompassing that it became unwieldy. The following passage is illustrative: "We have found that one cannot just set up artificial boundaries and rule out of the study of language such things as human reasoning, context, social interaction, deixis, fuzziness, sarcasm, discourse types, fragments, variation among speakers, etc. Each time we have set up an artificial boundary, we have found some phenomenon that shows that it has to be removed. That is not to say that there are no boundaries on the study of linguistics. I only suggest that at this point in history the boundaries are disappearing daily, and one should not be too surprised if the domain of the field continues to expand" (Lakoff 1974, 178). My claim is that although all those phenomena have something to do with language use, only a subset of the elements affecting use have effects on Grammar. In short, there are two major differences between Generative Semantics and the approach proposed here. First, the "deep" level where semantics is represented is not a syntactic level in the present proposal, so it is not directly accessible to syntactic processes like modification by a syntactic constituent. Second, the notion of semantics here is much narrower.

19. Both Ross and Jackendoff use the term "incorporation," but since it has been used to describe a syntactic process in recent studies (cf. Baker 1988), I will use the term "chunking" here to describe the process that merges semantic primitives into a single lexical item.

20. The example is given in Jackendoff's format, with his primitives and paraphrase methodology. It should be clear that this is for the sake of exposition and that I do not necessarily endorse any of these.

21. Reanalysis, as discussed in van Riemsdijk (1978) and Hornstein and Weinberg (1981), seems to be an operation similar to chunking, except that it, perhaps, maps one syntactic structure into another instead of having a semantic structure as input. Reanalysis has been said to be subject to a constraint that requires its output to be a "possible word." Some content can be given to this notion if we assume that both processes of chunking and reanalysis operate on similar kinds of structures and both fall under Homomorphic Mapping and the Endocentricity Principle.

22. A possible criticism is that the transparency of the linking regularities will be at the expense of the semantics: of course the linking is transparent, since the SRs are set up in such a way that they map fairly directly into the syntax. Such a criticism would come from a misunderstanding of the methodology involved. I cannot see how a linguist could elaborate on the matter of linking without looking at the most salient evidence there is. The methodology in approaching the linking problem is fairly simple (cf. Carter 1988, 7): one tries to find as simple a set of semantic representations and set of linking rules as possible, constantly going from one set to another. If sticking closely to the syntax allows one to propose a simpler linking procedure, and if that procedure additionally throws some light on the semantics and allows one to improve on the representation of meaning on empirical grounds, as I argue extensively in Part II below, then certainly the approach is justified. In fact, a similar objection could be levied against many thematic analyses, except that it is the syntax that is being manipulated, rather than the semantics. Thus, Dowty (1991, note 15) points out that if one wants to uphold the proposal that Incremental Themes are always linked to direct objects, a form of Unaccusative Advancement from underlying direct objects will have to be assumed in order to account for the cases where they appear in subject position: "[T]his is less plausible for *John entered the water (gradually)*, which has a visible, independent direct object. Even here of course, one can imagine a suggestion that the water originates as an underlying oblique and is advanced to direct object after John is advanced from direct object to subject. At that point, of course, one would have the right to ask whether the invariant association of Incremental Theme with syntactic direct object still had any empirical content or had been elevated from empirical hypothesis to methodological assumption, i.e. that one was in actuality prepared to postulate any syntactic abstractness necessary to maintain a uniform semantic association with a certain syntactic position. This would be, in other words, the methodology of generative semantics (and perhaps of some contemporary theorists), where meaning is the decisive arbiter of the deepest underlying structure and indirect syntactic argumentation is sought

post hoc to justify analyses suggested by such assumptions about semantic connotations of deep structure." Of course, the force of the criticism will depend on the ultimate value of the proposal. If it turns out that there is *independent* motivation for the syntactic analysis involving Unaccusative Advancement—not just syntactic encoding of some semantic effect, but actual syntactic evidence—the syntactic analysis is justified. My claim is that this is precisely the case for the proposal in the text about the semantic representations. The attempt to stick more closely to the syntactic evidence lead me to propose semantic representations that turn out to be empirically more justified than thematic notions.

23. Barbara Hall (1965) had already noted such differences between lexical and syntactic causatives. She gives the following examples:

(i)a.   A change in molecular structure caused the window to break.

   b.   *A change in molecular structure broke the window.

(ii)a. The low air pressure caused the water to boil.

   b.   *The low air pressure boiled the water.

(iii)a. The angle at which the door was mounted caused it to open whenever it wasn't latched.

   b.   *The angle at which the door was mounted opened it whenever it wasn't latched.

24. Ruwet attributes to Maurice Gross and Jean-Paul Boons an additional constraint, namely that lexical causatives are only possible when they have a corresponding intransitive sentence with auxiliary *être*. I return to this question in section 3.3 on auxiliary selection. Note furthermore that van Voorst (1988) argues that the notion of "direct responsibility" seems to vary across languages. In English, it corresponds to 'object of actualization,' whereas it corresponds to the more restrictive 'object of origin' in Dutch. Thus, the Dutch equivalent of *The key opened the door* is not grammatical because although the key actualizes the event (helps to bring it about), it is not at the origin of the event.

25. An example of proliferation of functional categories is studied in chapter 5. Note that effects such as those of Subjacency and ECP, because of the nature of the constraints, are more naturally associated with a binding analysis of Wh-constructions than with a transformational analysis. The domains of application of these constraints are defined in terms of dominance relations, as is explicitly expressed in Chomsky's (1985b) notion of L-marking, for example. In a binding analysis such as the V-chain analysis of Bouchard (1984a) or the Connectedness analysis of Kayne (1983), Wh-constructions involve an iteration of head-complement relations. It is therefore natural for dominance relations and the domains created by these to play a role in Wh-constructions. But in a transformational approach, a series of tree structures are related to one another, and it is unexpected that dominance properties internal to any of these structures should play a role in the transformational mapping (aside from those aspects of the structure that are affected by a term of the transformation). Hence, one must stipulate additional constraints of a very different nature from that of the transformational operations, such as constraints based on L-marking. Stating the restrictions in terms of constraints on variables as Ross (1967) did

was directly compatible with a transformational approach; but in generalizing the restrictions as a subjacency constraint on domains, Chomsky (1973) opened up a gap between the transformational operations and the constraints, a gap that has widened with the introduction of *Move* α, which eliminated variables from the formulation of transformations. In short, with constraints based on dominance relations—such as L-marking, Connectedness, and V-chains—and with binding relations between "moved" elements and their initial position, the actual transformational aspect of the analysis of long distance dependencies is redundant and has no independent effect in the grammar. Therefore, it is not an accident that traces are assumed to be easily deletable in current analyses; that is, since the introduction of L-marking in Chomsky (1985b). There is another way to look at movement transformations, but this will not help. In a chain approach to transformations such as Chomsky (1992), where the operation "Form Chain" may apply to a single tree structure, the operation creates a series of relations parallel to and dependent on the already present phrasal relations. The constraints on these additional relations are stated on the phrasal relations, so the constraints are of a different nature, again. On the face of it, therefore, a minimalist program should favor an analysis in which the operations and the constraints operative in Wh-constructions are based on elements of the same component—the construction should be analyzed as involving a binding relation in a single structure rather than as something like a movement transformation. These considerations bring additional support to the position taken in the text, where movement transformations are ruled out on general grounds in a minimalist approach because they are not sufficiently constrained.

26. As for the claim that raising verbs are not Case assigners, it faces two problems. First, an NP of the appropriate semantic class can appear as the direct object of *sembler* 'seem' in French (see Ruwet 1972):

(i)   Il me semble ceci: que l'empereur ne viendra pas ce matin.
        It seems to me this: that the emperor will not come this morning
        'It seems to me that the emperor will not come this morning'

Second, if the sentential complement of a raising verb must bear Case in order to be a "visible" argument and get a theta role, it must presumably get its Case from the raising verb.

Chapter Three

1. Another problem for a movement analysis based on prototypical use can be found in a sentence like (i), where it is not the subject of the "movement" verb that moves in the spatio-temporal situation in which the sentence would be used:

(i)   The motionless UFO came into view.

2. That is a bit too strong a statement: gender could change, as it does in English, depending on whether MAX is a person or a computer. But gender changes do not affect the properties under scrutiny here, namely the relational properties between actants.

3. A verb like *oscillate* might seem to be a counterexample to Boons's observation, but to oscillate is much more than moving back and forth, since a focal point is involved.

Similarly, a sentence like *La route s'étend entre Montréal et Québec* 'The road stretches between Montréal and Québec' also seems to refer to an axis with no orientation. But, in fact, there is no axis referred to by the sentence: *étendre* means to spread, hence in length and width, not on an axis, as can be seen in *Le mal s'est étendu* 'The damage/pain has spread.' Of course, for the road between Montréal and Québec, width is negligible in most cases. So, typically, given the distance between the two cities, we see the road in a certain orientation. But that is not necessarily the case, even for an object that has an orientation: a sentence like *Max s'est étendu entre deux arbres* 'Max laid down between two trees' (literally, 'Max stretched himself between two trees') says nothing about the orientation of Max with respect to the two trees. The verb *shuttle* is another potential counterexample. But, instead of having its definition based on space as in "to go to and fro," it is likely that the repetition involved is based instead on temporal iteration, as in "to go on a short route repeatedly." Thus, the *Concise Oxford Dictionary of Current English* defines a "space shuttle" as "a rocket for repeated use." So, it seems that the back and forth movement of *shuttle* is inferred pragmatically from temporal factors.

4. "Dans **Louis vient déjeuner, déjeuner** est non seulement prédicatif, mais encore sa valeur prédicative verbale vient se fondre, se télescoper en quelque sorte avec celle de **vient**, dont elle n'est que la prolongation en même temps que la justification. **Déjeuner** n'est pas le terme de la venue de Louis, c'en est plutôt la matière psychologique: l'action de déjeuner est en quelque sorte déjà entamée par les pas que fait Louis vers la maison où il doit manger. . . . Ce qu'il lui faut à lui, comme about, comme à tous les verbes de mouvement, c'est une virtualité verbale susceptible de se symphénoménaliser avec son propre phéno-mène: ce à quoi un infinitif seul est propre. Tel est le rôle de la progrédience." (Damourette and Pichon 1911–1950: #1055)

5. Lamiroy gives the constraint as a prohibition on stative predicates. It is better to state it as a constraint on individual-level predicates, since stative stage-level predicates are possible:

(i)   Jean vient/monte/entre avoir du plaisir.
        Jean comes/goes upstairs/comes in to have some fun.

6. This sentence is not to be confused with the one with *à*+ infinitive in (i):

(i)   Jean en est venu à ressembler à son père.
        'John came to look like his father.'

This construction is an example of the End-reaching use of *venir*, which I discuss in 3.1.1.6 below.

7. See the discussion of *Colorless green ideas sleep furiously* in section 1.5.2.2.1.

8. See chapter 4 and references therein for an extensive discussion of the effects of similar mismatches between reference to an individual as a substantive and as a concept. Note that if this account is on the right track, then the contrast between "the pencil is sad" and "the book is sad" is very relevant here, since the contextual properties of reference of John, pencils, and books—i.e., how one can refer to each of them—will provide a unified account of their potential to refer to a plausible situation when used with *sad*. Thus, *my*

pencil is sad today is possible if *my pencil* is used to refer to the content of what I am writing with my pencil. Similarly, *j'ai la plume triste aujourd'hui,* literally 'I have the pen sad today,' is fine in French, to express that everything I am writing today comes out as sad.

9. See Goldsmith and Woisetschlaeger (1982) for an extensive discussion of the schedule interpretation in English.

10. I extrapolate quite a bit from the proposal of Franckel and Lebaud here, and they should not be held accountable for what I do with it.

11. Note that explaining progredience by putting the infinitival phrase in x_2 in (25) bears some similarity to many analyses of the French causative construction, where *faire* + infinitive are said to form a complex predicate. I cannot go into the details here, but it could be worthwhile to explore an analysis of causatives in the vein of the present analysis of progredience, where at least in the case of the dative *faire* construction, one could correlate *Jean fait manger de la tarte à Marie* 'Jean makes Marie [dative] eat pie' with *Jean fait quelque chose à Marie* 'Jean does something to Marie [dative].' Morin and Saint-Amour (1977) discuss such a possibility on the basis of historical evidence. However, there are important differences between the progredience construction and the causative construction that would have to be explained, such as the availability of the *Tous*-à-gauche construction or clitic climbing.

12. Thanks to Rachel Panckhurst for pointing out this contrast to me. Another instance where *venir* is used predicatively is when its subject is a term that refers to a property, as discussed in Franckel and Lebaud (1990, p. 163):

(i)a.   La sagesse vient avec l'âge.
       Wisdom comes with age.
   b.   La souplesse vient avec l'entraînement.
       Flexibility comes with training.

The elements being centered, oriented toward the deicic center, are qualitative properties, so the centering is qualitative, as Franckel and Lebaud observed. We are talking about "real" wisdom here, a wisdom that deserves the name 'wisdom.'

13. I put spatio-temporal in quotes here because, of course, the street itself is not actually oriented. The orientation is virtual: motorists who use it must go in a certain direction determined by some official board and indicated by appropriate signs bearing arrows.

14. The future use of *venir* must not be confused with the effect found in infinitival relative clauses such as (i):

(i)a.   dans les jours à venir
       in the days to come
   b.   Les boîtes à venir sont/seront plus lourdes que celles-ci.
       The boxes to come are/will be heavier than these.

The effect here is due to the irrealis of the infinitive, as discussed in section 3.1.1.2, not to the future reading produced by *venir* that I discuss below. An indication of this irrealis effect comes from the fact that the boxes in (ib) might not even be made yet. There are two other indications that the effect does not depend on *venir.* First, it is not just *venir* that produces this effect, but any infinitival verb:

(ii)a.   J'ai des choses à faire.
         I have things to do.
   b.   J'ai des gens à voir.
         I have people to see.

Second, the irrealis effect disappears when the infinitival clause is replaced by a tensed one, as in (iii).

(iii)b.   Les boîtes qui viennent sont/??seront plus lourdes que celles-ci.
          The boxes that are coming are/will be heavier than these.

Thus, whereas the future *seront* is compatible with the irrealis in (ib), since the heaviness of the boxes is yet to be a reality, it is odd if the boxes are presumed to exist as in (iii), since we should already be aware of their heaviness.

   15. Lamiroy (1983, p. 134) notes an interesting restriction on infinitive clauses that follow *venir de:* some statives are not very good.

(i)   ?*Jean vient d'être de nationalité française/de savoir qu'Anne est venue/ de ressembler à son frère.
      Jean comes from to-be of French nationality/to-know that Anne has come/to-look like his brother.
      Jean has just been of French nationality/known that Anne has come/looked like his brother.

More precisely, the restriction seems to be that individual-level predicates are not very good here, since stage-level predicates are fine:

(ii)   Jean vient d'être malade.
       Jean comes from to-be sick.
       Jean has just been sick.

The restriction is understandable, if this use of *venir* expresses a change in time: individual predicates are not something that one becomes or comes to do, but something that one is or does. Note that this is the same stage-level/individual-level distinction as in the progredience constructions discussed in section 3.1.1.2.

   16. Lamiroy (1983, 130–31) and Traugott (1985, 28) also concur with the idea that, in the temporal uses of "movement" verbs, direction is preserved but no movement is involved, either of Ego moving to meet time or time to meet Ego.

   17. The orientation PAST→NOW is natural. Typically in our experiences, time spans are associated with movement across spatial expansions. Going from A to B takes time, and the time it took to reach point B is generally proportional to the distance between B and A in space.

   18. That English uses the same strategy as French, namely canonical face-to-face in-

teraction, is vividly illustrated by a line from Shelley: If Winter comes, can Spring be far behind?

19. The cognitive strategy of canonical face-to-face interaction does not affect the orientation of the temporal actants PARTIR and NOW in this case because their orientation with respect to one another is only indirectly mediated by the orientation of MAX, which holds strictly in the domain of grammar and, hence, is not subject to such cognitive strategies.

20. "La déchirure est donc postérieure au fait de voir. Mais, tandis que la contemplation de l'événement douloureux est présenté [sic] comme le début d'une succession vivante de faits à laquelle appartient encore le moment présent, la déchirure, elle, est présentée comme un acquêt définitif dont le coeur de la comtesse gardera toujours la plaie ou la cicatrice."

21. As for why these tense labels are associated with these particular morphosyntactic constructions, see Bouchard (1984b) and Cowper (1991).

22. As for why combining similar forms *have/avoir* + past participle seem to give very different Tense/Aspect results in English and French, I suspect that it depends on the definition of the moment of speech S, which would be only a point in time in English, but would be either a point or an interval in French. When S is seen as a point in French, we get the tense structure in (50b) E___R,S, which is equivalent to the English present perfect. However, if S is seen as an interval, S can stretch out to E, with the point R associated with S also possibly being situated close to E, so that the result is as in (i) (where interval S is represented as a bracketed series of points).

(i) $[_S.R. \ldots \ldots _S]$
         E ___ |

This closely resembles the English simple past E,R___S, as far as the positions of E and R with respect to one another, which explains why the French passé composé also covers the range of the English simple past tense. For now, I can only let the reader extrapolate this point for him or herself.

23. In Hausa, which has the "open-field" model for the front-back orientation of non-intrinsically oriented objects, a spatial situation like *the stone behind the tree* translates literally into English as *the stone in front of the tree* (cf. the discussion of (12)). As expected in the present analysis, this carries over to temporal situations: *the day after tomorrow* translates literally into English as *the day before/in front of tomorrow* (Hill 1978, 1982).

24. "La seule chose qui lui reste, c'est de marquer l'élan qui aboutissait au mouvement: élan qui, en l'absence d'un mouvement réel, se réduit à représenter la spontanéité vers une activité quelconque, l'efficience psychique personnelle." The passage actually refers to the involvement use of *aller*, but it applies equally well to *venir*, with only an orientation difference, as discussed in the text. See also Lamiroy (1983, 137ff) for relevant discussion.

25. This means that ME-PLACE-TIME is a better indicator of what the deictic center is, although I will continue to use ME-HERE-NOW for convenience, even if it contains a double redundancy.

26. "Avec l'auxiliaire venir, l'on intervient plus dans l'expression, on laisse entendre

qu'on est pour ainsi dire personnellement atteint par l'acte dérangeant . . ." This use of
venir is to be related to deictic uses of *here* and *there* in English (Lakoff 1987) and of *voici*
and *voilà* in French (Morin 1985; Bouchard 1988b) as in *Here we go again!* and *Voilà que
Jean est malade* 'There it is that Jean is sick.' Although the involvement use of these elements can correspond to a multiplicity of situations (see in particular Lakoff 1987), I believe there is only one meaning for each construction, and that the diversity of situations
depends on the referential nature of the arguments rather than on lexical properties of
venir, here, there, voici, or *voilà.*

27. "[L]e corps humain est interprété comme un lieu géographique où se déroule un
événement identifiable comme la transition d'une configuration spatiale à une autre. . . .
Pour que le corps soit interprétable comme un lieu, la transition spatiale ne peut affecter
qu'une partie de ce même corps: tout autre Thème dépasserait les limites du lieu au cours
de sa trajectoire."

28. Carter (1988, 295–96) characterizes *venir* and *aller* with respect to an endpoint.
However, his distinction is based on the spatial primitives HERE and THERE, whereas I
propose that the distinction is based on the broader notions of deictic center (ME-HERE-
NOW) and its complement. The fact that both of these verbs have multiple uses, many of
which are not spatial, indicates that the broader notions are more appropriate.

29. I assume that the French imperfect tense is not a past progressive (see Labelle
1994). As for the French morphologically marked future as in *ira,* it derives historically
from a combination of infinitival verb+AUX *avoir* in the present tense. (Presumably, it is
the difference between *avoir* and *aller* that explains the lack of temporal progredience in
the morphologically marked future.) So the French future does not receive the tense label
in (80c), but rather the label in (i):

(i)   S,R ____ E

See Bouchard (1984b) for a discussion of some consequences. I argue there that tense
representations are not labels, but structured representations that map homomorphically
to the morphosyntactic structure of the sentences. For example, the structured representation for the French future is argued to be as in (ii) rather than (i):

(ii)   S,R
        | ____ E

In this particular case, the two representations have very similar effects for tense interpretation, but a study of more complex tenses shows that structured representations are more
adequate. See Cowper (1991) for recent developments of similar ideas.

Note, finally, that this conflict with tense shifting holds only in temporal progredience,
that is, on centering specifically with the NOW aspect of the deictic/antideictic center. As
expected, it holds neither in spatial progredience (iii) nor in involvement (iv), which we
saw is a form of progredience (see sections 3.1.1.7 and 3.1.2.5).

(iii)   Tu iras déjeuner chez ta grand-mère.
        You will go and eat at your grand-mother's.

(iv)   Personne ne viendra me dire quoi faire.
         No one will come tell me what to do.
         I will not be told what to do by anyone.

30. The driver could be specified as in *Cette auto va bien à Gilles Villeneuve* 'This car
suits Gilles Villeneuve very well,' which says that the car is the kind of car that is well
suited for Villeneuve's driving style. One must also bear in mind that the car can be used
metonymically to refer to some of its parts, like the suspension or the motor.

31. The copula satisfies the Principle of Full Identification by being "obvious" and,
hence, not requiring an "outside" identifier. If *être* is not the copula itself but a support
for Tense, this predicts that if, for some reason, Tense is absent in a copular construction,
the presence of *être* should not be required (and by economy, *être* should not appear). It
is well known that this is what happens in languages like Arabic, where Tense is not obligatorily realized. In French, there are constructions where Tense is not realized and, as expected, we find bare copular sentences in those cases:

(i)   Je considère Paul très intelligent.
         I consider Paul very intelligent.

In keeping with the general position taken in this book, I assume that there is only one
copula (or one *be*), not three: whether the copula expresses existence, identity, or predication depends on the nature of the elements being related. Jackendoff (1983, 88–89) expresses a similar idea when he discusses the examples in (i):

(i)a.   Clark Kent is a reporter.
    b.   Clark Kent is Superman.

Whereas in a set-theoretic approach, (a) is an instance of inclusion and (b) one of
equality, with the odd result that two entirely unrelated relations are then expressed by the
same verb BE, Jackendoff suggests that the difference between the two is in the postverbal
NP, which can express either [THING TYPE] or [THING TOKEN]. Hence in (a), we
have a TOKEN INSTANCE OF TYPE and in (b) a TOKEN TOKEN-IDENTICAL TO
TOKEN. My position is more specific about the status of the grammatical representations.
The factor that distinguishes the two sentences is the manner of reference of the NP. This
is not a grammatical factor, and the representations should not differ at the level of Grammar. On the uniqueness of the copula and the relationships between existence, identity,
predication and ontological BE, see Rosen (1980, 105ff).

32. "L'accession du verbe *être* à cet emploi semble bien avoir pour racine le fait que,
quand on est allé dans un lieu, on se trouve nécessairement y avoir été, au sens ordinaire
du verbe *être,* pendant un certain temps."

33. Movement is not necessarily inferred, of course. It depends on the nature of the
arguments once again. If Jean is some famous personality—replace Jean with Hugo, for
example—*Hugo est à Paris désormais* may have an attributive use and expresses the fact
that Hugo now belongs to Paris. Note also that movement is much easier to infer from the
passé composé, as in (91b), than from the simple past, such as *Jean fut à Paris* 'Jean was

in Paris,' presumably because the relevance to the moment of speech is more salient in the passé composé. (See Reichenbach 1947 and Bouchard 1984b. See also the discussion of (51), above.)

34. This way of looking at the subject, the event, and time is the result of long discussions I had with Jacques Lamarche. I use it in Bouchard (1992b) to account for the choice of AUX. See also section 3.3, below.

35. From the beginning, this orientation problem has raised difficulties for thematic analyses. Its effects can still be seen in studies as recent as Jackendoff (1990a) who adopts the following "double-decker" notation for multiply specified Paths, where FROM and TO are indeterminated with respect to which one is the head of the Path:

(i) |FROM ([$_{\text{Thing}}$ HOUSE])|
       |TO ([$_{\text{Thing}}$ BARN]) |

I think that this quandary in hierarchically organizing the concepts of "Source" and "Goal" reflects the fact that they are not expressed by a hierarchical relation in a tree structure.

36. Besides the fact that negation of the lower part of the structure in (114) correctly expresses the meaning of *partir,* there may be another reason to put the negation there and not on the upper copular relation. If the scope of negation in semantic representations such as these is similar to the scope of negation in syntax in some respects, we could expect negation on the bottom relation to be similar to term negation, whereas negation on the top relation would be like sentential negation. Several properties distinguish the two types of negation. Thus, with term negation, a negative predicate is affirmed of the subject, and this presupposes the existence of the subject; whereas with sentential negation, there is denial of a predicate, and since denying a predicate of a nonexistent subject results in a true statement, the existence of the subject is not presupposed (see Horn 1989). Thus (i) is fine because the existence of Socrates is not presupposed, but his existence is presupposed in (ii), hence the oddness.

(i)   Socrates is not happy (of course, he is dead and dead people cannot be happy).

(ii)   #Socrates is unhappy (how could he be, since he is dead and dead people cannot have feelings and therefore cannot be unhappy).

Similarly, ascribing a negative property (e.g., being unhappy) to a subject (rocks) that cannot have such properties is bad (iii), but denying that such a subject has such properties is fine (iv):

(iii)   #Rocks are unhappy.

(iv)   Rocks are not happy.

Partir is like term negation in that the existence of its subject is presupposed: *Socrate est parti* 'Socrate is gone' is only possible in a context where the philosopher is alive, in contrast with *Socrate n'est pas arrivé* 'Socrate is not arrived.' A possible objection to this argument is that negation either of the upper or lower constituent in (114) should give the same result, since *partir* is eventually a word in the syntax. But it is not obvious that a verb containing negation necessarily behaves like term negation. In an example such as (v), with the verb *miss,* which is a good candidate for lexical negation, we do not have presupposition of the subject:

(v)   What is missing in your argumentation is a motivation for primitive P.

37.   In Québec French, there is also the transitive use in (i), with the corresponding *se-moyen* and inchoative constructions in (ii). This could be an anglicism.

(i)   Jean a parti le moteur d'un seul coup de manivelle.
       Jean started the motor with a single stroke of the crank.

(ii)a. Ce moteur se part très facilement/par ce bouton/avec cette clé.
       That motor self starts very easily/by that switch/with that key.
       That motor starts very easily/with that switch/with that key.

  b.   Ce moteur part très facilement/*par ce bouton/*avec cette clé.
       That motor starts very easily/by that switch/with that key.

38.   The same holds for *entrer.* Thus, only (i) can be used if Max went directly into the bathroom through a door (or window) that gives to the outside.

(i)   Max est entré dans la salle de bain de dehors.
       Max came in the bathroom from outside.

39.   In his discussion of *hors de* 'out of,' Vandeloise (1986) writes that it involves a previous inclusion. That does not seem to be correct, for reasons similar to the ones given for *sortir.* Although previous inclusion is by far the most frequent situation for pragmatic reasons, it is fairly easy to construct examples where it is not implied:

(i)   Il a encore la tête hors de l'eau.
       He still has his head out of the water.

(ii)   Je veux que ces gens restent hors de chez moi.
       I want that these people stay out of my home.

(iii) C'est hors de prix.
       It is out of price.
       It is very expensive.

(iv)   Hors de moi, point de salut.
       Out of me, no salvation.
       Apart from me, there is no salvation.

Compounds with *hors* such as (v) also do not imply previous inclusion (the absence of *de* is probably due to the compounding):

(v)   hors la loi, hors série, hors texte.
        out of the law, out of serie, out of texte.
        outlaw, special edition, inset plate.

40. Talmy (1985) claims that such a contrast holds between all Romance languages and all Germanic and Slavic languages; Jackendoff (1990a) cites Yoneyama (1986) for similar facts in Japanese.

41. None of these accounts necessarily draw us to the conclusion that languages can depart from strict compositionality. We could say that strict compositionality holds here, if we are willing to count these kinds of rules or features in the total computation, since, after all, they are triggered by specific lexical items.

42. Bear in mind that we are dealing with preferred readings throughout this discussion, not absolute readings.

43. Recall that the content of A, B, and *y* in (169) will determine the differences in meaning between *entrer* and the five other verbs that are the topic of this chapter.

44. This means that in *Mary floated under the bridge,* although the PP may remain neutral, the verb itself is directional. That a PP could remain neutral, even when combined with a directional verb, was already noted in the discussion of (167).

45. Since there are two ways for a verb to get a directional sense, a verb could combine both properties. We have already seen in (169) and (170) that *entrer* could be such a verb, since it is a "true" transitive verb (cf. (171)). French *glisser* also falls into the class of transitive directional verb that could also be three dimensional directional verbs. Thus, (i) can correspond to both (ii) and (iii), contrary to Emonds (1991, 388), who claims that only (ii) is possible (he attributes this claim to Talmy). Moreover, in (iv) *glisser* has a true transitive use:

(i)   La voiture a glissé en bas de la colline.

(ii)   The car skidded at the bottom of the hill.

(iii)   The car skidded to the bottom of the hill.

(iv)   Wayne a glissé la rondelle à Mario.
        Wayne slid the puck to Mario.

There are quite a number of verbs that behave like this (*monter, descendre,* etc.). Moreover, as expected if their direction is because of 3-D properties, French equivalents to *jump* and *swim*—*sauter* and *nager*—also allow a dynamic reading with neutral PPs, as also does 3-D *courir,* even though the only direct objects they allow as MMVs are measure phrases (or event phrases for *courir*):

(v)a.   Marie a nagé sous le pont.   (ambiguous)
        Marie swam under the bridge.
   b.   Il a sauté sous le pont.   (ambiguous)
        He jumped under the bridge.
   c.   J'ai couru derrière la maison.   (ambiguous)
        I ran behind the house.

(vi)a.   Marie a nagé trois kilomètres.
         Marie swam three kilometers.

   b.   Il a sauté six mètres.
         He jumped six meters.

   c.   J'ai couru 1500 mètres/ le marathon de Montréal.
         I ran 1500 meters/the Montreal marathon.

Note that (v.c) contrasts with *Je courais derrière la maison* 'I was running behind the house,'
for which it is harder to get the dynamic interpretation (but not impossible, as Talmy
claims: the dynamic interpretation is even the only one possible with a continuation like
. . . pour me cacher dans le hangar à chaque fois que tante Berthe nous rendait visite '. . . to
hide in the shed every time aunt Berthe came to visit us').

   46. Carter (1988, 178ff) discusses another entailment of MMV sentences that he says
cannot be attributed to any lexical item of the sentence: a causal connection is required
between the MMV and the final state described by the PP. Thus, (i) has the causative
entailment in (ii):

(i)   The bottle floated into the cave.

(ii)   The bottle moved into the cave by floating.

In the combination with a neutral preposition, as in (iii), the ambiguity about movement
gives a disjunctive entailment, as in (iv):

(iii)   The bottle floated under the wharf.

(iv)   Either the bottle was under the wharf and floating, or it came to be under the
        wharf by floating.

For Carter, it is clear that a causal connection is required, since "[i]f someone merely carried a vat in which the bottle was floating into the cave we could not say [(i)]" (179). Since
float is not a causative verb, and neither is *into* a causative preposition, says Carter, the
causative entailment cannot be traced to the lexical items. Although I am not sure what
his notion of causal entailment really is here, except at an intuitive level, it seems to me
simply to be expressing the fact that if a PP modifies a VP, it must be connected with it in
some fairly direct way. This connection need not be causal, however, and it need not be
related only to the dynamic reading. For example, one could not say (iii), with an intended
static interpretation, if someone merely held a vat in which the bottle was floating under
the wharf. As far as I can see, the Grammar merely states that the V and PP must be
connected, given their structural relationship; what counts as an appropriate connection
seems to be discourse governed. As it stands, this does not seem to be too serious a problem for strict compositionality.

   47. As Jan van Voorst pointed out to me (personal communication), it may be possible
to dispense with "actualizes" if we assume that this is expressed by the orientation towards
$[x_2 \text{ PRED}]$.

   48. There is probably no need to indicate that R_1 and R_2 must be COP in the case of
double recoverability, since COP is probably the only element that can take itself as head

of its own complement in $[x_1 \, R_1 \, [x_2 \, R_2]]$. See the discussion in Carter (1988, 231ff.) of the impossibility for CAUSE to take a CAUSE complement.

49. Following Vandeloise (1986), I assume that 3-D properties are expressed in dynamic terms rather than in terms of geometry or topology.

50. See Lavoie (1993), who shows that the semantic differences between Double Objects and Dative constructions derive from this difference in predication between the two constructions.

51. There is a very long tradition of having possessive constructions like (i) derive diachronically from a copular construction like (ii):

(i)   John has the car.

(ii)   The car is John's.

See Allan (1971, 6) for numerous references. He also gives several references from the sixties that transposed this analysis to a synchronic analysis of the constructions.

52. Additionally, it can be pointed out that this analysis goes against Chomsky's (1992) principle of Greed, which states that an operation applies to an element α only if it benefits α; the operation cannot apply to α to enable some different element, β, to satisfy its properties. In these cases, the incorporation at the head is not self-serving, since it is triggered by the need to solve the A/A-bar problem of the moved DP. Violating a principle proposed by another linguist is not in itself a major flaw, except that Greed is a principle that forces very local computations and thereby reduces complexity in the computational component; it is the kind of principle that should be given some consideration.

53. I assume that AP and NP predicates, as in (i), are instances of pure copula relations and that *his daughter* and *civilization* are not arguments here, but adjuncts.

(i)a.   John is $[_{AP}$ fond of his daughter].
   b.   World War III will be $[_{NP}$ the end of civilization].

54. See the discussion of DANS in 1.1.3 above for a similar notion of control. There are subtle differences between French and English in the main verb use of AVOIR, which I will not go into here. For example, the following sentences cannot be expressed with AVOIR in French:

(i)a.   I will not have any of that behavior here.
   b.   Bill had him make a copy.
   c.   We had him dismissed.

55. Many would introduce the primitive CAUSE here as in [x CAUSE [y BREAK]]. But the notion of causation is both too vague and too narrow (see section 1.5.2). As van Voorst (1992) observes, causation is nothing more than one of the many interpretations created by the interaction of a number of unrelated phenomena, such as the semantic specification of how the subject and the direct object participate in an event, the different referential possibilities of a noun phrase, the semantics relating to changes of states, and the semantics of agentivity. In short, "[a]lthough notions surrounding causation often seem to be clear in intuitive pragmatic terms, . . . it is impossible to give them enough linguistic

content to differentiate them from other semantic phenomena" (van Voorst 1992, 1). Therefore, I will assume the structure given in the text, in which the orientation of *x* toward the relation [y BREAK] in the semantic representation encodes part of what is linguistically relevant in causation.

56. "[Q]uand ces verbes veulent *être,* ils attirent l'attention sur le terme du phénomène en tant que ce terme est identique au début dudit phénomène, tandis que quand, avec *avoir,* ils expriment l'habitation, ils ne s'attachent qu'à marquer la durée du fait de loger en tel lieu."

57. It could also be the case that the manner expressed by WALK cannot be expressed by G-orientation because it involves complex 3-D properties that cannot be expressed using Grammatical tools, in which case English would be like French.

58. It is quite possible that R_I in $[x_1 \ R_1 \ [x_2 \ R_2]]$ is not a pure COP in the inchoative constructions, which would also explain the lack of COP conflation. Only a very detailed analysis of these verbs will allow us to choose between this option and the one in the text. It is also likely that the content of R_I is responsible for the metonymic reading of x_I.

59. A final comment on the data in (215) and (216): (216b) is not completely impossible. However, given the fact that control in unaccusatives is by a variable of an identical variable, it is less felicitous for pragmatic reasons: the level of a river is not likely to be strictly responsible for its own change in height.

60. The reason English does not have cliticization of pronouns could be that cliticization is an instance of a conflation in morpho-syntax, where a branching structure conflates into a nonbranching structure—the clitic and verb forming a single entity at the level of syntax—under cliticization. This passage from a branching relation to a point is precisely of the type that English seems to resist, as we saw in the discussion of conflation in 3.2 above. However, I am not at all sure that this is the correct correlation, since Spanish has clitics but does not have conflation of the type found in French (*habere* is the AUX used for unaccusatives, as we saw in table 1 above).

61. The analysis of the passive in Baker et al. (1989) is similar to the analysis of the French reflexive construction of Bouchard (1984a) in that, just as I did for *se,* they assume that the passive morpheme *-en* is the external argument of the verb. However, they also assume that *-en* is the head of INFL. Since INFL takes VP as its complement, *-en* both selects VP as a complement and is an argument of V, the head of the complement of *-en*. I fail to understand what it means for an element to be an argument of its own complement.

62. We can see immediately why there is an "implicit logical subject" in passives and *se*-middle, but not in inchoatives. Passive *-en* and *se* neutralize the highest argument so that it is present in Semantic Structure but not linked to a syntactic constituent; it is "implicit." In inchoatives, the highest argument binds the next-lowest one. The two arguments then have a single referent, which plays both roles, and no argument is left implicit.

63. There is an apparent problem if one compares the two sentences in (i):

(i)a.   Jean | a | | été | | à Québec |
   b.   Jean | est| | arrivé| | à Québec |

Why is *avoir* the AUX of *être* but *être* the AUX of *arriver,* when the relation between *Jean* and *été à Québec* seems to be so similar to the one between *Jean* and *arrivé à Québec?* In (a) *à Québec* is predicated of *Jean,* so the relation is simplex, but *été* introduces additional structure. This second relation is not simplex, and the AUX is *avoir,* as discussed for (223). In (b) I also assume that there is a double level of relations, namely $[x_1$ COP $[x_2$ COP y]], in the lexical entry of *arriver:* but although the highest relation is not simplex initially, conflation reduces it to a simplex relation, as we saw in the discussion of (203), so the AUX of *arrivé* is *être.* The difference between the two cases is that there is conflation in (b) but not in (a). The (b) structure $[x_1$ COP $[x_2$ COP y]] undergoes conflation at the level of the lexical entry of *arriver;* in (a), however, the double articulation of structure is not present at the lexical level, only at the syntactic level, and French does not allow conflation at the syntactic level (contrary to Italian, for example). Therefore, the difference in AUX choice in (i) is due to the different levels at which the double articulation of the structure is present: if it exists at the lexical level, conflation takes place and the AUX is *être,* as in (b); if it is only present at the syntactic level, conflation does not take place and the AUX is *avoir,* as in (a).

64. Binding theory has consequences for reference in many cases, but it is not about reference. For example, in Government and Binding theory, *it* is an expletive that has no reference but that binds a trace in (i).

(i)   It$_i$ seems [t$_i$ to be raining].

65. Note that there is agreement only on the participle that assigns a semantic role, not the AUX participle *été.* As noted in Bouchard (1987), we expect the argument to be coindexed with its role assigner, the coindexed participle which functions as a trace of the argument. No other verbal element but the role assigner may be coindexed with the argument since they do not bear any relation with the subject NP, except for the highest one which bears tense features, as discussed in 3.3.2.2. On the other hand, in an analysis of agreement based on movement through SPEC-AGR, it is not obvious how the AUX *été* is prevented from having a corresponding AGR (Chomsky 1991 has AGRAUX nodes) and how movement through its Spec can then be prevented in a nonstipulative way.

66. One does find examples that at first seem to be cases of sylleptic agreement of subject and verb, as in (i):

(i)a.   La plupart se sentent sentimentaux.
          The most part self feel sentimental+PLUR.
          Most of them feel sentimental.
   b.   La plupart d'entre nous sont/sommes sentimentaux.
          The most of us BE+3PLUR/BE+1PLUR sentimental+PLUR.
          Most of us feel sentimental.

However, I believe that these are false examples of sylleptic SPEC-HEAD agreement: *la plupart* functions as a Spec of a plural head here, like *plusieurs* in (ii):

(ii)   Plusieurs se sentent sentimentaux.
         Many feel sentimental.

On the other hand, *le monde* is very frequently used in Québécois, as in (iii), and cannot be explained as easily.

(iii)   Le monde sont donc fous.
         The world + SING *are so crazy* + PLUR.
         People are so crazy.

However, *le monde* is the only expression I have found with singular morphology that freely allows plural marking on the verb; it seems to be a true exception.

67. The hypothesis that a verbal stem can assign a Case to a suffix that will eventually be its head raises technical problems similar to those faced by the analysis of the passive morpheme *-en* in Baker et al. (1989), which I discuss in note 61.

68. Both French and Italian allow conflation; hence they favor simplex relations. But recall from section 3.3.1.3 that they differ, in that conflation can operate even in syntax in Italian. This could explain a difference that Kayne (1985) noted between the two languages in past participle agreement: whereas Italian clitic *ne* agrees with the participle, its French counterpart *en* does not.

(i)a.   *Il en$_i$ a [$_{SC}$ e$_1$ reprises [deux e$_2$]].
         He of-them has taken + FEM + PLUR *two.*
         He has taken two of them.

   b.   Ne$_i$ ha [$_{SC}$ e$_1$ riprese [due e$_2$]].

Both *ne* and *en* are complex synthetic clitics that correspond to a pro-PP rather than a pro-NP. It could be that this prevents *en* from functioning as an actant in French, hence the lack of agreement; whereas Italian, which is more permissive, would allow *ne* to function as an actant and trigger agreement effects. There are other cases discussed by Kayne (1985) in which there is no agreement with the past participle, although the direct object is in a "displaced" position that precedes the participle. I will not discuss these here, since I have already shown in Bouchard (1987) that Kayne's analysis of these facts can easily be transposed into an analysis based on coindexation.

69. Additional support comes from the fact that we will need an indexlike component of agreement, in any event, for the computation of number and gender in coordination.

70. The fact that passive participles and past participles have the same form suggests that something more general is going on. Following an idea by Jacques Lamarche, we could assume that there is only one participial morpheme. Suppose that this *−ed* morpheme suppresses something about the subject. That could be the link with the highest semantic role, as in standard analyses of passive. But if the subject is the actant of the event from which the whole event is related to time, as suggested in 3.1.3, this other link could be broken by the *-ed* suppressor: the event not being linked with the moment of speech S, it would then be linked with a moment in the past (presumably, future is not a tense but rather an aspectual notion of irrealis, as has often been suggested; cf. Vet 1980). A thorough study of participial properties will be needed to evaluate this hypothesis.

71. This relates to the general question of categorial membership. As Carter (1988, 76) observes, "[I]t is legitimate to ask whether there might not be, among the building blocks of semantic representations furnished by semantic theory, some which are more noun-like in nature, others verb-like, others adjective-like, etc. To put the question somewhat differently, we may ask whether there is any semantic basis for the widespread distinctions among lexical categories."

72. Labelle (1989) shows that *en*-cliticization is also not without its problems as a test to distinguish unaccusatives from unergatives. Contrary to what many have claimed, *en*-cliticization is possible with unergatives, as we can see in (266c–f). Similarly, auxiliary selection is also not a good criterion, since the verbs in (266) all take *avoir* as auxiliary. As Martin (1970) noted, the following verbs, which take *avoir,* also occur in the impersonal construction:

(i)a.   Il existe des ouvrages qui . . .
     There exists works that . . .

b.   Il manquerait l'essentiel si . . .
     There would miss the essential if . . .
     The essential would be missing if . . .

c.   Il gisait un homme sur le trottoir.
     There lay a man on the sidewalk.
     A man lay on the sidewalk.

If only unaccusative verbs are supposed to occur in the impersonal construction, and if unaccusative verbs take *être* as auxiliary verb, not *avoir,* it is a problem that the verbs in (i) participate in the impersonal.

73. In introducing his tiered approach, Jackendoff refers to similar work in phonology in recent years. But there are important differences between the two uses of tiers, specifically in how the links between the tiers are established. In phonological theory, the general format of linking conventions is that each element of one tier is linked to some element in another tier. But tiers in Jackendoff's representations are linked globally to other tiers, with the linking of individual elements from one tier to another left quite unclear so far.

Chapter Four

1. The scare quotes typically used for "open" syntactic position seem quite apt, since it cannot be properly defined within X-bar theory; its status is even more tenuous if one adopts the idea that C-selection derives from S-selection. Independent phrase structure rules do not exist in X-bar theory: a node is not licensed in PSRs in general, but rather it is licensed by selectional properties of a given lexical head (including semantically justifiable functional nodes like T, D, C) in each particular structure in which it appears. In other words, a rule like S→NP−TENSE−(Modal)−VP no longer exists to license an open subject position. In X-bar theory, if a node is in a "subject" relation with another element at DS, its presence must be licensed by the semantic (selectional) relation that exists between the two. So for example, if the subject position is SPEC of the Tense phrase TP, then an XP is licensed in that position if the XP is in the "proper" semantic relation with T. Under

these assumptions, the notion of "open" subject position is contradictory: an XP is licensed in DS if it can enter into a semantic relation, which presumably forces it to have features. How can an unfilled position have features? This criticism is reminiscent of the arguments for abandoning NP-postposing: in (i), *John* could not move to Δ because the object position of *by* is licensed at DS by a semantic relation established between the element in that position and *by;* such a relation is impossible here because Δ cannot enter into semantic relations (see, among others, Freidin 1978).

    i.   John stopped Bill by Δ.

    2. Given the highly situational nature of thematic notions, intuitions about underlying structures of sentences like those in (i) are really intuitions about the situation that is perceived as the most prototypical for such emotions:

    (i)a.   I enjoy movies.
       b.   Movies are enjoyable to me.

Thus, when Lakoff (1970a, 126) argues that these sentences are transformationally related and that (a) is the basic form, because "[w]e know this from our intuitions about what the underlying subjects and objects are," he can only be talking about his intuitions about the situation. I do not believe that anyone can have intuitions about Deep Structures.

    3. Chomsky has changed his mind a few times concerning whether Psych verbs like *strike* and *impress* are Raising verbs or Control verbs. For example, they are analyzed as Control verbs in Chomsky (1980), but as Raising verbs in Chomsky (1970) and (1981).

    4. Note that (9) does not directly ensure that the Cause argument will be the subject: it is logically possible that the Psych predicate could be higher than the CAUS predicate, in which case the Experiencer would be expected to appear as subject. Cases like this do not seem to arise, and this could be explained by general restrictions on the position of the CAUS predicate in semantic structures.

    5. On the notion of mental space, see Jackendoff (1975, 1976, 1983) and, of course, Fauconnier (1984).

    6. Nicolas Ruwet notes (personal communication) that (13a and b) contrast with (ia and b).

    (i)a.   Jean fait plaisir à Marie.
            Jean makes pleasure to Marie.
            Jean pleases Marie.
       b.   *Marie a plaisir en/de Jean.
            Marie has pleasure in/from Jean.

    7. Of course, we would also need many more entries for uses other than the prototypical one or the Psych one, such as *frapper des marchandises d'un droit* 'to impose a duty on goods' or *être frappé d'une maladie* 'to be struck down by a disease,' for example.

    8. Note that (17d) is peculiar, in that both the TRIGGER and the EXPERIENCER are subjects; this is possible because they are not coarguments.

    9. Pesetsky (1990), in his note 42, observes that the subject of an EO verb and the object of an ES verb differ in factivity.

(i)a.   Bill driving at night worries/concerns John. (Bill drives at night.)
  b.   John worries/is concerned about Bill driving at night. (He may not, in fact, drive at night.)

The contrast holds for pairs in (i) but not for others such as (ii), where the subject of the EO verb and the object of the ES verb agree in factivity (as Alain Villeneuve (personal communication) pointed out to me).

(ii)a.   Mary likes Bill's driving at night.
  b.   Bill's driving at night pleases Mary.

Pesetsky adds that presuppositions associated with what he calls the Cause argument in (iiib) differ from those associated for the object of (iiia) and account for its oddness.

(iii)a.   Mary feared/ was afraid of another possible tornado.
  b.   ??Another possible tornado frightened Mary.

   10. In fact, an "agentive" use of Psych *frapper* is not impossible in a sentence like (i), although it does require a special context.

(i)   Tu viens encore nous frapper par ton intelligence!
    You come again to strike us with your intelligence!

See the notion of progredience discussed in 3.1.1.2.
   11. "Il est évident qu'on a affaire ici à un phénomène productif, très général, et qu'il y a un rapport systématique entre les classes de verbes A et B; une grammaire du français qui n'en tiendrait pas compte serait inadéquate. De plus, dans la majorité des cas, tout sujet parlant natif du français a l'intuition d'un rapport sémantique entre les deux verbes homonymes. En gros, et d'une manière impressionniste, ce rapport peut s'exprimer de la manière suivante. Dans les exemples (a) comme dans les exemples (b), les verbes décrivent un processus dont le NP sujet désigne la cause, et ce processus affecte, ou a un effet, d'une manière ou d'une autre, sur l'être ou l'objet désigné par le NP objet. La différence est que, dans les exemples (a), l'effet en question est d'ordre purement physique, alors que, dans les exemples (b), il s'agit d'un effet psychologique, mental."
   12. Dowty (1979) also assumes that spatial relations are central. In his analysis of lexical decomposition, his basic idea is that statives are simpler or more limited in their interpretation and that it could be interesting to figure out how nonstatives derive from these. "The problem is to come up with some initial narrow constraint on the interpretation of statives that makes this a non-vacuous undertaking. . . . The meanings of many or perhaps most stative predicates are tied to physical properties of some sort—location in space, size, weight, texture, physical composition, color, etc. The suggestion is to add enough physical structure to the definition of a model to make stative predicates (or at least an interesting subclass of them) directly definable in terms of this physical structure. . . . We can constrain the interpretation of (physical) stative predicates by requiring that for each stative predicate there is a region of logical space such that at each index, an individual is in the extension of that predicate at the index if and only if the individual is assigned to a point within that region of space." (Dowty 1979, 126–27)

13. Roger Higgins (personal communication) points out that the hypothesis that so-called Psych verbs are instances of incorporation of a psy-chose argument is supported by the fact that these verbs are essentially denominals in Indo-European.

14. Partee and Rooth (1983) are concerned with problems of type ambiguity in conjunction. The fact that different types of elements can be conjoined makes it difficult to interpret them. For example, consider a conjunction of verbs. If two extensional verbs are conjoined, the interpretation is that the two verbs have the same direct object term phrase, so there is just one fish in (i), and the same three women are both hugged and kissed in (ii).

(i)   John caught and ate a fish.

(ii)   John hugged and kissed three women.

If two intensional verbs are conjoined, they are interpreted as having different direct object term phrases (see (iii)), and the same holds if an intensional and an extensional verb are conjoined (see (iv)).

(iii)   John wants and needs two secretaries.

(iv)   John needed and bought a new coat.

Conjoining NPs creates a similar problem. Thus, (v) is three-ways ambiguous:

(v)   The department is looking for a phonologist or a phonetician.
   a.   de re: specific person, who is either a phonologist or a phonetician
   b.   de dicto: they would be satisfied if they found one or the other
   c.   second de dicto: they have a particular kind of person in mind, but I don't know which kind (equivalent to The department is looking for a phonologist or looking for a phonetician).

Basing their work on Montague (1974) and Keenan and Faltz (1978), among others, where an individual is a set of term denotations, Partee and Rooth propose that an extensional phrase can always be "lifted" to a higher type intensional phrase. To put it in slightly different terms, an NP can be interpreted either as an individual or as the properties of an individual.

15. See Coppieters (1990) for a discussion of other contrasts that depend on this distinction. The idea that there is some form of conceptual relativism, and that an NP can be used to refer in different ways to the same object in the world, has been discussed in numerous other works. For example, Carlson (1977), Dowty (1979), and Kratzer (1988) propose a stage/individual distinction, where 'stage' refers to temporal slices of individuals, their manifestations in space and at individual times. By contrast, an 'individual' is whatever ties stages together and makes them a single unit. Cadiot (1988) discusses the reference of *ce/ça* and shows that when a NP can designate either an individual or the role of an individual like *le président,* only *il* can corefer with the NP, if it designates an individual, and only *ce/ça* can corefer with the NP, if it designates a role:

(i)a.   Le président, il/*ça change tous les sept ans. [individual]
        The president, he/it changes every seven years.

b.   Le président, *il/c'est Mitterrand. [role]
     The president, he/it is Mitterrand.

Ruwet (1991) argues that internal differentiations of the self, such as focusing on particular parts of the body, the soul, or their conflation in the person considered globally, affect the choice of pronouns.

Paul Kay (1983) discusses the fact that ordinary speakers of English have two conflicting theories of how we use words to refer to things in the world. The first one, which he refers to as "à la Frege," is when *words can fit the world by virtue of their inherent meaning,* as in (iia), whereas when one refers "à la Putnam or Kripke," one assumes that *there is some body of people in society who have the right to stipulate what words should designate, relative to some domain of expertise,* as in (iib).

(ii)a.   Technically, Ronald Reagan is a rancher. (true for the IRS)
    b.   Strictly speaking, Ronald Reagan is a rancher. (false)

The discussion of 'a sad book' and 'a sad person' in section 3.1.1.2 also relates to a distinction in way of referring and is taken up in Jackendoff (1983, 147), who notes that "book" has features of both a physical object and a body of information; similarly, "university" has features of both a physical object and a social organization. That these are not lexical ambiguities, but simultaneous possibilities, is shown by sentences such as (iiia-b), in which the words are used nonanomalously in both senses at once (Note that Jackendoff does not have the same qualms as Chomsky 1965 and considers such mismatches to be "nonanomalous," as does Bierwisch 1981, from whom Jackendoff took the examples).

(iii)a.   The book, which weighs ten pounds, ended sadly.
     b.   The university, which was built in 1896, has a left-wing orientation.

Lakoff (1987) says that such conceptual relativism is not restricted to language, but is very general. He gives the example of a chair, which can be viewed correctly from different points of view: at the molecular level, it is an enormous collection of molecules; from the point of view of wave equations in physics, the chair is a collection of wave forms; for me, it is the solid object on which I am sitting; and so on. The same is true of John: he can be a volitional individual I see acting, or a concept, or a type of person. Lakoff goes as far as to say that a *refusal* to recognize conceptual relativism where it exists has ethical consequences. "It leads directly to conceptual elitism and imperialism—to the assumption that our behavior is rational and that of other people is not, and to attempts to impose our way of thinking on others. Whorf's ethical legacy was to make us aware of this" (Lakoff 1987, 337). At present, there is no obvious way to reconcile all these distinctions in the ways of referring. In any event, whether some of these notions can be subsumed under others is not crucial for me, at this stage.

16. Note that self-to-other distancing is possible in (50a) in a proper context. For example, an actor just about to shoot a scene could say to the director:

(i)   Je veux bien que j'aime Marie, mais de là à l'embrasser avec tout ce maquillage dégoûtant, il y a une limite.

I don't mind if (lit., *I do want that*) *I love Marie, but to go as far as kissing her with all that disgusting make-up on, there is a limit.*

17. Further evidence in favor of an analysis based on matching properties of intentional notions can be found in Coppieters (1990). For example, consider the case of VP coordination, in which the same subject is selected by two different verbs. As the following examples show, if the two verbs require concurrently incompatible attitudes toward the same individual, the sentence is odd.

(i)   !Pongo struck Hermione as very intelligent and promised Mugsy to go to the
        movies.   [Concept + I-Subject = !]

(ii)   Pongo struck Hermione as very intelligent and promises to go far in his profes-
        sion.   [Concept + Concept = OK]

(iii)   !Pongo struck Hermione with his fist and promises to go far in his profession.
                                               [Substantive/I-Subject + Concept = !]

(iv)   Pongo struck Hermione with his fist and thinks that she will tell it to Mugsy.
                                           [Substantive/I-Subject + I-Subject = OK]

18. This possible objection was brought to my attention by James Higginbotham (personal communication).

19. Belletti and Rizzi discuss the examples in (i) but have failed to see the importance of the fact that this is a very productive alternation pattern.

(i)a.   Gianni si è colpito con un bastone.
        Gianni struck himself with a stick.
   b.   *Gianni si è colpito per la sua prontezza.
        Gianni struck himself with his speed.

20. This might be an overstatement on his part. As Alain Villeneuve (personal communication) pointed out to me, there are examples of action verbs that are used as ES verbs:

(i)a.   Jean digère mal d'avoir été banni du parti.
        Jean badly digests to have been excluded from the party.
        Jean does not accept having been excluded from the party.
   b.   Jean a très mal encaissé d'avoir été banni du parti.
        Jean has very badly collected to have been banned from the party.
        Jean can't stand having been banned from the party.
   c.   Marie ne supporte pas qu'on dise du mal de Jean.
        Marie does not bear that someone speak ill of Jean.
        Marie cannot bear to have someone speak badly of Jean.
   d.   Antoine a résisté à la tentation.
        Antoine resisted the temptation.

21. The oft-discussed example (i) should probably be considered part of the *frapper* class:

(i)   John turned the child against him/himself.

With the pronoun *him,* (i) is ambiguous between a literal meaning and the reading where the child becomes hostile to John. This second reading is very hard to get with *himself:* in the present analysis, this can be attributed to the fact that *John* is obligatorily interpreted as a Concept in order to get the Psych reading, so if *John* then binds the reflexive, a type mismatch results.

22. A sentence like (i) is an apparent counterexample to my analysis (Irene Heim, personal communication).

(i)   John strikes me as proud of himself.

Himself is bound by the subject of *strike,* with a Psych interpretation. If *strike* can only get a Psych reading by having a subject with a Concept interpretation, there should be a type mismatch here (the Concept subject of *strike* is binding the reflexive), yet the sentence is grammatical. What seems to be going on is that *strike* is not a good example of a verb of the *frapper* class in English. For many speakers, the verb *strike* is used almost exclusively as a Psych verb and rarely as an action verb (although these speakers might perfectly well understand its meaning in a passive way). If so, *strike* might be better classified as an EO verb such as *frighten,* in which case (i) comes as no surprise.

23. As Rosen (1980, 6) points out, from a very broad perspective, taking into account some referential properties of the self is unavoidable in any scientific endeavor: "The analysis of what I know is incomplete, and indeed, meaningless, if it makes no reference to how I know it, or that it is I who know it, namely, that meanings mean something only to knowers. Hence I become a problem in the attempt to establish the public or universal status of what I know. This problem is not resolved by pretending that it does not exist. In terms going back to Plato, the 'What is X?' question cannot be totally severed from the 'Who am I?' question."

24. I owe these examples to Jan van Voorst (personal communication).

25. Some of the relevant references are Kuroda (1965, 1973), Kuno (1972, 1975, 1983, 1987), Cantrall (1974), Banfield (1982), Sells (1987), and Pollard and Sag (1992), among many others. Zribi-Hertz (1989) gives a very thorough discussion of the key observations and proposals. In Bouchard (1984a, 1985a), I argue that long-distance reflexives do not behave like true anaphors for tests based on strict/sloppy distinctions, uniqueness, or locality of antecedent.

26. Additionally, an analysis based on the notion of Subject of Consciousness also explains why *myself* (and in certain contexts, *yourself*) can often be found without an apparent antecedent in the sentence. Speakers and the persons they are talking to are always Subjects of Consciousness.

27. Note that out of eighteen examples of putative unaccusatives used as adjectival passives in (94), only four are used strictly as intransitives: *elapsed, appeared, arrived,* and *lapsed.* The *Concise Oxford Dictionary of Current English* lists some transitive uses for all the others, which may mean that their adjectival passive might not be based on an unaccusative. Their intransitive uses are actually more like inchoatives, which I do not analyze as

unaccusatives. This means that examples of unaccusative adjectival passives may be very sporadic, indeed.

28. See also the discussion of *un-* in section 3.4. Given that *un-* is term negation, hence contrary negation (see Horn 1989), these adjectives are not compatible with *un-*, presumably because they do not have contraries.

29. Goldsmith and Woitsetschlaeger (1982) argue that the progressive is used to attribute phenomenological properties; these can presumably be attributed only to a Substantive. My analysis correctly predicts that verbs of the productive *frapper* class, which have a Psych use by virtue of their subject being interpreted as a Concept rather than a Substantive, will strongly resist the progressive in their Psych reading, since subjects interpreted as a Concept have a very low potential for activity:

(i)   *Ce paysage est en train de me frapper par sa beauté. (Ruwet 1972)

(ii)   *This scenery is striking me as beautiful.

30. One must be careful in using these tests. There seems to be some variation involved, since several English speakers have indicated to me that they disagree with Grimshaw's judgments in many of the tests.

31. In order to get unaccusatives not to have an external argument, Grimshaw must assume an absolute notion of prominence: "An unaccusative verb would have no external argument because the Theme would not count as maximally prominent even when there is no more prominent argument to compete for this assignment" (Grimshaw 1990, 39). She notes that *-ing* nominalization of unaccusatives seems to be limited to inchoatives. Thus, the two examples in (131) are inchoatives. If inchoatives are not unaccusatives, as I argue in sections 2.2.3 and 3.3.1.3, this contrast is not unexpected.

32. On this topic, recall the position taken in Chomsky (1975b, 84):

It is certainly correct that logic is indispensable for formalizing theories, of linguistics or anything else, but this fact gives us no insight into what sort of systems form the subject matter for linguistics, or how it should treat them. Neither from this fact, nor from the indisputable fact that work in logic has incidentally led to important insights into the use of language, can it be argued that the study of formal (or semantic) properties of natural languages should model itself on the study of the formal (or semantic) properties of logic and artificial languages.

33. Early proposals to relate syntactic categories to categories of symbolic logic were based on linguistic analyses. In the late 1960s, generative semanticists realized that what they had proposed as the deepest level of syntactic representation had a natural language-independent basis very close to proposals made by logicians like Carnap and Reichenbach (see among others Bach (1968, 121)). For example, it was suggested that all categories should be reduced to three basic ones—S, NP, and V, which correspond to proposition, argument, and predicate of logic, respectively. Such proposals have been abandoned as inadequate.

34. An important aspect of Davidson's analysis of the problem of polyadicity is that the adverbials are no longer considered added arguments, but rather added predicates,

which are predicated of the event *x*. This is closer to the linguistic description that I adopt here than Kenny's analysis is.

35. The reasoning seems to go as follows: on the one hand, NPs can have a reference, and, on the other hand, because of certain theoretical choices about argument structure, it would be interesting to have a variable available inside the NP. The conclusion is there is such a variable, *R,* the reference of the NP. But how does this help us understand reference in any way? Does it not duplicate indexing, or linking? Furthermore, if *R* is so different from other arguments, why even say that it is an argument?

36. This analysis owes much to work by Travis (1988) on adverbials and Lamarche (1990, 1992) on adjectives. The distinction between head-to-head and head-to-phrase relations also holds of adverb and verb relations, as I proposed in Bouchard (1990a). Lamarche (1990) shows that the hypothesis captures some interesting correlations in the distribution of adverbs and adjectives in both French and English. See note 41 below. I return to this topic in chapter 5 on Verb Raising.

37. In fact, I think that such a structural distinction is actually not necessary, except as a convenient diacritic reminder that different dynamic relations are involved. The W could be W^0 in (b), since I assume that heads only project if they have peripheral material, such as complements and modifiers; thus, *John* is an N^0 that is "phrasal," in the sense that it has the same distribution as more complex NPs (see section 2.1.1.1.3). Conversely, W in (a) need not be a W^0 (see note 38).

38. A phrase like *the very big boat* is not a counterexample because *very* and *big* enter into a head-to-head relation, and then this complex head in turn enters into a head-to-head relation with *boat.*

39. English does not allow bare adjectives to appear postnominally. Lamarche (1990, 1992) argues that this difference between French and English stems from the fact that adjectives must be in the scope of Number in NP in order to be properly interpreted and that Number is realized differently in French and in English. In French, Number is obligatorily realized on a syntactic node, independent from N, namely DET. Number is high in the structure and canonically governs to the right like other syntactic heads. It can, therefore, have both prenominal and postnominal adjectives in its scope. In English, Number is obligatorily realized morphologically on the head N. It is, thus, low in the structure and canonically governs to the left like other morphological heads, so cannot have postnominal adjectives in its scope.

40. Shape adjectives like *rond* 'round' and *carré* 'square' are also highly preferred in postnominal position, perhaps for similar reasons. On the other hand, some adjectives like *gros* and *bon* are generally found in prenominal position: grammarians and linguists generally agree that the reasons here are phonotactic, these adjectives being generally monosyllabic among others things. There remains the fact that a difference in interpretation is perceived when a color adjective is prenominal, but I cannot pinpoint what the difference is at this stage. It is an old problem, and it shows that the right system of decomposition to describe adjectives and nouns still has not been found.

41. We can now generalize the statement that a head must be in absolute left position in the NP in English and in French to the more general statement that all H+P combina-

tions are head initial in French and English. In work in progress, with Jacques Lamarche, we propose that the three combinations H + P, H + H, and P + P fall into two distinct classes. Class 1 (H + P) involves *selectional* heads, which have a whole-to-whole relation with their sister. Class 2 (H + H and P + P) does not involve a relation between two whole elements. We propose a linearization parameter, which states that selectional heads are initial in English and French. If an H is initial, it must be a selectional head, and the H + P combination results. If a head is not initial, the combination falls into class 2: the relation cannot be between two whole elements. This seems to correspond to the facts.

Thus, in head-to-head, a H relates not to another H as a whole, but rather to lexical sub-features of that H. As we saw in (155), this is clear in French where bare adjectives can appear both prenominally and postnominally: ADJ + N is a H + H, in which the ADJ can relate to a subfeature of N, whereas N + ADJ is a H + P in which the ADJ must relate to the N as a whole. As for phrase-to-phrase, the three cases in English where a phrasal element appears to the left of the element it relates to are (1) subjects, which relate to VP and to agreement features of T, (2) sentence-initial Wh-phrases, which relate "thematically" to a Sentence-internal element and to Wh agreement features of C; and (3) Possessive NPs which relate semantically to N and to Case features of D. In all three cases, the phrasal element is engaged in a relation which is not with a whole element, since it is split between two elements, one "thematic" and one functional. We now see why pre-X modifiers are generally not phrasal—they involve a nonwhole relation. Such a relation is generally held with a subset of lexical features, and only heads can have relations with such subfeatures. The only possibility for a nonwhole relation between phrasal elements is the case of split relations like the ones established by subjects, Wh-phrases, and Possessives.

42. Jackendoff (1990a) analyzes verbs of logical relations (*entail, imply, rule out,* etc.) and draws a conclusion that reinforces the idea that the logical vocabulary should not be used in core descriptions of linguistic facts: "If the present analysis is correct, verbs of logical relation express an abstract form of force-dynamic interaction, not too distantly related to verbs that express pushing things around in space. It is interesting that Piaget (1970) arrives at a similar hypothesis. He claims that concepts of logical relation, which appear relatively late in child development, are abstractions of concepts involved in motor activity, which appear very early. While one doesn't have to accept Piaget's theory of how development takes place, this particular point resonates with the present analysis. And I think Piaget's conclusion deserves to be taken seriously: that logical concepts, often taken to be the core of rational thought—the thing a theory of concepts must explain first—are really derivative. The real core of thought, according to Piaget, involves the principles by which we understand the physical world—cognitive principles that in evolutionary terms are much older than logic. To be slightly contentious, this conclusion demotes the logical vocabulary to a small and rather eccentric concern in semantic theory, while elevating the conceptualization of the physical world to a much more prominent status" (Jackendoff 1990a, 141–42).

43. This statement seems to contradict the "whenever possible" clause at the end of the Affectedness Condition. Since choosing π as the head causes the zero-CAUS morpheme to

violate the EMF, this seems to be an instance where the "whenever possible" clause should be invoked, so π is not chosen as the head. There should, in fact, be no problem with this derivation.

44. However, if the genitive is interpreted as agentive, actively involved in the annoyance of Mary, then (166b) is much better. Thus, changing *our nerves* to *her nerves* emphasizes the agentivity of *our* in *our constant annoyance* and makes the sentence more acceptable (Jennifer Ormston, personal communication). I return to this in the next section.

45. Grimshaw actually discusses the example in (i).

(i)   ?the arriving of the train

With a possessive, as in (169), the unaccusative seems to be significantly worse. See the discussion of (183) below.

46. In any event, even under the assumption that thematic notions play a role in Grammar, it is odd to deal with affectedness as some feature on thematic roles, since, as Gruber (1965) originally proposed, thematic roles are not primitives, but names for positions in a structure. In the approach assumed here, situational notions like affectedness play no role in the Grammar. In 4.3, I argued that the effects of affectedness are derived from an abstract notion of contact between points in a semantic representation. Affectedness may have some indirect effects on Grammar, just as the clearly situational notion of the frontal aspect of orientation in space was shown to have in chapter 3, but I do not think affectedness has any relevance to the cases in (170).

47. "[(174a)] est contradictoire, mais [(174b)] ne l'est pas; en effet, pour qu'Alice *remonte* Humpty Dumpty sur son mur, il faut qu'elle agisse sur lui directement, physiquement, en le prenant par exemple dans ses bras pour le déposer sur le mur; tandis qu'elle peut le *faire remonter* simplement par persuasion, sans agir elle-même directement."

48. Note also that *l'énervement* itself does not have sufficient control properties to be the causer in lexical causation (ia), only in syntactic causation (ib), whereas a physical element like *la poudre* can enter both types of causation (ii).

(i)a.   *L'énervement la pâlit.
        Nervousness pales her.
   b.   L'énervement la fait pâlir.
        Nervousness makes her pale.

(ii)a. La poudre la pâlit.
        Powder pales her.
   b.   La poudre la fait pâlir
        Powder makes her pale.

The meaning of the two causatives in (ii) is quite different. In the lexical causative *La poudre la pâlit,* there is direct causation and the interpretation is that powder on Mary's face makes her paler. Junker (1987) gives the syntactic causative *La poudre la fait pâlir* as ungrammatical; however, there is a possible use for this sentence. It can be used, for example, if she has an uncontrollable fear of powder, and becomes pale when she sees it.

This reading is clear in (iii), which contrasts with (iv). In this case, (iii) is fine, but (iv) is contradictory: blood (or the sight of blood) can make one become pale, but direct application of blood on oneself, as (iv) implies, has the opposite effect.

(iii)   Le sang la fait pâlir.
         Blood makes her pale.

(iv)   #Le sang la pâlit
         Blood pales her.

Essentially, in (iib) *La poudre la fait pâlir* 'Powder makes her pale,' *la poudre* is used as an indirect causer in the same way as *l'énervement* in (ib): it is not application of the powder that makes her pale, but a feeling or emotion it produces in her that makes her become paler, as in the contrast between (v) and (vi).

(v)   La simple mention du mot "poudre" la fait pâlir.
        Simple mention of the word "powder" makes her pale.

(vi)   *La simple mention du mot "poudre" la pâlit.
        Simple mention of the word "powder" pales her.

49. Some examples of "T/SM modification" are not very good without context, even with a subject that has the proper agentivity features:

(i)a.   Mary angered Bill.
   b.   ?*Mary angered Bill at the government.

But Jennifer Ormston (personal communication) pointed out to me that, if (ib) is set in a context where Mary is part of the government, and Bill's anger is directed at the government because of the behavior of one of its members, Mary, then the sentence is acceptable. The control factors involved are not yet as clear as one would like them to be, but whatever they are, Pesetsky's affectedness analysis is insufficient.

50. The identity relation is also determined by the nature of the head noun (the identified or "possessed" element). Massam (1990) gives the following examples: *hill, stone* (natural referential); *book, house* (cultural referential); *arm, head* (part/whole); *sister, friend* (relational); *story, picture* (depictive); *examination, destruction* (nominalization).

51. The fact that the experience of an emotion can be separated from the 3-D manifestation of that emotion is clear in examples like (i).

(i)   John concealed his love/anger from Mary.

The following passage from Kenny (1963) also suggests that such a distinction should be made: "But though one *can* experience an emotion only if one *can* manifest it, it does not follow that one *does* experience an emotion only if one *does* manifest it. There are indeed some emotions for which the stronger thesis holds: a man cannot be in a violent rage or extreme anguish if his countenance is serene and he talks composedly about indifferent topics. One of the criteria of intensity for such emotions is that they should be incapable of being concealed; as we talk of overmastering anger and overpowering grief. On the other hand, it is clearly possible to be afraid of something, or in love with someone, without telling anybody about it." (Kenny 1963, 63)

52. This could be problematic if theta-marking calculations *in general* proceed from the least prominent to the most prominent argument. If both theta and aspectual tiers determine the prominence relevant for these theta-marking calculations, it would be impossible to properly theta-mark arguments for EO verbs; it is impossible to begin the theta-marking with the argument that is the least prominent on both tiers at the same time because there is no such single argument with EO verbs.

53. If the source of (200b) is a Double-Object construction, no preposition is lost. However, recall from section 3.2 that I assume that in constructions like (i), the second NP object is predicated of the first one:

(i)a.   John gave Mary a headache.
   b.   John gave Mary a book.

I would argue that since *child* is predicative in (200b), it cannot be compounded because this would break up the predicative relation it has with *gifts*.

54. Some of the examples that are impossible with *-ing* are perhaps ruled out by blocking or semantic factors. It is also possible that some affixes may occur with either only N-bases or only V-bases and yet still be exceptional head-governors like *-er* and *-able*. For example, a verbalizing morpheme that did not add much semantic content to the base to which it was attached might never be found on a V-base because of blocking and yet still be a true head-governor. Similarly, a nominalizer that expressed the result or means of an action might not be found on N-bases because of blocking: N-bases often are a result or means of action. The affix *-ment* seems to be of this type, and the affix *-ion* might be another candidate. Neither of these is found on any N-base, perhaps because of blocking, but both still have the status of head-governors for the EMF. This analysis might explain the grammaticality of (121a) *John's public embarrassment/ humiliation of Mary.*

55. It is very likely that [*of* NP] is not an argument, but an adjunct. The fact that it is obligatory in certain cases derives from Full Identification.

56. It has often been noted that combinations of [V+N], where V is the head, cannot be used as a noun in English, in contrast with French.

(i)a.   *open-can (compare with 'can-opener')
   b.   ouvre-boîte

The analysis proposed in (218) seems to violate this generalization, but, in fact, it does not. As we saw in note 39, Lamarche (1990) argues that number is marked differently in French and English. In French, number is obligatorily realized on a syntactic node independent from N, namely DET, whereas in English, number is obligatorily realized morphologically on the head N. In an English compound like *open-can,* number would have to be realized on the V-head of the nominal compound, which is impossible. In French, *l'ouvre-boîte* is fine, since number has to be realized on the DET, not on the V-head of the compound. This requirement on number marking holds not word-internally, but at the level of syntax. Therefore, a compound with the structure in (218), such as *cookie-baking* or *can-opener*, is fine although part of its structure is a combination of N+V, with V as the head. The number-marking requirement does not hold for the N+V combination, but holds only for the noun formed by adding the suffix *-ing* or *-er*, which, being nominal, can take the number marking without any problem.

57. Another reason to distinguish the *-ing* that forms nominals from the *-ing* that forms adjectives is that the nominalizing *-ing* does not seem to form synthetic compounds, but rather root compounds. This can be seen by the fact that for nominal compounds like *wine-cooking* and *summer-gardening*, the condition that the compounded argument be an Object of Termination does not hold. Moreover, there seem to be aspectual conditions that actually prevent arguments that are Objects of Termination from compounding in *-ing* nominals, as in **music-hearing* and **angel-seeing*. Thanks to Jan van Voorst for these observations.

58. There is an additional possibility to bear in mind. Since the internal argument of EO verbs is an Experiencer, an I-Subject in my terms, reference to it as a person perceiving passions, emotions, and desires might be required, and it might not be possible to satisfy this kind of reference constraint from within a compound, given that compound-internal reference is, indeed, very restricted.

59. It seems to me that (i) is much better than (238a):

(i)   I can assure you that they'll get a phone call from me tomorrow.

60. Another way to state this is to say that the embedded predicate must be a stage level predicate. The condition discussed here may also rule out passive VPs embedded under *fare/faire*.

61. It is interesting to compare (252) with (251): the "raised" subject is acceptable under *faire*, which means that it has more control over the event. Intuitively, this is correct: we have no control over our height or the size of our eyes, but we could have control over the appearance of height or size of eyes. This indicates that a raising verb like *sembler* is not completely inert thematically, with respect to its subject: the subject of *sembler* in (252) has the potential for a certain degree of control over the event, which the subject of *être grand* 'be tall' or *avoir de grands yeux* 'have big eyes' does not have in (251). The same holds for *paraître* 'appear':

(i)a.   Ce costume te fait **être énorme.
          That suit makes you be enormous.
   b.   Ce costume te fait paraître énorme.
          That suit makes you look enormous.

(See the discussion in section 3.3.1.3, where I argued that verbs like *sembler* do not involve raising.)

62. The unaccusative analysis also has some difficulty accounting for a sentence like (249). Belletti and Rizzi, following Burzio (1985), suggest that this type of sentence is

grammatical because *fare*+V forms a complex verb capable of assigning accusative Case to the embedded NP in situ. This ad hoc assumption is not necessary in my analysis. For further difficulties with Burzio's proposal, see Ruwet (1991, 66ff) which provides additional support for the idea that the degree of potential control of the Causer over the Causee is a relevant factor here.

63. There is another set of data where the notion of "the most prominent I-Subject in the sentence" seems to play a role. Legendre (1989) provides the following data, where italics indicate that the argument can control the PRO subject of the participial clause.

(i)   Retrouvé par la police, *l'enfant* avait été confié à son père.
        Found by the police, the child was entrusted to his father.

(ii)   Déçu en amour, dorénavant la vie *lui* suffit/suffit à *Pierre*.
        Unfortunate in love, a solitary life was sufficient for him/for Peter from then on.

(iii)   Une fois déménagés, *nos amis nous* ont manqué.
        Once moved away, we missed our friends.

Legendre proposes the following principle to account for these facts:

(iv)   Only a matrix Working 1 can control Equi into a participial clause.

Travis (1990) suggests an account in line with Belletti and Rizzi's proposal: these empty subjects can be controlled by the SPEC of IP or the SPEC of VP. Experiencer objects can control in these cases because they are in the SPEC of VP. Although there are some problems with the data (some cases which are predicted to be impossible are not actually very bad), the cases given above can be accounted for by a condition such as (v):

(v)   Only the most prominent Substantive in the clause can control Equi into a participial clause.

A condition like this makes sense because there is an "aboutness" introduced by these participial clauses that could understandably require that they be anchored to a point of reference. In our terms, a point of reference is a whole self, as discussed with respect to the identification properties of genitives in 4.4.5.2.

64. Except, of course, if one is willing to propose different structures for each use of a verb. But then why not go even further and propose a different syntactic derivation for every single verb and each of its uses, to account for all the possible interpretations. History has shown that, in such an approach, one must eventually renounce any hope of explanation.

65. Erteschik-Shir marks sentence (281b) and other unacceptable examples of hers that I give in this section with an asterisk. However, the sentences discussed in this section are not strictly ungrammatical, but rather unacceptable in an unmarked context. Since context can improve them, I assume that they can be generated by the Grammar, and I, therefore, use the symbol "#" to mark all the unacceptable sentences discussed in this section.

66. This is the case, except in an imaginary society "in which every car came with a girl and buyers chose cars partly on the basis of the girls in them" (Erteschik-Shir 1981, 669).

67. This relates to the discussion of the 3-D properties of Pesetsky's SUG morpheme (see (185)). As expected, *worry,* the English equivalent of *preoccupare,* is not very good with that other 3-D use, either:

(i)   *John's manner was worried.

68. "Si *en* ou *y* se trouvent dans une proposition exprimant un contenu de conscience CC_i, *en* et *y* ne peuvent être coréférentiels du N" qui représente le sujet de conscience SC_i de ce CC_i." (Ruwet's 1990, 8).

69. Some sentences discussed by Ruwet are specially interesting because they contain verbs that allow their subject to alternate between I-Subject (which is an SC) and Concept (which is not an SC):

(i)   Ce grand malade$_i$ exige qu'on prenne grand soin de lui$_i$.
        That sick man requires that one take great care of him.
  a.   That sick man requires that people take care of him. (sick man = SC)
  b.   That sick man needs to be taken care of. (sick man = not SC)

(ii)   Ce grand malade$_i$ exige qu'on en$_i$ prenne grand soin.
        That sick man requires that one EN-take great care.
        That sick man needs to be taken care of. (sick man = not SC)

Sentence (i) has two possible interpretations: either it expresses the point of view of the sick man who tells us what he needs (a), or it expresses the point of view of someone else, such as his doctor, who tells us what he needs (b). But, as expected, given (318), (ii) is acceptable only with the second interpretation, in which 'sick man' is not a SC, since it corefers with *en* (other verbs that behave like *exiger* 'require' are *mériter* 'deserve,' *supposer* 'suppose,' *supporter* 'bear,' and *prévoir* 'foresee'). Moreover, given what I said above about the notions of SC and CC, we expect transparency to play a role here. The judgments are very subtle, but there seems to be an interpretation of (iii) where *en* can be coreferential with *Paul,* as long as the content of the proposition is not transparent, as indicated in the continuation.

(ii)   Paul croit que Sophie en a dit du mal . . . mais en fait c'était Albertine qui avait parlé.
        Paul believes that Sophie said nasty things about him . . . but, in fact, it was Albertine who had spoken.

70. We saw in section 4.3.4 some support for the idea that distantiation plays a role in Psych constructions, in the choice between infinitival and finite complements. That distantiation could also play a role in extraction is supported by an observation in Ruwet (1991, 49), who notes that nonbridge verbs do not easily allow infinitival complements (Ruwet puts a question mark in front of (ib), but, to my ear, this sentence is clearly unacceptable):

(i)a.　Elle murmurait qu'elle m'aimait.
　　　　She murmured that she loved me.
　b.　*Elle murmurait m'aimer.
　　　　She murmured to love me.

Nonbridge verbs also involve distantiation, which comes as no surprise, given that they are Manner-of-Speaking verbs (Stowell 1980). This means that the embedded clause does not count as part of the Content of Consciousness of the subject of the matrix clause, and, following (300), no constituent in that embedded clause can be Dominant; therefore, no constituent in the embedded clause can be extracted, as is well known for this class of verbs.

71. It should be clear by now that I am using the trace only for expository purposes here. Along the lines of what I said about Wh-extraction in 3.3.2.3, I assume that the index for the assignment of the semantic role inside the head of the SC-phrase actually functions as a trace.

72. Recall from the discussion of (263)–(268) that some Italian speakers consider sentences like (317b) acceptable and that the French equivalent of (317b) is perfectly grammatical.

73. For example, this postverbal subject might be in a situation of constructional focus (Rochemont 1978). I will not discuss these possibilities here.

Chapter Five

1. This is problematic, since later in the paper, when discussing the *there* construction, Chomsky assumes that agreement is checked at LF. He specifically refers to LF effects of Agreement, citing work by Mark Baker, in his note 46.

2. The relation between the verb and Tense has long intrigued me; I made a presentation on this topic at MIT in the spring of 1980 (later published as Bouchard 1984b). Reading Goldsmith's (1981) "Complementizers and Root Sentences" also triggered ideas about the possibility of a verb-movement account of the inversion facts, tying into the relation between the verb and Tense. I have presented some of these ideas on several occasions over the years, and I would like to thank the people present for their helpful comments: students in my classes at the University of Texas at Austin in 1986 and at Université du Québec à Montréal in 1990, audiences at the Association Linguistique du Maroc (particularly Jean-Yves Pollock), at the 7ème Colloque International de l'Université Paris 8 in 1987 ("L'inversion du sujet et de l'auxiliaire en français"), and at the 1990 annual meeting of the Canadian Linguistic Association at the University of Victoria (Bouchard 1990a).

3. There are also some technical problems with the analyses discussed above, but I will not dwell on them; the solution I will propose is quite different, and solving these problems becomes irrelevant for my analysis.

4. Similar structural problems arise in Ouhalla (1990). In the same note, Iatridou reports a problem that Noam Chomsky raises with Pollock's (129), given here in (i).

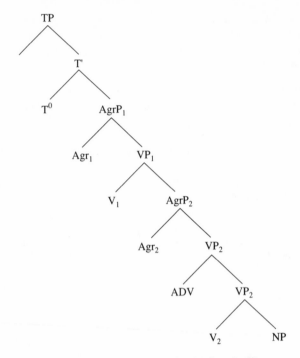

Pollock proposes this structure to account for the facts in (ii).

(ii)a.   Pierre a à peine vu Marie.
          Pierre has hardly seen Marie.
    b.   Pierre a vu à peine Marie.

Since in (iib) both the aspectual and the main verb precede the adverb, Pollock proposes the two Agr positions in (i), with *a* landing in Agr₁ and *vu* landing in Agr₂. Iatridou adds: "According to Noam Chomsky (personal communication), structure [(i)] by itself indicates that Pollock is mistaken about naming his proposed maximal projection 'subject-AgrP' (that is, 'carrying the agreement features for the subject'). What in fact would it mean for two such nodes to exist in a sentence with only one subject? Chomsky would claim that the (optional) order *vu à peine* of [(iib)] is due to movement of the participle *vu* out of its VP, over the VP-peripheral adverb *à peine,* and into the object-AgrP" (1990, 564, note 3). But Chomsky's analysis runs into exactly the same problem, if one adds an extra aspectual verb as in (iii).

(iii)   Marie a été soumise souvent à ce genre d'humiliation.
         Marie has been submitted often to that kind of humiliation.

Since all three verbs precede the adverb, Chomsky has to assume that *a* moves into AgrS and *vu* into AgrO, and an additional intermediate AgrAUX has to be postulated for *été.*

But what does it mean for three Agr nodes to exist in a sentence with only two agreeing elements, the subject and object? The node AgrAUX is even more problematic, given that intermediate auxiliary verbs like *été* never exhibit any form of agreement. One possible way around the problem would be to say that the adverb *souvent* is generated as in (i) above, with an extra VP for *été* above it. *Été* would thus be generated above the ADV in deep structure and need not move to an AgrAUX position. However, this will not work, because examples with two adverbials, as in (iv), would require the raising of *été* in this analysis, with the AgrAUX problems just noted.

(iv) Marie a été souvent soumise outrageusement à ce genre d'humiliation.
      Marie has been often submitted outrageously to that kind of humiliation.
      It is outrageous that Marie has often been subjected to that kind of humiliation.

Furthermore, the optional order *vu à peine* in (iib) requires an additional step in the derivation, which makes it more costly than the order *à peine vu,* so it should be ruled out on the grounds of economy. One way out of this last problem would be to say that lowering and raising have the same cost here: if the Agr lowers onto the participle, it does not have to raise back up at LF, since it has no LF properties. But this brings us right back to the selectional problems created by contentless elements: how can they select, and how can they be selected? The optional raising of the participle would also create agreement problems (see (15) below).

5. Iatridou actually uses (i) instead of (22), but the contrast is more salient with (22), since, for some speakers, (i) is a bit stilted.

(i)   To not have played football for many years is a disadvantage in a major game.

I made a similar change in (29) below.

6. I argued that contraction is not an appropriate test to distinguish between types of empty categories, such as between those that bear Case and those that do not, as proposed in Jaeggli (1980) and Chomsky and Lasnik (1978), since all instances of contraction are actually covered by the single structural condition. When a Case-marked trace appears to block contraction, it is because the structure required for a Case-marked trace actually blocks government of the contracting element (a point that seems to have escaped Aoun and Lightfoot 1984).

7. I assume that government into a maximal projection is never possible, contrary to Chomsky (1985b), except for "percolation government" of the head, as in Belletti and Rizzi (1981). The cases where Chomsky requires transparency for government are mainly due to his movement analysis of Wh-constructions, an analysis that I do not adopt. I opt, rather, for a V-chain or Connectedness-type analysis, for reasons given in Bouchard (1984a), (1985b), (1987), and section 3.3.2.

8. Although French creates many fewer empty verbal slots than English does, for reasons I return to below, there might be a few cases where there is *faire*-support in French, as in (i):

(i)   Il aboyait comme font les chiens.
          He was barking as dogs do.

9. The difference in structure between English and French correlates with another distinction between the two languages: complementizer *que* must be present in embedded clauses in French, but *that* is optional in English.

(i)   Marie pense *(que) Jean mange trop.

(ii)   Mary thinks (that) John eats too much.

Assuming that a French sentence has the basic structure in (51), in (i), the head of the complement of *que* only realizes properties of T. In (ii), on the other hand, the head of the complement of *that* is inflected *eats,* which realizes properties of both V and T. The following principle accounts for the contrast in (i and ii):

(iii)   Principle of Evolution: If a node is phonetically weak and substantively weak
          (i.e., if it lacks phonetic content and the substantive content of nouns or verbs
          and only has more functional content), and if its progeny is also weak, they tend
          not to survive (Where progeny of a node = its complement).

Thus, in (i), mother *que* has a substantively weak daughter T, so the mother cannot herself be weak. In (ii), mother *that* has a substantively strong daughter *is,* so the mother can be weak.

10. As we saw in note 39 of chapter 4, Lamarche argues that the same explanation holds for the absence of post-N bare adjectives in English, in contrast with French. In this case, it is Number that is a syntactic node in French because it is strong, but a morphological head in English because it is weak.

11. I am treating *tous* as an adverb because it has the distribution of an adverb. A logician would probably represent *tous* as a quantifier rather than an adverb, but that is not relevant for a linguistic analysis. See the quotation from Chomsky (1975b) in note 32 of chapter 4. *Tous* is an odd adverb in that it can appear as an N modifier, as in (ia), but other "degree" adverbs also appear in NPs (ib):

(i)a.   Tous mes amis sont venus me voir.
          All my friends came to see me.
    b.   Beaucoup/énormément/peu/trop de gens sont venus me voir.
          Many/enormously/few/too-many people came to see me.

The elements in (ib) are clearly adverbial, some by their morphology, like *énormément,* all of them by their distribution in sentences, like (ii), where there is no NP source for them:

(ii)a.   Jean a beaucoup/énormément/peu/trop pleuré.
          Jean has much/enormously/little/too-much cried.
          Jean has cried a lot/enormously/a little/too much.
    b.   Jean est beaucoup/énormément plus calme maintenant.
          Jean is much/enormously more calm now.
    c.   Jean est très peu/trop calme.

Jean is very little/too-much calm.
Jean is not very/too calm.

As for an analysis of *tous* on the basis of movement of a VP-internal subject into Spec of IP—which would strand the *tous,* as in Sportiche (1988)—it runs into two kinds of problems. First, in passives, a movement derivation predicts that there are three positions where *tous* could have been stranded in a sentence like (iii)—namely, where the three traces appear. But as indicated, the postverbal position is rather bad.

(iii)   Mes amis$_i$ ont (tous) t$_i$ été (tous) t$_i$ arrêtés (??tous) t$_i$.
         My friends have (all) been (all) arrested (all).

Moreover, there are sentences with *tous* where there is no source for it. Thus although the sentences in (iv) are fine, their counterparts with an "unstranded" *tous* are totally impossible (v).

(iv)a.   Le chat, le chien et le cheval sont tous sortis en vitesse.
         The cat, the dog and the horse all came out quickly.
    b.   Les jumeaux ont tous deux réussi à l'examen.
         The twins have all two passed the examination.
         The twins have both passed the examination.

(v)a.   *Tous le chat, le chien et le cheval sont sortis en vitesse.
   b.   *Tous deux les jumeaux ont réussi à l'examen.
   b'.   *Tous les deux jumeaux ont réussi à l'examen.

    12. The reason (72a') is not too bad could be that *to* is an AUX in English infinitivals (Postal and Pullum 1982), in which case (72a') would be similar to (72d').

    13. As expected, given the number of factors involved and their subtle semantic nature, there is variation in the judgments of acceptability. Pollock (1989) even gives sentences like (74b) as acceptable and contrasts them with (i):

(i)   *To forget almost one's name.

However, most speakers I have consulted in France and in Quebec consider the examples with the sequence [infinitive VADV] very bad for these head-to-head adverbs, and none found any of them on a par with the examples where these adverbs are in a pre-V position.

    14. The idea that *pas* was in modifier position in the earlier stage is defended in Hirschbüler and Labelle, following a suggestion made in Kayne (1991). They point out that this is also the analysis proposed by Pollock (1989) to account for the distribution of *point/ plus/rien* in examples like (i):

(i)   Pierre dit ne manger point/plus/rien.
         Pierre says NE to-eat not-at-all/no-more/nothing.
         Pierre says that he does not eat at all/anymore/anything.

However, they disagree with Pollock about the status of such examples in contemporary French: the judgments that they gathered suggest that such examples are not really part of contemporary French.

15. The analysis proposed here works for *ne* and *pas*. It is often claimed that there is more variation in order in the older texts than this analysis suggests, but this may be because such claims are made on the basis of the distribution of all negative elements. As Hirschbüler and Labelle (1993, 13) note, a comment about overgeneralization is in order: "Actually, a closer look at the data suggests that an adequate characterization of the facts requires a careful partition of various factors. In the early texts, the type of negative head plays a role in the respective positions of the verb, clitics and p-negative adverbs: there are differences between infinitives negated with *non* and those negated with *ne* (see Pearce 1990 and 1991, and Roberts 1991), as well as with those introduced by *sans* ('without'). Moreover, the type of adverb must be taken into account: *pas* and *point* for example, have a distribution different from that of other negative elements like *plus, rien, jamais,* which in turn pattern differently from each other and from positive adverbs; a complete picture of the syntax of infinitival clauses and of their evolution requires a detailed study of the individual distribution of each of these elements."

16. I will consider only contexts where English Subject-AUX inversion and French Subject-Clitic Inversion and Complex Inversion take place. French also has Stylistic Inversion (Kayne and Pollock 1978), which may occur in some of these contexts and in some other contexts specific to Stylistic Inversion. Since I am looking at inversion from the perspective of T-in-COMP, and since Stylistic Inversion does not fall under such an analysis, I will disregard it here.

17. Another example of the separation of T and the verbal base is VP ellipsis, as in (i), where *so* is a pro-V.

(i)   Bill left and John did so, too.

Although *so* is a pro-VP, it cannot be inflected. Therefore, *so* cannot be a base for T, and *do* must be inserted.

18. In an analysis with a Q-morpheme, one could assume that Q, just like T, is a weak morpheme in English, in the sense that it cannot be a syntactic preterminal node on its own. Therefore, *did* would bear both T and the Q morpheme and head the sentence.

19. This means that a Wh-phrase is not "operator-like," in the sense that it must bind a variable at some level of representation. It might be convenient from a logician's point of view to have operators and variables, since logicians are used to manipulating this kind of representation, but only linguistic facts will determine whether sentences *must* be so analyzed. That they can is no reason necessarily to adopt the analysis if another one without variables could do the job just as well. Only a global evaluation of both approaches, with and without variables, can settle the point. For an analysis of some scopal facts without LF binding of variables, see van Riemsdijk and Williams (1981) and Bouchard (1990b).

20. In using the notion of chain, I am not committed to a movement relationship between the external and internal T-nodes. As Chomsky (1981) notes, the distinction between interpretive and movement chains is generally impossible to make. Since a movement analysis requires additional theoretical tools, one who wishes to adopt such an analysis instead of the interpretive, binding, analysis of chains must argue for it.

21. In French, the only way to get a sentence like *Jean made us tell ourselves that story*

is to put one clitic on the causative verb and to leave one on the infinitival verb, as in *Jean nous a fait nous raconter cette histoire.*

22. It is always the lower clitic that appears, rather than the initial one, in order to distinguish a sentence with a special illocutionary force from a simple declarative sentence such as *il part*—the scope of the focused T must be as wide as possible.

References

Aissen, Judith. 1989. Agreement controllers and Tzotzil comitatives. *Language* 65: 518–36.

Allan, Keith. 1971. In reply to 'There$_1$, there$_2$'. *Journal of Linguistics* 8: 119–24.

Anderson, Stephen, and Paul Kiparsky. 1973. *A Festschrift for Morris Halle.* New York: Holt, Rinehart and Winston.

Andrews, Avery. 1983. A Note on the Constituent Structure of Modifiers. *Linguistic Inquiry* 14: 695–97.

Aoun, Youssef, and David Lightfoot. 1984. Government and Contraction. *Linguistic Inquiry* 15: 465–73.

Aoun, Youssef, and Dominique Sportiche. 1983. On the Formal Theory of Government. *The Linguistic Review* 2: 211–36.

Aristotle. 1984. *The Complete Works of Aristotle.* Volume one. J. Barnes (ed.). Princeton: Princeton University Press.

Aronoff, Mark. 1976. *Word Formation in Generative Grammar.* Cambridge: MIT Press.

Bach, Emmon. 1968. Nouns and Noun Phrases. In E. Bach and R. Harms (eds.), *Universals in Linguistic Theory,* 91–124. New York: Holt, Rinehart and Winston.

Bach, Emmon. 1977. Comments on the paper by Chomsky. In P. Culicover, T. Wasow, and A. Akmajian (eds.), *Formal Syntax,* 133–155. New York: Academic Press.

Baker, Carl L. 1970. Notes on the Description of English Questions: The Role of an Abstract Question Morpheme. *Foundations of Language* 6: 179–219.

———. 1989. *English Syntax.* Cambridge: MIT Press.

Baker, Carl L., and Michael Brame. 1972. Global Rules: A Rejoinder. *Language* 48: 51–77.

Baker, Mark. 1985. The Mirror Principle and Morphosyntactic Explanation. *Linguistic Inquiry* 16: 373–415.

———. 1988. *Incorporation: A Theory of Grammatical Function Changing.* Chicago: University of Chicago Press.

Baker, Mark, Kyle Johnson and Ian Roberts. 1989. Passive Arguments Raised. *Linguistic Inquiry* 20: 219–52.

Baltin, Mark. 1978. Toward a Theory of Movement Rules. Ph.D. dissertation, Massachusetts Institute of Technology.

Banfield, Ann. 1982. *Unspeakable Sentences.* London: Routhledge and Kegan Paul.

Belletti, Adriana. 1988. The Case of Unaccusatives. *Linguistic Inquiry* 19: 1–34.

Belletti, Adriana, and Luigi Rizzi. 1981. The Syntax of "ne": Some Theoretical Implications. *The Linguistic Review* 1: 117–54.

————. 1988. Psych-Verbs and Theta-Theory. *Natural Language and Linguistic Theory* 6: 291–352.

Benveniste, Emile. 1966. *Problèmes de linguistique générale.* Paris: Gallimard.

Bierwisch, Manfred. 1981. Basic Issues in the Development of Word Meaning. In W. Deutsch (ed.), 341–80. *The Child's Construction of Language.* New York: Academic Press.

Bloomfield, Leonard. 1933. *Language.* London: G. Allen and Unwin.

Boons, Jean-Paul. 1985. Préliminaire à la classification des verbes locatifs: les compléments de lieu, leurs critères, leurs valeurs aspectuelles. *Linguisticae Investigationes* IX: 195–267.

————. 1987. La notion sémantique de déplacement dans une classification syntaxique des verbes locatifs. *Langue Française* 76: 5–40.

Bouchard, Denis: 1979. Conjectures sur une grammaire indépendante du contexte pour les langues naturelles (master's thesis, Université de Montréal).

————. 1982. On the Content of Empty Categories. Ph.D. dissertation, Massachusetts Institute of Technology.

————. 1984a. *On the Content of Empty Categories.* Dordrecht: Foris Publications.

————. 1984b. Having a Tense Time in Grammar. *Cahiers Linguistiques d'Ottawa* 12: 89–113.

————. 1985a. On the Binding Theory and the Notion of Accessible SUBJECT. *Linguistic Inquiry* 16: 117–133

————. 1985b. Successive Cyclicity in Spanish. In O. Jaeggli and C. Silva-Corvalan (eds.), *Studies in Romance Linguistics.* 39–60. Dordrecht: Foris Publications.

————. 1986. Empty Categories and the Contraction Debate. *Linguistic Inquiry* 17: 95–104.

————. 1987. A Few Remarks on Past Participle Agreement. *Linguistics and Philosophy* 10: 449–74.

————. 1988a. En-Chain. In D. Birdsong and J. P. Montreuil (eds.), *Advances in Romance Linguistics,* 33–49. Dordrecht: Foris Publications.

————. 1988b. French voici/voilà and the analysis of pro-drop. *Language* 64: 89–100.

————. 1990a. La distribution des adverbes et de la négation en français et en anglais Paper presented at the Annual Meeting of the Canadian Linguistics Association, May 27–29, 1990, University of Victoria, Victoria, BC.

————. 1990b. Absorption à la S-structure. In A. M. Di Sciullo and A. Rochette (eds.), *Binding in Romance,* 77–95. Ottawa: The Canadian Linguistic Association.

————. 1991. From Conceptual Structure to Syntactic Structure. In K. Leffel and D. Bouchard (eds.), *Views on Phrase Structure,* 21–35. Dordrecht: Kluwer Academics.

————. 1992a. Psych Constructions and Linking to Conceptual Structures. In P. Hirschbühler and K. Koerner (eds.), *Romance Languages and Modern Linguistic Theory,* 25–44. Amsterdam: John Benjamins.

————. 1992b. Accord du participe passé et choix d'auxiliaire. In L. Tasmowski-De Ryck and A. Zribi-Hertz (eds.), *De la musique à la linguistique: Hommages à Nicolas Ruwet,* 191–204. Ghent: Communication & Cognition.

————. Directionality: Heading the Wrong Way. Unpublished manuscript, Université du Québec à Montréal.

Bouchard, Denis, and Paul Hirschbühler. 1986. French *Quoi* and its Clitic Allomorph *Que*. In C. Neidle and R. A. Nuñez Cedeño (eds.), *Studies in Romance Languages*, 39–60. Dordrecht: Foris Publications.

———. (In press). Primitives, Metaphor and Grammar. In J. Amastea and M. Montalbetti (eds.), *Proceedings of the Linguistic Symposium on Romance Languages*. Amsterdam: John Benjamins.

Bowerman, Melissa. 1978. The Acquisition of Word Meaning: An Investigation into Some Current Conflicts. In N. Waterson and C. Snow (eds.), *The Development of Communication*, 263–87. London: Wiley.

Bowers, John. 1990. The Syntax and Semantics of Predication. Unpublished manuscript, Cornell University.

Bresnan, Joan. 1978. A Realistic Transformational Grammar. In M. Halle, J. Bresnan, and G. A. Miller (eds.), *Linguistic Theory and Psychological Reality*, 1–59. Cambridge: MIT Press.

Burzio, Luigi. 1985. *Italian Syntax*. Dordrecht: Reidel.

Cadiot, Pierre. 1988. De quoi *ça* parle? A propos de la référence de *ça*, pronom-sujet. *Le Français Moderne* 56: 174–92.

Cantrall, William R. 1974. *Viewpoint, Reflexives, and the Nature of Noun Phrases*, The Hague: Mouton.

Carlson, Gregory. 1977. Reference to Kinds in English. Ph.D. dissertation, University of Massachusetts, Amherst.

Carter, Richard. 1988. *On Linking*. B. Levin and C. Tenny (eds.). Cambridge: Center for Cognitive Science, Massachusetts Institute of Technology.

Catlin, Jane-Carol, and Jack Catlin. 1972. Intentionality: A Source of Ambiguity in English? *Linguistic Inquiry* 3: 505–508.

Cattel, Ray. 1979. On Extractability from Quasi-NPs. *Linguistic Inquiry* 10: 168–72.

Champagnol, Raymond. 1992. Modèle d'acquisition des signifiés du langage. *Revue Québécoise de Linguistique* 22: 185–201.

Chapin, Paul. 1967. *On the Syntax of Word-Derivation in English*. Berford, Mass: The MITRE Corporation.

Chierchia, Gennaro. 1987. Aspects of a Categorical Theory of Binding. In R. Oehrle, E. Bach, and D. Wheeler (eds.), *Categorial Grammars and Natural Language Structures*, 72–128. Dordrecht: Reidel.

Chomsky, Noam. 1957. *Syntactic Structures*. The Hague: Mouton.

———. 1959. Review of *Verbal Behavior*, by B. F. Skinner. *Language* 35: 26–58.

———. 1965. *Aspects of the Theory of Syntax*. Cambridge: MIT Press.

———. 1970. Remarks on Nominalizations. In R. Jacobs and P. Rosenbaum (eds), *Readings in Transformational Grammar*, 184–221. Boston: Ginn and Co.

———. 1971. Deep Structure, Surface Structure, and Semantic Interpretation. In D. Steinberg and L. Jakobovits (eds.), *Semantics: An Interdisciplinary Reader*, 183–216. Cambridge: Cambridge University Press.

———. 1973. Conditions on Transformations. In S. Anderson and P. Kiparsky (eds.), *A Festschrift for Morris Halle*, 232–86. New York: Holt, Rinehart and Winston.

———. 1975a. Questions of Form and Interpretation. *Linguistic Analysis* 1: 75–109.

———. 1975b. *Reflections on Language*, New York: Pantheon.

———. 1977. On WH-movement. In P. Culicover, T. Wasow and A. Akmajian (eds.), *Formal Syntax*, 71–132. New York: Academic Press.

———. 1980. On Binding. *Linguistic Inquiry* 11: 1–46.

———. 1981. *Lectures on Government and Binding*. Dordrecht: Foris Publications.

———. 1985a. *Knowledge of Language*. New York: Praeger.

———. 1985b. *Barriers*. Cambridge: MIT Press.

———. 1991. Some Notes on Economy of Derivation and Representation. In R. Freidin (ed.), *Principles and Parameters in Comparative Grammar*, 417–54. Cambridge: MIT Press.

———. 1992. *A Minimalist Program for Linguistic Theory*. MIT Occasional Papers in Linguistics 1.

Chomsky, Noam, and Howard Lasnik. 1978. A Remark on Contraction. *Linguistic Inquiry* 9: 268–74.

Clark, Herbert. 1973. Space, time, semantics and the child. In T. E. Moore (ed.), *Cognitive Development and the Acquisition of Language*, 27–63. New York: Academic Press.

Comrie, Bernard. 1985. Causative Verb Formation and Other Verb-Deriving Morphology. In T. Shopen (ed.), *Language Typology and Syntactic Description* vol. 3, 309–48. Cambridge: Cambridge University Press.

Coppieters, René. 1982. Descriptions and Attitudes: The Problem of Reference to Individuals. *Studies in Language* 6: 1–22.

Coppieters, René. 1990. Individuals, Thematic Roles, and Semantic Interpretation. Unpublished manuscript, Pomona College.

Cowper, Elizabeth. 1991. A Compositional Analysis of English Tense. *Toronto Working Papers in Linguistics:* 53–64.

Cruse, D. A. 1973. Some thoughts on agentivity. *Journal of Linguistics* 9: 11–23.

Culicover, Peter, and Wendy Wilkins. 1986. Control, PRO and the Projection Principle. *Language* 62: 120–53.

Damourette, Jacques, and Emile Pichon. 1911–1950. *Des mots à la pensée*. Paris: D'Artrey.

Davidson, Donald. 1966. The Logical Form of Action Sentences. in N. Rescher (ed.), *The Logic of Decision and Action*, 81–95. Pittsburgh: University of Pittsburg Press.

———. 1980. *Essays on Actions and Events*, Oxford: Clarendon Press.

Desouvrey, Louis. 1994. Les classes de verbes en langue des signes québécoise. Master's thesis, Université du Québec à Montréal.

Di Sciullo, Anne-Marie, and Edwin Williams. 1987. *On the Definition of Word*. Cambridge: MIT Press.

Dowty, David. 1979. *Word Meaning and Montague Grammar*. Dordrecht: Reidel.

———. 1982. Grammatical Relations and Montague Grammar. In P. Jacobson and G. Pullum (eds.), *The Nature of Syntactic Representation*, 79–130. Dordrecht: Reidel.

———. 1991. Thematic Proto-roles and Argument Selection. *Language* 67: 547–619.

Dupuis, Fernande, Monique Lemieux, and Daniel Gosselin. 1992. Conséquences de la sous-spécification des traits de Agr dans l'identification de *pro. Language Variation and Change* 3: 275–99.

Emonds, Joseph. 1978. The Verbal Complex V'-V in French. *Linguistic Inquiry* 9: 151–75.

———. 1985. *A Unified Theory of Syntactic Categories.* Dordrecht: Foris Publications.

———. 1991. Subcategorization and Syntax-Based Theta-Role Assignment. *Natural Language and Linguistic Theory* 9: 369–429.

Ernst, Thomas B. 1984. *Towards an Integrated Theory of Adverb Positions.* Bloomington: Indiana University Linguistic Club.

Erteschik-Shir, Nomi. 1973. On the Nature of Island Constraints. Ph.D. dissertation, Massachusetts Institute of Technology.

———. 1981. More on Extractability from Quasi-NPs. *Linguistic Inquiry* 12: 665–70.

Erteschik-Shir, Nomi, and Shalom Lappin. 1979. Dominance and the Functional Explanation of Island Phenomena. *Theoretical Linguistics* 6, 41–86.

Ewing, A. C. 1937. Meaningless. *Mind* 46: 347–64.

Fabb, Nigel. 1984. Syntactic Affixation. Ph.D. dissertation, Massachusetts Institute of Technology.

Fauconnier, Gilles. 1974. *La coréférence: syntaxe ou sémantique.* Paris: Editions du Seuil.

———. 1977. *Quelques aspects de la quantification et de l'anaphore.* Ph.D. dissertation, Université de Paris VII.

———. 1984. *Espaces mentaux.* Paris: Editions de Minuit.

Fillmore, Charles. 1968. The Case for Case. In E. Bach and R. Harms (eds.), *Universals in Linguistic Theory,* 1–90. New York: Holt, Rinehart and Winston.

———. 1975. *Santa Cruz Lectures on Deixis, 1971.* Bloomington: Indiana University Linguistic Club.

Flynn, Michael. 1983. A Categorical Theory of Structure Building. In G. Gazdar, E. Klein, and G. Pullum (eds.), *Order, Concord and Constituency,* 139–74. Dordrecht: Foris Publications.

Fodor, Jerry. 1970. Three Reasons for Not Deriving "Kill" from "Cause to Die". *Linguistic Inquiry* 1: 429–38.

———. 1975. *The Language of Thought,* Cambridge: Harvard University Press.

Forsgren, Mats. 1977. *La place de l'adjectif épithète en français contemporain: Etude quantitative et sémantique.* Stockholm: Almqvist & Wiskell.

Franckel, Jean-Jacques, and Daniel Lebaud. 1990. *Les figures du sujet: A propos des verbes de perception, sentiment, connaissance.* Paris: Ophrys.

Freidin, Robert. 1978. Cyclicity and the Theory of Grammar. *Linguistic Inquiry* 9: 519–49.

George, Lelan. 1980. Analogical Generalization in Natural Language Syntax. Ph.D. dissertation, Massachusetts Institute of Technology.

Giorgi, Alessandra. 1984. Toward a Theory of Long Distance Anaphors. Unpublished manuscript, Instituto di Psicologia, Consiglio Nazionale delle Riserche, Rome.

Giry-Schneider, Jacqueline. 1978. *Les nominalisations en français: l'opérateur 'faire' dans le lexique.* Paris: Droz.

Goldsmith, John. 1978. Que c'est quoi? Que c'est QUOI. *Recherches linguistiques à Montréal* 11: 1–13.

———. 1981. Complementizers and Root Sentences. *Linguistic Inquiry* 12: 541–74.

———. 1989. Review of van Riemsdijk and Williams: *Introduction to the Theory of Grammar. Language* 65: 150–59.

———. 1991. Editor's Foreword. In N. Ruwet, *Syntax and Human Experience,* vii–xiii. Chicago: University of Chicago Press.

Goldsmith, John, and Eric Woisetschlaeger. 1982. The Logic of the English Progressive. *Linguistic Inquiry* 13: 79–89.

Grimshaw, Jane. 1979. Complement Selection and the Lexicon. *Linguistic Inquiry* 10: 279–326.

———. 1981. Form, Function and the Language Acquisition Device. In C. L. Baker and J. J. McCarthy (eds.), *The Logical Problem of Language Acquisition,* 165–82. Cambridge: MIT Press.

———. 1990. *Argument Structure.* Cambridge: MIT Press.

Gross, Maurice. 1968. *Grammaire transformationnelle du français: Syntaxe du verbe.* Paris: Larousse.

Gruber, Jeffrey S. 1965. Studies in Lexical Relations. Ph.D. dissertation, Massachusetts Institute of Technology.

Gruber, Jeffrey S. 1976. *Lexical Structures in Syntax and Semantics.* Amsterdam: North-Holland.

Guéron, Jacqueline. 1984. Inalienable Possession, *Pro*-inclusion and Lexical Chains. In J. Guéron, H.-G. Obenauer, and J.-Y. Pollock (eds.), *Grammatical Representation,* 43–86. Dordrecht: Foris Publications.

———. 1991. La possession inaliénable et l'aspect locatif. Unpublished manuscript, Université Paris X.

Guillaume, Gustave. 1970. *Temps et verbe: théorie des aspects, des modes et des temps.* Paris: Champion.

Haïk, Isabelle. 1982. On clitic *en* in French. *Journal of Linguistic Research* 2: 63–87.

Hale, Kenneth, Jeanne La Verne, and Paul Platero. 1977. Three Cases of Overgeneration. In P. Culicover, T. Wasow, and A. Akmajian (eds.), *Formal Syntax,* 379–416. New York: Academic Press.

Hall, Barbara. 1965. Subject and Object in Modern English. Ph.D. dissertation, Massachusetts Institute of Technology.

Hankamer, Jorge, and Ivan Sag. 1976. Deep and Surface Anaphora. *Linguistic Inquiry* 7: 391–428.

Harris, Zellig. 1951. *Methods in Structural Linguistics.* Chicago: University of Chicago Press.

Hellan, Lars. 1985. The Headedness of NPs in Norwegian. In P. Muysken and H. van Riemsdijk (eds.), *Features and Projections,* 89–122. Dordrecht: Foris Publications.

Herskovits, Annette. 1986. *Language and Spatial Cognition.* Cambridge: Cambridge University Press.

Higginbotham, James. 1985. On Semantics. *Linguistic Inquiry* 16: 547–93.

Higgins, Francis R. 1979. *The Pseudo-Cleft Construction in English.* New York: Garland Press.

Hill, Clifford A. 1978. Linguistic Representation of Spatial and Temporal Orientation. *Proceedings of the Fourth Annual Meeting of the Berkeley Linguistic Society,* 524–38. Berkeley: Berkeley Linguistic Society.

———. 1982. Up/down, Front/back, Left/right: A Contrastive Study of Hausa and English. In J. Weissenborn and W. Klein (eds.), *Here and There: Cross-linguistic Studies on Deixis and Demonstration,* 13–42. Amsterdam: John Benjamins.

Hirschbühler, Paul. 1979. The French Interrogative Pronoun Que. In W. Cressey and D. J. Napoli (eds.), *Linguistic Symposium on Romance Languages 9,* 227–47. Washington: Georgetown University Press.

Hirschbühler, Paul, and Marie Labelle. 1993. From *ne V pas* to *ne pas V* and the Syntax of *pas.* Unpublished manuscript, Université du Québec à Montréal.

Hjelmslev, Louis. 1961. *Prolegomena to a theory of language.* Madison, WI: University of Wisconsin Press.

Hoeksema, Jack. 1983. Plurality and Conjunction. In A. ter Meulen (ed.), *Studies in Model Theoretic Semantics,* 63–83. Dordrecht: Reidel.

Horn, Lawrence. 1989. *A Natural History of Negation.* Chicago: University of Chicago Press.

Hornstein, Norbert, and David Lightfoot. 1981. *Explanation in Linguistics,* London: Longman.

Hornstein, Norbert, and Amy Weinberg. 1981. Case Theory and Preposition Stranding. *Linguistic Inquiry* 12: 55–91.

Huck, Geoffrey, and John Goldsmith. Forthcoming. *The Ideological Structure of Linguistic Theory.* London: Routledge.

Iatridou, Sabine. 1990. About AgrP. *Linguistic Inquiry* 21: 551–77.

Jackendoff, Ray. 1972. *Semantic Interpretation in Generative Grammar.* Cambridge: MIT Press.

———. 1975. Morphological and Semantic Regularities in the Lexicon. *Language* 51: 639–71.

———. 1976. Toward an Explanatory Semantic Representation. *Linguistic Inquiry* 7: 89–150.

———. 1977. *X-Bar Syntax: A Study of Phrase Structure.* Cambridge: MIT Press.

———. 1983. *Semantics and Cognition.* Cambridge: MIT Press.

———. 1987a. The Status of Thematic Relations in Linguistic Theory. *Linguistic Inquiry* 18: 369–411.

———. 1987b. *Consciousness and the Computational Mind.* Cambridge: MIT Press.

———. 1990a. *Semantic Structures.* Cambridge: MIT Press.

———. 1990b. On Larson's Treatment of the Double Object Construction. *Linguistic Inquiry* 21: 427–56.

Jaeggli, Osvaldo. 1980. Remarks on *To* Contraction. *Linguistic Inquiry* 11: 239–45.

———. 1986. Passive. *Linguistic Inquiry* 17: 587–622.

Jongen, René. 1985. Polysemy, Tropes, and Cognition or the Non-Magrittian Art of Closing Curtains whilst Opening them. In W. Paprotté and R. Dirven (eds.), *The Ubiquity of Metaphor,* 121–39. Amsterdam: John Benjamins.

Junker, Marie-Odile. 1987. Les compléments prépositionnels des neutres. In P. Hirschbühler (ed.), *Syntaxe historique du français et catégories vides,* research report. 245–50. Ottawa: University of Ottawa.

Kay, Paul. 1983. Linguistic Competence and Folk Theories of Language: Two English Hedges. *Proceedings of the Ninth Annual Meeting of the Berkeley Linguistic Society,* 128–37. Berkeley: Berkeley Linguistic Society.

Kayne, Richard. 1975. *French Syntax: The Transformational Cycle.* Cambridge: MIT Press.

————. 1983. Connectedness. *Linguistic Inquiry* 14: 223–49.

————. 1984. *Connectedness and Binary Branching.* Dordrecht: Foris Publications.

————. 1985. L'accord du participe passé en français et en italien. *Modèles linguistiques* 7: 73–89.

————. 1990. Romance Clitics and PRO. In J. Carter, R.-M. Déchaine, B. Philip, and T. Sherer (eds.), *Proceedings of NELS 20,* 2: 255–302. Amherst, MA: Department of Linguistics, University of Massachusetts.

————. 1991. Romance Clitics, Verb Movement, and PRO. *Linguistic Inquiry* 22: 647–86.

————. 1993a. The Asymmetry of Syntax. Unpublished manuscript, Graduate Center, City University of New York.

————. 1993b. Toward a Modular Theory of Auxiliary Selection. *Studia Linguistica* 47: 3–31.

Kayne, Richard, and Jean-Yves Pollock. 1978. Stylistic Inversion, Successive Cyclicity, and Move NP in French. *Linguistic Inquiry* 9: 595–621.

Keenan, Edward. 1975. Some Universals of Passive in Relational Grammar. In R. E. Grossman, L. J. Sam, and T. J. Vance (eds.), *Papers from the eleventh regional meeting of the Chicago Linguistic Society,* 340–52.

Keenan, Edwin, and Leonard Faltz. 1978. *Logical Types for Natural Language,* Los Angeles: UCLA Occasional Papers in Linguistics No. 3.

————. 1985. *Boolean Semantics for Natural Language.* Dordrecht: Kluwer.

Kempson, Ruth. 1975. *Presupposition and the Delimitation of Semantics,* Cambridge: Cambridge University Press.

Kenny, Anthony. 1963. *Action, Emotion and Will.* London: Routledge and Kegan Paul.

Keyser, Samuel J. 1968. Review of *Adverbial Position in English,* by Sven Jacobson. *Language* 44: 357–74.

Kleene, Stephen. 1967. *Mathematical Logic.* New York: John Wiley and Sons.

Koopman, Hilda. 1982. Theoretical Implications for the Distribution of QUOI. In J. Pustejovsky and P. Sells (eds.), *Proceedings of NELS 12,* 153–162. Amherst, MA: University of Massachusetts.

Koyré, Alexandre. 1968. *Etudes newtoniennes.* Paris: Editions Gallimard.

Kratzer, Angelika. 1988. Stage-Level and Individual-Level Predicates. Unpublished manuscript, University of Massachusetts, Amherst.

Kuno, Susumu. 1972. Pronominalization, Reflexivization, and Direct Discourse. *Linguistic Inquiry* 3: 161–95.

————. 1975. Three Perspectives in the Functional Approach to Syntax. In R. Grossman et al (eds.), *Papers from the Parasession on Functionalism,* 276–336. Chicago: Chicago Linguistic Society.

———. 1983. Reflexivization in English. *Communication and Cognition* 16: 65–80.

———. 1987. *Functional Syntax: Anaphora, Discourse, and Empathy,* Chicago: Chicago University Press.

Kuroda, S.-Y. 1965. Generative Grammatical Studies in the Japanese Language. Ph.D. dissertation, Massachusetts Institute of Technology.

———. 1970. Some Remarks on English Manner Adverbials. In R. Jakobson and Y. Kawamoto (eds.), *Studies in General and Oriental Linguistics,* 378–96. Tokyo: T.E.C. Corporation.

———. 1973. Where Epistemology, Style, and Grammar Meet: A Case Study from Japanese. In S. Anderson and P. Kiparsky (eds.), *A Festschrift for Morris Halle,* 377–91. New York: Holt, Rinehart and Winston.

———. 1979. On Japanese Passive. In G. Bedell, E. Kobayashi, and M. Muraki (eds.), *Explorations in Linguistics: Papers in Honor of Kazuko Inoue,* 305–47. Tokyo: Kenkyusha.

Labelle, Marie. 1989. Unaccusative and Intransitive Inchoatives. Unpublished manuscript, Université du Québec à Montréal.

———. 1994. Predication on Times and the Semantics of the French Imparfait. Unpublished manuscript, Université du Québec à Montréal.

Labov, William. 1973. The Boundaries of Words and Their Meanings. In J. Fishman (ed.), *New Ways of Analyzing Variation in English,* 340–73. Washington: Georgetown University Press.

Lakoff, George. 1970a. Global Rules. *Language* 46: 627–39.

———. 1970b. *Irregularity in Syntax.* New York: Holt, Rinehart and Winston.

———. 1974. Interview. In H. Parret, *Discussing Language,* 151–78. The Hague: Mouton.

———. 1987. *Women, Fire, and Dangerous Things.* Chicago: University of Chicago Press.

Lamarche, Jacques. 1990. Tête-à-tête et autres relations: La position et l'interprétation des ADs. Master's thesis, Université du Québec à Montréal.

———. 1992. Problems for N⁰-movement to Num-P'. *Probus* 3: 215–36.

Lamiroy, Béatrice. 1983. *Les verbes de mouvement en français et en espagnol.* Amsterdam: Benjamins.

———. 1987. The Complementation of Aspectual Verbs in French. *Language* 63: 278–98.

———. 1988. Binding Properties of French *en.* In C. Georgopoulos and R. Ishihara (eds.), *Interdisciplinary Approaches to Language: Essays in Honor of S.-Y. Kuroda,* 397–413. Dordrecht: Kluwer.

Langacker, Ronald. 1986. *Foundations of Cognitive Grammar,* vol. 1. Stanford: Stanford University Press.

Lapointe, Steve. 1980. A Theory of Grammatical Agreement. Ph.D. dissertation, University of Massachusetts, Amherst.

Lappin, Shalom. 1982. Quantified Noun Phrases and Pronouns in Logical Form. *Linguistic Analysis* 10: 131–59.

Larson, Richard. 1988. On the Double Object Construction. *Linguistic Inquiry* 19: 335–91.

Lasnik, Howard. 1976. Remarks on Coreference, *Linguistic Analysis* 2: 1–22.

Lasnik, Howard, and Mamoru Saito. 1984. On the Nature of Proper Government. *Linguistic Inquiry* 15: 235–90.

Lavoie, Louise. 1991. Une approche sémantico-conceptuelle de l'alternance dative en anglais. In T. Wilson (ed.), *Toronto Working Papers in Linguistics,* 159–170.

———. 1993. De la sémantique à la syntaxe: le cas de l'alternance dative en anglais. Master's thesis, Université du Québec à Montréal.

Lee, Charles. 1994. The phonology and morphology of verbal agreement in American Sign Language. Unpublished manuscript, Stanford University.

Legendre, Géraldine. 1989. Inversion with Certain French Experiencer Verbs. *Language* 65: 752–82.

Lévi-Strauss, Claude. 1964. *Le cru et le cuit.* Paris: Plon.

Levin, Beth, and Malka Rappaport. 1986. The Formation of Adjectival Passives. *Linguistic Inquiry* 17: 623–61.

Lewis, David. 1970. General Semantics. *Syntheses* 22: 18–67.

———. 1975. Adverbs of Quantification. In E. Keenan (ed.), *Formal Semantics of Natural Language,* 3–15. Cambridge: Cambridge University Press.

Liberman, Mark. 1974. On Conditioning the Rule of Subject-AUX Inversion. E. Karose and J. Hankamer (eds.), *Papers from the Fifth Annual Meeting of the North Eastern Linguistic Society,* 77–91. Cambridge: Harvard University Press.

Lichtenberk, Frantisek. 1991. Semantic Change and Heterosemy in Grammaticalization. *Language* 67: 474–509.

Lieber, Rochelle. 1980. *On the Organization of the Lexicon.* Ph.D. dissertation, Massachusetts Institute of Technology.

Linebarger, Marcia. 1987. Negative Polarity and Grammatical Representation. *Linguistics and Philosophy* 10: 325–87.

Lois, Ximena. 1990. Auxiliary Selection and Past Participle Agreement in Romance. *Probus* 2: 233–55.

Long, Mark. 1974. Semantic Verb Classes and their Role in French Predicate Complementation. Ph.D. dissertation, Indiana University, Bloomington.

Lumsden, John. 1987. Syntactic Features: Parametric Variation in the History of English. Ph.D. dissertation, Massachusetts Institute of Technology.

MacLane, Saunders. 1981. Mathematical Models: A Sketch for the Philosophy of Mathematics. *American Mathematical Monthly:* 462–72.

Marantz, Alec. 1984. *On the Nature of Grammatical Relations.* Cambridge: MIT Press.

Marr, David. 1982. *Vision: A Computational Investigation into the Human Representation and Processing of Visual Information,* San Francisco: W. H. Freeman.

Martin, Jack. 1986. Towards a Modular Account of Psychological and Physical Predicates. Unpublished manuscript, University of California, Los Angeles.

Martin, Robert. 1970. La transformation impersonnelle. *Revue de linguistique Romane:* 377–94.

Martineau, France. 1990. La montée du clitique en moyen français: une étude de la syntaxe des constructions infinitives. Ph.D. dissertation, University of Ottawa.

Massam, Diane. 1990. Genitive Noun Phrases in English. Paper presented at the annual meeting of the Canadian Linguistic Association, May 27–29, 1990, University of Victoria, Victoria, BC.

McCawley, James D. 1968a. The Role of Semantics in Grammar. In E. Bach and R. Harms (eds.), *Universals in Linguistic Theory,* 125–70. New York: Holt, Rinehart and Winston.

———. 1968b. Concerning the Base Component of a Transformational Grammar. *Foundations of Language* 4: 243–69.

———. 1968c. Lexical Insertion in a Transformational Grammar without Deep Structure. *Papers from the Fourth Regional Meeting of the Chicago Linguistic Society,* 71–80. Chicago: Department of Linguistics, University of Chicago.

———. 1970. Where Do Noun Phrases Come From? In R. Jacobs and P. Rosenbaum (eds.), *Readings in English Transformational Grammar,* 166–83. Waltham, MA: Ginn and Co.

———. 1976. Some Ideas Not to Live By. *Die neueren Sprachen* 75: 151–65.

———. 1978. Conversational Implicature and the Lexicon. In P. Cole (ed.), *Syntax and Semantics,* vol. 9, 245–59. New York: Academic Press.

McConnell-Ginet, Sally. 1982. Adverbs and Logical Form: A Linguistically Realistic Theory. *Language* 58: 144–84.

Milner, Jean-Claude. 1978. *De la syntaxe à l'interprétation: quantités, insultes, exclamations.* Paris: Editions du Seuil.

———. 1982. *Ordres et raisons de langue.* Paris: Editions du Seuil.

———. 1989. *Introduction à une science du langage.* Paris: Editions du Seuil.

Milsark, Gary. 1974. Existential Sentences in English. Ph.D. dissertation, Massachusetts Institute of Technology.

Montague, Richard. 1970. Universal Grammar. *Theoria* 36: 373–98.

———. 1974. *Formal Philosophy,* R. Thomason (ed.). New Haven: Yale University Press.

Morgan, Jerry. 1969. On Arguing about Semantics. *Papers in Linguistics* 1: 49–70.

Morin, Yves-Charles. 1985. On Two French Subjectless Verbs *voici* and *voilà. Language* 61: 777–820.

Morin, Yves-Charles, and Marielle Saint-Amour. 1977. Description historique des constructions infinitives du français. *Recherches linguistiques à Montréal* 9: 113–52.

Mufwene, Salikoko. 1984. Stativity and the Progressive. Bloomington: Indiana University Linguistic Club.

Muller, Claude. 1991. *La négation en français.* Geneva: Droz.

Muysken, Pieter. 1983. Parameterizing the Notion Head. *Journal of Linguistic Research* 2: 57–76.

Myers, Scott. 1984. Zero-Derivation and Inflection. In M. Speas and R. Sproat (eds.), *MIT Working Papers in Linguistics 7: Papers from the January 1984 MIT Workshop on Morphology,* 53–69.

Newmeyer, Frederick. 1980. *Linguistic Theory in America.* New York: Academic Press.

Nöth, Winfried. 1985. Semiotic Aspects of Metaphor. In W. Paprotté and R. Dirven (eds.), *The Ubiquity of Metaphor,* 1–16. Amsterdam: John Benjamins.

Obenauer, Hans. 1976. *Etudes de syntaxe interrogative du français: quoi, combien et le complémenteur.* Tübingen: Niemeyer.

Ostler, N. D. M. 1979. Case-Linking: A Theory of Case and Verb Diathesis Applied to Classical Sanskrit. Ph.D. dissertation, Massachusetts Institute of Technology.

Ouhalla, Jamal. 1990. Sentential Negation, Relativised Minimality, and the Aspectual Status of Auxiliaries. *The Linguistic Review* 7: 183–231.

Partee, Barbara. 1975. Montague Grammar and Transformational Grammar. *Linguistic Inquiry* 6: 203–300.

Partee, Barbara, and Matts Rooth. 1983. Generalized Conjunction and Type Ambiguity. In R. Bäuerle, C. Schwarze, and A. von Stechow (eds.), *Meaning, Use, and Interpretation of Language,* 361–83. Berlin and New York: Walter de Gruyter.

Partee, Barbara, Alice ter Meulen, and Robert Wall. 1990. *Mathematical Methods in Linguistics.* Dordrecht: Kluwer.

Pearce, Elisabeth. 1991. Tense and Negation: Competing Analyses in Middle French. In *Parasession on Negation,* 218–32. Chicago: Chicago Linguistic Society.

Perlmutter, David. 1978. Impersonal Passives and the Unaccusative Hypothesis. *Proceedings of the Fourth Annual Meeting of the Berkeley Linguistics Society,* February 18–20, 1978, University of California at Los Angeles, 157–89.

Perlmutter, David and Paul Postal. 1984. The 1-Advancement Exclusiveness Law. In D. Perlmutter and C. Rosen (eds.), *Studies in Relational Grammar 2,* 81–125. Chicago: University of Chicago Press.

Pesetsky, David. 1982. Paths and Categories. Ph.D. dissertation, Massachusetts Institute of Technology.

———. 1988. Psych Verbs. Unpublished manuscript, Massachusetts Institute of Technology.

———. 1990. Experiencer Predicates and Universal Alignment Principles. Unpublished manuscript, Massachusetts Institute of Technology.

———. 1992. Zero Syntax. Unpublished manuscript, Massachusetts Institute of Technology.

Piaget, Jean. 1970. *Genetic Epistemology.* New York: Columbia University Press.

Piattelli-Palmarini, Massimo. 1980. *Language and Learning: The Debate Between Jean Piaget and Noam Chomsky.* Cambridge: Harvard University Press.

Pica, Pierre. 1987. Du caractère inaliénable de l'être. In T. Papp and P. Pica (eds.), *Hommages à Mitsou Ronat,* 207–21. Paris: Editions du Cerf.

Picallo, M. C. 1984. The INFL Node and the Null Subject Parameter. *Linguistic Inquiry* 15: 75–102.

Pinker, Steven. 1989. *Learnability and Cognition: The Acquisition of Argument Structure.* Cambridge: MIT Press.

Pinker, Steven, and Paul Bloom. 1990. Natural Language and Natural Selection. *Behavioral and Brain Sciences* 13: 707–27.

Piotrowski, David. 1991. Systèmes formels et théorie linguistique, quelques réflexions autour de H. B. Curry et L. Hjelmslev. Unpublished manuscript, Ecole des Hautes Etudes en Sciences Sociales, Paris.

Pollard, Carl, and Ivan Sag. 1992. Anaphors in English and the Scope of Binding Theory. *Linguistic Inquiry* 23: 261–303.

Pollock, Jean-Yves. 1984. On Case and the Syntax of Infinitives in French. In J. Guéron, H.-G. Obenauer, and J.-Y. Pollock (eds.), *Grammatical Representation,* 293–326. Dordrecht: Foris Publications.

———. 1989. Verb Movement, Universal Grammar, and the Structure of IP. *Linguistic Inquiry* 20: 365–424.

Postal, Paul. 1971. *Cross-Over Phenomena.* New York: Holt, Rinehart and Winston.

Postal, Paul, and Geoffrey Pullum. 1978. Traces and the Description of English Complements and Contraction. *Linguistic Inquiry* 9: 1–29.

———. 1982. The Contraction Debate. *Linguistic Inquiry* 13: 122–38.

Prigogine, Ilya, and Isabelle Stengers. 1984. *Order Out of Chaos.* New York: Bantam Books.

Pullum, Geoffrey. 1985. Assuming Some Version of X-bar Theory. In W. Eifort, P. Kroeber, and K. Peterson (eds.), *Chicago Linguistic Society* 21: 323–53. Chicago: Chicago Linguistic Society.

Putnam, Hilary. 1975. *Mind, Language, and Reality: Philosophical Papers,* vol. 2. Cambridge: Cambridge University Press.

Pylyshyn, Zenon. 1984. *Computation and Cognition.* Cambridge: MIT Press.

Raposo, Eduardo. 1987. Some Asymmetries in the Binding Theory of Romance. *The Linguistic Review* 5: 75–110.

Ratté, Sylvie. 1991. L'interface syntaxe-sémantique. Unpublished manuscript, Université du Québec à Montréal.

Reichenbach, Hans. 1947. *Elements of Symbolic Logic.* New York: Free Press.

Reinhart, Tanya. 1976. The Syntactic Domain of Anaphora. Ph.D. dissertation, Massachusetts Institute of Technology.

———. 1983. *Anaphora and Semantic Interpretation.* Chicago: University of Chicago Press.

Rizzi, Luigi. 1986. Null Objects in Italian and the Theory of pro. *Linguistic Inquiry* 17: 501–57.

———. 1990. *Relativized Minimality.* Cambridge: MIT Press.

Rizzi, Luigi, and Ian Roberts. 1989. Complex Inversion in French. *Probus* 1: 1–31.

Roberts, Ian. 1992. Restructuring in Old French. Paper presented at the *Second Diachronic Generative Syntax Workshop,* November 10, 1992, University of Pennsylvania, Philadelphia.

Rochemont, Michael. 1978. A Theory of Stylistic Rules in English (Ph.D. dissertation, University of Massachusetts, Amherst).

Rochette, Anne. 1988. Semantic and Syntactic Aspects of Romance Sentential Complementation. Ph.D. dissertation, Massachusetts Institute of Technology.

Roeper, Thomas, and Muffy Siegel. 1978. A Lexical Transformation for Verbal Compounds. *Linguistic Inquiry* 9: 199–260.

Rosen, Carol. 1984. The Interface between Semantic Roles and Initial Grammatical Relations. In D. Perlmutter and C. Rosen (eds.), *Studies in Relational Grammar 2,* 38–77. Chicago: University of Chicago Press.

Rosen, Stanley. 1980. *The Limits of Analysis.* New York: Basic Books.

Rosenbaum, Peter. 1967. *The Grammar of English Predicate Complement Constructions.* Cambridge: MIT Press.

Ross, John R. 1967. *Constraints on Variables in Syntax,* unpublished doctoral dissertation, MIT; reprinted with revisions as (1986) *Infinite Syntax!,* Ablex, New York.

———. 1972. Act. In D. Davidson and G. Harman (eds.), *Semantics of Natural Language,* 70–126. Dordrecht: Reidel.

———. 1981. Nominal Decay. Unpublished manuscript, Department of Linguistics, Massachusetts Institute of Technology.

Rothemberg, Mira. 1974. *Les verbes à la fois transitifs et intransitifs en français contemporain.* The Hague: Mouton.

Ruhl, Charles. 1989. *On Monosemy: A Study in Linguistic Semantics.* Albany: State University of New York Press.

Ruwet, Nicolas. 1972. *Théorie syntaxique et syntaxe du français.* Paris: Editions du Seuil.

———. 1982. *Grammaire des insultes et autres études.* Paris: Editions du Seuil.

———. 1983. Montée et contrôle: Une question à revoir? *Revue Romane* 24: 17–37.

Ruwet, Nicolas. 1990. EN et Y: Deux clitiques pronominaux antilogophoriques. *Langages* 97: 51–81.

———. 1991. *Syntax and Human Experience.* Chicago: University of Chicago Press.

———. 1993. Les verbes dits psychologiques: trois théories et quelques questions. *Recherches linguistiques de Vincennes* 22: 95–124.

Selkirk, Elizabeth. 1982. *The Syntax of Words.* Cambridge: MIT Press.

Sells, Peter. 1987. Aspects of Logophoricity. *Linguistic Inquiry* 18: 445–79.

Serres, Michel. 1977. *La naissance de la physique dans le texte de Lucrèce.* Paris: Les Editions de Minuit.

Shibatani, Masayoshi. 1976. The Grammar of Causative Constructions: A Conspectus. In M. Shibatani (ed.), *Syntax and Semantics,* vol. 6, 1–40. New York: Academic Press.

Simatos, Isabelle. 1986. Eléments pour une théorie des expressions idiomatiques. Ph.D. dissertation, Université de Paris VII.

Smith, Carlota. 1978. The Syntax and Interpretation of Temporal Expressions in English. *Linguistics and Philosophy* 2: 43–100.

Speas, Margaret. 1984. Saturation and Phrase Structure. *MIT Working Papers in Linguistics* 6: 174–98.

———. 1986. Adjunctions and Projections in Syntax. Ph.D. dissertation, Massachusetts Institute of Technology.

———. 1988. On Projection from the Lexicon. Unpublished manuscript, University of Wisconsin.

Sportiche, Dominique. 1988. A Theory of Floating Quantifiers and Its Corollaries for Constituent Structure. *Linguistic Inquiry* 19: 425–49.

Sproat, Richard. 1992. *Unhappier* is Not a "Bracketing Paradox." *Linguistic Inquiry* 23: 347–52.

Stowell, Timothy. 1980. Complementizers and the Empty Category Principle. In V. Burke and J. Pustejovsky (eds.), *Proceedings of NELS XI.* Amherst, MA: Department of Linguistics, University of Massachusetts.

———. 1981. Origins of Phrase Structure. Ph.D. dissertation, Massachusetts Institute of Technology.

———. 1982. The Tense of Infinitives. *Linguistic Inquiry* 13: 561–70.

Strawson, P. F. 1971. Identifying Reference and Truth-Values. In D. Steinberg and L. Jakobovitz (eds.), *Semantics: An Interdisciplinary Reader,* 86–99. Cambridge: Cambridge University Press.

Suñer, Margarita. 1987. On the Referential Properties of Embedded Finite Clause Subjects. In I. Bordelois, H. Contreras, and K. Zagona (eds.), *Generative Studies in Spanish Syntax,* 183–86. Dordrecht: Foris.

Szabolcsi, Anna. 1983. The Possessor that Ran away from Home. *The Linguistic Review* 3: 89–102.

———. 1985. Force Dynamics in Language and Thought. In W. Eilfort, P. Kroeber, and K. Peterson (eds.), *Papers from the Twenty-First Regional Meeting of the Chicago Linguistic Society.* 293–337. Chicago: University of Chicago Press.

Tasmovski-De Rijk, Liliane, and Paul Verluyten. 1981. Pragmatically Controlled Anaphora and Linguistic Form. *Linguistic Inquiry* 12: 153–54.

Tenny, Caroll. 1987. Grammaticalizing Aspect and Affectedness. Ph.D. dissertation, Massachusetts Institute of Technology.

Tesnière, Lucien. 1976. *Eléments de syntaxe structurale.* Paris: Editions Klincksieck.

Traugott, Elizabeth. 1985. Conventional and "Dead" Metaphors Revisited. In W. Paprotté and R. Dirven (eds.), *The Ubiquity of Metaphor,* 17–56. Amsterdam: John Benjamins.

Travis, Lisa. 1984. Parameters and the Effects of Word Order Variation. Ph.D. dissertation, Massachusetts Institute of Technology.

———. 1988. The Syntax of Adverbs. *McGill Working Papers in Linguistics,* 280–310.

———. 1990. The Nature of SPEC. Paper presented at the annual meeting of the Canadian Linguistic Association, May 27–29, 1990, University of Victoria, Victoria, BC.

van Oosten, Jeanne. 1977. Subject and Agenthood in English. In W. A. Beach, S. E. Fox, and S. Philosoph (eds.), *Proceedings of the XIIIth CLS Meeting,* 459–71. Chicago: University of Chicago Press.

van Riemsdijk, Henk. 1978. *A Case Study in Syntactic Markedness.* Dordrecht: Foris.

van Riemsdijk, Henk, and Edwin Williams. 1981. NP-Structure. *The Linguistic Review* 1: 171–217.

van Voorst, Jan. 1988. *Event Structure.* Amsterdam: John Benjamins.

van Voorst, Jan. 1990. The Aspectual Semantics of Psychological Verbs. Unpublished manuscript, Université du Québec à Montréal.

———. 1992. The Aspectual Semantics of Psychological Verbs. *Linguistics and Philosophy* 15: 65–92.

————. 1993. A Localist Model for Event Semantics. *The Journal of Semantics* 10: 65–111.

Vandeloise, Claude. 1986. *L'espace en français.* Paris: Editions du Seuil.

————. 1992. Les analyses de la préposition *dans:* faits linguistiques et effets méthodologiques. Lexique 11: 15–40.

Vendler, Zeno. 1967. *Linguistics in Philosophy,* Ithaca: Cornell University Press.

————. 1976. Causal Relations. *The Journal of Philosophy* 64: 704–13.

Verkuyl, Henk J. 1989. Aspectual Classes and Aspectual Composition. *Linguistics and Philosophy* 12: 39–94.

Vet, Co. 1980. *Temps, aspects et adverbes de temps en français contemporain.* Geneva: Droz.

Wall, Robert. 1972. *Introduction to Mathematical Linguistics.* Englewood Cliffs, NJ: Prentice-Hall.

Wasow, Thomas. 1972. *Anaphoric Relations in English.* Ghent: E. Story-Scientia.

Waugh, Linda R. 1977. *A Semantic Analysis of Word Order.* Leiden: E. J. Brill.

Willems, D. 1985. La construction impersonnelle. In L. Melis, L. Tasmowski, P. Verluyten, and D. Willems (eds.), *Les constructions de la phrase française.* Ghent: Communication and Cognition.

Williams, Edwin. 1980. Predication. *Linguistic Inquiry* 11: 203–38.

————. 1981. On the Notions "Lexically Related" and "Head of a Word." *Linguistic Inquiry* 12: 245–74.

Wittgenstein, Ludwig. 1953. *Philosophical Investigations.* New York: Macmillan.

Yoneyama, M. 1986. Motion Verbs in Conceptual Semantics. *Bulletin of the Faculty of Humanities of Seikei University, Tokyo* 22: 1–15.

Zribi-Hertz, Anne. 1982. La morphologie verbale passive en français: essai d'explication. In J. Guéron and T. Sowley (eds.), *Grammaire transformationnelle: Théorie et méthodologies,* 127–53. Paris: Université Paris VIII and Revue Encrages.

————. 1986. Relations anaphoriques en français: esquisse d'une grammaire générative raisonnée de la réflexivité et de l'ellipse structurale. Ph.D. dissertation, Université de Paris VIII.

————. 1987. La réflexivité ergative en français moderne. *Le français moderne* 55: 23–54.

————. 1989. Anaphor Binding and Narrative Point of View: English Reflexive Pronouns in Sentence and Discourse. *Language* 65: 695–727.

Zubizarreta, Maria-Luisa. 1987. *Levels of Representation in the Lexicon and in the Syntax.* Dordrecht: Foris.

Zwicky, Arnold, and Jerrold Sadock. 1975. Ambiguity Tests and How to Fail Them. In J. Kimball (ed.), *Syntax and Semantics,* vol. 4, 1–36. New York: Academic Press.

Le trésor de la langue française (dictionary). Paris: Gallimard.

Index